ANNUAL EDITIONS

Public Policy and Administration

Ninth Edition

D1622838

EDITOR

Howard R. Balanoff

Texas State University–San Marcos

Dr. Howard R. Balanoff is the William P. Hobby Professor of Public Service at Texas State University. He is also the Director of the University's William P. Hobby Center for Public Service and serves as the Director of the Texas Certified Public Manager (CPM) Program. He has taught at Texas State University for over 30 years and has also served as an adjunct professor of public affairs and educational administration at the University of Texas at Austin. He is the author of numerous articles in the area of public administration and planning and is the editor of the textbook, *Annual Editions: Public Administration*. He is a former member of the National Council of the American Society for Public Administration (ASPA) and a former President of the National Certified Public Manager (CPM) Consortium. He has also served as the Chair of ASPA's International Affairs Committees. He is currently Chair of ASPA's Section on Professional & Organizational Development.

His specialty areas are personnel administration, public policy and professional development, and education in the public sector. He also teaches courses and conducts research in the area of international and comparative public administration. For seven years he served on active duty as a communications-electronics officer and missile combat crew commander in the United States Air Force. He also served for 13 years as a member of the Air Force Reserves. He holds the rank of Major USAF-Retired. Dr. Balanoff received a bachelor of arts in political science and history from Hunter College of the City University of New York. He received a Master's and Ph.D. in urban and regional planning from Texas A&M University.

Contemporary Learning Series

2460 Kerper Blvd., Dubuque, IA 52001

Visit us on the Internet
http://www.mhcls.com

Credits

1. **Introduction and Overview**
   Unit photo—The McGraw-Hill Companies, Inc./Jill Braaten
2. **Government and Organizational Behavior**
   Unit photo—U.S. Air Force photo by Tech. Sgt. Jerry Morrison
3. **Human Resources Administration**
   Unit photo—Royalty-Free/CORBIS
4. **Finance and Budgeting**
   Unit photo—Steve Cole/Getty Images
5. **Technology and Information Systems**
   Unit photo—Royalty-Free/CORBIS
6. **Public Policy, Law, Community, and Environmental Planning**
   Unit photo—Photodisc Collection/Getty Images
7. **International Public Policy and Administration**
   Unit photo—Annie Reynolds/PhotoLink/Getty Images

Copyright

Cataloging in Publication Data
Main entry under title: Annual Editions: Public Policy and Administration. 9th Edition.
1. Public Policy and Administration—Periodicals. I. Balanoff, Howard R., *comp.* II. Title: Public Policy and Administration.

ISBN-13: 978–0–07–351626–4   ISBN-10: 0–07–351626–0   658'.05   ISSN 1052–7532

Ninth Edition

Cover image © 2007 Marvin Nauman/FEMA
Printed in the United States of America   1234567890QPDQPD9876   Printed on Recycled Paper

Editors/Advisory Board

Members of the Advisory Board are instrumental in the final selection of articles for each edition of ANNUAL EDITIONS. Their review of articles for content, level, currentness, and appropriateness provides critical direction to the editor and staff. We think that you will find their careful consideration well reflected in this volume.

EDITOR

Howard R. Balanoff
Texas State University – San Marcos

ADVISORY BOARD

Erik Bergrud
Park University

Ann Cobb
State of North Carolina Personnel Development Center

Jerrell Coggburn
University of Texas – San Antonio

David A. Gugin
University of Evansville

Arie Halachmi
Tennessee State University

Mary R. Hamilton
University of Nebraska – Omaha

Marc Holzer
Rutgers University

L. Douglas Kiel
University of Texas – Dallas

Gary A. Mattson
Northern Kentucky University

Jack Maykoski
US Dept. of Agriculture (USDA) Graduate School

Donald C. Menzel
American Society for Public Administration

Susan Paddock
University of Wisconsin – Madison

Charles Phelps
Cleveland State University

Jack M. Rabin
Pennsylvania State University

Mitchell F. Rice
Texas A & M University

Imelda Roberts
Metropolitan Washington Council of Governments

John Edward Rouse
Ball State University

Peter L. Sanzen
Hudson Valley Community College

Montgomery Van Wart
California State University – San Bernardino

Vera Vogelsang-Coombs
Cleveland State University

Terri Widick
University of Kansas

Staff

EDITORIAL STAFF

Larry Loeppke, Managing Editor
Jay Oberbroeckling, Developmental Editor
Jade Benedict, Developmental Editor
Nancy Meissner, Editorial Assistant

PERMISSIONS STAFF

Lenny J. Behnke, Permissions Coordinator
Lori Church, Permissions Coordinator
Shirley Lanners, Permissions Coordinator

TECHNOLOGY STAFF

Luke David, eContent Coordinator

MARKETING STAFF

Julie Keck, Senior Marketing Manager
Mary Klein, Marketing Communications Specialist
Alice Link, Marketing Coordinator
Tracie Kammerude, Senior Marketing Assistant

PRODUCTION STAFF

Beth Kundert, Production Manager
Trish Mish, Production Assistant
Kari Voss, Lead Typesetter
Jean Smith, Typesetter
Karen Spring, Typesetter
Sandy Wille, Typesetter
Tara McDermott, Designer
Maggie Lytle, Cover Graphics

Preface

In publishing ANNUAL EDITIONS we recognize the enormous role played by the magazines, newspapers, and journals of the public press in providing current, first-rate educational information in a broad spectrum of interest areas. Many of these articles are appropriate for students, researchers, and professionals seeking accurate, current material to help bridge the gap between principles and theories and the real world. These articles, however, become more useful for study when those of lasting value are carefully collected, organized, indexed, and reproduced in a low-cost format, which provides easy and permanent access when the material is needed. That is the role played by ANNUAL EDITIONS.

Public administration continues to be an exciting and dynamic field that offers a variety of stimulating challenges to public sector professionals both in the United States and abroad. Special emphasis has been placed on the problems of the public sector responses to emergencies such as hurricanes Katrina and Rita and the changes brought about by agency consolidations and privatization and the contracting out of public services. In the area of public policy, articles are provided that illustrate how public administrators have to deal with tough issues such as immigration, health care, and welfare reform.

September 11, 2001 was a "watershed" for the United States in general and for our public service in particular. In 2006, the public service is still being called upon to deal in an environment of uncertainty created by the continued potential for terrorism at home and the wars in Iraq and Afghanistan abroad.

As I was getting ready to do the research for the ninth edition of the book, I found myself focusing on articles that revolved around disaster, chaos, and uncertainly. I was drawn to articles that would help public administrators and public servants cope with the problems of our modern world. Therefore the ninth edition of this book not only contains articles about Katrina but also includes articles about other policy areas such as Iraq, immigration, and health care.

Special emphasis has been placed on finding articles that will help the reader acquire an improved understanding of the contemporary field of public policy and public administration. I am also hopeful that some of the articles will provide the readers with an understanding on how to improve their public policy and public administration skills.

With a view toward the future, the ninth edition includes almost all new articles. The articles in this edition have been selected to provide an insight into a very sophisticated and challenging field of study.

Each unit begins with an overview that provides an introduction to the articles that follow. The units and subunits in this book reflect many of the traditional subject areas of public administration, such as organizational behavior, human resources administration, public finance and budgeting, technology and information systems, public policy and international and comparative public administration. In addition, as mentioned previously, special emphasis has been placed on coping in an era of disaster and uncertainty. This is reflected in the articles on emergency planning and the governmental response to hurricanes Kartrina and Rita.

I would like to express my appreciation to those who have helped me get this book ready for publication. I would like to thank the members of the McGraw-Hill Advisory Board for their assistance. In addition, I would like to express my appreciation to colleagues, staff, public administration students, and alumni at Texas State University for their friendship and support.

I would also like to continue to recognize my friend and colleague, Rice University Professor and former Texas Lt. Governor, William P. "Bill" Hobby. *Texas Monthly* editor, Paul Burka once said that Bill Hobby has done more for public and higher education than any individual in Texas history. I agree with that assessment and I'm extremely proud to hold the William P. Hobby Professorship in Public Service at Texas State University.

Special thanks go to my wife, Marilyn, and my daughters, Emily and Amy, for assisting me and providing me with continuous moral support and encouragement. Emily is a Ph.D. student in Political Rhetoric at the University of Texas at Austin, and Amy is a Ph.D. student in Earth and Environmental Science at Colombia University in New York. I would also like to express my appreciation to Kerry Becket Dewitt, a student assistant in the Texas State University Department of Continuing Education for providing copying and logistical support.

This is the ninth edition of *Annual Editions: Public Policy and Administration,* and we would like to know what you think of it. Please take a few minutes to complete and return the article rating form at the back of the volume. Anything can be improved, and we need your help in order to publish future volumes of the highest quality.

Thank you for your continued use of the *Annual Editions: Public Policy and Administration* book.

Howard R. Balanoff

Howard R. Balanoff

Editor

Contents

UNIT 1
Introduction and Overview

Unit Overview   xvi

UNIT 2
Government and Organizational Behavior

Unit Overview   40

Part A. Productivity and Performance

The concepts in bold italics are developed in the article. For further expansion, please refer to the Topic Guide and the Index.

UNIT 3
Human Resources Administration

The concepts in bold italics are developed in the article. For further expansion, please refer to the Topic Guide and the Index.

UNIT 4
Finance and Budgeting

The concepts in bold italics are developed in the article. For further expansion, please refer to the Topic Guide and the Index.

UNIT 5
Technology and Information Systems

UNIT 6
Public Policy, Law, Community, and Environmental Planning

The concepts in bold italics are developed in the article. For further expansion, please refer to the Topic Guide and the Index.

The concepts in bold italics are developed in the article. For further expansion, please refer to the Topic Guide and the Index.

UNIT 7
International Public Policy and Administration

The concepts in bold italics are developed in the article. For further expansion, please refer to the Topic Guide and the Index.

Topic Guide

This topic guide suggests how the selections in this book relate to the subjects covered in your course. You may want to use the topics listed on these pages to search the Web more easily.

On the following pages a number of Web sites have been gathered specifically for this book. They are arranged to reflect the units of this *Annual Edition*. You can link to these sites by going to the student online support site at *http://www.mhcls.com/online/*.

ALL THE ARTICLES THAT RELATE TO EACH TOPIC ARE LISTED BELOW THE BOLD-FACED TERM.

Abu Ghraib
9. Abu Ghraib: A Case of Moral and Administrative Failure

Accountability
5. Performance Measurement: Test the Water Before You Dive In
9. Abu Ghraib: A Case of Moral and Administrative Failure

Administrative failure
8. "There Was No Plan"—A Louisiana Perspective
9. Abu Ghraib: A Case of Moral and Administrative Failure

Affordable housing
33. Getting to Yes

Auditing
18. Enron/Andersen: Crisis in U.S. Accounting and Lessons for Government

Balanced scorecard
5. Performance Measurement: Test the Water Before You Dive In

Budgets
19. Huge Rise Looms for Health Care in Local Budgets

Campaign finance web sites
11. Follow the Money

Campaign financing
11. Follow the Money

Certified Public Manager (CPM) program
14. The History of the Certified Public Manager

China
34. Urban Planning in China: Continuity and Change

Chinese planning
34. Urban Planning in China: Continuity and Change

Classical pragmatism
4. The Community of Inquiry: Classical Pragmatism and Public Administration

Community Communication Network
35. The Community Communication Network: New Technology for Public Engagement

Community of inquiry
4. The Community of Inquiry: Classical Pragmatism and Public Administration

Core ethical values
2. The State of Social Equity in American Public Administration
9. Abu Ghraib: A Case of Moral and Administrative Failure
10. Twelve Obstacles to Ethical Decision Making: Rationalizations

Crisis management
16. Governance and Risk Management: Challenges and Public Productivity

Cultural capitol
12. Leadership in Your Midst: Tapping the Hidden Strengths of Minority Executives

Digital document management
23. Find It Fast

Diversity
12. Leadership in Your Midst: Tapping the Hidden Strengths of Minority Executives

Economic development
32. Closing of Mine on Tribal Lands Fuels Dispute over Air, Water and Jobs

Electronic health records
24. Moving Medicine Forward

Emergency planning
8. "There Was No Plan"—A Louisiana Perspective

Employee discipline
13. Organization Culture as an Explanation for Employee Discipline Practices

Enron/Anderson scandal
18. Enron/Andersen: Crisis in U.S. Accounting and Lessons for Government

Environmental protection
32. Closing of Mine on Tribal Lands Fuels Dispute over Air, Water and Jobs

Ethical rationalizations
10. Twelve Obstacles to Ethical Decision Making: Rationalizations

Evidence based management
6. Evidence-Based Management

E-Waste
22. E-Waste Epidemic

Internet References

The following Internet sites have been carefully researched and selected to support the articles found in this reader. The easiest way to access these selected sites is to go to our student online support site at *http://www.mhcls.com/online/*.

AE: Public Policy and Administration

The following sites were available at the time of publication. Visit our Web site—we update our student online support site regularly to reflect any changes.

General Sources

Council for Excellence in Government
http://www.excelgov.org
The Council for Excellence in Government works to improve the performance of government at all levels as well as to better government's place in the lives and esteem of citizens.

ICMA: International City/County Management Association
http://www.iclei.org/index.php?id=636
The list of Web sites offered here by ICMA may be of interest to local public administrators. Included subjects are Community and Economic Development, Personnel and Human Resources, Public Safety, and Public Works.

Library of Congress
http://www.loc.gov
The nation's oldest federal cultural institution, the Library of Congress serves as the research arm of Congress. It is also the largest library in the world, with more than 126 million items on approximately 530 miles of bookshelves.

National Academy of Public Administration
http://www.napawash.org
Public policy and administration links at this site include Homeland Security, Government, Public Policy and Analysis, and Public Administration.

National Certified Public Manager Consortium
http://www.cpmconsortium.org
This consortium is the national organization responsible for setting standards and accrediting public sector management training programs across the United States.

New Federalism Home Page
http://newfederalism.urban.org
This site, dedicated to exploring the return of power to the individual states, discusses the federal budget, the Welfare Reform Bill, and the results of federal devolution.

State and Local Government on the Net
http://www.statelocalgov.net/index.cfm
Search individual states for elected officials, state government jobs, state organizations, and other links to local government sites.

UNIT 1: Introduction and Overview

American Society for Public Administration (ASPA)
http://www.aspanet.org
The ASPA is the focal point for intellectual and professional interaction, and its Web site is a rich source of information.

Public Administration Review (PAR)
http://www.blackwellpublishing.com/journal.asp?ref=0033-3352&site=1
The PAR, a major journal for those interested in public sector management, presents this Web page that contains book reviews, archives, a search mechanism, and related links.

UNIT 2: Government and Organizational Behavior

Government Accounting Standards Board (GASB)
http://www.gasb.org
The mission of the GASB is to establish and improve standards of state and local governmental accounting and financial reporting that will result in useful information for users of financial reports and also guide and educate the public, including issuers and auditors.

National Academy of Public Administration (NAPA)
http://www.napawash.org
NAPA is an independent, nonprofit organization chartered by Congress that responds to specific requests from public agencies and nongovernmental organizations.

Partnership for Public Service (PPS)
http://www.ourpublicservice.org
The PPS is a nonpartisan organization dedicated to revitalizing public service. It seeks to restore public confidence in and prestige of the federal civil service through an aggressive campaign of public-private partnerships as well as focused research and educational efforts.

Public Sector Continuous Improvement Site
http://curiouscat.com/psci/index.html
John Hunter's site, which aims to help public sector employees improve their organizations, includes online resources, lists of organizations, and important links, plus an online guide, a reading list, and a search capability.

Stateline.org
http://www.stateline.org
Stateline.org was founded to help journalists, policy makers, and engaged citizens become better informed about innovative policies.

UNIT 3: Human Resources Administration

Sexual Harassment in the Workplace: A Primer
http://www.uakron.edu/lawrev/robert1.html
This article is a very complete discussion of the subject, including statistics, tables, federal laws, case studies, employer liability, and guidelines for a sexual harassment policy.

Skill-Based Pay
http://www.bizcenter.com/skillpay.htm
The material at this site has been reproduced from the book, *Designing Skill-Based Pay,* by Donald F. Barkman.

U.S. Department of Labor
http://www.dol.gov/index.htm
This document, "Working Together for Public Service," is the report of the Secretary of Labor's Task Force on Excellence in State and Local Government through Labor-Management Cooperation.

Zigon Performance Group
http://www.zigonperf.com
This commercial company specializes in performance appraisal, management, and measurement systems for teams and hard-to-measure employees. The Web site offers measurement resources, performance measurement examples, publications, and how-to workshops.

UNIT 4: Finance and Budgeting

FirstGov
http://www.firstgov.gov

The official U.S. gateway to all government information, FirstGov.gov is the catalyst for a growing electronic government.

The U.S. Chief Financial Officers Council
http://www.cfoc.gov

CFOC is the organization of the CFOs and Deputy CFOs of the largest federal agencies and senior officials of the Office of Management and Budget and the Department of the Treasury who work collaboratively to improve financial management in the U.S. government. Events, links, documents, and initiatives can be found here.

UNIT 5: Technology and Information Systems

Activity-Based Costing (ABC)
http://www.esc-brest.fr/cg/cgkiosk3.htm

Created in France, this site leads to everything you might want to know about activity-based costing.

American Capital Strategies
http://www.americancapital.com/news/press_releases/pr/pr19961024.html

Malon Wilkus's article "ESOP Privatization," which is the historic account of the federal government's Office of Personnel Management's privatization of its Office of Federal Investigations, makes fascinating reading. It is the first privatization in the United States that transferred majority ownership to its employees through the use of an ESOP.

Brookings Institution
http://www.brook.edu

The Brookings Institution, a private, independent, nonprofit research organization, seeks to improve the performance of American institutions, the effectiveness of government programs, and the quality of U.S. public policies. Through its Web site, explore the Centers on Social and Economic Dynamics and on Urban and Metropolitan Policy.

Putting Technology to Work for America's Future
http://sunsite.unc.edu/darlene/tech/report3.html

Here is an excellent paper on the technology policy issued on February 22, 1998, by the Clinton administration, entitled "Technology for America's Economic Growth."

Reason Foundation
http://www.reason.org/policystudiesbysubject.shtml

The Reason Public Policy Institute's Privatization Center has been at the center of the debate on streamlining government. Their Web site is filled with interesting information.

UNIT 6: Public Policy, Law, Community, and Environmental Planning

Capitol Reports: Environmental News Link
http://www.caprep.com

This excellent source of environmental news links to federal and state agencies, courts, Congress, state legislatures, and federal regulations.

Innovation Groups (IG)
http://www.ig.org

IG is a network of city, town, and county government leaders that provides support for pioneering new approaches to managing cities. The group provides networking, research, and training opportunities to local government administrators.

National Association of Counties
http://www.naco.org/counties/index.cfm

The National Association of Counties offers this entry into county government sites by state.

National League of Cities
http://www.nlc.org

The NLC Web site leads to Legislative Priorities, Local Government Access, Policy Process, News and Events, Other Resources, and a search capability.

UNIT 7: International Public Policy and Administration

Division for Public Administration and Development Management
http://www.unpan.org/dpepa.asp

This United Nations site is a source for international information on management innovation and development, public economics, public policy, and public and private partnerships.

European Group of Public Administration (EGPA)
http://www.iiasiisa.be/egpa/agacc.htm

EGPA's page leads to study groups on personnel policies, productivity and quality in the public sector, and the development of contracting in the public sector.

Governments on the WWW
http://www.gksoft.com/govt/en/

This site offers access links to government Web sites throughout the world.

Institute of Public Administration of Canada (IPAC)
http://www.ipaciapc.ca

IPAC is a national bilingual (English/French) nonprofit organization that is concerned with the theory and practice of public management.

Latin American Center for Development Administration (CLAD)
http://www.clad.org.ve/siare/index.htm

CLAD hosts an online database containing thousands of public administration documents and resources. Although the site is written in Spanish, many of the resources contained within the database are in English.

Section on International and Comparative Administration (SICA)
http://www.uncc.edu/stwalker/sica/

SICA, a division of ASPA, specifically aims to facilitate professional networking globally through a series of programs.

UNPAN
http://www.unpan.org

The mission of UNPAN is to promote the sharing of knowledge, experiences, and best practices throughout the world in sound public policies, effective public administration, and efficient civil services through capacity-building and cooperation among member states, with emphasis on south-south cooperation and UNPAN's commitment to integrity and excellence.

We highly recommend that you review our Web site for expanded information and our other product lines. We are continually updating and adding links to our Web site in order to offer you the most usable and useful information that will support and expand the value of your Annual Editions. You can reach us at: *http://www.mhcls.com/annualeditions/*.

UNIT 1
Introduction and Overview

Unit Selections

1. **What's New About the New Public Management?: Administrative Change in the Human Services**, Stephen Page
2. **The State of Social Equity in American Public Administration**, H. George Frederickson
3. **A New Approach to Regulatory Reform**, Murray Weidenbaum
4. **The Community of Inquiry: Classical Pragmatism and Public Administration**, Patricia M. Shields

Key Points to Consider

- Define and discuss the concept of the New Public Management. How is this concept reflected in the human services area?

- What is "social equity?" What is the "social equity gap?" Why are these important concepts for public administrators to understand?

- What did you learn about the history of regulatory reform? What are some recommendations for improving the regulatory environment?

- Define and discuss the following terms: (a) classical pragmatism, (b) community of inquiry, (c) participatory democracy.

Student Web Site

www.mhcls.com/online

Internet References

Further information regarding these Web sites may be found in this book's preface or online.

American Society for Public Administration (ASPA)
http://www.aspanet.org

***Public Administration Review* (PAR)**
http://www.blackwellpublishing.com/journal.asp?ref=0033-3352&site=1

The initial articles are provided as an introduction and a brief overview to some of the major movements in public administration. They are designed to give the reader an understanding of some of the major concepts and movements that public administrators will experience during their careers in public service.

As seen in the first article, one of the important areas of public administration is the emergence of the New Public Management Movement. Among other areas, the New Public Management Movement has been reflected in recent innovations in human services.

The next article discusses how Social Equity has become one of the key areas in American public administration. The evolution of social equity in the United States illustrates a widening social equity gap in U.S. public administration.

The process of regulatory reform in the United States is explored in the following article. The escalation of the number and types of government regulations, past and recent government reform efforts, and specific recommendations that are necessary for future regulatory reform are reviewed.

The concepts of classical pragmatism, the concept of a community of inquiry, and the recognition of participatory democracy are all explored in the article *The Community of Inquiry: Classical Pragmatism and Public Administration.* This article defines and discusses how all of these concepts relate to modern public administration theory and practice.

What's New About the New Public Management? Administrative Change in the Human Services

Interpretations of the emergence of the New Public Management are split. The champions of the movement present it as a new administrative paradigm that departs sharply from past thinking and practice, whereas skeptics argue it has evolved incrementally from past administrative traditions. To assess these views, this article examines recent administrative innovations in the human services that broadly reflect the New Public Management. The findings suggest that these innovations have built incrementally on past reforms in the human services field, supporting the skeptics' claim that the New Public Management represents an evolution and renewal of historical trends in public administration.

STEPHEN PAGE
University of Washington

The field of public administration has been rife with debate about the New Public Management over the past decade. Interpretations of its origins and evolution, in particular, have become polarized. Champions of the New Public Management argue that pressing demands for change have overridden the historical traditions of public administration, resulting in a global revolution favoring postbureaucratic forms of government (e.g., Barzelay 1992; Caiden 1991; Kettl 2000; Osborne and Plastrik 1997). Skeptics, however, link the principles of the New Public Management directly to long-standing administrative traditions and contend that recent changes in government are more incremental and historically contingent than discontinuous and universal (Dobel 2001; Lynn 1998, 2001; Wolf 1997). Has a new generation of reforms replaced earlier traditions with a universal postbureaucratic paradigm?

This article addresses this question by analyzing the process and content of recent administrative reforms in the human services that broadly reflect the principles of New Public Management. By scrutinizing the historical roots of these reforms and comparing them to the New Public Management, the article seeks to answer two specific questions:

1. Do today's human services reforms represent discontinuous or incremental developments in the human services field?
2. Which aspects of the reforms draw explicitly on the principles of New Public Management?

The investigation proceeds in six parts. The first part lays out in detail the debate between the champions and skeptics of the New Public Management. The second part describes recent human services reforms and the rationale for comparing them with the New Public Management. The third part outlines the methodology of the study. The fourth part traces the origins and evolution of human services reforms. The fifth part interprets this evolution by characterizing the process and content of administrative change in the human services field, and the conclusion discusses the implications for the debate about the New Public Management.

New Public Management: A Universal New Paradigm?

Since the 1980s, administrative reforms have emerged to considerable fanfare under the banner of "New Public Management" in New Zealand, the United Kingdom, and elsewhere and "reinventing government" in the United States (Kettl 2000). Although the specifics vary from country to country, all the initiatives seek to improve governmental performance by emphasizing customer service, decentralization, market mechanisms, cross-functional collaboration, and accountability for results (Barzelay 1992; Caiden 1991; Osborne and Plastrik 1997; Peters 1996).

The quest to improve performance is most pronounced in the performance contracts of cabinet ministers in New Zealand and the exposure of public programs to market competition in the United Kingdom (Kettl 2000). It also appears in the U.S. Government Performance and Results Act and public agencies' efforts to "do more with less." Either through clear incentives to "make the managers manage," or by removing impediments to innovation so as to "let the managers manage," governments have given administrators discretion to improve the performance of their agencies while requiring them to measure the outcomes they produce (Behn 2001; Kettl 2000).

The champions of the New Public Management see this emphasis on performance as a sharp break with past approaches to administration. Earlier eras, they argue, were conducive to Max Weber's (1947) ideal of centralized, bureaucratic monopolies, in which laws and regulations dictated standardized services and accountability entailed compliance with procedures (Barzelay 1992; Osborne and Plastrik 1997). In recent decades, major changes in politics, economics, society, and government itself have challenged those administrative traditions: Voters and elected officials now demand effective programs that do not consume excessive tax revenues; globalization requires adaptive economies supported by nimble public agencies; and diverse citizenries seek responsive services—all from governments facing regulatory burdens and cross-cutting political pressures (Cullen and Cushman 2000; Kettl 2000; Peters 1996).

In light of these new demands, many proponents of the New Public Management are "convinced that the appearance of ... entrepreneurial organizations in the late twentieth century is no accident. We believe that it represents an inevitable historical shift from one paradigm to another" (Osborne and Plastrik 1997, 15). This sense of inevitability, in turn, has led the champions to argue that governments around the world have converged on the principles of the New Public Management because they are useful in virtually any political setting, geographic region, or policy area (Caiden 1991; Osborne and Plastrik 1997).

This view of the New Public Management as a universal new paradigm is consistent with a discontinuous understanding of change in management strategies and problem-solving approaches. Discontinuous change occurs when a crisis prompts reformers to abandon obsolete concepts and practices in favor of new ones that solve pressing problems more effectively (Gersick 1991; Kuhn 1970; Miller and Friesen 1980). Some scholars of public administration refer to discontinuous change as reform by the "roots" (e.g., Lindblom 1959). The alternative to discontinuous change is incremental or "branching" reform, which occurs when reformers make successive comparisons among a limited array of historically contingent options (Lakatos 1970; Lindblom 1959; Miller and Friesen 1980; Popper 1970).

In keeping with an incremental understanding of change, skeptics of the New Public Management see recent reforms as building directly on historical traditions of public administration. Laurence Lynn, for example, argues that the New Public Management is neither a distinct paradigm nor particularly new. He contends that the label "New Public Management" encompasses too many varied concepts and practices to support the champions' claims of global convergence (Lynn 1998). He reviews the work of seminal scholars of public administration from the early and middle twentieth century to show that a number of their ideas—including managerial discretion, cross-functional collaboration, and policy-making roles for civil servants and citizens—are now central to the New Public Management (Lynn 2001).

Even the emphasis on performance that appears to distinguish the New Public Management from past administrative traditions is nothing new. Characteristics that foster effective governmental performance—adaptability, efforts to build capacity and resources, customer service, and a sense of mission—appear in federal organizations during different eras of the twentieth century and were common before 1950 (Wolf 1993, 1997).[1] Although these characteristics are consistent with the New Public Management, none are unique to the present era, suggesting that the U.S. government has long featured key principles of the New Public Management (Wolf 1997).

To understand the wide variety of New Public Management practices, as well as the persistence of administrative principles across historical eras, Patrick Dobel (2001) calls attention to the rich tradition of discourse in the field of public administration. Because different sets of ideas in that tradition jockey for influence and cross-fertilize one another, Dobel sees the New Public Management not as a wholly new paradigm, but as one of many schools of thought within a lengthy, rancorous debate. Paul Light's study of the "tides" of reform supports this view by showing that trends in administration ebb, flow, and intersect over time. Different trends accumulate over time, so none ever dominates or leaves an indelible imprint, but trends may combine with one another in distinct ways during particular eras (Light 1997).

In combination, the skeptics suggest that the recent ferment in public administration is less a discontinuous departure from past traditions than an incremental evolution of thinking and practice that varies across governments and policy areas. For them, the principles of the New Public Management are simply part of the diverse history of public administration.

To break the impasse between the champions and the skeptics, this article examines the evolution of administrative reforms in the human services field. In recent years, human services agencies have emphasized customer service, decentralization, cross-functional collaboration, and accountability for results, all of which are core principles of the New Public Management. Hence, the reforms offer a rich basis for assessing the champions' and skeptics' views of the origins of the New Public Management and the process of administrative change.

New Public Management in the Human Services

Parallel to the rise of the New Public Management, a new wave of human services reforms has emerged in states and communities in the United States over the past two decades (Kagan 1993; Waldfogel 1997). These initiatives seek to improve human services performance by streamlining the implementation of related programs (Schorr 1997). Some states and communities have concentrated on restructuring child welfare, children's mental health, and juvenile justice programs; others, early childhood, public health, and children's mental health programs; and still others, welfare-to-work and employment training programs (Kahn and Kamerman 1992; Knitzer 1997).

Although the programmatic focus of the reforms varies from site to site, the administrative thrust is similar. Consistent with the New Public Management, the innovating states grant increased discretion to local actors in exchange for performance agreements to track and improve outcomes (Page 2003). The discretionary aspect of the reforms encourages the local coordination of program design and delivery across multiple human

Table 1 Selected Statewide Human Services Reforms, 1987–Present

State	Year started	Vision	Target programs
Georgia	1991	Children are healthy, ready to start school, and perform well in school. Families are stable and self-sufficient.	Various programs for children and families
Iowa	1987	Child welfare services are family centered, preventive, and community based. Children are healthy and ready to succeed in school. Communities are safe and supportive. Families and child care settings are secure and nurturing.	Child welfare, children's mental health, juvenile justice, early childhood, public health
Maryland	1989	Children and families thrive in their homes and communities.	Various
Missouri	1989	Children have strong families and communities in which parents are working. Children succeed in school and grow up healthy, safe, and prepared to be productive adults.	Schools, health care, behavioral health, and other services in disadvantaged neighborhoods
Minnesota	1993	Children are healthy. Children enter school ready to learn. Families are healthy and stable. Children excel at academics. Children's mental health services are flexible, family centered, preventive, and coordinated.	Schools, public health, Community Action, mental health, corrections
North Carolina	1993	Every child enters school healthy and ready to succeed.	Public health, mental health, early childhood
Ohio	1992	Expectant parents, infants, and toddlers thrive. Children are ready for school. Children and youth succeed in school. Youth are healthy. Youth transition successfully to adulthood.	Various programs for children and families
Oregon	1991	Citizens and professionals work together to improve the lives of children and families. Students stay in school and succeed. Adults are employed and increase their earnings. Individuals and families live successfully in their communities.	Public health, welfare-to-work, early childhood, behavioral health, services for the elderly and disabled
Vermont	1990	Children, families, and individuals thrive.	Various programs for children and families
Washington	1989	Risky behaviors related to youth violence decrease.	Various programs for children and families

services organizations (Waldfogel 1997), and the performance agreements promote systemwide accountability for community-level outcomes (Kagan et al. 1995). More specific descriptions of today's reforms suggest that they include at least four discrete components (Morrill 1996b; Page 2000):

- At the front line, the reforms promote *family-friendly services*, in which providers work with families as partners to address the full range of challenges they face.

- To support the collaboratives' efforts, states offer flexible funding and regulatory relief.

- Innovating states have authorized *local governance collaboratives* to design and manage the new family-friendly services. Most collaboratives include representatives from public and nongovernmental agencies, civic and neighborhood leaders, and service recipients.

- In exchange for this increase in discretion, the states hold each collaborative *accountable for achieving broad outcomes* for children and families, such as family self-sufficiency, family health, children's success in school, and family and community safety. The states measure

local progress toward these outcomes by tracking social indicators in each community.

Since the late 1980s, these components have emerged piecemeal in Alaska, California, Florida, Georgia, Illinois, Iowa, Maryland, Michigan, Minnesota, Missouri, North Carolina, Ohio, Oregon, Texas, Vermont, Washington, West Virginia, and other states (Cauthen, Knitzer, and Ripple 2000; Center for the Study of Social Policy 2001). Table 1 outlines the aims of the reforms in 10 states whose initiatives are especially ambitious and sweeping. The Vision column shows how these initiatives share an emphasis on improving outcomes for clients; the Target Programs column illustrates how the programmatic focus of the reforms varies from state to state.

The current wave of human services reform is especially noteworthy because leading states have aligned the components in mutually reinforcing ways (Page 2003). Georgia, Maryland, and Missouri, for example, have created performance agreements requiring local collaboratives to develop regular strategic plans that identify the social indicators they will improve, specific timelines and targets for improvement, family-friendly services that will enable them to achieve their targets, and the funds and other resources required for implementation (DeLapp 2002; Georgia Family Connection Partnership 2003; Tsakalas

2002). As they implement their plans, the collaboratives must account for their performance in meeting their indicator targets, identify strategies for future improvements, and propose changes in targets, services, or funding necessary to implement their new strategies. A team of state officials reviews the collaboratives' strategic plans and self-assessments and allocates rewards or sanctions based on each collaborative's performance (DeLapp 2002; Watson 2000).

Because these reforms reflect core principles of the New Public Management, examining their origins and evolution can illuminate key influences on administrative thinking, as well as changes and continuities in practice. Of course, generalizing from a longitudinal case study of human services reforms to the overall field of public administration is risky, but examining multiple cases risks glossing over subtle yet important distinctions in administrative thinking and practice that have evolved over time. This study, therefore, can serve as an initial reference point for comparing the champions' and the skeptics' views, and future research can examine administrative changes in other policy areas. The field of human services is especially well suited to this purpose: The reforms sketched here parallel the New Public Management in three central ways.

First, the inherited system of human services administration that the reforms seek to alter embodies the administrative traditions that the champions of the New Public Management consider obsolete. Human services agencies tend to operate as specialized, hierarchical monopolies—distinguishing characteristics of Weberian administration (Weber 1947)—with specific rules, standard operating procedures, and procedural reporting requirements (Brodkin 1997; Lipsky 1980; Sandfort 2000; Wilson 1989). Agency line staff, for example, tend to receive training specific to their own subdiscipline of human services (Yessian 1995). Most programs operate through distinct functional units and hierarchical command, and most public human services agencies originated as monopolies—the sole recipients of public funds appropriated to serve particular client populations (Gardner 1994). Although the hierarchical and monopolistic nature of this system has eroded since federal social spending exploded during the 1960s, rigidity and specialization persist (Thomas 1994; Schorr 1997): Many human services agencies continue to define their missions narrowly around specific human needs (Gardner 1994; Kusserow 1991; Yessian 1995).

Second, like the broader inherited system of public administration, changing conditions have created new performance challenges for human services agencies. Voters and elected officials of both major political parties now expect most recipients of human services to work or move toward self-sufficiency in exchange for receiving public assistance (Blendon et al. 1995). The problems associated with disadvantaged families have become more concentrated and isolated in specific communities in recent decades, increasing the need to coordinate the delivery of separate programs that address closely related human needs (Halpern 1995; Wilson 1996). At the same time, the number of public human services programs has grown, complicating cross-program coordination and increasing the number of line staff, service providers, and clients with vested interests in the system's operations (Thomas 1994). In 1994, for example, the

Los Angeles public schools offered 238 separate programs for students defined as "at risk" in one way or another. Each program had its own separate eligibility requirements, application forms, and intake processes; many used different service providers (Gardner 1994, 4).

Third, many human services reformers join the champions of the New Public Management in calling for a new paradigm to improve performance. State officials in Vermont, for example, seek a "conceptual shift ... from program accountability ... to outcomes responsibility" (Hogan and Murphey 2002). Other reformers want to change the aim of human services—from correcting client problems to preventing their emergence in the first place—and to shift frontline work from individual professionals to teams of professionals, community members, and parents (Schorr 1997).[2]

These parallels permit the current wave of human services reforms to serve as a testing ground for competing views of the New Public Management. If the reforms draw directly on the principles of the New Public Management and depart starkly from past practices in the human services field, the champions' interpretation of universal, discontinuous change will gain support. If the reforms instead draw heavily on long-standing practices in the human services and have emerged through an incremental, historically contingent process of change, the skeptics' position will gain support.

Research Methods

To conduct this comparison, the article combines primary and secondary data to develop an intellectual history of recent human services reforms. The primary sources included more than 160 semistructured interviews conducted since 1995 with actors involved in the reforms, as well as documents from participating states, private foundations, and think tanks. The secondary data came from a review of existing research on past and current human services reforms.

The primary research examined the emergence and growth of today's reforms—specifically, the following elements:

- Their origins and focus—Where did the ideas come from? What services, populations, and agencies are included? How and why did they get involved? What are their aims?
- Their institutional architecture—How much authority over programming and funding have the states delegated to the local collaboratives? How much guidance and oversight do the states provide? How have these elements changed over time?
- The processes used to build and sustain this architecture—Which participants and components of the reform agenda emerged first? When, how, and why did others join them?

Insights into the development of the current wave of reforms came from interviews with staff and consultants to philanthropic foundations and applied research organizations that offer funding and technical assistance to help states and communities foster collaboration for children and families.

These organizations included the Annie E. Casey Foundation, the Center for the Study of Social Policy, the National Governors' Association, the Finance Project, the Institute for Educational Leadership, the National Civic League's Program for Community Problem Solving, and the National Center for Service Integration, among others. Many of them have published comparative studies or reports on their efforts to assist states and communities that also served as valuable primary sources.[3] These national informants and documents provided a synthetic, cross-site view of the origins and evolution of the reforms.

A detailed understanding of specific instances of reform came from interviews with informants and analyses of documents from the 10 states listed in table 1, which a national survey identified as pursuing especially ambitious reforms (Knitzer and Page 1996).[4] Officials in those 10 states set out to transform and align their systems of service delivery, governance, funding, and accountability to improve the lives of children and families. Examining their efforts revealed emerging concepts and practices in the field with the potential to diffuse to additional states.

Specific information on the origins and focus, institutional architecture, and developmental processes of the reforms in each of the 10 states came from interviews with the following informants:

- The governor's policy advisor on issues related to children and families

- Commissioners, assistant commissioners, or collaborative liaisons in public agencies such as social services, education, public health, and, in some cases, economic development

- The staff of local collaboratives in three to five communities

- Participants from key collaborating agencies in those same communities

Table 2   Origins and Evolution of Four Reform Components, 1900–2000

Family-friendly service delivery	Flexible funding	Local governance	Accountability for outcomes
1900s: Settlement houses pioneer comprehensive, neighborhood-based services.	**1900s:** Charitable societies coordinate fund-raising and grant allocation across local charities.	**1900–20:** A Few local "social centers" bring providers and community members together to plan and deliver education and health services.	**1900s:** Progressive movement boosts the policy analysis role of the social sciences.
1960s: War on Poverty creates Head Start and comprehensive, neighborhood-based service centers.	**1960s:** War on Poverty and Model Cities delegate modest amounts of program funds to local organizations.	**1960s:** War on Poverty delegates program decisions to neighborhood groups. Model Cities creates broad-based local planning councils.	**1930s:** Evaluation research emerges to assess some New Deal social programs.
1970s: HEW service-integration projects pilot colocated services.	**1970s:** Revenue sharing and block grants offer general-purpose funds to states. HEW service-integration projects pilot flexible use of program-specific funds.	**1970s:** HEW service-integration projects and selected states pilot interagency teams and community planning councils.	**1960s–70s:** War on Poverty, Great Society, and Federal Program Planning and Budgeting System make broad use of quantitative, controlled evaluation to isolate the impact of individual social programs. Social indicators movement emerges to track broad human outcomes.
1980s–90s: Family support movement encourages broad use of family-friendly case work. Subdisciplines build their own service continuums. Local sites colocate services.	**1980s–90s:** States and local collaboratives refinance services and reallocate funds across program and agency lines. Some states pass flexible pools of funds to local collaboratives.	**1980s–90s:** States grant local collaboratives authority to assess local service needs, design comprehensive plans to address them, and (in some cases) allocate funds to implement the plans.	**1990s:** Evaluation of individual programs supplemented by tracking broad social indicators in states and communities. Some states hold local collaboratives accountable for improving indicators in exchange for discretion in programming.

Data to supplement these interviews came from a review of proposals, plans, evaluations, and other reports from the states, their consultants, and the foundations and research organizations supporting their efforts.[5]

Content analyses of these interviews and documents elicited the four components of the current reforms as well as the processes by which they developed. A review of existing research on past human services reforms (e.g., Gans and Horton 1975; Gilbert and Specht 1977; Halpern 1995; Kagan 1993; Kusserow 1991; Lynn 1980; Marris and Rein 1973; Mittenthal 1976; Yessian 1995) illuminated the origins and evolution of each component.

The Origins and Evolution of Today's Human Services Reforms

The research uncovered both changes and continuities in human services administration. Table 2 identifies precursors of each component of today's reforms from the past century; the sections that follow summarize their refinement during the past two decades and trace their historical evolution.

Family-Friendly Service Delivery

Recent efforts to promote family-friendly services stem from the family support movement, which took shape among progressive human services practitioners in the 1970s. The movement's premise is that treating severe client problems after they surface is less humane and more expensive than crafting effective front-end services that prevent the emergence of problems in the first place. The principles of family support suggest that services are most effective when they are comprehensive, community driven, responsive, easy to access, and preventive and when providers trust and respect clients and treat individuals as part of their families and families as part of their communities (Schorr 1988). The movement gained momentum in 1981, when a national practitioners' forum founded the Family Resource Coalition, an intermediary organization that nurtures and assists family support programs around the country (Kagan et al. 1987).

To disseminate the principles of family support across the different subfields of human services, initiatives emerged during the mid-1980s to help providers prevent severe family problems. The federal Child and Adolescent Service System Program and the Robert Wood Johnson Foundation offered grants and technical assistance to help states and counties coordinate services for children with severe emotional disturbances (Stroul and Friedman 1986). Part H of the federal Individuals with Disabilities Education Act required states to provide comprehensive services to families who have infants and toddlers with disabilities (Agranoff 1991). The Edna McConnell Clark Foundation and later the 1993 federal Family Preservation and Support Act funded states to provide preventive child welfare services to help troubled families stay together (Schorr 1997; Stevenson 1998). All of these initiatives sought to build a continuum of care for groups of children and families that are difficult and costly to serve (Knitzer 1997, 7–8).

As these national initiatives took root, interagency relationships emerged in communities across the country. Case conferences brought providers from different agencies serving the same families together to review the families' situations, divide service delivery and reporting tasks, and coordinate activities (Knitzer 1996; Overdorff 2000). To provide "wraparound" services for children with emotional or behavioral disorders, multiple agencies worked jointly with families to design individualized service plans (Knitzer 1997; Springer, Sharp, and Foy 2000).

New "colocation" efforts and comprehensive programs, meanwhile, offered multiple services to children and families at schools, child care centers, and public housing developments. Models emerged during the 1980s in cities such as San Diego,

Baltimore, and St. Louis (Melaville and Blank 1993). By the mid-1990s, states such as California, Florida, Kentucky, Missouri, and New Jersey had funded programs offering health, behavioral counseling, and other services linked to schools (Dryfoos 1994). During the 1990s, an increasing number of states began to fund comprehensive early childhood programs linking health, nutrition, and family support services to the provision of child development assistance (Blank, Schulman, and Ewen 1999; Cauthen, Knitzer, and Ripple 2000).

As table 2 indicates, all of these frontline changes recall previous innovations in human services delivery. The settlement houses of the early twentieth century offered comprehensive, family-friendly services in urban neighborhoods (Halpern 1995). During the 1960s, War on Poverty programs such as Head Start, Community Action, and neighborhood service centers offered comprehensive, community-based assistance to families (Marris and Rein 1973). Other federal programs of that era, such as community mental health centers and special education grants, encouraged client and family participation in service delivery (Kagan 1993). Finally, service-integration pilot projects launched by the federal Department of Health, Education, and Welfare (HEW) during the 1970s promoted the colocation of services (Kusserow 1991; Yessian 1995).

Flexible Funding

As the experiments with family-friendly services took shape, states and local governments sought ways to finance them. However, the majority of federal and state human services programs were designed to remediate severe problems facing children and families rather than provide family-friendly assistance to prevent such problems from arising (Gardner 1994; Schorr 1997). Innovating states and communities, therefore, had difficulty using existing program funds to support the new family-friendly services (Friedman 2000).

In response, creative financing strategies emerged during the late 1980s that used flexible state policies or federal Medicaid or child welfare waivers. Oregon and Vermont delegated responsibility for allocating funds for preventive services for young children and families to local collaboratives (Cutler, Tan, and Downs 1995). Missouri used a consolidated, cross-agency budget to fund school-linked services and other family-friendly interventions (O'Brien 1997; Rozansky 1998). Iowa and Maryland pooled funds for child welfare, mental health, juvenile justice, and related programs and delegated them to local collaboratives, which they charged with designing services and allocating funds based on the needs of local families. These two states also granted their local collaboratives a share of any savings they achieved by assisting severely troubled families without resorting to expensive crisis services such as foster care (O'Brien 1997; Waldfogel 1997).

Table 2 shows how these fiscal innovations built on earlier precedents. During the late nineteenth and early twentieth centuries, before government began to provide substantial support for human services, charitable organization societies coordinated the funds raised and services delivered by myriad local charities (Lynn 1980). Decades later, the War on Poverty and

Model Cities provided modest amounts of flexible funding to neighborhood organizations and local planning commissions, respectively (Gans and Horton 1975; Gilbert and Specht 1977; Marris and Rein 1973). During the early 1970s, federal policy makers' concerns about the proliferation of narrow categories of similar programs led to attempts to consolidate related programs into block grants (Conlan 1988; Derthick 1975; Kagan 1993). Some of these initiatives, such as the Comprehensive Employment and Training Act and the Community Development Block Grant, featured explicit provisions for local planning (Kagan 1993). In the same spirit, revenue-sharing programs implemented under President Nixon offered grants to the states with "no strings attached" (Conlan 1988, 65; see also Derthick 1975). The HEW service-integration projects of that era gave selected states and local governments flexibility to use federal funds to integrate the administration and delivery of services across agency and program lines (Agranoff 1991; Kagan 1993; Kusserow 1991). Several states also delegated programming and funding decisions to regional authorities during the 1970s (Lynn 1980). In the late 1970s and early 1980s, the movement toward more flexible federal funding gained even more momentum as Congress passed a number of block grants through to the states (Conlan 1988).

Local Governance

To ensure that family-friendly services and flexible funds responded effectively to diverse community conditions and priorities, many of the states at the fore of the current wave of human services reforms sponsored local governance collaboratives. Most of these collaboratives included a cross-section of professional service providers and public agency representatives, as well as civic leaders, community members, and clients. During the early 1990s, states such as Georgia, Maryland, Missouri, Ohio, Oregon, Vermont, and Washington authorized local collaboratives to assess community needs, develop comprehensive service plans, and marshal resources to implement their plans (Brunson 1998; Schorr et al. 1995).

In addition, a number of states created state-level interagency teams to monitor local decisions and activities and to provide assistance and examples of promising practices to build capacity. Some states also created waiver provisions permitting local collaboratives to request changes in state regulations or administrative operations that hindered implementation of their comprehensive plans (Center for the Study of Social Policy 1996; Page 2000, 2003).

Like family-friendly services and flexible funding, these experiments with local governance have historical precedents. Early in the twentieth century, Cincinnati, Rochester, and other cities attempted to build "social centers" that brought service providers and community members together to plan and deliver education and health services (Dorf and Sabel 1998, n. 468). During the 1960s, the War on Poverty and Model Cities involved citizens and community groups in planning and implementing human services programs (Gilbert and Specht 1977; Marris and Rein 1973). States such as Oregon and Minnesota established interagency teams and coordinating councils during the 1970s under the aegis of the HEW pilot projects or through state or local initiatives (Mittenthal 1976).

Accountability for Outcomes

With local collaboratives designing services and allocating resources, innovating states needed to hold them accountable for their use of public funds. At the same time, a number of reformers wanted to track client outcomes to demonstrate the need for human services and to counter public skepticism about social programs by showing their tangible benefits for children and families. In the states with the most elaborate reform initiatives, these impulses came together in performance agreements that held local collaboratives accountable for improving key social indicators.

When their initiatives first began, states such as Georgia, Missouri, and Vermont used outcomes simply to inspire and convene collaborators rather than to measure performance. They fostered broad dialogues about common aims for children and families to identify outcomes that all the participants wanted to achieve (Brunson 1998; Farrow 1998). These conversations enabled public officials to bring service recipients, business and civic leaders, and other lay citizens into joint discussions about what human services agencies ought to accomplish. During the early 1990s, Georgia, Missouri, and Vermont used this kind of participatory process to agree on core outcomes for children and families, as well as data indicators to measure progress toward them (Center for the Study of Social Policy 1995; Hogan 1999; Rozansky 1997a).[6] Iowa, Maryland, and Ohio later followed suit (Ayer 2003; Bell 2003; Cannon 2003).

Georgia, Maryland, Missouri, and Washington ultimately created performance agreements with their local collaboratives, in which the collaboratives target specific indicators for improvement and report regularly to the state on their progress (DeLapp 2002). Information on their efforts is preliminary but promising so far: Data from these four states (as well as Vermont) reveal consistent improvements in the well-being of children and families that correlate with the duration, focus, and intensity of family-friendly services and local collaboration (Family Policy Council 2001a, 2001b; Family and Community Trust 2003; Georgia Family Connection Evaluation Team 2001; Hogan and Murphey 2002; Hyde 2003; Tsakalas 2002).

As the right column of table 2 indicates, these accountability arrangements draw on various strands of administrative history. Some of the earliest systematic attempts to assess the effectiveness of social programs date back to evaluations of school programs in the early twentieth century (Haveman 1987). Such efforts grew during the 1930s as the expansion of federal social spending under the New Deal prompted evaluations of the new programs (Haveman 1987). The 1960s saw the emergence of the modern forebears of today's trend toward results—based accountability as federal initiatives such as the War on Poverty, the Great Society, and Program Planning and Budgeting drove the development of capacity for program evaluation (Haveman 1987; Schorr 1997). Meanwhile, the social indicators movement arose among social scientists interested in tracking human outcomes and documenting the effectiveness of social programs (e.g., Bauer 1966). As the foregoing description of today's reforms shows, program evaluation and indicator measurement remain critical tools for human services practitioners seeking to demonstrate accountability and improve program design (Schalock and Bonham 2003).

Interpreting the Current Wave of Human Services Reform

This sketch of the four components of the current wave of human services reforms indicates they evolved out of administrative traditions that date back at least a century. Drawing further on the interview data, this section analyzes whether today's reforms represent incremental or discontinuous changes in human services administration, and assesses how explicitly they draw on the principles of the New Public Management.

An Incremental Process of Change

The informants interviewed for this study indicated that the current wave of reform emerged through an experimental process of self-reflection and discovery. The changes in thinking and practice sketched previously are less the result of an application of universal, new principles of administration to human services programs than the product of a series of exchanges between two groups of human services reformers—practitioners and analysts. The practitioners have worked in state and local positions to design and implement the reforms. The analysts have worked in national organizations supporting and analyzing the practitioners' efforts. The two groups share a commitment to helping children and families, as well as considerable experience in human services administration. This common background led them to similar views of the challenges facing families with disadvantages, the value and limitations of the inherited system of human services, and the risks and opportunities of various reform options (Chynoweth 1998). Strengthening the ties between the two groups, a number of practitioners moved into analyst roles as the reforms developed (Farrow 1998; Stark 1998).

Among the practitioners, veteran agency executives such as Jim Ledbetter in Georgia, Charles Palmer in Iowa, Gary Slangier in Missouri, Con Hogan in Vermont, and Gary Weeks in Oregon played key roles (Rozansky 1998). Holding office for years, surviving changes in partisan control of state government, and developing historical perspectives on their state bureaucracies gave these leaders the knowledge and the contacts to undertake major reforms (Ledbetter 1996).

The analysts, for their part, have worked mostly in philanthropic foundations and applied research organizations that specialize in issues related to children and families.[7] To support the practitioners, they have provided consultation and written working papers, planning documents, and evaluation materials to document and disseminate promising ideas and practices.

The practitioners and analysts initially set out to improve the performance of human services programs and to demonstrate their impact by tracking outcomes. Judy Chynoweth. who managed the state Family Policy Academies for the National Governors Association, noted, "In the 1980s, funding was scarce,

and the political climate was conservative.... The old way of getting good ideas funded—design a plan, line up the interest groups, get the Governor's ear, and wait for a good fiscal year—wouldn't work anymore. [M]arketing wasn't enough; we needed to show that what we were proposing could generate better results" (Chynoweth 1998). The initial attempts to change service delivery, for example, gained support when evidence emerged that family-friendly services could be more effective for clients than standardized programs.[8]

Despite—or perhaps because of—the reformers' intentions, they encountered a series of setbacks. Although the practitioners' early experiments with family-friendly services enabled the analysts to identify promising practices in the field (e.g., Kagan et al. 1987; Schorr 1988), many proved hard to sustain because of regulatory, fiscal, and organizational obstacles (Schorr 1997). Some attempts to combine Head Start and child care services to create comprehensive, full-day child development programs, for example, foundered on differences in program standards and pay rates (Kagan et al. 2000). In other places, family-friendly services faltered because providers failed to develop supportive relationships with clients.[9] More generally, waiver authorizations and grants proved unable to sustain family-friendly services across entire counties or states (Bruner 1994). Even local pilot sites had trouble surviving over time, and a number of the early model programs that the analysts had identified were defunct within several years of their inception (Schorr 1997).

By 1990, the reformers recognized that further administrative changes were necessary to support family-friendly services, but they were unsure exactly how to proceed. Doug Nelson, president of the Annie E. Casey Foundation, noted, "We all assumed that somebody somewhere knew ... what a new comprehensive, community-based, integrated support system really looked like.... And we were wrong" (quoted in Walsh 1997, 300). The early proposals for comprehensive systems of care for children and families turned out to be "only a rough blueprint for change"—a vision and general principles (Knitzer 1996, 221). Consequently, the remaining reform components—local governance, flexible funding, and results-based accountability—took shape gradually as the analysts and practitioners exchanged additional ideas and experiences and discovered new reform possibilities and solutions.

Some of these exchanges were smooth, as the two groups worked together to shape emerging experiments. Implementation of the 1993 Family Preservation and Support Act, for example, featured extensive consultation among federal officials, policy and program analysts, and state and local practitioners (Schorr 1997, 227–29).

Other exchanges entailed more conflict. When the National Governors Association offered Family Policy Academies to help states develop their governance collaboratives, for example, "The states consistently said the most valuable thing ... was coming together as a team. They consistently rejected ... the substantive content [of the Academies]" (Chynoweth 1998). Rather than take advice from the analysts, the practitioners sought to customize their own initiatives to mesh with the particular settings in which they were working, "with room for additions and revisions as experience and changing circumstances dictate[d]" (Stroul and Friedman 1986, 116). In time, some analysts came to sympathize with the practitioners' feelings about the need to adapt the reforms to specific local contexts. Doug Nelson of the Annie E. Casey Foundation noted. "The idea that you can develop a standardized template for this kind of fundamental political and social change ... impos[es] a kind of bureaucratic daydream on reality" (Annie E. Casey Foundation n.d., 19). Hence, one study recommended, "Rather than thinking of systemic reform as the construction and replication of a single ... model, [reformers] should focus on building many approaches, each of which is embedded in communal problem-solving" (Kagan et al. 1995, 68).

Additional conflict developed around the role of outcomes and indicators in the reforms. In 1990, in response to an emerging interest in data, the Annie E. Casey Foundation began funding the compilation of the KIDSCOUNT report, which tracks indicators of children's well-being in every state. Many service providers and program managers valued KIDSCOUNT as a tool to persuade legislators to fund social programs. They were uncomfortable, however, using outcomes to assess performance and establish accountability for the well-being of children and families because they feared being penalized for an inability to counteract social conditions that were beyond their control (Schorr et al. 1995; Brunson 1998). State officials in Georgia, Vermont, and elsewhere eventually allayed these fears by stating that the new measurement efforts would serve to improve the collaboratives' plans and operations rather than to penalize poor performance (Page 2003). Local collaborators remained skeptical, but some were willing to commit to the new performance agreements, and as state officials made good on their promises, more and more collaboratives made similar commitments (Gerstein 1998; Rozansky 1998; Tsakalas 2002).

The setbacks, uncertainty, and conflicts described here demonstrate the challenges of innovation that the analysts and the practitioners encountered in the course of their efforts. The ways in which they overcame those challenges, in turn, suggest that they learned more by monitoring their own experiments in the field than by looking outside the human services for universal reform principles or prescriptions.[10] This iterative process of administrative change looks especially incremental if we trace the ideas informing today's innovations back to lessons that the analysts and practitioners gleaned from human services reforms of the recent past.

The Historical Contingence of Today's Reforms

In addition to refining their innovations in light of their own experiments in the field, the analysts and practitioners consciously built their initiatives on concepts and practices that were familiar from prior eras of human services administration. From the HEW service-integration projects of the 1970s, for example, they learned about the limited impact of administrative reorganizations and time-limited funding on the actual delivery of services and outcomes for clients (Agranoff 1991). They concluded that subsequent reforms should focus on specific services for clearly defined groups, foster fiscal and regulatory flexibility, develop strong leadership and support, measure out-

comes, and create local governance authorities to implement change (Kusserow 1991; Yessian 1995).

The recent innovations in local governance responded in particular to the local power struggles, lack of focus, and limited capacity that plagued the War on Poverty and Model Cities programs. Those initiatives suffered from disagreements about program priorities and competition for resources between community organizations and local governments (Gans and Horton 1975; Marris and Rein 1973). In addition, "[N]o one in the field knew enough ... to request waivers and programs from the federal government" (Joe 1998).

By contrast, today's local collaboratives receive assistance to enhance their capacity from state officials, applied research organizations, and peer collaboratives (Center for the Study of Social Policy 1996, 2001; Page 2000). They also pursue clear outcomes, make decisions by consensus or through structured negotiations, and include a variety of public officials, business representatives, community leaders, and service recipients. Because they receive technical assistance and encompass a wide range of human services organizations, the collaboratives have the potential to mobilize the professional expertise and resources needed to design and implement comprehensive community plans. At the same time, they include nonprofessional lay citizens and track outcomes to limit self-dealing by human services professionals and to foster accountability to service recipients and the general public (Center for the Study of Social Policy 1996, 2001).

Emerging shifts in accountability also build consciously on past traditions in human services administration. Since the growth of evaluation research and policy analysis during the 1960s, governments and philanthropic funders have assessed the performance of individual human services programs primarily to determine whether to continue funding them (Schorr 1997). The most capable of today's collaboratives, though, link evaluations of individual programs with the measurement of social indicators at the community level to assess the overall performance of their local service systems (Georgia Family Connection Evaluation Team 2001; Hobbs, Schondelmeyer, and Shively 2003; Hyde 2003; Schorr 1997). Tracking both community-wide indicators and program-specific impacts enables collaborators to identify the contributions of individual programs to community well-being and then to adjust the design and funding of programs to improve the performance of their local systems (DeLapp 2002). Thus, accountability is evolving, focusing less on evaluating individual programs to inform specific funding decisions and more on identifying strengths and weaknesses of entire service systems to enhance aggregate performance (Schorr 1997, 128).

In addition, the new performance agreements between states and local collaboratives deliberately address weaknesses in the flexible funding initiatives of the 1960s and 1970s. Phyllis Rozansky, an architect of Missouri's recent reforms, noted, "We explicitly sought to avoid [emulating] Model Cities, because it lacked accountability for outcomes and mechanisms to build local capacity. We wanted local ... decision making, but we didn't want [local] authority without accountability and capacity" (Rozansky 1998). While granting local discretion in program design and resource allocation, the new agreements foster accountability for performance by establishing joint state and local commitments to track and improve social indicators (Morrill 1996a).

At a general level, the current wave of human services innovations mirrors the New Public Management's combination of managerial discretion with accountability for outcomes. In spite of the parallels, this study suggests that the human services reforms arose independent of the New Public Management. Although analysts and practitioners in the reform movement recognized the potential benefits of the principles of the New Public Management for human services administration, they did not consciously adopt those principles (Rozansky 1998). Rather, as one foundation officer noted, "The [new] structures emerged because ... [human services agencies] created joint teams to solve particular problems, not because people ... set out to ... transplant management ideas" from outside the field (Barbell 1998). Another analyst observed that today's human services reforms are "largely the invention of the field—of those struggling to better meet the needs of children and families" (Knitzer 1997, 15).

Instead of drawing on the principles of the New Public Management or creating a discontinuous break with past traditions of human services administration, then, the analysts and the practitioners refined concepts and practices that were familiar from prior reforms in their own field. Their incremental efforts to build and improve on the history of human services administration support the skeptics' view that the discourse of New Public Management represents an evolution and renewal of administrative traditions (Dobel 2001; Lynn 2001). Their accomplishments also echo Light's (1997) finding that familiar administrative concepts of the past can combine with one another in new ways. By contrast, the champions' view of the New Public Management as a novel set of administrative principles fails to acknowledge the substantial debt that today's human services reforms owe to prior innovations that are specific to the field.

Conclusion

This interpretation of recent human services reforms points to several tentative conclusions about the New Public Management. First, the emergence of New Public Management principles in the human services lends partial support to the champions' hypothesis of convergence: Governments and agencies in different states and programmatic subdisciplines of the human services have adopted the principles of the New Public Management, albeit with some variation.

The portrait of human services reform offered here nevertheless suggests that the champions need to be cautious in claiming that the New Public Management represents a global shift in administrative paradigms. Rather than deriving from universal principles for improving governmental performance, today's administrative changes may have grown out of experiences that are specific to particular policy areas, such as human services. Consequently, "There is a real need to understand that the success of the various [New Public Management] initiatives are

contingent on the context in which they are initiated" (Ferris and Graddy 1998, 226).

Furthermore, this interpretation of innovation in the human services supports the skeptics' contention that the New Public Management has developed through a continuous process of evolution rather than a discontinuous revolution. Therefore, the champions of the New Public Management may oversell the novelty of emerging changes. If administrative traditions can renew themselves by refining old concepts and practices—as today's human services reforms show—then most instances of administrative change will likely trace their origins to familiar ground.

Finally, the possibility that the New Public Management represents evolution in the discourse of public administration rather than a wholly new paradigm takes nothing away from its utility for administrators. In the case of human services, social indicators have improved in communities in Georgia, Maryland, Missouri, Vermont, and Washington since the current reforms began, and the improvements covary with the duration, robustness, and focus of local collaborative work (Family Policy Council 2001a, 2001b; Family and Community Trust 2003; Georgia Family Connection Evaluation Team 2001; Hogan 1999; Hyde 2003). Thus, the reforms may have had a positive impact above and beyond the general improvements in the well-being of children and families that emerged across much of the United States during the late 1990s (Page 2003).

Even if recent administrative changes are largely old wine in new bottles—or familiar concepts combined in an innovative synthesis—the current blend of varietals in the human services appears fruitful so far. The efforts of today's reformers to build and improve on the past demonstrate that administrative discourse can be revitalized by combining lessons from history with experimentation in the field. The human services experience suggests that the New Public Management is an integral part of the history of public administration rather than a stark departure from past traditions.

Acknowledgments

The author extends many thanks to the human services professionals who took the time to share their experiences and interpretations of the reforms this article describes. Helpful comments on earlier drafts came from Nancy Cohen, Jocelyn Crowley, Pat Dobel, Frank Farrow, Bill Gormley, Peter May, Phyllis Rozansky, Chuck Sabel, Tom Sample, Steven R. Smith, and the *PAR* editorial team.

Notes

1. The literature suggests that effective government organizations have attractive missions, support from political authorities, autonomy to pursue their missions, strong cultures focused on their missions, and leadership that motivates staff (Rainey and Steinbauer 1999). Specifically, Wolf's (1993) historical study of federal agencies found that autonomy, competition, a sense of mission, adaptability, and presidential support predicted effec-

tiveness. Brewer and Selden (2000), using data from a 1996 survey of federal employees, found that elements of a high-involvement workplace influenced organizational performance most.

2. A typical combination of proposals comes from Pottowattamie County, Iowa, where principles for changing the child welfare system include moving from a procedural focus to a vision focus, from agency to client priorities, from program requirements to individual needs, from specific to integrated community services, from restrictive to flexible policies and funding, from service tracks to service adaptations, from a focus on processes to a focus on results, and from bureaucratic to community ownership (Farrow and Bruner 1993, 14).

3. Space constraints preclude a complete list of sources, but useful comparative studies included the Annie E. Casey Foundation (n.d.), Cauthen, Knitzer, and Ripple (2000), Center for the Study of Social Policy (1995, 1996, 2001), DeLapp (2002), Farrow and Bruner (1993), Friedman (2000), Kagan et al. (1995), O'Brien (1997), Schorr et al. (1995), and Watson (2000).

4. The sample omits some states that are considered to be innovators in human services, such as Massachusetts, New York, and California, because they had not launched sweeping reforms resembling the New Public Management when the research began. Because of the study's focus, sample selection centered on ambitious administrative innovations rather than historical or demographic variation. The sample nevertheless varies a bit in terms of programming history, size, and geography (e.g., Georgia, Missouri, Minnesota, Oregon, and Vermont).

5. Some of the most helpful state documents were those of the Family Policy Council (2001a, 2001b), Georgia Family Connection Evaluation Team (2001), Georgia Family Connection Partnership (2003), Hogan (1999), Hogan and Murphey (2002), and Rozansky (1997a, 1997b).

6. Missouri, for example, tracks 19 indicators corresponding to six broad outcomes—parents working, children and families safe, children and families healthy, children ready to enter school, children succeeding in school, and youth ready for productive adulthood (Family and Community Trust 2003).

7. For examples of these organizations, see the list in the Research Methods section.

8. Schorr found that "The programs that work best ... typically offer comprehensive and intensive services. Whether they are part of the health, mental health, social service, or educational systems, they are able to respond flexibly to a wide variety of needs" (1988, xxii). Analysts at the Association for Marriage and Family Therapy, the Center for the Study of Social Policy, the Harvard Working Group on Early Life and Adolescence, and the Family Resource Coalition were instrumental in making this case (Preister 1997; Schorr 1988).

9. Don Crary, the director of New Futures for Little Rock Youth, observed, "Our case managers' ... job was to refer young people to services.... They found there wasn't much out there to refer kids to. Most services weren't culturally sensitive, and most were about 'treatment,' and the case managers did not see that as what these kids needed" (Walsh n.d., 7).

10. On "learning by monitoring," see Sabel (1994). For its role in human services reform, see Waldfogel (1997).

References

Agranoff, Robert. 1991. Human Services Integration: Past and Present Challenges in Public Administration. *Public Administration Review* 51(6): 533–42.

Annie E. Casey Foundation. n.d. *The Path of Most Resistance.* Baltimore, MD: Annie E. Casey Foundation.

Ayer, David. 2003. Maryland Office for Children, Youth, and Families. Telephone interview with the author.

Barbell, Ira. 1998. Annie E. Casey Foundation. Interview with the author, Baltimore, MD.

Barzelay, Michael. 1992. *Breaking through Bureaucracy.* Berkeley: University of California Press.

Bauer, Raymond. 1966. *Social Indicators.* Cambridge, MA: MIT Press.

Behn, Robert. 2001. *Rethinking Democratic Accountability.* Washington, DC: Brookings Institution.

Bell, Kris. 2003. Iowa Department of Management. Telephone interview with the author.

Blank, Helen, Karen Schulman, and Danielle Ewen. 1999. *Seeds of Success: State Prekindergarten Initiatives.* Washington, DC: Children's Defense Fund.

Blendon, R. J., D. E. Altman, J. M. Benson, M. Brodie, M. James, and G. Chervinsky. 1995. The Public and the Welfare Reform Debate. *Archives of Pediatrics and Adolescent Medicine* 149(10): 1065–74.

Brewer, Gene, and Sally Coleman Selden. 2000. Why Elephants Gallop. *Journal of Public Administration Research and Theory* 10(4): 685–711.

Brodkin, Evelyn. 1997. Inside the Welfare Contract. *Social Service Review* 71(1): 1–33.

Bruner, Charles. 1994. State Government and Family Support. In *Putting Families First*, edited by Sharon Lynn Kagan and Bernice Weissbourd, 338–57. San Francisco: Jossey Bass.

Brunson, Phyllis. 1998. Center for the Study of Social Policy. Interview with the author, Washington, DC.

Caiden, Gerald. 1991. *Administrative Reform Comes of Age.* New York: Walter de Gruyter.

Cannon, Jessie. 2003. Ohio Family and Children First. Telephone interview with the author.

Cauthen, Nancy, Jane Knitzer, and Carol Ripple. 2000. *Map and Track.* New York: National Center for Children in Poverty.

Center for the Study of Social Policy. 1995. Trading Outcome Accountability for Fund Flexibility. Unpublished manuscript.

———. 1996. *Toward New Forms of Local Governance.* Washington, DC: Center for the Study of Social Policy.

———. 2001. *Building Capacity for Local Decisionmaking.* Washington, DC: Center for the Study of Social Policy.

Chynoweth, Judy. 1998. Foundation Consortium for School-Linked Services, Sacramento, CA. Telephone interview with the author.

Conlan, Timothy. 1988. *New Federalism.* Washington, DC: Brookings Institution.

Cullen, Ronald, and Donald Cushman. 2000. *Transitions to Competitive Government.* Albany: State University of New York Press.

Cutler, Ira, Alexandra Tan, and Laura Downs. 1995. *State Investments in Education and Other Children's Services: Case Studies of Financing Innovations.* Washington, DC: The Finance Project.

DeLapp, Lynn. 2002. *Accountability Systems.* Washington, DC: The Finance Project.

Derthick, Martha. 1975. *Uncontrollable Spending for Social Services.* Washington, DC: Brookings Institution.

Dobel, J. Patrick. 2001. Paradigms, Traditions, and Keeping the Faith. *Public Administration Review* 61(2): 166–71.

Dorf, Michael, and Charles Sabel. 1998. A Constitution of Democratic Experimentalism. *Columbia Law Review* 98(2): 267–473.

Dryfoos, Joy. 1994. *Full-Service Schools*. San Francisco: Jossey-Bass.

Family and Community Trust. 2003. Missouri Community Partnership Benchmark Database. **www.mofact.org/benchmark/ countyidx.asp.**

Family Policy Council. 2001a. Dependency and Termination in Counties Where Community Health and Safety Networks Focus on Child Abuse and Neglect. Olympia, WA: Family Policy Council.

———. 2001b. Juvenile Justice Data in Counties Where Community Health and Safety Networks Focus on Youth Violence. Olympia, WA: Family Policy Council.

Farrow, Frank. 1998. Center for the Study of Social Policy, Washington, DC. Interview with the author.

Farrow, Frank, and Charles Bruner. 1993. *Getting to the Bottom Line*. NCSI Resource Brief No. 4. New York: National Center for Service Integration Information Clearinghouse.

Ferris, James, and Elizabeth Graddy. 1998. A Contractual Framework for New Public Management Theory. *International Public Management Journal* 1(2): 225–40.

Friedman, Mark. 2000. Reforming Finance and Financing Reform for Family and Children's Services. *What Works Policy Brief*. Sacramento, CA: Foundation Consortium.

Gans, Sheldon, and Gerald Horton. 1975. *Integration of Human Services*. New York: Praeger.

Gardner, Sid. 1994. *Reform Options for the Intergovernmental Funding System: Decategorization Policy issues*. Washington, DC: The Finance Project.

Georgia Family Connection Evaluation Team. 2001. *Family Connection as a Catalyst for Community Change*. Atlanta: Georgia Family Connection.

Georgia Family Connection Partnership. 2003. Family Connection Three-Year Community Strategic Plan: FY 2004 Guidelines. **www.gafcp.org/tools/forms/FY2004Guidelines.doc.**

Gersick, Connie. 1991. Revolutionary Change Theories: A Multilevel Exploration of the Punctuated Equilibrium Paradigm. *Academy of Management Review* 16(1): 10–36.

Gerstein, Ellen. 1998. Gwinnett County Coalition for Health and Human Services, Lawrenceville, GA. Telephone interview with the author.

Gilbert, Neil, and Harry Specht. 1977. *Coordinating Social Services*. New York: Praeger.

Halpern, Robert. 1995. *Rebuilding the Inner City*. New York: Columbia University Press.

Haveman, Robert. 1987. Policy Analysis and Evaluation Research after Twenty Years. *Policy Studies Journal* 16(2): 191–218.

Hobbs, Gayle, Brett Schondelmeyer, and John Shively. 2003. Local Investment Corporation, Kansas City, MO. Telephone interview with the author.

Hogan, Cornelius. 1999. *Vermont Communities Count*. Baltimore, MD: Annie E. Casey Foundation.

Hogan, Cornelius, and David Murphey. 2002. *Outcomes: Reframing Responsibility for Well-Being*. Baltimore, MD: Annie E. Casey Foundation.

Hyde, Kelly. 2003. Accountability Solutions, Inc., Santa Fe, NM. Telephone interview with the author.

Joe, Tom. 1998. Center for the Study of Social Policy. Interview with the author, Washington, DC.

Kagan, Sharon Lynn. 1993. *Integrating Services for Children and Families: Understanding the Past to Shape the Future*. New Haven, CT: Yale University Press.

Kagan, Sharon Lynn, Stacie Goffin, Sarit Golub, and Eliza Pritchard. 1995. *Toward Systemic Reform*. Falls Church, VA: National Center for Service Integration.

Kagan, Sharon Lynn, Doug Powell, Bernice Weissbourd, and Edward Zigler, eds. 1987. *America's Family Support Programs*. New Haven, CT: Yale University Press.

Kagan, Sharon Lynn, Marce Verzaro-O'Brien, Una Kim, and Megan Formica. 2000. *Head Start-Child Care Partnership Study*. New Haven, CT: Yale University Bush Center.

Kahn, Alfred, and Sheila Kamerman. 1992. *Integrating Services Integration*. New York: National Center for Children in Poverty.

Kettl, Donald. 2000. *The Global Public Management Revolution*. Washington, DC: Brookings Institution.

Knitzer, Jane. 1996. Children's Mental Health. In *Children, Families, and Government*, edited by E. Zigler, S. L. Kagan, and N. Hall, 207–32. Cambridge: Cambridge University Press.

———. 1997. Service Integration for Children and Families: Lessons and Questions. In *Integrated Services for Children and Families*, edited by R. J. Illback, C. T. Cobb, and H. M. Joseph, Jr., 3–21. Washington, DC: American Psychological Association.

Knitzer, Jane, and Stephen Page. 1996. *Map and Track: State Initiatives for Young Children and Families*. New York: National Center for Children in Poverty.

Kuhn, Thomas. 1970. *The Structure of Scientific Revolutions*. 2nd ed. Chicago: University of Chicago Press.

Kusserow, Richard P. 1991. *Services Integration for Families and Children in Crisis*. Washington, DC: Department of Health and Human Services, Office of the Inspector General.

Lakatos, Imre. 1970. Falsification and the Methodology of Scientific Research Programmes. In *Criticism and the Growth of Knowledge*, edited by Imre Lakatos and Alan Musgrave, 91–196. Cambridge: Cambridge University Press.

Ledbetter, James. 1996. Director, Georgia Health Policy Center. Telephone interview with the author.

Light, Paul. 1997. *The Tides of Reform*. New Haven, CT: Yale University Press.

Lindblom, Charles. 1959. The Science of Muddling Through. *Public Administration Review* 19(2): 79–88.

Lipsky, Michael. 1980. *Street-Level Bureaucracy*. New York: Russell Sage Foundation.

Lynn, Laurence. 1980. *The State and Human Services*. Cambridge, MA: MIT Press.

———. 1998. A Critical Analysis of the New Public Management. *International Public Management Journal* 1(1): 107–23.

———. 2001. The Myth of the Bureaucratic Paradigm: What Traditional Public Administration Really Stood For. *Public Administration Review* 61(2): 144–60.

Marris, Peter, and Martin Rein. 1973. *Dilemmas of Social Reform*. 2nd ed. Chicago: Aldine.

Melaville, Atelia, and Martin Blank. 1993. *Together We Can*. Washington, DC: U.S. Department of Education/U.S. Department of Health and Human Services.

Miller, Danny, and Peter Friesen. 1980. Momentum and Revolution in Organizational Adaptation. *Academy of Management Journal* 23(4): 591–614.

Mittenthal, Stephen. 1976. A System Approach to Human Services Integration. *Evaluation* 3(1–2): 142–48.

Morrill, William. 1996a. Getting Beyond the Micro Gee Whiz. In *Children and Families in Big Cities*, edited by Alfred Kahn and Sheila Kamerman, 186–210. New York: Columbia University, School of Social Work.

———. 1996b. Implications for the Future of Service Delivery System Reform. In *New Directions for Evaluation* 69, edited by J. Marquart and E. Konrad, 85–95. San Francisco: Jossey-Bass.

O'Brien, Mary. 1997. *Financing Strategies to Support Comprehensive, Community-Based Services for Children and Families*. Portland, ME: National Child Welfare Resource Center for Organizational Improvement.

Osborne, David, and Peter Plastrik. 1997. *Banishing Bureaucracy*. Reading, MA: Addison-Wesley.

Overdorff, Randall. 2000. Building Effective Multi-Agency Teamwork for High-Risk Child Abuse Cases. *California Journal for the Community Approach* 1(1): 17–20.

Page, Stephen. 2000. State Human Services as Disciplined Intergovernmental Collaboration. In *Privatization, Democratization, and Decentralization in Cross-National Public Administration*, edited by Stuart Nagel, 215–45. Westport, CT: Quorum Books.

———. 2003. Entrepreneurial Strategies for Managing Interagency Collaboration. *Journal of Public Administration Research and Theory* 13(3): 311–40.

Peters, B. Guy. 1996. *The Future of Governing*. Lawrence: University Press of Kansas.

Popper, Karl. 1970. Normal Science and Its Dangers. In *Criticism and the Growth of Knowledge*, edited by Imre Lakatos and Alan Musgrave, 51–58. Cambridge: Cambridge University Press.

Preister, Steve. 1997. Association for Family-Based Services. Interview with the author, Washington, DC.

Rainey, Hal, and Paula Steinbauer. 1999. Galloping Elephants. *Journal of Public Administration Research and Theory* 9(1): 1–32.

Rozansky, Phyllis. 1997a. *Missourians Working Together: A Progress Report*. St. Louis, MO: Family Investment Trust.

———. 1997b. *Navigating the River of Change*. St. Louis, MO: Family Investment Trust.

———. 1998. Independent Consultant. Interview with the author, Washington, DC.

Sabel, Charles. 1994. Learning by Monitoring. In *Handbook of Economic Sociology*, edited by Neil Smelser and Richard Swedberg, 137–65. Princeton, NJ: Princeton University Press.

Sandfort, Jodi. 2000. Moving Beyond Discretion and Outcomes. *Journal of Public Administration Research and Theory* 10(4): 729–56.

Schalock, Robert, and Gordon Bonham. 2003. Measuring Outcomes and Managing for Results. *Evaluation and Program Planning* 26(3): 229–35.

Schorr, Lisbeth. 1988. *Within Our Reach*. New York: Anchor/Doubleday.

———. 1997. *Common Purpose*. New York: Anchor/Doubleday.

Schorr, Lisbeth, with Frank Farrow, David Hornbeck, and Sara Watson. 1995. *The Case for Shifting to Results-Based Accountability*. Washington, DC: Center for the Study of Social Policy.

Springer, D. W., D. S. Sharp, and T. A. Foy. 2000. Coordinated Service Delivery and Children's Well-Being. *Journal of Community Practice* 8(2): 39–52.

Stark, Donna. 1998. Annie E. Casey Foundation. Interview with the author, Baltimore, MD.

Stevenson, Carol. 1998. David and Lucile Packard Foundation. Interview with the author, Los Altos, CA.

Stroul, Beth, and Robert Friedman. 1986. *A System of Care for Severely Emotionally Disturbed Children and Youth*. Washington, DC: CASSP Technical Assistance Center.

Thomas, George. 1994. *Travels in the Trench between Child Welfare Theory and Practice: A Case Study of Failed Promises and Prospects for Renewal*. Binghamton, NY: Haworth Press.

Tsakalas, Roann. 2002. Maryland Office for Children. Youth, and Families. Telephone interview with the author.

Waldfogel, Jane. 1997. The New Wave of Service Integration. *Social Service Review* 71(3): 463–84.

Walsh, Joan. 1997. Community Building in Theory and Practice. *National Civic Review* 86(4): 291–314.

———. n.d. *The Eye of the Storm*. Baltimore, MD: Annie E. Casey Foundation, **www.aecf.org/publications/eyeofstorm/newfutures.htm**.

Watson, Sara. 2000. *Informed Consent*. Washington, DC: The Finance Project.

Weber, Max. 1947. *The Theory of Social and Economic Organization*. Edited by Talcott Parsons. New York: Free Press.

Wilson, James Q. 1989. *Bureaucracy*. New York: Basic Books.

Wilson, William Julius. 1996. *When Work Disappears*. New York: Alfred A. Knopf.

Wolf, Patrick. 1993. A Case Survey of Bureaucratic Effectiveness in U.S. Cabinet Agencies. *Journal of Public Administration Research and Theory* 3(2): 161–81.

———. 1997. Why Must We Reinvent the Federal Government? *Journal of Public Administration Research and Theory* 7(3): 353–88.

Yessian, Mark. 1995. Learning from Experience. *Public Welfare* 53(3): 34–42.

STEPHEN PAGE is an assistant professor at the Daniel J. Evans School of Public Affairs at the University of Washington. He has also worked as a consultant to state and local governments and nonprofit organizations that serve children and families. His research focuses on interorganizational issues in the design and management of social and health policies. E-mail: sbp@u.washington.edu.

From *Public Administration Review*, Vol. 65 Number 6, Nov/Dec 2005, pp. 713–727. Copyright © 2005 by American Society for Public Administration. Reprinted with permission. www.blackwell-synergy.com

The State of Social Equity in American Public Administration

H. GEORGE FREDERICKSON

Over the years, public administrators have contributed much in helping to create a more equitable, fairer, and more just America. Yet we have much more to contribute. As a core value in public administration, social equity is no longer novel or new. Nevertheless, during the past thirty years, as social equity has grown in importance in public administration, there is an irony: Americans have become less equal in virtually all aspects of social, economic, and political life. In our literature, in our classrooms, and in our administrative practices we have learned to talk the social equity talk. But if the data on the growing gap between the haves and have-nots in American are any clue, we are not walking the social equity talk. In this essay, I attempt to describe the changing terrain of public administration and sketch the challenges administrators face as they navigate both the theory and the reality of that terrain. Finally, I offer some suggestions for walking the social equity talk in the years ahead.

The Evolution of Social Equity in American Public Administration

In his seminal essay of almost a century ago, "General Principles of Management," Henri Fayol listed equity as one of fourteen general principles. His description of equity was entirely internal, having to do with equitable or fair treatment of employees. Fayol put it this way: "Desire for equity and equality of treatment are aspirations to be taken into account in dealing with employees. In order to satisfy these requirements as much as possible without neglecting any principles of losing sight of the general interest, the head of the business must frequently summon up his highest faculties. He should strive to instill a sense of equity throughout all levels of the scalar chain" (p. 58).

Though claiming equity to be a primary principle of management, Fayol did not consider the details of how to achieve equity in the context of the "scalar chain," or hierarchy, which contains such obvious inequalities as difference in pay, authority, and responsibility. Furthermore, because his founding essay had primarily to do with business organization, Fayol did not wrestle with the unique public administration challenges of equity in public policy or service delivery. Except for an essay by

Woodrow Wilson, none of the other founding documents consider what we now call social equity in public administration.

Wilson pointed out that it is "harder to run a constitution than to frame one" and claimed that "administration lies outside the proper sphere of politics"; nevertheless, he describes a form of public administration social equity. Consider these words from his founding essay, "The Study of Administration": "The ideal for us is a civil service cultured and self-sufficient enough to act with sense and vigor, and yet so intimately connected with the popular thought, by means of elections and constant public counsel, as to find arbitrariness or class spirit quite out of the question" (p. 24).

Aside from these glancing blows, and the more considered treatment of justice in the early literature, for the first several generations of the field of public administration it was simply assumed that good administration of government was equally good for everyone. It was during the 1960s that it became increasingly evident that the results of governmental policy and the work of public administrators implementing those policies were much better for some citizens than for others. Issues of racial and class inequality and injustice were everywhere evident and the subject of open anger, indignation, outrage, and passion. Riots in the streets over racial injustice and an unpopular war tend to concentrate the mind. It was in this state of concentration that the phrase *social equity* entered the literature and later the practices of public administration. Certainly there had always been concern for fairness in the better practices of public administration, but it was not until the 1960s that the phrase *social equity* became a feature of public administration with an attendant set of concepts and a cluster of shared values.

In a brief and summary form, the initial elements of the concept of social equity are found in the claim that justice, fairness, and equality have everything to do with public administration. First, laws do not carry out themselves; implementation is our work. As one of the early leaders of our field wrote, "public administration is the law in action." Second, if public administrators implement the law, can we not bring the law simply and precisely to life as it is written? No, we cannot. The law is seldom so clear, so precise, or so evident that it can uniformly be applied from case to case to case. Third, in the early years of our field it was written that public administration should be neutral implementation of law and policy. We know that this is not strictly possible. Public administration is the law in action and involves, indeed requires, interpretation of that law and discretion in its application. Fourth, our public institutions are the setting in which our elected leaders, working in our system of democratic self-government, struggle with issues of fairness, justice, and equality. But because public administrators are responsible for carrying out the laws and policies, we too have important struggles with fairness, justice, and equality. As a nation, we are not as fair, as just or equal, as we should be. Public administrators cannot say that these problems belong only to lawmakers.

In the early stages of the development of social equity in public administration, it was assumed that other academic fields or disciplines and other bodies of professional practice were also developing and embracing self-aware concepts of social equity. We now know that this was not the case. Only in recent years have other fields, disciplines, and bodies of professional practice stepped up to consideration of social equity.

> **Because public administrators are responsible for carrying out the laws and policies, we too have important struggles with fairness, justice, and equality. As a nation, we are not as fair, as just or equal, as we should be. Public administrators cannot say that these problems belong only to lawmakers.**

So it could be said that, at least with respect to social equity, public administration has led the way.

In the early years of applying concepts of social equity to public administration, emphasis was on issues of race and gender in employment, democratic participation, and service delivery. Efficient and economical management of government agencies characterizes the ethics that guided much early reasoning in American public administration. The logic of those ethics allowed public administrators to assume that the effects of good management, efficiency, and economy would be evenly and fairly distributed among our citizens. Gradually, however, public administration began to acknowledge that many public programs were implemented much more efficiently and effectively for some citizens than for others. Indeed, public administrators could not logically claim to be without responsibility for some practices that resulted in obvious unfairness and injustice, so an argument emerged for social equity as an added ethic in public administration. Eventually, social equity took its place along with efficiency and economy as the "third pillar" of public administration. Indeed, by the late 1990s these words were in Shafritz and Russell's standard text:

"The ethical and equitable treatment of citizens by administrators is at the forefront of concerns in public agencies. Reinforced by changing public attitudes, the reinventing government movement and civil rights laws, the new public ad-

ministration has triumphed after a quarter century. Now it is unthinkable (as well as illegal), for example, to deny someone welfare benefits because of their race or a job opportunity because of their sex. Social equity today does not have to be so much fought for by young radicals as administered by managers of all ages" (p. 436).

Over the years the phrase *social equality* has come to encompass the many complex issues associated with fairness, justice, and equality in public administration. Shafritz and Russell list three qualities of social equity:

> First is the obligation to administer the laws they work under in a fair manner. It is hard to believe today that this first obligation was once controversial.
>
> The second way of interpreting obligations to advance social equity is to feel bound to proactively further the cause—to seek to hire and advance a varied workforce. The attitude requires a specific approach: It is not enough to go out and find qualified minorities. You must go out, find them, and then qualify them. This is why the U.S. armed forces have been so much more successful in their affirmative action efforts than the society as a whole.
>
> Third, government can go only so far in forcing social equity. But there is no limit to the amount of inspiration it can provide to encourage people to do the right, decent, and honorable thing. This encouragement has a name. It is called moral leadership. [pp. 436–437]

Over the years both the subject of social equity and its language have changed. Equity is now more broadly defined to include not just race and gender but ethnicity, sexual preference, certain mental and physical conditions, language, and variations in economic circumstances. The words *multiculturalism* and *diversity* are now often used to suggest this broader definition of social equity.

There is little doubt that inequality in America would be worse were it not for pubic administrators dedicated to social equity in their practice, but there is no question that the broader context of American politics has tilted the playing field toward the privileged and away from the underprivileged, making contemporary commitment on the part of public administrators to social equity particularly difficult.

Some Examples of the Widening Social Equity Gap

The growing acceptance of social equity in public administration over the past thirty-five years has occurred during a time when the actual status of social equity in America has been in steady decline. Although we have been promoting democracy abroad and even fighting to bring it to others, democracy at home is in trouble. The recent report of the Task Force on Inequality in America of the American Political Science Association puts it this way: "Our country's ideals of equal citizenship and responsive government may be under growing threat in an era of persistent and rising inequality. Disparities of income, wealth, and access to opportunity are growing more sharply in the United States than in many other nations, and gaps between races and ethnic groups persist. Progress toward realizing American ideals of democracy may have stalled, and in some arenas reversed" (p. 651).

At the time of the emergence of social equity in public administration, racial and gender inequality and discrimination were widespread. But in our time "the scourge of overt discrimination against African Americans and women has been replaced by a more subtle but still potent threat—the growing concentration of the country's wealth and income in the hands of the few" (p. 651). Rising economic inequality is accompanied by other forms of democratic privation—highly unequal voices in political affairs and government processes that are much more responsive to the privileged than to other Americans. "Disparities in participation," the task force goes on to say, "mean that the concerns of lower- or moderate-income Americans, racial and ethnic minorities, and legal immigrants are systematically less likely to be heard by government officials. In contrast, the interests and preferences of the better-off are conveyed with clarity, consistency, and forcefulness" (p. 658). In addition to the gap between the poor and the rest of society, there is a growing gap between privileged professionals, managers, and business owners on the one hand and the middle strata of white, African American, and Latino workers and blue-collar employees on the other. Put bluntly, despite our claimed commitment to social equity, important elements of professional public administration are part of the problem. All of the contemporary social equity research and data seem to indicate that the terrain of social equity has shifted from more-or-less exclusive concentration on the equity issues of minorities to broad consideration of how to achieve social equity in the context of growing disparity between the haves and have-nots, recognizing that minorities constitute a disproportionate percentage of the have-nots.

The APSA task force concludes their report with these words:

> The Declaration of Independence promised that all American citizens would enjoy equal political rights. Nearly every generation has returned to this promise and struggled to elevate the performance of American democracy to its high ideals. The promise of American democracy is threatened again. The threat is less overt than the barriers of law or social custom conquered by earlier generations. Today the risk is that rising economic inequality will solidify longstanding disparities in political voice and influence, and perhaps exacerbate such disparities. Our government is becoming less democratic, responsive mainly to the privileged and not a powerful instrument to correct disadvantages and look out for the majority. If disparities of participation and influence become further entrenched and if average citizens give up on democratic government-unequal citizenship could take on a life of its own, weakening American democracy for a long time to come. [p. 662]

> **"If disparities of participation and influence become further entrenched—and if average citizens give up on democratic government—unequal citizenship could take on a life of its own, weakening American democracy for a long time to come."**
> —APSA TASK FORCE ON INEQUALITY IN AMERICA

In the manner of political science, the APSA Task Force on Inequality in America report calls for research on matters of social equity and for "the engagement of political science with improving American democracy through scholarship" (p. 661). For two reasons, however, those identified with public administration, either as a field of political science or as a freestanding academic field and body of professional practice, are inclined to a less passive and more engaged approach to the problems of inequality in America. First, the argument that issues of inequality belong to politics and policy and not to public administration must be rejected. Virtually all empirical research in the field indicates that public administration is highly influential in policy making and implementation. Second, as an academic field, a body of research, and a field of professional practice, public administration has always been applied. After all, how can we run the constitution and carry out the laws if we do not get our hands dirty? Because our work tends to be applied, it is not a surprise that public administration wrestled with issues of social equity for thirty years before our political science colleagues looked into it. It is also not a surprise that our political science colleagues have chosen to attempt to improve democracy through scholarship, a distinctly "clean hands" approach to the subject. This is good. Let political scientists and others keep their hands clean and study in minute detail exactly how unequal America has become. We need their good work. But in public administration, I insist that we engage with the problem of inequality, that we dirty our hands with inequality, that we be outraged, passionate, and determined. In short, I insist that we actually apply social equity in public administration.

Walking the Social Equity Talk

It is easy, of course, to exhort one and all to apply social equity in all aspects of public administration. But how should it be done?

First, like our environmental friends, when it comes to social equity we should think globally and act locally. Indeed I argue that all important matters of social equity are local, in the sense of consequences. The results of national policies are all manifest locally, in our neighborhoods, our families, our cities and our work places.

Many of the elements of inequality are influenced by the unique patterns of jurisdictional fragmentation in American metropolitan areas. The concentration of poor African Americans, and to a lesser extent Latinos, in low-income urban areas has had a spiraling effect on inequality as the basic elements of opportunity—access to good schools, jobs, transportation, housing, and safety—have become largely unavailable to residents of these neighborhoods. Large-scale federal government policies such as public housing, transportation, welfare reform, and educational reform have tended either to be ineffective or to exacerbate the problems of inequality. Census data now indicate that poverty is moving into the suburbs and our metropolitan areas are becoming more geographically diverse. Public administrators at the local level are increasingly in a position to either influence policies or implement already established policies in a way that ameliorates some of the effects of poverty and opens opportunities. Metropolitan migration is so pronounced that the us-versus-them patterns of an inner city and its suburbs is giving way to "us and us" patterns of similarity between inner cities and suburbs. Like-minded public administration professionals should be working together on their collective social equity issues because it is increasingly evident that few jurisdictions can claim to be isolated from the consequences of poverty and inequality.

Second, it is time for everyone in public administration to be engaged in the war of ideas. We are, as Weir explains, still citizens: "Ceding the ideological terrain to antigovernmental messages like 'the era of big government is over' is not good enough in a polity in which simple media messages are not counterbalanced by organizational politics. In fact, simple antigovernmentalism amounts to endorsing unchecked inequality. A strong, big message about how government is 'on your side' or is 'here to help you' is essential to counteract antigovernment messages" (p. 680). Americans may be philosophical conservatives, but they are programmatic liberals, in the sense of support for rural electrification, environmental protection, Medicare, Social Security, and so forth. The problem is that simple defense of the programmatic status quo is defensive and bereft of new ideas. It is time for public administrators of all kinds to relentlessly ask the so-called second question. The first question is whether an existing or proposed public program is effective or good. The second question is more important: For whom is this program effective or good? Answer any class-warfare charge immediately with the understanding that the second question can be deferred if it can be demonstrated that a program is universally good. If that doesn't work, try this retort: "You say that I am practicing class warfare. Nonsense. I am engaged in the war of ideas, and my idea is fair and yours is not. Stop tossing around class-warfare slogans and engage me in the war of ideas." To effectively engage in the war of ideas requires knowledge, courage, and a quick wit. We public administrators have the knowledge and most of us have a quick wit. But do we have the courage?

Third, it is important to remember that it isn't necessarily good ideas that win the war of ideas. Determination, organization, money, and persistence behind an idea are likely to win the war. Public administrationists know how to organize, and we are determined and persistent. We are natural social equity warriors. We are passionate advocates for policy specialization and we can be equally passionate advocates for fairness in implementing it. Those of us committed to social equity should pick our cause and enlist in the organizations most likely to turn the levers of policy in the direction of fairness and justice.

It is time for public administrators of all kinds to relentlessly ask the so-called second question. The first question is whether an existing or proposed public program is effective or good. The second question is more important: For whom is this program effective or good?

Fourth, when public administration is practiced at the street level it employs a form of social equity. As Steven Maynard-Moody and Michael Musheno suggest in their book *Cops, Teachers, Counselors,* social service officers, cops on the beat, and teachers in the classroom all live in a world of scarce resources, limited time, ambiguous expectations, and conflicting rules. To manage their way through these limitations, street-level bureaucrats apply a form of public service delivery and distribution based on what the authors describe as "client worthiness." Client worthiness is based on stories and master narratives that enable street-level workers to affix particular identity to their clients. The day-to-day practices of street-level public servants is all about the search for fairness, equity, and justice. "Fixing and enforcing citizen-client identities forms the premise for street-level workers' judgments," they write:

> Their stories reveal how street-level decision making is complexly moral and contingent rather than narrowly rule-bound and static. Cops, teachers, and counselors first make normative judgments about offenders, kids, and clients and then apply, bend, or ignore rules and procedures to support the moral reasoning. Identity-based normative judgments determine which and how rules, procedures and policies are applied. Morality trumps legality in terms of which rules, procedures, and policies are acted on; who gets what services and who is hassled or arrested; and how rules, procedures and policies are enacted. [p. 155]

Maynard-Moody and Musheno describe street-level bureaucrats as the coal miners of policy: they do the hard, dirty, and dangerous work of the state. Sometimes they get it all wrong, as in examples of racial profiling and police abuse. Still, most of the time and in most street-level settings "small acts of normative improvisation by forgotten streetwise workers sustain the state; they are acts of statecraft on which the institutions of governing depend." (p. 165) When it comes to social equity in action, supervisors, managers, and super grades could take some lessons from street-level bureaucrats.

Fifth, like it or not, senior public administrators and those of us who study public administration are part of the elite, the privileged. In much of our literature and ideology there is a distinctly patronizing tone to social equity. A commitment to social equity obliges us to look after the interests of those who are denied opportunities or are disadvantaged regardless of their competence. At the intermediate and upper levels of public administration, we tend to avoid the uncomfortable issue of competence, although street-level workers have no illusions about competence. I am partial to the blunt words of Lawrence M. Mead on this subject. In an article in *Perspectives on Politics,* he wrote: "To recover democracy, government must assume greater competence in lower-income Americans than the elite finds comfortable. We would rather lay the burden of change on ourselves than on the less fortunate. We believe in our own abilities; we are less sure about theirs. But, unless some minimal capacities are expected of the less privileged, change becomes unimaginable, and a caste society will emerge" (p. 674).

> ## "To recover democracy, government must assume greater competence in lower-income Americans than the elite finds comfortable. We would rather lay the burden of change on ourselves than on the less fortunate."
> —LAWRENCE M. MEAD

There are two interesting lessons on this subject. One is the lesson and life of Mohandas Gandhi, who insisted in collective nonviolent expression of demands for fairness on the part of the least advantaged acting together. Another is the lesson of the Roundheads or Puritans, British citizens below the elite who asserted a belief in the individual, independent of class; insisted on egalitarian politics; and were suspicious of elites in their hierarchical polity. The founding of the United States of America was a denial of aristocracy and the triumph of Roundhead reasoning. In much of social equity there is democratic rhetoric but aristocratic assumptions. We search still for versions of social equity that are truly from the bottom up.

Sixth, it is high time for moral indignation, for passion and anger. The moral high ground, often put passionately as Christian doctrine, has tended toward those interested in issues such as abortion, gay marriage, human cloning, stem-cell research, and euthanasia, and those mobilized in pursuit of these issues have proven to be formidable. Issues of poverty, at least from the biblical Christian perspective, are at least as central to doctrine as are these other issues. But it is far more difficult to bring indignation and passion to matters of poverty. Still, this is what needs to be done. Describing "sinful inequalities," John Dilulio writes in *Perspectives on Politics,* "Bible-believing Christians are supposed to heed the call to 'be not afraid' of any worldly challenge. . . . Inequality is a moral problem, and [if] you are convinced that it is a real problem in America today, you should not be afraid to say so—and not be afraid to recommend whatever policies or programs you believe might make a real lasting difference. . . . It is liberals, not conservatives, who have normally lacked the courage of their true convictions, some for fear of being accused of favoring 'big government' or having other thoughts out of season" (p. 669). Persistent and grinding poverty is a profoundly moral issue, and social equity is part of a moral stance on that issue. But how shall we most effectively put the social equity of public administration in practice?

In addition to applying social equity in our day-to-day public administration work, I suggest that we more broadly engage issues of racial, gender, and ethnic inequality and issues of inequality in economic opportunity, jobs, housing, transportation, and health care. I respect those who are working on social eq-

uity indicators, social equity benchmarks, and other forms of statistics, but the prospects of such labor for success seem to me to be limited. Furthermore, statistics and data lack passion and smother indignation. It does the cause of social equity little good to be able to know exactly how poor the poor are.

Instead we should turn to the media most likely to stir an interest in social equity. Think of the statistics regarding the grossly disproportionate percentage of incarcerated African Americans. We know those appalling statistics forward and backward, and it seems to make little difference. Stories, films, videos, essays, and personal descriptions of the ravages of an overly long sentence for a drug offence have the power to move people, and also to move policy makers. Stories, films, and videos of single mothers working two jobs and still falling behind hold some prospect for moving watchers and readers. There is a desperate need to dramatize social equity issues, to bring them to life. I am convinced that if the general population understood more fully the effects of discrimination and poverty on American lives they would respond by supporting candidates committed to social equity. Through their neighborhoods, churches, and social groups, mobilized citizens who understand poverty and inequality would personally do their part to even up the economic and political playing field.

If politics is all about majority rule—and it is—then public administration should be all about seeing after the interests of minorities and the poor. It seems to me we are long past needing to defend this proposition. It is time to walk the social equity talk.

References

Dilulio, J. J. "Attacking 'Sinful Inequalities.'" *Perspectives on Politics,* 2004, 2(4), 671–675.

Fayol, H. "General Principles of Management." In C. Storrs (trans.), *General and Industrial Management.* London: Pitman, 1949. (Original work published 1916). Reprinted in J. M. Shafritz, J. S. Ott, and Y. S. Jang. *Classics of Organizational Theory.* Belmont, Calif.: Wadsworth, 2005.

Maynard-Moody, S., and Musheno, M. *Cops, Teachers, Counselors: Stories from the Front Lines of Public Service.* Ann Arbor: University of Michigan Press, 2003.

Mead, L. M. "The Great Passivity." *Perspectives on Politics,* 2004, 2(4), 671–675.

Shafritz, J. M., and Russell, E. W. *Introducing Public Administration.* Upper Saddle River, N.J.: Pearson Education, 2005.

Task Force on Inequality in America (American Political Science Association). "American Democracy in an Age of Rising Inequality." *Perspectives on Politics,* 2004, 2(4), 651–663.

Weir, M. "Challenging Inequality." *Perspectives on Politics,* 2004, 2(4), 677–681.

Wilson, W. "The Study of Administration." *Political Science Quarterly,* 1887, 2, 197–222. Reprinted in J. M. Shafritz and A. C. Hyde, *Classics of Public Administration.* Belmont, Calif.: Wadsworth, 1992.

H. GEORGE FREDERICKSON is the Edwin O. Stene Distinguished Professor of Public Administration at the University of Kansas.

Social Science and Public Policy

A New Approach to Regulatory Reform

MURRAY WEIDENBAUM

Over the years, many attempts have been made to reform government regulation, but success has been very limited. These efforts have been severely hampered by distrust on both sides of the regulatory debate. Individuals committed to protecting public health, safety, and the environment are suspicious of any effort that is seen as possibly obstructing or delaying their objectives. In contrast, people advocating the reduction of "big government" decry those who would proceed rapidly to address various problems with costly or ill-designed remedies.

To reconcile these two polar extremes, or at least to narrow the gap between them, it is necessary to raise the level of understanding of the galaxy of issues involved. That objective, in turn, requires a far better flow of information, one based on sound science and professional analysis. Moreover, a broader approach is in order in the regulatory process than has been customary.

The most carefully constructed and well-grounded analysis, however, can antagonize citizen groups, which may jump to the conclusion that wetlands are about to be paved over or national forests sold to the highest bidder. Any successful and comprehensive reform must have a perspective that is not threatening to the widespread concerns of citizens—and that positive approach to achieving the nation's social priorities must be translated into reality.

In that spirit, the various parties to the regulatory debate should recognize that the American people believe there is a legitimate need for government regulation to achieve economic and social goals of high priority to the nation. There are many areas in which regulation is accepted without question. Airline safety is an obvious example; the public is reassured by the licensing of pilots. Similarly, restrictions on child labor in the United States are no longer controversial. Agencies such as the Environmental Protection Agency (EPA), the Equal Employment Opportunity Commission (EEOC), the Food and Drug Administration (FDA), the Federal Trade Commission (FTC), and the Occupational Safety and Health Administration (OSHA) may be viewed as bureaucratic and burdensome "alphabet soup" by those subject to their rulings, but the public at large strongly supports continuing government involvement in their areas of responsibility. Serious shortcomings in market outcomes and in the conduct of business often generate or increase public support for government intervention in private-sector decision making.

However, the process of regulation—the way in which a national priority or concern is translated into a specific rule—is not widely understood. It does not begin when a government agency issues a ruling. Rather, it starts much earlier, when Congress passes a law establishing a regulatory agency and gives it a mandate to issue rules governing some activity. The writing of the specific statute, which has been largely ignored by most organized efforts at regulatory reform, is usually the most important action in what is an extended rule-making process. Basic defects in the enabling legislation cannot be cured by the regulatory agency concerned or anywhere else in the executive branch.

Regulations are promulgated by agencies in response to laws passed by Congress to address some perceived "market failure" or to achieve a social goal. Regulatory proceedings are not, for the most part, mere matters of procedure and conformance. Rather, they spring from the desire for clean air, safe drinking water, safe workplaces, reliable financial markets, improved medicines, and competitive industries.

Yet, achieving these desirable results is far more complicated than is commonly understood. It is not simply a matter of Congress proclaiming worthy goals or an executive branch agency promulgating rules to that effect. The regulatory process is fundamentally bureaucratic, with all the powers and shortcomings associated with government. Even at its best, regulation is a blunt and imperfect tool. Far too often, it imposes costs that greatly outweigh the benefits achieved, often unnecessarily.

In seriously considering the subject of regulation, an important distinction needs to be made between two types: *economic regulation*, historically used by such agencies as the Federal Communications Commission (FCC), the Maritime Commission, and two agencies which Congress has terminated, the Civil Aeronautics Board (CAB) and the Interstate Commerce Commission (ICC), and *social regulation*, performed by EPA, OSHA, and similar government agencies of fairly recent origin. The characteristics of the two types of regulation are very different and so are the ways of improving them.

Economic regulation relates primarily to such aspects of business as prices, profits, entry, and exit. Typically, an agency or commission regulates a specific sector of the economy, such as transportation, communications, utilities, or banking. Social regulation, in contrast, is characterized by the use of agencies organized along functional or issue lines (ecology, discrimination, product safety) rather than industry categories. Many of these agencies have power to regulate across all industries, although their jurisdiction is limited to one aspect of business activity.

Since the 1970s there has been a strong and consistent effort to reform or eliminate economic regulations where competition adequately serves the public interest. Thus, the CAB and the ICC have been terminated; the Securities and Exchange Commission (SEC) no longer regulates brokers' commission rates; and the FCC is beginning, somewhat fitfully, to let competition replace rate regulation in the rapidly changing telecommunications industry.

The staffing of federal economic regulatory agencies (nearly 30,000 persons in 1997) is dwarfed by the much larger array of inspectors, reviewers, and other officials of federal agencies engaged in social regulation (almost 94,000 in number). However, there has been no sustained effort to reduce social regulations. On the contrary, the recent tendency has been to *expand* the scope of this activity.

In some cases, citizens become so used to regulation that they forget the value of marketplace competition in protecting consumers. For decades, regulation by the ICC was accepted by the trucking industry as a fact of life. But since the effective dismantling of these controls in the early 1980s, thousands of additional firms have entered this market, and the cost of transporting goods in the United States has been reduced by billions of dollars a year. The demise of the ICC goes unmourned.

Thus, substantial progress has been made in deregulating some key sectors of the economy—notably transportation, communication, and financial services—in which competition does an effective job of protecting consumer interests. The United States has enjoyed large productivity gains in these sectors relative to other industrial economies because it has successfully challenged the traditional approach of selecting regulation or public ownership for utilities and related industries and opted instead for the relatively "radical" solution of competition.

It is helpful to recall the limits as well as the advantages of reliance on the market mechanism. Market-place competition is not an effective way of directing people to follow very specific courses of action. Control of automobile traffic provides an example. Traffic lights, stop signs, and similar command-and-control devices are an accepted part of everyday life. However, for producing changes in behavior that are less specific or that differ among individuals or organizations, economic incentives can be useful. For example, lower fees for toll bridges and toll highways during off-peak hours can reduce the road congestion facing the command-and-control traffic system at peak hours of usage. Likewise, a statutory or administrative command-and-control apparatus can set a specific level of air or water purity for society to strive to achieve, but emission fees or tradable permits can achieve this same level of purity at lower cost than conventional regulatory control mechanisms.

The marketplace does not function perfectly. But the relevant question in any given instance is whether it works better than regulation. The response is less a matter of philosophy than of practicality. The answer can be "yes" or "no," depending on such factors as the type of regulation and the state of technology.

The costs imposed by regulation also are often broader than many people realize. In addition to specific equipment that may have to be added to an automobile or to a production line to meet a federal requirement, the government directive may also have powerful indirect influences. A case in point is the value of time that people must spend waiting in line for permits and inspections or filling out forms.

Using information from the U.S. Office of Management and Budget for fiscal year 1996, if we value the time of those filling out the forms very conservatively at the national average hourly earnings of about $16 an hour, the cost of the 6.8 billion hours consumed was about $110 billion. Since those actually performing much of the paperwork are likely to have earnings substantially above the average, the actual economic cost was no doubt even higher.

The impact on consumers can be even less transparent, especially since regulations often have unintended consequences. Take the case of a federal requirement that the household ladder be made safer. Such an action not only increases the cost of the product, but may make it more difficult to use. As a result, many families may forgo purchasing this more expensive and less convenient item and stand on chairs or tabletops instead. The unintended adverse result, the reduction of safety in the home, would not be apparent from merely reading the proposed rule.

In another ironic example, the current narrow tolerance standards on pesticide residues on fresh fruits and vegetables do more than merely increase the costs of nutritious foods. A diet rich in fruits and vegetables may reduce cancer rates far more than would eliminating trace pesticides on those foods. Because the standards are so tight, many low-income persons, in particular, do not eat sufficient fruits and vegetables; these foods have become too costly. On balance, cancer rates may actually be higher because pesticide restrictions are too rigid. That unintended result only becomes apparent when we trace through the effects of the government's rule-making. Clearly, the rhetorical claim that onerous regulation is always justified because "lives are more important than dollars" is far too simplistic.

On the other hand, critics of regulation must keep in mind the many instances in which regulations, sometimes with very large costs, have served the public interest. Thus, EPA's two-decade-old regulation requiring refiners to stop adding lead to gasoline was an effective way to eliminate hazardous lead particles from exhaust fumes. The costs were substantial; the rule required refiners to adopt more expensive refining techniques, since lead had been a low-cost octane booster. But these costs were exceeded by the important public health gains that resulted from lower levels of lead in the environment.

It is heartening to realize that changes in the regulatory process do not have to start at square one. The appropriate question no longer is, "Are you for or against environmental or workplace regulation?" That question has long been answered. The relevant questions relate to how those regulatory mandates are carried out—to the degree of rule making and the specific approaches directed by a statute or a government agency. Most studies of government regulation conclude that adopting sensible reforms could result in greater social benefits being achieved with the same resources now committed to complying with regulations—or equivalent benefits at much lower economic cost. In this regard, regulatory failure in the public sector can be as costly as market failure in the private sector.

The Need for Change

Leaving aside for the moment the question of benefits (an important subject to which we shall return), the dollar costs of regulation are too large to be ignored. In the aggregate, the costs of government regulations exceed the budgetary cost of all federal domestic discretionary programs. The widely used estimate prepared by CSAB adjunct scholar Thomas Hopkins shows that complying with federal regulation cost $677 billion (or over $3,000 per capita) in 1996 and will cost $721 billion in the year 2000. Moreover, those regulatory costs fall disproportionately on small businesses; the burden of compliance for firms with fewer than 20 workers in 1992 was about 90 percent higher per employee than for companies with 500 or more workers.

From a more aggregate viewpoint, regulation impairs economic growth. It is estimated that, when the Clean Air Act of 1990 is fully implemented in 2005, it (in combination with pre-existing environmental regulation) will have reduced the nation's capital stock by four percent, increased the cost of capital by five percent, and reduced the real gross domestic product, as conventionally measured, by more than three percent. Moreover, this analysis does not include the effects of costly new air quality standards for ozone (smog) and particulates established in late 1997.

Many people find it hard to comprehend such important, but abstract, aggregate effects. For this reason, the micro analysis may be helpful. A business firm becomes subject to more and more regulation as it grows in size. Hiring a fifteenth employee, for example, means that the firm must comply with Title VII of the Civil Rights Act and the Americans With Disabilities Act. Hiring five more people subjects the employer to the Age Discrimination Act, the Older Worker Benefit Protection Act, and COBRA (requiring the continuation of medical benefits for up to 18 months after a job termination). Expanding the firm's labor force by still another five workers brings it under the purview of the Health Maintenance Organization Act and the Veterans Reemployment Act. Some companies have stated that they refrain from increasing employment specifically to avoid becoming subject to the next level of regulation.

When the entire body of federal regulation is examined—something that is rarely done in the executive, legislative, or judicial branches—it becomes apparent that the resulting burdens of compliance are enormous. The typical business firm in this country is subject to regulation of virtually every aspect of its activity. For each box on its organizational chart, from the board of directors down to first-line management, there is at least one government agency, and often more, with the power to shape, review, change, or veto the company's decisions. In the new, global marketplace, complying with this vast array of rules handicaps American companies that compete against foreign firms with lower cost structures.

Regulatory costs, of course, are only half the equation. Were it evident that the benefits of most of the vast array of current regulations justified their economic costs, we should consider these costs well spent. But there is no sound basis for jumping to this conclusion.

It is widely acknowledged that the positive results of many regulatory activities are subject to sharply diminishing returns. Benefits may greatly exceed costs for early interventions, but subsequent actions tend to produce smaller benefits at sharply rising costs. In such circumstances, as a careful survey of environmental economics noted in 1992, "It will be quite easy…to enact new, more stringent regulations that impose large costs on society, well in excess of the benefits."

Recent reports on major environmental regulations reinforce these concerns. A study using the government's own regulatory impact analyses (taken from Robert Hahn, *Risks, Costs, and Lives Saved*) reveals that only 38 of the 83 major regulations analyzed by five major federal agencies from 1990 to 1995 met a benefit-cost standard. EPA leads the parade in promulgating rules whose costs exceed their benefits; 40 of their 61 regulations flunk a benefit-cost test. This, perhaps, should not be surprising given the high and often uncritical public support for environmental protection recorded in opinion polls. But the public is ill-served when new rules produce more costs than benefits.

In addition to generating direct costs, regulation often retards the innovation process. Thus, reliance by the Department of Agriculture on continuous inspections instead of on modern sampling techniques discourages or delays adoption of new food safety technologies. Another example is new medical software that models the reaction of cancerous tumors when treated with a specific dose of radiation. The FDA has ruled that this software must be approved as a "medical device." As a result, even a slight change in computer code can require time-consuming and expensive reapproval. Yet, the FDA regulations on medical devices surely did not contemplate the inclusion of medical computer software.

The extensive regulatory reviews to which many new products are subjected in the United States inevitably raise the cost of product innovation and increase the uncertainty of financial success. However, many companies bypass these barriers to innovation by establishing research laboratories and production facilities abroad. Pharmaceutical and medical equipment firms provide striking illustrations. Companies moving to the Netherlands, for example, are not seeking a weak or ineffective regulatory environment, but one that is more flexible and efficient (nor are firms locating in Holland looking for low-cost labor). In many instances, contemporary regulatory activity is a vestige of responses to problems that have long since passed. A clear example is the Davis-Bacon Act, which prescribes "prevailing" wages on government construction contracts that are generally above the market wages received by other workers in construction jobs. The statute, which was enacted in the depths of the Great Depression of the 1930s, was designed to prevent sweatshop conditions in the building trades. Sixty years later, the original justification has long since disappeared, but the statute and its regulations survive in full force. Any sound economic reason to continue such wage regulation has yet to be articulated.

Another striking example of the persistence of obsolete rules is found in the administration of the Resource Conservation and Recovery Act (RCRA). EPA's Office of Solid Waste (which administers RCRA) originally placed silver on its toxic characteristic list because silver was so listed by EPA's Office of Drinking Water. However, in January 1991, the Office of Drinking Water eliminated the standard for silver because it determined that silver in drinking water had no adverse effects on humans. Yet, silver remains on RCRA's list of toxic substances. Such examples dramatically illustrate the need for periodic reviews of regulations to ensure that their original purpose remains valid and that shortcomings that emerge from the reviews be corrected.

It is easy to identify regulatory programs that have serious deficiencies and elicit widespread objections. But the problem is more fundamental than suggested by lists of silly regulations. No one sets out deliberately to create burdensome and ineffective rules. Many of the underlying statutes have created huge and unnecessary costs because Congress responded to the concerns of some citizen groups without sufficiently analyzing the problems and the proposed solutions. Powerful examples are asbestos removal and superfund legislation. The shortcomings of these laws are too serious to be brushed off by a general appeal to the universal desire for a healthy environment.

It is useful to remind Congress that it passed a sweeping law that led cities and states to spend nearly $20 billion removing asbestos from public buildings, although EPA concluded, after some research, that ripping out asbestos was an expensive and dangerous mistake: the removal effort *increased* the asbestos fibers circulating in the air. Obviously, the analysis should have *preceded* the legislation. Similarly, the congressionally enacted superfund law has turned out to be a costly bonanza for lawyers because the statute emphasized determining liability rather than reducing health risks.

Compounding the problem, many regulatory statutes, especially in the areas of environment and job safety, prohibit or severely restrict any use of economic analysis in the executive branch's rule making process. The courts have supported EPA's position that costs should not be considered in establishing air quality standards.

One universal shortcoming of standard rulemaking is apparent. Each statute or rule is promulgated in isolation, as if no others existed. If there is any lesson that we have learned in recent decades, it is that regulation is a powerful remedy that should be used only in situations where markets do not work adequately. Given the huge amount of regulation in force today, a compelling case can be made for economizing on the government's regulatory power. Like any strong medicine, regulation should be used carefully and with full attention to its adverse side effects.

Some people argue that regulatory review itself is costly and burdensome. Exactly the opposite is true. The United States substantially *underinvests* in information on regulatory programs and should significantly increase the resources devoted to that purpose. Government regulatory activities involve hundreds of billions of dollars annually in benefits and costs. Yet, the unelected decision makers who issue and enforce these regulations usually have little knowledge of the magnitude of their impact—especially who bears the costs and who receives the benefits. Government agencies and OMB now spend $50 million or less each year to deal with these issues. Expenditures of several times this amount on such informational and analytical activities would be fully justified.

Benefit-cost analysis can also serve broader purposes such as thinking systematically about social issues and more fully understanding the implications of selecting one plan of action over another. Alternative approaches may not involve regulatory powers at all. However used, a careful calculation of advantages and disadvantages provides an essential discipline to improve the current arbitrary procedure.

To avoid problems inherent in placing monetary values on human lives, benefit-cost analysis sometimes can be structured in terms of lives themselves. For example, sodium nitrite, which is used to preserve food, is a mild carcinogen. Its use creates the possibility that a limited number of people will develop cancer. On the other hand, a far larger number of people would die of botulism if nitrites were not used as a preservative in meat. A comparison of the costs and benefits of restricting the use of nitrites in meats indicates that more lives are saved by its continued use. This type of comparison was the basis for the FDA's sensible decision not to ban nitrites in meat and, instead, merely to urge a reduction in their use.

The recent experiences with air bags further demonstrate that neither the benefits nor the costs of regulation need be measured in dollars but at times should focus directly on human life. The National Highway Traffic Safety Administration issued air bag standards based on automobile tests that made no distinctions about the occupants' age, sex, or height, although car manufacturers had informed the agency of the importance of this difference. As a result, children under the age often have experienced a net increase in fatality risk because of air bags. At least 40 children in that age group have been killed by air bags in crashes that otherwise would not typically have been fatal. In that case, the regulatory shortcoming was not an excess of analysis but a shortage of it.

Previous Attempts

A brief examination of previous attempts at reform provides a useful background for preparing recommendations to reform the regulatory system.

Since 1974 every president of the United States has attempted to improve the regulatory process. President Gerald Ford launched an effort to modernize economic regulation, particularly with respect to rate regulation of the transportation and financial industries. President Jimmy Carter maintained the momentum with the elimination of the CAB, the reduction of restrictions imposed by the ICC, and the creation of intense price competition in the financial industry. Both presidents also established formal systems to review new government regulations before they were issued. Every subsequent president has carried forward this general approach. Important lessons can be learned from their successes as well as their failures.

President Ford's concerns about the inflationary impact of federal activities, especially regulation, marked the beginning of an organized, comprehensive effort at regulatory reform. His Executive Order 11821 established procedures for preparing "inflation impact statements" to illuminate the economic impact of regulatory proposals. The statements were prepared by the various executive agencies and reviewed by the Council on Wage and Price Stability.

The Ford Administration focused on four reforms: (1) measuring and considering the benefits and costs of proposed regulations, (2) reducing the backlog and delays in regulatory proceedings, (3) suggesting changes in legislation under which regulatory programs operate, and (4) ensuring that consumer interests prevail in regulatory proceedings. (Because the so-called independent agencies are not subject to the jurisdiction of presidential executive orders, Ford and his staff could only try to coax them into following the spirit, if not the letter, of his directive.) With some exceptions, the agencies paid merely lip service to this initiative. Nevertheless, this basic way of performing regulatory reviews has continued under successive administrations, with revisions in the details reflecting experience gained over the years.

To formalize regulatory review, President Carter issued Executive Order 12044, replacing Ford's "inflation impact statement" with a new "regulatory analysis." For all new regulations with an estimated economic impact of $100 million or more, preparation of a regulatory analysis was required prior to the publication of the regulation in the *Federal Register*. Each analysis included a description of the proposed rule, an identification of alternative ways of achieving the policy goal, and an examination of the economic impact of the regulation. A rudimentary cost-effectiveness test was also required to enforce the requirement that "the least burdensome of acceptable alternatives has been chosen."

On balance, however, the 1970s will be remembered for an outpouring of new federal rules and an expansion of the number and size of regulatory agencies. The agencies subject to presidentially-ordered regulatory review generally considered cost-benefit analysis merely to be the final hurdle to clear *after* they had completed the regulation design.

Two procedural reforms were enacted by Congress in the last year of the Carter Administration. The Regulatory Flexibility Act of 1980 required rule-making agencies to write regulations in a manner that would minimize burdens on small business. Compliance was minimal. Many agencies simply attached a perfunctory statement to new rules to meet the law's formal requirements.

The second and far more useful procedural law was the Paperwork Reduction Act of 1980, which took effect after President Carter left office. The statute created the Office of Information and Regulatory Affairs (OIRA) in the Office of Management and Budget to supervise enforcement of the law's objective of reducing federal reporting requirements. Early in 1981, President Reagan expanded OIRA's mission to encompass review of regulations promulgated by executive branch agencies.

Regulatory reform was a basic component of President Reagan's economic agenda. One of his most important actions was to establish the Task Force on Regulatory Relief, chaired by Vice President George Bush, to oversee the reform effort. Executive Order 12291, issued in 1981, stated, "Regulatory action shall not be undertaken unless the potential benefits to society from the regulation outweigh the potential costs to society." The presidential directive required agencies to prepare a "regulatory impact analysis" subject to review by OIRA for each "major rule" pending. A federal agency could not publish a notice of proposed rule making until an OIRA review was complete and its concerns had been addressed.

Executive Order 12291 had two real powers: (1) It required regulatory agencies to demonstrate that the benefits of a proposed regulation exceeded the costs, and (2) it gave OIRA power to delay rule making until regulatory agencies had appropriately addressed these broader economic concerns. Another strength of the order was that it allowed OIRA to identify any rule as a major rule, not just those imposing estimated costs of more than $100 million a year.

The regulatory review process during the Reagan Administration had a substantial impact, as indicated by the large number of proposed regulations returned, changed, or withdrawn. During 1981–1989, over 40 percent of the regulations of the Department of Labor failed, at least initially, to obtain OIRA approval. At the statutory level, President Reagan avoided new regulation. He neither proposed nor authorized a new regulatory agency or a new major regulatory program.

President George Bush continued President Reagan's reforms. The Council on Competitiveness, which replaced the Task Force on Regulatory Relief in 1989, was also headed by the Vice President. Like the Task Force, the Council was authorized to review regulations with the aim of eliminating those that inhibited U.S. competitiveness, and it intervened in many specific regulatory matters. The Council's procedures were frequently criticized, especially those permitting businesses to oppose pending regulations in special *ex parte* presentations.

Presidential review of regulatory decisions was also questioned on constitutional grounds. The Bush administration's response emphasized that the Constitution empowers the president to see that laws are "faithfully executed." The incoming Clinton administration, in 1993, rescinded the existing executive orders on regulatory review and abolished the Council on Competitiveness. Nevertheless, regulatory reform continued to have a significant place on the federal agenda.

President Bill Clinton replaced the Reagan-Bush directives with Executive Order 12866. He reaffirmed OMB (via OIRA) as the central agency to review proposed regulations. However, the new executive order made the process more accessible to the public by requiring OIRA to identify publicly its recommended changes for regulatory actions. Under the order, OMB retains no formal power to hold up rule making or to require a demonstration that the estimated benefits of a regulation exceed its costs. Regulatory agencies have to find only that the benefits of the intended regulation "justify" its costs.

The Clinton executive order requires agencies to do many sensible things in drafting rules. They must identify alternative ways of meeting government objectives, consider benefits and costs, and use market-based alternatives and performance standards. The elimination of thousands of pages of environmental and pharmaceutical regulations is a positive result of that effort. However, new regulations have been added at such a rapid rate that they more than offset the reductions.

Like its predecessors, the Clinton administration has issued formal guidelines on performing and using economic analysis, but recent rule making often appears to have honored them more in the breach than in the observance. In the case of EPA, the largest regulatory agency, only 6 of 45 "significant" rules issued from April to September 1994 contained the required determination that the benefits justified the costs, only three were based on a compelling public need, and only 9 considered alternative approaches to regulating. Of the other 177 EPA rules issued during that period (including those not considered to be "significant"), none was supported by a determination that the benefits justified the costs.

Meanwhile, the aggregate federal rule-making list has grown. The April 1998 semiannual regulatory plan (an innovation instituted in the Carter administration) requires over 1,500 pages merely to list short summaries of the regulatory actions that the federal departments and agencies are working on, including nearly 250 entries by EPA alone. The staffs of federal regulatory agencies have also grown; the total of nearly 125,000 in 1996 represented a 26 percent increase from the 1985 low.

On balance, the formal systems of review put in place by presidents from Ford through Clinton have helped convince often reluctant officials of government agencies to analyze the implications of their rules before issuing them. That approach has been somewhat successful in getting regulators and their supporting interest groups to develop data on the costs and the benefits they impose on society. However, the impact of such analyses on the actual decision making of the regulatory agencies has been very limited.

Congressional Efforts

In response to the shortcomings of executive branch efforts to improve the regulatory process, many members of Congress have introduced bills to legislate generic regulatory reform. In 1995, the proposed Comprehensive Regulatory Reform Act, which would have required each regulatory agency to show a detailed cost-benefit analysis prior to issuing a major new rule, failed by one vote in the Senate. The Congressional Budget Office estimated the cost of complying with the proposed law at a modest $180 million a year (compared to the nearly $700 billion that regulation costs Americans each year).

Not all provisions of the various legislative proposals would have truly improved the regulatory process. In quite a few instances, the requirements to be imposed would have greatly complicated rule making. Although these changes would likely have slowed down the issuance of new rules, they also would have made it more difficult to simplify or eliminate existing ones.

Some of the proposed reform bills would have required detailed analysis of any regulation imposing annual costs of $25 million or more (or an average of $500,000 a state); other versions would set the threshold at $50 million. The benefit-cost ratio of performing the innumerable studies required by such a low threshold likely would not be favorable. Critics, perhaps justifiably, charged that the federal government does not possess the analytical resources that would be required, and that such a provision would swamp any reform effort in an overwhelming paperwork burden. Two decades ago, President Carter focused the analysis effort on those rules generating costs of $100 million or more a year and President Reagan maintained that size cutoff.

Several important reforms have been legislated in recent years, nonetheless. The Unfunded Mandates Reform Act of 1995 requires federal agencies to prepare written assessments of the costs and benefits of significant regulatory actions that may result in the expenditure by state and local governments or the private sector of at least $100 million annually. Independent regulatory agencies were exempted, as were a few politically sensitive programs such as civil rights. The new law requires that an agency consider a "reasonable" number of regulatory alternatives and select the least costly, most cost-effective, or least burdensome alternative that achieves the proposed rule's objectives. The law also requires that Congress have a CBO cost estimate before taking action on such legislation.

Pursuant to the Regulatory Accounting Act of 1996, OMB issued in September 1997 a report on the costs and benefits of federal regulations. The report, prepared by OIRA, estimates the total benefits and costs of federal regulation but provides no supporting detail by agency or program. Congress has now required OMB to issue another such report by September 30, 1998. This report, if extended to include the necessary detail, could become the genesis of a regulatory budget (a mechanism to control the total regulatory costs that federal agencies impose, akin to the limits on direct agency spending set by the fiscal budget). A major stumbling block to a regulatory budget to date has been the absence of an adequate database.

A promising generic reform statute, the Small Business Regulatory Enforcement and Fairness Act (SBREFA), was passed in late 1996. Among its numerous provisions is one establishing a procedure for congressional review of major rules (those involving annual costs of $100 million or more) before they become effective. Congress is given 60 days from the publication of the final rule in the *Federal Register* to review and reject it, subject to presidential veto. SBREFA also requires each regulatory agency to submit to Congress and the General Accounting Office, before the rule takes effect, a complete copy of any cost-benefit analysis.

Congress, however, has not yet used the provisions of SBREFA to challenge any major regulatory proposal. Among the notable lost opportunities was the highly debated new standards for ozone, which will produce comparatively small benefits at very high cost.

While potentially very useful, the new laws, like the presidential executive orders, focus on the middle stage of the regulatory process, when the agencies issue rules, rather than the birth stage, when Congress passes the basic regulatory statutes. In any event, it will take a strong follow-up effort by congressional leaders to ensure that government agencies take these tough new provisions seriously. To achieve the benefits envisioned by the framers of this legislation, hearings should be scheduled on every major regulatory proposal that a regulatory agency sends to Congress, and the agencies' justifications for new regulations should be subjected to rigorous congressional examination. This would require increased analytical capacity for Congress.

Specific proposals for reforming regulation need to be developed within a broader framework. The following four basic standards for justifying and evaluating regulation are an attempt to provide such a useful framework:

Regulation is warranted only when private markets do not work as well as regulation to protect citizens and consumers. A worthy objective does not necessarily create a need for regulation. Government regulation is already a very large presence in the American economy, and clearly the American people believe that it is needed to achieve many important economic and social goals. But the ability of competitive markets to protect the public is very powerful. Therefore, the burden should be on those who would replace the market with additional regulation to demonstrate with solid information and careful analysis that the public would benefit from a further extension of government into the private sector.

Regulatory authority should not be exercised capriciously, and the delegation of such authority by Congress to regulatory bodies should be limited to ensure this. Small businesses are especially vulnerable to arbitrary actions by regulators. The Wisconsin toy producer who went out of business following an erroneous report by the Consumer Product Safety Commission is a classic example of a little firm unable to cope with large bureaucracy. The agency had refused to correct its error in a timely fashion even after acknowledging the mistake—and the company lost key sales as a result.

Often, officials lack the authority to correct an error quickly, even when they would like to do so. For example, the EPA admitted it erred in listing the household antibiotic Bacitracin as an "extremely hazardous" substance. However, the agency was precluded from deleting that erroneous listing without going through the same burdensome process that it does in listing a very hazardous product.

Congress and the regulatory agencies should publicly and objectively evaluate the expected benefits and costs of proposed major regulatory efforts, using unbiased, professional, scientific advice. Such an evaluation also should be applied periodically to major existing regulations. Government decision makers involved in the regulatory process necessarily perform a rudimentary form of cost-benefit analysis when they make judgments about programs, whether they know it or not. It is vital that they think hard and analytically about these important decisions, using the best available information. The regulatory process would be improved if decision makers relied more heavily on sound science, including peer review of the technical basis for new regulations. Too often, regulators are influenced more by emotional and widely publicized fears and claims of interest groups than by professional analysis. As a result, priorities of federal agencies frequently do not reflect the relative seriousness of the numerous hazards and risks to which the public is subjected.

Where feasible and effective, regulations should be applied with a "soft touch" that allows flexibility of response, including the use of market incentives, instead of command-and-control directives. A regulatory system based on incentives to "do the right thing" can be both more effective and less costly. In pollution control, this means changing people's incentives so that not polluting becomes cheaper and easier than polluting. This approach also is far less onerous when government is dealing with the average citizen than the more traditional approach, which imposes highly specific and often extremely complex directives and then emphasizes seeking out wrongdoers for punishment. On occasion, simply setting performance standards may suffice, with the private sector having the flexibility to use the most cost-effective approach in achieving those standards.

The basic thrust of regulatory reform should be shifted. Virtually all reforms to date have focused on improving the way in which government agencies write regulations to carry out laws already enacted. Although this activity is useful, it ignores the compelling fact that the key decisions occur earlier in the process—when Congress writes an Occupational Safety and Health Act or an amendment to the Food, Drug, and Cosmetics Act or any other important regulatory law, usually with hundreds of pages of detailed specifications.

Each congressional committee should be required, when drafting a regulatory statute, to present estimates of the expected benefits and costs of the regulatory program in the report accompanying the legislation. The committee should affirm that these benefits justify the program in light of its estimated costs. Such a statement, and the benefit-cost analysis supporting it, should be required before a legislative proposal can be reported to the full House or Senate. To the extent feasible, this report should include a monetary evaluation of costs and benefits as well as a description of other advantages and disadvantages of the regulatory proposal.

The way regulatory statutes are now written frequently precludes the agencies from even considering the most cost-effective approaches. Key provisions of the Occupational Safety and Health Act, the Federal Food, Drug, and Cosmetics Act, the Clean Air Act, the Safe Drinking Water Act, and the Superfund Act implicitly, or explicitly, prohibit the regulators from taking account of economic impacts when setting standards. Despite well-intended presidential directives, it is impossible for regulators to strike any sensible balance between the costs they impose and the benefits they generate when the basic regulatory laws prohibit costs from being considered at all.

Congress should eliminate provisions in existing regulatory statutes that prevent or limit regulatory agencies from considering costs or comparing expected benefits with costs when designing and promulgating regulations. Regulations that seek to reduce health or safety risks should be based on scientific risk-assessment and should address risks that are real and significant rather than hypothetical or remote.

From time to time, Congress should enact statutes making technical corrections of provisions of regulatory legislation that are widely recognized as inappropriate or generating unintended negative consequences. The successful experience with the technical correction of tax laws provides a good model for such a process. (Of course, these problems could be minimized in the first instance if regulatory laws were written in clear and simple English.)

To help it carry out the expanded reviews of regulatory laws and rules proposed here, Congress should establish its own professional, nonpartisan regulatory analysis organization to provide it with reliable data, including the required estimates of benefits and costs. This organization could be a part of the CBO. This new organization also should evaluate the costs and effectiveness of existing regulatory programs. Each year it should analyze a limited number of current major regulatory programs.

The CBO itself provides a good precedent for such an organization. In carrying out their respective functions, it would be helpful if OIRA (the regulatory office of OMB) and its new congressional counterpart would develop a cooperative attitude on exchanging statistical and technical information, consistent with the separation of powers between legislative and executive branches. Such an effort would be similar to existing cooperation between CBO and OMB on budget matters.

Congress should also require OMB to continue on an annual basis its report on the costs and benefits of federal regulations, with supporting detail by agency and program. When regulatory cost data become more fully developed, Congress should establish on an experimental basis a regulatory budget for the federal government.

Regulatory Agencies

The current efforts of government agencies to examine the impacts of proposed regulations before they issue them need to be strengthened. By statute, these requirements should be extended to the so-called independent commissions, such as the Federal Energy Regulatory Commission, the Federal Trade Commission, the International Trade Commission, and the Nuclear Regulatory Commission.

Congress should legislate provisions for regulatory review by OIRA similar to those contained in the executive orders promulgated by Presidents Reagan and Clinton. A firm statutory basis would help to provide continuity in this important activity. In addition, Congress should codify in a single statute a requirement that regulatory agencies analyze the impact of significant regulatory initiatives before they are undertaken. Such an analysis of expected benefits and costs should be made a routine part of the drafting of new regulations by the various federal agencies.

Difficulties in estimating costs and benefits should not deter efforts to analyze the impact of regulations before they are issued. For example, uncertainty about the dollar benefits of air pollution control is not primarily a problem of statistical measurement. Rather, it may mainly reflect the unpleasant fact that we are unsure how many asthma attacks will be prevented or how much agricultural crop damage will be avoided by a specific emissions reduction. Such uncertainty should be recognized in the analysis, but should not be used as an excuse to proceed without analysis.

Furthermore, in making decisions and setting priorities based on risk, agencies should use best estimates rather than worst-case projections of risk. OSHA has based occupational cancer risks on the unrealistic assumption that a hypothetical worker is exposed to the risk eight hours every day, five days a week, for 50 weeks a year for 45 years. Similarly, the EPA sometimes assumes that an individual is exposed to emissions at a distance of 200 meters from the factory, 24 hours a day, every day for 70 years.

None of the procedural changes proposed here will succeed in truly improving the regulatory process unless they have the support of the public. It is the public who receives the benefits and pays the costs generated by the very substantial involvement of government in business decision-making. Thus, the emphasis in considering these proposals should not be on the effects on either business or government—but on the American people.

Nevertheless, despite the most careful preparation, reformers must be ready for vehement criticism from defenders of the *status quo*. Ironically, when benefit-cost analysis is used to justify large government water projects, local beneficiaries rarely challenge the calculations. But when the analysis contradicts the position of active interest groups, the analysis quickly comes under attack.

A final barrier to careful analysis is the common and erroneous perception that the costs of government regulation are of little concern to citizens because they are simply "paid by business." That is not so. By and large, those costs are ultimately borne by the individual workers and consumers who make and purchase the products and services produced under regulation. Moreover, much of the rule making extends to all employers, be they profit or nonprofit, in the public sector or in the private sector. Many regulations disproportionately affect smaller enterprises and organizations. In the case of paperwork, for example, each firm, regardless of size, may have to fill out the same burdensome form.

The criticism in this report of the government's response to public concerns about worker safety, the environment, and similar issues does not imply that those public concerns are not legitimate or should be ignored. The analysis here, rather, leads to the compelling conclusion that the American people deserve better results from the very substantial amounts of resources, time, and effort devoted to government regulation than is now the case. Air ought to be cleaner, water purer and workplaces safer, at the same time that consumer living standards are higher. The motivating force for the reforms proposed here is to improve the lives of our citizens.

Suggested Further Reading

Modernizing Government Regulation: The Need for Action New York: Committee for Economic Development, 1998.

Weidenbaum, Murray. 1997. "Regulatory Process Reform." *Regulation*, Winter.

Weidenbaum, Murray. 1999. *Business and Government in the Global Marketplace*, Sixth Edition. Englewood Cliffs, N.J.: Prentice-Hall.

MURRAY WEIDENBAUM is Mallinckrodt Distinguished University Professor at Washington University in St. Louis. He is the author of *One-Armed Economist*, available from Transaction.

The Community of Inquiry: Classical Pragmatism and Public Administration

This article argues that the community of inquiry notion of the classical pragmatists has much to offer public administration theory and practice. The community of inquiry is an ideal position from which public administrators can effectively examine how they approach problems, consider data, and communicate. Participatory democracy is a vital component of the community of inquiry developed by John Dewey and Jane Addams. The recognition of participatory democracy's place in public administration is underdeveloped. The community of inquiry context provides a useful lens to show how participatory democracy can nurture a creative public service.

PATRICIA M. SHIELDS
Texas State University

"So he killed her, washed the knife and himself, took a knife from the kitchen . . . Is that how you see it?"

"It's a working hypothesis," (p. 310)

Yet she knew that Dalgliesh was right in not hurrying Mrs. Buckley. She had information they needed, and too many *inquiries go wrong,* Kate knew, because the police had *acted in advance of the facts.* (p. 367) (italics added)

P. D. James, *A Certain Justice* (1999)

The community of inquiry is a powerful idea developed by classical pragmatists[1] that has wide application to many contexts within public administration. The detectives in P. D. James's novels, for example, may become a community of inquiry as they investigate a homicide. Community justice councils may form communities of inquiry as they deliberate about a just sentence. If they are lucky, university faculties form communities of inquiry as they consider curriculum change. In practice, the community of inquiry is an ideal position to which public administrators should strive. It is the position from which public administrators can most effectively examine how they approach problems, consider data, and communicate.

The purpose of this article is first, to clarify the meaning of the community of inquiry concept as developed by classical pragmatists. The community of inquiry notion is powerful because it is an organizing principle that can be applied to diverse public administration contexts. It also reconciles some of the prominent controversies in public administration (PA), such as the practice/theory dichotomy, the role of expertise, and ways to include democracy in practice. Second, this article shows how the community of inquiry concept can be applied to both PA theory and PA practice. Links to PA theory and issues (lead-

ership and role of expertise) are made throughout the text, and specific practice applications are developed in the conclusion.

Brief Definition

Common to all communities of inquiry is a focus on a problematic situation. The problematic situation is a catalyst that helps or causes the community to form and it provides a reason to undertake inquiry. Most problematic situations require further investigation and action (i.e., inquiry). Second, members of the community of inquiry bring a scientific attitude to the problematic situation. The scientific or experimental attitude is a willingness to tackle the problem using working hypotheses that guide the collection and interpretation of data or facts. Both theory and method are viewed as tools to address the problematic situation. In addition, the community is linked through participatory democracy. The parameters of the problematic situation and approaches to resolution are shaped by the interaction of the community and the facts. The democratic community also takes into account values/ideals such as freedom, equality, and efficiency as it considers goals and objectives. The three key ideas—problematic situation, scientific attitude, and participatory democracy—reinforce each other.

Many movements or trends in public administration (scientific management, rational decision-making model, planning programming budgeting systems, management by objectives, reinventing government, performance measurement) emphasize one or two aspects of the community of inquiry. Unfortunately, these reforms often divorce the benefits of science from the democratic community. The emphasis for many of these techniques is data collection and analysis. They are also viewed as methods to rationalize government. Their proponents often offer the technique as a solution to some government problem, such as inefficiency. The community of inquiry organizing principle should enable reflective public administrators to use and modify these tools as they approach problems. There is no deterministic faith that these techniques offer a definitive solution. Rather, these techniques offer data for the community to consider and use. The community of inquiry has special appeal for public administration because it is an orientation that uses a democratic approach to problem definition and interpretation of consequences.[2] At the same time, it is conducive to the development and use of methods for fact finding, analysis, and democratic decision making.

The community of inquiry is not a method, such as total quality management and others; rather, it is an organizing principle that provides fertile grounds for methods to be developed and tried. It is conducive to making mistakes, and making progress. And it reinforces founding ideals such as democracy, freedom, and equality. Thus it is an organizing principle that encourages better method, better theory, and democracy. I propose that it may be the missing link in public administration discourse.

Classical Pragmatism

Classical American pragmatism, the philosophy that is the source of the community of inquiry concept has recently received significant attention by public administration scholars.[3] For example, Karen Evans (2000, p. 308) suggests that public administration should "reclaim the philosophy of John Dewey as a guiding ethos for practice."

Charles Sanders Peirce originally conceived of pragmatism as a philosophy of science with inquiry at its center. To Peirce, the scientific method unlocks or at least leverages the power of individualism as people work together to address problems. Science is distinguished from all other methods of inquiry by its cooperative or public character (as cited in Buchler, 1955, p. x).

The classic Buddhist story of the three blind men confronting the problem of describing an elephant illustrates the need for a community of inquiry. Each blind man characterized the elephant from his own limited perspective ("It's a rope"—tail, "It's a fan"—ear, etc.) (Kyokai, 1966/1993, p. 148). The story's moral is that we are all trapped inside our limited selves and cannot know the truth. If, however, the three blind men were members of a community of inquiry, they would behave very differently. They would talk to each other, compare perspectives, argue, and test hypotheses as they touched, smelled, and listened to the elephant (gathered facts). Under these circumstances, it is possible to imagine that the blind men will eventually overcome their limited perspectives and come to a truer sense of the elephant.[4]

For example, take TQM, one method that ideally employs the community of inquiry idea. The power of TQM lies in its primary goal of reducing the psychological and organizational barriers to people sharing their thoughts and ideas, many of which boil down to the single barrier of fear. For example, fear of contradicting or embarrassing one's boss. TQM is an approach to gelling the blind men to speak—both directly, by reducing the fear of speaking, and indirectly, by gelling them to use the benchmark approach to measurement. In other words, it

does not matter if folks are completely accurate or honest; the focus is the direction the measurements take over time.

A community of inquiry is difficult to form if members are fixed in their belief system and impervious to fresh evidence. Charles Sanders Peirce (1958) draws a distinction between doubt and belief and the impact each has on action:

> Doubt is an uneasy and dissatisfied state from which we struggle to free ourselves and pass into the state of belief; while the latter is a calm and satisfactory state. . . . The irritation of doubt causes a struggle to attain a state of belief. I shall term this struggle *inquiry.* (p. 99)

Classical pragmatism argues that inquiry using the methods of science is the best way to "satisfy our doubts" (Peirce, 1958, p. 107). Ideally, members of the community of inquiry recognize the value of uncertainty.

The rich community of inquiry concept that pertains to public administration grew out of the writing and experiences of Jane Addams and John Dewey. In the late 1890s, they were both in their midthirties and worked in Chicago (Dewey at University of Chicago, Addams at Hull-House). Although they came from different backgrounds and had different life experiences, they had independently come to recognize many similar philosophic organizing principles (Westbrook, 1991). Subsequently, their shared experiences at Hull-House, their social activism, and their respectful, enduring friendship helped to propel classical pragmatism into full fruition.

> John Dewey had visited Hull-House in his Michigan years, and when he arrived in Chicago he became a trustee. Jane Addams became an extremely close personal friend; she was a profound influence on Dewey and he on her. The goals of progressive education and the settlement house movement, of Jane Addams and John Dewey, were intertwined at every point. (Dearborn, 1988, p. 54)

Camilla Stivers (2000) has persuasively argued that the settlement movement at the turn of the century is a part of public administration's heritage that should be synthesized and embraced. Jane Addams and John Dewey's community of inquiry notion is clearly a vehicle to do this.

Critical Optimism

Before moving on to a detailed discussion of the key components of the community of inquiry (problematic situation, scientific attitude, and participatory democracy) we take a detour to examine the fundamental notion of critical optimism.[5] The members of a community of inquiry proceed with a sense of critical optimism. Critical optimism is the faith or sense that if we put our heads together and act using a scientific attitude to approach a problematic situation, the identified problem has the potential to be resolved. This is faith in the human capacity for progress. Clearly, the "spirit of public administration" identified by George Frederickson (1997) is infused with a sense of critical optimism. In addition, the overriding theme in Charles Goodsell's (1994) classic *The Case for Bureaucracy* is one of critical optimism. Without some faith in the possibility of progress, public administrators would be trapped in a static world of standard operating procedures.

Critical optimism avoids the pitfalls of both optimism and pessimism. "Optimism, untempered by criticism, declares that good is already realized and as a result glosses over the evils that concretely exist" (Dewey 1920/1948, p. 178). The optimist easily becomes "callous and blind to the suffering of the less fortunate" or adopts a Pollyanna attitude and is unwilling to listen to the concerns of others. On the other hand,

> pessimism is a paralyzing doctrine. In declaring that the world is evil wholesale, it makes futile all efforts to discover the remedial causes of specific evils and thereby destroys at the root every attempt to make the world better and happier. (Dewey, 1920/1948, p. 178)

Both unfettered optimism and pessimism are consistent with dogmatism and perhaps determinism. Critical optimism, on the other hand, embraces uncertainty and change but with a skeptical attitude. Critical optimism (meliorism)

> is the belief that the specific conditions which exist at one moment, be they comparatively bad or comparatively good, in any event may be bettered. It encourages intelligence to work to improve conditions and it arouses reasonableness and confidence as optimism does not. (Dewey, 1920/1948, p. 179)

Jane Addams led the Hull-House experiment with a sense of critical optimism. She and the residents were clearly aware of all the social ills around them. Obviously, they approached their work with faith that their efforts could in some measure ameliorate pressing community problems and concerns. Indeed, it was the social problems that drew them together.

Critical optimism should surround the application of any idea to public administration or any organized effort to achieve the public good. If a public administrator is not a critical optimist as defined here, they have no business being a public administrator; no more than that one should be a doctor who does not believe in the sanctity of life. Critical optimism orients the practitioner toward his obligations to his duty and to his supervisor. A mature community of inquiry (one infused with a spirit of critical optimism) should mitigate or steer even selfish impulses toward results of general benefit; as a pragmatist, one would never count on self-motivation alone to accomplish this goal.[6]

Today's modern public administrator is daily confronted with new challenges (problematic situations). She is also called on to collect and analyze data. Finally, every day, public administrators communicate with people. The community of inquiry approach has immediate relevance to PA because it touches all aspects of the PA workaday world.

Essential Components

There are three essential components to the community of inquiry: problematic situation, scientific attitude, and community as participatory democracy. Neither Addams nor Dewey identified these components in a separate discussion. Rather, each element is found consistently within their published works and

actions. The three components were distilled for their immediate relevance to public administration theory and practice.

Problematic Situation

Approaches to public administration have often used the "problem" as a focus. A classic example is Hitch and McKean's (1965/1978) *Economics of Defense in the Nuclear Age.* Hitch and McKean conceptualized the defense of our nation as an "economic efficiency problem." They demonstrated how the problem could be addressed using economic theory and decision-making techniques such as cost and optimization analysis, Robert McNamara adopted many of their ideas during his tenure as secretary of defense.[7] Perhaps because of policies such as that during the Vietnam War, in which the problem orientation and the use of efficiency techniques were applied with disastrous effect, the focus on a problem has been criticized in the PA literature (See Hummel & Stivers, 1998; Adams & Balfour, 1998; Goodsell, 1994). Critics point to the natural tendency to link problems to final (often, technical) solutions. Technical solutions may appear value free and are not questioned because they promote efficiency. Problem solving linked to definitive solutions can close off discussion and debate and may put a public bureaucracy in an untenable position because it is expected to solve insolvable problems. Classical pragmatism's focus on the problematic situation is fruitful because it is not solution as end-of-quest oriented and thus addresses critics' concerns. An all knowledgeable expert, for example, would never have a final solution, rather a useful approach to the problematic situation. Simultaneously, the commonsense, practitioner-friendly focus on the problem is retained.

John Dewey's term *problematic situation* is appealing because it speaks to practitioner's experience. Practitioners daily find themselves in problematic situations. Examples range from developing a meeting agenda, evaluating employee performance, developing rules and regulations consistent with new legislation, negotiating a contract, initiating a program, developing a budget, or responding to an emergency. Most of the above situations involve a blend of standard operating procedures and new issues. Each can be conceptualized as more or less a problematic situation imbedded in practitioner experience. Each has the opportunity to provide learning through inquiry.

The importance of practitioner experience is recognized both in the day-to-day practice of public administration and in formal public administration training (e.g., internships, choosing deans of schools of public affairs based on their executive-level federal experience). One might even argue that historically, PA education traces its distinctiveness to the role of practitioner experience (Stivers, 2000, p. 104).

Classical pragmatism places the nature of experience as a point of departure and as the crucial link to the problematic situation. Dewey's focus on the problematic situation

> recognizes that we are always beginning in the middle of things. Experience inescapably involves some kind of existential situation before language or reflection is brought to bear. . . . Dewey chooses the situation as a *theoretical starting point* [Webb's emphasis] for his analysis of experience. (Webb, 1999, p. 26)[8]

The situation and experience are given meaning during the process of defining/understanding the problem. The problem is imbedded in a past and is linked to the future because a problem implies that "something that needs to be done is not yet done" (Webb, 2000, p. 5). Every situation's being contingent on the problematic situation brings a focus to certain elements of the situation. Nevertheless, there is always background that recedes into the horizon. As the problematic situation is confronted, some of the background "may come into focus as pertinent to the issue at hand." In fact, from the viewpoint of the community of inquiry, "the focus will inevitably shift" (Webb, 1999 p. 13). Thus, the problematic situation is usually connected to a historical context. Aside from the influence of past decisions, for the public administrator, the problematic situation is tied to deadlines and budget constraints.

Jane Addams's philosophy is problem centered. Her approach to social analysis was comprehensive, synthetic, and problem centered, as compared to profession or discipline centered. Her problem-centered perspective encouraged fundamental rethinking of seemingly settled issues. The problem orientation allowed her to envision communities in which cooperation crystallized around a quest to address common problems.

Inquiry is a process that has direction and organization (Dewey, 1938, p. 104). Dewey defines inquiry as a "controlled or directed transformation of an indeterminate situation." The transformation converts the "original situation into a united whole" (Dewey, 1938, p. 104). The definition of the problematic situation emerges as part of the transformations of inquiry. "A problem that does not grow out of the original situation. . . is . . . busy work mere excuses for seeming to do something intellectual" (Dewey, 1938, p. 108). In a community of inquiry, the transformation is directed with a scientific attitude.

Scientific Attitude

John Dewey drew on Percian themes to connect the problematic situation to the scientific attitude:

> A disciplined mind takes delight in the problematic, and cherishes it until a way out is found that approves itself upon examination. The questionable becomes an active questioning, a … quest for the objects by which the obscure and unsettled may be developed into the stable and clear. The *scientific attitude* [italics added] may almost be defined as that which is capable of enjoying the doubtful; scientific method is, in one aspect, a technique for making a productive use of doubt by converting it into operations of infinite inquiry. (Dewey, 1929, p. 228)

Dewey notes that attainment of the relatively secure and settled can take place "with respect to *specified* problematic situations," but a larger (universal) quest for certainty is destructive. "One question is disposed of; another offers itself and thought is kept alive" (Dewey, 1929, p. 228).

Dewey and Addams also extended Peirce's scientific logic of inquiry to practical reasoning and social problems. The struggle to see the elephant becomes the struggle to *use* the elephant

in everyday life.[9] Science is not privileged but is an unusually successful intellectual enterprise whose success relies on openness to criticism, fallibilism, and an "explicit belief that knowledge is irrevocably and inescapably embedded in experience" (Webb, 1999, p. 16).

The hypothesis is a tool of science brought to the problematic situation. "A hypothesis is not about 'what is' but about 'what will happen'—that is, an expectation that certain events will occur in specified circumstances. Even what are commonly called 'data' are not 'given' but 'taken' in a process involving many hypotheses." In other words, nothing is above criticism. "No hypothesis or class of hypotheses is singled out as the foundation upon which all else rests" (Webb, 1999, p. 1). Of course, some (many) hypotheses are accepted provisionally to conduct inquiry. Dewey often used the term *working hypothesis* to emphasize the provisional nature of hypotheses. The working hypothesis may be particularly suited to PA inquiry because it explicitly takes into account uncertainty and the ongoing process of discovery. A working hypothesis would appear to be a natural tool for a PA practitioner in the midst of dealing with a problematic situation. A working hypothesis is one that is more or less imbedded in experience, in contrast to formal hypotheses that are often tested in laboratories or conditions with more controls. Time and money constraints as well as the fluid nature of PA problems give the flexible, contextual working hypotheses great appeal.

A practitioner who uses a working hypothesis as a tool of inquiry must be prepared for the unexpected. In other words, evidence that does not adhere to expectations is allowed to emerge. When contrary evidence emerges, the practitioner may be in the uncomfortable position of telling their boss what they do not want to hear. This possibility is the strength of the scientific attitude. Note that evidence may take many forms—both quantitative and qualitative.

John Dewey's process of inquiry begins and ends in experience. Empirical consequences, not popularity, consensus, or rhetorical prowess, control inquiry. Dewey has "faith that the conclusions yielded by the process of inquiry that he describes will be persuasive to those who engage in it for precisely the same reason that scientific explanations are persuasive. There is a community engaged in inquiry." Inquiry is an open-ended process with positive feedback. "The knowledge yielded by this process—what Dewey calls warranted assertibility—is not infallible, simply the best currently available" (Webb, 2000, p. 5).[10] From the perspective of classical pragmatism, public administration decisions that use a scientific attitude are not perfect (or truth). They are just the best available (at the time) and are subject to revision.

John Dewey's discourse on the scientific attitude generally had a theoretical tone. In contrast, Jane Addams applied and extended Dewey's theories to her work at Hull-House. For example, Addams's definition of a settlement[11] includes both the scientific attitude (experimental effort) and the problematic situation.

> The Settlement, then is an *experimental effort* to aid in the solution of the social and industrial *problems* which are engendered by the modern conditions of life in a great city. (italics added) (Addams, 1910/1930, p. 125)

The settlement residents cannot be fixated on a single belief system or a single method. The settlement must welcome all perspectives and be flexible in its approach to problem solving.

Furthermore, its residents (the core community) should have "scientific patience in the accumulation of facts."

> From its very nature [the Settlement] can stand for no political or social propaganda. It must in a sense, give the warm welcome of an inn to all such propaganda, if perchance one of them be found an angel. The one thing to be dreaded in the Settlement is that it lose its flexibility, its power of quick adaptation, its readiness to change its methods as its environment may demand. It must be open to conviction and must have a deep and abiding sense of tolerance. It must be hospitable and *ready for experiment.* It should demand from its residents a *scientific patience in the accumulation of facts* and the steady holding of their sympathies as one of the best instruments for that accumulation. (italics added) (Addams, 1910/1930, p. 126)

The collection of data is linked to the scientific attitude component of the community of inquiry. Sometimes data collection techniques must be developed (tailored to the problematic situation). Data collection is an often-overlooked activity of the Hull-House experience.

This belief in the necessity of depending on factual data for scientific inquiry led to innovative research design and cartographic techniques developed by the residents of Hull-House. In the early 1890s, Jane Addams and her colleague Florence Kelley supervised the writing and production of *Hull-House Maps and Papers* (Residents of Hull-House, 1895/1970). The complete *Hull-House Maps and Papers* contains two large multicolored maps that depict the demographic characteristics within a third of a square mile near Hull-House. One map provided information on the distribution of 18 nationality groups who resided in the area. The other large map focused on the residents' wages, occupations, and housing conditions. The field-based research methods and the innovative mapping techniques developed by the residents of Hull-House has been suggested as a prototype for ideas later espoused by the Chicago Department of Sociology (Deegan, 1988).

Hull-House Maps and Papers also contained chapters that delved into some of the most important problems facing the immediate community. Florence Kelley (1895/1970) detailed the many problems with employment in the garment industry in "The Sweating System."[12]

The aim of both the maps and subsequent narrative chapters (papers) was to present

> conditions rather than advance theories—to bring within reach of the public exact information concerning this quarter of Chicago rather than to advise methods by which it may be improved. While vitally interested in every question connected with this part of the city, and especially concerned to enlarge the life and vigor of the immediate neighborhood, *Hull House offers these facts more with the hope of stimulating inquiry* and *action,* and *evolving new thoughts and methods* [italics added], than with the idea of recommending its own manner of effort. (Holbrook, 1895/1970, p. 13)

Jane Addams was the overseer of the entire project. The mapping of social and demographic characteristics of a population was a methodology first adopted at Hull-House. Not only was this landmark methodological approach first used to create and publish *Hull-House Maps and Papers,* researchers at Hull-House continued using and refining this approach after the book's publication and national dissemination. Thus, the Addams neighborhood and surrounding areas became a place of ever-increasing study and ever-increasing cartographic analysis. In addition, the maps became part of the community, an integral component of the settlement's goals of encouraging and promoting education and democracy among neighborhood residents.

Jane Addams also stressed two key elements of the experimental approach (or scientific attitude). First, people must be willing to forgo preconceived belief systems and they must listen carefully. This was a lesson learned early while working among the immigrants.

> The experience of the coffee-house taught us not to hold preconceived ideas of what the neighborhood ought to have, but to keep ourselves in readiness to modify and adapt our understandings as we discovered those things which the neighborhood was ready to accept. (Addams, 1910/1930, p. 132)

Second, the scientific attitude involves a willingness to see and learn from experimental failures. "There was room for discouragement in the many unsuccessful experiments in cooperation which were carried on in Chicago during the early nineties" (Addams, 1910/1930, p. 141). And, "in spite of failures, cooperative schemes went on, some of the same men appearing in one after another with irrepressible optimism" (Addams, 1910/1930, p. 142).

The scientific attitude that characterizes classical pragmatism's approach to addressing problems is different from the technical rationality that Adams and Balfour (1998) link to administrative evil. Adams and Balfour[13] harshly criticize the dominance of technical rationality as "a way of thinking and living that emphasizes the scientific-analytic mindset and the belief in technical progress" (Adams & Balfour, 1998, p. xx). They argue that the scientific-analytic approach inevitably led to the use of experts (professionals) to solve problems. In addition, technical rationality associates with expertise emphasized efficiencies that could be gained through science. The technical-rational approach rewards professionals dedicated to their specialized field. It also disconnects the technical expert from the people and an ethical framework. They maintain that Germany's efficient, technical, rational, and disconnected public administration professionals contributed to the evil of the Holocaust. Indeed, the support of the efficient, technically trained professionals made the scale of the human tragedy so massive.

Adams and Balfour (1998) trace technical rationality to the Progressive Era. Taylor's scientific management is perhaps the most well-known example. Ironically, this is just the time when the pragmatism of John Dewey and William James was receiving widespread attention. Clearly, the technical rationality described by Adams and Balfour is consistent with Ayer's (1952) positivism, not Dewey's pragmatism. Positivism is disconnected from values and is individualistic. In contrast, classical pragmatism links the scientific attitude with a rich participatory community.

Community as Participatory Democracy

The community as participatory democracy is both the simplest and the most profound component of the community of inquiry for public administration practice. Most practitioners and scholars immediately associate democracy with the representative democracy and its methods, such as voting (both citizen and legislative behavior). For the most part, the methods of representative democracy fall outside public bureaucracies. Participatory democracy, on the other hand, is a way of communicating. It is a way of communicating that, according to McSwite (1997), was part of our colonial heritage. Town meetings and conversations across fences are historical examples of participatory democracy cited by McSwite. Clearly, bureaucracies are places where conversations occur continuously and where participatory democracy can be employed daily.

Dewey's conception of community is also closely connected to his understanding of democracy as a kind of cooperative experiment (Seigfried, 1996, p. 92). The values of democratic community—"mutual respect, mutual toleration, give and take, the pooling of experience" (Dewey, as cited in Campbell, 1998, p. 40)—pervade all aspects of his thought. For Dewey, the success of the community depends on cooperative efforts to seek the common good in a democratic way. We may be drawn together to solve our problems, but it is the togetherness, not the solution, that is the primary result (Campbell, 1998, p. 40).

Dewey's notion of community is not necessarily based on physical proximity. It is rather rooted in intellectual and cultural neighborhoods that interact with shared membership. The community might also be anchored in the desire to address a common problem. "Associated or joint activity is a condition of the creation of a community. But association itself is physical and organic, while communal life is moral, that is emotionally, intellectually, consciously sustained" (Dewey, 1927/1954, p. 151).

Dewey does not see democracy as simply giving everyone a say in a squabble over cutting up a pie of given size. Rather, his conception includes the capability of designing a better pie or imagining and constructing something other than a pie. This characteristic requires the capability for inquiry on the part of the participants.

John Dewy reiterates the theme that democracy is not political democracy. We act "as if democracy were something that took place mainly at Washington and Albany—or some other state capital" (Dewey, 1938/1998, p. 342). Dewey viewed democracy as "a way of life controlled by a working faith in the possibilities of human nature," and human nature as being "exhibited in every human being irrespective of race, color, sex, birth and family, of material or cultural wealth." Dewey's conceptualization of democracy also incorporated a "faith in human equality" or the "belief that every human being, independent of the quality or range of his personal endowment, has the right to equal opportunity with every other person for development of whatever gifts he has" (Dewey, 1938/1998, p. 342).

Democracy as a way of life includes an overarching personal faith in the

day-by-day working together with others. Democracy is the belief that even when needs and ends or consequences are different for each individual, the habit of amicable cooperation—which may include, as in sport, rivalry and competition—is itself a priceless addition to life. (Dewey, 1938/1998, p.342)

Dewey (1927/1954, pp. 218–219) stresses that listening is a critical component of participation. "The connection of the ear with vital and outgoing thought and emotion are immensely closer and more varied than those of the eye. Vision is a spectator; hearing is a participator."

Camilla Stivers (1994) discusses the role of the "listening bureaucrat" as an agent of democracy. She argues that listening as an "embodied ability, way of knowing, moral capacity and potential administrative practice" helps to shape a "revived responsiveness, one that avoids passivity and partisanship" (p. 365). Mutual responsiveness is an essential component of *participatory* in participatory democracy.

Again, Jane Addams consciously used and refined participatory democracy at Hull-House. She also incorporated carefully crafted conceptualizations of participatory democracy into her pragmatism. Addams's ideal democracy was egalitarian. It was also generic enough to apply to both large and small groups (Farrell, 1967, p. 63). Further, Addams's democracy was not solely associated with government. "Democracy was a method of discovering truth through the combination of rational thought with equal participation of all citizens in community process" (Addams, as cited in Deegan, 1988, p. 275). She incorporated a scientific method as part of the method for discovering the truth. "Democracy was weakened by excluding any group from the democratic ideal" (Farrell, 1967, p. 78). She viewed the settlement (in all its complexity) as a "tangible expression of the democratic ideal" (Addams, 1910/1930, p. 122). The settlement was also an expression of "the desire to interpret democracy in social terms" (Addams, 1910/1930, p. 125).

Addams's democracy links to a larger, moral "common good." And part of the settlement's job is to articulate an end-in-view associated with the common good.

> *The settlement is pledged* to insist upon the unity of life, to gather to itself the sense of righteousness to be found in its neighborhood, and as far as possible in its city; *to work towards* the betterment not of one kind of people, but for *the common good*. (italics added) (Addams, 1895/1970. p. 203)

Jane Addams may have articulated an ideal democracy in her philosophy; nevertheless, she had an abiding reverence for the flawed U.S. democracy for which Lincoln "had cleared the title" (Addams, 1910/1930, p. 41).[14] "We must learn to trust our democracy, giant-like and threatening as it may appear in its uncouth strength and untried applications" (Addams, 1895/1970, p. 198).

Much of her social reform efforts involved ways to make U.S. democracy more inclusive—more egalitarian. At the local level, she and the residents of Hull-House worked to effect reform within the political framework of a corrupt Cook County.

Ironically, they did not even have the right to vote. Although Addams's reform efforts[15] may have appeared radical at the time, she always respected and worked within the existing democratic governmental framework.

The kind of democratic community envisioned by Dewey and Addams is consistent with Frederickson's (1997) *Spirit of Public Administration* and King and Stivers's (1998) *Government Is Us.* Both influential books argue for a reconceptualizing of the role of the public administrator. George Frederickson (1997) maintains that public administrators should view themselves as "representative citizens." King and Stivers (1998, p. 196) advocate "active citizenship and active administration." Public administration should emphasize citizen engagement and the facilitator role vis-à-vis the technical expert role. King and Stivers call for a world where scientific and technical approaches are balanced with "experienced based knowledge and personal skills like listening" (1998, p. 196). Addams obviously worked to achieve this balance.

Dewey and Addams have an idealized vision of democracy more radical than the one depicted in *Government Is Us* and *The Spirit of Public Administration.* They saw democracy as a way of life that extended to all kinds of human ways of organizing for example, family, school, and church. In the case of PA, one would extend this vision to life inside a bureaucracy where problematic situations are purely internal. Thus, the community of inquiry organizing principle is implied when public administrators confront problematic situations (evaluate a program, develop performance measures, negotiate a contract) and consciously incorporate principles of participatory democracy into their practice. Examples include everything from active listening to seeking out greater community support—all the while, paying attention to the problematic situation, working hypotheses, and the nature and meaning of evidence. In other words, engaging in a cooperative experiment.

Leadership

The community of inquiry sounds great in theory. Unfortunately, Dewey's insight about practical questions such as who leads or directs the community of inquiry is unclear. John Dewey's insights perhaps give us a clue to what a leader should *not* be. Leaders who are fixed in their belief systems, unwilling to confront evidence they do not expect, unwilling to listen, and uncomfortable with uncertainty and doubt undermine the formation or a community or inquiry. Further, leaders who adopt a pessimistic attitude foreordain failure. Alternatively, leaders who are unfettered optimists are unwilling to see problems or are ill prepared to adjust their approach when negative/unexpected information needs to be processed. Note, Dewey would maintain that leaders (and the community) ground their inquiry in values such as equality, freedom, and justice. Further, some of the most challenging problematic situations facing leaders involve conflicts between these cherished values.

Fortunately, both the writing and the actions of Jane Addams are informative about the nature of leadership in a community of inquiry. Jane Addams's designation as a founder of pragmatism has been recently rediscovered.[16] More important, from the perspective of practice, she is an acknowledged early leader of social work, the settlement movement, the Suffrage movement, Progressive politics, and the peace movement. She was also cofounder of the famous Chicago settlement Hull-House. In addition, Camilla Stivers (2000) makes a strong case that she is also an undiscovered founder of public administration. Thus, her insights and actions about leadership have much to offer the larger PA literature.

Jane Addams's actions and writings demonstrate the role of leadership in a community of inquiry. Moreover, Hull-House is a living example of a community of inquiry guided by Addams, the caring leader-mediator. She used a facilitator/mediator approach to dealing with the problematic situations at Hull-House (a community of inquiry). Her actions and writings show how leader-facilitators in a community of inquiry use reflection and listening to bridge problematic communication dualisms and articulate the larger often-evolving end-in-view. Thus, leaders in a community of inquiry have a responsibility to keep the big picture in mind as inquiry proceeds (discussion, data collection, and problem definition).

The community of inquiry has by implication an open-ended quality. Both the problem definition and the end-in-view may change as deliberation and data collection proceeds. The leader-facilitator must be flexible and capable of adaptation. Leaders must also keep the community of inquiry focused on data collection and interpretation.

It must be emphasized that Addams guided the experimental effort. She was the leader who directed and, probably most important, held Hull-House together for over 40 years. Addams guided the work at Hull-House by stressing important components of the community of inquiry—cooperation and the mediator role. In some ways, she was the personification of the pragmatic mediator role described by William James (1907) in *Pragmatism.* Her personality was nonjudgmental and she encouraged diversity in points of view at Hull-House.

Communities of inquiry need leader-mediators because there are often language and other barriers that discourage cooperation. Mediators build bridges between different points of view and different experiential references. Addams used a labor museum as a mediation device.

> It seemed to me that Hull-House ought to be able to devise some educational enterprise, which should build a bridge between Europe and American experiences in such ways as to give them both more meaning and a sense of relation. I meditated that perhaps the power to see life as a whole, is more needed in the immigrant quarter of a large city than anywhere else, and that the lack of this power is the most fruitful source of misunderstanding between European immigrants and their children, as it is between them and their American neighbors. (Addams, 1910/1930, pp. 235–236)

The immensely successful labor museum built a bridge by including traditional Old-World methods of clothes making alongside new technology (sewing machines). Further, the museum bridged dichotomies (Europe/America; young/old), enabling learning and reconstructing experience and thus resolving problems. Addams hoped that

> if these young people could actually see that the complicated machinery of the factory had been evolved from simple tools, they might at least make a beginning towards that education which Dr. Dewey defines as "continuing reconstruction of experience." They might also lay a foundation for ... sound progress (Using the elephant). (Addams, 1910/1930, pp. 236-237).

Jane Addams was often called on to negotiate complicated and passionate labor disputes. Although she was associated with the causes of immigrant labor, industry accepted her because she was fair and she listened. As the mediator, she was able to hear words that blocked productive discussion. Terms such as *friend* and *enemy* fixated discourse and should be replaced by words such as *manager* and *employee*. She listened so that others might hear and reach a negotiated settlement. Addams's faith in participatory democracy as a template for negotiation was often rewarded. "And democracy did save industry. It transformed disputes about wages from social feuds into business bargains" (Addams, 1895/1970, p. 197).[17] At their best, leaders in the community of inquiry facilitate the transformations of inquiry. Because leaders and members of the immediate community may lack technical expertise, they may call on experts to join the discourse. The role of the expert is particularly relevant to PA, in which many problematic situations require technical expertise.

The Role Of Expertise

The public-administrator-as-expert role has recently been harshly criticized. There is concern that large elements of both policy and management are turned over wholesale to experts. Scholars such as McSwite (1997), King and Stivers (1998), and Adams and Balfour (1998) posit that experts enamored with their technical knowledge and skills often become detached from larger public purposes. How is expertise considered within the community of inquiry?

One might argue that their criticism of expertise is nonsense. What is the alternative? It is hard to imagine that the country would be better off if people with specialized expertise did not inspect our meat, plan and oversee the building of roads, lead our peacekeeping forces, and prepare personnel policies. From Dewey's perspective, the key is not whether expertise is necessary but rather what role expertise plays in the community of inquiry.

Indeed, Dewey speaks directly to these issues in *The Public and Its Problems*. He makes a distinction between administrative matters and politics: "Is not the problem at the present time that of securing experts to manage administrative matters. . . . The important governmental affairs at present, it may be argued, are also technically complicated matters to be conducted properly by expert" (Dewey, 1927/1954, p. 123).

He also identifies problematic situations such as sanitation, public health, healthful and adequate housing, planning of cities, transportation, regulation and distribution of immigrants, selection and management of personnel, preparation of competent teachers, efficient management of funds, and adjustment of taxation that are relevant even today.

> These are technical matters as much so as the construction of an efficient engine for purposes of traction or locomotion. Like it, they are to be settled by inquiry into facts: and as the inquiry can be carried on only by those especially equipped, so the results of inquiry can be utilized only by trained technicians. (Dewey, 1927/1954, pp. 123–125)

Dewey anticipates the current criticism of expertise in PA. Experts have the potential to become "a specialized class . . . shut off from knowledge of the needs which they are supposed to serve" (Dewey, 1927/1954, p. 206). He is concerned that the class of experts could inevitably be so removed from common interests as to become a class with private interests and private knowledge. Ideally, these experts are connected to a process of popular government and comfortable with the "common interest," even if the recognition of common interest is confused. He notes that discussion and publicity help to clarify the expert's purpose. "The man who wears the shoe knows best that it pinched and where it pinches, even if the expert shoemaker is the best judge of how the trouble is to be remedied" (credited to De Tocqueville by Dewey, 1927/1954, p. 207).

He warns that a government by experts in which the masses do not have a chance to inform the experts about their needs will become

> an oligarchy managed in the interests of the few. A government that incorporates expertise must proceed in ways that force the administrative specialist to take account larger common purposes.... The world has suffered more from leaders and authorities than from the masses. (1927/1954, p. 208)

The crucial component of the community of inquiry that addresses the expertise problem is "participatory democracy." Dewey notes that there is an essential need to improve "the methods and conditions of debate, discussion and persuasion. That is *the* problem of the public." (Dewey, 1927/1954, p. 208) As Paul Appleby (1962, p. 175) noted in his classic *Public Administration Review* essay, experts should be "on tap not on top."

Dewey asserts that progress depends

> upon freeing and perfecting the processes of inquiry and of dissemination of their conclusions. Inquiry, indeed, is a work which devolved upon experts. But their expertness is not shown in framing and executing policies, but in discovering and making known the facts upon which the former depend. (1927/1954, p. 208)

"They are technical experts in the sense that scientific investigators and artists manifest *expertise*. It is not necessary that the many should have the knowledge and skill to carry on the needed investigations; what is required is that they have the ability to judge of the bearing of the knowledge supplied by others upon common concerns" (Dewey, 1927/1954, p. 209). Dewey has identified and addressed the same issues as current critics of PA. Thus, one contribution of the community of inquiry notion to PA is that the role and value of expertise is automatically contextualized through the emphasis on participatory democracy. Ideally, there is a listening expert at the table.

In the above discussion, the role of expertise within a participatory democracy was emphasized. Keith Snider (2000) stresses another aspect of the community of inquiry (experimentalism or scientific attitude) in his investigation of pragmatism and the role of expertise in PA:

> Since the late 19th century, mainstream public administration has been characterized by the pursuit of certainty through administrative expertise, whether through techniques, principles or empiricism. Since that time as well, pragmatism has offered the field a more modest alternative of experimenting that holds out no such promise of administrative 'Truth' but, rather merely the opportunity for administrators to craft themselves legitimate roles based on experience and context. (p. 351)

One might also add a participatory community.

So What!

One might ask, So what? The community of inquiry notion is just too remote or ideal to contribute anything to PA. The community of inquiry is subject to attack from all sides. Scholars who want PA to distance itself from the scientific way of knowing can find fault. Others can point to the world of power politics (bureaucratic and others) and dismiss the community of inquiry as a pipe dream. Economists might ask, Where is self-interest?

From the point of view of classical pragmatism, all of these issues are points of departure for further inquiry. Patricia Shields (1996) argues that the pragmatism of James and Dewey resonates with practitioner experience. The community of inquiry is a conceptual tool that practitioners can use to help them interpret and shape experience.[18] In addition, public administrators who consciously use the community of inquiry as a conceptual structure should be better able to tap into the collective and historical experience of their organizational community. Analogous to the useful efficiency fable of the 90% untapped brain, the aware administrator may be able to extract more from a less-knowledgeable community than the unaware administrator might from a crack troupe. Further, he seeks to institute (or improve current) methods to continuously increase the intelligence of the community. He seeks to motivate an inquiring community to listen, share, learn, and persuade (Brom, 2000).

There are many seemingly disparate problematic situations in PA in which a practitioner (or group of practitioners) might use the community of inquiry as a beneficial conceptual lens. The following examples (methods) show that the community of inquiry is an organizing principle that can be used in a variety of settings to help administrators understand what they do and how to forward the public interest (progress).

Any time a problem is referred to a committee, the community of inquiry model could be employed as a conceptual framework. If the spirit of participatory democracy prevailed, meetings would be civil. This alone might improve work life in

PA. A committee or a task force is an ideal forum to employ many of the organizing principles found within the community of inquiry. Committees usually form to address some problem. The members of the committee often are tasked to make recommendations (it is hoped by gathering and analyzing facts). It is easy to see how the leader or chair of the committee could make a difference. If the meeting is guided by a leader who encourages discourse, is centered on the problematic situation (but open to redefinition of the problematic situation), is comfortable with uncertainty, and encourages active listening, the work of the committee should closely adhere to the community of inquiry ideal.

The crafting of performance measures is another example. If performance measures are developed using a community of inquiry approach, one would expect that the outcome or process measured would be tied to a deliberative process that defines the problematic situation, taking into account larger/different contexts and goals. Performance indicator development is tied to an ongoing process of hypothesis development and testing. In addition, the meaning of performance measures is interpreted through the eyes of participatory democracy. The community of inquiry model mirrors a continuous quality improvement approach to management at its best (Wilson, 2002).

The negotiated rulemaking process offers another opportunity to apply the community of inquiry notion. Negotiated rulemaking is "a consensus based process in which a proposed rule is initially developed by a committee composed of representatives of all those interests that will be affected by the rule, including those interests represented by the rulemaking agency" (Center for Public Policy Dispute Resolution, 1996, p. 11). The committee composed of representatives of all those interested could act like a community of inquiry. If so, the goal of greater citizen participation by citizen and administrator would be furthered (Beechinor, 1998).

Something very close to a community of inquiry has been legislated by the Individuals with Disabilities Act of 1997. When disabled students become consistently disruptive in class, the teacher, parents, counselor, and other specialists must work together (form a community that crystallizes around a problem). They are mandated to do a Functional Behavioral Assessment. The Functional Behavioral Assessment requires the team to approach the disruptive behavior by developing and testing causal hypotheses. Interventions are suggested, tried, and assessed. If the intervention fails, the process begins again. Perhaps the community of inquiry could be called a team with a scientific attitude (Pratt, 2000).

The field of juvenile justice is beginning to use councils akin to communities of inquiry to wrestle with sentencing (problematic situation) of youthful nonviolent offenders. The model generally includes a panel of volunteer community members who have received training. These "community justice councils" examine the crime and sentencing options with the offender, the parents, the victim (if applicable—vandalism), and criminal justice professionals. The sentencing process involves deliberations with all involved (participatory democracy). The council may mandate community service or drug awareness classes. Importantly, the progress is monitored (it is hoped, with a scientific attitude, e.g., evidence of compliance) using a process that requires follow-up and continued contact with the youth (Raffray, 1997).

Three hundred sixty-degree performance evaluations can be approached using the community of inquiry. The 360-degree system uses input from the individual, peers, and supervisor. This group forms the community that addresses the problematic situation (the evaluation of the employee). Using the community of inquiry model, the evaluation is approached with a spirit of critical optimism. Thus, the focus is development (improvement of employee performance). Ideally, evidence of current performance is collected with a scientific attitude. Working hypotheses for improvement are proposed (and tested over time). Members of the evaluation team also approach the assessment discourse with the spirit of participatory democracy (Garza, 2000). Indeed, even a performance evaluation system limited to a smaller community (supervisor and employee) would benefit from a community of inquiry approach.

The detectives in P. D. James's (1999) novel use a process similar to the community of inquiry. They work together to understand the problematic situation—who killed the victim. They find evidence, formulate hypotheses, and search for more evidence. If they fail to keep an open mind (scientific attitude), they will miss or misinterpret evidence. If all are free to talk and participate, multiple points of view about how to interpret evidence and form new hypotheses are considered. Even an ideal community of inquiry might arrest an innocent woman. There is no certainty.

The contributors of *Government Is Us* all want to see greater participatory democracy between citizen and public administrator. If citizen and administrator act as part of a community of inquiry, PA would move closer to the framework that King, Stivers (1998), and contributors advocate.

Participatory democracy is not a replacement for representative democracy. The two should work together. Nevertheless, participatory approaches are better equipped to reach win-win solutions. The awareness and practice of participatory democracy is probably underdeveloped in public administration. It is hoped that the community of inquiry context provides a useful lens to see how more participatory democracy can enter and influence our field. In that way, participatory democracy has the potential to bridge fixed belief systems that separate us from each other and the citizens we serve.

Finally, as public administrators, we are committed to serving a democratic state. There is something at once liberating and exciting about conceptualizing our conversations as a form of democracy. The community of inquiry places our conversations within an experiential context of budgets and deadlines. It also focuses our conversations on problematic situations and subsequent data collection and interpretation. Overriding all is critical optimism—the sense that we have the potential to make a difference and connect to the common good.

Notes

1. For purposes of this article, classical pragmatists include Charles Sanders Peirce, William James, John Dewey, and Jane Addams.

2. Public administration has long struggled with the seemingly conflicting roles of bureaucracy and democracy. See Redford (1969) and Garofalo and Geuras (1999). One of the final issues that Key (1964, p. 709) dealt with in his classic *Politics, Parties, and Pressure Group* was the place of the bureaucracy in democracy.

3. See, for example, Garrison, 2000; Stever, 2000a, 2000b; and Snider 2000.

4. Thanks to Jeff Knepp, a contributor to the Peirce list serve, for the elephant and the blind men example (pierce-1@ttacs6.ttu.edu). Peirce maintained that over a long time horizon (hundreds of years), it was possible for communities of inquiry to discover scientific truth (nature's eternal laws). At any point in time, however, results using the scientific method are provisional. The uneven course of progress (a better description of the elephant) proceeds over time. Peirce describes this aspect of the scientific method as "fallibilism," which holds that "people cannot attain absolute certainty concerning questions of fact" (Peirce, 1955, p. 59).

5. Critical optimism is a synonym for meliorism. Much of this material is drawn from Dewey's (1920/1948) *Reconstruction in Philosophy*.

6. James Stever (2000b) makes a similar point in *The Path to Organizational Skepticism*. He shows how skepticism is a destructive trend in the theory of public organizations. He contrasts organizational faith and skepticism. Organizational faith is linked with modernism and the pragmatism of John Dewey. He maintains that the managerial ism of modernism, while imperfect. is checked by criticism. On the other hand. the post modern path of organizational skepticism is akin to Dewey's description of pessimism and is worse than a dead end.

7. It should be noted that Hitch and McKean's (1978) model differs from Dewyan instrumentalism because the analysis is separated from experience. Thus, abstractions are never brought to the experiential context, so body counts have lives of their own.

8. See David Hildebrand (1997) for more discussion on the importance of experience as the starting point of analysis.

9. Hence, unlike earlier philosophers such as Plato, Aristotle, Decartes, and Kant, Dewey's real interest is not truth but rather the social grounds of belief. He used "warranted assertibility" as the test for the social grounds of belief (Dewey, 1938, p. 14). The methods of science retain their centrality, but the focus of science is no longer the "discovery of nature's eternal laws."

Dewey hoped that philosophy would be a tool of social progress, in which the "scientific method in some generalized form, is applied to problems of public policy and social morality." Thus, he believed that philosophy should take the latest scientific knowledge into account. Unlike the Platonists, Positivists, and Cartesians preceding him, Dewey did not construe philosophy as a kind of superscience or source of knowledge superior to ordinary fallible experience. But, unlike the postmodern and the End of Philosophy movements, Dewey does not see science as merely one narrative among many competing narratives (Webb, 1999).

10. A scientific attitude is difficult to achieve if thinking is dominated by absolutist dualisms. Nevertheless, relevant distinctions grounded in particular problematic situations—and subjected to critical scrutiny and revision—are crucial to successful inquiry. Dewey maintained that common dualisms associated with the enlightenment, such as mind and body, subject and object, perception and reality, and form and substance, have had the effect of fixating belief systems (Flower & Murphy, 1977). Dualisms in public administration, such as politics and administration, fact and value, theory and practice, and policy and administration, may also fixate our views. If people use a philosophy that suspends or connects dualisms, they can be more open to the benefits

and insights from each perspective. The process of forging a community of inquiry is difficult (impossible) when members of the group are fixated in opposite belief systems.

11. A common, understandable misconception is that Hull-House was an 1890s version of a modem soup kitchen/homeless shelter. Hull-House had a broader objective. It quickly became a large complex that addressed the needs of the nearby immigrant community in a vast variety of ways. There were college extension courses, (that emphasized art, literature, language, music, history, mathematics, and drawing), a summer school, Sunday concerts, a choir, at least 25 clubs, cooking classes, free kindergarten and day nursery, facilities for organized labor to meet, speaker series, dances, a gymnasium, a coffee house, a public dispensary (drug store), labor bureau, and a labor and art museum (Residents of Hull-House, 1895/1970, Appendix, p. 208). John Dewey, Susan B. Anthony, and Theodore Roosevelt lectured at Hull-House. Some of the services were self-supported (coffeehouse, dispensary) whereas others were subsidized through private funding sources.

12. She was also able to document that the decentralized "sweating system" increased the likelihood of labor abuses and health risks. For example, "sweaters" with typhoid often illegally worked on suits that later infected the purchaser. Florence Kelley and Alzina Steven (1895/1970), both inspectors of workshops and factories for the State of Illinois, reported on the enforcement of recently passed Illinois child labor laws. They documented the increased dangers of mutilation and death faced by children because they were less cautious and often unable to read directions.

13. The problem with Adams and Balfour (1998) is related to what John Dewey called the philosophic fallacy. A philosophic fallacy is an abstract construct derived and distilled from experience but then placed in a realm separate from experience, accessible only to those who possess a special language and knowledge (usually of a technical realm). Modernity is just such an abstract construct that is embraced with great enthusiasm but which lacks a cutting edge. Citing "modernity" as the problem is like saying "capitalism" is the problem: The solution then depends primarily on ideology, not on relevant experience. Discussion relics primarily on appeals to accepted authority and a specialized jargon. Facts and history are malleable anecdotes, selectively employed to confirm what one already believes.

Part of the problem that the authors see in modernity, besides technical rationality, is the attempt at the progressive development of knowledge. One does not have to swallow Whiggish histories and rational reconstruction to be engaged in an effort to develop knowledge. Why should *progress* be a dirty word? The problem with neoclassical economics (which exemplifies problems of modernity in social sciences) is not that it is progressively developing knowledge but that the discipline is not only ahistorical, it has been empirically regressive in terms of explaining the real world economy. Indeed, do the authors not see what they are doing as better than some alternative and representing therefore progress?

14. Addams's devotion to democracy stemmed from her devotion to her father, who was a state senator and a friend of Lincoln. Some of her earliest and most vivid memories were of Lincoln's death (she was 4 years old). In *Twenty Years at Hull-House,* Addams describes her attraction to democracy: "There was growing within me an almost passionate devotion to the ideals of democracy" (Addams, 1910/1930, p. 79).

15. Causes that Addams championed included women's right to vote, child-labor laws, safety regulations for the workplace, restrictions on hours worked, social security for the elderly and sick, civil service reform, juvenile justice, mandatory education for teenagers (up to age 16), and better and more available care for the mentally ill.

16. Both Deegan (1990) and Seigfried (1996) attribute the delayed recognition to a sexist tradition within academia (and philosophy in particular) and the unorthodox institutional setting of Hull-House. Addams's works, most notably *Twenty Years at Hull-House,* is filled with her philosophy. Nevertheless, *Twenty Years* is unlike most philosophy texts because it is in narrative form. (See, for example, Audi, 1995, p. 638; Seigfried, 1996; Deegan, 1990; Menand, 2001; and Luizzi & McKinney, 2001. Deegan also argues persuasively that Addams is one of the founders of Chicago Sociology.

17. Note that Jane Addams did not always succeed in negotiating a settlement. The community of inquiry approach includes uncertainty.

18. See Shields (1998) for other ways in which classical pragmatism can bring conceptual frameworks to public administration.

References

Adams, G., & Balfour, D. (1998). *Unmasking administrative evil.* Thousand Oaks, CA: Sage.

Addams, J. (1930). *Twenty years at Hull-House.* New York: McMillan. (Original work published 1910)

Addams, J. (1970). The settlement as a factor in the labor movement. In Residents of Hull-House, *Hull-House maps and papers* (pp. 183–206). New York: Arno Press. (Original work published 1895)

Appleby, P. (1962). Making sense out of things in general. *Public Administration Review, 22,* 175–181.

Audi, R. (Ed.). (1995). *The Cambridge dictionary of philosophy.* Cambridge, England: Cambridge University Press.

Ayer, A. J. (1952). *Language, truth and logic* (2nd ed.). New York: Dover.

Beechinor, J. R. (1998). *Negotiated rulemaking: A study of state agency use and public administrator opinions* (Applied Research Project). San Marcos: Southwest Texas State University.

Brom, R. (2000). *Workplace diversity training: A pragmatic look at an administrative practice* (Applied Research Project). San Marcos: Southwest Texas State University.

Buchler, J. (1995). Introduction in J Buchler (Ed.) *Philosophical writings of Peirce.* pp. ix–xvi. New York: Dover.

Campbell, J. (1998). Dewey's conception of community. In L. Hickman (Ed.), *Reading Dewey: Interpretations for a postmodern generation* (pp. 23–42). Bloomington: Indiana University Press.

Center for Public Policy Dispute Resolution. (1996). *Texas negotiated rulemaking deskbook.* Austin: University of Texas Law School.

Dearborn, M. (1988). *Love in the promised land: The story of Anzia Yezierska and John Dewey.* New York: Free Press.

Deegan, M. J. (1990). *Jane Addams and the men of the Chicago School, 1892–1918.* New Brunswick, NJ: Transaction Books.

Dewey, J. (1929). *The quest for certainly: A study of the relation of knowledge and action.* New York: Minton Blach & Co.

Dewey, J. (1938). *Logic: The theory of inquiry.* New York: Holt, Rinehart and Winston.

Dewey, J. (1948). *Reconstruction in philosophy* (enlarged ed.). Boston: Beacon Press. (Original work published 1920)

Dewey, J. (1954). *The public and its problem.* Chicago: Swallow Press. (Original work published 1927)

Dewey, J. (1998). Creative democracy: The task before us. In L. Hickman & T. Alexander (Eds), *The essential Dewey: Volume I Pragmatism, education, democracy* (pp. 340–344). Bloomington: Indiana University Press. (Original work published 1938)

Evans, K. (2000). Reclaiming John Dewey: Democracy, inquiry, pragmatism, and public management. *Administration & Society, 32,* 308–328.

Farrell, J. (1967). *Beloved lady:* A *history of Jane Addams' ideas on reform and peace,* Baltimore, MD: The John Hopkins Press.

Flower, E., & Murphy, M. (1977). *A history of philosophy in America.* New York: Capricorn

Frederickson, G. (1997). *The spirit of public administration.* San Francisco: Jossey-Bass.

Garofalo, C., & Geuras, D. (1999). *Ethics in public service: The moral mind at work.* Washington DC: Georgetown University Press.

Garrison, J. (2000). Pragmatism and public administration. *Administration & Society, 32,* 458–477.

Garza, M. (2000). *360 degree performance evaluations: An assessment of the attitudes of human resource directors in the state of Texas* (Applied Research Project). San Marcos: Southwest Texas State University.

Goodsell, C. (1994). *The case for bureaucracy: A Public administration polemic* (3rd ed.). Chatham, NJ: Chatham House.

Hildebrand, D. (1997). *Undercutting the realism-antirealism debate: John Dewey and the neopragmatists.* Unpublished dissertation, University of Texas at Austin.

Hitch, C., &, McKean, R. (1978). *The economics of defense in a nuclear age* (10 ed.). Cambridge, MA: Harvard University Press. (Original work published 1965)

Holbrook, A. (1970). Map notes and comments. In Residents of Hull-House, *Hull-house maps and papers* (pp. 3–23). New York: Arno Press. (Original work published 1895)

Hummel, R., & Stivers, C. (1998). Government isn't us: The possibility of democratic knowledge in representative government. In C. King & C. Stivers (Eds.), *Government is us: Public administration in an anti-government era* (pp. 28–48). Thousand Oaks, CA: Sage.

Individual With Disabilities Act of 1997, Pub. L. No. 105–17.

James, W. (1907). *Pragmatism:* A *new name for some old ways of thinking.* Cambridge, MA: The Riverside Press.

James, P. (1999). *A certain justice.* New York: Ballantine Books.

Kelley, F. (1970). The sweating system. In Residents of Hull-House, *Hull-House maps and papers* (pp. 27–48). New York: Arno Press. (Original work published 1895)

Kelley, F. & Steven, A (1970) Wage earnings children. In Residents of Hull-House, *Hull-House Maps and Papers* (pp. 49–78). New York: Arno Press. (Original work published 1895)

Key, V. O., Jr. (1964). *Politics, parties, and pressure groups* (5th ed.). New York: Thomas Y. Crowell.

King, C. S., & Stivers, C. (1998). *Government is us: Public administration in an anti-Government Era.* Thousand Oaks, CA: Sage.

Kyokai, B. (1993). *The teaching of Buddha.* Tokyo: Society for the Promotion of Buddhism. (Original work published 1966)

Luizzi, V., & McKinney, A. (2001). *New and Old World philosophy* New York: Prentice Hall.

McSwite, O. (1997). *Legitimacy in public administration: A discourse analysis.* Thousand Oaks, CA: Sage.

Menand, L. (2001). *A story of ideas in America.* New York: Farrar, Straus and Giroux.

Peirce, C. S. (1955). The scientific attitude of fallibilism. In J. Buchler (Ed.), *Philosophical writings of Peirce* (pp. 42–59). New York: Dover.

Peirce, C. S. (1958). The fixation of belief. In P. Wiener (Ed.), *Charles Sanders Peirce: Selected writings* (pp. 91–112.) New York: Dover.

Pratt, J. W. (2000). *The behavioral assessment and intervention mandates of the 1997 amendment to IDEA and implications for special education programs* (Applied Research Project). San Marcos: Southwest Texas State University.

Raffray, L. (1997). *The Cascade County, Montana, community youth justice council program: A new citizenship model* (Applied Research Project). San Marcos: Southwest Texas State University.

Redford, E. (1969). *Democracy in the administrative state.* New York: Oxford University Press.

Residents of Hull-House. (1970). *Hull-House maps and papers.* New York: Arno Press. (Original work published 1895)

Seigfried, C. (1996). *Pragmatism and feminism: Reweaving the social fabric.* Chicago: University of Chicago Press.

Shields, P. M. (1996). Pragmatism: Exploring pubic administration's policy imprint. *Administration & Society* 28, 390–411.

Shields, P. (1998). Pragmatism as philosophy of science: A tool for public administration. In J. White, *Research in public administration* (Vol. 4, pp. 195–226). Stamford, CT: JAI Press.

Snider, K. F. (2000). Expertise or experimenting? Pragmatism and American public administration, 1920–1950, *Administration & Society 32,* 290–354.

Stever, J. (2000a). The parallel universe: Pragmatism and public administration. *Administration & Society, 32,* 453–457.

Stever, J. (2000b). *The path to organizational skepticism.* Burke, VA: Chatelaine Press.

Stivers, C. (1994). The listening bureaucrat. *Public Administration Review, 54,* 364–369.

Stivers, C. (2000). *Bureau men, settlement women: Constructing public administration in the Progressive Era.* Lawrence: University of Kansas Press.

Webb, J. (1999, April). *Dewey and discourse: Some implications for institutionalism and postmodernism.* Paper presented at the meeting of the Western Social Science Association, Denver, CO.

Webb, J. (2000, June). *Warranted assertibilty: Economics and reality and the continuing relevance of Dewey.* Paper presented at the meeting of the International Network of Economics and Methodology, Vancouver, B.C., Canada.

Westbrook, R. (1991). *John Dewey and American democracy.* Ithica, NY: Cornell University Press.

Wilson, T. (2002). *Pragmatism and performance measurement: An exploration of pragmatic principles* (Applied Research Project). San Marcos: Southwest Texas State University.

AUTHOR'S NOTE: I would like to thank Robert Brom, Vince Luizzi, Tim Wilson, Nancy Warren, George Glaser, and James Webb for encouragement and comments while this article was in draft form.

PATRICIA M. SHIELDS is the MPA Director at Southwest Texas State University. She has been investigating the link between pragmatism and public administration for about 13 years. She is also the editor of Armed Forces & Society.

From *Administration & Society,* Vol. 35 No.5 November 2003, pp. 510–538. Copyright © 2003 by Sage Publications. Reprinted by permission.

UNIT 2

Government and Organizational Behavior

Unit Selections

Key Points to Consider

- Identify and discuss some of the major problems with implementing a performance-based system in a public sector organization. What are some of the things a manager must consider prior to implementing such a system?

- What are some of the major principles of "evidence-based management?" How can these principles help improve public and private sector management skills?

- Define and discuss the concept of "outsourcing." How can managers learn the difference between high-risk and low-risk outsourcing?

- Identify and discuss the major failings of the government as related to the response to hurricane Katrina. How can these failures be avoided in future emergencies?

- What are some of the major lessons related to ethics and values that can be learned from Abu Ghraib? Describe and discuss the major administrative failures that are reflected by Abu Ghraib.

- Review the 12 major obstacles to ethical decision making that are identified by Michael Josephson. Identify and discuss your top 4 major obstacles.

- Identify some of the major issues with campaign financing. What is wrong with the system, and what can be done to correct these problems?

Student Web Site

www.mhcls.com/online

Internet References

Further information regarding these Web sites may be found in this book's preface or online.

Government Accounting Standards Board (GASB)
http://www.gasb.org

National Academy of Public Administration (NAPA)
http://www.napawash.org

Partnership for Public Service (PPS)
http://www.ourpublicservice.org

Public Sector Continuous Improvement Site
http://curiouscat.com/psci/index.html

Stateline.org
http://www.stateline.org

The articles in this unit focus on governmental and organizational behavior including productivity and performance. Special attention is paid to the importance of ethics and values in public sector organizations.

In the first subsection, articles center on the topic areas of performance measurement, planning, and results-based management. The articles try to answer the question of how do you achieve higher productivity in the public sector while facing diminishing resources.

The articles in the second subsection are centered on the area of ethics and values. Ethics and values are essential elements for a democratic government. Ethical behavior and ethical decisions maintain citizen trust and ensure effective and efficient use of resources. How can we ensure ethical behavior when we are faced with a high-stress and crises-filled environment?

Productivity and Performance

In today's world we are dealing with not only improving productivity and performance of public organizations during normal times but we are focusing on keeping the public sector going in the face of chaos and disaster.

Arie Halachmi, in his article *Performance Measurement: Test the Water Before You Dive In*, points out that according to conventional wisdom, performance measurement is a management concept that can help administrators and elected officials address the issues of productivity and accountability. According to the author, performance measures should be used with caution. This article explores many of the things that can go wrong when managers use performance measures and balanced scorecards without a full understanding of their limitations.

Evidence-Based Management by Jeffrey Pfeffer and Robert I. Sutton defines and discusses the concept of Evidence-Based Management. This concept works for both public and private sector managers. It proceeds from the premise that using better, deeper logic and employing facts, to the best extent possible, will permit leaders to do their jobs more effectively. This article also explores how managers can use these techniques to improve organizational productivity and performance.

Outsourcing is a strategy used by local governments in an effort to provide high-quality public services at low costs. The article *Managing High-Risk Outsourcing* by Emanuele Padovani and David Young explores some of the ways in which government organizations must manage their vendors to have a successful outcome. The success or failure of outsourcing is essentially a risk management operation, which identifies the key area that can be analyzed to help achieve success in this area.

Hurricanes Katrina and Rita brought a new meaning to the concept of emergency planning. According to authors Evan M. Berman, Thomas D. Lynch, Cynthia E. Lynch, and Maria D. Berman in their article, *"There Was No Plan"—A Louisiana Perspective,* planning without implementation meant that "There Was No Plan." This article explores administrative failure of the planning effort and what the government needs to do in order to successfully respond to an emergency.

Ethics and Values

The scandal of Abu Ghraib has directed attention on the need for Americans to focus on our core ethical values. The articles in this section point out that ethics is more than just what is legal and illegal. Saundra J. Reinke in her provocative article *Abu Ghraib: A Case of Moral and Administrative Failure* argues that "Abu Ghraib" represents a case of moral and administrative failure at the highest level. Core ethical values were severely tested and responsibility and accountability of the military were challenged. From the standpoint of public administration, this article explores the connection between administrative failure and individual behavior.

The article *Twelve Obstacles to Ethical Decision Making: Rationalizations,* by Michael Josephson, founder and president of the Josephson Institute of Ethics, identifies many of the key ethical rationalizations we use in making tough decisions. He argues that public managers need to explore their core ethical values when examining the fallacies of these rationalizations in order to avoid poor decisions.

The article *Follow the Money* by Rachel Smolkin reviews and discusses the issue of how money is raised for political campaigns. The blurred line between big money, coveted access, and impropriety or its appearance is explored. Campaign-financed websites are also identified.

Performance Measurement: Test the Water Before You Dive In

Performance measurement and reporting are promoted in various publications as a management concept that can help administrators and elected officials address the issues of productivity and accountability. This article challenges this general assertion for two reasons. First, because the cost of performance score cards is always significant while the benefits, in many instances, may be only tentative. Second, because of possible problems that result when measuring performance is used for two different and potentially competing functions: accountability versus productivity. The article concludes that while performance measurement has a potential, its use should be encouraged but not mandated by external bodies. The article asserts that a more prudent introduction and use of performance score cards may result from better understanding of two things: first, what can go wrong when compiling performance reports; and, second, that there might be a need for other corresponding changes, within and outside government agencies, in order to facilitate meaningful performance reports.

ARIE HALACHMI

Continuing pressure for greater accountability, better value-for-money, and improved performance have prompted elected officials, particularly during the last decade of the 20th century, to endorse the use of performance measurement (Allen, 1996; Halachmi, 1996a; Radin, 2000). However, studying the evolution of various accounting practices worldwide reveals that, as a public management concept, the quest for accountability and efficiency by collecting and analyzing input, output and outcome data is not new.

In the case of the USA (Williams, 2003, 2004), the New York Bureau of Municipal Research and other related organizations had, by the early 20th century, begun to promote the desirability of such a practice. As cited by several writers (Bouckaert, 1990, 1992; Williams, 2003, 2004; Gianakis, 2004), Ridley and Simon's Measuring Municipal Activities (1938) advocated performance measurement. However, like the earlier efforts of the New York Bureau of Municipal Research, these 'progressive' ideas did not become common management practices in the USA.

The success of highly publicized performance measurement efforts such as Thatcher's Financial Management Initiative (FMI) in the UK (Carter, 1995) or the Government Performance and Results Act (GPRA) of 1993 in the USA is questionable (Halachmi, 1996a, 1999). This suggests that little was learned from the earlier experiences of the Bureau of Municipal Research. Some of the Bureau's ideas about relating productivity to allocation of resources and the use of performance data for accountability, planning, and management (Williams, 2003, 2004) were incorporated into the public management fad of the 1960s, namely the Planning, Programming, and Budgeting System (PPBS) (Halachmi 1996a, b). Yet, even the lessons from the dubious success of PPBS in America were never reviewed in the UK before the launching of Thatcher's FMI nor were the lessons of this British initiative studied in the USA before compiling and launching GPRA in the 1990s.

The stream of articles, books, and official reports on performance measurement that began in the early 1990s continues to flow. Using Google, a 2004 internet search returned 2.6 million entries, indicating the enduring saliency of this concept on the public agenda. The flair of performance measurement initiatives around the globe towards the end of the 20th century have been attributed by Halachmi (2002) to reasons such as

- a need to review the allocation of resources rigorously due to the inability of many governments to generate new sources of revenue to underwrite the growing cost of existing programs and services or to finance new ones;
- demands by a better educated public, in the aftermath of scandals concerning waste and corruption, for information about the use of tax money;
- the evolution of a global village in which a report about an alleged good practice in one place may generate local media reports influencing public opinion in favor of imitating and transplanting such a desired practice;
- pressure from donor states and international organizations, such as the World Bank on governments of developing countries to introduce such measures to facilitate better decisions by donors; and
- the desire of legislatures to re-establish their credibility and accountability and create solutions to serious social issues.

The purpose of this article is to highlight some of the reasons why performance measurements in the service sector, in general and in public agencies, in particular, are likely to fail. This, it is hoped, may lead to further scholarly debate and inspire academics and practitioners alike to develop more effective strategies to increase the odds for success of future schemes.

The premise of the discussion that follows is based on two arguments. First, that there is an inherent problem with the way performance measurement is commonly understood, implemented, and used. In most cases, performance measurement involves the study of data to facilitate decisions. Specifically, performance measurement assists in the allocation of resources for future operations by passing judgement on past achievements. However, this practice has all the risks of driving a car on an unfamiliar winding road while looking too long in the rear-view mirror. Such a practice must be based on two questionable assumptions. First, that optics or other factors are not distorting that view. Second, that the road traveled holds reliable clues for the rest of the way. By using this analogy, we aim to highlight one of the basic issues with performance measurement, namely its usefulness for managers. For auditors, the media, legislative oversight, and accountability-seeking public performance measurements have a lot to offer. But what can they offer managers? True, better understanding of past performance may hold important clues for improving future performance—that is where glancing at the rear-view mirror comes in handy. However, the risk is that by studying the past one may lose a proper perspective with which to gauge a future that may be very different from the past. Given the current pace of change within and outside organizations, dwelling too much on the past may distort the vision of the future. Also, for the practicing manager who is faced with ever-decreasing budgets for field operations, justifying the transfer of more resources to overhead is both an operational and moral dilemma. The problem with performance measurements is that they are needed because we have yet to come up with better alternatives to make up for their possible dysfunctions.

Second, most of the recipes in the 'cookbook' approach to performance measurement are wrong. Thus, for example, McGregor's (1960) 'human side' of the enterprise plays an important role in determining the fate of any performance measurement effort but gets little attention. Compiling an exhaustive list of contextual and behavioral factors that should be considered before designing a performance measurement scheme is beyond the scope of this article. However, a few key issues that should be considered by public managers and elected officials will be discussed.

The discussion starts by exploring some of the issues relating to the need to examine performance data in context in order to avoid misinterpretations. It asserts that because the cost of performance measurement is a certainty but its benefits are not, greater care should be given to calculating those probable costs before commitments are made. It notes that since performance measurement does not happen in a vacuum, politics plays a role in the selection and use of performance measurement and issues of validity and methodology are covers for clashes over values. It urges caution in the selection of performance measurements because schemes that can bring about greater accountability may not be good instruments for enhancing productivity. It argues that by being more cognizant of the possible problems relating to performance measurement, managers and elected officials may take a more prudent approach to the introduction and the use of performance measurement as a means of improving public productivity.

The Context of Performance Measurement

In 1936, Lasswell observed that politics had to do with who gets what, when, and how. In recent years, the 'how' in Lasswell's equation has sometimes been equated with performance reports which are expected to influence funding. Furthermore, debates over priorities have been metamorphosed into disputes over the selection of the proper methodology for measuring performance. In the zero-sum-like situations of many countries, such 'technical issues' are now widely used to justify disagreements over the allocation of resources for competing programs. Methodological disputes serve as pretexts for the real struggles over control, ideology, norms of governance, and protection of partisan interests. For example, in the case of education in the USA, the debate is allegedly about the justification for the use of one common battery of tests in all schools. For those opposing this idea, there are alternative tests and other ways to measure student competency. The debates and controversies among educators, teachers' unions, elected officials (at state and federal level), and various interest groups (Toppo, 2001; Wilgoren, 2001; Mui, 2004) illustrate that what is measured and how it is measured (e.g. level of aggregation) can influence the perceived quality of education. By the same token, the current debate about performance measurement in education also uncovers uncomfortable issues of control and partisan interests that have nothing to do with education.

Disagreements about what constitutes a proper approach to the selection and use of performance measurement to establish accountability, efficiency, effectiveness, or any other important value, such as egalitarianism, are not uncommon. The availability of information about performance may be a necessary condition for improving performance but is not sufficient to bring it about. In particular, when the selection, intended uses, or methodologies are challenged on any grounds, performance reports are not likely to effect an improvement.

Those who wish to use performance results to introduce a change in procedures or funding, to re-define goals, missions or desired results must deal with those wishing to preserve the status quo. In his Systems Model of the political process, David Easton (1953, 1957) used the term 'feedback' to denote part of what we now call performance measurement. His model captures the notion that the output or outcomes of one political cycle influence the demand (for change) or support (of the status quo), which become the input for subsequent cycles of the political process. By nature, the political process is geared to produce a compromise, which is preferred, by all parties, to an impasse. However, any compromise is inherently only a temporary solution to a problem. The reason is that at least one of the involved parties may feel they could have done better and is likely to start undermining the compromise in the hope of securing that better deal. Under these circumstances, the necessary support for any scheme of performance measurement is not likely to materialize. Because such developments are so common and the introduction and use of performance measurement is so likely to involve compromises, experienced politicians and managers have an incentive to drag their feet They prefer being accused of moving too slowly over the risk of the consequences of being politically on the defense when the 'official' (but silently contested) measurement scheme fails to produce the intended results.

Performance measurements are supposed to protect and isolate funding decisions from political pressure. As articulated in President George W. Bush's Message to Congress with his Fiscal Year 2003 Budget Proposal: 'Where government programs are succeeding, their efforts should be reinforced—and the 2003 Budget provides resources to do that And when objective measures reveal that government programs are not succeeding, those programs should be reinvented, redirected, or retired (Bush, 2002; Peckenpaugh, 2001). While Bush's message about the normative way to allocate resources seems logical, the likelihood of consensus for its use is slim.

One reason for this relates to the selection of the proper time frame for measuring success. In the early years of many programs, there may not be enough clues as to how successful they may eventually become. According to Bush's 2003 Budget Message, such programs are likely to be terminated prematurely. This practice of equating early indications of desired results with ultimate success has been labeled 'the Awakening Syndrome' (Halachmi, 1996b) after the book (Sacks, 1973) and 1990 namesake movie *Awakenings* staring Robert De Niro and Robin Williams.

The second reason is that the polity is made up of multiple groups with differing objectives. Each of these objectives has the potential to influence the eventual distribution of costs and benefits among the different segments of society, with various political and economic consequences. For example, health or education providers define the objectives of their respective organizations differently to the recipients of their services. Taxpayers who are not consumers of such services may have still other ideas about the objectives that should be pursued by such agencies. It is no surprise that these differing perspectives result in disagreements about what should be funded and, thus, about what should be measured (to establish merit) and how to measure it.

If the environmental context of performance measurement is so important, what is being done to make sure that any proposed performance measurement scheme is consistent with it?

The national coastal management performance measurement system states:

> The National Coastal Management Performance Measurement System consists of a suite of performance indicators to track how well the states are achieving the Coastal Zone Management Act (CZMA) objectives and contextual indicators to track environmental and socioeconomic factors that influence program actions. This quantification of coastal management outcomes re-

sponds to Congressional requests for improved accountability and also facilitates adaptive management, enhances communication, and informs planning and resource allocation decisions by federal and state coastal managers. (Coastal Zone Management Act, n.d.)

Including contextual information with performance reports to assist with the interpretation of various performance data is not a matter of choice. However, there is, as yet, no proven strategy for dealing with the environmental context of an agency without risking questions about the external validity of a proposed performance measurement scheme.

Users of performance measurements want to be able to make comparisons across agencies and among programs. Thus, they push for common measures such as per capita cost or rate of client satisfaction which can be used to make comparisons. They opt for a simple methodology for collecting data and compiling performance reports so they can understand what is going on, explain it to others (e.g. constituents), and defend its use if necessary. However, the use of plain measurements and simple protocols for collecting and analyzing data may result in methodological vulnerabilities.

Unfortunately, most elected officials are not aware of the various methodological issues that may be used to challenge and compromise the value of performance reports. Ignoring this reality, many current writings use a 'cookbook' approach to promote performance measurement as a worthy and simple management tool. They make it look easy as they gloss over the many possible questions about validity. Dwelling too much on such issues, they insinuate, is simply too complicated and may discourage the use of performance measurement altogether.

For example, performance measurement writings do not alert their readers to the fact that insufficient attention to the particular attributes of an agency's environment during any given period may render performance data useless whenever these attributes are expected to change. Thus, when the population is aging or when the local economy is rapidly changing, the performance of local services may fluctuate even without any change in the mode of their delivery. Alerting prospective users of performance measurement to such problems would require still another warning. The warning would be that too much attention to contextual variables, such as the agency's environment during the period under study, may prevent meaningful benchmarking and possible comparisons, reducing the value of any performance report to anecdotal information. The delicate balancing of the two considerations providing enough 'technical' information for proper selection of methodology without confusing the reader—is a test which many performance measurement 'cookbooks' fail.

Establishing the balance between the need to consider particular contextual attributes yet allowing for meaningful comparisons is only one of the hard questions to be considered. Two other important questions are: 'Can the cost of performance measurement always be justified?' and 'Can the instruments that established whether a planned action was carried out as promised be as useful for generating new ideas and innovations to improve productivity and help its user assume a proactive posture in anticipation of future problems or circumstances?' With such questions in mind, this article asserts that performance measurement can have some serious dysfunctions that should be considered when organizations review existing performance measurement schemes or decide to introduce them in the first place. These two important questions will be discussed in the following sections.

Performance Measurement: Sure Costs but Only Tentative Benefits

The question of cost justification is not an easy one. While the cost of performance measurement is a certainty, its benefits are tentative (Halachmi, 2004). It should be noted that developing the capacity to generate any kind of a report card (Gormley and Wiemer, 1999) about organizational performance is never without cost The literature about the most recent performance measurement fad, *The Balanced Score Card* (Kaplan and Norton, 1996), praises at length the virtues of the said approach but devotes little space to its possible costs. The aggregate cost for any performance measurement effort may defy a simple calculation of the involved resources (i.e. money or time).

First, the cost involves the value of any loss of operational capacity due to the transfer of resources from 'production' to 'overhead'. Shifting resources from 'line' functions to 'staff' functions—from doing what the agency is expected to do (production) to 'housekeeping' (overheads)—leaves any agency with less capacity for action. Until such time when the agency is able to extract some new insights from performance data and make better use of its resources, the ratios of input to output, which are used to measure efficiency (Strassmann 1994), will be tilted the 'wrong' way. In practical terms, in the case of a school or a public health facility, the cost per capita will increase without corresponding improvement in care quality, clients' satisfaction, or employees' morale.

For critics of government operations, the only thing that is certain to be visible in the immediate aftermath of an attempt to introduce performance measurement is further bureaucratization. For students of public management, the implication is that, at least in the short term, the introduction of a performance measurement scheme undermines efficiency. Second, in addition to the loss of operational capacity (due to the shifting of resources from production to overhead), many agencies experience additional loss of operational capacity due to the developmental cost involved.

The introduction of performance measurement is akin to administrative reform (Pierce and Puthucheary, 1997) in its ability to generate ill will and opposition in-house. Selling the concept to employees, training, the incentives to pre-empt possible opposition, and any lost goodwill come at a price. To get an accurate estimate of the total cost for using performance measurement, the expenditures of these activities should be added to those of collecting, analyzing, and compiling periodic performance reports. For service recipients, this aggregate cost may not be justified.

Can Measures for Bringing About Greater Accountability Be Used to Improve Productivity?

Broadly speaking, most arguments in support of performance measurement are in two categories: accountability and improved productivity. Yet, measurements for accountability and productivity may not be compatible with each other for any of the following reasons:

- Accountability is living up to performance standards that existed when the use of resources/authority was authorized.
- Accountability is primarily about relationships: Who is superior to whom? Who is answerable to whom? What must be reported and who decides it?
- Productivity is more than keeping with past trends or marginally improving on them.
- Productivity relates to progress, innovation, and change, preferably moving to a higher curve rather than moving to a higher point on the same productivity curve.
- Productivity is about management, adaptation, creativity, and breaking away from the past or from the group, while accountability is about staying within the four corners of the contract.
- Productivity results from thinking outside the box, while from an accountability point of view, all such activities suggest deviation and a disregard for the rules.
- Productivity involves feeling good about alleged results and having a sense of achievement, whereas accountability is about feeling right, safe, and capable of defending an official (formal) record.
- Productivity has to do with a continuous free-form process of self-examination and an internal search for new insight, whereas accountability involves external scrutiny and a relatively rigid use of pre-established legal or professional standards.

If this list is valid, performance measurement of accountability and of performance for productivity cannot be the same. As noted in some earlier writings by Halachmi (1996b, 2004), and as re-iterated more recently by Behn (2003), there may be a need, for various purposes, to use different kinds of measures. However, is it possible that the use of one kind of measure for a specific purpose can undermine the usefulness of other measures or the attainment of another goal? Can performance measurement for accountability undermine efforts to improve productivity?

This article argues that performance measurement for accountability may be inconsistent with performance measurement for enhancing productivity because the two have different orientations. Performance measurement for accountability attempts to answer the question 'Was it done right?'; while performance measurement for improved productivity is an attempt to answer the question 'Was the right thing done?'.

Performance measurement for accountability is about keeping the promise to work hard towards achieving a goal. It is about book-keeping and verification of the various 'accounts', about whether resources have been used as intended and in the most economic way, and a guarantee that agreed accounting standards have been applied. Best Value and Best Value for Money (Bovaird, 2000; Halachmi and Montgomery, 2000) are meaningful tools for establishing accountability but only when the 'books' are not 'cooked'. Performance data are the evidence to support claim(s) of alleged achievements so that consumption of resources can be meaningfully related to results. This is the logic of the so-called Service Effort and Accomplishments reporting (Halachmi and Bouckaert, 1996; Christensen and Yoshimi, 2003).

Alternatively, performance measurement for productivity is about exploration and learning from experience. Performance data are for analysis but constitute only a portion of the input that goes into the effort to derive the lessons and the ideas to be tested in the future. Benchmarking, the comparison with one's own past with the best in the industry or with the best-performing organizations in the sector, is a promising tool for carrying out this effort because it puts achievements in perspective and allows for discussion of future actions.

Gendron et al. (2001: 278) offer a dichotomy between what they call progressive public administration (PPA) and New Public Management (NPM). For supporters of PPA, they note that 'public management is mainly aimed at limiting corruption and the waste and incompetence that are held to go with it. The emphasis, they argue, is:

> control through compliance to rules and regulations, such as ensuring that spending is within approved levels and for authorized purposes. Accountability of the executive is therefore essentially a procedural process, in that if the requirements with regard to inputs are satisfied, the intended results are assured.

Among its benefits, Gendron et al. (2001: 278) assert: 'PPA offers consistency in policy and reliability in execution. It is likely to be effective in departments where organized crime and corruption pose a major threat to the integrity of public service.' However, they note that 'reliance on PPA in other departments may be problematic since it lacks flexibility and discourages individual initiative'.

For supporters of NPM, Gendron et al. (2001: 278) suggest that it 'shifts the emphasis from process accountability towards a greater element of accountability for results'. They note that while there is considerable diversity about the specific components and purposes of NPM across jurisdictions, it is generally seen as advocating that governmental organizations be split into business units and assigned performance targets for which managers are held accountable.

The author's position relating to the use of performance measurement for accountability is consistent with Gendron et al. (2001), with PPA-related measures. However, when it comes to productivity, or what they label NPM-related issues, expecting managers to attain just the pre-approved outcomes shortchanges the public. What is articulated at the planning, programming, and budgeting stages of many public policies may fall short of what is being desired when results materialize. Managers should strive

to meet the valuation of the end result rather than be in simple compliance with the initial plan.

Henry Mintzberg's (1994) description of the relationship between strategic management and strategic planning offers further insight into the relationship between the use of performance measurement to improve accountability and the use of performance measures to improve productivity. In 'The Fall and Rise of Strategic Planning', Mintzberg suggests that 'strategic thinking' (the term he uses for strategic management) and 'strategic planning' are inconsistent, although many use the term strategic planning for both concepts.

According to Mintzberg (1994: 108), strategic thinking calls for the use of tacit knowledge soft data, and synthesis, which involve intuition and creativity. Strategic thinking resembles key attributes of performance measurement, while strategic planning involves rational and systematic analysis using hard data. Mintzberg's (1994) notion of planning seems to be consistent with what auditors are looking for to establish accountability, suggesting that it is 'about breaking down a goal or a set of intentions into steps, formalizing those steps so that they can be implemented almost automatically, and articulating the anticipated consequences or result of each step' (Mintzberg, 1994: 108). Such an effort is conducive to and consistent with performance audits and, therefore, with the notion of accountability.

Thus, strategic planning is conducive to the way mechanistic (bureaucratic) organizations operate. Strategic thinking is akin to the notion of an organic organization—an important characteristic of organizations that have the capacity to enhance productivity. Bureaucratic organizations, which are the opposite of organic organizations, are likely to have a diminished capacity in that respect. The reason is simple: innovation, improvisation, change, and experimentation are incompatible with the bureaucracy and cannot be tolerated, let alone encouraged. Organic organizations generate random streams of communication. Members of an organic non-bureaucratic organization mobilize their collective insights in an attempt to deal with an ever-changing environment. Multiple and simultaneous activities by members of the organization—interactions, reactions, and counteractions—create an impression of chaos. To the order- and pattern-seeking auditor, establishing accountability in an organic organization is impossible. To establish accountability, auditors need a clear picture of who makes the decision, who implements the decision, what is the basis for the decision, and what are the functional relations between any achievement and specific organizational actions (such as consumption of resources). Without the formalization and the small steps that characterize strategic planning, auditors are at a loss.

Thus, the organizational structure and process most likely to facilitate strategic thinking and enhanced performance may not be consistent with basic notions of accountability such as transparency, complete disclosure, and minimizing deviations from the approved plan.

Concluding Remarks

In the quest for greater productivity and better accountability, we have witnessed, during the last decade of the 20th century, a new stream of initiatives to mandate performance measurement. Although not a new idea, performance measurement has been rediscovered and embraced globally. The emergence of an internet-connected global village, with global media coverage around the clock, facilitated public demands for an affirmative action to improve public productivity. Elected officials, in search of quick fix solutions in response to such pressure, embraced the concept of performance reporting as the panacea. They were attracted to this concept because it seemed to have a low price tag but a high symbolic significance for dealing with other issues such as declining public confidence in government and growing demands for accountability by a more educated public.

On face value, performance measurement is promising. Its many virtues have been promoted by academicians, management consultants, auditors, and legislators as they search for new relevancy within the hollowed government. Indeed, it has a lot to offer public managers, government employees, elected officials, and the public at large when it is implemented by people who are well trained and believe in it. However, in most instances, this is not the case.

There are many reasons why performance measurement may not be successful. These include human behavior, the nature of government agencies as institutions, and the shaky assumption at the heart of performance measurement that studying the past is a sure way to navigate into a better future.

Many writers on performance measurement do not highlight the political risks, the methodological problems, and the certainty of the cost versus the tentative benefits of performance measurement. What is lost on many of them is that while having some kind of a performance measurement scheme in-house may be very desirable, mandatory measures can be dysfunctional. Hence, such writers do not offer answers that can help managers make moral and responsible choices between doing things 'right' and doing the 'right things'.

Being cognizant of the possible problems relating to performance measurement can help managers and elected officials take a more prudent approach to the introduction and the use of performance measurement as a means of improving either accountability or public productivity.

References

Allen, J.R. (1996) 'The Uses of Performance Measurement in Government', *Government Finance Review* 12(4): 11–16.

Behn, R.D. (2003) 'Why Measure Performance? Different Purposes Require Different Measures', *Public Administration Review* 63(5): 586–606.

Bouckaert, G.(1990) 'The History of the Productivity Movement', *Public Productivity and Management Review* 14(1): 53–89.

Bouckaert, G. (1992) 'Public Productivity in Retrospective', in M. Holzer (ed.) *Public Productivity Handbook,* pp. 15–46. New York: Marcel Dekker.

Bovaird, T. (2000) 'Best Value in the United Kingdom: Using Benchmarking and Competition to Achieve Value for Money', *International Review of Administrative Sciences* 66(3): 415–32.

Carter, N. and Klein, R. (1995) *How Organizations Measure Success: The Use of Performance Indicators in Government.* London: Routledge.

Christensen, M. and Yoshimi, H. (2003) 'Sector Performance Reporting: New Public Management and Contingency Theory Insights', *Government Auditing Review* 10(Mar.): 71–83.

Coastal Zone Management Act (n.d.) *The National Coastal Management Performance Measurement* http://www.ocrm.nos. noaa.gov/pdf/CMPerfMeas.pdf

Easton, D. (1953) *The Political System: An Inquiry into the State of Political Science.* New York: Alfred A Knopf.

Easton, D. (1957) 'An Approach to the Analysis of Political Systems', *World Politics* 9: 393–400.

Gendron, Y., Cooper, D.J. and Townley, B. (2001) 'In the Name of Accountability: State Auditing, Independence and New Public Management', *Accounting, Auditing & Accountability Journal* 14(3): 278–310.

Gianakis, G.A. (2004) 'The Promise of Public Sector Performance Measurement: Anodyne or Placibo', *Public Administration Quarterly* 26(1): 35–65.

Gormley, W.T. and Weimer, D.L. (1999) *Organizational Report Cards.* Cambridge. MA: Harvard University Press.

Halachmi, A. (1996a) 'Promises and Possible Pitfalls on the Way to SEA Reporting', in A. Halachmi and G. Bouckaert (eds) *Organizational Performance* and *Measurement in the Public Sector,* pp. 77–100. Westport, CT: Quorum Books.

Halachmi, A. (1996b) 'Measure of Excellence', in Hill et al. (eds) *Quality Innovation* and *Measurement in the Public Sector,* pp. 9–23. Frankfurt am Main.

Halachmi, A. (1999) 'Mandated Performance Measurement: A Help or a Hindrance', *National Productivity Review* 18(2): 59–67.

Halachmi, A. (2002) 'Performance Measurement, Accountability, and Improved Performance', *Public Performance & Management Review* 25(4): 370–4.

Halachmi, A. (2004) 'Performance Measurements, Accountability and Improving Performance', in M. Holzer and S.H. Lee (eds) *Public Productivity Handbook,* 333–53. New York: Marcel Dekker.

Halachmi, A. and Montgomery, V.L. (2000) 'Best Value and Accountability: Issues and Observations', *International Review of Administrative Sciences* 66(3): 393–414.

Kaplan, R. and Norton, D. (1996) *The Balanced Score Card: Translating Strategy into Action.* Boston, MA: Harvard Business School Press.

Lasswell, H.D. (1936) *Politics: Who Gets What, When, How.* New York: McGraw-Hill.

McGregor, D.M. (1960) *The Human Side of the Enterprise.* New York: McGraw-Hill.

Mintzberg, H. (1994) 'The Fall and Rise of Strategic Planning', *Harvard Business Review* (Jan.–Feb.): 107–14 (Reprint 94107).

Mui, Y.Q. (2004) 'Md. Union Opposes Mandatory "Exit" Tests', *The Washington Post,* 26 May, p. B03, URL: http://www. washingtonpost.com/wp-dyn/articles/A55989-2004May25.html

Peckenpaugh, J. (2001) 'Bush to Link Agencies' Budgets to Performance in 2003', *GovExeccom,* 10 April, URL: http://www. govexec.com/dailyfedl0401/041001p2.htm

Pierce, J. and Puthucheary, N. (1997) 'Using Performance Measures to Drive Change Within the Public Sector The NSW Experience', NSW Treasury TRP 97–3, URL: http://www.treasury.nsw.gov. au/pubs/trp97_3/nswexper.htm

Radin, B. (2000) *Beyond Machiavelli: Policy Analysis Comes of Age.* Washington, D.C.: Georgetown University Press.

Sacks, O.W. (1973) *Awakening.* London: Ducksworth.

Strassmann, P.A. (1994) 'How We Evaluated Productivity', *Computerworld* Premier 100 Issue, 19 September, p. 45, URL: http//www.strassmann.com/pubs/cw/eval-productivity.shtml

Toppo, G. (2001) 'Teachers: Tests Might Harm Learning', Associated Press–21 February, URL: www.interversity.org/lists/am-I/archives/feb2001/msg00967.html

Wilgoren, J. (2001) 'In Reconciling School Bills, 2 Chambers Agree on Tests', *The New York Times,* 15 June, URL: www.nytimes.com/2001/06/15/national/15SCHO.html?ex=993707377&ei=1&en=81a07f06231b4381)

Williams, Daniel W. (2003) 'Measuring Government in the Early Twentieth Century', *Public Administration Review* 63(6): 643–59.

Williams, Daniel W. (2004) 'Evolution of Performance Measurement until 1930', *Administration and Society* 36(2): 131–65.

ARIE HALACHMI is Professor at Zhongshan University (China) and Tennessee State University (USA).

From *International Review of Administrative Sciences,* Vol. 71(2) 2005, pp. 255–266. Copyright © 2005 by Sage Publications, Ltd. Reprinted by permission.

Evidence-Based Management

Executives routinely dose their organizations with strategic snake oil: discredited nostrums, partial remedies, or untested management miracle cures. In many cases, the facts about what works are out there—so why don't managers use them?

JEFFREY PFEFFER AND ROBERT I. SUTTON

A bold new way of thinking has taken the medical establishment by storm in the past decade: the idea that decisions in medical care should be based on the latest and best knowledge of what actually works. Dr. David Sackett, the individual most associated with *evidence-based medicine,* defines it as "the conscientious, explicit and judicious use of current best evidence in making decisions about the care of individual patients." Sackett, his colleagues at McMaster University in Ontario, Canada, and the growing number of physicians joining the movement are committed to identifying, disseminating, and, most importantly, applying research that is soundly conducted and clinically relevant.

If all this sounds laughable to you—after all, what else besides evidence *would* guide medical decisions?—then you are woefully naive about how doctors have traditionally plied their trade. Yes, the research is out there—thousands of studies are conducted on medical practices and products every year. Unfortunately, physicians don't use much of it. Recent studies show that only about 15% of their decisions are evidence based. For the most part, here's what doctors rely on instead: obsolete knowledge gained in school, long-standing but never proven traditions, patterns gleaned from experience, the methods they believe in and are most skilled in applying, and information from hordes of vendors with products and services to sell.

The same behavior holds true for managers looking to cure their organizational ills. Indeed, we would argue, managers are actually much more ignorant than doctors about which prescriptions are reliable—and they're less eager to find out. If doctors practiced medicine like many companies practice management, there would be more unnecessarily sick or dead patients and many more doctors in jail or suffering other penalties for malpractice.

It's time to start an evidence-based movement in the ranks of managers. Admittedly, in some ways, the challenge is greater here than in medicine. The evidence is weaker; almost anyone can (and often does) claim to be a management expert; and a bewildering array of sources—Shakespeare, Billy Graham, Jack Welch, Tony Soprano, fighter pilots, Santa Claus, Attila the Hun—are used to generate management advice. Managers seeking the best evidence also face a more vexing problem than physicians do: Because companies vary so wildly in size, form, and age, compared with human beings, it is far more risky in business to presume that a proven "cure" developed in one place will be effective elsewhere.

The use and defense of stock options as a compensation strategy seems to be a case of cherished belief trumping evidence, to the detriment of organizations.

Still, it makes sense that when managers act on better logic and evidence, their companies will trump the competition. That is why we've spent our entire research careers, especially the last five years, working to develop and surface the best evidence on how companies ought to be managed and teaching managers the right mind-set and methods for practicing evidence-based management. As with medicine, management is and will likely always be a craft that can be learned only through practice and experience. Yet we believe that managers (like doctors) can practice their craft more effectively if they are routinely guided by the best logic and evidence—and if they relentlessly seek new knowledge and insight, from both inside and outside their companies, to keep updating their assumptions, knowledge, and skills. We aren't there yet, but we are getting closer. The managers and companies that come closest already enjoy a pronounced competitive advantage.

What Passes for Wisdom

If a doctor or a manager makes a decision that is not based on the current best evidence of what may work, then what is to blame? It may be tempting to think the worst. Stupidity. Laziness. Downright deceit. But the real answer is more benign. Seasoned practitioners sometimes neglect to seek out new evidence because they trust their own clinical experience more than they trust research. Most of them would admit problems with the small sample size that characterizes personal observation, but nonetheless, information acquired firsthand often feels richer and closer to real knowledge than do words and data in a journal article. Lots of managers, likewise, get their companies into trouble by importing, without sufficient thought, performance management and measurement practices from their past experience. We saw this at a small software company, where the chair of the compensation committee, a successful and smart executive, recommended the compensation policies he had employed at his last firm. The fact that the two companies were dramatically different in size, sold different kinds of software, used different distribution methods, and targeted different markets and customers didn't seem to faze him or many of his fellow committee members.

Another alternative to using evidence is making decisions that capitalize on the practitioner's own strengths. This is particularly a problem with specialists, who default to the treatments with which they have the most experience and skill. Surgeons are notorious for it. (One doctor and author, Melvin Konner, cites a common joke amongst his peers: "If you want to have an operation, ask a surgeon if you need one.") Similarly, if your business needs to drum up leads, your event planner is likely to recommend an event, and your direct marketers will probably suggest a mailing. The old saying "To a hammer, everything looks like a nail" often explains what gets done.

Hype and marketing, of course, also play a role in what information reaches the busy practitioner. Doctors face an endless supply of vendors, who muddy the waters by exaggerating the benefits and downplaying the risks of using their drugs and other products. Meanwhile, some truly efficacious solutions have no particularly interested advocates behind them. For years, general physicians have referred patients with plantar warts on their feet to specialists for expensive and painful surgical procedures. Only recently has word got out that duct tape does the trick just as well.

Numerous other decisions are driven by dogma and belief. When people are overly influenced by ideology, they often fail to question whether a practice will work—it fits so well with what they "know" about what makes people and organizations tick. In business, the use and defense of stock options as a compensation strategy seems to be just such a case of cherished belief trumping evidence, to the detriment of organizations. Many executives maintain that options produce an ownership culture that encourages 80-hour workweeks, frugality with the company's money, and a host of personal sacrifices in the interest of value creation. T.J. Rodgers, chief executive of Cypress Semiconductor, typifies this mind-set. He told the *San Francisco Chronicle* that without options, "I would no longer have employee shareholders, I would just have employees." There is, in fact, little evidence that equity incentives of any kind, including stock options, enhance organizational performance. A recent review of more than 220 studies compiled by Indiana University's Dan R. Dalton and colleagues concluded that equity ownership had no consistent effects on financial performance.

Ideology is also to blame for the persistence of the first-mover-advantage myth. Research by Wharton's Lisa Bolton demonstrates that most people—whether experienced in business or naive about it—believe that the first company to enter an industry or market will have a big advantage over competitors. Yet empirical evidence is actually quite mixed as to whether such an advantage exists, and many "success stories" purported to support the first-mover advantage turn out to be false. (Amazon.com, for instance, was not the first company to start selling books online.) In Western culture, people believe that the early bird gets the worm, yet this is a half-truth. As futurist Paul Saffo puts it, the whole truth is that the second (or third or fourth) mouse often gets the cheese. Unfortunately, beliefs in the power of being first and fastest in everything we do are so ingrained that giving people contradictory evidence does not cause them to abandon their faith in the first-mover advantage. Beliefs rooted in ideology or in cultural values are quite "sticky," resist disconfirmation, and persist in affecting judgments and choice, regardless of whether they are true.

Finally, there is the problem of uncritical emulation and its business equivalent: casual benchmarking. Both doctors and managers look to perceived high performers in their field and try to mimic those top dogs' moves. We aren't damning benchmarking in general—it can be a powerful and cost-efficient tool. Yet it is important to remember that if you only copy what other people or companies do, the best you can be is a perfect imitation. So the most you can hope to have are practices as good as, but no better than, those of top performers—and by the time you mimic them, they've moved on. This isn't necessarily a bad thing, as you can save time and money by learning from the experience of others inside and outside your industry. And if you consistently implement best practices better than your rivals, you will beat the competition.

Benchmarking is most hazardous to organizational health, however, when used in its "casual" form, in which the logic behind what works for top performers, why it works, and what will work elsewhere is barely unraveled. Consider a quick example. When United Airlines decided in 1994 to try to compete with Southwest in the California market, it tried to imitate Southwest. United created a new service, Shuttle by United, with separate crews and planes (all of them Boeing 737s). The gate staff and flight attendants wore casual clothes. Passengers weren't served food. Seeking to emulate Southwest's legendary quick turnarounds and enhanced productivity, Shuttle by United increased the frequency of its flights and reduced the scheduled time planes would be on the ground. None of this, however, reproduced the essence of Southwest's advantage—the company's culture and management philosophy, and the priority placed on employees. Southwest wound up with an even higher market share in California after United had launched its new service. The Shuttle is now shuttered.

We've just suggested no less than six substitutes that managers, like doctors, often use for the best evidence—obsolete knowledge, personal experience, specialist skills, hype, dogma, and mindless mimicry of top performers—so perhaps it's apparent why evidence-based decision making is so rare. At the same time, it should be clear that relying on any of these six is not the best way to think about or decide among alternative practices. We'll soon describe how evidence-based management takes shape in the companies we've seen practice it. First, though, it is useful to get an example on the table of the type of issue that companies can address with better evidence.

An Example: Should We Adopt Forced Ranking?

The decision-making process used at Oxford's Centre for Evidence-Based Medicine starts with a crucial first step—the situation confronting the practitioner must be framed as an answerable question. That makes it clear how to compile relevant evidence. And so we do that here, raising a question that many companies have faced in recent years: Should we adopt forced ranking of our employees? The question refers to what General Electric more formally calls a forced-curve performance-ranking system. It's a talent management approach in which the performance levels of individuals are plotted along a bell curve. Depending on their position on the curve, employees fall into groups, with perhaps the top 20%, the so-called A players, being given outsize rewards; the middle 70% or so, the B players, being targeted for development; and the lowly bottom 10%, the C players, being counseled or thrown out of their jobs.

Without a doubt, this question arose for many companies as they engaged in benchmarking. General Electric has enjoyed great financial success and seems well stocked with star employees. GE alums have gone on to serve as CEOs at many other companies, including 3M, Boeing, Intuit, Honeywell, and the Home Depot. Systems that give the bulk of rewards to star employees have also been thoroughly hyped in business publications—for instance, in the McKinsey-authored book *The War for Talent*. But it's far from clear that the practice is worth emulating. It isn't just the infamous Enron—much praised in *The War for Talent*—that makes us say this. A couple of years ago, one of us gave a speech at a renowned but declining high-technology firm that used forced ranking (there, it was called a "stacking system"). A senior executive told us about an anonymous poll conducted among the firm's top 100 or so executives to discover which company practices made it difficult to turn knowledge into action. The stacking system was voted the worst culprit.

Would evidence-based management have kept that company from adopting this deeply unpopular program? We think so. First, managers would have immediately questioned whether their company was similar enough to GE in various respects that a practice cribbed from it could be expected to play out in the same way. Then, they would have been compelled to take a harder look at the data presumably supporting forced ranking—the claim that this style of talent management actually has caused adherents to be more successful. So, for example, they might have noticed a key flaw in *The War for Talent*'s research method: The authors report in the appendix that companies were first rated as high or average performers, based on return to shareholders during the prior three to ten years; then interviews and surveys were conducted to measure how these firms were fighting the talent wars. So, for the 77 companies (of 141 studied), management practices assessed in 1997 were treated as the "cause" of firm performance between 1987 and 1997. The study therefore violates a fundamental condition of causality: The proposed cause needs to occur *before* the proposed effect.

Next, management would have assembled more evidence and weighed the negative against the positive. In doing so, it would have found plenty of evidence that performance improves with team continuity and time in position—two reasons to avoid the churn of what's been called the "rank and yank" approach. Think of the U.S. Women's National Soccer Team, which has won numerous championships, including two of the four Women's World Cups and two of the three Olympic women's tournaments held to date. The team certainly has had enormously talented players, such as Mia Hamm, Brandi Chastain, Julie Foudy, Kristine Lilly, and Joy Fawcett. Yet all these players will tell you that the most important factor in their success was the communication, mutual understanding and respect, and ability to work together that developed during the 13 or so years that the stable core group played together. The power of such joint experience has been established in every setting examined, from string quartets to surgical teams, to top management teams, to airplane cockpit crews.

In a recent survey of more than 200 HR professionals, respondents reported that forced ranking had consequences such as lower productivity, inequity, damage to morale, and mistrust in leadership.

If managers at the technology firm had reviewed the best evidence, they would have also found that in work that requires cooperation (as nearly all the work in their company did), performance suffers when there is a big spread between the worst- and best-paid people—even though giving the lion's share of rewards to top performers is a hallmark of forced-ranking systems. In a Haas School of Business study of 102 business units, Douglas Cowherd and David Levine found that the greater the gap between top management's pay and that of other employees, the lower the product quality. Similar negative effects of dispersed pay have been found in longitudinal studies of top management teams, universities, and a sample of nearly 500 public companies. And in a recent Novations Group survey of more than 200 human resource professionals from companies with more than 2,500 employees, even though over half of the companies used forced ranking, the respondents reported that this approach resulted in lower productivity, inequity, skepticism, decreased employee engagement, reduced collaboration, damage to morale, and mistrust in leadership. We can find plenty of consultants and gurus who praise the power of dispersed pay, but we can't find a careful study that supports its value in settings where cooperation, coordination, and information sharing are crucial to performance.

Negative effects of highly dispersed pay are even seen in professional sports. Studies of baseball teams are especially interesting because, of all major professional sports, baseball calls for the least coordination among team members. But baseball still requires some cooperation—for example, between pitchers and catchers, and among infielders. And although individuals hit the ball, teammates can help one another improve their skills and break out of slumps. Notre Dame's Matt Bloom did a careful study of over 1,500 professional baseball players from 29 teams, spanning an eight-year period, which showed that players on teams with greater dispersion in pay had lower winning percentages, gate receipts, and media income.

Finally, an evidence-based approach would have surfaced data suggesting that average players can be extremely productive and that A players can founder, depending on the system they work in. Over 15 years of research in the auto industry provides compelling evidence for the power of systems over individual talent. Wharton's John Paul MacDuffie has combined quantitative studies of every automobile plant in the world with in-depth case studies to understand why some plants are more effective than others. MacDuffie has found that lean or flexible production systems—with their emphasis on teams, training, and job rotation, and their de-emphasis on status differences among employees—build higher-quality cars at a lower cost.

Becoming a Company of Evidence-Based Managers

It is one thing to believe that organizations would perform better if leaders knew and applied the best evidence. It is another thing to put that belief into practice. We appreciate how hard it is for working managers and executives to do their jobs. The demands for decisions are relentless, information is incomplete, and even the very best executives make many mistakes and undergo constant criticism and second-guessing from people inside and outside their companies. In that respect, managers are like physicians who face one decision after another: They can't possibly make the right choice every time. Hippocrates, the famous Greek who wrote the physicians' oath, described this plight well: "Life is short, the art long, opportunity fleeting, experiment treacherous, judgment difficult."

Teaching hospitals that embrace evidence-based medicine try to overcome impediments to using it by providing training, technologies, and work practices so staff can take the critical results of the best studies to the bedside. The equivalent should be done in management settings. But it's also crucial to appreciate that evidence-based management, like evidence-based medicine, entails a distinct mind-set that clashes with the way many managers and companies operate. It features a willingness to put aside belief and conventional wisdom—the dangerous half-truths that many embrace–and replace these with an unrelenting commitment to gather the necessary facts to make more informed and intelligent decisions.

As a leader in your organization, you can begin to nurture an evidence-based approach immediately by doing a few simple things that reflect the proper mind-set. If you ask for evidence of efficacy every time a change is proposed, people will sit up and take notice. If you take the time to parse the logic behind that evidence, people will become more disciplined in their own thinking. If you treat the organization like an unfinished prototype and encourage trial programs, pilot studies, and experimentation—and reward learning from these activities, even when something new fails—your organization will begin to develop its own evidence base. And if you keep learning while acting on the best knowledge you have and expect your people to do the same—if you have what has been called "the attitude of wisdom"—then your company can profit from evidence-based management as

you benefit from "enlightened trial and error" and the learning that occurs as a consequence.

Demand evidence. When it comes to setting the tone for evidence-based management, we have met few chief executives on a par with Kent Thiry, the CEO of DaVita, a $2 billion operator of kidney dialysis centers headquartered in El Segundo, California. Thiry joined DaVita in October 1999, when the company was in default on its bank loans, could barely meet payroll, and was close to bankruptcy. A big part of his turnaround effort has been to educate the many facility administrators, a large proportion of them nurses, in the use of data to guide their decisions.

To ensure that the company has the information necessary to assess its operations, the senior management team and DaVita's chief technical officer, Harlan Cleaver, have been relentless in building and installing systems that help leaders at all levels understand how well they are doing. One of Thiry's mottoes is "No brag, just facts." When he stands up at DaVita Academy, a meeting of about 400 frontline employees from throughout the organization, and states that the company has the best quality of treatment in the industry, that assertion is demonstrated with specific, quantitative comparisons.

A large part of the company's culture is a commitment to the quality of patient care. To reinforce this value, managers always begin reports and meetings with data on the effectiveness of the dialysis treatments and on patient health and well-being. And each facility administrator gets an eight-page report every month that shows a number of measures of the quality of care, which are summarized in a DaVita Quality Index. This emphasis on evidence also extends to management issues—administrators get information on operations, including treatments per day, teammate (employee) retention, the retention of higher-paying private pay patients, and a number of resource utilization measures such as labor hours per treatment and controllable expenses.

The most interesting thing about these monthly reports is what *isn't yet* included. DaVita COO Joe Mello explained that if a particular metric is deemed important, but the company currently lacks the ability to collect the relevant measurements, that metric is included on reports anyway, with the notation "not available." He said that the persistent mention of important measures that are missing helps motivate the company to figure out ways of gathering that information.

Many impressive aspects of DaVita's operations have contributed to the company's success, as evidenced by the 50% decrease in voluntary turnover, best-in-industry quality of patient care, and exceptional financial results. But the emphasis on evidence-based decision making in a culture that reinforces speaking the truth about how things are going is certainly another crucial component.

Examine logic. Simply asking for backup research on proposals is insufficient to foster a true organizational commitment to evidence-based management, especially given the problems that bedevil much so-called business research. As managers or consultants make their case, pay close attention to gaps in exposition, logic, and inference. This is particularly important because, in management research, studies that use surveys or data from company records to correlate practices with various performance outcomes are far more common than experiments. Such "nonexperimental" research is useful, but care must be taken to examine the logic of the research design and to control statistically for alternative explanations, which arise in even the best studies. Managers who consume such knowledge need to understand the limitations and think critically about the results.

When people in the organization see senior executives spending the time and mental energy to unpack the underlying assumptions that form the foundation for some proposed policy, practice, or intervention, they absorb a new cultural norm. The best leaders avoid the problem of seeming captious about the work of subordinates; they tap the collective wisdom and experience of their teams to explore whether assumptions seem sensible. They ask, "What would have to be true about people and organizations if this idea or practice were going to be effective? Does that feel true to us?"

Consultant claims may require an extra grain of salt. It is surprising how often purveyors of business knowledge are fooled or try to fool customers. We admire Bain & Company, for example, and believe it is quite capable of good research. We do wonder, however, why the company has a table on its Web site's home page that brags, "Our clients outperform the market 4 to 1" (the claim was "3 to 1" a few years back). The smart people at Bain know this correlation doesn't prove that their advice transformed clients into top performers. It could simply be that top performers have more money for hiring consultants. Indeed, any claim that Bain deserves credit for such performance is conspicuously absent from the Web site, at least as of fall 2005. Perhaps the hope is that visitors will momentarily forget what they learned in their statistics classes!

Evidence-based management is conducted best not by know-it-alls but by managers who profoundly appreciate how much they do not know.

Treat the organization as an unfinished prototype. For some questions in some businesses, the best evidence is to be found at home—in the company's own data and experience rather than in the broader-based research of scholars. Companies that want to promote more evidence-based management should get in the habit of running trial programs, pilot studies, and small experiments, and thinking about the inferences that can be drawn from them, as CEO Gary Loveman has done at Harrah's. Loveman joked to us that there are three ways to get fired at Harrah's these days: steal, harass women, or institute a program without first running an experiment. As you might expect, Harrah's experimentation is richest and most renowned in the area of marketing, where the company makes use of the data stream about customers' behaviors and responses to promotions. In one experiment reported by Harvard's Rajiv Lal in a teaching case, Harrah's offered a control group a promotional package worth $125 (a free room, two steak dinners, and $30 in casino chips); it offered customers in an experimental group just $60 in chips. The $60 offer generated more gambling revenue than the $125 offer did, and at a reduced cost. Loveman wanted to see experimentation like this throughout the business, not just

in marketing. And so the company proved that spending money on employee selection and retention efforts (including giving people realistic job previews, enhancing training, and bolstering the quality of frontline supervision) would reduce turnover and produce more engaged and committed employees. Harrah's succeeded in reducing staff turnover by almost 50%.

Similarly, CEO Meg Whitman attributes much of eBay's success to the fact that management spends less time on strategic analysis and more time trying and tweaking things that seem like they might work. As she said in March 2005, "This is a completely new business, so there's only so much analysis you can do." Whitman suggests instead, "It's better to put something out there and see the reaction and fix it on the fly. You could spend six months getting it perfect in the lab … [but] we're better off spending six days putting it out there, getting feedback, and then evolving it."

Yahoo is especially systematic about treating its home page as an unfinished prototype. Usama Fayyad, the company's chief data officer, points out that the home page gets millions of hits an hour, so Yahoo can conduct rigorous experiments that yield results in an hour or less—randomly assigning, say, a couple hundred thousand visitors to the experimental group and several million to the control group. Yahoo typically has 20 or so experiments running at any time, manipulating site features like colors, placement of advertisements, and location of text and buttons. These little experiments can have big effects. For instance, an experiment by data-mining researcher Nitin Sharma revealed that simply moving the search box from the side to the center of the home page would produce enough additional "click throughs" to bring in millions more dollars in advertising revenue a year.

A big barrier to using experiments to build management knowledge is that companies tend to adopt practices in an all-or-nothing way—either the CEO is behind the practice, so everyone does it or at least claims to, or it isn't tried at all. This tendency to do things everywhere or nowhere severely limits a company's ability to learn. In particular, multisite organizations like restaurants, hotels, and manufacturers with multiple locations can learn by experimenting in selected sites and making comparisons with "control" locations. Field experiments at places such as McDonald's restaurants, 7-Eleven convenience stores, Hewlett-Packard, and Intel have introduced changes in some units and not others to test the effects of different incentives, technologies, more interesting job content, open versus closed offices, and even detailed and warm (versus cursory and cold) explanations about why pay cuts were being implemented.

Embrace the attitude of wisdom. Something else, something broader, is more important than any single guideline for reaping the benefits of evidence-based management: the attitude people have toward business knowledge. At least since Plato's time, people have appreciated that true wisdom does not come from the sheer accumulation of knowledge, but from a healthy respect for and curiosity about the vast realms of knowledge still unconquered. Evidence-based management is conducted best not by know-it-alls but by managers who profoundly appreciate how much they do not know. These managers aren't frozen into inaction by ignorance; rather, they act on the best of their knowledge while questioning what they know.

Cultivating the right balance of humility and decisiveness is a huge, amorphous goal, but one tactic that serves it is to support the continuing professional education of managers with a commitment equal to that in other professions. The Centre for Evidence-Based Medicine says that identifying and applying effective strategies for lifelong learning are the keys to making this happen for physicians. The same things are surely critical to evidence-based management.

Another tactic is to encourage inquiry and observation even when rigorous evidence is lacking and you feel compelled to act quickly. If there is little or no information and you can't conduct a rigorous study, there are still things you can do to act more on the basis of logic and less on guesswork, fear, belief, or hope. We once worked with a large computer company that was having trouble selling its computers at retail stores. Senior executives kept blaming their marketing and sales staff for doing a bad job and dismissed complaints that it was hard to get customers to buy a lousy product—until one weekend, when members of the senior team went out to stores and tried to buy their computers. All of the executives encountered sales clerks who tried to dissuade them from buying the firm's computers, citing the excessive price, weak feature set, clunky appearance, and poor customer service. By organizing such field trips and finding other ways to gather qualitative data, managers can convey that decisions should not ignore real-world observations.

Will It Make a Difference?

The evidence-based-medicine movement has its critics, especially physicians who worry that clinical judgment will be replaced by search engines or who fear that bean counters from HMOs will veto experimental or expensive techniques. But initial studies suggest that physicians trained in evidence-based techniques are better informed than their peers, even 15 years after graduating from medical school. Studies also show conclusively that patients receiving the care that is indicated by evidence-based medicine experience better outcomes.

At this time, that level of assurance isn't available to those who undertake evidence-based management in business settings. We have the experience of relatively few companies to go on, and while it is positive, evidence from broad and representative samples is needed before that experience can be called a consistent pattern. Yet the theoretical argument strikes us as ironclad. It seems perfectly logical that decisions made on the basis of a preponderance of evidence about what works elsewhere, as well as within your own company, will be better decisions and will help the organization thrive. We also have a huge body of peer-reviewed studies—literally thousands of careful studies by well-trained researchers—that, although routinely ignored, provide simple and powerful advice about how to run organizations. If found and used, this advice would have an immediate positive effect on organizations.

Does all this sound too obvious? Perhaps. But one of the most important lessons we've learned over the years is that practicing evidence-based management often entails being a master of the mundane. Consider how the findings from this one little study could help a huge organization: An experiment at the University of Missouri compared decision-making groups that stood up during ten- to 20-minute meetings with groups that sat down. Those that stood up took 34% less time to make decisions, and the quality was just as good. Whether people should sit down or stand up during meetings may seem a downright silly question at first blush. But do the math. Take energy giant Chevron, which has over 50,000 employees. If each employee replaced just one 20-minute sit-down meeting per year with a stand-up meeting, each of those meetings would be about seven minutes shorter. That would save Chevron over 350,000 minutes—nearly 6,000 hours—per year.

Leaders who are committed to practicing evidence-based management also need to brace themselves for a nasty side effect: When it is done right, it will undermine their power and prestige, which may prove unsettling to those who enjoy wielding influence. A former student of ours who worked at Netscape recalled a sentiment he'd once heard from James Barksdale back when he was CEO: "If the decision is going to be made by the facts, then everyone's facts, as long as they are relevant, are equal. If the decision is going to be made on the basis of people's opinions, then mine count for a lot more." This anecdote illustrates that facts and evidence are great levelers of hierarchy. Evidence-based practice changes power dynamics, replacing formal authority, reputation, and intuition with data. This means that senior leaders—often venerated for their wisdom and decisiveness—may lose some stature as their intuitions are replaced, at least at times, by judgments based on data available to virtually any educated person. The implication is that leaders need to make a fundamental decision: Do they want to be told they are always right, or do they want to lead organizations that actually perform well?

If taken seriously, evidence-based management can change how every manager thinks and acts. It is, first and foremost, a way of seeing the world and thinking about the craft of management; it proceeds from the premise that using better, deeper logic and employing facts, to the extent possible, permits leaders to do their jobs more effectively. We believe that facing the hard facts and truth about what works and what doesn't, understanding the dangerous half-truths that constitute so much conventional wisdom about management, and rejecting the total nonsense that too often passes for sound advice will help organizations perform better.

JEFFREY PFEFFER (pfeffer_jeffrey@gsb.stanford.edu) is the Thomas D. Dee II Professor of Organizational Behavior at Stanford Graduate School of Business in California. **ROBERT I. SUTTON** (robert.sutton@stanford.edu) is a professor of management science and engineering at Stanford School of Engineering, where he is also a codirector of the Center for Work, Technology, and Organization. Pfeffer and Sutton are the authors of *The Knowing-Doing Gap: How Smart Companies Turn Knowledge into Action* (Harvard Business School Press, 1999) and *Hard Facts, Dangerous Half-Truths, and Total Nonsense: Profiting from Evidence-Based Management* (Harvard Business School Press, forthcoming in March 2006).

Managing High-Risk Outsourcing

EMANUELE PADOVANI AND DAVID YOUNG

Outsourcing is a strategy used by local governments in an effort to provide high-quality public services at a low cost. The underlying idea is that a locality can take advantage of a vendor's considerable experience and economies of scale. The result will be comparable or better-quality services than provided by the locality itself, at a reduced cost to taxpayers, while still allowing the vendor to earn a reasonable profit.

During the past three decades, local governments in both the United States and abroad have undertaken such disparate outsourcing activities as animal control, legal services, fire protection, trash collection, health care, snow plowing, building maintenance, bill collection, data processing, street cleaning, street repair, and recycling. Unfortunately, outsourcing has not always achieved the dual goals of high quality and reduced cost. In part, this is because of poor vendor management by localities.

The way in which a locality must manage its vendors depends on the risk associated with the outsourced activity. The purpose of this article is to present two frameworks that can assist local governments in outsourcing. The first framework is designed to assess the nature of the risk of a potentially outsourced activity. The second, on which we place most of our emphasis, comprises techniques that can be used to manage the vendor of a high-risk outsourced activity.

In this regard, it is important to note that many communities tend to avoid high-risk outsourcing. Yet, just because an activity is high-risk is not a good reason to avoid it; rather, it must be managed differently from a low-risk outsourced activity if it is to achieve cost-effective results for the citizenry.

Framework 1.
Assessing Outsourcing Risk

The nature of risk in a potentially outsourced activity can be viewed from three perspectives: citizen sensitivity, the supplier market, and the costs of switching.

Citizen sensitivity. From the citizens' perspective, a city's sanitation service clearly is much more important than, say, its publications department. Citizens are extremely concerned about the timely removal of waste and only minimally concerned about printing quality. In large part, this is because they are the final clients, so that, for the local government, the risk of nonperformance is much higher. As a result, any external out-

sourcing decision must weigh the impact of poor performance or nonperformance on residents.

Supplier market. Competitiveness in the supplier market can range from many potential suppliers (high competition) to few, or perhaps only one, potential supplier. For example, there usually are many printing companies competing for a community's publication business, but there may be few vendors offering sanitation services or nursery schools. With only a few potential vendors, the community's ability to negotiate on price and features is low.

Switching costs. Occasionally, outsourced activities are carried out using some highly unusual resources that cannot be transferred easily from one vendor to another. When this happens, a community will have difficulty, and no doubt incur substantial costs, in replacing an existing vendor. Finding a new vendor for, say, a sanitation service or nursery school could be difficult because of a variety of investments that must be replicated if a new vendor is selected. In a nursery school, teachers have learned about the children's needs, established relationships with parents, and so forth. In instances like this one, the switching costs are high.

From the vendor's perspective, the cost of losing a contract can be great. For many high-risk outsourced activities, the vendor has purchased expensive equipment and incurred training and other start-up costs to carry out the contract. For this reason, if problems arise some managers will give the vendor time to improve; other managers may be unconcerned with the vendor's onetime costs and decide to use a new vendor before the situation worsens. Much depends on the terms of the contract and the nature of the relationship between the local government and the vendor.

In contrast, if a service like snow removal is outsourced, the locality's switching costs are likely low, as are the vendor's start-up costs. If one vendor does not perform according to the contract, the locality usually has little difficulty in replacing that vendor. Indeed, the city or county may have contracts with several other providers as well, to protect it from any sort of "vendor holdup."

The low-risk embodies services such as a publication department, with a combination of low citizen sensitivity, high market competition, and low switching costs—a situation with a high probability of successful outsourcing and without the need for careful vendor management. A service like snow removal might fall into the upper-left, front corner, where citizen sensitivity is high but where a poorly performing vendor can be replaced easily and quickly.

At the other end of the spectrum (high citizen sensitivity/low competition/high switching costs) are services for which outsourcing poses a high risk. An example was seen some years ago when the commonwealth of Massachusetts outsourced its Medicaid Management Information System, which mailed several hundred thousand checks each month to indigent citizens. Citizen sensitivity was high, and there were almost no vendors, other than the one chosen, having computer systems of sufficient size and sophistication to undertake the various activities needed (only one of which was sending out checks).

Moreover, because of the need to transfer software (or rewrite code, in some instances), plus the difficulty of moving data files from one vendor to another and performing needed audits, the switching costs were high. When the vendor went bankrupt, Massachusetts and several hundred thousand Medicaid recipients learned, quite painfully, the true meaning of high-risk outsourcing.

Framework 2. Managing High-Risk Outsourcing

Even though an outsourced service may fall into the high-risk area, it still may have considerable potential for improving the cost-effectiveness of public services. To achieve this potential, the local government must manage the vendor carefully. In some cases, vendors, while abiding by the "letter" of a contract, may make reductions in quality and features in an attempt to save costs. Or they may not be responsive to citizen concerns. Or they may attempt to raise switching costs to make it difficult for the local government to consider competitors at the time of contract renegotiation.

To address these sorts of problems, a city or county must focus on three distinct activities: performance measurement, ongoing communication and coordination, and links to the management control process. A high-risk outsourcing contract requires multiple performance measures; a high level of ongoing communication and cooperation to fill the gaps that are inevitable in any high-risk contract; and a full linkage with the management control system, including process measures concerning the contract manager's activities.

Performance Measurement

With high-risk outsourcing, contract monitoring must involve a variety of activities to ensure not only service effectiveness, but also responsiveness of the vendor to citizen needs and problems. These activities must include taking steps to ensure that problems are resolved quickly. In effect, a local government must shift from traditional *regulatory contracting* (whereby it specifies inputs, or processes, in detail) to *performance contracting* (whereby it simply states the outputs wanted and allows the vendor to determine the appropriate mix and quantity of inputs). Thus, the community is no longer concerned with

processes, or their measures, but with the vendor's ability to achieve the agreed-upon results at a lower cost than if it had undertaken the activity itself.

To illustrate, consider a decision by the department of public safety to outsource traffic-light maintenance. The department is unconcerned with how often the vendor inspects each plant or the efficiency of the vendor's employees in conducting the inspections—both of which are process measures. Instead, the department focuses on such results measures as the percentage of operating traffic lights or the amount of time needed to restore a broken light. In effect, the department is purchasing functioning traffic lights, not inspections.

Clearly, not all types of results measures can be included in a contract. Many qualitative aspects, such as cleanliness in a street-cleaning contract or the effectiveness of an outsourced social service, can be measured by subjective evaluation only. Sometimes, surrogate measures of vendor performance can be used, like citizen complaints, length of assistance period, and so forth.

Finally, unless the community is careful, a vendor may develop a rigid focus on the results measures specified in the contract, rather than on creative thinking about how the service might be improved at no or minimal additional cost. To avoid this sort of focus, community staff must engage in ongoing communication and coordination with the vendors.

Ongoing Communication and Coordination

One characteristic of many high-risk outsourcing arrangements is that the contract cannot define all future contingencies, especially when the task to be completed is complex and evolving. Here, the relationship between the community and the vendor must be tightly linked, ideally characterized by mutual trust, altruism, cooperation, and a close working relationship.

To illustrate, consider the outsourcing of some printing needs of a publications department. In a "spot market" relationship, a locality would make a one-time purchase of, say, 5,000 copies of a brochure about a youth program. It would call several local printing companies for bids and choose the lowest one, knowing from prior experience that the quality would be acceptable and the delivery made on time. Alternatively, the community might have some short-term contracts with several local printing companies to meet needs like this one. If one company were unavailable, a request to another could be made.

Another possibility is a long-term contract with a single printing company, with the idea that the company would be the sole provider of printing needs. This sort of contract might evolve into a strategic alliance if the locality had some uncertain printing needs for which the vendor agreed to provide service as demanded without knowing in advance exactly what requests it would receive. The contract might be a loosely worded one, calling for, say, quarterly discussions and a settling-up of balances due.

Going even further, a joint venture might take place in which the company becomes a partner with the community and perhaps is guaranteed a certain percentage profit each year. Finally, vertical integration would exist if the community obtained all of its printing needs from an in-house department with no reliance on outside vendors. In effect, vertical integration returns the service to in-house provision.

More generally, with high-risk outsourcing, a shift to the right is essential to assure citizen satisfaction. While routine problems can be solved by daily contacts (phone calls, e-mails, and so on), structural problems (ones that are or could become repetitive) require a working relationship characterized by a high level of communication and coordination. In effect, with high-risk outsourcing, the working relationship between the community and its vendor is at least as important as the specific terms of the contract, perhaps more important.

Links to the Management Control Process

Outsourcing a service does not mean excluding it from a community's ongoing process of programming, budgeting, reporting, and evaluating. Changes in its strategy, for example, may mean that a vendor—as an integral part of the community—needs to consider new or different programmatic activities, such as a program to pick up recyclable waste or one to synchronize traffic lights along a major artery.

Similarly, if new programmatic activities will begin in the upcoming year, the budgeting phase of the management control process must incorporate a revised vendor budget; otherwise, the community's budget will be unrealistic.

Perhaps most important, the various results measures for the outsourced services need to be an integral part of the reporting phase of the management control process, as does information concerning the department charged with managing the vendor. For this reason, the reporting phase focuses on both the results being produced by the vendor and the monitoring activities of the internal department. Otherwise, senior management may learn too late of emerging problems.

Finally, recognizing that outsourcing is a matter of trade-off choices, and that the environment in which these choices are made is constantly evolving, a local government needs to evaluate the outsourced service periodically. In part, this is because results measures may fail to capture some of the more subjec-

tive elements of citizen satisfaction. Also, however, for any number of reasons an outsourced activity may have moved from one to another, which might call for a change in the outsourcing strategy.

Similarly, technology may have changed, such that it would be more beneficial to return from outsourcing to in-house service provision. Alternatively, it is possible that another vendor, working in another city or county, has developed some considerable expertise in the outsourced activity, such that a change in vendors would improve the quality of the service, lower its cost, or both.

In general, these sorts of problems and opportunities will not become apparent during day-to-day operations or even during the budgeting phase of the management control process. Ordinarily, only a thorough program evaluation can identify new opportunities or as-yet-unseen problems.

In short, when a community engages in high-risk outsourcing and wishes to assure its citizens that the savings realized from the outsourced activity are not matched by a reduction in service quality and features, it must develop an appropriate set of outsourcing-management activities. Given that a considerable number of outsourcing arrangements are of a high-risk nature, a focus on these activities is essential for those localities that wish to assure their citizens of effective services at a reasonable cost.

EMANUELE PADOVANI, Ph.D., is assistant professor at Forli Campus Facolta di Economia, University of Bologna, Italy (emanuele.padovani@unibo.it). **DAVID W. YOUNG, D.B.A.,** is professor of management in the public and nonprofit management program at the Boston University School of Management, and visiting professor at Forli Campus Facolta di Economia, University of Bologna, Italy (DWY204@cs.com).

This article is based on a paper prepared for the Ninth International Research Symposium on Public Management (IRSPM IX) held April 8, 2005, at Bocconi University, Milano, Italy. Authors retain the copyright. Copy can't be cited or reproduced in whole or in part without the written permission of the authors.

"There Was No Plan"—A Louisiana Perspective

Evan M. Berman, Thomas D. Lynch, Cynthia E. Lynch, and Maria D. Berman

The most commonly heard plight of people in the immediate aftermath of the hurricane landfall and later was that they felt abandoned. They were. Among residents, emergency workers and the media, the commonly heard assessment was that "There was no plan." The present estimate of the quantified cost associated with this event is about $300 billion in damage and 1,000 deaths. This is a high price to pay for poor human decision-making and leadership.

Facts are facts: the American emergency preparedness system failed. This was a public administration failure on a remarkable scale. Government agencies should have been there immediately or soon, but they were not. The National Guard failed to arrive in meaningful numbers for about five days. The Corps of Engineers did not immediately and effectively tend to catastrophic levee breaks.

The tragedy of Hurricane Katrina lies less in the storm itself than in the failed decisions of people and organizations with responsibilities for managing and planning such events. Women were raped at emergency shelters. Looters outgunned the local police. Children, infirm and old people were abandoned—some dying in nursing homes and hospitals. People without cars and the handicapped were not assisted in their evacuation efforts and, hence, left in harm's way. Survivors sometimes walked 40 miles for help. Patients sat in airport baggage areas for hours in their own urine. In this American disaster, rescuers from Canada arrived days before the American National Guard and the Federal Emergency Management Agency (FEMA).

Public Management Lessons

Some lessons for public management are already in evidence. The public is wrong to state that there was "no plan." The State of Louisiana's Emergency Operations Plan, is posted on the State's website. When printed, it stands about two inches tall, and was last updated in April 2005, just before the start of the hurricane season.

The plan assigns responsibilities for state and local governments throughout the State of Louisiana. A supplement discusses specific emergency operations in Southeastern Louisiana for evacuation and sheltering associated with cata-strophic hurricanes. These are defined as slow moving category three hurricanes, and categories four and five hurricanes—Katrina, a category four hurricane at landfall, is such an event. A plan existed, and it can be assessed. What follows should cause every community in the United States, to re-assess their own emergency plans and every professor of strategic planning to re-think what is being taught. The following is based on facts as they are presently known; while future investigations may reveal additional facts and circumstances, it is likely that the following considerations will remain important.

Lack of Implementation

The plan calls for announcing the location of staging areas for people who need public transportation in order to evacuate. However, no such call seems to have been made, nor is there evidence that adequate public transportation was provided for those without cars or having special needs. For example, Amtrak has a station in downtown New Orleans near the Superdome where trains regularly depart for Chicago and Los Angeles. It could have been used to transport a massive number of people out of harm's way.

Amtrak offered its trains, but the offer was not accepted by State officials. Quite simply, the public transportation needs of people, such as those with low incomes, were known and ignored by emergency and other officials. Only a few, inadequate number of buses were used.

One emergency planner, who was also an evacuee, waited for public transportation on I-10. She was stunned by what happened. The problem of inadequate public transportation reoccurred when evacuees were stranded waiting for days, often without food or water in the hot sun on the high ground of the Interstate highway. Emergency workers needed busses to take thousands of very needy people out of the area to Baton Rouge, Houston and other places. They were not available. The scene was cruel and embarrassing.

What is the lesson? Planning is more than putting something on paper. Planning includes delivering on plans; planning requires a commitment of resources, human and physical assets and regularly scheduled training. Planning, without implementation and without follow through, is a paper exercise that, in this instance, turned out to be a deceit that caused immense human suffering and loss of life.

Lack of a Plan for Foreseen Events

The State emergency plan acknowledges that above normal water levels and hurricane surge may cause levee overtopping or breaches. However, the plan is silent as to how the State will deal with such a crisis and, surprisingly, when the levees broke, the State response was absent and confused. Maybe planners assumed that the Army Corps of Engineers would take control and repair the breaks, but that was not spelled out in the plan. Neither the State, the Army Corps or local levee boards reacted quickly or adequately enough.

Another foreseen event was the extent of the flooding. The LSU Hurricane Center forecasted the extent of possible damage, as did the local newspaper, the Times-Picayune a few years earlier. No one can claim that the extent of possible damage was unforeseen—it was. Yet, the State plan is silent about how it might address situations that outstrip state and local capabilities and resources—the plan notes that such situations may occur. Another foreseeable event was that the mayor would have to declare a mandatory evacuation, and that the governor would have to request federal assistance. Yet, both seemed unprepared for making these decisions, and they lost valuable time considering these decisions. What is the lesson? Watch out for loose ends. Planners must identify every foreseeable phenomenon and develop appropriate responses. They must be prepared to seek multi-government responses as needed. Security must be present both within the shelters and on the streets to stop gangs fighting over food and looting stores. Medical services must be adequate to save lives. Places are needed to accommodate pets.

Failure to Identify Foreseeable Events

The State plan talks about the operation of emergency shelters. It addresses the special attention needed for medical and mental health needs. However, the plan does not mention the need to ensure safety in shelters, nor was public safety within the shelters provided for in the State plan. What did planners think would happen inside these shelters? The case histories of emergency shelters in other situations are well-known and clearly public safety is always a problem. The lawlessness, killings and rapes that occurred in the Superdome and Convention Center were execrable, but foreseeable. In the immediate aftermath of the hurricane landfall. Mayor Nagin prioritized rescue over law enforcement, which further exacerbated lawlessness.

There were other foreseeable events, as well. Many (if not most) people did not want to leave their pets behind. Among those who did, several people went back later to rescue them, clandestinely sneaking past security. It is also foreseeable that handicapped and elderly might be left alone. For example, one of the authors of this article talked to a diabetic elderly lady, who bad one leg amputated due to diabetes, who was left alone in her apartment for nine days in the dark without any means to communicate before rescuers finally found her. Offers of help are also foreseeable-public officials turned down such offers from many nonprofit organizations. What is the lesson? Planners need to creatively imagine what might go wrong, and not be quick to dismiss scenarios. They need to think through the smallest details. Clearly, in the future security must be provided both within the shelters and on the streets to stop gangs fighting over food and looting stores. Medical services and supplies must be adequate. And so on.

Questionable Assumptions

A plan cannot escape being based on assumptions, and it is now standard practice to state these. One of these is that all local, city and parish preparedness offices will be in communication with the state, federal and each other before, during and following the emergency. Such an assumption is questionable, especially following experience with the terrorist acts of September 11, 2001. The breakdown in communications in the Gulf states was foreseeable. Also, while the Superdome was not planned as a refuge of last resort, anyone who has ever visited New Orleans knows it is an imposing structure that people naturally view as a place of refuge. The population of New Orleans and especially those living in its broader vicinity flocked to it as a beacon of safety.

What is the lesson? Planners must check and verify the reality of their planning assumptions. They must be realistic and understand natural human behavior. They must communicate the pleas clearly and often to the general public well in advance of the crisis. During and immediately after a major event, they must get the facts from people on the ground as they continually update and adapt their planning document.

Planning Successes

Clearly, Katrina severely tested the Southeastern Louisiana hurricane plan. But there were planning successes, too. Local leaders were very successful at getting many people out of the New Orleans area on the three bridges and one main road that connect the city with the rest of Louisiana. Following last year's Hurricane Ivan, state officials developed a "contra flow" traffic system that increased traffic lanes by making all lanes outward bound, only. Tropical Storm Cindy, a month before Katrina, caused local political officials to pressure the governor to give them more time to activate this plan. Local officials can congratulate themselves for having saved many lives by developing a better evacuation plan for those with cars. Last year it took eight hours to get from New Orleans to Baton Rouge (about 75 miles) in order to evacuate for Hurricane Ivan, but in Katrina it took only four hours. Normally, the drive takes about one hour and fifteen minutes. Two of the authors benefited from this plan.

We also note the many heroic acts of individual public servants and agencies. The Louisiana Department of Wildlife and Fisheries was heroic in its effort to organize many private, shallow boats to navigate the flooded streets of New Orleans. Police officers worked tirelessly in very extreme conditions to rescue people. The jail evacuated all of its inmates—not a single one died. It might also be noted that the mayor of New Orleans, in the days following the landfill, was extraordinary in castigating state and federal officials and getting them to respond. But all these individual acts cannot make up for the absence of a well-considered and implemented emergency plan.

There is no reason to believe that Louisiana's state hurricane emergency plan is any better or worse than any other such plan in the country. We hope that communities throughout the country are taking the lessons of Louisiana to heart, rather than hoping that they will be spared from having their plan tested. If Katrina occurred in Houston, damages would also be in the hundreds of billions. If a major earthquake hit Los Angles, damages would be in the same magnitude or worse. If a major terrorist attack hit any major city, then again the damages could be in the hundreds of billions. How real are the assumptions in your state plan? Would your state plan be implementable? Are your first responders adequately trained? What intergovernmental relations are necessary to properly coordinate the rescue activity, and are these in place and recently tested? Your community's plan is likely not as good as you would like to think it is.

We need to anticipate far greater federal involvement in emergency operations in the future. There should not be state emergency plans but rather there should be intergovernmental emergency plans that clearly present, coordinate and integrate the federal, state and local roles. Katrina taught us that state and local governments cannot cope with the magnitude of a major disaster. It might be wise for the federal government to oversee the quality and implementation of some of the plans.

While the landfall location of any catastrophic hurricane is uncertain, it is highly certain that every year one or more will occur somewhere in the Southeastern United States. The federal government should pre-position supplies and assets that can be deployed within hours of the disaster to ensure law enforcement and rescue until a larger force arrives some days later. The federal government must also provide adequate emergency communications (including mobile transmission towers, satellite telephones and other needed equipment) within three hours to the affected areas. In every large disaster since Hurricane An-drew, a lack of communication has been the most often cited complication to the rescue effort. Federal forward deployment is essential for areas in which disaster is likely to occur.

In New Orleans, the levee system must be rebuilt, but in a manner that fits today's state of the art. Some politicians argue that New Orleans should not be rebuilt because it is below sea level. The Dutch have proven that living below sea level can be achieved. Their result is a very viable society and healthy economy. New Orleans is a national and historic treasure. In addition, the nation needs a major city near the mouth of its greatest river. This has been the historic role of the city. Can the United States not achieve what the Dutch can? Louisiana senators and representatives have requested upgrades to the levees for decades and cries of pork barrel politics have killed the U.S. Army Corps of Engineers requests. Because Congress refused to act and pay the needed $6-10 billion to upgrade the levees, it will now pay this, and perhaps $300 billion more.

Hurricane Katrina brought devastation to many people in Southeastern Louisiana, but the shortfalls in planning made the cost, death toll and human and animal suffering that much higher in the immediate aftermath. Let us hope that we act on the lessons from this monumental failure in public administration. Let us help our elected leadership learn these important lessons. Clearly, the United States needs to develop better approaches to disaster relief based on the lessons of Katrina.

ASPA member **EVAN BERMAN** is professor of public administration at Louisiana State University. **MARIA BERMAN** is a psychotherapist in private practice. Evan and Maria Berman live in Metairie, LA, located just outside of New Orleans. E-mail: berman@lsu.edu.

ASPA member **THOMAS D. LYNCH** is a professor of public administration at Louisiana State University. He is a former president of ASPA and has written many books and articles primarily on public budgeting and ethics. E-mail: tlynch@lsu.edu.

ASPA member **CYNTHIA E. LYNCH** is an assistant professor the MPA program in the Nelson Mandela School of Public Policy and Urban Affairs at Southern University. E-mail: CYNTHIA_LYNCH@cxs.subr.edu.

From *Public Administration Times*, Vol. 28, No. 10, November 2005. Copyright © 2005 by American Society for Public Administration. Reprinted by permission.

Abu Ghraib: A Case of Moral and Administrative Failure

The special expertise of the military professional is in combat—the controlled application of violence to achieve political goals. This unique expertise gives the military a special social responsibility to apply violence only for socially approved purposes in a socially approved manner. However, the violence of combat also places extreme pressures on individuals to depart from accepted values and professional standards. When such stress is combined with administrative failure, the stage is set for atrocities. This article seeks to understand the role of administrative failure in creating the conditions leading up to the torture and abuse of Iraqi prisoners at Abu Ghraib. It is not intended to excuse the behavior but to illuminate the relationship between administrative failure and individual behavior. The systemic problems identified in the many investigation reports paint a picture of administrative failure that stretches from Abu Ghraib prison to Washington, D.C.

SAUNDRA J. REINKE

When faced with evil, what do we do? As individuals, we may fall back on our religious or moral upbringing, hoping it will tell us what to do. Professionals, however, also have a set of values that lie at the heart of what it means to follow and belong to their particular profession. The military is no exception. In fact, the U.S. military may have one of the best-articulated, most consistent set of professional values today. Nonetheless, the military faces unique challenges. Specifically, the violence of combat places extreme pressures on individuals to depart from the accepted value set of the military professional.

A profession is more than an occupation: A profession implies a lifelong commitment to a specific way of life. Huntington (1957) describes a profession as a type of vocation. A vocation, or "calling," is a way of life grounded in a set of values (Palmer 2000). This definition is similar to Moskos's (1977) distinction between an institution and an occupation. An institution is centered on a purpose that transcends individual self-interest for a higher good. Members of an institution are following a calling, and they see themselves as different from the mainstream of society. An occupation is none of these things. Military service has traditionally been seen as an institution.

The special, central expertise of the military professional is in combat—the controlled application of violence to achieve political goals (Clausewitz 1989; Huntington 1957). This places a special social responsibility on the military—the obligation to apply violence only for socially approved purposes in a socially approved manner (Huntington 1957). In a democracy, because of the emphasis placed on civil liberties and rights, the military's responsibility to behave in a socially responsible fashion becomes even more critical. Toner (2000) argues that the es-

sence of military professionalism is responsible choice. Thus, all the military services stress the importance of discipline as well as adherence to established codes of behavior (AFDD 1–1, 2004; FM 22–100, 1999; MCWP 6–11, 2002; NLCM, 2004). The codes of each service include sets of "core values" espoused by the service. In the case of the Army, the core values include loyalty, duty, respect, selfless service, honor, integrity, and personal courage (FM 22–100, (999). In addition, soldiers are expected to comply with service rules and regulations and the Geneva and Hague conventions.

These codes of behavior were violated at Abu Ghraib, resulting in major embarrassment to the U.S. government. The Army's investigation into the abuse of Iraqi prisoners concluded that systematic and illegal abuse of detainees occurred (Taguba 2004). The abuse shocked the world. In addition to the now-famous photograph of the prisoner with the sandbag on his head and electric wires attached to his fingers, toes, and penis, Taguba's report found evidence of punching, slapping, and kicking detainees, videotaping and photographing naked male and female detainees, arranging detainees in sexually explicit poses, forcing male detainees to masturbate while being photographed and videotaped, using military working dogs without muzzles to intimidate and frighten detainees (with one reported biting and injuring of a detainee), and one instance of a guard having sex with a female detainee.

Why did this happen? What role did administrative failure play in the atrocities at Abu Ghraib? Administrative failure at Abu Ghraib will be examined first by looking at responsibility and accountability in organizations. Next, the subject of combat stress will be introduced to place the actions of the guards in the proper context. Then, the specifics of what occurred at

Abu Ghraib will be examined, with emphasis on administrative actions that led to prisoner abuse. The article concludes with a discussion of where responsibility and accountability the for the torture and abuse of prisoners at Abu Ghraib. It is not the intent to condone or ignore individual moral responsibility in the torture and abuse of Iraqi prisoners—individuals who tortured and abused prisoners, or stood by and ignored such behavior, must accept their personal responsibility and, hopefully, punishment. From the standpoint of public administration, however, it is critical to explore the connection between administrative failure and individual behavior.

Responsibility and Accountability

"Responsibility may well be the most important word in all the vocabulary of administration, public and private" (Mosher 1968, 7). Terry Cooper (1998) suggests that there are two kinds of responsibility, objective and subjective. The former concerns externally imposed standards and norms of behavior; the latter flows from one's beliefs, values, and character.

Objective responsibility has two major components (ibid.). Accountability acknowledges one's responsibility to others, whether to a specific individual, a group, an organization, or even the Citizenry at large. It presupposes a structure of superior subordinate relationships designed to facilitate the accomplishment of the organization's mission. But objective responsibility does not imply blind obedience to orders. Indeed, it cannot, because public administrators may find it difficult to determine just who they are accountable to—their supervisor, elected officials, or the public at large (Gawthrop 1998). All of these parties can demand conflicting things of an administrator, creating an ethical quandary. Obedience is an important virtue, particularly in a military setting, but it is not the only virtue.

The second component of objective responsibility is obligation, the responsibility to complete assigned tasks, care for subordinate personnel, and achieve the goals of the organization (Cooper 1998). Public administrators are expected to be both efficient and effective in the execution of their duties (Gawthrop 1998). Accountability and obligation may conflict, for "doing one's job" may entail ignoring what is in the best interest of the public. Ultimately, an administrator's actions will be judged not only on the basis of efficiency or effectiveness, but also on ethical grounds.

Responsibility will be the most important word in all the vocabulary of administration, public and private.

Subjective responsibility refers to individual beliefs flowing from the values individuals are taught in their families and in religious and school settings (Cooper 1998). In addition, professions develop ethical standards that shape the attitudes and behavior of their members. These standards help create and sustain trust among organizational members. Unethical behavior damages the civic order in an organization and destroys trust between employees and supervisors (Bies and Tripp 1996).

Romzek and Ingraham proposed that there are four types of accountability: hierarchal accountability (which comes through bureaucratic structure and supervision), legal accountability (external oversight or review of work through audits or legislative hearings), professional accountability (based on "internalized norms of appropriate practice" [2000, 242]), and political accountability (responsiveness to external stakeholders, including elected officials and the public). All of these sources of accountability exist in the military: the military chain of command, military directives governing the treatment of prisoners of war, and international standards of behavior in the Hague and Geneva conventions.

The first principle of the international body of law in this area is humanitarianism. It requires that "persons who are in the power of a party to the conflict shall be treated humanely in all circumstances." Humanitarianism requires that all parties to a conflict respect the "person, honor, conviction, and religious practices" of those in custody. One does not have to be a prisoner of war to be covered by the principle of humanitarianism (Green 2000, 349).

The responsibility to treat prisoners humanely rests on everyone. "Every individual, regardless of rank or governmental status, is personally liable for any war crime or grave breach that he might commit" (ibid., 303). The Geneva Conventions and Protocol require signatory nations to ensure that all their military personnel are trained in the laws of armed conflict, including the proper treatment of prisoners (ibid.).[1] The military does this during initial training and annually thereafter. In addition to a review of the laws of armed conflict, the training covers the obligation to refuse to obey an illegal order. Thus, the claim "I was just following orders" is not a viable defense under either American or international law. Receipt of an illegal order may, however, mitigate the subsequent punishment (ibid.).

Persons in command, regardless of rank, have an obligation to exercise proper control over their forces and therefore are held accountable for all illegal actions by their subordinates. This includes actions they ordered, permitted, tolerated, or observed. A commander who claims not to have known about violations of the laws of war is presumed to have failed to exercise proper control and is still held responsible (ibid.).

The responsibility to treat prisoners humanely rests on everyone.

These outside standards of international law are reinforced in military directives and through the training process. In addition, the military deliberately socializes each of its members into a professional ethic through the initial training process and reinforces that ethic in further training programs and the promotion process. Much of this professional ethic is also expressed in written directives or doctrinal manuals. Thus, in the military setting, it is difficult to make Cooper's (1998) distinction between subjective and objective responsibility.

Samuel Huntington (1957) argues that military personnel share a particular *weltanschauung,* or professional military ethic. This "ethic" consists of the values, attitudes, and perspectives military members share. These values, attitudes, and perspectives flow logically from the unique role of the military in society and are as essential to combat effectiveness as good training or weaponry (Hillen 1999; Huntington 1957; Toner 2000). Central to the professional military ethic is a shared set of values—discipline, tradition, unity, and cohesion (Huntington 1957). Miller (1995) adds putting the group before individual needs. Discipline has always been understood to be at the heart of combat effectiveness. Some 2,500 years ago, Sunzi pointed out that method and discipline were one of the five key factors that predicted success in military operations. He claimed that "soldiers must be treated with humanity, but kept under control by means of iron discipline" (1983, 49). The Roman military writer Vegetius said that "victory in war does not depend entirely upon numbers or mere courage; only skill and discipline will insure it" (1985, 75). In the nineteenth century, Clausewitz (1989) put discipline first in his description of the military virtues.

This professional ethic is repeated in modern military directives. All of the services stress the importance of discipline, tradition, unity, cohesion, and selfless service in their leadership manuals (AFDD 1–1, 2004; FM 22–100, 1999; MCWP 6–11, 2002; NLCM, 2004) and in the training environment. Leaders have a special responsibility to care for the needs of subordinates. The Army's leadership manual (FM 22–100, 1999) also emphasizes the importance of accomplishing the mission honorably, in accordance with international standards governing the conduct of war. The rationale for this is that waging war "honorably" helps the United States "win the peace." Consequently, both in this document and in the training process, military personnel are taught that they have a positive duty to disobey illegal orders.

In sum, both objective and subjective responsibility exist within the American military. Objective responsibility is manifested in a clearly established chain of command and in directives specifying what constitutes appropriate behavior. Subjective responsibility is shown in a clearly articulated set of core values that includes discipline, selflessness, and honor. Leaders are singled out as responsible for the well-being and behavior of subordinates.

Combat Stress

Before engaging in an examination of the administrative failure behind Abu Ghraib, combat stress must be discussed. Bartone (2004) considers it imperative to examine both the contextual/ situational and individual/personality influences at work in order to understand what happened at Abu Ghraib. Stress levels are high among military personnel, whether in combat, supporting combat, or awaiting combat (Miles 2002). A psychologist who treats combat veterans states that "we must grasp what is at stake: lethal danger and the fear of it" (Shay 1994, 10). Combat stress may be defined as the "constantly changing result of all the stressors and stress processes inside the soldier as

he performs the combat-related mission. At any given time in each soldier, stress is the result of the complex interaction of many mental and physical stressors" (FM 22–51, 1994, 2–2g), including exposure to weather, sleep deprivation, extreme fatigue, fear, time pressure versus what may seem to be endless waiting, grief, guilt, frustration, and injury. These stressors work in combination and can produce both positive and negative responses in individuals (FM 22–51, 1994). Positive responses help individuals adjust to the combat environment, whereas negative or dysfunctional responses include battle fatigue and misconduct.

> **The dependency of the modern soldier on a distant organizational structure that provides him with all essentials of survival . . . creates a moral structure, a fiduciary relationship that makes trust in leadership critically important to psychological survival.**

Stress-induced misconduct can range from minor violations of orders up to violations of the laws of armed conflict. Such misconduct can include killing or torturing prisoners, mutilating enemy dead, rape, looting, "fragging" (killing one's own leader), and desertion. Bartone, Adler, and Vaitkus (1998) identify five psychological stressors in military operations: ambiguity, isolation, a feeling of powerlessness, boredom, and danger. Similarly, Shay (1994) proposes that the dependency of the modem soldier on a distant organizational structure that provides him with all the essentials of survival—orders, weapons, ammunition, food, water, training, and fire support—creates a moral structure, a fiduciary relationship that makes trust in leadership critically important to psychological survival. Soldiers expect a certain amount of deprivation. Indeed, the endurance and courage of soldiers under such conditions is legendary. But when deprivation is seen as the outcome of indifference or disrespect by superiors, it becomes an unbearable offense and can spark misconduct (ibid.).

The Army (FM 22–51, 1994) finds that misconduct is more common in poorly trained, undisciplined units. Other factors that may increase misconduct stress behavior include the availability of alcohol or drugs, boredom or monotonous duties, commission of atrocities by the enemy, perceptions that the civilian populace is hostile or untrustworthy, lack of expected support leading to a feeling of abandonment by senior leaders, lack of unit cohesion, and loss of confidence in leadership (ibid.). Seven of these nine factors: (training, discipline, availability of alcohol or drugs, monotonous duties, expectations of support, unit cohesion, and confidence in leadership) can either be controlled or significantly shaped by administrative processes and actions.

In short, combat stress can lead to violations of both U.S. policy and international law. This is especially likely when commanders fail in their obligation to care for the needs of subordinates. Soldiers are dependent on the military bureaucracy for all the essentials of survival. When the bureaucracy and its leaders fail to provide these essentials, stress-induced misconduct becomes much more likely.

Abu Ghraib

Were the conditions at Abu Ghraib stressful? Were there administrative failures that match the preconditions for misconduct responses to combat stress? These questions will be answered by exploring the conditions under which American military personnel worked. First, the situation in Iraq will be reviewed, followed by an examination of administrative behavior from Washington, D.C., down to the local level.

Clearly, the situation in Iraq, then and now, is highly stressful. The initial euphoria of Saddam's overthrow was quickly replaced by a sense of disappointment and deepening frustration with the U.S. occupation forces among the Iraqi populace. This fact, along with the continuing infiltration of terrorists from outside Iraq, led to an increasing number of ambushes and assaults on American military personnel (Schlesinger et al. 2004; Taguba 2004). Abu Ghraib came under mortar attack twenty-five times in July, 2003 alone. It quickly became impossible, and possibly deadly, for a U.S. soldier to assume that an Iraqi civilian was a friend. In short, soldiers were, and are, living and working in a stressful, dangerous place, under circumstances that foster a sense of distrust and dislike for the local populace.

In addition to this "background stress," the Department of Defense (DoD) did not provide consistent or timely guidance on appropriate interrogation techniques as DoD policy was revised several times between 2001 and 2003. Behind the confusion in DoD lay the debate within the Bush administration over what interrogation practices should or could be used. During this time, memos circulated between the Justice Department, DoD, and the White House establishing legal arguments for using harsh interrogation techniques on suspected terrorists (Mangan 2005). There is no indication in the Schlesinger et al. (2004) report that these memos made it down the chain of command to commanders in Iraq, but the arguments at the higher levels undoubtedly led to delay in getting clear guidance on the treatment of detainees.

What guidance DoD did provide was often published well after battlefield commanders needed it, forcing them to improvise. Policies that were approved at Guantanamo Bay were copied in Iraq by the Joint Task Force (CJTF-7) without authorization. When Central Command leaders ordered these policies rescinded, CJTF-7 published a new set of guidelines that rely heavily on the Army's Field Manual 34–52, which complies with the Geneva and Hague conventions. Nonetheless, the "existence of confusing and inconsistent interrogation technique policies contributed to the belief that additional interrogation techniques were condoned" (Schlesinger et al. 2004, 10).

Moreover, the Army did not train the members of the 800th Military Police Brigade or its subordinate unit, the 372nd. Military Police Company, in detention or prison operations. The training of soldiers is ultimately the responsibility of the brigade commander, in this case Brigadier General Janis L. Karpinski. Such training for a reserve unit would normally be conducted during the mobilization period, before the unit deploys to the theater of operations. Training would have been essential for this unit because detainee and prison operations are not part of its regular duties.[2] However, the unit was ordered to Iraq without being informed of its specific mission (Schlesinger et al.

2004; Taguba 2004). As a consequence, Karpinski did not have the opportunity to conduct training before her soldiers actually had to perform their duties.

Even had such training been provided, it might have proved inadequate. Army training prepares military police to operate prisoner of war camps, where detainees are relatively self-regulated and compliant. This situation is much different from operating a facility such as Abu Ghraib, where common criminals were mixed in with prisoners of war. Taguba (2004) concluded that the failure to separate these two populations, coupled with a lack of training, forced soldiers to make rules on-the-job. In a separate report, Schlesinger and his colleagues (2004) stated that this problem was exacerbated by the confusing shifts in interrogation-technique policy coming from DoD. As a consequence, procedures varied from unit to unit, cell block to cell block, and even shift to shift.

A vigorous and competent leader would have corrected the training problem once discovered and set clear standards for behavior, but Karpinski had a laissez-faire approach to leadership (Bartone 2004). Taguba (2004) documents numerous instances where even the most simple and normal military standards (uniform wear and saluting) were not enforced. Worse, after an earlier investigation into abuse at another location under her command (Camp Bucca), Karpinski disciplined the subordinate commander responsible but left him in command. The same subordinate commander was later in charge of the company abusing prisoners at Abu Ghraib. This failure to relieve the responsible commander sent a clear message to everyone that prisoner abuse would be tolerated. Moreover, after the Camp Bucca investigation was completed and abuse confirmed, Karpinski took no steps to ensure that her soldiers were trained or informed of Geneva Convention rules (ibid.).

In addition to training deficiencies, soldiers suffered as a result of other leadership oversights. For example, soldiers at Abu Ghraib lacked the basic amenities American military personnel routinely receive, and that are and were widely available in other areas of Iraq (ibid.). When soldiers in one unit do not receive what soldiers in other units receive, they correctly see this as a result of leadership that is not concerned about their welfare (FM 22–100, 1999; Shay 1994). Leaders who are indifferent to the needs and concerns of their subordinates break the critically important bond of trust between leader and follower. Shay (1994) notes that such breaches of trust are seen as "betrayals" and are frequently the precursor for stress-induced misconduct.

Another incident that damaged soldiers' trust in the Army concerned the timing of their return home. When it first arrived in Iraq, the brigade was given the mission of guarding prisoners of war at Camp Bucca. Unit members believed they would be going home as soon as all the detainees were released. However, in late May to early June 2003, they were given a new mission—managing the entire Iraqi penal system and several detention centers. Predictably, morale suffered as soldiers' hopes disappeared. From the evidence, it appears that Karpinski and her subordinate commanders made no special effort to explain to the soldiers why the mission change was essential or to otherwise raise morale (Taguba 2004).

To compound matters, Abu Ghraib held too many prisoners for its size, and the brigade, overall, was under-strength. In part, the lack of personnel occurred because Army reserve units do not have an established system for replacing individuals who become unfit for duty (as a result of injury, for example) and must be returned home. This systemic problem was exacerbated by Karpinski's failure to properly manage what manning she had. Taguba (2004) reports that while Abu Ghraib held 6,000–7,000 inmates, it was operated by one battalion of soldiers. Schlesinger and his colleagues (2004) noted that in October 2003, there were 7,000 detainees at Abu Ghraib and only ninety MPs to guard them and defend the installation. At the same time, another facility under Karpinski's command, holding 100 detainees, was operated by a unit of the same size. She could have reassigned subordinate units to better balance the workload, but did not.

The manning problem was one that applied across all units in Iraq. The joint task force in Iraq was never fully resourced to meet the size and complexity of its mission (Schlesinger et al. 2004). Ultimately, the responsibility for ensuring that American forces in Iraq had sufficient resources to perform their mission rests with the secretary of defense. He failed to provide the resources, with tragic consequences.

Another systemic problem dealt with the unclear command relationship between Karpinski and Colonel Thomas Pappas, the commander of the 20Sth Military Intelligence Brigade, also located at Abu Ghraib. According to CJTF-7 Fragmentary Order 1108, issued November 19, 2003, Pappas was given responsibility for operations at Abu Ghraib.[3] Military intelligence and military police have very different missions. Placing military police under the authority of military intelligence is doctrinally unsound, from the Army's standpoint (Taguba 2004). Worse, it technically placed a brigadier general under the authority of an officer she outranked. Taguba concluded that neither officer paid any attention to the directive, but nonetheless it left all parties confused about the relationship between the two units and their respective commanders. This situation also contributed to the friction between the two commanders and their units, according to Schlesinger and his colleagues (2004).

Adding to these problems, alcohol was not only available but may have been abused by soldiers at Abu Ghraib. Just weeks before Major General Taguba began his formal investigation at the prison, commanders there launched a crackdown on alcohol use. Although possession of alcohol was prohibited by U.S. regulations in Iraq, local vendors regularly provided soldiers with alcohol. At least one (unnamed) military intelligence officer alleged that the military police liked to drink, and the atmosphere on the cellblock where the abuse occurred was like a "fraternity party" (Miller 2004).

The soldiers who abused the prisoners at Abu Ghraib have all claimed they were "ordered" to do so to "soften up" prisoners for interrogation. The Army's own appointed investigator, Major General Taguba (2004), concluded that soldiers were led to believe they should "soften up" prisoners, although he found no evidence that they were given direct orders to abuse prisoners. Green (2000) comments that everyone accused of war crimes makes this plea, and it is never an adequate defense. If true, however, it adds immeasurably to the evidence already presented that persons higher in the chain of command bear much of the responsibility for the prisoner abuse at Abu Ghraib.

Discussion

In the midst of fear and uncertainty, where death is a real possibility, misconduct in response to combat stress is always possible. But in the case of Abu Ghraib, administrative failure created a situation that greatly and unnecessarily increased both the stress level on soldiers and the likelihood of prisoner abuse and mistreatment. These failures stretched from Washington, D.C., all the way to Iraq. The DoD failure to develop and publish a set of consistent guidelines for interrogation led to unnecessary confusion in the field (Schlesinger et al. 2004). Taguba (2004) concluded that MPs were under the impression that they were expected to "soften up" detainees for interrogation. Confusing and untimely guidance from the DoD level down through to the local command no doubt contributed to this perception.

The Army's failure to give the 800th Military Police Brigade some advance notice of their duties in Iraq resulted in an untrained unit facing a difficult mission. By not providing reserve units with some sort of personnel-replacement system, the Army unnecessarily aggravated the manning problem. The unclear order giving the 205th Military Intelligence Brigade's commander authority over operations at Abu Ghraib resulted in needless confusion between the military police and the military intelligence units he commanded. Finally, and most important, the Army's failure to provide competent leadership resulted in an undisciplined unit, under extreme stress and feeling abandoned by both the Army and its leaders.

Collectively, these failures resulted in an untrained, undisciplined, and undermanned unit. The Army's own manual on the subject of controlling and preventing combat stress (FM 22–51, 1994) claims that these are precisely the conditions that foster misconduct. Under these conditions, it seems clear that soldiers lost trust in leadership and turned to alcohol, and in some cases, abuse of prisoners as ways to cope with the situation. This fact does not excuse the behavior of those who mistreated and abused prisoners—such behavior is inexcusable. But if their individual behavior is not excusable, then neither can one excuse the administrative failures that created the conditions that led to abuse and torture.

Having said this, it is clear from the evidence that most of the soldiers assigned to Abu Ghraib did not abuse or mistreat prisoners (Bartone 2004; Schlesinger et al. 2004; Taguba 2004). Bartone points out that while contextual and situational factors are very important to an understanding of prisoner abuse, individual factors cannot be overlooked. Milgram's (1983) classic experimental study of obedience and conformity found that some individuals resist pressure to inflict pain and abuse others.

Subsequent research has found that personality "hardiness" (Kobasa 1979) and psychological maturity (Kegan 1994) are related to the ability to resist pressure to conform or succumb to stressors. Personality hardiness refers to a personality style or trait that includes a strong sense of commitment in life, an internal locus of control, and the ability to see change as challenging or fun (ibid.). Kegan's (1994) theory of psychological development incorporates cognitive, moral, and social dimensions of experience to describe how individuals construct their worldviews.[4] In this framework, most young people are at stage three, meaning that they define themselves based upon the people and organizations around them, which makes them quite susceptible to group influences and pressures. A recent study on Army officers and cadets suggests that this framework fits well within the military (Forsythe et al. 2002). An additional implication for the Abu Ghraib case is that a stage four perspective—one that recognizes different approaches to understanding the world as legitimate—is essential in respecting cultural differences.

Under these circumstances, organizations have an even greater responsibility to focus on what they can influence and control—specifically, their own policies for training personnel, selecting leaders, and setting performance standards. Schlesinger and his colleagues concluded that "the abuses were not just the failure of some individuals to follow known standards, and they are more than the failure of a few leaders to enforce proper discipline. There is both institutional and personal responsibility at higher levels" (2004, 5). The Army's own appointed investigator, Major General Taguba (2004), concluded that there were "systemic problems" at Abu Ghraib that led to prisoner abuse. In this case, the DoD and the Army fell short and must shoulder much of the blame for the shocking abuse of prisoners at Abu Ghraib.

The blame need not stop with DoD and the Army. The recent confirmation hearings of Alberto Gonzales for attorney general gave the general public an opportunity to examine his role in creating American policy toward detainees. As the primary author of the administration's official policy on torture, Gonzales developed the legal rationale that supported the detention of "enemy combatants" in Guantanamo without the prisoner of war protections of the Hague and Geneva conventions. He worked to narrow the definition of torture and justify the use of coercive interrogation techniques. Gonzales created the policies that lay behind the DoD interrogation policies, and thus helped create the conditions that led to the torture and abuse of Iraqi prisoners in Abu Ghraib prison.

"There is both institutional and personal responsibility at higher levels."

By the Pentagon's count, eleven investigations of the mistreatment of prisoners have been commissioned, and eight of them have been completed. All eight have confirmed abuse. Not one has found evidence of any official policy sanctioning abuse. More than 130 members of the armed forces have been disciplined or convicted in connection with the killing or mistreatment of prisoners or civilians in Afghanistan, Iraq, and Guantanamo Bay. Many more cases are pending. Every one of these cases involves junior-ranking personnel—the actual killers or abusers ("Just a Few Bad Apples" 2005).

After the Abu Ghraib pictures were published, Secretary of State Colin Powell announced, "Watch how America will do the right thing" ("Hearts, Minds and Shameful Pictures" 2005, 13). The military has aggressively prosecuted killers and abusers, including the alleged ringleader at Abu Ghraib, Specialist Charles Graner. He was sentenced on January 15, 2005, to ten years in prison to go with his dishonorable discharge. Four other soldiers have already been convicted, while three are awaiting trial in the Abu Ghraib case ("Just a Few Bad Apples" 2005). But none of these trials involves the higher-ranking personnel

responsible for creating the conditions that led to the abuses at Abu Ghraib and elsewhere.

Is torture and abuse still going on? The U.S. Justice Department did not rescind the memo liberalizing the definition of torture (the "torture memo") until recently (Ibid.). The information coming out of Guantanamo Bay suggests that detainees are still being abused ("Gitmo Soldier Details Sexual Tactics" 2005). And there is no publicly available evidence to suggest that the Army or the Defense Department has taken action to address the systemic problems identified in Major General Taguba's (2004) report. Until such action is taken, the public should be prepared for more revelations of torture and abuse.

Conclusion

The torture and abuse of prisoners has had repercussions far beyond a few military courtrooms. The reputation of the United States has suffered enormously as a result and provided a rationale for the Iraqi insurgents that has undoubtedly helped them gain support and may well have led to more American casualties. Ultimately, the question of who was responsible for the torture and abuse at Abu Ghraib must still be asked. The simple answer is that those who perpetrated the abuse are responsible. Under international law, everyone has the responsibility to treat detainees humanely. Even if a soldier has been given an order to torture or abuse prisoners, there is a positive duty to refuse to obey the order.

But this simple answer obscures the responsibility that everyone in the chain of command had to provide the soldiers at Abu Ghraib with the guidance, training, manning, and leadership essential for them to properly carry out their duties. Everyone in the chain, from Iraq to Washington, D.C., was responsible and accountable for the illegal actions of their subordinates. This is particularly true when those in the chain failed to fulfill all their obligations to those subordinates.

Limiting punishment to lower-ranking personnel is not an adequate response. It is not just, and it does not satisfy world or American public opinion. If the American government is to live up to Secretary Powell's claim that it will "do the right thing" and restore the country's image as a law-abiding nation, it can do no less.

Notes

1. The requirement to conduct such training is codified in directives at the DoD level and in each of the individual services. In the author's experience (twenty years' service in the Air Force), the training was conducted as required. This does not mean that one can generalize that all military personnel always get the training as required.

2. Every Army unit has a "mission essential task list" (METL). The METL lists each and every task the unit must be prepared to perform. The 800th MP Battalion's METL did not include detainee or prison operations, although doctrinally such tasks are assigned to military police units (Taguba 2004).

3. The 205th Military Intelligence Battalion was given TACON for security of detainees and force protection. TACON is "command authority over assigned or attached forces" that is limited to "direction and control of movements or maneuvers within the 'operational area necessary to accomplish assigned missions or tasks" (JP 0–2, 2001).

4. Kegan (1994) proposes five stages of development or orders of consciousness. In the first stage, the person (infant) behaves on sheer impulse. In the next stage, needs, wishes, and desires order behavior (children). In the third, interpersonal relationships order behavior, as is typical of teens. In the fourth stage, one acquires a respect for the beliefs and behavior of others. The fifth stage, according to Kegan, is very rare. In this stage, the individual integrates the beliefs and behaviors learned in childhood with lessons learned over a lifetime to arrive at personally unique level.

References

Bartone, Paul T. 2004. "Understanding Prisoner Abuse at Abu Ghraib: Psychological Considerations and Leadership Implications." Washington, D.C.: National Defense University. Available at www.apn.org/divisions/div19/documents/prisonabusefactors2June04-AbuGhraib.pdf.

Bartone, Paul T., Amy Adler, and Mark A. Vaitkus. 1998. "Dimensions of Psychological Stress in Peacekeeping Operations." *Military Medicine* 163:587–593.

Bies, Robert J., and Thomas M. Tripp. 1996. "Beyond Distrust: 'Getting Even' and the Need for Revenge." In *Trust in Organizations: Frontiers of Theory and Research,* edited by Roderick M. Kramer and Tom R. Tyler, pp. 246–261. Thousand Oaks, Calif.: Sage.

Clausewitz, Carl von. 1989. *On War.* Edited and translated by Michael Eliot Howard and Peter Paret. Princeton: Princeton University Press.

Cooper, Terry L. 1998. *The Responsible Administrator.* 4th ed. San Francisco: Jossey-Bass.

Forsythe, George B., Scott Snook, Paul Lewis, and Paul T. Bartone. 2002. "Making Sense of Officership: Developing a Professional Identity for 21st Century Army Officers." In *The Future of the Army Profession,* edited by Don M. Snider and Lloyd J. Matthews, pp. 357–378. New York: McGraw-Hill.

Gawthrop, Louis C. 1998. *Public Service and Democracy.* New York: Chatham House. "Gitmo Soldier Details Sexual Tactics." 2005. *Fox News,* January 28. Available at www.foxnews.com/0.3566.145659,00.html.

Green, Leslie C. 2000. *The Contemporary Law of Armed Conflict.* 2d ed. Manchester, UK: Manchester University Press.

"Hearts, Minds and Shameful Pictures." 2005. *Economist,* January 22: 13–14.

Hillen, John. 1999. "Must U.S. Military Culture Reform?" *Orbis* 43, no. 1:43–58.

Huntington, Samuel P. 1957. *The Soldier and the State.* Cambridge, Mass.: Harvard University Press.

"Just a Few Bad Apples?" 2005. *Economist,* January 22:29–31.

Kegan, Robert. 1994. *In Over Our Heads: The Mental Demands of Modern Life.* Cambridge, Mass.: Harvard University Press.

Kobasa, Suzanne C. 1979. "Stressful Life Events, Personality and Health: An Inquiry into Hardiness." *Journal of Personality and Social Psychology* 37: 1–11.

Mangan, K. 2005. "Torture's Paper Trail." *Chronicle of Higher Education* 51 (20): A12, January 21, 2005.

Miles, Donna. 2002. "Stress Levels High Among Service Members." Washington, D.C.: Air Force Print News. Available at www.af.mil/news/story_print.asp?storyID=1230007165.

Milgram, Stanley. 1983. *Obedience to Authority: An Experimental View.* New York: Harper/Collins.

Miller, Greg. 2004. "Alcohol Cited as Problem at Prison." *Los Angeles Times,* June 13. Available at www.latimes.com/la-fg-prison13jun 13,1,1266693.story/.

Miller, Laura. 1995. "Feminism and the Exclusion of Army Women from Combat." Project on U.S. Post–Cold War Civil-Military Relations. Working paper no. 2. John M. Olin Institute, Cambridge, Mass.

Mosher, Frederick C. 1968. *Democracy and the Public Service.* New York: Oxford University Press.

Moskos, Charles C. Jr. 1977. "From Institution to Occupation: Trends in Military Organization." *Armed Forces and Society* 4, no. 1:4 1–50.

NLCM. 2004. *Navy Leadership Competency Model.* Available at www.au.af.mil/au/awc/awcgate/navy/navy-ldr-comp.htm.

Palmer, Parker J. 2000. *Let Your Life Speak: Listening for the Voice of Vocation.* San Francisco: Jossey-Bass.

Romzek, Barbara, and Paul Ingraluim. 2000. "Cross Pressures of Accountability: Initiative, Command, and failure in the Ron Brown Plane Crash." *Public Administration Review* 60, no. 3:240–253.

Schlesinger, James R., Harold Brown, Tillie K. Fowler, and Charles A. Homer. 2004. *Final Report of the Independent Panel to Review DoD Detention Operations.* Washington, D.C: Department of Defense.

Shay, Jonathan. 1994. *Achilles in Vietnam: Combat Trauma and the Undoing of Character.* New York: Scribner's.

Sunzi [Sun Tzu]. 1983. *The Art of War.* Edited by James Clavell. New York: Delacorte Press.

Taguba, Antonio M. 2004. Article 15–6 Investigation of the 800th Military Police Brigade. Available at www.npr.org/iraq/2004/prison_abuse.report.pdf.

Toner, James H. 2000. *Morals Under the Gun: The Cardinal Virtues, Military Ethics, and American Society.* Lexington: University Press of Kentucky.

U.S. Department of the Air Force. 2004. *Leadership and Force Development.* Air Force Doctrine Document 1–1. Washington, D.C. (cited as AFDD 1–1).

U.S. Department of the Army. 1994. *Leader's Manual for Combat Stress Control.* Field Manual 22–51. Washington, D.C. (cited as FM 22–51).

———. 1999. *Army Leadership.* Field Manual 22–100. Washington, D.C. (cited as FM 22–100).

U.S. Joint Chiefs of Staff. 2001. *Unified Action Armed Forces.* Joint Publication 0–2. Washington, D.C. (cited as JP 0–2).

U.S. Marine Corps. 2002. *Leading Marines.* Marine Corps Working Publication 6–11. Washington. D.C. (cited as MCWP 6–11).

Vegetius. 1985. "De Re Militan." In *Roots of Strategy,* edited by Thomas R. Phillips, pp. 66–175. Harrisburg, Pa.: Stackpole Books.

SAUNDRA REINKE is an associate professor and director of the M.P.A. Program at Augusta State University. She has a B.B.A. from the University of Texas, Arlington (1978), an M.S. in management from Troy State University (1988), and a D.P.A. from the University of Alabama (1993). Her articles on leadership, trust, and performance appraisal have appeared in the *Review of Public Personnel Administration* and the *Journal of Political and Military Sociology.* Her research on civic engagement and service learning has appeared in the *Journal of Public Affairs Education.*

From *Public Integrity,* Volume 8 Number 2, Spring 2006, pp. 135–147. Copyright © 2006 by American Society for Public Administration. Reprinted by permission of M.E. Sharpe, Inc.

Twelve Obstacles to Ethical Decision Making: Rationalizations

MICHAEL JOSEPHSON

We judge ourselves by our best intentions, our noblest acts and our most virtuous habits. But others tend to judge us by our last worst act. So in making tough decisions, don't be distracted by rationalizations. Here are some of the most common ones:

If It's Necessary, It's Ethical

This rationalization rests on the false assumption that necessity breeds propriety. The approach often leads to ends-justify-the-means reasoning and treating non-ethical tasks or goals as moral imperatives.

The False Necessity Trap

As Nietzsche put it, "Necessity is an interpretation, not a fact." We tend to fall into the "false necessity trap" because we over-estimate the cost of doing the right thing and underestimate the cost of failing to do so.

If It's Legal and Permissible, It's Proper

This substitutes legal requirements (which establish minimal standards of behavior) for personal moral judgment. This alternative does not embrace the full range of ethical obligations, especially for individuals involved in upholding the public trust. Ethical people often choose to do less than the maximally allowable, and more than the minimally acceptable.

It's Just Part of the Job

Conscientious people who want to do their jobs well often fail to adequately consider the morality of their professional behavior. They tend to compartmentalize ethics into two domains: private and occupational. Fundamentally decent people thereby feel justified doing things at work that they know to be wrong in other contexts. They forget that everyone's first job is to be a good person.

It's All for a Good Cause

People are especially vulnerable to rationalizations when they seek to advance a noble aim. "It's all for a good cause" is a seductive rationale that loosens interpretations of deception, concealment, conflicts of interest, favoritism and violations of established rules and procedures.

I Was Just Doing It for You

This is a primary justification for committing "little white lies" or withholding important information in personal or professional relationships, such as performance reviews. This rationalization pits the values of honesty and respect against the value of caring. An individual deserves the truth because he has a moral right to make decisions about his own life based on accurate information. This rationalization overestimates other people's desire to be "protected" from the truth, when in fact most people would rather know unpleasant information than believe soothing falsehoods. Consider the perspective of people lied to: If they discovered the lie, would they thank you for being thoughtful or would they feel betrayed, patronized or manipulated?

I'm Just Fighting Fire with Fire

This is the false assumption that promise-breaking, lying and other kinds of misconduct are justified if they are routinely engaged in by those with whom you are dealing. Remember: when you fight fire with fire, you end up with the ashes of your own integrity.

It Doesn't Hurt Anyone

Used to excuse misconduct, this rationalization falsely holds that one can violate ethical principles so long as there is no clear and immediate harm to others. It treats ethical obligations simply as factors to be considered in decision-making, rather than as ground rules. Problem areas: asking for or giving special favors to family, friends or public officials; disclosing non-public information to benefit others; using one's position for personal advantage.

Everyone's Doing It

This is a false, "safety in numbers" rationale fed by the tendency to uncritically treat cultural, organizational or occupational behaviors as if they were ethical norms, just because they are norms.

It's OK If I Don't Gain Personally

This justifies improper conduct done for others or for institutional purposes on the false assumption that personal gain is the only test of impropriety. A related but narrower view is that only behavior resulting in improper financial gain warrants ethical criticism.

I've Got It Coming

People who feel they are overworked or underpaid rationalize that minor "perks"—such as acceptance of favors, discounts or gratuities—are nothing more than fair compensation for services rendered. This is also used as an excuse to abuse sick time, insurance claims, overtime, personal phone calls and personal use of office supplies.

I Can Still Be Objective

By definition, if you've lost your objectivity, you can't see that you've lost your objectivity! It also underestimates the subtle ways in which gratitude, friendship and the anticipation of future favors affect judgment. Does the person providing you with the benefit believe that it will in no way affect your judgment? Would the person still provide the benefit if you were in no position to help?

From *Texas Town & City*, Vol. XCII, Number 9, September 2005, pp. 26–27. Copyright © 2005 by Texas Town & City. Reprinted by permission of the publisher and author.

Follow the Money

The campaign finance beat is important—and challenging. The tangled web of rules that govern fundraising and spending can be hard to penetrate, and doesn't necessarily make for sparkling copy. How are the news media doing this time around?

RACHEL SMOLKIN

Hundreds of moneyed republicans converged at the refined Ritz-Carlton Lodge on Lake Oconee near Greensboro, Georgia, joined by President Bush, Vice President Cheney and a couple of uninvited journalists.

On Friday night, April 2, after Bush and Cheney had departed, two Washington Post reporters appeared at the Ritz-Carlton. Thomas B. Edsall and James V. Grimaldi—who together "looked like Mutt and Jeff," the shorter Grimaldi says—walked into the lobby and started interviewing Bush "Pioneers" who had raised at least $100,000 each for Bush's reelection campaign from friends and associates and "Rangers," who had solicited $200,000 each. The Pioneers and Rangers looked uncomfortable. A hotel staffer asked if the reporters were guests, and they said no. They were asked to leave.

They returned the next morning and found discarded papers, including a list of attendees and a schedule of events, in the hotel and in a spacious tent outside. Grimaldi, a projects reporter less recognized by many of the fundraisers and campaign staff than beat reporter Edsall, walked into a session in a windowless conference room and sat down. There, more than 300 of Bush's Pioneers and Rangers were learning that the Rangers would lose their star status, just as the Pioneers had before them. To qualify as a "Super Ranger," they would need to raise an additional $300,000 for the Republican National Committee, where the individual contribution limit is $25,000.

The April "appreciation weekend" for fundraisers and the insights from that session formed the beginning and end of a May 16, front-page Post story about "The Bush Money Machine" by Edsall, Grimaldi and Post database editor Sarah Cohen. It was the first of a two-day series that explored links between fundraising and access to the administration and included a memorable "Spheres of Influence" graphic showing ties between Bush and his fundraisers.

More than two decades ago, Deep Throat advised another pair of Post reporters to "follow the money," and their diligence helped topple a president. Seldom is the link between money and political corruption so clear-cut, and the Post series on Pioneers did not establish any wrongdoing. But the search for connections among big dollars, coveted access and impropriety or its appearance remains a priority at the nation's top newspapers.

The 2004 presidential race has presented fresh challenges as reporters scramble to chronicle not only the mammoth fundraising operations of Bush and challenger John Kerry, but also to understand and document the ramifications of the campaign finance bill that Congress passed two years ago. Dubbed the McCain-Feingold law after its two main sponsors, it raised the limit on individual contributions to federal candidates from $1,000 to $2,000 and banned unlimited "soft money" contributions from labor unions, corporations and wealthy individuals to political parties.

The money-and-politics beat has yielded illuminating and important stories during this election season, but also bewildering and even mind-numbing accounts. "Confusing" is a criticism leveled repeatedly at the media's sometimes-conflicting political money coverage. Following the money is a daunting and often thankless task, and getting tossed out of posh, private fundraisers is the least of reporters' troubles.

"It really is a thicket of legalistic rules and regulations and laws that are so complicated that half the people involved in fundraising can't follow them themselves," says Grimaldi, who covered the subject at the Orange County Register and Seattle Times before joining the Post in 2000. "Unless you follow it constantly, you're at an extreme disadvantage."

Even for the regulars, it isn't easy. Reporters often succumb to jargon—or ignore it at their own peril. "It's a beat with too many technicalities, but the problem is, when you oversimplify those, you can really distort the truth," says Edsall, who has covered money and politics intermittently for more than three decades. "It's very hard to figure out the balance between readability and real accuracy."

Reporters' intense interest in money—an "obsession" in the eyes of some critics—has led to some misapprehensions about presidential nominees.

What really matters, longtime campaign finance reporter Brooke Jackson says, is for a challenger to raise enough money to compete effectively.

"For a profession so deeply worried about the corrupting influence of money, we spend an awful lot of time and energy pumping the fundraising angle—not just following the money, as we should, but allowing money to dominate and frame the entire conversation about who should run the country," National Journal media critic William Powers wrote last July. Noting a wave of stories about Howard Dean's fundraising prowess and sudden viability as a candidate, Powers observed that in assessing presidential candidates, "the media place one qualification above all others: the ability to raise dough."

His commentary proved prescient: After overlooking the former Vermont governor's powerful antiwar message, the media then proclaimed a cash-flush Dean the front-runner, only to see his formidable war chest fail to translate into votes.

Brooks Jackson, who covered money and politics for three decades at the Associated Press, the Wall Street Journal and CNN, says that reporters operate "from a set of unexamined assumptions that are not always correct. For example, 'Money is always decisive.' That's just false, and yet I bet you that every reporter who covers this has at one time or another written stories to that effect." What really matters, Jackson adds, is for a challenger to raise enough money to compete effectively.

Even framing a debate as being about campaign finance "reform" can open reporters to charges that they're siding with groups advocating stricter rules.

"Basically, the Washington press corps cannot be educated on this subject," says Terry Michael, executive director of the Washington Center for Politics & Journalism. Michael, who opposes campaign finance regulations on First Amendment grounds, except for strong disclosure requirements, says the press is "basically enthralled with the idea that money drives everything." He contends stories hint at corruption "without every really showing the nexus" and argues reporters "often seek overheated quotes from ethics industry spokesmen to suggest the appearance of corruption they can't prove factually."

Jack Shafer, Slate's media critic and editor at large, last July exhorted journalists to purge the "crappy, meaningless" word "reform" from their copy. "Newspapers shouldn't feel obliged to repeat the pointless R word just because politicians label their every action 'reform,'" Shafer wrote. "A Nexis dump and unscientific study of news stories from the past two years reveals the mediocre records the New York Times, Los Angeles Times and Washington Post have compiled in policing the R word. These papers generally treat the word as if it were value-neutral when reporting the campaign finance, Medicare and tort debates."

A Lexis-Nexis search of news stories from the past six months shows improved performances by the New York Times and Washington Post, but Los Angeles Times reporters continue to scatter the "R word" through their campaign finance stories, frequently citing the 2002 "campaign finance reform law." USA Today avoids the word, as Shafer noted in his column.

"There are words that have value judgments implicit, and 'reform' tends to be one of those," says Jim Drinkard, who launched the money-and-politics beat at the Associated Press in 1993 and now covers it for USA Today. "There are people opposed to it who did not see it as reform."

When journalists lean too heavily on the "R word," it is perhaps because many terms associated with the campaign-finance debate are so esoteric. Choked off from the political parties, some of the old soft money is gushing into nonparty political organizations called 527s, named for the section of the tax code that governs them.

Threatened with a story about a subject named for the federal tax code, most reporters would rather flee. "That's why God created the AP," or "It's too inside-the-Beltway" are serviceable excuses. Those who try face inevitable criticism for lack of clarity.

In February, the Federal Election Commission voted to limit the nonparty political groups but stopped short of severely curtailing their activities. Conflicting headlines followed. "Advocacy Groups Win Fund Ruling," said the New York Times on page one. "FEC Moves to Regulate Groups Opposing Bush," said the Washington Post on page 6.

"I remember reading those stories," The Weekly Standard's David Tell wrote March 8, after referencing the Post and an early Times edition with a slightly different headline. "I remember being totally confused by them ... the coverage itself was confused."

Nick Confessore, an editor at The Washington Monthly, a politics and policy magazine, expresses empathy for reporters writing about complex developments on deadline, but says of the press' coverage, "It did not give readers a clear picture of the issues at hand."

The Post's Edsall defends his reporting, saying he was a "little bothered" by The Weekly Standard story, which "basically affirmed that my piece was accurate, but it never said so. In fact, one [story] was right and one was wrong. At that stage, [the groups] did not win the ruling and there was still plenty of possibility that there could be restrictions applied."

Times reporter Glen Justice also stands by his story. "You're dealing with interpretations of the law, not necessarily questions of legal, hard fact," he says. His follow-up story the next day was headlined "Final Word Still to Come On Interest Group Money"—a point Edsall made in his lead the previous day.

USA Today's Drinkard wrote a short story that avoided the term "527s," referring instead to "non-party political committees." The headline was similar to the Post's but clearer and more specific: "FEC OKs limits on non-party political committees."

Drinkard explained in his lead that the FEC had taken a step toward "limiting the activities of political groups that seek to help or defeat" Bush and then explained the action in simple, declarative language. "The commission voted 4–2 to advise some groups that they may not use unlimited contributions known as 'soft money' for TV ads, mailings and other communications that 'promote, support, attack or oppose' a candidate for federal office," he wrote.

On May 13, the FEC rejected a plan that would have reined in the heavily pro-Democratic 527 groups. As Drinkard anticipated in a front-page story published that day, commissioners indicated they might later adopt new rules but those would not take effect until after the election.

The next day, the coverage again perplexed. Edsall's lead plainly stated the commission "cleared the way for liberal groups yesterday to continue to raise and spend millions of dollars in unrestricted contributions." But the Post headline proclaimed, "In Boost for Democrats, FEC Rejects Proposed Limits on Small Donors." While all terms are relative, billionaires such as George Soros, cited in the story for giving $7.5 million to two prominent liberal groups, scarcely seem to qualify as "small" donors.

Some coverage of the 527 groups has been clear and insightful. The Post's Dan Balz and Edsall wrote a March 10, front-page story on the parallel Democratic campaign underway by a coalition of interest groups "led by veterans of presidential and congressional campaigns" and "armed with millions of dollars in soft money." Justice wrote in a page-one Times story May 29 that after months of trying to close down Democratic groups, Republicans were "scrambling to set up similar organizations."

And a June 7 Wall Street Journal article by Jeanne Cummings surveyed the top 20 corporate donors to national political party committees during the 2002 election cycle and found that more than half—including Citigroup, Pfizer and Microsoft—were "resisting giving big-dollar donations to the new, independent organizations." Cummings wrote that this corporate reticence "to get sucked back into the world of unlimited political contributions" places Republicans at a fundraising disadvantage against well-financed groups bolstering the Democrats.

As reporters try to explain the volatile situation surrounding the 527 groups, they have come under fire for overlooking the role of other tax-exempt groups. In May, The Washington Monthly's Confessore explored another category of nonprofit organizations called 501(c)s, which include groups such as the AARP and the Nature Conservancy. Most of these groups, established under another section of the tax code, are allowed to raise and spend a limited amount of money for political purposes, including broadcasting "issue ads" about candidates.

In his story, "Bush's Secret Stash," Confessore noted that some of these groups, including the National Rifle Association and the National Right to Life Committee, are "vital allies of the GOP." He asked why "the press and campaign finance groups haven't blown the whistle, even as they pound away at the Democrats' 527s."

Confessore then suggested several explanations, including Republicans' success in defining the debate and different disclosure requirements. "Because 527s must disclose their donors and expenditures every quarter, it's easier for political reporters and watchdog groups to blow the whistle on them in real time, issuing reports and press releases about the latest soft-money outrage," he wrote. "The 501(c)s disclose virtually nothing—and by the screwy rules of Washington, no data, no foul."

With such complex issues to untangle and good visuals hard to come by, the money chase remains the province of print journalists. "You don't get TV shots of lobbyists handing big bags of loot to politicians," says Jackson, a pioneer in TV follow-the-money stories and now director of Annenberg Political Fact Check, a project of the University of Pennsylvania's Annenberg Public Policy Center. "It just doesn't happen that way."

When possible, Jackson would cover lavish parties at the national conventions or extravagant fundraisers, his camera crew shooting video over fences or through restaurant windows of lobbyists and wealthy donors "sipping Chablis and eating canapes." But he was always at a disadvantage to print. "It's really tough to get the pictures that tell the story."

From January to May, the networks' weekday nightly newscasts devoted a combined 11 minutes to issue ads by independent activist groups including 527s like MoveOn.org; five minutes to presidential fundraising and zero to the campaign finance law, according to Andrew Tyndall, publisher of a weekly newsletter monitoring broadcast television news.

Tyndall says the fundraising prowess of Dean and Bush has been mentioned as part of broader political coverage, but fundraising during Campaign 2004 "has been little covered as a separate story." The Justice Department's investigation into alleged abuses during the 1996 presidential campaign generated by far the most television news on these topics in the last seven years—481 minutes combined on the networks' weekday newscasts.

With such complex issues to untangle and good visuals hard to come by, the money chase remains the province of print journalists.

Lisa Myers, a senior investigative correspondent for NBC, followed the Justice Department's 1997 investigation. In her money stories, she has tried to pinpoint the relationship between large contributions and government action, particularly when such actions benefit only one or two people. Myers finds it easier to translate these stories for television when they revolve around a central character or theme, such as Democratic fundraiser Johnny Chung—who in 1998 pleaded guilty to charges stemming from illegal campaign contributions—or President Clinton's opening of the Lincoln bedroom to big donors.

"There was a tremendous amount of coverage in '97, a tremendous amount of coverage when [Sen. John] McCain was fighting to get McCain-Feingold through," Myers says. She believes TV's coverage of money stories may have trailed off in part because after the Justice Department probe, "the fact that no one of any importance was indicted for misconduct left the impression, I think, that anything goes."

Ironically, the success of McCain and his allies in rewriting the campaign finance laws also may have diminished television's appetite for chasing the money. "The public doesn't really understand and isn't really interested in the details of the laws that govern campaign finance and how money is raised and spent," says Linda Douglass, the chief Capitol Hill correspondent for ABC News. "It's a much greater challenge to get those stories on TV now that McCain-Feingold has passed."

During the 1996 campaign, Douglass, then at CBS News, established a campaign finance feature called "Follow the Dollar." She says before the new law, she could track soft money wending its way from corporations and businesses to elected officials through the political parties. She reported on donors proud to admit they "successfully got the ear of an officeholder" they wanted to persuade.

"Now what you have is a murkier connection between people who give money and people who benefit from that donation," Douglass says. "When you ask me how I get these stories on the air, well, guess what? I haven't done these stories this year."

Douglass says she's tried to pitch stories about the "obvious stuff" such as the activism of financier Soros, but "it's not as clean a hit as it used to be, and we have to be more creative about how to tell these stories on TV." Adds Myers, "It was hard enough when it was soft money, and now you have to explain what a 527 is—hello?! ... It's not just TV. If you read the print stories, they're almost indecipherable. By the time you put in all the nuances and caveats and the denials, they're very difficult for readers to get through."

A s journalists ferret out new trends in giving and spending, the Internet provides an invaluable resource. Reporters who once trudged to the FEC and spent bleary-eyed hours combing through microfilm or copying smudged papers now can surf myriad Web sites, including the Center for Responsive Politics (www.opensecrets.org), PoliticalMoney-Line.com (www.politicalmoneyline.com) and the FEC's own site (www.fec.gov).

Perusing the Center for Responsive Politics' Web site, the Wall Street Journal's Cummings noticed that Wal-Mart's political action committee ranked as the largest corporate donor. Curious why the "famously apolitical retailer" had plunged into the political money game, she produced a front-page, March 24 story that explored Wal-Mart's transformation, including its heavy giving to Republicans and to Bush.

"Not only has the number of stories about campaign finance grown significantly because of the Web, but the nature of those stories has changed," according to a 2002 study commissioned by George Washington University's Institute for Politics, Democracy & the Internet. In early June, GW's Institute for Politics and its School of Media and Public Affairs held a conference on the changed landscape of the 2004 election (tran-

script available at www.smpa.gwu.edu/changedlandscape). "In the old days, just getting the number [for how much cash a candidate raised] was a victory," USA Today's Drinkard said there. "That was news. Now the number's out there and it's easy. So what do you do?"

Drinkard's answer is to adopt a more sophisticated approach, drawing the "tightest picture you can of cause-and-effect, fundraising and lobbying, and then how a donor or that person's business or industry or interest benefited from it."

Although the Internet has revolutionized campaign finance reporting, the press was slow to catch on to the Web's influence on fundraising itself. After Dean shocked journalists by raising more than $7 million last summer, much of it over the Internet, a spate of page-one stories followed.

But Al May, principal author of the GW study and interim director of its School of Media and Public Affairs, says "most of the attention has been on this quirky, coffee klatch society of people meeting and the Internet as an organizing tool." What's been overlooked, in his view, is the Internet's role in spurring people to give for the first time and to give modest sums.

Fred Wertheimer, president of the nonprofit group Democracy 21 and a major supporter of the McCain-Feingold bill, agrees that while stories covering presidential fundraising have been comprehensive and generally well done, the media are missing an opportunity to explore Internet giving more fully.

"One area that hasn't had as much attention as it should is the Internet success of Howard Dean and then John Kerry, because that is one of the most significant campaign-finance developments in years in terms of its potential long-term impact on the way campaigns are financed," Wertheimer says. "If in fact substantial numbers of candidates can figure out how to raise substantial amounts of money through the Internet, you will have a brand-new dynamic in the financing of campaigns."

Kent Cooper, cofounder and vice president of PoliticalMoney-Line.com, a Web site that tracks money and politics, says reporters outside Washington also could do a better job tracking new trends in campaign finance. With "a national story about 527s, people's eyes glaze over," says Cooper, who ran the public records office at the FEC for 22 years. But a local reporter can tackle fundraising from a perspective more compelling to local readers or viewers. If a local business leader suddenly decides to give $2,000 to a political candidate, Cooper says, a reporter "should talk to the person and say, 'What caused you to give this time around?'"

W hen wealthy Republicans flocked to the Ritz-Carlton Lodge on the Reynolds Plantation for the "appreciation weekend," Atlanta Journal-Constitution reporter Moni Basu wrote an April 1 feature about the event, although the resort staff wouldn't release details about preparations or even the "culinary delights." That day, Basu's colleague Matthew C. Quinn waited in the lobby at the resort, reading "The Da Vinci Code" and chatting with guests.

He saw Mercer Reynolds III, Bush's national fundraising chairman and owner of the hotel and golf resort, introduced himself and said he'd like to ask some questions. Reynolds said he wasn't sure Quinn was supposed to be there but sat down and politely entertained a few queries.

Soon after, someone from hotel security asked Quinn whether he was a registered guest. He had spent the night, he said, but no longer was. The official told him he would need to leave. Quinn dictated a brief story to his editor about his Reynolds interview while he drove away.

"Showing up at these events is how you bring it alive," Grimaldi says of campaign finance reporting. He and Edsall showed up the next day after the Secret Service had departed. Before the paper published their story, the reporters called the Bush campaign to read the quotes they were using from the Saturday session and allow the campaign to comment.

"They were quite angry that we were there," Edsall recalls. "They said we had gone into a private meeting and implied that a good reporter would not do that."

"A Post reporter walked into the session, which the campaign described later as an event closed to the media," their story stated. "The speakers 'were under the belief that they were speaking privately with our contributors,'" campaign communications director Nicolle Devenish said in the article.

The story described how "Wall Street mingled with Texas" as Pioneers and Rangers sipped imported mineral water and coffee. Travis Thomas, the Bush-Cheney finance director, told those assembled that they could hold fundraisers in their homes, which "are more comfortable for the president," the story said. "And, Thomas added, 'If it is in a private residence, it can be closed to the press.'"

The press has been guilty of some missteps in its money coverage, including a preoccupation with dollars as the decisive characteristic in the presidential race and a tendency toward pro-"reformer" bias in its coverage. Some stories rely too heavily on jargon or fail to offer clear enough explanations for readers not steeped in the arcana of campaign finance law.

But holding presidential fundraisers in private residences or channeling money into more secretive organizations is unlikely to stifle journalists' interest in a beat that inspired a generation of reporters and remains a priority at the nation's top papers. Where the money goes, the press will follow.

Senior writer **RACHEL SMOLKIN** writes frequently about political coverage for AJR.

UNIT 3

Human Resources Administration

Unit Selections

Key Points to Consider

- Identify and discuss some of the major reasons for identifying and using minorities for executive positions in your organization.

- Why is organizational culture an important concept to understand in relation to employee discipline?

- What is the Certified Public Manager (CPM) Program? Identify and discuss some of the things that you learned about the history of the CPM Program in the United States.

- Go to the GovBenefits.gov website. Identify and discuss at least two major government benefit programs that you reviewed on this website.

- Discuss the concept of risk management as it relates to public accountability and productivity.

Student Web Site

www.mhcls.com/online

Internet References

Further information regarding these Web sites may be found in this book's preface or online.

Sexual Harassment in the Workplace: A Primer
http://www.uakron.edu/lawrev/robert1.html

Skill-Based Pay
http://www.bizcenter.com/skillpay.htm

U.S. Department of Labor
http://www.dol.gov/index.htm

Zigon Performance Group
http://www.zigonperf.com

Articles in this unit focus on human resource administration issues such as leadership, organizational culture, professional development/training, sexual harassment, and benefits in the workplace. The emphasis of these articles is on how to improve the human resources function in the public sector workplace.

The article *Leadership in Your Midst: Tapping the Hidden Strengths of Minority Executives* by Sylvia Ann Hewlett, Carolyn Buck Luce, and Cornel West explores the area of diversity and leadership development. Minority professionals often hold leadership roles outside of work. According to the authors, employers need to recognize the accomplishments and cultural capital of minority managers and utilize them on the job.

Poorly designed discipline systems cause problems in any organization. The authors Aimee L. Franklin and Javier F. Pagan in their article *Organization Culture as an Explanation for Employee Discipline Practices* focus on the problems of employee discipline in the public sector workplace and discuss how a better understanding of organizational culture can provide guidance for improving discipline procedures.

The National Certified Public Manager (CPM) Program began almost 30 years ago in Georgia and has evolved into one of the most important public manager training and professional development programs in the United States. The authors, Thomas H. Patterson and Kenneth K. Henning in their article *The History of the Certified Public Manager,* trace the history of the CPM Program in the United States and discuss how the application of management principles contributed to the growth and development of the organization.

The next article, *GovBenefits.gov: A Valuable E-Government Tool for Citizens,* provides a user friendly review of the GovBenefits.gov website, which is a valuable interactive tool managed by the U.S. Department of Labor in partnership with a network of federal and state agencies. This website lets people immediately determine their eligibility for a wide variety of available government benefit programs.

To complete this unit author Arie Halachmi, in his article *Governance and Risk Management: Challenges and Public Productivity,* explores the issue of public accountability for crisis management and how to improve productivity through the process of outsourcing traditional government functions. The article also explores the shift from governing to governance for risk management and the development of risk culture.

Leadership in Your Midst

Tapping the Hidden Strengths of Minority Executives

Minority professionals often hold leadership roles outside work, serving as pillars of their communities and churches and doing more than their share of mentoring. It's time their employers took notice of these invisible lives and saw them as sources of strength.

SYLVIA ANN HEWLETT, CAROLYN BUCK LUCE, AND CORNEL WEST

All companies value leadership—some of them enough to invest dearly in cultivating it. But few management teams seem to value one engine of leadership development that is right under their noses, churning out the kind of talent they need most. We're referring to the deeply substantive outside lives of their minority executives.

If you know many minority professionals—particularly women of color—then you know that these are the people who are called upon inordinately to lend their energies, perspectives, and guidance to activities outside their jobs. (We use the term "minority" in the statistical sense to denote people who in terms of race or ethnicity are not in the majority in their corporations or organizations.) Because they have "made it," and because often they have done so against heavy odds, they are mentors of choice to young people in their communities. Within their workplaces, they serve on numerous diversity-seeking task forces and spearhead minority recruitment efforts. They play high-profile volunteer roles in their towns, schools, and churches, and the amount of time they invest in these roles is substantial. In the words of Ella Bell, a professor at Dartmouth's Tuck School of Business, "They comprise the backbone of religious organizations and provide a significant part of the energy driving community service in the United States."

For many minority professionals, involvement in such activities is an important, inherently satisfying part of their lives. For some, it's a way of giving back—or, more accurately, giving in turn the kind of help that benefited them early on. But it's also a fertile source of continued personal growth. In these myriad roles, minority professionals hone valuable leadership skills. The problem is that those skills are not properly recognized by their employers. And no conscious attempt is made to transfer them into the corporate environment and develop them further. The disproportionate load of care that minority professionals bear in their extended families is also invisible to employers, and neither acknowledged nor supported by corporate benefits packages. The result: Too many high-potential employees end up feeling ignored and diminished, overextended and burned out. At the same time, organizations are being deprived of the strong and diverse leadership they could so easily draw upon.

In 2004, the Center for Work-Life Policy formed a private-sector task force called the Hidden Brain Drain to investigate the challenges faced by female and minority talent over the life span. In the spring of 2005, three member companies—Unilever, General Electric, and Time Warner—sponsored a cross-sectoral national survey and series of focus groups to discover the facts about minority professionals' outside leadership work and why it remains unrecognized. A companion study, which targeted the global executives of a large multinational corporation, attests to the resonance of this research in other countries.

The U.S. research, which we share here for the first time, underscores that the lives of minority professionals are rich with experience that goes unleveraged by their employers. But it also reveals a startling fact: These lives remain invisible largely by choice. For many reasons, minority professionals are reluctant to speak of their outside pursuits and accomplishments to colleagues and managers. We are left with a dual challenge: Companies can't leverage what they don't see—and they can't see what is purposely concealed.

Cultural Capital

One of the impressive professionals we encountered in our research is Sheryl Battles, an African-American vice president of corporate communications at a major global corporation. In addition to her primary responsibility managing executive and investor communications, she coordinates the corporation's communications on issues of diversity and in that capacity supports 30 to 40 events a year. It's a task that constitutes just 5% of her official job description but consumes roughly 25% of her 50-hour workweek. In her personal life, she speaks at community events and career seminars for minority students and is involved in the church that she, her husband, and their daughter attend. She is also on the board of a local organization for the arts and has been active in its African-American Cultural Heritage Series since its inception a decade ago.

Over the years, Sheryl has accumulated substantial cultural capital, sociologist Pierre Bourdieu's term for nonmonetary wealth and relationship capital generated outside the workplace. Cultural capital is impossible to measure with any precision but is undeniably vital for anyone who wishes to exert influence in a neighborhood, a company, or a nation. Everyone accumulates a measure of cultural capital in their lives, but in the case of minority professionals, it is unusually rich. Consider, for example, the value of Joyce's cultural capital. (All research participants referred to in this article by a first name only are disguised at their request.) Joyce is a change agent to be reckoned with in her community. In her church, she was recently inspired by a progressive pastor's vision for transforming the congregation's stance on a divisive social issue. At the same time, she knew he would face resistance—and that the intensity of his enthusiasm was blinding him to the harsh realities of making change happen. He needed a pragmatic strategist, and in her, he found one. Together they guided the church through the transition, crunching the numbers, outlining a plan, initiating a series of meetings with congregants, and evaluating progress. When we talked with Joyce, she reflected on the experience, noting the difficulty of simultaneously unleashing and controlling the energy that flows from transformational change.

Does all this sound like valuable leadership training? The irony is that, despite being a strategic planner at a *Fortune* 100 company, Joyce never heads up such comprehensive initiatives at work. "Sure, I develop strategic plans here," she reflects, "but my hands are tied half the time. [At church] I have an audience that says, 'Yeah, do your thing.'"

Beyond personal stories like these, statistics do even more to make the point. Among highly educated African-American female professionals, 25% are active leaders in their religious communities (compared with 16% of white men) and 41% are involved in social outreach activities (compared with 32% of white men). Most frequently, they volunteer in schools, hospitals, libraries, shelters, and other organizations in their communities. Minority women are also on the front lines helping young people in their communities as mentors, tutors, and "big sisters." A quarter of African-American businesswomen (25%) take on these roles. (The figure for white businesswomen is 14%).

Such substantive community involvement develops strategic and interpersonal skills, hones core values, and builds organizational and communication capabilities—all of which are transferable to and highly valued in the workplace. Yet our research shows that these skills remain invisible to managers.

Under the Radar

Why aren't companies more attuned to the untapped leadership in their ranks? First, because they haven't looked for it. Traditionally, to the extent that management takes an interest in employees' "extracurricular" lives, the focus has been on activities that have long been sanctioned by white male executives and are thought to burnish a company's image or enhance client relationships: United Way drives, symphony orchestra sponsorships, and sporting events, for example. Most companies do not bother to note the kind of pursuit that Stephanie, a bright, young African-American manager we interviewed, is involved in: running an award-winning Girl Scout troop in a homeless shelter. "These kids are not going to Harvard, they don't have a place to live, and they don't know how many times they're going to eat today," she told us. Stephanie's commitment to these homeless girls is expanding her leadership skill set as she navigates public- and nonprofit-sector bureaucracies while serving a population with myriad needs.

But Stephanie is convinced that her boss disapproves of her involvement in scouting, because it means she must leave work at 5:30 PM a few times a month. Despite the fact that she arrives at 7 AM on those days, she is acutely concerned about being thought of as less than fully committed to her job. She refrains from talking about her Girl Scouts program at work—even though this initiative earned her a Future Leader Today award at a ceremony at the White House.

Stephanie's reticence suggests a second reason that minority professionals' lives remain invisible to their managers: because they are deliberately hidden. Sometimes this is simply because professionals themselves don't recognize their outside affiliations as legitimate leadership development venues. One highly accomplished woman we met is on the board of an active and growing nonprofit organization, where she is gaining valuable skills in fundraising and finance. But she told us, "I have not made the choice to share my board involvement at work…. I have never found a natural segue to make it relevant to what I do for the firm."

Sometimes the conversation doesn't occur because it would necessarily touch on religion, an important part of many minorities' nonwork lives. Joyce, the strategic planner we introduced earlier, feels she can't talk about the change effort she managed for her church, which is a different denomination from that of the apparently homogeneous hierarchy of leaders at her company. The same fear makes Michael, an Asian-American executive at a large California-based energy company, reluctant to share with colleagues his involvement on the board of a prominent charity. His reticence stems from the fact that the charity supports faith-based organizations and targets minority families. According to Michael, colleagues are likely to react negatively to his involvement because it raises "the big taboo subjects of the workplace: religion and ethnicity." In his view, it leads them to think, "You're *different*. I have always suspected that—and now you're confirming it." Michael admits that if people, himself included, talked more openly, then the taboos might be lifted, and his charity work might gain legitimacy and heft. But his short-term view is strictly pragmatic: "Why give anyone ammo?"

The fact that many minorities fear giving employers "ammunition" to use against them is among the most disturbing findings of our research. Many minority women professionals feel they cannot trust their employers with even basic information about their private lives. In large corporations, the percentage rises to more than half.

The survey data show that the distrust and reluctance to discuss private lives are deeply rooted in minorities' experiences of "hidden bias" in corporate cultures. Many avoid discussing their nonwork lives because they don't want to run the risk of reinforcing negative stereotypes. Latisha, an African-American executive at a global consumer products company, described growing up in the Newark projects, her mother on welfare and both parents eventually succumbing to AIDS. "When I do try and open up personally, people just don't get it…So you stop trying." Others worry about a perception that they got their jobs through affirmative action rather than on the grounds of merit.

Some feel hemmed in by "style compliance" issues, such as speaking style, hand gestures, and appearance. Nearly one-third of minority female executives (32%) in large corporations worry that their quiet speaking style is equated with lack of leadership potential, while 23% worry that their animated hand gestures are perceived as inappropriate. Fully 34% of African-American women in the business sector believe that promotion at their companies is based on appearance rather than ability.

According to Sears executive Angela Williams, hidden biases can be debilitating because they lead minority professionals to "deny their authenticity" in their efforts to fit into the prevailing white male model. Indeed, our research shows that almost one-fifth of professional women of color (19%) perceive hidden biases severe enough for them to consider quitting. Focus group participants talked about "teetering on the edge" (thinking about quitting, looking for a new job, trying to figure out whether there is less bias elsewhere) for months, or even years, meanwhile downsizing effort and expectations. One participant told us she had "quit but stayed on the job"—with predictable effects on performance.

Leveraging Unseen Strengths

Companies stand to benefit enormously if they can learn to nurture and support the cultural capital that minority professionals routinely develop outside work. Our research reveals four ways companies can discover and leverage these hidden skills: Companies need to build a greater awareness of the invisible lives of their minority professionals; they need to appreciate and try to lighten the outsize burdens these professionals carry; they must build trust in their ranks by putting teeth into diversity goals and encouraging more latitude in leadership style; and they should finish the job of leadership development begun in minorities' off-hours activities so that those nascent skills can make a difference to workplace performance and competitive strength.

Shine a light. First, greater awareness and appreciation of community work is key. A large number of minority women professionals (45%) do not feel that their roles and responsibilities outside the workplace are recognized or understood by their employers. Minority women in larger companies (56%), young

women of color (50%), and Asian women (49%) are the most likely to feel that their lives are "invisible" to their employers.

Community involvement develops skills that are transferable to and highly valued in the workplace.

Demitra Jones, on the other hand, has no such concern. A dedicated human resource generalist at Pitney Bowes, she feels her employer is fully supportive of the evenings and weekends she spends with her sorority sisters. When Demitra says "sorority," she's talking about Delta Sigma Theta, an African-American organization founded in 1913 that "places more emphasis on service than on socializing." Her membership in the organization is a strenuous commitment, demanding 30 hours a month on top of 60-hour workweeks. It's a win-win situation for her and for Pitney Bowes and has been since the beginning. It was a Delta Sigma Theta member who matched Demitra with the company even before she entered college through Inroads, a leadership development institute for minority youth. Since then, Pitney Bowes has continued to support Delta Sigma Theta in many ways, from purchasing advertising space in fund-raising souvenir journals to matching Demitra's own donations. More important, it has kept an eye on the cultivation and training of Demitra as a leader in both worlds. It's no coincidence that her rapid rise in the company paralleled her progress through the leadership structure of the sorority, which she joined as a junior at Trinity College in Hartford, Connecticut.

What Pitney Bowes has done is not difficult; the company merely shined a light on an aspect of employee life that is often left in the shadows. This kind of light can take many forms. Some specific suggestions that came out of our survey include, for example, ensuring that recruiting activities are recognized explicitly in job descriptions and performance evaluations. Also, allowing employees to set aside time for volunteer activities—even a few hours a month—would send a message that employers recognize and value social outreach and community involvement. An overwhelming majority of our survey participants would welcome training from their companies in fundraising for volunteer activities. Companies could even take an active role in helping young minority professionals access nonprofit boards, thereby giving them an early opportunity to develop leadership skills they can bring back to their workplaces.

Lessen the load. Companies that are truly invested in seeing their diverse talent flourish must be better attuned to the extra burdens carried by many minorities—particularly minority women, whose load of care reaches beyond the nuclear family to extended family and the community. Over half of minority professional women are working mothers (51%), compared with 41% of professional white women. Many, too, are single moms or prime breadwinners. African-American professional women in our survey are more than twice as likely as white women to be single mothers (18%, compared with 7%). In addition, minority women spend significant amounts of time caring for elders and extended family. Seventeen percent of African-American female professionals care for elders and extended family, spending an average of 12.4 hours per week on this care. (The figures for professional white men and women are 6.6 and 9.5 hours, respectively.)

Given this heavy burden of care, some well-established practices like flextime and telecommuting may be especially attractive to minority professionals. Beyond these, there are forms of assistance that few companies have considered, but that might, at small expense, be of tremendous benefit. For example, in our survey there was considerable support for company initiatives that "widen the tent," such as employee benefits that go beyond the nuclear family. Nearly three-quarters (74%) of minority women want help paying for health insurance for up to two members of their extended families. Many minority women (72%) want a few days of annual leave for the purpose of elder care or extended-family care. And 74% of minority women say they would appreciate help in accessing state and federal services for a range of nuclear- and extended-family needs.

Time Warner is one company that has begun to address the issue. Patricia Fili-Krushel, executive vice president of administration, explains, "I wanted to check if we were looking through a white lens in terms of how we organize benefits—and, sure enough, we were." The company recently extended its employee assistance program (which includes, for example, access to child care referral services and company scholarship programs) to other reliant family members (perhaps an aunt or uncle). "In the last five months, there's been a 200% increase in uptake," she says. "There's a lot we can do that doesn't cost a lot of money. It just takes some different thinking."

Reimagine inclusion. The research data underscore the need to expand and amplify what is meant by inclusion. We're not talking here about the same old diversity initiatives, but specifically about innovative policies that build trust and foster workplace environments where minorities feel able to share the full round of their lives. Our survey revealed a widespread wish that companies establish "safe harbors"—places where employees can discuss issues, challenges, or opportunities in their private lives while maintaining anonymity. (Support for this notion was highest among Hispanic women professionals, at 75%, but it was also favored by majorities of African-American women, white women, and African-American men.)

Respondents in our survey also emphasize the need to "walk the talk" in diversity initiatives and put in place financial incentives to motivate managers. Fully 71% of minority businesswomen support the idea of evaluating managers on their track records in recruiting minority talent and favor linking this evaluation to compensation.

This was particularly important to Marie, a Wall Street professional coming back to the financial world after a few years doing client work. She wanted a company that not only had a diversity program, but had one with teeth. As an African-American woman, she was all too familiar with diversity initiatives that never seemed to amount to anything and diversity goals that were never evaluated past their inception. When Marie started work at Lehman Brothers, she was encouraged by the firm's sizable diversity bonus pool—an incentive that recognizes individual managers and teams for their innovative diversity initiatives. The fact that her new firm encouraged investment bankers

to take diversity seriously by providing meaningful incentives was a source of reassurance for Marie.

At Time Warner, there is a policy that for any hire at the vice president level or above, the slate of candidates must be diverse. In 2002, the company created the role of executive connector to make sure that there are viable candidates available for consideration. The connector uses contacts in numerous social and professional circles to develop an extensive pool of diverse candidates. Since taking on this role, Debra Langford has been instrumental in the hiring of 65 minority senior executives. She travels frequently to events and conferences looking for talented high-potential candidates. Once Debra has facilitated a minority hire, she monitors his or her progress. She knows that, unlike their white counterparts, the individuals may not have preexisting relationships within the company. Debra organizes formal and informal gatherings of employees with similar backgrounds—for instance, a lunch for African-American fathers or a dinner for minority lawyers.

Minority professionals are also reassured when they see companies actively combating hidden bias. According to DeAnne Aguirre, a senior vice president at Booz Allen Hamilton, a good way to begin is to "examine the prevailing mode of managerial behavior, determine where it is narrowly drawn, and reenvisage a much more inclusive model." In our survey, 72% of minority women back cultural sensitivity training for managers to break down stereotypes.

One company that has historically welcomed diversity and champions the notion of bringing one's whole self to work is Unilever. Through its Getting into the Skin program, introduced in 2002 as a key part of the company's leadership development program, Unilever takes direct aim at hidden biases by asking selected groups of current and future leaders to spend time outside the realm of their normal experiences. Former Unilever co-chairman Niall FitzGerald helped create the program and was also a participant. Of a 2002 journey to Croatia, he remarked, "I lived the life of a Salvation Army volunteer and picked up an unkempt, uncared-for man off the street…we talked about his life. In an eerie twist of fate, he turned out to be from my hometown. We were two people who fate had dealt very different hands. He taught me, in a way no other experience has, the power of generous listening—without judgment." Other participants have spent time at a rural hospital in Mexico, an AIDS clinic in Ireland, and a prison in Germany. The current CEO Patrick Cescau continues to build on Unilever's mission of inclusion and has established a diversity board, which he chairs.

Finish the job of leadership development. Companies will reap the most benefit from the outside leadership experiences of their employees when they begin to consider this cultural capital explicitly as a form of leadership "action learning." What this means is that they should observe established pedagogical practice, helping minority executives reflect on their experiences, extract and generalize the lessons, and apply what's been learned to other settings.

Some leading corporations are beginning to view afterhours work as leadership training. Goldman Sachs is one, says Aynesh Johnson, an investment banker at Goldman. With the firm's full knowledge and encouragement, Aynesh is sharpening her people skills by working as a board vice president for the Lincoln Square

Neighborhood Center, a nonprofit organization that supports public housing residents who happen to share a zip code with some of the richest people in the world. In the process of figuring out how to fund-raise for these families, Aynesh has taken on a marketing task so challenging it would serve admirably as a business school case study. "It's a very rich and wonderful opportunity," Aynesh says, carefully. "But it's not glamorous." Nevertheless, Aynesh is proud to call her position on the center's board "part of my career." Describing her volunteer work, Aynesh says "it has taught me how to work with a wide range of individuals…maximizing their contributions." She's also learned how to listen gracefully when a prospective donor says no and how to refuse (also gracefully) to take no for an answer. These are skills her superiors at Goldman Sachs think are important. As a result, at work she does not hesitate to be open about this outside commitment. "Managers know, all the way up to the executive suite."

Another way to transfer cultural capital to the workplace is through networks of mentors. Many minority businesswomen are skilled mentors themselves, having reached out to young people in their own communities. They therefore know the potential of these relationships and feel frustrated when they lack mentors in their own organizations. In our survey, a significant proportion of minority professionals (66%) supported the creation of mentoring programs across divisions and the matching of minority employees with senior colleagues from similar ethnic and cultural backgrounds. When mentors build trusting, open relationships with minority protégés, companies gain an important window on leadership talent that is often hidden from view. Mentors can actively engage their protégés in discussions about their outside roles and work with them to apply and enhance those skills in their everyday jobs.

General Electric provides much-needed access to mentors and actively fosters leadership along the way through affinity networks. The African-American Forum is a case in point. It began informally—15 black managers coming together to study retention problems—and has grown into a major initiative that both serves as a vehicle through which minority employees find mentors and holds an annual meeting that draws nearly 1,400 people and features top executives. GE has integrated the AAF into succession planning. As Deborah Elam, manager of diversity and inclusive leadership, explains, "The practice of taking high-potential employees and placing them in leadership roles within the AAF allows top executives to better see the strengths of talented minority professionals."

Lives Made Visible

In 1952, Ralph Waldo Ellison published his classic novel, *Invisible Man*. His central insight remains relevant more than 50 years later: Those rendered "invisible" may well be the key to maintaining America's prosperity and integrity. This past half century has seen a sea change in terms of the opportunities available to minorities—especially female minorities. In response to the antidiscrimination laws of the 1960s and 1970s and the global talent shifts of the past 15 years, the face of

About the Research

Statistics in this article are the findings of a 2005 survey, fielded by Charney Research under the auspices of the Center for Work-Life Policy. The targeted survey sample comprised 1,601 professionals in the United States, ages 28 to 55, with college or professional degrees. This included 1,001 minority women (of whom one-third were African-American, one-third were Hispanic, and one-third were Asian), 200 minority men (also equally divided among the three groups), 198 white women, and 202 white men. The survey targeted people equally in four professional areas: medicine, law, education, and business and accounting. Interviews averaged 20 minutes and were conducted by telephone between January 2005 and February 2005. (A detailed report of the findings will be available at www.work-lifepolicy.org in late 2005.)

power has begun to change. One only need look around the workplace. Whether you're talking Wall Street, Main Street, or the White House, most management teams now include powerful and conspicuous nonwhite talent. Secretary of State Condoleezza Rice, Avon CEO Andrea Jung, and Time Warner CEO Dick Parsons are cases in point.

Still, the belief among many minority professionals that they must somehow cloak their real identities has been extremely debilitating. Every professional, no matter what color or creed, wants to be recognized, appreciated, and supported. As we can see from these new data, for a substantial number of minority professionals, covering up outside lives and staying below the radar has produced isolation, alienation, distrust, and disengagement, all of which helps explain why progress has stalled. According to Catalyst and other research organizations, the data show that minorities are not being promoted or advanced at a rate commensurate with their representation in the talent pool. They remain bunched in the early stretches of the career highway. Few make it into the fast lane.

Any company that hopes to compete on the world stage using superior leadership talent must look squarely at the problem of hidden lives and resolve to overcome it. The key is to value the cultural capital that minorities routinely develop in their communities and bring this to bear in their workplaces. Think of the extraordinary energy and purpose that will be released when minority professionals are finally able to speak openly and proudly of their lives, their core values, and their skills. It might well be transformative—of individuals, of companies, and of society.

SYLVIA ANN HEWLETT is the president of the Center for Work-Life Policy, a New York-based nonprofit organization. She also heads the Gender and Policy Program at the School of International and Public Affairs at Columbia University in New York. **CAROLYN BUCK LUCE** is the global partner for Ernst & Young's health sciences industry practice in New York. **CORNEL WEST** is the Class of 1943 University Professor of Religion at Princeton University in New Jersey. The authors are founding members of the Hidden Brain Drain task force.

Organization Culture as an Explanation for Employee Discipline Practices

Most supervisors dread employee discipline and often employ strategies not officially sanctioned by the organization. Poorly designed discipline systems cause this variation in discipline practices. Inconsistent discipline can cause losses in productivity and reduce employee morale. Extant literature offers little in the form of guidance for improving this important human resource activity. This article explores where normative literature on organizational culture may have explanatory value for understanding variation in discipline practices. The article suggests two groups of factors that have causal effects on discipline practices. The tangible factors are those describing the formal practices the organization wishes its employees to follow. The intangible factors provide cues for explaining why informal strategies emerge as successful practices for getting things done. Using this conception of organization culture, the article proposes hypotheses for future testing to validate the suspected influence of culture on decisions regarding employee discipline.

AIMEE L. FRANKLIN
University of Oklahoma

JAVIER F. PAGAN
University of Puerto Rico

Every day, first-line supervisors face the challenge of deciding what action to take when faced with employee performance problems. A common supervisory complaint is about employees who waste and misuse time. When employees persistently extend the time they take for coffee and lunch breaks, for example, by spending more than 25 to 30 minutes on each of the two 10 minute coffee breaks in the day, productivity suffers. One supervisor may document the problems, counsel the employee, and note the action taken in the employee's personnel folder; another supervisor may choose to look the other way and take no action.

Why do supervisors use different strategies in some cases and avoid formal disciplinary action in others? The most frequently cited reason is the amount of time documentation requires (Ban, 1995). Other common explanations include a lack of managerial support evidenced by supervisory actions that are later overturned through the grievance and arbitration process. Consistent practices that follow organization policies avoid a loss of productivity associated with the administration of discipline, such as managerial time spent pursuing the steps in the discipline process, processing grievances, and hiring new employees. They also foster equity in employee treatment and prevent a demoralized workforce (Kearney & Carnevale, 2001). Assuming that organizations value consistent disciplinary practices, discovery of factors causing supervisors to vary their discipline strategies is a valuable endeavor.

We suggest that explanations for variation in discipline practices can be discerned by exploring the influence of cultural cues supervisors receive regarding appropriate behavior. Recognized as a means for organization members to interpret and make sense of the work environment, symbols such as language, metaphors, objects, and rituals can influence employee actions (Goffman, 1967; Morgan, Frost, & Pondy, 1983). The literature abounds with descriptions of behavioral cues found in an organization's culture. Schein (1992) used the term *artifacts* to describe the visible organization structures and processes that influence employee behavior. Hofstede (2001) described the symbols of an organization, for example, words, gestures, pictures, or objects, that carry a particular meaning. Cultural cues can also be characterized as stories and folklore surrounding watershed events that reinforce a code of conduct (Ingersoll & Adams, 1992; Organ, 1987); symbols such as uniforms, works paces, and building architecture (Goodsell, 1984; Pagan, 1998); or language, jargon, and rituals that differentiate members of different workgroups and organizations (Kunda, 1992; Martin, Hatch, & Sitkin, 1983; Turner, 1971). Khademian (2002) labeled patterns of communication and language, rules of thumb, reference points for decision making, shared symbols, and stories as commitments associated with an organization.

Culture inside an organization defines the boundaries of acceptable action. It signals what work should be done and how that work is to be carried out (Kaufman, 1960). In terms of employee discipline, then, an organization's culture could define what a supervisor should consider as a problem that must be addressed. It could also prescribe what an acceptable response is, given that the supervisor faces a range of choices regarding what action to take.

To explore the relationship between employee discipline practices and organization culture, the first section of the article reviews the employee discipline literature. The second section identifies tangible and intangible factors described in the organization culture literature that may have utility when considering variation in employee discipline. We organize these factors into two categories of cultural cues: those representing the official culture the organization wishes to foster and those reflecting pragmatic responses to disciplinary issues that have been developed by supervisors (in the third section of the article). Finally, we suggest hypotheses that can be tested to validate causal relationships between employee discipline strategies and variables representing the cultural cues supervisors receive.

Employee Discipline in the Literature and in Practice

Every day first-line supervisors are confronted with employee behaviors that do not comply with the letter or the spirit of what the organization expects its employees to do and how that work is to be done. Employee infractions can range from innocuous behaviors such as failing to respond to a client inquiry quickly or being abrupt with a coworker to more egregious violations such as persistent insubordination, theft, or even sexual harassment. In this section, we define *discipline* and describe typical approaches to employee discipline. Then, we present the practical challenges supervisors experience when faced with discipline problems, and we review the formal and informal discipline strategies used by supervisors in response to these challenges.

Employee discipline has many definitions. Some focus on fostering productivity, others on ensuring compliance with policies or controlling behavior. Belohlav (1985) emphasized that making and keeping people productive is the function of the disciplinary process. Werther and Davis (1993) defined discipline as "management action to encourage compliance with organizational standards" (p. 548). Robbins (1994) argued that the term refers to "actions taken by a manager to enforce the organization's standards and regulations" (p. 544). Greer and Labig (1987) suggested that "[d]iscipline is an important, albeit distasteful function in almost every manager's job as he or she attempts to control undesired behavior in the work place" (p. 507).

Organizations typically have elaborate policies and procedures to guide the supervisor in responding to a wide range of employee performance problems. Two formal approaches to discipline systems are identified in the literature: the progressive sanctions approach and the positive approach. Many organizations have a formal disciplinary system featuring progressive sanctions, starting with verbal counseling and moving to written reprimands, suspension, and even termination. In some organizations, a positive discipline approach supplements the progressive approach with coaching and the development of

supervisor-employee agreements to modify problem behavior. Under both systems, supervisors are encouraged to work with their managers and with their human resource departments (and union representatives, if applicable) to take the appropriate course of action in the correct sequence and to fully document the problem and the organizational response. In organizations with a union presence and collective bargaining agreements, uniform disciplinary practices are vital to ensure that supervisors handle cases consistently across time, increasing the likelihood that disciplinary actions will be upheld in grievance and, ultimately, arbitration actions (Klingner, 1980). An empirical study of public and private firms finds that organizations with a union presence do, in fact, have greater consistency. This is explained, in part, because the disciplinary system is made more transparent as supervisors carry a portable copy of the collective bargaining agreement. Furthermore, managers, human resource department personnel, and the union representative place high emphasis on abiding by the agreement (Pagan, 1998).

Supervisors may resist the assessment of subordinates and utilization of the discipline system, progressive or positive, given the difficulty of adequately expressing the performance contract and the desired results and job-related employee behavior (Nalbandian, 1981). When employee performance falls outside prescribed standards, supervisors may not feel comfortable substituting subjective judgments for formal evaluation tools. As described by Klingner and Nalbandian (2003), the psychological contract governing the relationship between employee and employer helps one to understand expectations and behaviors—tangible as well as intangible—that occur when supervisors face discipline problems.

Of course, the supervisor has discretion in determining what constitutes a discipline problem requiring action and in choosing what course of action to take in response. Defining the behavior as a problem can be influenced by the employee's pedigree (e.g., a history of problem behavior). According to Bellizzi and Hasty (2000), "At times, however, similar or identical behaviors are met with different disciplinary actions and, in some cases, the cause of the differential action is tied to the personal characteristics of the subordinate" (p. 159).

In addition to variation in the definition of what a discipline problem is, there is also variation in the supervisor's response. Although disciplinary systems are supposed to guide discipline actions "because those policies are often quite nebulous, it is the managers within the organization" (Klaas & Dell'Omo, 1991, p. 814) who seem to create or put into place strategies for dealing with disciplinary cases. Disciplinary actions taken in organizations vary greatly, and formal and informal methods, such as written warnings and off-the-record discussions between supervisors and subordinates, are widely employed (Greenberg & Baron, 1995).

The use of sanctions and rewards may help to explain variation in disciplinary actions. There can be inadequate incentives or even disincentives that affect motivation to perform the work as expected (Argyris, 1964). Barnard (1938) described sanctions and rewards as basic factors in inducing individuals to work. Argyris (1964) argued that these will reinforce described activities and increase control over individual behavior. The rewards and penalties can be tangible and intangible. Those that relate directly to the work performed will be more robust (P. B. Clark & Wilson, 1961). Organ (1987) documented the influence of cultural expectations when someone handles subordinates too harshly and is assigned to the penalty box-a meaningless job at the same level but in an undesirable location. Outsiders may view this as another job rotation; however, insiders know that the benched supervisor is temporarily "out of the game" (Organ, 1987, p. 473).

According to a U.S. Government Accountability Office (U.S. GAO; 1978) study, public organizations have similar informal tactics: Isolating, reassigning, long-term training, special assignments, early retirement offers, and promoting unsatisfactory employees are some examples of the informal methods of disciplining or getting rid of problem employees within some federal government agencies. Other research supports the findings that informal methods such as these are widely employed, in spite of the existence of formal rules and regulations for dealing with disciplinary issues (Ban, 1995; Beyer & Trice, 1984; U.S. GAO, 1989, 1990; U.S. Merit Systems Protection Board [U.S. MSPB], 1992). Pagan and Franklin (2003) reported that 83% of supervisors interviewed in a public organization in Puerto Rico relied on informal rather than formal strategies when dealing with disciplinary issues.

This reliance on informal strategies is of concern because it suggests that formal systems are being circumvented; and, as a result, there is little consistency in the treatment of problem employees. Adhering to formal discipline policy is important because it ensures that supervisors are abiding by relevant laws and collective bargaining agreements (Kearney & Carnevale, 2001). Such adherence can also be helpful in justifying disciplinary actions in grievance and arbitration processes. According to a study by Wheeler (1976), the vast majority of cases going through the grievance and appeal processes are related to disciplinary issues and problem employees. As Klingner (1980) pointed out, "Procedures are developed to … ensure equity of disciplinary and grievance actions by both parties" (pp. 390–391). Fostering equity in treatment can prevent a demoralized workforce and a resultant loss in productivity (Ban, 1995; Kaufman, 1960).

We suggest that the use of informal strategies can be better understood by examining the cultural cues that supervisors receive regarding how they should handle discipline problems. The role of culture in explaining variation in discipline practices has received some attention in the literature. Norms on discipline are shaped in practice by a whole range of informal practices, and supervisors may select informal approaches because their organization's culture supports them over formal approaches of dealing with employee discipline (Edwards & Scullion, 1982; Gaertner & Gaertner, 1984). Ban (1995) supported this statement when she pointed out that "managers learn by watching … and seeing 'how things are done' in their organizations. Their decisions are also based … on what is valued in their organizations" (pp. 69–70). We can conclude, then, that the choice of discipline strategies may be based on cultural cues suggesting that formal strategies are not really the way things are done in an organization. This possibility is explored in the next section.

Organization Culture Literature

Culture provides guidance on what an organization's employees can do and how they can do it. Argyris and Schon introduced the concept of espoused values in 1974. They argued that an organization will prescribe desired behavior as what employees ought to do; however, actual practice will differ based on the situation, relevant assumptions, and intended outcomes, even though employees claim they behave according to corporate espoused values. These differences result in theories of action that determine the actual behavior of professional practitioners (Argyris & Schon, 1974). Thus, there can be a disconnect between what the organization officially prescribes, what the employee accepts as reasonable behavior, and what the employee does. Explanation of what causes these differences among espoused values, theories of action, and theories in use, we argue, can be discerned through greater examination of organization culture. Schein (1992) also used the concept of espoused values to represent the midrange level of culture that consisted of justifications of strategies, goals, and philosophies of the organization.

One can discern culture in any organization by looking for tangible and intangible cues (Schein, 1992; Smircich, 1983). Tangible cues can be found in things such as the characteristics of the physical facilities; appearance of the employees and their workspaces; the structure of the organization; the formality and clarity of discipline manuals, rules, and processes; and the emphasis on management-related education and training. The intangible cues are more relationship based, as employees working in a group learn acceptable responses to problems they encounter (Schein, 1985). Intangible cues can be found by studying employee interactions, such as the day-to-day relationships supervisors have with their managers, other supervisors, employees, the human resource department, and union delegates.

Czarniawska-Joerges (1992) addressed the tangible and the intangible components of culture: "Culture is the actual ways of doing things as contrasted to those prescribed in documents, decisions, and regulations" (p. 174). Others focused on the tangible cues as well. Khademian (2002) suggested tangible cues describe how work should be done. Kunda (1992) defined *culture* as "rules for behavior, thought, and feeling, all adding up to what appears to be a well-defined and widely shared member role" (p. 7).

Extant literature that focuses more on the intangible component often defines culture in terms of group dynamics. Perhaps one of the most frequently cited definitions of the concept has been offered by Edgar Schein. In his perspective, culture is seen as the "basic assumptions and beliefs that are shared by members of an organization, that operate unconsciously, and that define in a basic 'taken for granted' fashion an organization's view of itself and its environment" (Schein, 1985, p. 6). Imundo (1985) suggested that "[culture] is most readily observed by the ways employees behave in their roles" (p. 21). Along this line, Kilman, Saxton, and Serpa (1986) defined the concept as

the shared philosophies, ideologies, values, assumptions, beliefs, expectations, attitudes, and norms that knit a community together. All of these interrelated psychological qualities reveal a group's agreement, implicit or explicit, on how to approach decisions and problems. (p. 89)

For Barley (1983), culture within organizations "is best understood as a set of assumptions or an interpretative framework that undergirds daily life in an organization or occupation." (p. 399)

There is little consensus regarding the definition of culture (Frost, Moore, Louis, Lundberg, & Martin, 1985; Ingersoll & Adams; 1992; Martin, 2002). Literature on organizational sociology suggests culture is a combination of formal and informal norms that create a psychological contract between employees and employers (Nalbandian, 1981). Others have characterized it as the personification of national culture (Hofstede, 2001; Ingersoll & Adams, 1992). Another line of literature restricts culture to that found within organizations. Through meta-analysis, Martin (1992) developed three organizing perspectives for cultural studies, attributing differences in conceptual definition to different units of analysis, orientation, and interpretation of subjectively examined empirical facts.

For this article, we operationalized culture as a system of shared values and beliefs constructed by an organization and by its employees through tangible and intangible cues. These values and beliefs serve as the general guides through which the organization directs its members' behaviors to be able to solve their problems and work productively. Extant literature suggests several cultural factors that may have explanatory value in understanding variation in employee discipline. In this section, we review the literature on the tangible and intangible components of culture to determine where they may be applicable to the issue of employee discipline.

New employees learn culture after they enter the organization, and this learning process can continue indefinitely as the employee gains more experience and the organization's culture evolves over time (Louis, 1980; Seidman & Gilmour, 1986; Wanous, 1980). Depending on the organization, the induction process may be very timely and detailed, such as providing a new-employee orientation session and making reference documents (such as employee handbooks or the collective bargaining agreement) and discipline policies available and accessible. Alternatively, it may be just the opposite, with little or no effort expended by managers or human resource personnel to ease the new employee's entry into the organization (Pagan & Franklin, 2003; Wanous, 1980). Instead, socialization may occur through subtle changes and adjustments as the new employee becomes an accepted member of a work group (Adkins, 1995) and tests lessons in a socialization chain (Van Maanen, 1984).

The socialization, or acculturation, process helps people adapt to their new jobs as they learn the assumptions, beliefs, values, norms, and behaviors necessary to function effectively in the organization (Fisher, 1986; On, 1989; Schein, 1968; Van Maanen, 1976). This introduction signals how the organization expects supervisors to handle employee infractions. In terms of employee discipline, ensuring consistency in supervisors' actions can depend, largely, on the resources committed to a systematic acculturation process. Thus, we expect that variation in employee discipline will decrease when the organization offers a timely, detailed orientation and makes important documents outlining the discipline process available.

Written documents play a very important role in setting expectations regarding discipline practices in an organization. As described previously, each organization will have detailed policies and procedures outlining the steps of the discipline process. In addition to the organization's specific policies, the supervisor must also follow formal civil service regulations and collective bargaining agreements when taking disciplinary actions. These documents often complicate the disciplinary process in the public sector (Ban, 1995; Ban, Goldenberg, & Marzatto, 1982; Ban & Riccucci, 1991; Shafritz, Riccucci, Rosenbloom, & Hyde, 1992). For example, collective bargaining agreements usually prescribe in detail the actions for which supervisors may subject employees to disciplinary actions and terminations (Freeman & Medoff, 1984; Katz & Kochan, 1992; Rosenbloom & Shafritz, 1985). As Rivas (1991) put it "[T]he organization of the work force and the presence of labor unions tend to require managers to exercise due process in disciplinary actions" (p. 191). When policies are clear, understood, and accepted as valid, supervisors are more likely to follow formal disciplinary policies (Pagan & Franklin, 2003). Of course, the supervisor may utilize formal discipline practices because higher management has signaled, through the allocation of resources and time, that it supports formal actions and will sanction those who do not conform. Therefore, we expect written documents to influence supervisors' approaches to employee discipline, especially when upper-level management reinforces these actions.

It has been recognized that a systematic and formal transmission of organizational disciplinary standards is important for effective operations (Imundo, 1985). Training is one way to accomplish this objective. However, research shows that supervisors within their respective organizations rarely receive training in supervisory skills (Klingner, 1980). Moreover, when supervisors receive training, it appears to be highly superficial in nature and does not teach them how to handle the difficulties usually associated with disciplinary cases (Bryant, 1984). Studies conducted by Ban (1995) indicate that a "dearth of adequate training means that many people have to learn how to manage informally, on the job" and "never really get a firm grasp on the complex personnel system" (pp. 60–61). Inadequately trained supervisors have considerably more problems in dealing with poor performers (Robisch, 1996). Therefore, another tangible aspect of organization culture that may influence disciplinary practices is the organization's commitment to training on formal discipline policies.

The structure of the organization may also influence employee discipline practices. When looking at structure, things such as the lines of authority and span of control must be considered. Authority may be limited during a probationary period as superiors judge the qualifications of the employee (Kaufman, 1960). As another example of how organizational and environmental factors can influence supervisors' performances, many federal organizations do not delegate much authority to first-line supervisors to make decisions and take actions. This leaves "supervisors out in the trenches with little authority to do the things that they deem necessary for the effective and efficient operation of the work unit" (U.S. MSPB, 1992, p. 27). Many first-line supervisors feel that the real authority, particularly on a matter as controversial as discipline, lies above them—sometimes several levels above them (Ban, 1995). Unfortunately, although first-line supervisors are responsible for conducting many of the activities related to employee discipline and problem employees, they are sometimes denied authority over them (U.S. Navy Personnel Research and Development Center, 1984).

The number of employees that a supervisor oversees is another structural issue that affects discipline practices. Supervisors who frequently use formal warnings as a method of correcting problem employees are usually those who have more subordinates under their direct supervision (Podsakoff, 1982). In this sense, as the span of control increases, supervisors may be more inclined to fire problem employees than to counsel them. Therefore, first-line supervisors' handling of employee discipline can also be affected by unclear delegation of authority or variation in the span of control.

Over time, empirical studies have found that culture is heavily dependent on history or the actions of a specific individual and/or leader (Barnard, 1938; Kaufman, 1960; Kunda, 1992; Riccucci, 1995; Schein, 1992). Thus, the people inside the organization can provide intangible cues about expected employee behaviors. There are four types of individuals or groups that can influence the supervisor's choice of disciplinary actions: organization management (including the HR department), the problem employee, the supervisor's peers, and groups providing overlapping value systems. Normative prescriptions for each of these as they relate to employee discipline are considered next.

In a GAO (U.S. GAO, 1978) report, it was found that "supervisors and managers perceive firing as a difficult chore which often lacks top-level management support" (p. ii). Managers "are likely to go through the lengthy and complex formal process only if they have strong support from their superiors (sometimes several layers up) and from the employee relations staff" (Ban, 1995, p. 81). Decisions made by supervisors are often overruled by higher levels of management or by staff specialists (Imundo, 1985, pp. 5–6). Campbell, Flemming, and Grote (1985) argued that "not only do they catch flak from below but supervisors also discover that maintaining discipline may produce reversed decisions 'upstairs'" (p. 168). Such a situation leads to a condition where "supervisors and employees perceive their agencies as non supportive should they want to fire someone" (U.S. GAO, 1978, p. 17). From this, we can conclude that when considering the relationship between the supervisor and organization management, if there is a sense of support, it is more likely that supervisors will pursue formal disciplinary actions. If supervisors fear their decisions will not be supported and will perhaps be overruled, the use of informal strategies is more likely.

The relationship between the supervisor and the subordinate may also affect the choice of discipline strategies. Research conducted by Rosen and Jerdee (1974) found that offenders' (subordinates') characteristics, such as status and talent, appear to influence supervisors' judgments and application of disciplinary sanctions. Participants in this study tended to be more lenient in applying sanctions, for the same rule violation, if positive characteristics were present. The approach supervisors take to someone with inadequate skills can differ from that taken to an employee

with personal problems (Ban, 1995). Based on these observations, it is likely that formal strategies will be favored when the employee has unsatisfactory personal skills.

The norms of referent, or reference, groups can be highly influential in shaping employee behaviors. A referent group is a group whose values, norms, and perspectives guide the employee's behavior in social situations (R. E. Clark, 1972). In 1957, Merton suggested that a person compares herself or himself with others in the same situation when deciding how to interpret an experience. Others argued that role models are necessary to have adequate role performance (Ingersoll & Adams, 1992; Kemper, 1968). This is part of the identification process through which people respond to social influence. When identification occurs, compliance and internalization serve to align group member behavior (Kelman, 1961). Bion (1961) reinforced this notion in his finding that there are "basic assumptions" or dynamics that operate within groups and guide member behavior and reactions to other members. Failure to conform can lead to sanctions or removal (R. E. Clark, 1972).

Studies off acuity members by Gouldner (1957, 1958; later replicated by Flango & Brumbaugh, 1974) examined the influence of manifest and latent social roles on organization loyalty, commitment to professional skills and values, and reference group orientations. Two general types of organization members are identified in the university setting: cosmopolitans and locals. Locals use an inner reference group orientation and are highly identified with the current organization. They are so-called company men who seek to get along with others to make the organization succeed. Cosmopolitans are less concerned with the internal operations of their current organization and more concerned with establishing themselves as experts in, and gaining recognition from, the professional community at large. These findings suggest that referent groups occur inside and outside the organization's boundaries.

For supervisors, their peers, that is, other supervisors (inside and outside the organizations) and managers are the primary referent groups. As Klaas and Dell'Omo (1991) pointed out, although disciplinary systems are supposed to guide general behavior "because those policies are often quite nebulous, it is the managers within the organization" (p. 814) who seem to create or put into place adequate strategies and/or approaches to help them navigate through the complexities usually associated with disciplinary cases. Others comment that supervisors' individual and peer group norms are ingrained and/or programmed into each employee (Argyris, 1967) and passed on and/or transmitted from generation to generation (Harrison & Carroll, 1991; Kaufman, 1960). Research by Podsakoff (1982) supports this assumption in the conclusion that "less experienced supervisors are more likely to refer their problems to someone else" (p. 73). If supervisors, as a group within an organization, tend to follow formal discipline policy, we expect to find that individual supervisors will be more likely to use formal approaches as well. The opposite, a prevalence of informal strategies will foster approaches that are more informal, is predicted as well.

Overlapping cultural influences on an individual, such as those held by professional, social and/ or affiliation, religious, family, and societal groups, constitute additional referent groups that may influence disciplinary practices (Franklin & Raadschelders, 2004; Hofstede, 2001; Van Maanen & Barley, 1984). Existing empirical literature does not test the influence of these external referent groups in the discipline process. The literature on culture, however, does suggest that the norms, values, and beliefs of an organization need to closely align with an individual's preexisting beliefs to be self-enforcing (Argyris, 1989; Blau & Scott, 1962). If there are conflicts in value systems, then there may be differences in employees' perceptions of expected behavior (French & Bell, 1999; Martin, 1992). As a result, disciplinary actions may vary because employees will resist values that are dissonant with those they hold outside work (Deal & Kennedy, 1982; Juran, 1964). Therefore, we can infer that the choice of discipline strategies can also be influenced by the values the supervisor holds that are reinforced by individuals and groups outside the workplace.

In reviewing the literature, it appears that several tangible and intangible cultural factors representing the formal or officially sanctioned behaviors, and the informal or unofficially developed norms, respectively, may influence the choice of discipline strategies. Assuming that it is desirable for all supervisors to be consistent in the employee discipline process and that formal strategies are favored for productivity, equity, and morale reasons, we offer these hypotheses regarding the influence of culture on employee discipline.

Tangible Factors (Formal or Officially Sanctioned)

- Socialization and/or acculturation experience: If the organization provides an orientation that is timely and detailed, the supervisor will be more likely to use the formal discipline process.
- Written documents: If the relevant policies and procedures are given to the supervisor and are useful, the supervisor will be more likely to use the formal discipline process.
- Training: If the organization provides training on discipline, the supervisor will be more likely to use the formal discipline process.
- Organization structure: If the organization vests authority with the supervisor and if the supervisor has a larger span of control, the supervisor will be more likely to use the formal discipline process.

Intangible Factors (Informal or Unofficially Developed)

- Problem employees: If the employee does not have good job skills or high status, the supervisor will be more likely to use the formal discipline process.
- Socialization/acculturation occurring through referent group HR department): If supervisory decisions are supported and not overturned by organizational management, the supervisor will be more likely to use the formal discipline process.
- Peers: If other supervisors follow the formal discipline process, the supervisor will be more likely to use the formal discipline process.

- Groups outside work: If overlapping value systems fostered by groups outside work reinforce the expectations supported by the organization's culture, the supervisor will be more likely to use the formal discipline process.

Although these tangible and intangible factors are thought to be important for explaining bivariate relationships, we suspect that there may also be interaction effects between the two types of cultural cues (tangible and intangible). We explore this possibility in the next section.

Organization Culture as an Explanatory Factor

From these observations regarding different cultural factors, we suggest that an organization's culture can be thought of as being composed of two distinct dimensions: one that constitutes the official culture of what we do and how we do it, and the operating culture of how work is really done. Supervisors can rely on stated and unstated assumptions of what constitutes appropriate behavior. One is overt and explicit, and the other is tacit and implicit (Gibson, Ivancevich, & Donnelly, 2000; Ingersoll & Adams, 1992). The organization attempts to prescribe formally what employees are expected to do and how they are expected to do it through the tangible factors. We label this the *official culture* and propose that it is signaled through tangible cues as the organization attempts to guide (and regulate) supervisors' actions. The intangible factors, as a group, are given the label *operating culture* because they prescribe allowable behaviors for how work really is done. These behaviors are negotiated through interpersonal interactions as employees, working in a group, learn successful responses to resolving problems (Argyris & Schon, 1974; Schein, 1992). The operating culture provides cues suggesting the rules of thumb for acceptable behavior given different problems. It defines how things are really done and outlines where there is flexibility in following official standards. In this section, we suggest that the two types of factors influencing culture, tangible and intangible, provide important cues as the supervisor searches the official and operating dimensions of culture for information regarding appropriate behavior.

We can combine the cues a supervisor receives regarding the two dimensions of culture, official standards and operating guidance, in three ways: (a) providing the same prescription for action, (b) providing similar prescriptions with slight inconsistencies, or (c) providing different prescriptions. Expectations regarding these combinations are described below; however, these are untested hypotheses that warrant empirical testing. One might assume that based on these three conditions, the supervisor experiences different levels of congruence or dissonance (Argyris & Schon, 1974), and that may explain variation in the use of formal or informal discipline strategies. Cognitive dissonance (Argyris, 1989) occurs when there are discrepancies between the official statements describing expectations for employee actions and normal employee behaviors. In terms of discipline systems, the optimal situation is the alignment and

Table 1   Managing the Official and Operating Dimensions of Cultures

	Operating Guidance (Based on Intangible Cues)	Supervisor Experiences	Disciplinary Strategies Used by Supervisors
Official standards (based on tangible cues)	Same	No dissonance	Consistent, formal strategies
	Similar	Discretion	Unpredictable, mixed strategies, but bias toward formal
	Different	Dissonance	Inconsistent, informal strategies dominant

integration of the tangible cultural cues received from official standards with the intangible cues received in the form of operating guidance from others in the organization. This framework, presented in Table 1, provides a starting point for the development of hypotheses that can be tested empirically as the next stage of theory development.

In the first combination, there is no dissonance in the cues received from the official and operating cultures regarding what disciplinary actions are expected. In this case, it is likely that formal strategies will be used because the tangible and intangible cues suggest that policies and procedures should be followed. In addition, there is a greater likelihood that there will be consistency between supervisors, with a tendency to favor formal strategies that are clearly described in written documents and reinforced in orientation and training events.

When the two dimensions provide similar cues, the supervisor is now faced with a choice of following the formal policy stated in the official standards or choosing other strategies learned through interactions with other groups. In this situation, the choice of discipline strategies is unpredictable; however, it may be reasonable to expect that the supervisor will follow official policy and try a formal strategy to avoid jeopardizing his or her job. The effectiveness of cultural cues to guide behavior decreases when the messages between the official and operating dimensions are inconsistent because the employee has to determine what factors (cues) are assigned greater weight relative to the others and decipher which signals are correct in the view of a majority of members in most situations. In short, the problem is that intangible cues are more subjective and lead to greater variations in perceptions and interpretations.

In the third combination, the cues received regarding official standards and operating guidance are in conflict. When this occurs, the supervisor experiences dissonance. The discrepancy between what is expected and what is actually being done will be evaluated by the supervisor to determine how important the difference is and if there is a strategy that will accommodate both sets of cues. However, we hypothesize that in this situation, supervisors will favor informal strategies that ignore the problem, hoping it will go away; or they will take steps proactively to make the problem go away. Recall that common informal strategies are ignoring, isolating, reassigning, transferring, offering early retirement, and promoting unsatisfactory employees. None of these takes a great deal of effort from the supervisor. On the other hand, formal strategies are described as time-consuming and seldom successful. Thus, we speculate that the supervisor's bias will be toward the self-interested behavior supported by informal strategies. In addition, because supervisors learn informal strategies through interactions, and not all supervisors interact with all other supervisors and managers, the highest level of variation in discipline practices is expected.

Discussion

In this article, we suggest two dimensions of culture that provide cues to employees regarding acceptable behavior. In elaborating these dimensions, we do not seek to provide the ultimate definition of culture; rather, we attempt to provide a framework for empirical confirmation and theory extension. Using the two dimensions of culture, official and operating, to analyze how supervisors choose between formal and informal strategies can be useful for decreasing variation in employee discipline practices. It can be assumed that official organizational efforts designed to make desired employee discipline practices transparent to supervisors can increase the likelihood that formal, rather than informal, disciplinary strategies prevail.

To improve the consistency between the official standards and the operating guidance dimensions and to reduce variation in employee discipline practices, organizations can identify the cues employees receive (Sackmann, 1991) regarding both dimensions of culture. For situations where the cues are contradictory or inconsistent, this line of inquiry can be informative for identifying what types of targeted interventions (Detert, Schroeder, & Mauriel, 2000) may have utility in terms of encouraging a unified and consistent approach to discipline. If it is observed that the official culture is sending inconsistent signals, then actions such as rewriting the discipline manual to make it more user friendly or offering training focusing on disciplinary processes will be beneficial.

Attempts to modify an inconsistent operating culture may include teambuilding or communication exercises (although it is acknowledged that changes of this nature are more difficult to attain and can take a long time; see Selznick, 1948). Changes to the official standards can focus on institutional structure and/or mechanisms and can be based in traditional or authority-based leadership and are forcible in the short term (Senge, 1990). Changes to the operating guidelines require that acceptance be gained through charismatic leadership, dialogue, and negotiation with the organization's members (Selznick, 1948; Van

Blijswijk, Van Breukelen, Franklin, Raadschelders, & Slump, 2004); and as Carnevale (2003) pointed out, this may take longer than other actions to change organization culture.

The definition of culture as being composed of two dimensions representing the official standards (as described in tangible cues) and operating guidance (as learned through intangible cues) can be useful in assessing why supervisors prefer certain disciplinary strategies. Of course, implying a strict demarcation between tangible and intangible cues is false; the categories are not mutually exclusive. However, it does serve to illustrate the difference between the official and the operating dimensions of culture. The hypotheses predicting bivariate relationships between each of the cultural factors in the tangible and intangible groups need deductive validation. Then, research can be undertaken to test the predictive validity of the model presented in Table 1, suggesting interaction effects between the factors representing the two dimensions of an organization's culture. Future studies should test these causal relationships across a large-scale, representative sample of organizations.

Conclusion

Organizations struggle to create employee discipline systems that are used by their supervisors. When supervisors follow formal policies, productivity is enhanced and equity is preserved. However, empirical evidence suggests that informal strategies are common when supervisors confront discipline problems. Using extant literature, we suggest that there are cultural factors that can explain why there is variation in the selection of discipline strategies. These factors are grouped into two categories, tangible and intangible cues, describing what are expected and what are acceptable behaviors, respectively. The tangible cues represent the official expectations of the organization. These cues are present in the employee induction process, written documents, training events, and the structure of the organization. The intangible cues give guidance on what is really done in daily operations. Relationships and interactions with organization management, other supervisors, problem employees, and other referent groups outside of work are the source of intangible cues for acceptable behaviors. We argue that these two dimensions interact in three combinations influencing the choice of discipline strategy and the likelihood that there will be consistency between supervisors. Without mutually reinforcing cues, the strategies supervisors use may not be in accord with organizational preferences and may vary widely, leading to unsatisfactory outcomes. Given the high levels of dissatisfaction that already exist with employee discipline practices, we suggest that the proposed influence of culture is one that deserves greater attention among public management scholars.

References

Adkins, C. L. (1995). Previous work experience and organizational socialization: A longitudinal examination. *Academy of Management Journal, 38*(3), 839–862.

Argyris, C. (1964). *Integrating the individual and the organization.* New York: John Wiley.

Argyris, C. (1967). *Executive leadership: An appraisal of a manager in action.* Harnden, CT: Archon.

Argyris, C. (1989). The individual and the organization. In W. E. Natemeyer & J. S. Gilberg (Eds.), *Classics of organizational behavior* (2nd ed., pp. 21–35). Oak Park, IL: Moore.

Argyris, C., & Schon, D. A. (1974). *Theory in practice: Increasing professional effectiveness.* San Francisco: Jossey-Bass.

Ban, C. (1995). *How do public managers manage? Bureaucratic constraints, organizational culture, and the potential for reform.* San Francisco: Jossey-Bass.

Ban, C., Goldenberg, E. N., & Marzano, T. (1982). Firing the unproductive employee: Will civil service reform make a difference? *Review of Public Personnel Administration, 2*(2), 87–100.

Ban, C., & Riccucci, N. (1991). *Public personnel management: Current concerns–future challenges.* White Plains, NY: Longman.

Barley, S. R. (1983). Semiotics and the study of occupational and organizational cultures. *Administrative Science Quarterly, 28*(3), 393–413.

Barnard, C. I. (1938). *The functions of the executive.* Cambridge, MA: Harvard University Press.

Bellizzi, J. A., & Hasty, R. (2000). The effects of hiring decisions on the level of discipline used in response to poor performance. *Management Decision, 38*(3), 154–159.

Belohlav, J. A. (1985). *The art of disciplining your employees: A manager's guide.* Englewood Cliffs, NJ: Prentice Hall.

Beyer, J. M., & Trice, H. M. (1984). A field study of the use and perceived effects of discipline in controlling work performance. *Academy of Management Journal, 27*(4), 743–764.

Bion, W. R. (1961). *Experiences in groups.* London: Tavistock.

Blau, P. M., & Scott, W. R (1962). *Formal organizations: A comparative approach.* San Francisco: Chandler.

Bryant, A. W. (1984). Replacing punitive discipline with a positive approach. *Personnel Administrator, 29*(2), 79–87.

Campbell, D. N., Flemming, R. L., & Grote, R. C. (1985). Discipline without punishment at last. *Harvard Business Review, 63*(4), 162–174.

Carnevale, D. G. (2003). *Organizational development in the public sector.* Boulder, CO: Westview.

Clark, P. B., & Wilson, J. Q. (1961). Incentive systems: A theory of organizations. *Administrative Science Quarterly, 6*(2), 134–135.

Clark, R. E. (1972). *Reference group theory and delinquency.* New York: Behavioral Publications.

Czarniawska-Joerges, B. (1992). *Exploring complex organizations: A cultural perspective.* Newbury Park, CA: Sage.

Deal, T. E., & Kennedy, A. A. (1982). *Corporate cultures: The rites and rituals of corporate life.* Reading, MA: Addison-Wesley.

Detert, J. R., Schroeder, R. G., & Mauriel, J. J. (2000). A framework for linking culture and improvement initiatives in organizations. *Academy of Management Review, 25*(4), 850–872.

Edwards, P. K., & Scullion, H. (1982). Deviancy theory and industrial praxis: A study of discipline and social control in an industrial setting. *Sociology, 16*(3), 322–340.

Fisher, C. D. (1986). Organizational socialization: An integrative review. *Research in Personnel and Human Resources Management, 4*, 101–145.

Flango, V. E., & Brumbaugh, R. B. (1974). The dimensionality of the cosmopolitan-local construct. *Administrative Science Quarterly, 19*(2), 198–210.

Franklin, A. L., & Raadschelders, J. C. N. (2004). Ethics in local government budgeting—Is there a gap between theory and practice? *Public Administration Quarterly, 27*(4), 456–490.

Freeman, R. B., & Medoff, J. L. (1984). *What do unions do?* New York: Basic Books.

French, W. L., & Bell, C. (1999). *Organization development: Behavioral science interventions for organizational improvement* (6th ed.). Upper Saddle River, NJ: Prentice Hall.

Frost, P. J., Moore, L., Louis, M., Lundberg, C., & Martin, J. (Eds.). (1985). *Organizational culture.* Beverly Hills, CA: Sage.

Gaertner, G. H., & Gaertner, K. N. (1984). Formal disciplinary actions in two federal agencies. *Review of Public Personnel Administration, 5*(1), 12–24.

Gibson, J. L., Ivancevich, J. M., & Donnelly, J. H. (2000). *Organization: Behavior, structure, processes.* Boston: Irwin, McGraw-Hill.

Goffman, E. (1967). *Interaction ritual.* New York: Anchor.

Goodsell, C. T. (1984). Welfare waiting rooms. *Urban Life, 12*, 467–477.

Gouldner, A. W. (1957). Cosmopolitans and locals: Toward an analysis of latent social roles—I. *Administrative Science Quarterly, 2*(3), 281–306.

Gouldner, A. W. (1958). Cosmopolitans and locals: Toward an analysis of latent social roles—II. *Administrative Science Quarterly, 2*(4), 444–480.

Greenberg, J., & Baron, R. A. (1995). *Behavior in organizations* (5th ed.). Englewood Cliffs, NJ: Prentice Hall.

Greer, C. R., & Labig, C. E. (1987). Employee reactions to disciplinary actions. *Human Relations, 40*(8), 507–524.

Harrison, J. R., & Carroll, G. R. (1991). Keeping the faith: A model of cultural transmission in formal organizations. *Administrative Science Quarterly, 36*(4), 552–582.

Hofstede, G. (2001). *Culture's consequences: Comparing values, behaviors, institutions, and organizations across nations* (2nd ed.). Thousand Oaks, CA: Sage.

Imundo, L. V. (1985). *Employee discipline: How to do it right.* Belmont, CA: Wadsworth.

Ingersoll, V. H., & Adams, G. B. (1992). *The tacit organization.* Greenwich, CT: JAI.

Juran, J. M. (1964). *Managerial breakthrough: A new concept of the manager's job.* New York: McGraw-Hill.

Katz, H. C., & Kochan, T. A. (1992). An *introduction to collective bargaining and industrial relations.* New York: McGraw-Hill.

Kaufman, H. (1960). *The forest ranger: A study in administrative behavior.* Baltimore: Johns Hopkins University Press.

Kearney, R. C., & Carnevale, D. G. (2001). *Labor relations in the public sector* (3rd ed.). New York: Marcel Dekker.

Kelman, H. C. (1961). Process of opinion change. *Public Opinion Quarterly, 25*(1), 55–77.

Kemper, T. (1968). Reference groups, socialization and achievement. *American Sociological Review, 33*(1), 31–45.

Khademian, A. M. (2002). *Working with culture: The way the job gets done in public programs.* Washington, DC: CQ Press.

Kilman, R. H., Saxton, M. J., & Serpa, R. (1986). Issues in understanding and changing culture. *California Management Review, 28*(2), 87–94.

Klaas, B. S., & Dell'Omo, G. (1991). The determinants of disciplinary decisions: The case of employee drug use. *Personnel Psychology, 44*(4), 813–835.

Klingner, D. E. (1980). *Public personal management: Contexts and strategies.* Englewood Cliffs, NJ: Prentice Hall.

Klingner, D. E., & Nalbandian, J. (2003). *Public personnel management: contexts and strategies* (4th ed.). Englewood Cliffs, NJ: Prentice Hall.

Kunda, G. (1992). *Engineering culture: Control and commitment in a high-tech corporation.* Philadelphia: Temple University Press.

Louis, M. R. (1980). Surprise and sense making: What newcomers experience in entering unfamiliar organizational settings. *Administrative Science Quarterly, 25*(2), 226–251.

Martin, J. (1992). *Cultures in organizations: Three perspectives.* New York: Oxford University Press.

Martin, J. (2002). *Organizational culture: Mapping the terrain.* Thousand Oaks, CA: Sage.

Martin, J. F., Hatch, M. J., & Sitkin, S. B. (1983). The uniqueness paradox in organizational stories. *Administrative Science Quarterly, 28*(3), 438–453.

Merton, R. K. (1957). *Social theory and social structure.* Glencoe, IL: Free Press.

Morgan, G., Frost, P. J., & Pondy, L. R. (1983). *Organizational symbolism.* Greenwich, CT: JAI.

Nalbandian, J. (1981). Performance appraisal: If only people were not involved. *Public Administration Review, 41*(3), 392–396.

Organ, D. W. (1987). *The applied psychology of work behavior: A book of readings.* Plano, TX: Business Publications. On, J. S. (1989). *The organizational culture perspective.* Chicago: Dorsey.

Pagan, J. (1998). *Discipline and first line supervisors: An ethnographic approach to the study of how supervisors handle employee discipline.* Unpublished doctoral dissertation, State University of New York at Albany.

Pagan, J., & Franklin, A. L. (2003). Understanding variation in the practice of employee discipline. *Review of Public Personnel Administration, 23*(1), 16–25.

Podsakoff, P. M. (1982). Detetminants of a supervisor's use of rewards and punishment: A literature review and suggestions for further research. *Organizational Behavior and Human Performance, 29,* 58–83.

Riccucci, N. (1995). *Unsung heroes: Federal execucrats making a difference.* Washington, DC: Georgetown University Press.

Rivas, R. F. (1991). Dismissing problem employees. In R. L. Lewis & J. A. Yarkey (Eds.), *Skills for effective human services management* (pp. 186–203). Washington, DC: NASW.

Robbins, S. P. (1994). *Management.* Englewood Cliffs, NJ: Prentice Hall.

Robisch, T. G. (1996). The reluctance of federal managers to utilize formal procedures for poorly performing employees. *Review of Public Personnel Administration, 16*(2), 73–85.

Rosen, B., & Jerdee, T. H. (1974). Factors influencing disciplinary judgments. *Journal of Applied Psychology, 59*(3), 327–331.

Rosenbloom, D. H., & Shafritz, J. M. (1985). *Essentials of labor relations.* Reston, VA: Reston Publishing.

Sackmann, S. A. (1991). Uncovering culture in organizations. *Journal of Applied Behavioral Science, 27*(3), 295–317.

Schein, E. H. (1968). Organizational socialization and the profession of management. *Industrial Management Review, 9*(2), 1–16.

Schein, E. H. (1985). *Organizational culture and leadership.* San Francisco: Jossey-Bass.

Schein, E. H. (1992). *Organizational culture and leadership* (2nd ed.). San Francisco: Jossey-Bass.

Seidman, H., & Gilmour, R. (1986). *Politics, position, and power: From the positive to the regulatory state* (4th ed.). New York: Oxford University Press.

Selznick, P. (1948). Foundations of the theory of organization. *American Sociological Review, 13*(1), 25–35.

Senge, P. M. (1990). *The fifth discipline: The art and practice of learning organization.* New York: Doubleday.

Shafritz, J. M., Riccucci, N. M., Rosenbloom, D. H., & Hyde, A. C. (1992). *Personnel management in government: Politics and process.* New York: Marcel Dekker.

Smircich, L. (1983). Concepts of culture and organizational analysis. *Administrative Science Quarterly, 28*(3), 339–358.

Turner, B. A. (1971). *Exploring the industrial subculture.* New York: Herder and Herder.

U.S. Government Accountability Office. (1978). *A management concern: How to deal with the nonproductive federal employee* (FPCD-78-71). Washington, DC: Author.

U.S. Government Accountability Office. (1989). *Poor performance: How they are identified and dealt with in the Social Security Administration* (GAO/GGD-89-28). Washington, DC: Author.

U.S. Government Accountability Office. (1990). *Performance management: How well is the government dealing with poor performers?* (GAO/GGD-91-7). Washington, DC: Author.

U.S. Merit Systems Protection Board. (1992). *Federal first-line supervisors: How good are they?* Washington, DC: Author.

U.S. Navy Personnel Research and Development Center. (1984). *The first-line supervisor: Literature review* (MPRDC TR 84-18). San Diego, CA: Author.

Van Blijswijk, J. A. M., Van Breukelen, R. C. J., Franklin, A. L., Raadschelders, J. C. N., & Slump, P. (2004). Beyond ethical codes: The management of integrity. The case of the Netherlands tax and customs administration. *Public Administration Review, 64*(4), 718–727.

Van Maanen, J. (1976). Breaking in: Socialization to work. In R. Dubin (Ed.), *Handbook of work, organization, and society* (pp. 67–130). Chicago: Rand McNally.

Van Maanen, J. (1984). Doing new things in old ways: The chains of socialization. In J. L. Bess (Ed.), *College and university organization* (pp. 211–245). New York: New York University Press.

Van Maanen, J., & Barley, S. R. (1984). Occupational communities: Culture and control in organizations. *Research in Organizational Behavior, 6,* 287–365.

Wanous, J. P. (1980). *Organizational entry: Recruitment, selection and socialization of new comers.* Reading, MA: Addison-Wesley.

Werther, W. B., & Davis, K. (1993). *Human resources and personnel management.* New York: McGraw-Hill.

Wheeler, H. N. (1976). Punishment theory and industrial discipline. *Industrial Relations, 15*(2), 235–243.

AIMEE L. FRANKLIN is an associate professor and graduate program director at the University of Oklahoma. Her research and teaching focuses on improving public management, with areas of interest in strategic planning, budgeting, evaluation, performance measurement, and ethics.

JAVIER F. PAGAN is an associate professor at the University of Puerto Rico in San Juan. He teaches courses in management, human resources, and organizational behavior. His research focuses on labor-management relations and human resource practices in public and private organizations.

The History of the Certified Public Manager

How the Application of Management Principles Contributed to Success and Sustained Growth over a Three Decade Organizational Journey

This history describes the birth of the Certified Public Manager concept, the establishment of the Society concept in Georgia, and the transfer of the model to other states. It also details the formation of the National Certified Public Manager Consortium as the higher education instructional and program standards organization, and the formation of the American Academy of Certified Public Managers as the national association of State CPM Societies and their professional members. In addition, Mr. Henning identifies major management concerns as the organizational process evolved and the strategies that were successful in their resolution.

THOMAS H. PATTERSON, CPM
Louisiana Department of Environmental Quality
Past-President, American Academy of Certified Public Managers

KENNETH K. HENNING, CPM (HON.)
University of Georgia (Ret.)

Foreword

This is the story of an organizational journey. While, here and there, it focuses on some individuals and organizational entities, it also provides the opportunity to observe some of the principles of management in practice and demonstrates their validity.

While we often think of organizations as inherently stable, Chester Barnard, the former President of the New Jersey Bell Telephone Company, hypothesized the opposite. In his classic management book *The Functions of the Executive*, he suggested that successful cooperation of people in organizations is abnormal and that failure of organizations is highly likely. He further suggested that while organizations of all sorts are everywhere, what is observed are "the successful survivors among innumerable failures." (Barnard 1948)

That the Certified Public Manager Organization, from its genesis to the present, has not only survived but has expanded and developed for nearly three decades, is a substantial achievement. —Kenneth K. Henning

Introduction

In the early-1970s, the Service Division of the University of Georgia recognized that the state's government was beginning to be significantly affected by accelerating change increasingly characteristic of the American society. Along with the rest of the country, the state was experiencing the effects of rapid population growth, an almost explosive growth in information and knowledge, significant new social legislation and rapidly altering social values.

During this time, the Institute of Government and the Center for Continuing Education of the University of Georgia, and the Georgia Merit System, independently, and in some instances, collaboratively, had offered management training to agencies of Georgia state government (Henning and Wilson 1979).

In early 1974, representatives of the University of Georgia's Institute of Government and Center for Continuing Education and the Georgia State Merit System of Personnel Administration initiated a series of informal meetings to explore ways of broadening and focusing their individual and collaborative efforts to assist Georgia state government in meeting the challenges of a rapidly changing state and society (Henning and Wilson 1979).

Specifically, Ken Henning, Senior Management Development Associate in Governmental Training at the University of Georgia, and Douglas Wilson, Assistant Division Director on the Georgia State Merit System's Training Division, began to meet informally to brainstorm ways to enhance the educational efforts of both organizations for the benefit of Georgia State government. It was quickly agreed that management in state government needed to become more professional. During these meetings, the two reviewed the broad outline of the impact of rapid change on the public service suggested by Chapman and Cleaveland in their 1973 study conducted for the National Academy of Pubic Administration (Chapman and Cleaveland 1973). This article was an indication of support for the project. The authors anticipated that public managers would:

- Be required to develop and implement new standards for effectiveness, efficiency, and accountability;
- Be required to make more decisions in open meetings and, therefore, be subjected to broader and more varied participation as well as more substantial and diverse external evaluation and intervention;
- See more actions taken by their agencies and therefore be subjected to legal challenges and judicial review and intervention;
- Need to implement more widespread and effective collaboration between and among agencies at all levels of government and between the public and private sectors (Henning and Wilson 1979).

Henning and Wilson concluded that formal planning should be undertaken to design and implement a truly collaborative joint venture in management education.

Ken Henning's professional experience prior to 1970 provided an excellent background for the establishment of the Certified Public Manager concept. He had previously served as Deputy Director, Center for Advanced Study in Organization Science at the University of Wisconsin; Associate Director, Center for Programs in Governmental Administration, University of Chicago; Chairman of the Department of Management, College of Commerce at DePaul University and had extensive consultations in this country and abroad. In each of these settings, he served as an instructor, lecturer, researcher or course designer.

The Vision

During the months of informal brainstorming, Henning also was conducting management development programs for stats agencies. On many of these occasions, he observed that employees had placed certificates for the workshops that they had attended on the walls of their offices. It occurred to him that instead of separate courses whose content varied significantly from one topic to another, it would be better to have an integrated, sequential program. Drawing upon his earlier observations of the Certified Public Accountant credential that Accounting faculty possessed and many students were pursuing, he proposed it as a model for a management credential. The CPA program involved elements of study and preparation, practice and application of learning, examination, and

prestigious recognition (Henning and Wilson 1979). The accounting profession also featured state societies with the American Institute of Certified Public Accountants as a central capstone organization, a concept that would later provide the pattern for the formation of the individual state societies and the American Academy of Certified Public Managers. Henning then discussed his concept with Wilson and he agreed. The two then prepared a detailed proposal of the long-range intentions and broad guidelines of the program leading to the designation of Certified Public Manager (C.P.M.) and presented them to their respective organizations, which endorsed their recommendations.

The long-range intentions of the program were:

- To achieve and subsequently to maintain a level of national recognition for the CPM designation similar to that accorded the Certified Public Accountant (CPA) designation; and
- To foster and encourage the highest possible levels of competence and ethical practice by managers in state and other levels of government through a national body of professionally trained and oriented Certified Public Managers (Henning and Wilson 1979).

Beyond these long-range objectives, the formal planning process delineated seven broad guidelines that were believed to be imperative to successful functioning and therefore needed to be embodied within the administrative and programmatic components of the plan. The following guidelines were published in Henning and Wilson (1979):

First, the management development program should be specifically developed for, and not adapted to, state government. It was the observation of the joint planning group, based on member's personal knowledge and experience, that in-service state programs in many states often were functionally oriented and designed to meet the perceived needs of a single agency. These programs were not, in many instances, focused on the current and developing management requirements of state government as a whole. It also had been observed that a substantial number of university-based management development programs either were modifications of programs originally designed for industry and offered by business school faculty, or off-campus modifications of public administration programs originally designed for graduate students and substantially oriented to federal government management.

Second, the programs of study leading to certification should be officially recognized by the state that should award the certification. The credentialing would not be merely a designation by a university, the state's civil service system, or by another agency of state government.

Third, the program of preparation should be substantially professional in focus rather than largely academic in character and, therefore, complementary to and not competitive with the Master of Public Administration degree.

Fourth, the program should be operated under the active policy guidance and administrative oversight of an officially constituted board with broad, official representation.

Fifth, the course content and subject presentation should challenge candidates with high levels of academic preparation and, simultaneously, be sufficiently reality-oriented and job-related to enable those with relatively limited formal education to satisfy the requirements for certification.

Sixth, the candidate's competence should be tested in rigorous examination so that certification would not be merely a designation for attendance.

Seventh, graduates should be able to continue in an ongoing relationship with the program of study to ensure that their knowledge would be kept abreast of new developments and technologies in the field of administration and their professional competency maintained as a high level.

At that point in time, mid-1975, the Henning-Wilson joint venture planning team, which later became the Curriculum and Standards committee of the Georgia C.P.M. Program, expanded to four members. John Pine, Coordinator of State Government Programs at the Institute of Government and Quinn Spitzer, Merit System Management Development Team Leader, were added as members.

This group was assigned the task of planning the details of integrating the courses offered by the University and the Merit System within the framework of the Certified Public Manager model (Holtz, 2001a).

At the same time, Harold Holtz, Director of the Training Division at the Institute of Government and the Center for Continuing Education and Grady Huddleston, Director of the Merit System's Training Division, began to investigate the degree of support which might be provided by the governor, the University System of Georgia, and the Regional I.P.A. Office of the U. S. Civil Service Commission (Henning and Wilson, 1979)

The Early Program Planning and Development Process

In the early stages of the formal planning process, the planners determined that a truly innovative and rigorous program of study, application of knowledge, examination and certification should be developed and implemented to provide for and recognize professional and educational attainment in the field of public management.

A workgroup was formed that began discussing the marriage of the University courses with the Merit System courses to develop a framework for integrating both programs into a consolidated program with the intent of minimizing duplication and maximizing the efforts of both agencies. The workgroup consisted of two representatives from the Georgia Merit System and two from the University of Georgia. The workgroup included Ken Henning, Senior Management Development Associate in Governmental Training; Doug Wilson, Assistant Division Director; Quinn Spitzer, Management Development Team Leader in the Georgia State Merit System; and John Pine, Coordinator of State Government Training in the Governmental Training Division of the Institute of Government/Georgia Center for Continuing Education, University of Georgia (Holtz 2001a).

Agreements made between the Merit System and the University of Georgia on how the two programs would interact, including dedication of funds granted by the legislature for implementation of the Certified Public Manager Program, assignment of teaching responsibilities, co-sponsoring all training for Georgia Government Employees, including all presentations of Levels I-VI and other arrangements (Huddleston 1974).

Relying heavily on the structure and content of existing courses taught by both organizations, the planners developed a program of six courses that was unique at that time because of the logic that tied them together (Wilson 2002). The arrangements that were made are contained in the Huddleston-Holtz letter dated October 16, 1974 (Huddleston 1974).

The Merit System government management trainers, under the direction of Doug Wilson and Quinn Spitzer, taught the following three-course series.

- Level I Management: Management of the Individual (1 week)
- Level II Management: Management within the State Government Environment (1 week)
- Level III: Management of the Small Group (1 week)

The University of Georgia would teach the following three courses that were made up of elements of existing courses, taught primarily by Ken Henning with occasional involvement from other University instructors:

- Level IV: Management of the Large Organization (2 weeks)
- Level V: Management Systems (1 week)
- Level VI: Management Decision Making and Ethics (2 weeks)

The embryonic Curriculum and Standards Committee also undertook the task of developing a comprehensive and detailed description of the proposed program elements, including admission requirements and application procedure; objectives, sequencing, duration and content of the core course curriculum; course and hour substitution criteria and procedures; the objectives and nature of the application projects; elective course requirements and specification and the specifics of the certification examination requirements and procedures. This planning document became the basis for the CPM brochure subsequently published (Certified Public Manager Program 1976). This committee also proposed that the program, once initiated, should be under the policy direction of a Certified Public Manager Board, and that IPA funding should be sought to assist in the initiation of the program (Henning 1978).

This planning effort was partially funded by a $5,000 grant from Title I of the U. S, Department of Education's Higher Education Act. This grant was among several grants that were eventually used to expand the concept.

After an initial series of meetings, the planning committee undertook the task of drafting a comprehensive and detailed description of the proposed program elements, including admission requirements and application procedure; objectives, sequencing, duration and content of the core course curriculum; course and hour substitution criteria and procedures; the objectives and nature of the application projects; elective course requirements and specifications; and the specifics of the certification examination requirements and procedures. The planning document became the basis for the CPM brochure subsequently published (Certified

Public Manager Program 1976). The planning committee proposed that the program, once initiated, should be under the policy direction of a Certified Public Manager Board, and that IPA funding should be sought to assist in the implication of the program (Henning 1978). The effort was partially funded by a $5,000 grant from Title I of the U. S. Department of Education's Higher Education Act. This grant was among several grants that were eventually used to expand the concept.

Gathering Support for the Concept

Representatives from the Institute of Government and the Merit System undertook a series of meetings with Norman Underwood, the Governor's Executive Secretary, legislative leadership, the Chancellor and the Vice-Chancellor for Services of the University System of Georgia and the state and regional IPA offices to ensure their interest and commitment to this concept (Henning 1978).

Once it was known that the Governor, legislative leadership, the top management of state agencies, the University System of Georgia, and the Regional IPA Office of the U.S. Civil Service Commission were willing to strongly support the initiation of the program, the University of Georgia's Institute of Government and Center for Continuing Education and the Georgia State Merit System of Personnel Administration jointly presented a formal, detailed proposal for initiation of the Georgia Certified Public Manager Program to the Governor and also submitted a formal proposal through the State Merit System to the U.S. Civil Service Commission Regional IPA Office and to the State of Georgia's IPA Review Committee for initial funding support (Henning and Wilson 1979).

The detailed plan was presented to Governor Busbee, who gave his approval to the planners to go ahead with the implementation of the Certified Public Manager Program prior to his request for approval of the program in the January 13, 1976 State of the State address. When the planners received this approval from the Governor, they were told to have graduates in six months. Because the six levels of management development were already in place, the six months were devoted to accomplishing the following (Wilson 2002):

- Developing all the tests for the six levels

- Developing all the projects for each level

- Developing the elective coursework criteria

- Communicating with the graduates of Level VI to see if they were interested in the CPM concept

- Developing and teaching refresher courses for this group

- Testing the graduates

- Designing the CPM certificate

- Conducting the first graduation ceremony

The Official Establishment of the Georgia Certified Public Manager Program

In Governor Busbee's January 13, 1976 State of the State Address to the Joint Session of the Georgia General Assembly, he recommended the establishment of the CPM program as prepared by the University of Georgia-Governmental Training Division and the Merit System and called on the General Assembly to authorize its initiation. Speaking of the CPM Program, the Governor said, "I'm going to ask for your approval of a new program which will begin to strengthen the management function in state government... If we are going to raise the caliber of state government, we must have managers with more professionalism and skill... It will be a professional training program used to develop management skills, and the state government—through the Merit System—will recognize that training and reward it with higher management responsibility..." (Busbee 1976). It is of special note that Fiscal Year 1977 was a year of budgetary austerity in Georgia, and the Certified Public Manager Program was the only new program recommended by Governor Busbee for implementation in that fiscal year (Henning 1978).

On February 9, 1976, in response to the Governor's request, the Georgia House of Representatives passed Resolution Act No. 97 authorizing and directing the State Personnel Board and the State Merit System of Personnel Administration to implement a Certified Public Manager Program in the State Government of Georgia. The Georgia Senate adopted this resolution on February 19, 1976. The Georgia Legislature unanimously passed a joint resolution directing the State Personnel Board to implement the CPM Program as a means of upgrading the capability, efficiency and administrative expertise of management personnel throughout the State government. The resolution was signed on February 26, 1976 (Georgia 1976). On March 1, 1976, the Georgia Merit System for Personnel Administration sent a memorandum to all state training officers announcing the formal establishment of the CPM Program (Henning 1978).

Responding positively to the recommendations of the planning group, the governor agreed to place the joint Institute of Government/Merit System staff of the Certified Public Manager Program under the policy guidance and administrative oversight of a six-member official board. Membership on the board included the governor's Executive Secretary, Vice Chancellor for Services of the University System of Georgia, the Director of the Training and Staff Development Division of the Georgia State Merit System, the Administrator of Governmental Training of the Institute of Government of the University of Georgia, a Commissioner representative of the executive branch agencies of state government, and the Director of the Certified Public Manager Program, ex officio. The Assistant Director of the Training and Staff Development Division of the State Merit System was designated Secretary of the Board and Associate Director of the CPM Program.

Observations by Mr. Henning

From the perspective of nearly thirty years later, Mr. Henning shares some thoughts on why and how the Georgia CPM Program moved smoothly from an idea to a fully functioning professional management development program.

Management Commentary by Mr. Henning

This effort involved the on-going collaboration of two organizations, the cooperation of the executive and legislative branches of Georgia State Government, and the participation of all agencies of Georgia State government.

The first leg of this journey was accomplished successfully largely as a result of two factors. First, we did comprehensive, detailed strategic and operational planning. Specifically,

- We did comprehensive environmental screening. Fortunately, I had been the moderator in executive development seminars at the University of Wisconsin in which programs the focus was innovation and change. I was able to hear presentations by distinguished scholars in areas related to change and had gathered their research findings into a paper titled *The Changing Managerial Environment*. These materials became the first day of the Level IV classes that preceded the CPM Level IV. This simplified our task somewhat.
- We *anticipated* the impacts of rapid change on our state, our state government, our managers, and on managerial development.
- We had a *vision*
- We specified our *values*
- We established *objectives* and then *goals*
- And we divided these goals into *tasks* to be accomplished.

This was no more than utilizing the elements of strategic planning that I had learned in the course of my management education and subsequently taught in my classes.

Second, we organized our efforts in planning for and subsequently in managing the C.P.M. Program through what I have called the "expert/team" model. This approach was, for me, the result of observations I made while serving as a navigator on a B-24 bomber in World War II.

On combat missions, I had observed that while there was an officer-enlisted distinction and though the pilot was the officer in charge, real authority shifted while in the air. The pilot was in charge during taxi out and take-off; the navigator was in charge enroute to the target; the bombardier was in charge on the bombing run; the engineer was in charge during fuel transfer, and so on. This was more than authority. It was an actual shift in authority based on expertise.

Also, I thought that having formal establishment under gubernatorial and legislative authority and a broadly representative board would provide stability for the program should key members be lost or replaced.

The Formation of the Georgia Society of Certified Public Managers

The minutes of the Georgia Certified Public Manager Program meeting on February 7, 1977, show that Mr. Henning challenged the group to elect a temporary chairman, a temporary secretary, and to become involved in the idea of "establishing a Georgia Society of Certified Public Managers affiliated with a national organization to be known as the American Academy of Certified Public Managers" (Wilson and Kraft 1977).

After the first graduation, the planning group formed the Georgia Society of Certified Public Managers, which was incorporated in the State of Georgia on June 20, 1977. The Articles of Incorporation were submitted with a letter signed by Kenneth K. Henning as Incorporator. The Society played a vital role as the alumni association for the graduates of the program (Henning 1977). The Georgia Society of Certified Public Managers held its first meeting in Atlanta, GA., on September 29, 1977 (Weiskittel 1977).

Management Commentary by Mr. Henning

The Georgia Society did an excellent job of organizing itself. Officers were elected and a Board of Directors was established. The Director of the Georgia C.P.M. Program was assigned an ex officio seat on the Board. Both the Society and I thought this would facilitate communication between the Society and the Program.

The Society also erected a number of committees to better distribute the work that the Society would be doing. These committees included Continuing Membership and Ethical Practice, Candidate Advisory, Marketing/Publications, Ways and Means, Society Archives, By-Laws and Awards.

In addition, the Society worked with the Internal Revenue Service to establish a not-for-profit Educational Foundation to conduct seminars and to accomplish some long-range professional intentions.

The Society also established a membership publication *Management Update* to keep members informed about the Society and developments regarding the C.P.M. program and its expansion; and to provide a vehicle for the publication of management articles by members, Program faculty, State government officials and others.

A major contribution that the Society made to the C.P.M. concept was the work on the American Academy noted later in this paper.

The Initial Expansion of the CPM Concept

The transfer of the concept to the initial states was a direct result of the combined work of Henning, Wilson, Spitzer, Huddleston and Holtz.

In 1978, Ken Henning prepared a grant proposal for the expansion of the concept. The proposal was titled "A Proposal to Develop a Transfer Process and Implementation Plan for the Effective Transfer of the Georgia Certified Public Manager Program to Other State Jurisdictions" (Henning 1978). The acceptance of this plan by the U. S. Civil Service Commission led to a three-year $132,000 implementation grant (Weiskittel 1978). Early in 1979, this grant, provided through the U. S. Civil Service Commission's Intergovernmental Personnel Act, funded the exploration with other states to assess interest in the concept and the national transfer of the program (Beckman 1978). This included inviting trainers from interested states to visit Georgia to become familiar with the Georgia CPM program.

The IPA funding allowed for the participation of five states in the transfer implementation. The five states that indicated an interest in the program and appeared to have the necessary training capability and top-level executive and legislative support to initiate and sustain the implementation of a CPM program were Arizona, Florida, Kansas, North Carolina, and Vermont. Subsequent to the awarding of the grant, the state of Louisiana indicated a desire to collaborate with Georgia and the five transfer states, even though not included in the grant funding. Kansas was not able to participate at that time (Henning1979).

Following a preliminary meeting of CPM planners and NTDS staff in Washington in early April 1979, an initial multistate planning meeting was held in Atlanta on April 19, 1979. At this meeting, a tentative date was set for conducting a demonstration session of Level I for administrators and trainers from the collaborating states. This demonstration was conducted in Atlanta, during the week of June 18, 1979, with a second session scheduled for Atlanta during the week of October 22, 1979 (Henning 1979).

The states selected for the initial expansion of the concept had to meet many requirements, but the most important one was the personal commitment of the states' governors (Holtz 2001b). After considerable discussion, the planning group agreed on initial requirements that included:

- 240 hours of management development courses
- 60 hours of elective courses
- 6 management-related projects
- Testing to cover the material
- Ongoing re-certification education to maintain the CPM designation

Though the University of Georgia and other universities were concerned that the Certified Public Manager would compete with the Masters in Public Administration, the process of expansion continued. This concern remained for years and was discussed by Conant and Housel (1995).

The Formation of the National Certified Public Manager Consortium

In June 1979, a meeting was held in Atlanta where the initial work of drafting the Constitution and By-laws of the National Certified Public Manager Consortium (Consortium) began. While there was no actual formalization of the Consortium at this meeting, the groundwork was laid for later formative meetings and the work of setting the standards and orienting the state's trainers with the program of instruction proceeded.

Subsequent to the meeting in June 1979, other meetings were held regularly in Georgia and the states to orient the state program instructors from Arizona, Florida, Georgia, Louisiana, North Carolina, and Vermont with course content. Representatives from each member state program traveled regularly to Georgia for these training programs to become familiar with the course materials through Level V.

The completed Constitution of the Consortium was signed by 10 individuals from member programs at a meeting in Raleigh, N.C., on July 9, 1980 (Consortium 1980).

On October 6, 1980, the Certified Public Manager National Policy Board met for the first time in Washington, D.C. and ratified the Constitution of the Consortium (Wilson 1980). The meeting was held to illustrate to Washington supporters how far the Consortium had come with the help of the grant and to explore future funding opportunities for the Consortium. Indeed, the grant support provided by the Carter Administration (1977–1981) played an integral role in the formation of the Consortium. Dr. Howard Jordan, Vice-Chancellor for Services for the Board of Regents of the University System of Georgia and Chairman of the Georgia Certified Public Manager Board was elected as the first chairman of the Program Administration Committee (Wilson, 1980).

The National Certified Public Manager Consortium was formed with the participation of six CPM states: Arizona, Florida, Georgia, Louisiana, North Carolina, and Vermont. Its purpose was to establish and preserve standards for the Certified Public Manager (CPM) designation. Specifically, the Consortium was to promote state CPM programs by providing and monitoring accreditation standards, facilitating program development, encouraging innovation and developing linkages with programs and organizations having similar concerns (Hays and Duke 1996).

The Consortium was formed to provide a framework within which each program should operate, not to dictate curriculum or administrative specifics for each Certified Public Manager program. The Consortium would establish standards by which CPM programs were to be reviewed, including administrative and program design requirements, a demonstration of adequate funding and governing structure to support the program, and a demonstration that each program would provide opportunities for participants to apply the training to their work environment. At the present time, twenty-eight colleges and universities are affiliated with the Consortium.

Management Commentary by Mr. Henning

The early days of the Consortium were difficult ones for Doug Wilson and me. For the first time, we were undertaking a fusion of an existing state program with varied states training and development organizations, and colleges and universities.

One of the definitions of "consort" is ". . . to come into accord." At first, we served an undercurrent of 'Georgia is trying to sell its product,' and more than once I felt apprehensive about our ability to achieve cohesion.

Complicating interaction was some turnover of representatives from some states. But as we proceeded, trust and genuine affection developed. Subsequent discussions were quite often vigorous but nearly always collaborative and the action agreed upon turned out to be sound.

The Formation of the American Academy of Certified Public Managers

In anticipation of the reality of a large number of graduates from several formally accredited CPM programs, the Georgia Society proceeded with the establishment of the American Academy of Certified Public Managers in 1984 (Henning 1984b). One of the highlights of the year was the reservation of the name for the American Academy of Certified Public Managers with the Georgia Secretary of State's Office on March 2, 1984 (Cleland 1984).

Ken Henning and Glen Williamson drafted the first version of the Constitution and By-laws, which was accepted in principle, by the Consortium's Executive Committee in September of 1983 in Oklahoma City. Following that meeting, the draft was provided to the American Academy Initiation Committee, a committee of the Georgia Society of Certified Public Managers. The product of this committee was used in the incorporation of the Academy (Askew 1984).

On May 7, 1984, the Articles of Incorporation, accompanied by a letter from Ken Henning, was mailed to the Georgia Secretary of State Max Cleland, resulting in the incorporation of the Academy as a not-for-profit professional society in the State of Georgia with an incorporation date of May 8, 1984 (Henning 1984a). Incorporation of the Academy was undertaken to reserve the name and provide an organizing mechanism to establish it. (Williamson 2003).

The American Academy of Certified Public Managers (AACPM) was established in Georgia as a professional association of public sector managers who had earned the designation of Certified Public Manager (CPM) through a management program accredited by the National Certified Public Manager Consortium and were members of an accredited state society of Certified Public Managers (Laubsch 1988a).

The Academy was established to:

- Unite Certified Public Managers
- Encourage the acceptance of management in government as a profession established upon an underlying body of knowledge
- Promote a high professional, educational, and ethical standard in public management
- Improve communication, cooperation, and coordination among public entities
- Foster leadership through example and innovation
- Facilitate positive changes to enhance the delivery of public services

After incorporation of the Academy and designation of graduates by the accredited state programs, the work of organizing the Academy became the responsibility of the graduates. On August 2–5, 1987, AACPM representatives from Florida, Georgia, Louisiana, and New Jersey met in Tallahassee, Florida, in conjunction with the Consortium to form the framework for a national society. The Academy Constitution, Bylaws, Mission Statement, Vision, Goals, Objectives, as well as the majority of the Academy's business processes, were products of that meeting. In 1988, all five states ratified the document that became, and remains, the basis for the operations of the Academy (Laubsch 1988b). At the February 4, 1989 House of Delegates Meeting, the Bylaws were adopted (Laubsch 1989).

The Henning Award

In 1990, the Academy authorized the Henning Trophy, in honor of Kenneth K. Henning, the former Director of the Georgia Certified Public Manager Program and "Father" of the Certified Public Manager concept. This recognition has been presented annually to an active Academy member who, through his or her efforts, had made the greatest contribution to the Academy, his or her state Society, or the prestige of the CPM image (Askew 1990).

The Fran L. Wilkinson Scholarship

On April 30, 1993, members of the House of Delegates unanimously voted to designate the Academy's existing annual scholarship as the Fran L. Wilkinson Memorial Scholarship as a token of remembrance, affection, and esteem for her involvement at the state and national level, in both graduate and Consortium capacities. This scholarship was developed in support of one of the objectives of the American Academy of Certified Public Managers—*"to promote a high professional, educational and ethical standard in public management"* (Norman 1993). Fran Wilkinson was instructor in the Training Division of Georgia's Merit System. She became the Management Team Leader when Quinn Spitzer left the Merit System to become a management consultant, and assumed Doug Wilson's position as Director of the Training Division when he left the Merit System. She passed away suddenly.

The George C. Askew Award

At the November 9, 1996, Board of Directors Meeting, the Board authorized the presentation of up to three awards per year to recognize exemplary CPM projects (Hagler 1996). At the May 17, 1997 HOD Meeting in Utah, the Board was directed to work with the Consortium, to develop a special award program in honor of George C. Askew, the "first" CPM, because of his unwavering commitment to exceptional management practices. The Management Practices Committee was charged with defining nomination criteria for the Askew Award, with the expectation that the first awards would be presented at the 1998 AACPM Conference in Mississippi. The criteria established that the award be given to one participant (or team) from each Consortium member's state training program. It was to be selected from projects reviewed from the prior year that exemplified the management practices philosophy of the Academy. The Askew Awards are presented annually at the Academy educational conferences (Gough 1997).

The Past and the Future

This history describes the development of the Certified Public Manager Concept from its earliest vision through program development and implementation resulting in its expansion to twenty-five state or regional Certified Public Manager Programs as of December 31, 2002. Throughout the history of the Certified Public Manager concept, it has been described as a relatively recent program (Finkle 1985).

In 1996, S. W. Hays and Bruce Duke commented that the accomplishments of the Program had surpassed anything that might reasonably have been expected when the first CPM program was initiated in 1979 (Hays and Duke 1996). They went further to comment that the spread of the CPM program to the number of states that had developed formal certification programs in an environment that lacked conditions for vibrant growth was truly remarkable.

Despite obstacles described in various articles about the CPM (Conant and Housel 1995; Finkle 1985; Hays and Duke 1996), the programs accredited by the Consortium and their graduates continue to increase in number. According to Conant and Lado in 1991, the factors contributing to the creation of CPM programs include a desire to fill important gaps in public sector training, to provide an incentive for continuing education, to "officially certify a manager's competence," and to improve management practice through targeted employee development activities (Hays and Duke 1996). The current budget-challenged management environment of doing more with less, improving the efficiency, effectiveness and competence of today's government managers makes these early factors even more viable.

From the beginnings of the National Certified Public Manager Consortium in 1979, it has grown to include twenty-six state or territorial programs, including the USDA. The Consortium's continued promotion of the program is vital to maintenance and expansion of the concept.

From its 1984 incorporation as the alumni association of CPMs, the American Academy of Certified Public Managers has grown to include 20 separate Certified Public Manager Societies in 20 states. In late 2002, CPM Program graduates from three additional states are developing applications for membership as Certified Public Manager Societies. The Iowa graduates predict their application will be completed by June of 2003. In addition, as of this writing, the possibility of membership by certain tribal nations is being discussed. The CPM Societies, including the American Academy of Certified Public Managers and member Societies, were described as a potentially powerful force for change in the public management field, if they follow the lead of other professional societies by lobbying for gradual strengthening of certification requirements and formal recognition of CPM recipients (Hays and Duke 1996).

The future of the Certified Public Manager is directly dependent on the CPM certification earning public manager's respect by distinguishing itself as a true achievement and being perceived as a prestigious accomplishment that is worthy of recognition and reward (Hays and Duke 1996). The following quote from an unknown source can be used to tell the story of this journey: "An organization succeeds, not because it is long-established, but because there are people in it who live it, sleep it, dream it, and build future plans for it." The authors wholeheartedly agree.

References

Askew, G.C. (1984) "American Academy Initiation Committee Report." *Georgia Society of Certified Public Managers* (23 April 1984) Gainesville, GA.1–5.

Askew, G.C. (1990) Henning Trophy: Board of Elections Committee Report, *American Academy of Certified Public Managers* (29 March 1990) 1.

Barnard, C. I. (1948) *The Functions of the Executive.* Cambridge, Mass.: Harvard University Press, 1948.

Beckman, Norman (1978) to G. W. Watt. Bureau of Intergovernmental Personnel Programs (1 June 1978) 1–2.

Busbee, George (1976) "State of the State Address to the Georgia General Assembly by Governor George Busbee." *Journal of the Georgia House of Representatives* (13 January 1976) 36–41.

Certified Public Manager Program (1976) "Certified Public Manager". *Georgia State Merit System of Personnel Administration* (1976) 1–36.

Chapman, Richard L. and Frederic N. Cleaveland (1973). "The Changing Character of the Public Service and the Administrator of the 1980's." *Public Administration Review* (July/August) 358–366.

Cleland, Max (1984). Receipt for Name Reservation for American Academy of Certified Public Managers. *Secretary of State: Corporations Division.* Atlanta (2 March 1984) 1.

Conant, James K. and S. Housel (1995) "MPA and CPM Programs: Competitors or complements in Public Service Management Education." *Public Personnel Administration* (Fall 1995) 5–21.

Consortium (1980) "Constitution". National Certified Public Manager Program Consortium (6 October 1980) 1–4.

Finkle, Arthur (1985) "CPM-Professionalizing Professionalism" *Public Administration Quarterly.* Vol. 9 (Spring) 47–54.

Georgia (1976) Resolution Act Number 97. House Resolution 537–1462 (1976). Georgia House of Representatives (26 February 1976) 1–5.

Georgia Merit System of Personnel Administration (1975) "Management Development for State Government Officials" (Atlanta) 1–9.

Gough, Brian (1997) Minutes of House of Delegates Meeting. *American Academy of Certified Public Managers* (17 May 1997) 1–9.

Hagler, Patricia J. (1996) Minutes of House of Delegates Meeting. *American Academy of Certified Public Managers* (9 November 1996) 1–12.

Hays, S. W. and Bruce Duke (1996) "Professional Certification in Public Management: A Status Report and Proposal." *Public Administration Review.* Vol. 56, no. 5 (September/October 1996) 425–432.

Henning, Kenneth K. (1977). Articles of Incorporation: *Georgia Society of Certified Public Managers.* Atlanta (20 June 1977) 1–5.

Henning, Kenneth K. (1978). "A Proposal to Develop a Transfer Process and Implementation Plan for the Effective Transfer of the Georgia Certified Public Manager Program to Other State Jurisdictions." University of Georgia. Athens (23 March 1978) 1–22.

Henning, Kenneth K (1979). "National Extension of the CPM Program." *Georgia Society of Certified Public Managers*. Vol.1 No.1. Athens (October 1979) 3.

Henning, Kenneth K (1984a). Articles of Incorporation: *American Academy of Certified Public Managers*. Atlanta (7 May 1984) 1–20.

Henning, Kenneth K (1984b). "The American Academy." Management Update. *Georgia Society of Certified Public Managers*. Athens (September, 1984) 1–2.

Henning, Kenneth K. and L. Douglas Wilson (1979). "The Georgia Certified Public Manager (CPM) Program." *SRPA* (March 1979) 424–435.

Holtz, Harold F. (2001a) to T.H. Patterson. Transcript in the hand of Thomas Patterson. Historical Documents. *American Academy of Certified Public Managers* (4 Sept 01) 1–2.

Holtz, Harold F. (2001b) to T.H. Patterson. Undated transcript in the hand of Thomas Patterson. Historical Documents. *American Academy of Certified Public Managers* (15 Nov 01) 1–2.

Huddleston, Grady L. (1974) to Harold F. Holtz. *Georgia Merit System for Personnel Administration* (16 October 1974) 1–2.

Laubsch, Paulette (1988a) Minutes of House of Delegates Meeting. *American Academy of Certified Public Managers* (1 October 1988) 1–4.

Laubsch, Paulette (1989) Minutes of House of Delegates Meeting. *American Academy of Certified Public Managers* (4 February 1989) 1–34.

Norman, S.M. (1993) Minutes of House of Delegates Meeting. *American Academy of Certified Public Managers* (30 April 1993) 1–12.

Weiskittel, Richard. (1977) Meeting Minutes. *Georgia Society of Certified Public Managers*. Atlanta. (29 September 1977) 1–4.

Weiskittel, Richard. (1978) Minutes of Board of Directors Meeting *Georgia Society of Certified Public Managers*. Atlanta. (4 August 1978) 1–3.

Williamson, Glen (2003) to T.H. Patterson. Personal communication in the hand of Thomas Patterson. Historical Documents. *American Academy of Certified Public Managers* (24 January 2003) 1.

Wilson, L. Douglas (1980). "CPM Program Associate States Report." Management Update. *Georgia Society of Certified Public Managers*. Vol. 2 Number 1. Athens (October 1980) 1–2.

Wilson, L. Douglas (2002) to T.H. Patterson. Personal communication in the hand of Thomas Patterson. Historical Documents. *American Academy of Certified Public Managers* (10 Dec 02) 1–3.

Wilson, L. Douglas and E. Kraft (1977) Minutes of Certified Public Manager Society Meeting. *Center for Continuing Education: University of Georgia* (7 February 1977) 1–3.

From *Public Administration Quarterly*, Vol.28, Number 2, Fall 2004, pp. 255–283. Copyright © 2004 by Southern Public Administration Education Foundation, Inc. Reprinted by permission.

GovBenefits.gov: A Valuable E-Government Tool for Citizens

Learn how this interactive government Web site—launched in 2002 and managed by the U.S. Department of Labor in partnership with a network of federal and state agencies—lets people immediately determine their eligibility for the benefit programs that best meet their needs.

PATRICK PIZZELLA

As a government official, caseworker, or representative, how can I help American citizens learn about the government benefit programs they need without making them navigate through hundreds of Web pages?

The answer to this question, on the mind of those who want to fulfill their public service, is a one-stop Web site called GovBenefits.gov (www.govbenefits.gov). It is the official one-stop benefits Web site of the U.S. government and includes over 400 federal benefit programs and some 600 benefit programs from all fifty states.

In three years, GovBenefits.gov has referred more than three million citizens—veterans, college students, new citizens, and parents—to benefit programs that meet their needs.

GovBenefits.gov, which recently celebrated its third anniversary, is managed by the U.S. Department of Labor, in partnership with the U.S. Departments of Agriculture, Education, Energy, Health and Human Services, Housing and Urban Development, State, Veterans Affairs, and Homeland Security, and the Social Security Administration. It is part of President George W. Bush's E-Government Strategy to make it easier for citizens and businesses to interact with and obtain information from the government, save taxpayer dollars, and streamline citizen-to-government communications.

Before the GovBenefits.gov launch in April 2002, federal benefit information was spread across thirty-one million Web pages on hundreds of sites. Today, over 300,000 visitors a month discover the value of the site. In three years, GovBenefits.gov has referred more than three million citizens—veterans, college students, new citizens, and parents—to benefit programs that meet their needs. As of April 2005, more than seventeen million people have visited the site.

GovBenefits.gov is an efficient tool for helping citizens find and access government benefit programs for which they may be eligible. The site's powerful search and screening tools allow users to find benefit programs that suit their needs in less than six minutes. Its eligibility prescreening tool provides users with a higher success rate in receiving benefits when they apply and reduces the burden on agency call centers and staff time dedicated to processing ineligible applications.

Getting Online

So how does the site work? It's simple:

Get online. Open your Internet browser.

Type **www.govbenefits.gov** into your address bar or search engine.

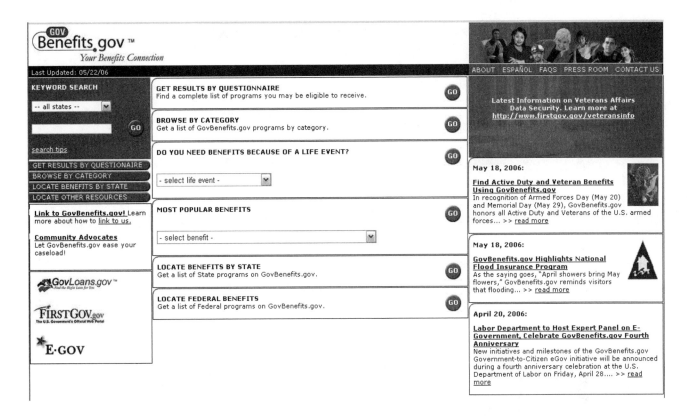

Press **Enter,** and the GovBenefits.gov home page is displayed.

There are many different ways to search for benefits on GovBenefits.gov—by keyword, benefit category, specific state, life event, or answering questions on a confidential questionnaire.

Searching by Keyword

Select the state from which you want to search for benefits from the drop-down list. You may also select to search among **all states**.

Enter the keyword for the type of benefit you want to find or that describes your circumstance, such as **veteran** or **senior**, and then click **GO**. A list of benefit programs displays that relate to the keyword and state, or states, entered.

Searching by Questionnaire

To get a list of benefit programs tailored to your constituent's particular needs, you may select the "Get Results By Questionnaire" option, also located on the home page. All answers are completely confidential and no identifying information is ever stored.

Open the www.govbenefits.gov homepage. Select **GET RESULTS BY QUESTIONNAIRE**. A list of questions displays.

At any point during the questionnaire, you can stop and view the applicable benefit programs based on the answers you have already given. When you have completed the questionnaire, or elected to **stop and view results**, a list of benefit programs for which you may be eligible is displayed.

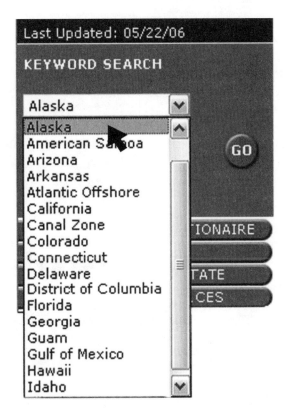

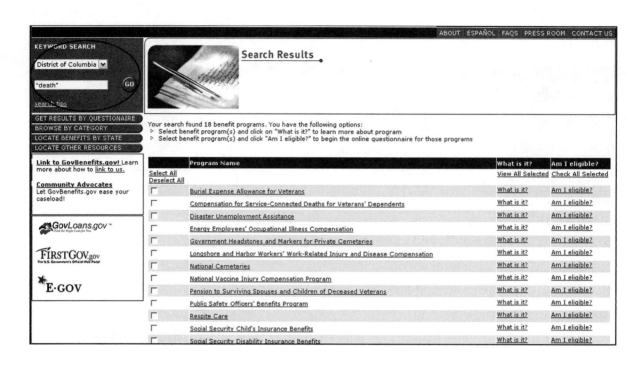

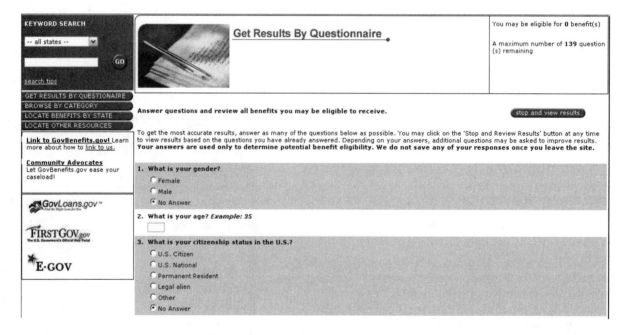

Program Name

Grants for Public Works and Economic Development Facilities

Eligibility criteria
In order to qualify for this benefit program, you must characterize your financial situation as low income or very low income , or you must be under-employed (work for very low wages), unemployed or about to become unemployed.

Description
The Public Works and Economic Development Program supports locally-developed projects that encourage long-term economic self-sufficiency and global competitiveness. The program empowers distressed communities in economic decline to revitalize, expand, and upgrade their physical infrastructure to attract new industry, encourage business expansion, diversify local economies, and generate or retain long-term, private sector jobs and investment.

Managing Organization
U.S. Department of Commerce
http://www.doc.gov/

Program contact information & web resources
For more information please visit:
http://www.eda.gov

For contact information and field offices visit:
http://www.eda.gov/InvestmentsGrants/FFON.xml

To get more information about a particular benefit program, just click it. A program description displays, along with eligibility and corresponding agency contact information.

Comprehensive Utility

GovBenefits.gov is a valuable resource for all American people. The site, available in English and Spanish, includes information on a variety of benefit and assistance programs for veterans, seniors, students, teachers, children, people with disabilities, dependents, disaster victims, farmers, caregivers, job seekers, prospective homeowners—practically something for everyone. Encourage your constituents to visit this site regularly, particularly when life events occur—such as applying for college, seeking food or nutrition services, sustaining property damaged by a storm, retirement, or starting a business—that could make them eligible for assistance programs.

GovBenefits.gov and Customized Connections

During the site's third anniversary event, U.S. Deputy Secretary of Labor Steven J. Law unveiled a revolutionary concept called GovBenefits.gov Customized Connections. This new initiative enables federal agencies and state governments to use GovBenefits.gov eligibility screening and search functionality from their Web sites while retaining their Web site design and brand. Customized Connections offers an Office of Management and Budget-endorsed solution to eliminate redundant information technology investments, save costs, and make better use of taxpayer dollars.

This revolutionary approach to reuse this functionality was leveraged to successfully create and launch the GovLoans.gov Web site (www.GovLoans.gov) in April 2004. GovLoans.gov, a Web site that features a variety of federal loan programs, was developed in partnership with the U.S. Department of Education and reuses the GovBenefits.gov architecture to provide a consolidated source for federal loan information. The Customized Connections approach was developed from industry best practices similar to toolbars made available by sites such as Amazon.com and Google.

GovBenefits.gov is a leading example of the way government services can—and should—be delivered to citizens in the twenty-first century. With Customized Connections, GovBenefits.gov raises the bar for true intergovernmental collaboration by allowing government to integrate efforts and eliminate redundancy. In addition, GovBenefits.gov illustrates effective use of taxpayer dollars by redefining and expanding the American public's access to information about eligibility for government benefit programs. Thanks to GovBenefits.gov, citizens have a comprehensive connection to benefits that can improve their quality of life and can easily search the universe of benefit programs available to them.

Please visit www.GovBenefits.gov today to help citizens or your own loved ones find out which benefit or assistance programs they may be eligible to receive. To request additional information, brochures, or placement on the GovBenefits.gov Connection newsletter mailing list, contact the GovBenefits.gov team at 202-693-4219 or e-mail GovBenefits@dol.gov.

PATRICK PIZZELLA is the Assistant Secretary of Labor for Administration and Management and serves as the chief information officer and chief human capital officer.

Governance and Risk Management: Challenges and Public Productivity

Purpose—This paper has two purposes. The first is to help elected officials address the issue of public accountability for crises and improve productivity and risk management in the process by outsourcing some traditional government functions to civil society based organizations that can do a better job. The second is to mobilize researchers to explore the implications of the shift from "governing" to "governance" for risk management and the development of risk culture.

Design/methodology/approach—After exploring some case studies, the paper examines some leading resources on the shift from "governing" to "governance". The paper goes on to present an alternative approach for managing public risks.

Findings—In order to improve the management of public risks, and given the financial constraints faced by most governments, there is a need for a deliberate effort to entice civil society based organizations to help government identify and alert the public to possible risks. In other words, civil society based organizations that make claims for public resources in the name of good governance should, as necessary, play the role of a watchdog when it comes to public safety and guarding of the public interest in that regard.

Practical implications—Use of market forces and non-governmental entities to replace government agencies and regulations that cannot assure the public safety because they are difficult to implement, expensive or likely to be compromised due to various forms of corruption and politics.

Originality/value—The paper advocates substitution of "management by exception" by a "management by risk" approach and the fostering of an administrative culture that is more mindful of the need to recognize and address possible risks. Such an approach, the paper claims, is a more promising approach than an increase in government regulation.

ARIE HALACHMI

Zhongshan University, Zhongshan, China and Tennessee State University, Nashville, Tennessee, USA

At approximately 4.00 pm EDT on Thursday August 14, 2003, a series of unexpected and undesired events began unfolding. At the end of it, a domino effect produced the largest electric system failure in history. Approximately 50 million consumers in the Northeast and parts of the Mid-West in the USA and Canada experienced a blackout when the interconnected electric grid of Eastern North America collapsed (Synapse, 2003). According to a CBS TV news report that evening:

> The blackouts affected a broad swath of the Northeast stretching west to Ohio and Michigan and into southern Canada, starting shortly after 4 pm EDT. In Toronto, Canada's largest city, workers fled their buildings when the power went off. There also were widespread outages in Ottawa, the capital.

> Nine nuclear power reactors—six in New York and one each in New Jersey, Ohio and Michigan—were shut down because of the loss of offsite power, according to the Nuclear Regulatory Commission in Bethesda, MD.

Flights in and out of JFK Airport in New York, as well as airports in Toronto and Ottawa were grounded, leaving passengers stranded. Flights also were halted for more than three hours in and out of New York LaGuardia, Cleveland and Newark, NJ, but those airports reopened before 8 pm EDT.

The blackout closed the Detroit-Windsor Tunnel, which 27,000 vehicles use daily, and silenced the gambling machines at Detroit's Greektown Casino. Patrons filed into the afternoon heat carrying cups of tokens.

Traffic lights were out throughout downtown Cleveland and other major cities, creating havoc at the beginning of rush hour. Cleveland officials said that without the power needed to pump water to 1.5 million people, water reserves were running low.

Gov. Pataki said more than half of New York State was without power. He said there were supposed to be backup systems to prevent blackouts from snowballing, and that "there have to be some tough questions asked."

In New York City, subways and elevators lost electricity or resorted to limited backup power. Thousands of people streamed into the streets of lower Manhattan in 90-degree heat, and some subway commuters were still stuck underground hours after the blackout hit.

Amtrak suspended passenger rail service between New Haven, Conn., and Newark. Some northbound trains from Washington, a city that did not lose power, turned around at Newark.

There were outages in northern New Jersey and in several Vermont towns. Lights flickered at state government buildings in Hartford, Conn. (CBS, 2003).

On August 15, 2003, at a news conference in Moscow, Anatoly Chubais, the former Deputy Prime Minister and now Head of the Russian Federation energy monopoly, pointed to a "principle difference" between the US and Russian energy systems. In particular, he noted, the Russian system is highly centralized and the ties between its parts are firmer (*Pravda*, 2003).

Central to any discussion of what took place on August 14, 2003, is the role of the North American Electric Reliability Council (NERC), a non-governmental (NGO) not-for-profit organization. The American and Canadian governments allowed the evolution of NERC, a decentralized, fragmented and self-regulated alliance of electric utility companies (both public and private), precisely in order to prevent such an occurrence from taking place.

NERC was formed by the "industry" after the Northeast blackout in 1965. Its mission (Gent, 2003a) is to ensure that the bulk electric system in North America is reliable, adequate, and secure. NERC works with all segments of the electric industry as well as electricity consumers and regulators to set and encourage compliance with rules for the planning and operation of reliable electric systems. NERC is an independent organization, governed by a board of ten independent trustees. In the words of Gent, NERC's CEO, "[W]e bring together the best electrical system technical expertise available in the world. We are also an international organization, integrating electric system reliability across North America's electricity grids" (Gent, 2003a).

Since the inception of NERC in 1968, compliance with its reliability standards has been voluntary (Gent, 2003b). While NERC monitors the utilities for compliance with certain operating and planning standards, it has no means to enforce compliance with those standards. Indeed, the Interim Report (2003) on the possible causes of the "greatest blackout in history" (*Pravda*, 2003) suggests that violation of NERC's reliability standards (Interim Report, 2003, pp. 22, 29) by a utility company in Ohio and a regional coordinating NGO started the unfortunate domino effect that resulted in this massive power outage. As would have to be concluded after reading this paper, "governance", in the case of the "greatest Blackout in History" failed to replace "governing". The term "governance", as will be explained below, refers to the results of the interactions within a decentralized structure of governmental and non-governmental elements of civil society under non-binding arrangements. The term "governing" refers to the outcomes of activities within a centralized structure with sole government control. The

difference between the two arrangements was highlighted by the observation of Anatoly Chubais about the differences between the management of the two power-grids as cited above.

Given the early findings of the Interim Report (2003), it seems that Adam Smith's (1776) "hidden hand" in this particular market has failed to produce the desired results and may have to be replaced by the old-fashioned long hand of government, as suggested by Anatoly Chubais, if service is to be reliable. Rules of supply and demand and voluntary cooperation among various players, which are part of what we now refer to as "governance", seem to have failed on August 14, 2003.

Without the benefits of additional discussion, this unfortunate case may suggest that governments should increase their regulatory involvement if they are to live up to their basic responsibility of assuring safety and basic services. The problem is that from an economic (i.e. efficiency) point of view, government regulations have negative effects when it comes to productivity due to the resulting increase of the cost of production. However, in the case of utilities, as in many other cases, the loss of productivity due to the higher cost of production cannot assure better reliability. It is possible to think about several reasons for this state of affairs. For example, no government has the resources or the capacity to enforce genuine compliance not only with the letter of the law but with its spirit. That means that compliance cannot be assumed to be 100 percent under any circumstances. Another possible reason is that the body of regulations in most cases is less than optimal due to the compromises that result from political dynamics inside and outside government agencies that are entrusted to write and enforce various regulations. Without such compromises the feasibility of any regulatory effort is questionable. In short, assuring service or lower risk through regulatory action is sure to reduce efficiency but cannot ascertain the desired results.

As viewed by this writer, the great blackout of August 14, 2003 is just one case that illustrates the importance of questions about the relationship between governance, risk management, accountability and public productivity. Even lack of direct governmental involvement, as illustrated by this case does not absolve government, as an "institution" in the sociological sense, from its responsibility to protect the public. Elected officials are going to be held accountable on election day every time something goes wrong because of the common belief that it is their job to be ready for, if not to prevent, any threat to life or property. For that reason, this paper argues, it behooves elected officials and government agencies to make a deliberate effort to manage the risks that may threaten life or property in their respective areas of operations. This reality was not overlooked by the US Congress in the rush to organize (in September 2003), within less than a month of the blackout, formal hearings in the House and in the Senate to investigate what took place and how to prevent it in the future. However, such an effort to re-establish the traditional roles of the government bureaucracy due to the failure of markets and networks (Rhodes, 1996) is problematic for three reasons. First, it is counter-intuitive to the current exhilaration with the concept of "governance" as a way of overcoming structural, legal, and administrative limitations (Halachmi, 2003a). Second, the added regulatory cost increases the cost of producing goods and services, resulting in lower productivity. Third, for a variety of reasons, the certainty of the regulatory cost does not assure the quality or dependability of any critical service. As illustrated time and again in various countries around the world (e.g. Canada, France, Japan, India, or Australia) blood tainted with AIDS was distributed in spite of government regulations to prevent it. The reason in all these cases was greed and politics (Picard, 2002; Pollard, 2003; BBC, 1999, 2001; *British Medical Journal*, 1995; Mizoguchi, 2000). This underscores the need to find ways to reduce risks to the public by more reliable means than government regulations.

The paper starts with a brief review of some current writings about the concept of "governance" and the alleged paradigm shift (Adshead and Quinn, 1998; Halachmi, 2003a) from "governing" to "governance". It goes on to discuss briefly the renewed interest in risk management in the public sector in general and following the events of September 11, 2001 in particular. This serves as a reminder that the traditional roles and reason for government have to do with protection of life and property. The paper concludes by pointing out that since elected officials are likely to be held responsible whenever something goes wrong, they need to pay more attention to risk management. To help them address this issue, the paper suggests that government adopt a two-pronged approach, on the one hand fostering a culture of risk management, and on the other hand, the government should be encouraging elements of the civil society and the market to serve as watchdogs and as a catalyst to induce public and private organizations to develop plans for risk management. Such an approach, the paper claims, is more promising than an increase in government regulation for three reasons:

1. it would not add to the current cost of government operations as would be the case if new regulations were issued to address the management of risk;
2. the overhead for the production of services is not increased due to the cost of complying with new regulations; and
3. this approach takes advantage of the public support of the migration from "governing" to "governance".

In short, the proposed approach suggests a way of improving public productivity by addressing the management of risk without interfering with the evolvement and functions of markets and civil society organizations.

Governance as an Emerging Paradigm

Doornbos (2003) points out that for a long time the word "governance" had a "somewhat obscure dictionary existence, primarily carrying legalistic connotations, as in respect to bodies having boards of governors whose institutional role required a designation that was more grand than 'administration,' less business-like than 'management'". Yet he notes (Doornbos, 2003) "all at once, the notion of good *governance* was there, referring to the way in which cities, provinces, or whole countries

were being governed, or should be governed. Thus Doornbos (2003) asserts:

> As is often true with new buzzwords, though, there has hardly been a consensus as to its core meaning, and less and less of a common idea as to how it could be applied more concretely. Still, it is there, and it has gained a key function by virtue of its capacity all at once to draw attention to a whole range of often largely unspecified issues concerning processes of public policy-making and authority structures. In that sense it has appealed to the imagination of analysts as well as practitioners, and become a focal point for intellectual and policy discourses.

Doornbos (2003) echoes the earlier observation of Rhodes (1996, p. 652) that "governance signifies a change in the meaning of government, referring to a *new* process of governing; or a *changed* condition of ordered rule; or the *new* method by which society is governed". For Rhodes (1996), governance has to do with self-organizing inter-organizational networks that substitute and complement the functions of hierarchies (i.e., bureaucracies) and markets or co-exist with them. Rhodes (1996) asserts that these networks are characterized by interdependence between organizations, continuing interaction between network members, and game-like interactions rooted in trust and subject to rules negotiated by network participants. Rhodes (1996) also notes that because of the significant degree of autonomy of these networks from the "state", it can steer them only indirectly, because the "state" is not in the role of the sovereign any more. Rhodes (1996, p. 653) adds to any possible confusion about the essence of governance by pointing out that, in fact, the term "governance" may be used in at least six different meanings, namely as minimal government, as corporate government, as new public management, as "good governance", as a socio-cybernetic system, or as a self-organizing network. Rhodes (1996, p. 667) goes on to note that inter-organizational networks are already widespread. This trend is not widely recognized and has widespread implications not only for the practice of British government but also for democratic accountability. Thus, Rhodes (1996, p. 667) concludes, "governance as self organizing networks is a challenge to governability because the networks become autonomous and resist central guidance".

Walti and Kubler (2003) observe that during the 1990s, self-governing networks for various reasons replaced hierarchical administrative governing structures. One of these reasons is to improve the authenticity and democratic quality of public decisions. Thus, they note, "new governance" has been praised for its propensity to provide a plurality of civil society organizations with access to the decision process. They go on to assert that:

> Be it from the point of view of making government more efficient and responsive to social needs or from the normative perspective of making it more democratic, the central argument advanced in favor of self-organizing networks "involving complex sets of organizations from the public and private sectors" (Rhodes, 1996, p. 658), is

its capacity to enhance the responsiveness and quality of public policies by bringing together a wide range of public agencies and private organizations. A crucial element to reach these goals is the participation of service users via associations. These developments depend on increased decentralization and devolution (Walti and Kubler, 2003, p. 500).

Reading such opinions, one may assume that the recent interest in exploring the concept of governance as it relates to civil society, and concerns about the capacity to govern, is one that is unique to writers in the West or in the so-called "developed" countries. In fact, the opposite is true. The recent utilization of the term "governance" in the context of democratization, civil society, accountability, governing capacity, and development started in connection with the case of aid by international donor to "developing" countries (Doornbos, 2003; Hout, 2002). Thus, for example, Stern (2000, p. 1) notes, "by the 1990s a subtle new concept was making its way through development seminars and research studies. This concept was 'governance'". The term "governance", he notes, "began to be used in the development literature in the late 1980s, particularly in Africa" (Stern, 2000, p. 1). According to Stern (2000), the Report of the Governance in Africa Program of the Carter Center in Emory University in Atlanta spoke of governance as "a broader, more inclusive notion than government" and "the general manner in which a people is governed". As cited in McCarney *et al.* (1995, p. 94), "governance" "can apply to the formal structures of government as well as to the myriad institutions and groups which compose civil society in any nation". According to Carmichael (2002), whereas "government" is concerned with the formal institutions of government, "governance" signifies a change in the meaning of government, focusing on wider processes through which public policy is effected. It refers to the development and implementation of public policy through a broader range of private and public agencies than those traditionally associated with elected government. Thus, Carmichael (2002) argues, government is increasingly characterized by diversity, power interdependence, and increased reliance on policy networks. The result of this development is the hollowing out of the nation-state as functions are either pooled upwards to supranational bodies like the EU, downwards to devolved administrations and regional bodies, and outwards to civil society agencies or even removed from direct public sector involvement altogether by privatization.

According to a publication of the US Department of State (US Agency for International Development, 1998) "[G]overnance issues pertain to the ability of government to develop an efficient and effective public management process [...] [that is able] to deliver basic services". According to the (United Nations Development Programme 1997), "[G]overnance is the exercise of economic, political, and administrative authority to manage a country's affairs at all levels and the means by which states promote social cohesion, integration, and ensure the well-being of their populations. It embraces all methods used to distribute power and manage public resources, and the organizations that shape government and the execution of policy". The United Nations Development Programme definition contains an additional

quality, one that can be considered the essence of inclusiveness and broad base participation: "[I]t encompasses the mechanisms, processes, and institutions through which citizens and groups articulate their interests, exercise their legal rights, meet their obligations, and resolve their differences". The World Bank (1992, p. 3) defines governance as "the manner in which power is exercised in the management of a country's economic and social resources". Kooiman (1996, p. 8) suggests "for the World Bank and the developmental literature, the governance concept is the essence of broadening its traditional technical capacity-building scope to a base in which there is room for civil society and participation as well. Building a pluralistic institutional structure (creating an enabling environment) can be seen as one of the key contributions to this shift in the World Bank's policy approach". Kooiman (1996) points out that the World Bank's use of the term is only one of several possible uses. Describing two other possible uses of the term, he says:

> The second concept is that of using governance to develop a broad theory of social-political interaction. The central argument is that because modern societies are diverse, dynamic and complex, the problems in those societies have these same characteristics. And, likewise, so does solving those problems. Traditional problem approaches neglect diversity, do not cope with dynamics and unsatisfactorily reduce complexity. New ways of interaction between public and private are needed to cope with solving diverse, dynamic and complex collective action problems. A third example is a recent usage of the concept in terms of a broad administrative reform program in the USA. Key dimensions are participants in the provision of public services; purposes of public action; the means used to accomplish these purposes; and finally the politics of determining the basic purposes, structure and funding levels of governmental activities (Kooiman, 1996, p. 8).

According to Halachmi (2003a), "the notion of governance has been used by various writers to refer to a possible paradigm shift" in the last part of the twentieth century (Neu, 1996; Adshead and Quinn, 1998; Mayntz, 2002; Rhodes, 1996). The shift involved a transition from "governing" and into "governance"—a term depicting the evolvement of a new "order" and a different interface among operators whose traditional basis of operation used to be either government, civil society organizations or markets. This new "order" was labeled interchangeably either "governance" or "good governance" (Bovaird and Loffler, 2003). Yet, it should be noted that in addition to the above, "governance" is now used to depict an effort to meet the welfare needs of citizens in a better way through partnerships with other elements of the "civil society" for the purpose of overcoming limits on action due to governmental structures, legal issues, or administrative procedures. While some of these partnerships are explicit, others are implicit.

Explicit partnerships involve some kind of designation or official recognition of non-governmental entities, like NERC, as leading players in addressing some important issues or, as providers of an essential community service for a fee, as is the case with private garbage collection or fire protection services. These players are free agents to a lesser or greater degree. They may have to be in compliance with fewer (or some times even more) governmental regulations to carry out their mission but they can move their operations from one place to another on a relatively short notice. Thus, such players may have to be licensed, incorporated, or regulated in some way by the central government. The lesser is the role of the central governing *vis-à-vis* each of the said players, the greater is the move from "governing" to "governance". This, in turn, reduces the high profile of agencies. It is a common element of the effort to deregulate and reduce the cost of government as a political ideology as it is a response to the growing inability of governments to mobilize new resources or to launch new activities.

Implicit partnerships result when central government agencies deliberately overlook local level initiatives to provide (or to experiment with the provision) of services that complement, augment, or replace those that are provided by government or its declared partners in the public or private sector. In the case of the USA, for example, these may include church-based programs for adoption and placement of children or the sponsorship and settlement of refugees. In China, and in other countries, such programs may include various neighborhood-based initiatives that originate as a result of campaigns by local residents with no involvement or support from the "authorities". Reflecting on these partnerships, Sabel and O'Donnell (2000, p. 1) note that the central government tolerance of such developments by lower level authorities or initiatives seems to suggest that the center is reforming itself not by changing its mode of operations but through a change in its role as provider of certain goods and services. Sabel and O'Donnell (2000, p. 1) also note that such view of the central government is remarkable more in its capacities for self-limitation and dis-entrenchment than its positive abilities to co-ordinate and construct.

From a pragmatic point of view, the transition from governing to governance translates into contracting out and load sharing by agencies at all levels of government. However, while more activities that used to be performed by government and others that should have been performed by government became the domain of "for-profit" and "not-for-profit" organizations, little has been done to address the issue of comprehensive risk management. Thus, the current literature about public sector productivity, finance or welfare is missing critical discussions about one important question, namely, "how current governance practices enhance (or undermine) the management of risk".

Addressing this issue is important beyond its immediate implications for homeland security of every country, since the management of risk, broadly defined, includes (or should include) issues of financial solvency of pension funds and other welfare, health, education, and public works accounts.

Governance and Risk Management

One question that comes to mind at this juncture is why is it, that in an area of renewed calls for government to be managed more like a business, has so little been done until recently about risk management in comparison with the intensive development of such initiatives at well-managed corporations in the private sector? By the same token, one must ask why so little has been done to address the question of how the existing governance practices in various countries enhance (or undermine) the management of risk within and outside government.

Addressing risk has been part of the old rationale for having government in the first place (Narayan, n.d.; Kalaw, 2002). Protecting the public is the mandate that must be observed by all levels of government. Human society has created the unique institution of the organized state in order to maintain public order, defend frontiers, and ensure harmony among individuals and groups (Narayan, n.d.; Kalaw, 2002). The Great Wall of China, management of water projects in ancient Egypt or Mesopotamia, the Hammurabi Code and the Law of Moses are a few illustrations of the traditional role of government, namely the protection of life and property. If, as asserted by various writers, and as noted above, governance is a way to improve the polity's (i.e. a country, state, province, city, etc.) capacity to meet its citizens' needs, one must wonder what are the implications of governance to the management of risk? Such an inquiry is not an academic exercise. This assertion can be supported in two ways:

1. by the case of the Great Blackout of August 14, 2003, as described above; and
2. by the results of a recent survey (Cole, 2003) suggesting that as the world becomes a riskier place, British citizens are increasingly distrustful of how their government handles risks.

Hood *et al.* (2001) addressed the issue of risk regulation by government. The starting point for their discussion is that government is the key player in the effort to manage risk. Schneider (1987) addressed the questions involving the co-production of safety services with citizens. The starting point of that discussion is that, on occasion, governments enter into some kind of agreement or partnership with elements of the civil society to manage risk. However, what about the role of government in managing risk when governance replaces governing? That is, what is the responsibility of government, if any, when it allows a non-governmental entity to become the focal point for managing risks involved in the provision of a public service? For the purpose of this paper, some of the possible implications for risk management, as a result from migration or paradigm shift from governing to governance, can be summarized in the following way:

- "Governing" has to do with control, while "governance" has to do with steering. Governing is the sole prerogative of governments because it involves the possible use of coercion while governance involves cooperation and collaboration among multiple governmental and non-governmental actors with diverse economic and non-economic interests. The implication for risk management is that under "governing" the authorities can force all entities to manage risk using its regulatory powers. Under "governance" the authorities must find other ways to induce risk management by other means to preserve the advantages of governance over governing. Thus, in the context of governance, risk management is a more challenging task than it is when it comes to governing. Any attempt to use the direct or indirect authority of the state can undermine the governance structure that evolved as a result of free interactions among all the involved parties. The temptation to resort to the state authority to overcome any weakness in the governance structure is illustrated by our August 14, 2003 Blackout case. For example, the use of state authority was suggested by Mr Gent, CEO of NERC, in his testimony before Congress. Mr Gent pointed out that provisions in the Energy Bill that are pending before Congress would influence future compliance with NERC standards of operation (Gent, 2003a). Yet, one might ask, at what cost?

- Governing is state-centered while governance assumes a polycentric (or at least a decentralized) institutional structure with the government apparatus as only one of several centers. Simultaneously, in concert or independent of each other, these centers are seeking legitimacy, initiating a variety of programs, competing for and mobilizing public and private resources. The implication for risk management is that there is no reason to assume that risk management plans, which are developed independently of each other, would somehow be synchronized, be consistent with each other, or would not undermine each other. There is no invisible hand to coordinate risk management efforts unless government steps in to do it.

- Governing takes place within the national or internationally recognized borders of a given polity while governance results from interactions within and across such borders. Governing assumes the existence, sovereignty, sole jurisdiction, and a clear hierarchy of norms (i.e. a legal system). In the governing framework, actors play either primary or subsidiary roles *vis-à-vis* each other. Governance, on the other hand, is multidimensional. It tolerates multiple jurisdictions, co-existence of alternative sets of values with actors playing primary or subsidiary role in some public policy arena, and a different role in other public policy arenas. The implication for risk management is that it cannot be based on any assumption that has to do with territoriality. Risk cannot be associated with any specific geography, as illustrated by the SARS epidemic of winter 2003, which affected Hong Kong and Toronto independently of each other. Since current risks cannot be defined by a reference to a unique source or confined to an area that can be defined by borders that fall under specific laws/ jurisdiction or by whether it is (or can be) controlled by any one government there is a need for a new approach to public risk management. The December 2004 Tsunami that hit countries in South East Asia illustrates the fact that in the new millennium the risk to life in one place is a concern and matter for action by official and non-official agencies in other places. The decision of President Bush to ask two former American Presidents,

his father and Bill Clinton, to lead the effort to raise funds from the public to augment the US Government relief effort (Loven, 2005) demonstrates that *governance*, rather than *governing*, is the promising strategy for addressing risk.

First Do No Harm

During graduation ceremonies, medical students in some countries take a professional vow using a version of the Hippocratic Oath. In the original oath, a would-be doctor swears, before others, "I will prescribe regimen for the good of my patients according to my ability and my judgment and never do harm to anyone" (Bibliotheque Nationale, n.d.). Recent activities by many governments around the world to address and develop an in-house capacity of risk management follow the logic of the Hippocratic Oath. This risk management capacity is meant to minimize the risk to the community due to government operations.

Historically, the "state" evolved as a societal institution or as an instrument for protecting life and property. Thus, the last thing one would expect is for the state to be the cause, the origin, or the perpetrator of any such threats. However, as demonstrated by many environmental fiascos around the world, good intentions may not translate to good deeds from some citizens' point of view. In the United States, such fiascos include the draining of swamps and marshlands in Florida and Louisiana that resulted in floods, industrial and urban development that resulted in contamination of drinking water, etc. In their eagerness to foster economic development, defense capability, or short-term political gains, elected officials in various countries may create hazardous situations and problems down the road. In some cases, such problems may evolve to be larger than their creator's ability to handle them. The clear-cutting of parts of the rain forest (leading to mud slides), the sinking in the high seas of barrels of radioactive waste (leading to pollution of fishing areas), the releasing of untreated sewage into bodies of water (leading to contamination of drinking water), or the construction of buildings, roads, dams, canals and bridges that change the water flow (leading to floods) are a few examples that are applicable to the case of many countries. In all of these examples, lack of a deliberate effort by government agencies to manage the risk that may result from their own operations (or from what they allowed others to do) amounts to violation of the "first do no harm" dictum.

A recent review of the fires of the fall of 2003 in California (USA) suggests that risk management is not value-free. Thus, the governance arrangements (i.e. the division of labor between civil society based organizations and government) are likely to be influenced by political inclinations. A liberal inclination, at least in the American context, would imply that government should play a greater role in the production of services while a conservative inclination would suggest that more should be left to markets and non-governmental organizations. According to Allen (2003), in the politically conservative San Diego County, "where they like their tax low and government small", 16 people died and 2,400 homes were destroyed in the fires of fall 2003. In comparison, neighboring Los Angeles County fared better. With two specially fitted helicopters plus two Super Scoopers leased from Quebec to douse fires by scooping water from the ocean, Los Angeles County was able to do a better job containing the fires.

In Los Angeles, a stronghold of the Democratic Party in Southern California, a lot of the citizens' tax money went to pay for this fire preparedness, meeting public demands for government capacity to address safety issues. In conservative San Diego County, taxes were kept low. Though citizens paid dearly for their saving on taxes, the county was attempting to meet another set of demands—less government is better. While San Diego County did not start the killing fires, the decision about the use of resources, in the context of risk management, was a clear factor contributing to the high magnitude and cost of the damage (Allen, 2003).

On the face of it, one of the differences between the risk management approaches of the two counties seems to be related to the extent and involvement of civic and community organizations in the management of local affairs. According to the US Census Bureau (1997a), there were more than 2,000 tax-exempt (NAICS code 813) establishments in the Metropolitan Statistical Area (MSA) of Los Angeles in 1997. These organizations, with more than 20,300 salaried employees, served a population of more than nine million. In San Diego County MSA, according to the US Census Bureau (1997b) in the same year there have been only 766 tax-exempt establishments (NAICS code 813) with about 7,000 paid employees serving a population of 2.8 million residents. In both cases the *per capita* ratio of civic organizations is about 1:400. However, in the case of Los Angeles County the sheer number of civic organizations with enough human resources on board could assure greater pressure on the authorities to make the preparedness for emergency a high priority. These civic organizations, however, did not leave the management of emergency to market forces and by supporting budget allocation for emergency preparedness voted for the "governing" model.

The lack of fire preparedness in San Diego County had to do with lack of pressure for abundant budget allocation to emergency management (Allen, 2003). This, in turn, suggests that trusting government with this task was not an option for residents of San Diego County. The lack of a significant evidence of civic organization based pressure on the authorities in San Diego was consistent with the belief in this conservative county that whenever possible "market forces" and elements of civil society (i.e. "networks" in Rhodes's (1996) terminology), would prove to be more efficient and effective way than government bureaucracies (i.e. hierarchies) for addressing matters of public concerns.

For our purposes the end results, in the case of the fall 2003 fires in California or the case of the Great Blackout of 2003, raise the same set of questions about the current transition from "governing" to "governance". These questions include the following:

- What are the limits of "governance", if any?
- To what extent can a government abdicate some of its traditional "governing" responsibilities without risking

questions about the legitimacy and the rationale for its existence?

- How can the "state" remain effective while it is reducing its capacity for action and involvement in other areas by contracting out and acceleration of a shift from governing to governance?
- Who should decide and what process should be used to decide what areas of government should be "opened" to joint arrangements with non-governmental entities or even be left altogether to them to take care of without any direct governmental intervention?
- Whose responsibility is it to guard the public interest, when it comes to risk management, in areas where all the actors are non-governmental entities due to a deliberate plan of government devaluation?
- The answers to such questions may have a direct bearing on the role(s) public bureaucracies will play in the future and how they interface with other elements of the civil society and market forces. However, when it comes to risk management and protecting citizens and their assets, the question goes directly to the heart of the issue of sovereignty and the rationale for having government in place.

It's the Government's Fault!

As illustrated by the case of the Great Blackout of August 14, 2003, even though government agencies were not involved in any direct capacity, elected officials felt the heat. Whether the accusatory fingers within and outside the United States were real or imagined, whether members of Congress were trying to contain the developing political fallout or be proactive, the quick onset of the Congressional inquiry into the reasons for the Great Blackout highlights the issue of accountability. In a related fashion, a similar accusatory finger was pointed at governments in the aftermath of disasters in other countries (Halachmi, 2003b). The universality of this observation suggests that when something bad happens, government officials are very likely to be held accountable for what took place on their watch. Such accountability is expected regardless of whether the elected officials in question had any prior involvement, knowledge, or influence on any aspect of the process leading to the unfortunate development.

Hahn and Kleiner (2002, p. 1) assert that "public perception of government ineffectiveness and waste of taxpayer dollars have resulted in a continual need to downsize and reduce budgets". Coupled with growing difficulties to mobilize new resources to underwrite the increasing cost of government operations, elected officials may opt to reduce the size of bureaucracies by contracting out and devaluation. Allegedly for the sake of catering to greater diversity of opinions and broader participation, agencies may try to foster the end results of government programs that must be phased out by encouraging and tolerating related activities by non-governmental entities. By facilitating the migration from governing to governance, and by cultivating a "civil society", governments can foster alternatives to bureaucracies and markets. However, such efforts, even when they are very successful, cannot relocate accountability from the polity point of view. So far, there is no empirical evidence that elected officials can escape the responsibility for anything that goes wrong on their watch. Such responsibility translates to votes on election day and to trust in government every day. With this in mind, the question is what can government do to harvest many of the possible benefits of the migration from *governing* to *governance* while mitigating some of the involved dysfunctions? This paper refers to this issue as the question of governance and accountability.

The tentative answer offered in this paper to the question of governance and accountability consists of two elements. These elements are related but involve separate efforts to address the issue of risk management.

The first element of the proposed answer involves an effort to change management posture, within and outside government, so that risk management becomes a common practice in all organizations. As I have pointed out in an earlier paper, there used to be a time when the "in" thing was management by exceptions (Halachmi, 2003a). Now, it is asserted, the time has come for organizations to adopt "management by risk" as part of any management approach. The reason for that needed change is the growing complexity of the environment of any given governmental or non-governmental organization and, given the greater functional dependencies among social, economic and, political systems that used to be independent of each other. With the evolution of the global village and the interconnectedness of societies all over the world, getting prepared to address potential risks must start with the development of the business plan for any governmental or non-governmental entity. Indeed, one way of measuring management excellence and an important consideration in auditing organizations should involve the study of the organization's risk management plan.

Developing a better risk management plan for an agency may require mobilization, if not a synthesis of a large interdisciplinary body of knowledge. In fact, such planning may be a function of better insights that can be gained only through more comprehensive efforts of fact-finding and more in-depth analysis of questions like the following:

- What is the agency actually doing? (This may involve "re-engineering"-like studies.)
- What can go wrong and why? (This may involve the use of exploratory studies using methods like Delphi or simulations.)
- What can be done if something does go wrong? (This may involve proactive moves to sell or share risks as part of any strategic planning effort.)

The chances are that better insight being gained in the effort to develop a better risk management plan would enhance the quality of management and planning within the agency, in turn reducing the odds for some risks.

The second element of the proposed answer to the question about accountability and governance involves facilitating, encouraging, and mobilizing elements of civic society to serve as watchdogs when it comes to risk management. Such elements of civil society can over time develop greater expertise than

government. The reasons for this are simple. To start with, in areas that are of interest or concern to them, they are free from some of the characteristics of government operations, such as politics and corruption (broadly defined), bureaucratic entrenchment and reluctance to admit wrong judgment or poor past performance, sudden alteration of agency priorities due to changes in leadership or budget constraints, loss of expertise due to personnel changes, etc. At the same time, civic groups can act alone or call on government for assistance as needed. Thus, such civil society groups can do a better job of monitoring and assuring compliance with common elements of risk management than any government agency. This prospect was the basis of the story for movies like *The China Syndrome* or *Erin Brockovich*. Recent, questions about the safety of various drugs like Aleve, Vioxx or Celebrex that were approved by government regulators and their hasty withdrawal from the markets (Heavey, 2004; Barrett, 2004) is another case in point. According to media reports:

> Two-thirds of Food and Drug Administration [FDA] scientists surveyed two years ago lacked confidence that the FDA adequately monitors the safety of prescription drugs [...] And 18% of the almost 400 respondents said they had been pressured to approve or recommend a drug despite reservations about its safety, effectiveness or quality (Schmit, 2004).

The questionable safety of various drugs followed the publication of research reports outside of government. This recent case illustrates the possible shortcomings of any government oversight and regulation of possible risks to the public. The recent questions about the way the government regulates the safety of drugs resembles too much the earlier case of car safety, where the "industry" made sure that public safety issues were not interfering with its business. The review of government shortcomings in the approval and oversight of car safety resulted only after a non-governmental entity (i.e. Ralph Nader's 1965 bestseller *Unsafe at Any Speed*) put the issue on the public agenda forcing Congress to take action.

Yet, this paper goes one step further to suggest that civil society based groups can effect changes that serve public safety while by-passing government. Groups like Greenpeace, who have mastered the art of media campaigns, can use market forces such as the financial interest of insurance companies to foster a prudent management of risk. Highlighting possible risks or possible deficiencies in preparedness to handle risk can make it very difficult for any non-governmental entity to obtain insurance. Coupled with the negative publicity this can undermine the credibility of any non-governmental entity. Alerting the underwriters to possible issues of risk management in the case of any organization can be carried out without new government regulations for management of alleged risks. When insurance executives need to answer their own stakeholders why they take chances and issue an insurance policy they are going to be much more prudent about it. To secure their own portfolio and reputation they are likely to insist that any organization that seeks to purchase an insurance policy maintains a proper level of risk management, which meets the underwriters' professional standards. Thus, the monitoring of activities by civic groups or insurance providers for detecting possible risks may even replace exiting regulations that aim to achieve the same results, i.e. assuring the safety of life and property.

Underlining the promise of this element of the answer to the question about accountability and governance is a simple observation: the migration from *governing* to *governance* is a fact of life and cannot be reversed. Thus, governments need to use the mechanisms of governance (i.e. partnerships, coordination, collaboration, and persuasion) as the means for accomplishing what it used to do by regulation and central enforcement.

Due to growing constraints on government actions and direct involvement, such as fiscal pressures, government accountability is going to become an issue more than it used to be in the past. The reason is that governments are now being held accountable not only for what they do wrong but for everything that goes wrong, as illustrated by the case of the 2003 Blackout. The proposition advanced in this paper is that in the new millennium the issue of government accountability when it comes to risk management may be served better when the "state" facilitates the evolution of civil society based organizations than if the "state" attempts to address it as the sole or main player.

Concluding Remarks

Governments around the world experience pressures to expand and upgrade services on the one hand and the demands to keep the existing level of taxation stable (or even to reduce it) on the other. The result is that many activities that should be performed by government and some that used to be performed by governments are now provided by non-governmental organizations. Several writers described this development as part of the migration from "governing" to "governance", where networks replace the markets that were expected to replace inefficient bureaucracies. Yet the change in the manner by which society is served does not absolve government officials from responsibility when something goes wrong. Government loses some control over risk management when "governance" replaces "governing", yet it is still being held responsible for adequate risk management. Government can regain lost control over risk management in two ways. First, a government can do so by issuing regulations that would assure greater compliance with common elements of risk management by non-governmental entities. However, such legislative initiatives, as proposed now to avoid another experience like the Great Blackout of 2003, may be counter-productive. Second, a government may be able to achieve the same results by the use of a two-pronged approach that avoids much of any possible increase in the cost of government operations. The two-pronged approach is offered as part of the tentative answer of this paper to the question about risk management and accountability when it comes to governance. First, this paper advocates an effort to create a culture of risk management where management by attention to possible risks is common at all levels of any organization and is part of developing and implementing the business plan. Second, this paper advocates encouraging the development and mobiliza-

tion of elements of civil society to serve as a watchdog to oversee that all organizations manage risk and comply with reasonable safety standards. Such watchdogs are likely to entice insurance companies to play a more active role in assuring that their clients have reasonable risk management plans in place beyond the mere insurance of property or simple liabilities. Greater involvement of market forces (i.e. underwriters) and networks (community watchdogs) may prove to be more effective and efficient than direct government involvement in assuring an acceptable level of risk preparedness. After all, over time such players (i.e. underwriters and community watchdogs) are less likely to be pressured by bribes or short-term political considerations.

References

Adshead, M. and Quinn, B. (1998), "The move from government to governance: Irish development policy's paradigm shift", *Policy & Politics*, Vol. 26 No. 2, pp. 209–25.

Allen, J.T. (2003), "Call it protection money", *US News and World Report*, November 17, p. 47.

Barrett, A. (2004), "Why drugs need a longer look", available at: www.yourlawyer.com/practice/news.htm?story_id=8757&topic=Vioxx

BBC (1999), "Europe: blood scandal ministers walk free", available at: http://news.bbc.co.uk/1/hi/world/europe/293367.stm

BBC (2001), "Japan blood scandal official convicted", available at: http://news.bbc.co.uk/1/hi/world/asia-pacific/1568626.stm (accessed September 28, 2001).

Bibliotheque Nationale (n.d.), "The Hippocratic Oath", *circa* 380BC, Greek Manuscript 2144, f 10v, c. 1342, Bibliotheque Nationale, Paris, available at: www.hal-pc.org/~ollie/hippocratic.oath.html

Bovaird, T. and Loffler, E. (2003), "Evaluating the quality of public governance: indicators, models and methodologies", *International Review of Administrative Sciences*, Vol. 69 No. 3, pp. 313–28.

British Medical Journal (1995), "India hit by contaminated blood scandal", *British Medical Journal*, available at: http://bmj.bmjjournals.com/cgi/content/full/311/7003/467

CBS (2003), "Massive blackout hits US, Canada", available at: www.cbsnews.com

Carmichael, P. (2002), "Review of public administration briefing paper: Multi-Level Governance", available at: www.rpani.gov.uk/multilevel.pdf

Cole, C. (2003), "Britons distrust government on key risk issues", *Futurist*, Vol. 37 No. 4, available at: www.wfs.org/futindexdeps.htm

Doornbos, M. (2003), "Good governance: the metamorphosis of a policy metaphor", *Journal of International Affairs*, Vol. 57 No. 1, pp. 3–18.

Gent, M.R. (2003a), Summary of testimony of Michel R. Gent, President and CEO of North American Electric Reliability Council (NERC), House Committee on Energy and Commerce, September 3.

Gent, M.R. (2003b), Letter to John Dingell, US House of Representatives Committee on Energy and Commerce, Washington, DC.

Hahn, R.M. and Kleiner, B.H. (2002), "Managing human behaviour in city government", *Management Research News*, Vol. 25 No. 3, pp. 1–10.

Halachmi, A. (2003a), "Governance and risk management: the challenge of accountability, transparency and social responsibility", *International Review of Public Administration*, Vol. 8, pp. 1–10.

Halachmi, A. (2003b), "Risk management accountability and governance", available in Korean translation by the Korea Research Institute for Local Administration (KRILA) at: www.krila.re.kr/forum/menu_01/menu_6.html

Heavey, S. (2004), "Naproxen joins list of questionable drugs", available at: www.usatoday.com/money/industries/health/drugs/2004-12-21-naproxen-warning_x.htm (accessed December 21, 2004).

Hood, C., Rothstein, H. and Baldwin, R. (2001), *Government of Risk: Understanding Risk Regulation Regimes*, Oxford University Press, Oxford.

Hout, W. (2002), "Good governance and aid: selectivity criteria in development assistance", *Development and Change*, Vol. 33 No. 3, pp. 511–28.

Interim Report (2003), "US-Canada Power System Outage Task Force Interim Report: causes of the August 14th blackout in the United States and Canada", available at: https://reports.energy.gov/814BlackoutReport.pdf

Kalaw, M. (2002), "Global governance, civil society and Earth Summit 2002", available at: www.ncsdnetwork.org/knowledge/global_governance.pdf

Kooiman, J. (1996), "Research and theory about new public services management: review and agenda for the future", *International Journal of Public Sector Management*, Vol. 9 Nos. 5/6, pp. 7–22.

Loven, J. (2005), "Ex-presidents ask for tsunami aid", *Chicago Sun-Times*, January 4, available at: www.suntimes.com/output/news/cst-nws-tsuaid04.html

McCarney, P., Halfani, M. and Rodriguez, A. (1995), "Towards an understanding of governance: the emergence of an idea and its implications for urban research in developing countries", in Stren, R. (Ed.), *Perspectives on the City*, Vol. 4, Centre for Urban and Community Studies, University of Toronto, Toronto, pp. 91–141.

Mayntz, R. (2002), "The state and civil society in modern governance", paper presented at the VI Congreso Internacional del CLAD, available at: www.clad.org.ve/anales6/mayntz.html

Mizoguchi, K. (2000), "Japan tainted blood execs jailed", Associated Press, February 24, available at: www.aegis.com/news/ap/2000/AP000210.html

Narayan, J. (n.d.), "Civil society and governance", available at: www.loksatta.org/civil%20society.pdf

Neu, C. (1996), "Local governance: the next 'change' frontier", *Illinois Municipal Review*, March, available at: www.lib.niu.edu/ipo/im960313.html

Picard, A. (2002), "The blood scandal", *Globe and Mail*, November 21, available at: www.andrepicard.com/scandal.html

Pollard, R. (2003), "Red Cross audit after release of tainted blood", *Sydney Morning Herald*, September 13, available at: www.smh.com.au/articles/2003/09/12/1063341768099.html?from = storyrhs

Pravda (2003), "RAO UES Head comments on power outage in USA", *Pravda,* available at: http://newsfromrussia.com/main/2003/08/15/49319.html

Rhodes, R.A.W. (1996), "The new governance: governing without government", *Political Studies*, Vol. 44 No. 3, pp. 652–67.

Sabel, C.F. and O'Donnell, R. (2000), "Democratic experimentalism: what to do about wicked problems after Whitehall", paper presented at the OECD Conference on Devolution and Globalization Implications for Local Decision-Makers, Glasgow, February 28–29.

Schmit, J. (2004), "Survey: FDA scientists question safety", *USA Today*, December 16, available at: www.usatoday.com/news/health/2004-12-16-fda-survey-usat_x.htm

Schneider, A.L. (1987), "Co-production of public and private safety: an analysis of bystander intervention, 'protective neighboring' and personal protection", *Western Political Quarterly*, Vol. 40 No. 4, pp. 611–30.

Smith, A. (1776), *The Wealth of Nations*, Edinburgh.

Stern, R.E. (2000), "New approaches to urban governance in Latin America", available at: www.internationalbudget.org/cdrom/papers/systems/ParticipatoryBudgets/IDRCEng.htm

Synapse (2003), "August 14th blackout", Synapse-Energy, August 18, available at: www.synapse-energy.com

United Nations Development Programme (1997), *Governance for Sustainable Human Development, A UNDP Policy Document*, United Nations Development Programme, New York, NY.

US Agency for International Development (1998), "Democracy and governance: a conceptual framework", US Agency for International Development, PN-ACC-395, November, available at: www.usaid.gov/democracy/pdfs/pnacd395.pdf

US Census Bureau (1997a), 1997 Economic census: other services Los Angeles—Long Beach, CA, PMSA, available at: www.census.gov/epcd/ec97/metro4/M4480_81.HTM

US Census Bureau (1997b), 1997 Economic census: other services San Diego, CA, MSA, available at: www.census.gov/epcd/ec97/metro7/M7320_81.HTM

Walti, S. and Kubler, D. (2003), "'New governance' and associative pluralism: the case of drug policy in Swiss cities", *Policy Studies Journal*, Vol. 31 No. 4, pp. 499–526.

World Bank (1992), *Governance and Development*, World Bank, Washington, DC.

From *The International Journal of Public Sector Management*, Vol. 18, Number 4, 2005, pp. 300–317. Copyright © 2005 by Emerald Group Publishing Ltd. Reprinted by permission.

UNIT 4

Finance and Budgeting

Unit Selections

Key Points to Consider

- Identify and discuss some of the major fiscal and financial issues facing the United States. What are some of the major impacts of these issues on the federal budget?

- What are some of the structural flaws in the U.S. government accounting system that still exist after the Enron/Andersen scandal? What additional action may be necessary in order to prevent a future crisis of this type?

- What are some of the major reasons for the huge increases in health care costs for local government budgets?

Student Web Site

www.mhcls.com/online

Internet References

Further information regarding these Web sites may be found in this book's preface or online.

FirstGov
http://www.firstgov.gov

The U.S. Chief Financial Officers Council
http://www.cfoc.gov

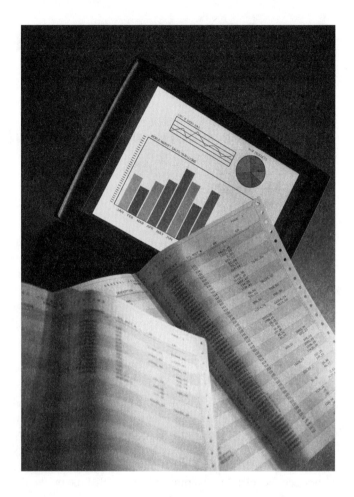

Articles in this unit focus on the U.S. financial condition and fiscal outlook with a special emphasis on the impact of health care cost increases on public budgets. Also featured in this section are articles that discuss the importance of contracting for public organizations and an update on lessons for governmental accounting systems that were negatively impacted by the Enron/Andersen scandal.

David M. Walker, Comptroller General of the United States and head of the U.S. Government Accountability Office, in his article *Our Nation's Financial Condition and Fiscal Outlook: Shaping the Future of the Federal Government* discusses our nation's financial condition and fiscal outlook. He also identifies the challenges of a long-term structural deficit, which will shape the future of the federal government.

In the article *Enron/Andersen: Crisis in U.S. Accounting and Lessons for Government,* Richard Brown discusses that the Enron/Andersen scandal is not an isolated case. This scandal exposed structural flaws that may be present in governmental accounting and auditing systems. The Sarbanes-Oxley Act of 2002 may not be enough to fix these flaws. In the author's opinion, additional action may be necessary to prevent a future crisis.

Health care is now one of the fastest growing components in local budgets. In the article *Huge Rise Looms for Health Care in Local Budgets*, Mary Williams Walsh and Milt Freudenheim explore the reasons for the large increases and look at how a new accounting rule could send the costs of health care for cities and states through the roof.

Our Nation's Financial Condition and Fiscal Outlook

Shaping the Future of the Federal Government

DAVID M. WALKER

I have been speaking out lately on a subject that deserves far more attention: the U.S. government's worsening financial situation and long-term fiscal imbalance. Despite the current economic recovery and the reassuring messages conveyed by some government officials, the truth is that our nation faces a long-term structural deficit that is set to increase significantly as the baby boomers retire.

Crunch Is Coming

A crunch is coming, and eventually all of government will feel its impact. Although defense and homeland security have so far avoided the budget constraints affecting other discretionary spending, these areas also face lean times ahead. As budgetary pressures build, federal managers will be uniquely challenged to provide the level of government services that the public demands and deserves.

It seems only yesterday that many economists and government officials were projecting surpluses for years to come. Several of the underlying conditions for a long-term structural deficit, however, existed even during the recent years of annual budget surpluses. Namely, largely because of rising health care costs, a looming demographic tidal wave unprecedented in American history, and reduced federal revenue as a percentage of the economy, we now face decades of deficits. Difficult choices are inevitable.

If we look at changes in federal spending over time, the powerful effects of long-term trends become clear. In 1964, two-thirds of the federal budget was discretionary, and nearly half was spent on national defense. In 2004, less than 40 percent of the federal budget was discretionary, and about 20 percent was spent on national defense. Steady growth in entitlement programs has crowded out other government expenditures: Two out of every five federal dollars are spent now on Social Security, Medicare, and Medicaid.

The status quo, however, is unsustainable. Take Social Security, for example. In 1950, more than sixteen workers were paying into the system for every retiree drawing benefits. By 2040, that ratio will have dwindled to two to one. Without changes to current policy, the twin burdens of paying for costly medical care and supporting a growing elderly population will put increasing pressure on the nation's spending and tax policies.

Keeping Score

Unfortunately, the way in which our government keeps score provides an incomplete and misleading picture of our true financial condition and fiscal outlook. For instance, the Congressional Budget Office's (CBO's) "baseline" projections, which are designed to be a reference point against which to measure policy changes, are often misinterpreted as projections of likely budget outcomes. But CBO is required to assume that discretionary spending will rise at the rate of inflation, that recent tax cuts will be phased out, and that there will be no changes to current law. Historically, however, discretionary spending has generally exceeded the rate of inflation, and considerable support exists to extend at least some of the tax cuts passed in recent years. Moreover, spending pressures continue to mount for such big-ticket items as the war in Iraq and homeland security. On the revenue side, current law assumes that a growing number of taxpayers will pay higher taxes under the alternative minimum tax—an assumption with which many taxpayers and elected officials are likely to take issue.

Timely, reliable, and useful financial and management information on current government operations can also be difficult to come by. This year, my agency, the U.S. Government Accountability Office (GAO), was unable for an eighth consecutive year to express an opinion as to whether the U.S. government's consolidated financial statements were fairly stated. The good news was that eighteen of the twenty-four major federal agencies received an unqualified opinion on their individual financial statements, which they issued in record time. The bad news was that GAO was unable to express an opinion on the federal government as a whole because of continuing financial management weaknesses at the Department of Defense, the government's inability to properly account for intragovern-

Table 1.   Selected Fiscal Exposures: Sources and Examples, 2005

Type	Example ($ billion)[a]
Explicit liabilities	Publicly held debt ($4,297) Military and civilian pension and post-retirement health ($3,059) Veterans benefits payable ($925) Environmental and disposal liabilities ($249) Loan guarantees ($43)
Explicit financial commitments	Undelivered orders ($596) Long-term leases ($39)
Financial contingencies	Unadjudicated claims ($4) Pension Benefit Guaranty Corporation ($96) Other national insurance programs ($1) Government corporations, e.g., Ginnie Mae
Exposures implied by current policies or the public's expectations about the role of government	Debt held by government accounts ($3,071)[b] Future Social Security benefit payments ($4,017)[c] Future Medicare Part A benefit payments ($8,561)[c] Future Medicare Part B benefit payments ($12,384)[c] Future Medicare Part D benefit payments ($8,686)[c] Life-cycle cost, including deferred and future maintenance and operating costs (amount unknown) Government-sponsored enterprises, e.g., Fannie Mae and Freddie Mac

[a] All figures are for end of fiscal year 2004, except Social Security and Medicare estimates, which are as of January 1, 2005.

[b] This amount includes $845 billion held by military and civilian pension and post-retirement health funds that would offset the explicit liabilities reported by those funds.

[c] Figures for Social Security and Medicare are net of debt held by the trust funds ($1,687 billion for Social Security, $268 billion for Medicare Part A, and $19 billion for Medicare Part B) and represent net present value estimates over a 75-year period. Over an infinite horizon, the estimate for Social Security would be $11.1 trillion, $24.1 trillion for Medicare Part A, $25.8 trillion for Medicare Part B, and $18.2 trillion for Medicare Part D.

Source: GAO analysis of data from the Department of the Treasury, Office of the Chief Actuary, Social Security Administration, and Office of the Actuary, Centers for Medicare and Medicaid Services.

mental transactions, and various technical obstacles to preparing the consolidated financial statements. In addition, eleven federal agencies had to restate their prior year financial statements, up from five in the previous year.

Results

Ultimately, we should not settle for anything less than a "clean opinion" on timely financial statements that are free from prior year restatements. Real financial management success, however, means no material control weaknesses, no compliance issues, and systems that generate timely and reliable information policymakers can use with confidence.

Beyond current federal financial reporting, too few agencies clearly show the results that they are getting with the taxpayer dollars they spend, and too many significant government commitments and obligations are not fully disclosed. Particularly troubling are the many promises for future spending made in connection with several major programs and policies: Social Security and Medicare, veterans' health care, and contingencies arising from a range of government activities and entities. (See Table 1.) Despite their sobering implications for future budgets, tax burdens, and spending flexibilities, these unfunded commitments are inadequately addressed in the government's current financial statements, budget processes, and legislative deliberations.

The official U.S. gross debt now stands at more than $7 trillion, which works out to about $25,000 for every man, woman, and child in this country. But if you factor in the federal government's other obligations, liabilities, and commitments, including unfunded promises for future Social Security and Medicare benefits, the burden for every American rises to more than $150,000. Believe it or not, our government has already committed itself to more than $45 trillion in debt and other obligations and commitments in current dollars—an amount about eighteen times the current federal budget, or almost four times the current gross domestic product. According to the most recent Medicare trustees' report, the long-term cost to the federal government of the new Medicare prescription drug benefit alone exceeds $8 trillion in current dollars over seventy-five years. That is more than the current outstanding debt of the U.S. government—a fact that never came up during the related legislative debate in Congress.

Although an improving economy will help, we will not be able to grow our way out of the problem. In fact, using reasonable assumptions, closing our projected fiscal gap would require on average real double-digit economic growth every year for the next seventy-five years. Such a growth rate is unprecedented and unrealistic. Even during the boom years of the 1990s, the economy on average grew at only a 3.2 percent real annual rate.

Long- and Short-Term Projections

Long-term simulations from GAO paint a chilling picture. By 2040, assuming discretionary spending grows with Gross Domestic Product (GDP) and all expiring tax provisions are extended, we will have to cut federal spending by more than half or raise taxes to more than two and one-half times today's level to balance the budget. Absent action, the federal government

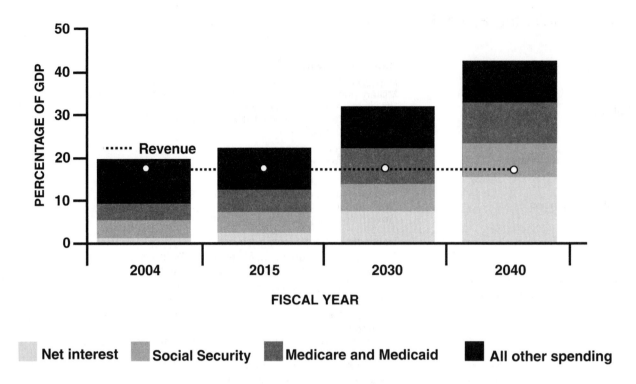

Note: *Although expiring tax provisions are extended, revenue as a share of GDP increases through 2015 due to (1) real bracket creep, (2) more taxpayers becoming subject to the AMT, and (3) increased revenue from tax-deferred retirement accounts. After 2015, revenue as a share of GDP is held constant.*

Source: *GAO's March 2005 analysis.*

Figure 1. Composition of Spending as a Share of GDP (Assuming Discretionary Spending Grows with GDP After 2005 and All Expiring Tax Provisions Are Extended)

could be reduced to doing little more than paying off the interest on the national debt. (See Figure 1.)

Despite the assertions by some, deficits do matter—in both the short and the long term. More immediately, if we fail to act, no one can predict how far interest rates will rise or whether or when foreign investors may lose confidence in U.S. securities as the world's safest investment. Further down the road, we are sure to face a fiscal crisis if we fail to act.

Digging Out

It is time to recognize that we are in a fiscal hole and to stop digging. The sooner we get started, the better. Prompt action will reduce the need for drastic steps and give individuals more time to adjust to any changes. It will also allow the miracle of compounding to start working for us rather than against us. Perhaps most important, prompt action will help us to avoid a dangerous upward spiral of debt and inflation that would ultimately harm every American.

We can begin by insisting on truth and transparency in government financial reporting and the federal budget process. More than 200 years ago, Thomas Jefferson wrote to his Secretary of the Treasury, "We might hope to see the finances of the Union as clear and intelligible as a merchant's books so that every member of Congress, and every man of any mind in the

Union, should be able to comprehend them, to investigate abuses, and consequently to control them." Today, consistent and accurate financial information can seem as elusive as it was in Jefferson's time. But the fiscal risks I have mentioned can be managed only if they are properly accounted for and publicly disclosed.

A crucial first step is to identify the significant commitments facing our government. GAO and other budget experts continue to encourage reforms in government financial reporting and the federal budget process to better reflect the government's commitments and to signal emerging problems. Among other things, GAO has recommended that the government issue an annual report on major fiscal exposures—explicit and implicit promises for future government spending.

We also need to revise current scorekeeping practices across government to emphasize the long-term implications of current policy choices. Too often, annual deficit forecasts and even ten-year budget projections fall short of capturing the long-term costs of federal programs and tax provisions. New budget metrics and mechanisms are needed to assess how spending and tax proposals are likely to play out over time and to manage those risks. For example, our elected representatives should have more explicit information on the long-term costs of pending legislation—including legislation with sunset provisions—on both the spend-

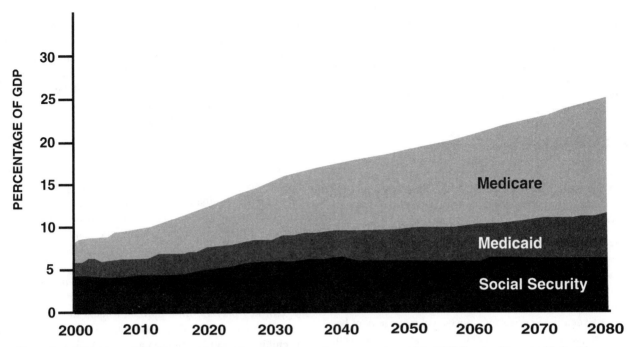

Note: *Social Security and Medicare projections based on intermediate assumptions of the 2005 Trustees' Reports. Medicaid projections based on CBO's January 2005 short-term Medicaid estimates and CBO's December 2003 long-term Medicaid projections under mid-range assumptions.*

Source: *GAO analysis based on data from the Office of the Chief Actuary, Social Security Administration, Office of the Actuary, Centers for Medicare and Medicaid Services, and Congressional Budget Office.*

Figure 2. Social Security, Medicare, and Medicaid Spending as a Percentage of GDP

ing and the tax sides, before they are voted on. The time has also come to consider reinstating budget controls, such as spending caps and "pay-go" rules on both sides of the ledger.

Some specific steps have already been taken to improve federal financial reporting. The latest annual report of the federal government focuses more on the nation's long-range fiscal imbalance, and *The President's Management Agenda* is bringing greater attention to several important management areas. The Federal Accounting Standards Advisory Board (FASAB), which sets accounting and reporting standards for federal entities, is making similar progress. For example, FASAB's beefed-up reporting requirements for social insurance programs such as Social Security and Medicare provide better information on the present value of the net long-term costs facing the federal government. FASAB has also taken steps to enhance disclosure requirements that would provide greater transparency on the collection, use, and remaining balance of "earmarked funds," such as airline ticket surcharges intended to fund improvements at the nation's airports and payroll taxes destined for the Social Security and Medicare trust funds.

Three-Pronged Approach

Looking forward, I believe that a three-pronged approach could significantly reduce our long-term fiscal gap.

First, we need to undertake a top-to-bottom review of government activities to ensure their relevance for the twenty-first century and to free up scarce resources. Today, many if not most of these activities are based on conditions that existed when Harry Truman or Dwight Eisenhower were in the White House. Congress and the president will ultimately need to determine which programs and policies remain priorities, which should be overhauled or consolidated, and which have outlived their usefulness.

Being on the front lines of government operations, federal managers should play a key role in transforming government to address current and future needs. They are in a strong position to help ensure that current programs are getting real results, realign government programs to better meet their objectives, point out instances of waste and mismanagement, and suggest ways to fine-tune government services so that the taxpayer gets maximum value for his or her money. In an environment of increasing budgetary constraints, we will need federal managers who can think strategically and creatively. To this end, agencies will, among other things, need to better identify their own workforce needs. The future success of government will depend in great measure on its ability to recruit, retain, and reward top talent. Modernizing and linking performance systems for institutions and individuals will also be essential.

Second, entitlement reform is unavoidable. We need to put Social Security and Medicare on a sound footing and make these programs solvent, sustainable, and secure for future generations. (See Figure 2.) Actually, the problems with Social Security should not be that difficult to solve. In fact, a window of opportunity now exists in which we can exceed the expectations of all Americans, regardless of whether they will be receiving benefits thirty days or thirty years from now. It will, however, take leadership, courage, and conviction to get the job done.

Third, we need to revisit existing tax policy, including the hundreds of billions of dollars in annual tax preferences. Among other things, we must streamline and simplify existing tax laws while giving closer scrutiny to our tax enforcement efforts.

Conclusion

In the final analysis, the nation's growing fiscal imbalance is not a partisan issue. Overcoming our fiscal challenges will take the combined efforts of both sides of the aisle and both ends of Pennsylvania Avenue.

Elected and appointed officials come and go in Washington, so the responsibility for carrying out many of the program and policy changes I discussed earlier will fall to dedicated civil servants. Given our fiscal challenge and the frequent changes at the top of most federal agencies, it is critically important that the career Senior Executive Service and upper-level management begin to take steps to review and reengineer what the government does, how it does business, who does that business, and how it is financed. It is their efforts that will directly shape the government of the future and help close our fiscal gap. After all, career public servants are, in many cases, the only persons who will be around long enough to see through the process of real government transformation.

More broadly, the understanding and support of the American people will be critical in providing a foundation for action. The public needs to become more informed and involved in the debate over our fiscal future and make their views known. Younger Americans, especially, need to become active in this discussion because they and their children will bear the heaviest burden if today's leaders fail to act. Ignorance and apathy are not viable options. Educating the public about our true financial condition and fiscal outlook is, I believe, the best hope for meaningful and lasting change today.

The price of passivity is steep. The longer we wait, the more onerous our options become. To avoid a range of unacceptable options, from eliminating vital government programs to raising taxes to unreasonable levels to shifting a crushing burden of debt onto future generations, we must act, and act soon.

The task before us is both serious and substantial, but I believe that we can succeed if we start soon and work together in a professional, objective, fact-based, and non-partisan manner. The key to success will be a concerted effort over time by a range of key players, from opinion leaders to policymakers to federal managers. All of us should make every effort to leave our children and grandchildren a world that is more secure and better positioned for the future than it was when we found it. That is what fiscal statesmanship and stewardship are all about.

DAVID M. WALKER is the Comptroller General of the United States and head of the U.S. Government Accountability Office.

From *The Public Manager*, Vol. 34, Number 1, Spring 2005, pp. 29–33. Copyright © 2005 by The Bureaucrat, Inc. Reprinted by permission.

Enron/Andersen: Crisis in U.S. Accounting and Lessons for Government

Accounting and auditing play a key role in the belief of ordinary taxpayers and investors in their institutions. This is equally true of the private and governmental sectors. The Enron/Andersen scandal, regrettably, is not an isolated case, but rather merely indicative of underlying, structural flaws in our financial systems. Moreover, there is evidence that some of these flaws may be present in governmental accounting and auditing. The Sarbanes-Oxley Act of 2002 is an attempt to address these problems in the private sector, but does not address concerns in the public sector. Public sector accounting issues that need to be addressed and monitored include substandard audit work and related liability issues, the appropriate funding of GASB so as to ensure its independence, auditor fees, and auditor independence questions including protection of elected and appointed state auditors.

RICHARD E. BROWN

Introduction

During the past few years, the failure of fundamental U.S. financial processes, checkpoints, and institutions has been staggering and on such a scale as to be difficult to fully absorb. The near failure of Enron and total failure of Andersen, the world's largest and richest personal services firm, shocking as this may seem, is but the tip of the iceberg. One corporate scandal after another has occurred—Adelphia, Waste Management, Global Crossing, Health South, Tyco, Rite Aid, Xerox, WorldCom, and Boston Chicken, to name a few—and in many cases, the public accounting firms performing the corporations' audits have been brought into these scandals.

In the midst of all this financial turmoil there is a great inclination for those in government service, whether local, state, or federal, to view the problems as relating only to the private sector of the economy and as not really impacting or having implications for the governmental sector. There is also a tendency to believe that "these things could not happen to us." It is the goal of this paper, after reviewing some of the financial meltdowns of the past few years, especially those of Enron and Andersen, to try to explain some of the underlying causes for these breakdowns, indicate the widespread and sometimes hidden costs of these failures and, most importantly, review the possible lessons contained in these events for both scholars and practitioners of governmental finance and accounting.

What Happened (and Is Still Happening)?

When one considers the near collapse of Enron and the total demise of Andersen, one of the then Big Five of U.S. public ac-

counting firms, the story of the sinking of the Titanic comes to mind. The Titanic was damaged by fire before it left port, and left without all repairs fully completed. There were not enough lifeboats on the ship to handle all passengers. The ship continued at high speed in an attempt to set records despite warnings of icebergs in the area. And, even after being mortally damaged, many in charge refused to believe that the ship could or would sink. One senses, in both cases, a strong sense of misplaced confidence, perhaps even arrogance. In the case of Enron/Andersen, and the many other similar failures, one also detects much of the "go-go spirit" of the 1990s, flowing, perhaps, out of the Reagan years, with the emphasis on private initiative, entrepreneurial zeal, a buoyant economy, and a general lifting of governmental control and regulation. Indeed, it could be held up as a leading example of why just the right amount of governmental intervention is needed in some key areas of society and the economy.

In the case of Enron, as well as in nearly all the other financial failures, the specifics are enlightening, but hardly new or especially creative. Such financial gimmickry goes back a very long way. Enron created "The Raptors," four special purpose entities. In so doing, the corporation was able to keep the financial details of these entities off the corporate balance sheet, presumably because an independent party owned at least 3 percent of each partnership and this treatment was thus allowed under generally accepted accounting principles (GAAP), as set forth by the Financial Accounting Standards Board (FASB).[1] The problem was that the losses of these entities quickly rose into billions of dollars and when, under pressure, the entities were brought into the core financial statements, it became clear that, after all, Enron itself had huge losses. The corporation's stock price plummeted, and the company went into bankruptcy in December 2001. About 5,000 employees were laid off, and were owed around $140 million in severance pay but would ultimately negotiate a settlement capping payments at $13,500 each, and investors lost millions of dollars. Creditors were owed at least $67 billion, but would likely receive less than 20 cents on the dollar.[2]

Andersen had been Enron's auditor for many years and the question was immediately raised as to why the firm did not in some fashion either work with management to correct the problems or retire as auditor. Andersen's official response was to point out that most of Enron's more controversial treatments of financial issues were within established GAAP. Unofficially, the firm began to destroy important audit-related documents, was charged by the U.S. Department of Justice, ultimately found guilty of the felony charge in court, and dissolved as a firm in the fall of 2002.[3]

As startling as these developments are, they are but the surface of the story. It is other, related developments and events that may well turn out to be more instructive. For example, Enron's financial difficulties apparently went well beyond ''The Raptors'' alone, since a few months after its bankruptcy filing, Enron posted a further $14 billion write down in the value of its assets.[4] Questions inevitably surfaced about the oversight role played by Enron's Board of Directors and Audit Committee, and evidence began to mount that several members of the Board had debatable ties to Enron and its management. And last, but by no means least, fundamental issues arose regarding both auditing procedures and, of equal import, the appropriateness of ties and relationships between auditor and auditee. In addition to serving as Enron's auditor, Andersen conducted important consulting assignments for Enron. In 2001 Andersen earned $55 million in fees from Enron, and over half of that amount was for consulting work, raising basic questions about auditor independence. Moreover, this blend of audit and consulting was not unusual for Andersen (nor for other firms, it should be noted), and in fact was dubbed an ''integrated audit'' within the firm. Auditors who did raise objections to Enron's accounting were taken off the engagement. Finally, Andersen's continued relationship with Enron had let to a situation in which auditors and Enron employees shared offices for long periods, and socialized together, all of which, if not violating auditing standards regarding personal relationships, certainly pushed them to the limit.[5]

One would wish that the Enron/Andersen fiasco could be dismissed as rare and unique. Unfortunately, as indicated earlier, this is far from the case. The business news has seemed filled, if not daily, then weekly, with financial failures approaching and perhaps even exceeding Enron/Andersen over the past year or two. The list is a long one, including some of the nation's largest corporations and CPA (audit) firms. And, to no great surprise, many of the same elements are to be found. For example, in February 2003, KPMG sent out a letter to university accounting faculties and others, which stated:

> On Wednesday, January 29th, the Securities and Exchange Commission filed a complaint in federal district court against the firm, three current partners, and

one former partner in connection with KPMG's audits of the 1997–2000 financial statements of Xerox Corporation, a former client.

> We're confident that, when all the facts are reviewed through the appropriate legal processes, the Firm's position and that of our partners will be vindicated. While we would have preferred to resolve this matter without litigation, we firmly believe we did the right thing. The anticipated action by the SEC will in no way affect our ability to continue to serve our clients. It will not impede our efforts to help restore shareholder confidence in the capital markets, nor will it interfere with our ability to work with the SEC.

> KPMG stands firmly behind our audits of Xerox's financial statements and the professional judgments made during the course of the audits. Our audits for Xerox were performed with professionalism and independence, and pursuant to the high standards KPMG sets for itself every day.

In June 2003, it was reported that the Securities and Exchange Commission (SEC) was filing civil fraud charges against KPMG.[6]

Another ''Big Five'' firm, Ernst & Young (E & Y), ran into its own set of recent difficulties with audit services and the SEC. The SEC has accused Health South of artificially inflating earnings and profits over five years by a total of $1.4 billion, and E & Y was the auditor during much of this time. Also in 2003, E & Y ran into difficulty with the SEC over providing nonaudit services to Sprint, an E & Y audit client.[7]

The pervasiveness of the problem is illustrated by the results of a study showing that auditors gave a ''clean'' (unqualified) audit opinion to nearly half of the 228 public companies that later filed for bankruptcy within the year. Such findings raise fundamental questions about both auditing procedures and processes, and the value that investors derive from audits and audit fees.[8]

How and Why Did Enron/Andersen Happen?

Many of those involved in things financial during the past decade or two would likely have predicted the current situation. The storm clouds have been gathering for a very long time. A former chairman of the SEC, Arthur Levitt, had been warning anyone who would listen that allowing public accounting firms to provide both auditing and consulting services to the same client was growing to an unacceptable level in terms of both dollars and mix of services, and was undermining the integrity of the audit and the ability of investors to rely on the audits. Levitt's attempts to correct this situation met—again, no great surprise—stiff resistance from many in the CPA community, especially the larger, richer, and more powerful CPA firms. Eventually these lobbying efforts succeeded in preventing Congress from taking needed corrective action, action that was eventually taken with the collapse of Enron.[9]

The good news for the SEC and Congress is that they were not the only institutions to let down the American public and investors. One would have thought that the larger accounting community could have counted on the American Institute of CPAs (AICPA) to help avoid such a calamity. The AICPA is the leading trade association representing member CPAs and their interests in the U.S. In fact, the AICPA has been under harsh criticism throughout this same time period for being deeply involved in other ventures, including an expensive and controversial effort to create a new more all-encompassing credential to include non-CPAs, and a new venture called CPA 2 Biz to promote and sell a wide array of accounting services.[10]

Nor is the American Accounting Association (AAA), the nation's leading membership organization representing educators, without blame. One could argue that it is just such a role—objective analysis and criticism—that academics are supposed to perform (and what tenure is all about). However, one would need to look long and hard to find any such counsel emanating from the AAA and academic community during this period. This silence could be explained in large measure by the close ties between the academic and practice communities in the form of student internships and employment, firm funding of student scholarships and faculty professorships, and the fact that many accounting faculty members are themselves CPAs and have practiced public accounting. A sad but vivid reminder of these ties is evidenced by the letter sent to university accounting faculties as Andersen was going out of existence. Andersen student scholarships and faculty professorships continue in accounting programs at many universities.[11]

The extent to which many of these influential bodies not only did not criticize accounting and auditing developments over the past several years, but even bought into those developments, is well illustrated by a book that appeared in August 2000, authored by two leading scholars and entitled, *Accounting Education: Charting a Course Through a Perilous Future*. Published by the AAA, and funded by the AICPA, Institute of Management Accountants (IMA), and Big Five firms, one could easily argue that the book's purpose was to chastise accounting educators for teaching too much accounting and teaching too few of the skills needed for consulting. In short, one could argue that the book was following the then party line of the large firms that the future, and money, rested more in consulting than auditing.[12]

Thus, the warning signs had been out there for decades, and either fell on deaf ears or were ignored or resisted often for reasons of self-interest. And, in all this, nearly every leading political, practice, and academic institution having a role in U.S. accounting and auditing must share the responsibility for the ultimate accounting crisis. As if to reinforce the cliché, "better late than never," prominent accountants are only now beginning to document the crisis in the profession in detailed and knowledgeable accounts. One of the most complete accounts is contained in a two-part series entitled, "How the U.S. Accounting Profession Got Where It Is Today," by Stephen Zeff of Rice University. Several of the topics discussed, covering the period to about 1980, are instructive: "Scandals, Lawsuits, and Criticism of the Profession"; "More Scandals and Attacks from Congress"; "Under the Gun, the Institute [AICPA] Reforms";

and "Management Advisory Services [Consulting] Come Under SEC Fire." Zeff makes the point that "The body proposed in Rep. Moss' bill, which died in committee at the end of 1978, foreshadowed … the Public Company Accounting Oversight Board, established by the Sarbanes-Oxley Act of 2002."[13]

Fallout: The Price We Pay

The costs associated with these developments are both qualitative and quantitative, and are large and widespread. As seen, few relevant institutions (and belief in them) are left unaffected. The list is a long one including FASB, the SEC, Congress, the AICPA, the AAA, etc. The investing public must also be left wondering about the roles of boards of directors, audit committees, and internal auditors and accountants and what they do to earn their pay.

The cost to the investing public is enormous. Anecdotally, each of us knows one or more people who now plan to keep working because at least half of their investments evaporated in the wake of corporate scandals (along with other economic problems, to be sure). The simple fact is that over 80 million Americans own stocks or mutual funds and were thus adversely impacted. Not surprisingly, polls show that Americans have little confidence in U.S. institutions, and a long list of influential leaders, both individuals and organizations, including Paul Volcker, *The Wall Street Journal*, Lou Dobbs, the New York Stock Exchange, and the chairman of Goldman Sachs, have noted this crisis of confidence and its importance. The international implications of the financial scandals are described in one newspaper in this way: "U.S. Loses Sparkle As Icon of Marketplace: Wave of Corporate Scandals Could Tilt World Business Away From American Model."[14]

Other costs are witnessed daily, but are often overlooked. University endowments are suffering and so are students who now as a result receive reduced or no scholarships. As public, state, and local retirement systems experience the impact of these losses—California is suing Enron, and Florida lost $282 million in the Enron collapse—benefits to retirees are reexamined and often reduced. The Ohio Public Employees Retirement System has made substantial reductions in health benefits for retirees. And, of course, as tax revenues decline, public entities must reduce employment and, it follows, services. Most American states are struggling to cut budgets and thus avoid deficits, and at least a part of this is owing to the breakdown of, and confidence in, our financial institutions. John Biggs, then chairman of TIAA-CREF, one of the nation's largest retirement systems stated: "Did Enron's collapse affect TIAA-CREF? Of course it did."[15]

Alan Greenspan, chairman of the Federal Reserve Board, summed up the interdependence of all this in a speech to the Gerald R. Ford Foundation:

> I do not deny that many in our society appear to have succeeded in a material way by cutting corners and manipulating associates, both in their professional lives and personal lives, but no economy can function properly if dishonesty is widespread. Trust is at the root of any economic system based on

mutually beneficial exchange. In virtually all transactions, we rely on the word of those with whom we do business. If a significant number of business people violated the trust upon which our interactions are based, our court system and our economy would be swamped into immobility. It is critically important that all Americans believe that they are part of a system they perceive as fair and worthy of their support.[16]

Ultimately (and few will lose much sleep over it), one of the greatest losses is to the accounting profession itself. With passage of the Sarbanes-Oxley Act of 2002, the accounting profession lost the right to regulate itself, a privilege which until now the SEC had delegated to the profession since the passage of the Securities Exchange Act in 1934. Sarbanes-Oxley is to a great extent—and long overdue—based on the reforms suggested years earlier by Arthur Levitt. Among other things, the Act creates a five-member Public Company Accounting Oversight Board (PCAOB), including three non-CPAs, and all appointed by the SEC. The Board must register accounting firms, adopt auditing standards, conduct inspections of accounting firms, and, if needed, impose sanctions on firms. Eight specific consulting services cannot be performed by the auditing firm, and other services must be approved by the corporation's audit committee. Corporation executives must certify, under criminal sanctions, as to the accuracy of financial statements. The lead audit partner must rotate off the audit every five years. And FASB has been made more independent of corporations and CPA firms through a change in its funding mechanism. The significance of this legislation cannot be overstated: the accounting profession has lost the right to regulate itself. Most key concerns of reformers have been addressed in the legislation. However, indications are that the CPA firms will not go down without a fight. Even as this paper is written there are signs that the firms are negotiating to retain important consulting services, and the U.S. Congress, under enormous lobbying pressure, is attempting to pass legislation relating to the expensing of stock options, which would undermine the independence of the FASB.[17]

Lessons for Government

The good news is that Sarbanes-Oxley goes a long way toward correcting most of the structural problems inherent in the way in which accounting–auditing practices have evolved over the past couple of decades as they pertain to public corporations. The bad news may be that Sarbanes-Oxley does not apply to large sectors of the U.S. economy, including privately held companies, not-for-profit organizations, and governmental entities. It is the latter, government, which is our concern here. The governmental sector may indeed be experiencing some of the same underlying problems we have seen in the case of public corporations.

Some gains have been made recently in the public arena. At the federal level, in January 2002 the GAO adopted new auditing standards relating to auditor independence, in an effort to address many of the same concerns relating to an auditor providing both auditing and consulting services.[18] For example, the all-too-frequent practice of CPA firms both assembling and opining on financial statements for small- and medium-sized public entities will be discouraged under the revised auditing standards. And there is some evidence that the provisions in Sarbanes-Oxley may ultimately impact private companies, not-for-profit organizations, and governmental entities.[19] However, the fact is that governmental finance and accounting officials may still face many of the same practices and dangers we have observed in the pre-Sarbanes-Oxley era. The following concerns are intended to be merely illustrative and include substandard audit work, the level of audit fees, the funding of GASB, and the independence of government auditors.

Substandard Audit Work

The governmental sector has had its own share of problems with audit "failures," or substandard audit work. In March 1986 the GAO released a study, *CPA Audit Quality: Many Governmental Audits Do Not Comply with Professional Standards*. Significantly, this study was but the last in a series of such reviews spanning nearly two decades. The 1986 report used widely accepted sampling techniques and included audit work performed by large and small CPA firms in many regions of the nation. As important as the GAO study itself was the debate it created over self-regulation of accountants. Indeed, the report became the focal point of congressional hearings on the accounting profession. Perhaps the most significant thing about the 1986 study and its immediate aftermath was the degree to which the accounting profession refused to accept the findings of the study and take swift corrective action. In a sense this event, staged in the public arena, became a predictor of the future leading to Sarbanes-Oxley. An earlier conference called jointly in Cherry Hill, NJ, by the GAO and AICPA, presumably to discuss substandard governmental audit work, had turned instead into a discussion of how and why more such audits currently performed in-house, by government auditors, should not instead be contracted out to CPA firms.[20]

While more recent studies of the quality of CPA firm audits of governmental entities are lacking, the earlier series of GAO studies clearly indicate that in the area of substandard audit work the public sector is no less vulnerable than the private sector. This reality is made all the more dangerous because there tends to be less oversight and scrutiny by direct investors and their representatives in the case of the public sector. In short, audit "failures," lacking a GAO-type review, are more apt to go undetected.

Exacerbating this situation is the pressure exerted on auditors by low audit fees. Many CPA firms refuse to do governmental auditing because of the low fees paid by governmental entities. For national firms some local offices, for the same reason, do not do government audits. In some areas smaller firms, specializing in government audits, do a great deal of the contracted work. Fees at 50 percent or even less of usual fees are not uncommon for governmental work. This fee structure is owing to the fact that such work can often be done in a period when audit staff are not otherwise occupied. Whatever the reasons for the lower fees there may also be a further reason to do substandard audit work as firm partners and staff rush to stay within the lower budget.

Funding

Created in 1984, it took the GASB about fourteen years to issue Statement 34, which in effect is the adoption of entity-wide financial statements (versus fund by fund) and full accrual accounting. This is fairly elementary accounting and the delay was undoubtedly due in no small measure to strong political opposition by vocal constituency groups and to the fact that GASB is dependent upon these same groups for its support and funding. Service efforts and accomplishments reporting (performance reporting), remains on GASB's research agenda nearly twenty years after its start-up, due in no small degree to strong opposition by a number of influential constituency groups, including the Government Finance Officers Association (GFOA). In many ways these realities remind one of FASB and the problems it encountered in establishing a stronger, more realistic GAAP. Independence often translates into funding, and GASB funding needs reexamination.[21]

Until passage of the Sarbanes-Oxley Act, the FASB, founded in 1973, was funded for the most part from contributions from accounting firms, the AICPA, corporations, and other organizations. The Act requires that public companies pay a mandatory fee to support FASB and the Public Company Accounting Oversight Board.[22]

Unfortunately, GASB's funding problems have not yet been solved. The Financial Accounting Foundation (FAF), the unit which oversees both the FASB and GASB, is committed to independence from federal funding and control while providing adequate financial resources. To date, the FAF has been successful in achieving the first goal, but is still experiencing difficulty with the second. An unintended consequence of Sarbanes-Oxley was to decrease contributions, a major source of funding for GASB as well as FASB. Thus, with the passage of the Sarbanes-Oxley Act, GASB is faced with implementing a new funding model. Provisions of Sarbanes-Oxley are such that FASB will now receive funding from all publicly traded firms based on a fee based on their market capitalization. Prior to this the FAF received voluntary contributions from corporations and public accounting firms. This change in funding has adversely impacted GASB finances because of both higher mandated cost allocations between the FASB and GASB and the fact that public accounting firms and some other organizations are no longer making contributions. As a result, GASB's finances have become precarious.

Contributions have normally been GASB's main source of funding ($2,176,000 in fiscal year [FY] 2002), followed closely by subscription and publication sales ($1,946,000). Contributions decreased over $100,000 between FY 2001 and 2002. Major categories of contributions in FY 2002 include state governments ($963,000), the public accounting profession ($435,000), foundations ($407,000), financial organizations such as securities, investor, and insurance companies ($189,000), and the GFOA ($182,000). To alleviate GASB's funding problems the FAF plans to change this mix somewhat and make assessments of local units of government based on budget size and an assessment on municipal debt issues. GASB had the option under Sarbanes-Oxley to accept funding from the new mandatory assessment, but it was decided that to rely on federally controlled funding would impair the Board's independence. Thus, new funding solutions were investigated. The FAF is now in the process of finalizing a funding mechanism that would include a one half-cent assessment on municipal debt issues. Contributions from governmental units and the continued sale of publications and memberships would be other key parts of funding. However, the challenge remains the same as it was and is for FASB: how to raise sufficient funds to retain a top-notch professional staff while remaining independent of those who pay the salaries. In his farewell message outgoing GASB Chairman Tom Allen stated:

> My biggest regrets are related to the lack of a stable funding base for the GASB and the fact that despite our efforts, we have not been able to establish as close a working relationship as the GASB needs with a few of the GASB's constituent organizations....
>
> On a positive note, some key GASB constituent organizations recently have established a mechanism to collect a small fee on municipal debt issuances. This program should help provide some much-needed funding stability to the Board; however, it will not resolve all of the GASB's funding issues. The FAF is seeking to increase the financial support from the larger city and county governments impacted by the GASB standards and from financial statement users that benefit from those standards. In the meantime, I am very appreciative of the FAF's willingness to help cover the GASB's operating deficits through Foundation reserves until a more stable funding base can be provided.[23]

Independence of Government Auditors

The GAO, the nation's and Congress' audit agency, is headed by the U.S. Comptroller General who has a fifteen-year term of office, presumably to attract high-quality individuals in a difficult and complex political environment, and to allow this individual to act without regard to politics. Initially, as state audit agencies were growing in stature, size, and funding, the GAO pressed for a set term of office for state auditors with difficult removal provisions. However, the GAO quickly and quietly withdrew this "model legislation." The result is that today about a fifth of the state auditors serve without a constitutional or contractual term of office. Perhaps of greater importance is the fact that about one-half or more of state auditors can be removed from office for unspecified or very general causes. These conditions raise fundamental concerns about the independence of these auditors. Similarly, if a state audit staff serves at the pleasure of a state auditor who himself/herself is without a term of office, how independent can such an audit operation truly be? A series of other, audit-related questions follow. If public accounting firms are used to perform audits of governmental entities, are they rotated every three to five years (or, as in Ohio, are auditors merely requested to rebid every five years?). Must firm partners rotate off the audit? If state audit agency teams are used, are they rotated? These fundamental issues of audit independence remain a problem in many state and local units of government.[24]

A Summing Up

This is a good time for governmental financial officials to ask hard questions of themselves in the wake of Enron/Andersen. Most of those in the governmental financial community have personally witnessed or are aware of stories similar to Enron's "creative accounting": moving special entities in and out of the financial reports as needed (i.e., bridges, tunnels, airports); creating bonds with the "moral" backing of the governmental entity (but perhaps not the legal backing); changing the fiscal year as needed; booking grant revenues as needed instead of when they should be booked; etc. While in most cases such devices are clearly not within government GAAP, auditors must be positioned in such a way, in terms of independence, resources, time, and fees, to identify such problems in audits should that prove necessary.[25]

Indeed, because of the great importance and sensitivity of these financial issues, it is often difficult to learn from and build on lessons from the past. Even as the business press is filled with enormous financial disasters, we read for example that Congress is considering legislation which would impose a ban on FASB action to create new rules for recording and reporting stock options.[26]

Accounting and auditing play a key role in the belief of ordinary taxpayers and investors in their institutions. This is equally true of the private and governmental sectors. The Enron/Andersen scandal, regrettably, is not an isolated case, but rather may be suggestive of underlying, structural flaws in our accounting, auditing, and related financial systems. Moreover, there are indications that some of these flaws might be present in governmental accounting and auditing. The Sarbanes-Oxley Act of 2002 is an attempt to address these problems for public corporations, but much remains to be done in the public sector.

Kenneth Arrow, the Nobel laureate in economics, wrote nearly 30 years ago: "Trust is an important lubricant of a social system. It is extremely efficient; it saves a lot of trouble to have a fair degree of reliance on another person's word."[27]

Robert Fulghum stated it in more basic terms:

> Think of what a better world it would be if we all—the whole world—...had a basic policy to always put things back where we found them and cleaned up our own messes....[28]

Only because of federal action, and unhappily, not to the accounting profession itself, accounting in the private sector is in the process of cleaning up some of its own messes. Governmental accounting is in a position to benefit from this experience. A reality we must confront is that many private sector accounting and audit failures will at last be ultimately caught as profits and stock prices deteriorate and investors become aware of underlying problems. In the public sector, such failures may be allowed to linger indefinitely as the taxpayers continue to pay the bill unaware of what lies beneath.

Notes

1. Anite Raghavan, "How a Bright Star at Andersen Fell along with Enron," *The Wall Street Journal*, May 15, 2002, sec. A: 1.

2. Bloomberg News, "Severance Package from Enron Is Set," *The New York Times*, August 29, 2002, sec. C: 2; Edward Iwata, "Enron Creditors' Possible Take? 14–18 Cents on Dollar," *USA Today*, July 14, 2003, sec. B: 3.

3. Ken Brown and Ianthe Jeanne Dugan, "Andersen's Fall from Grace Is a Tale of Greed and Miscues," *The Wall Street Journal*, June 7, 2002, sec. A: 1.

4. Tom Fowler, "The Fall of Enron," *The Houston Chronicle*, August 12, 2002, sec. A: 1.

5. Brown and Dugan, "Andersen's Fall from Grace Is a Tale of Greed and Miscues," sec. A: 1.

6. Letter from James E. Buckley, Partner in Charge, University Relations, KPMG, February 6, 2003; Bloomberg News, AP, "Former Xerox Chiefs Settle," *The Gazette* (Montreal), June 6, 2003, sec. B: 8.

7. Jonathan Weil, "Did Ernst Miss Key Fraud Risks at Health South?" *The Wall Street Journal*, April 10, 2003, sec. C: 1; Edward Alden and Andrew Parker, "E & Y Fined in IRS Clampdown," *Financial Times* (London), July 3, 2003: 25.

8. Cassell Bryan-Low, "Auditors Failed to Warn Companies," *The Wall Street Journal*, July 11, 2002, sec. C: 9; Ken Brown, "Auditors' Methods Make It Hard to Catch Fraud by Executives," *The Wall Street Journal*, July 8, 2002, sec. C: 1.

9. See, for example, comments by former President Clinton in "News Briefs," *Accounting Today*, May 5–18, 2003: 3; Scott Bernard Nelson, "Healing the Accounting Industry," *The Boston Globe*, June 23, 2002, sec. C: 1.

10. For a discussion of some of the issues/distractions confronting the accounting profession during the past several years, the best (most objective) coverage may be included in the newspaper, *Accounting Today*. See, for example, columns by Eli Mason, "An Open Letter to AICPA Council," May 6–19, 2002: 6, and "CPA 2 Biz—On a Consistent Basis," January 6–26, 2003: 6; see also, in the same newspaper, the column by J. Edward Ketz, "Why Didn't the Private-Sector Watchdogs Bark?" November 25–December 15, 2002: 8, and the column by Paul B. W. Miller and Paul R. Bahnson, "Nature Abhors a Vacuum...," January 6–26, 2003: 14.

11. Relatively little has been written on the role of, or lack of involvement by, scholars in the current problems of the accounting profession. For a critique of this, see Richard E. Brown, "What Will Public Administration Do?" *PA Times*, May 2003: 8.

12. W. Steve Albrecht and Robert J. Sack, *Accounting Education: Charting the Course through a Perilous Future* (Sarasota, FL: American Accounting Association, 2000).

13. Stephen A. Zeff, "How the U.S. Accounting Profession Got Where It Is Today," *Accounting Horizons* 17, nos. 3 and 4 (September 2003 and December 2003): 189–205 and 267–286, respectively. See also Arthur R. Wyatt, "Accounting Professionalism—They Just Don't Get It!" *Accounting Horizons* 18, no. 1 (March 2004): 45–53.

14. All in *The Wall Street Journal*; see "U.S. Loses Sparkle as Icon of Marketplace," June 28, 2002, sec. A: 10; "Corporate Governance: How to Fix a Broken System," February 24, 2003, sec. R: 1; and "Americans Distrust Institutions in Poll," June 13, 2002, sec. A: 4.

15. See, for example, Kathryn Kranhold, "Florida Panel May Sue Alliance over Pension's Enron Losses," *The Wall Street Journal*, April 23, 2002, sec. B: 2; John H. Biggs, "Enron and TIAA-CREF," *TIAA-CREF Perspective*, May 2002: 2; *STRS Ohio News*, May 2003: 1–3.

16. ''Honesty Good for Business,'' *The Morning Journal* (Lorain, OH), AP Wire, September 9, 1999, sec. D: 1.

17. Gila N. Fox and Madeline Mohanco, ''A Crisis in Confidence,'' *Catalyst* (Ohio Society of CPAs), (September/October 2002), 14–20; ''FAF Blasts House Options Reform Bill,'' *Accounting Today*, June 7–20, 2004: 4.

18. Comptroller General of the United States, *GAO Press Statement* (Washington, DC: U.S. General Accounting Office, January 25, 2002).

19. ''PCAOB Chair Signals Expansion of SOX to ''Other Contexts,'' *Catalyst* (July–August 2004): 50–51; ''States Mull Tighter, Tougher Auditing Rules and Penalties,'' *Accounting Today*, June 21–July 11, 2004: 5.

20. U.S. General Accounting Office, *CPA Audit Quality: Many Governmental Audits Do Not Comply with Professional Standards* (Washington, DC: GAO/AFMD-86–33, March 1986); Richard E. Brown, The Expectations Gap: An Added Dimension—The Case of Government Auditing, in *Research in Accounting Regulation*, ed. Gary John Prints (Volume 1, Greenwich, CT, JAI Press, 1987): 139–164.

21. Timothy Greive, President, Government Finance Officers Association, ''Editorial: The GASB's Mission and Performance Measurement,'' *Government Finance Review* 17, no. 5 (October 2001): 4–5.

22. Glenn Cheney, ''No More Donations: FASB Readies for Shift in Funding,'' *Accounting Today*, July 7–20, 2003: 14.

23. William Voorhees, ''Commentary: Funding GASB after Sarbanes-Oxley,'' *PA Times* (June 2004): 7–8; Douglas R. Ellsworth, William H. Hansell, and Richard D. Johnson, ''The Role of Local Governments in Ensuring the Financial Viability of the GASB,'' Financial Accounting Foundation, undated; Financial Accounting Foundation, ''Fulfilling Our Critical Mission,'' *2002 Annual Report*, see especially pp. 30–34; GASB, *The GASB Report*, ''GASB Chairman Reflects on Its Ten Years as a Member of the Board,'' No. 231-B, June 2004: 2–3.

24. These independence issues are discussed in Richard E. Brown, ''On the State of State Auditing: Analysis; Reflections,'' *Public Budgeting & Finance* 5, no. 2 (Summer 1985): 75–78 and Karen Schuele Walton and Richard E. Brown, ''State Legislators and State Auditors: Is There an Inherent Role Conflict?'' *Public Budgeting & Finance* 10, no. 1 (Spring 1990): 3–12. Information on state auditors is taken from National Association of State Auditors, Comptrollers and Treasurers, *Auditing in the States: A Summary* (Lexington, KY: 2003 Edition), Table 18.

25. A recent reminder of the relevance and importance of such issues is Statement No. 39 of the Governmental Accounting Standards Board, ''Determining Whether Certain Organizations Are Component Units'' (Norwalk, CT: GASB, May 2002).

26. Marilyn Geewax, ''Bill Would Halt Ruling on Options,'' *The Atlanta Journal and Constitution*, June 4, 2003, sec. D: 1.

27. David Wessel, ''Invisible Hand Works because of Invisible Handshake,'' *The Wall Street Journal*, July 11, 2002, sec. A: 2.

28. Robert Fulghum, ''All I Ever Really Needed to Know, I Learned in Kindergarten,'' reprint from *Kansas City Times*, September 17, 1986.

RICHARD E. BROWN is Professor and Chair, Department of Accounting, Kent State University. He may be reached at dbrown@bsa3.kent.edu.

From *Public Budgeting and Finance*, Vol. 25, Number 3, Fall 2005, pp. 20–32. Copyright © 2005 by Blackwell Publishing, Ltd. Reprinted by permission.

Huge Rise Looms for Health Care in Local Budgets

A New Accounting Rule

Cost of Meeting Promises Could Soon Quintuple for States and Cities

MARY WILLIAMS WALSH AND MILT FREUDENHEIM

When the Metropolitan Transportation Authority proposed making new workers chip in more to its pension fund than current workers do, it was enough to send the union out on strike and bring the nation's largest mass-transit system to a halt for three days.

But the cost of pensions may look paltry next to that of another benefit soon to hit New York and most other states and cities: the health care promised to retired teachers, judges, firefighters, bus drivers and other former employees, which must be figured under a new accounting formula.

The city currently provides free health insurance to its retirees, their spouses and dependent children. The state is almost as generous, promising to pay, depending on the date of hire, 90 to 100 percent of the cost for individual retirees, and 82 to 86 percent for retiree families.

Those bills—$911 million this year for city retirees and $859 million for state retirees out of a total city and state budget of $156.6 billion—may seem affordable now. But the New York governments, like most other public agencies across the country, have been calculating the costs in a way that sharply understates their price tag over time.

Although governments will not have to come up with the cash immediately, failure to find a way to finance the yearly total will eventually hurt their ability to borrow money affordably.

When the numbers are added up under new accounting rules scheduled to go into effect at the end of 2006, New York City's annual expense for retiree health care is expected to at least quintuple, experts say, approaching and maybe surpassing $5 billion, for exactly the same benefits the retirees get today. The number will grow because the city must start including the value of all the benefits earned in a given year, even those that will not be paid until future years.

Some actuaries say the new yearly amount could be as high as $10 billion. The increases for the state could be equally startling. Most other states and cities also offer health benefits to retirees, and will also be affected by the accounting change.

"It's not likely that New York City has a way to fund current costs, its pension obligation and fund retiree health care without raising taxes or cutting services," said Jan Lazar, an independent consultant specializing in city retirement finances. "These are huge numbers, not a one-time cost."

The pay-as-you-go accounting method that New York now uses greatly understates the full obligation taxpayers have incurred because it does not include any benefits to be paid in the future. Most other state and local governments that offer significant health benefits to retirees use the same method and will also have to bring newer, larger numbers onto their books in the next two or three years.

The increases will vary from place to place, but New York is expected to be at the high end because it offers richer benefits than many other cities and has many police officers, firefighters and sanitation workers who can retire with full pension at age 50.

At the transit talks, pensions were pulled off the table in the end, and the final settlement is likely to reflect an increased health care payment by current workers, not retirees. But even though New York was pushed to a standstill over proposed changes in transit workers' pensions, virtually no one in government, outside of a tiny group of experts, is talking publicly about the far more daunting bill for citywide retiree health insurance.

The total value of the pensions promised is probably bigger, but money has already been set aside to pay the pensions, to a significant degree. For retiree health care, nothing stands behind those promises except the expectation that taxes will be raised enough in the future to cover them.

At last count, the city's biggest pension fund—the one for about 300,000 workers not covered by police, firefighter, teacher or school workers plans—said it had $42 billion set aside in trust for the $42.2 billion it owed. No money at all has been set aside for that same group of city employees' post-retirement health care.

Determining the correct amount will be "a tremendous undertaking," a city official said, adding that rapid changes in the overall health care environment, including the Medicare and Medicaid programs, make it extremely difficult to see what future costs will be.

No one really knows what the total health care obligation is for the 836,000 people already retired or now working for the city and state, much less who will pay for it. Neither side in the transit dispute, for example, has publicly mentioned retiree health care.

A small group of city officials has been quietly working for months, gathering data on the dozens of city retiree health plans, large and small, but the process is not expected to be complete for months.

Meanwhile, a handful of other states and cities have already done the same calculations. If their results are any guide, New York City and the state could ultimately find that they have each promised their retirees health care worth tens of billions of dollars. The transportation authority, a state entity whose retiree health care costs are partially borne by New York City, could find that it has already promised more than $5 billion worth of benefits to its current and future retirees.

At the moment, the transportation authority is spending about $380 million a year on health care for its unionized workers. That covers both active workers and retirees; while a precise breakdown does not exist, citywide demographics suggest that about $165 million of that may be for retirees.

Once the new accounting rule is in force, the transportation authority may find itself scrounging for 5 to 10 times that amount every year, $825 million to $1.6 billion, if an accounting rule of thumb devised by one of the chief credit rating firms, Fitch Ratings, holds up. By the time anybody knows for sure, the authority will probably be halfway through the union contract it is still struggling to complete.

To find the money, the authority will have to turn to "higher fares, less service, or more pressure on the city government to fork over subsidies," said Robert A. Kurtter, an analyst with Moody's Investors Service who monitors New York's finances. The city's retirement system, meanwhile, will be struggling with the same problem on a much larger scale.

Failing to allow for the future expenses will undercut cities' ability to borrow.

The city has been offering free health care to its retirees for decades. In the private sector, companies that once offered health insurance for retirees began to stop doing so in the 1990's, for a number of reasons, including accounting rule changes like those now coming into effect for states and cities. Today, only 38 percent of companies with more than 200 workers offer retiree health insurance, according to the Citizens Budget Commission, a group that analyzes city and state finances.

An even smaller number of companies, 9 percent, pay any part of the premiums that can be used to buy optional supplements to Medicare for retirees over 65. New York City and the state both pay the full cost of Medicare supplements for their retirees.

"They've stuck with that, although the rest of the world has changed," said Charles M. Brecher, research director of the Citizens Budget Commission and a professor of public and health administration at New York University's Wagner School of Public Service.

While the private sector was curtailing retiree benefits, New York City and the state have been preserving and even expanding benefits in bargaining with their unions. Both sides focused mainly on the current cost of the benefits. No one was paying much attention to the deferred cost of the benefits that would come due once current workers retired. Meanwhile, health costs resumed rising at double-digit rates, and a large share of the public work force began to reach retirement age. Currently, the city administers a big health plan for its workers and retirees and contributes to dozens of smaller retiree health plans that are run by individual unions and supplement the city's coverage.

The calculations are now being done, privately, because of the accounting rule change. In 2004 the Governmental Accounting Standards Board, a nonprofit body that writes accounting rules for governments, issued a new standard for retiree medical plans. It roughly follows a similar standard issued in 1994 for public pension plans.

But rather than requiring local governments to finance their retiree medical plans, the rule simply requires them to lay out a theoretical financing framework, then report how they are dealing with it. Localities that create trust funds will get certain financial rewards. Localities that do not put money behind their promises risk being punished by falling credit ratings. When a city's credit rating falls, it becomes harder and more expensive to issue bonds or otherwise borrow money.

Municipal bond analysts at Moody's and Standard & Poor's said they were taking a wait-and-see stance. "How the city addresses the burden is another question—by reducing the benefit or funding the cost, or allowing this liability to mount," said Mr. Kurtter, of Moody's. If the amount grows, "at some point it will create a credit issue," he said.

Mr. Kurtter said city officials have acknowledged privately that the amounts will be large, "in the billions, they say."

Labor officials say that even though the change is just a new way of accounting, not a price increase in the conventional sense, they fear that putting a number on the city's promises for future retiree health care will lead to sticker shock and renewed calls to cut benefits.

"There's a lot of fear that this kind of disclosure will reignite the whole battle of who assumes retiree health costs," said Randi Weingarten, the president of the United Federation of Teachers and the chairwoman of the Municipal Labor Committee. "Even though it should be a data point, it will be used as a hammer."

MICHAEL COOPER contributed reporting for this article.

UNIT 5

Technology and Information Systems

Unit Selections

Key Points to Consider

- Identify and discuss the positive and negative aspects of posting extensive amounts of public information on the Web. What are some of the ways in which you can balance the desire for open government with the need for privacy?

- Discuss how DeKalb County, Georgia, is using radio-frequency identification (RFID) technology for its juvenile justice system. Do you think that this is an appropriate use of RFID technology? Why or why not?

- Why is e-waste such a major problem? Identify and discuss some of the ways that the e-waste problem can be mitigated.

- Discuss some of the ways in which the city of Garland is implementing its digital document management program. What are some of the major advantages of this program?

- Identify and discuss some of the ways in which the U.S. health care system can be improved through high-tech methods and procedures.

Student Web Site

www.mhcls.com/online

Internet References

Further information regarding these Web sites may be found in this book's preface or online.

Activity-Based Costing (ABC)
http://www.esc-brest.fr/cg/cgkiosk3.htm

American Capital Strategies
http://www.americancapital.com/news/press_releases/pr/pr19961024.html

Brookings Institution
http://www.brook.edu

Putting Technology to Work for America's Future
http://sunsite.unc.edu/darlene/tech/report3.html

Reason Foundation
http://www.reason.org/policystudiesbysubject.shtml

The articles in this unit review the impact of technology on such diverse topics as privacy and dealing with an "e-waste epidemic." Additional articles also discuss the strategic application of technology at the county level and digital document management.

How do you balance open government with the concern for privacy? Merrill Douglas in his article *Privacy Concerns* reviews the fear that persons have for the safety of judges, police officers, and other officials with the public's right to access information that is on the Web and is readily available at the courthouse.

The article *Strategic Applications of Technology: County-Level Case Study in the State of Georgia* discusses how the De-Kalb County Juvenile Court is using radio-frequency identification (RFID) technology to obtain prompt and reliable access to information for appropriate judicial decision making.

We are experiencing an epidemic of E-waste of tremendous proportions. Computers, especially cathode ray tube (CRT)

monitors, contain a number of elements that are harmful to people and the environment. Sherry Watkins in her article *E-Waste Epidemic* proposes a number of ways including recycling by which this E-waste can be cleaned up.

Digital document management is moving forward at such a pace that many public sector organizations are looking to eventually digitize all documents throughout the organization. According to Adam Stone in his article *Find It Fast*, the city of Garland, Texas, is an excellent example of the successful implementation of a digital document management program.

Electronic health records are one of the major keys to upgrading and improving our health care system. Shane Peterson, in his article *Moving Medicine Forward*, reviews many of the ways in which the health care system can be improved through high-tech methods including the development of a nationwide health information network that would link health records throughout the country.

Privacy Concerns

Fears for the safety of judges, police officers and other officials spark debates over personal information on e-government sites.

MERRILL DOUGLAS

A t first, it sounds obvious: If citizens can read public records in the county courthouse, surely those citizens are entitled to read the same information on the Web.

But as more governments put public records online, protests from certain quarters prompt public-sector officials to think long and hard about how to balance open government and the right to privacy.

For those who need some of the information contained in transactions such as tax payments and real-estate sales, it's much easier to tap an e-government site than appear in person and leaf through paper files. But the thought that people who may want to harm others can, in a few clicks, locate home addresses and Social Security numbers of potential victims turns the stomachs of some public-sector leaders.

Among those who feel most alarmed are some government officials who fear that putting their personal details online makes them easy targets for criminals.

In the Public Eye

In May 2005, Dan Onorato, chief executive of Allegheny County, Pa., agreed to take the names of about 100 federal, state and local judges off a county real-estate Web site.

According to news reports, he did this at the behest of a federal judge, who expressed safety concerns after the husband and mother of U.S. District Judge Joan Lefkow were murdered in Lefkow's Chicago home in February 2005.

In testimony before the U.S. Senate Judiciary Committee in May, Lefkow asked for a law that would prohibit the posting of personal information about judges and other public officials on the Internet without their written consent.

In July, the county refused a request that it also remove police officers' names. Then, County Council member Bill Robinson introduced legislation to suppress the names of all property owners, not just public officials. It required that any member of the public seeking the name of a property owner make a formal request via letter or e-mail.

In September, the county started testing a version of the real-estate Web site on which a person searching property records by address would not see the owner's name, and a person searching

by name would not see the address. Allegheny County officials did not know when or if the site would go public, and did not respond to requests for an interview.

Missouri Makes a List

In Missouri, concern about government officials' privacy also sparked a controversy over government Web sites.

The state passed a law in 2005 prohibiting courts and state and local agencies from posting the home address, Social Security number or telephone number of any elected or appointed public official on the Internet without that person's written consent.

The law listed 13 categories of officials to be protected, including state legislators, judges, county commissioners, mayors and city council members, police chiefs, sheriffs, and peace officers, among others.

Four Missouri counties—Boone, Cass, Jackson and Platte—sued the state over the law. The counties said it would force them to shut down databases of public information on their Web sites, since gaining permission from every relevant public official would be absurdly difficult and expensive.

The four counties developed e-government services because that's what citizens asked for, said Ken Evans, director of e-government and public relations for Jackson County.

"This law, because of the unfortunate way it was worded, put that whole initiative in jeopardy," Evans said.

> **"If you really have a safety issue, you don't solve it just by taking the data offline. If it's still in the public record, [a person] can just come to the courthouse, request it and get it."**
>
> **—Ken Evans, Director of e-Government and Public Relations, Jackson County, MO.**

The law would have affected two databases providing tax records and information on real-estate sales on Jackson County's Web site. Following the outcry from the counties, the state Legislature repealed the law, replacing it with a law containing language that covers both private citizens and government officials.

The new law makes it illegal for anyone to post personal information about any person on the Internet "with the intent of doing harm," Evans said, which is a critical change because it allows Jackson County officials to feel confident in continuing with e-government efforts.

"Jackson County would have no problem proving that what we're doing is with the intent of serving citizens," he explained.

Ever since it first put its tax and real-estate databases online, Jackson County has fielded occasional complaints from public officials and private citizens who fear that easy access to their personal information could aid assassins or stalkers, Evans said. In response, the county points out that this information is already available to anyone motivated to search it out.

"If you really have a safety issue, you don't solve it just by taking the data offline," he said. "If it's still in the public record, [a person] can just come to the courthouse, request it and get it."

One change Jackson County officials *would* like to make is to keep Social Security numbers out of not just electronic records, but all public records, to protect citizens from identify theft. It's illegal, however, under Missouri law for a county deed recorder to "cleanse" Social Security numbers from real-estate documents before making them part of the official government record.

"I think we can fix that," Evans said. "I just don't think the amount of attention necessary has been given to it yet."

Practical Obscurity

Though Jackson County officials—and many others—maintain that posting a public record online is the same as providing it on paper, not everyone agrees.

"There's a difference in 'practical obscurity,'" said Daniel Solove, associate professor at the George Washington University Law School in Washington, D.C., and author of *The Digital Person: Technology and Privacy in the Information Age.*

"Practical obscurity" refers to the privacy an individual enjoys when personal information contained in public records is relatively hard to obtain. If a would-be harasser must travel some distance, wait in line and deal face-to-face with clerks to obtain a victim's home address and phone number, he or she might think twice about taking action.

"When you put it on the Internet, I can get information about anyone at any time, at the click of a mouse," Solove said, meaning that one can quickly and anonymously assemble a dossier on a person with information from different sources in different states, or even assemble databases of information about individuals.

Laws about personal information on the Internet vary from state to state, and governments that put public records on the Web often act without understanding the legal ramifications, Solove said.

"We're in an area where the law is not entirely clear," he continued. "I think some government officials said, 'Let's just put it up there. Let's make it all public.'"

But that's not always allowable, he said.

Although the controversies in Pennsylvania and Missouri both started with requests from public officials, in each case the argument broadened to address privacy for all citizens. It's only fair, said Evans, and Jackson County Executive Katheryn Shields has stressed that point.

"She believes that to the extent that her information is out there, too," Evans explained. "It's all or nothing with e-government."

Though Evans said government should be careful about posting personal information on the Web, Solove agreed that government officials should not receive special treatment.

"It's true that they do need privacy," he said, adding a caveat. "I don't think it's fair that they just protect their own and leave everyone else out to dry."

MERRILL DOUGLAS is a freelance writer based in upstate New York. She specializes in applications of information technology.

Strategic Applications of Technology: County-Level Case Study in the State of Georgia

How the DeKalb County Juvenile Court is using radio-frequency identification (RFID) technology to obtain prompt and reliable access to information for appropriate judicial decision making.

DALE PHILLIPS

Technologies are emerging at a dizzying pace from the marketplace, and they are rapidly changing, making it difficult for anyone, including the court manager, to integrate the best of them into a coherent and strategic fit in their respective court operation.

However, the court manager must make the effort anyway, separating the technological wheat from the chaff—knowing that technology directly links with accelerated court performance—to improve effectiveness, enhance accountability, and help court officials get better information within increasingly complex court operations. The court manager has to operate with the understanding that the correct application of any technology will, at a primary level, support and assist the decision-making process. Any decision-making process, particularly appropriate judicial decision making, requires complete, accurate, and timely information. Prompt and reliable access to this information motivated the DeKalb County Juvenile Court to adopt RFID technology.

The DeKalb County Juvenile Court is the second-largest juvenile court in the state of Georgia. Its mission is to restore and redirect, as law-abiding citizens, children who have admitted to or been found in violation of the law, while protecting the best interests of each child and the community, leaving the children in their homes when possible. To accomplish this mission, DeKalb juvenile judges employ a broad array of methods and programs for addressing juvenile offenders, including taking into account the severity of the offense and the background of the offender. These approaches include fines, treatment programs, informal probation, formal probation, detention, incarceration, and community supervision.

Given these circumstances, proper filing and quick retrieval of court records are critical in providing up-to-date and accurate information to the judges as they make decisions that drastically affect the future of the individuals who come before them. In 2004, the DeKalb County Juvenile Court

- conducted over 17,000 court hearings,
- recorded over 15,000 juvenile offenses,
- investigated more than 2,300 cases of neglect, and
- heard reviews related to 1,200 youths in foster care and over 1,000 youths under active court supervision.

These figures underscore the fact that the court has to account for nearly 12,000 active file folders on more than 9,000 children processed through the court system each year. In addition, nearly 8,000 inactive files are usually on hand as required by legal file retention schedules for juvenile court cases (particularly dependency cases). On any given day, scores of files move through the hands of the court staff, judges, and others.

The Need

DeKalb County Juvenile Court files are initially logged into the records department of the clerk of court's office. These files are then pulled for court hearings once the cases are set on the court calendars. Delinquent case files go to court an average of five times each before the case is concluded. Dependency case files go to court approximately five times before the case is disposed of and then are returned to court for judicial reviews every six months. In addition to hearings, case files are pulled for other reasons, including motions, appeals, and requests for information. Because these case files are constantly pulled for different courts, different judges, calendar clerks, the clerk of court, and various other court personnel, they are not always in their original destination and "file put-away" and location errors often result.

No activity disrupts the normal flow of court and case management operations more than a lost or misfiled court record. When looking for a file that is temporarily lost and is needed immediately for a scheduled court hearing the next morning, everything and everyone enters a "hypercritical" mode. At 8:30 a.m., the sight of a judge's secretary (or worse yet, a judge) scouring the central record room for a file for a 9:00 a.m. hearing is enough to drive the court manager to distraction. Thus begins a cycle of frustration that includes an infuriated judge (because he or she lacks the critical information needed to render a fair and appropriate decision), an angry clerk of court (because the file or records staff can't find the file), and, finally, angry staff members (because they have to drop everything, including helping other customers, and direct all their energies to finding the file—one which may already have been checked out to someone on the judge's staff or the judge himself or herself).

The court case flow process essentially shuts down to find the file, and the impact ripples throughout the court system. At the DeKalb County Juvenile Court, the clerks in the record room were spending an estimated ten hours a week trying to track down lost or misplaced files. These files could be in an office on any of the three floors of the courthouse, or even in the remote transitional file area, which the record room file clerks derisively refer to as "the dungeon," where files are stored until they can be moved to an off-site area. Even at the juvenile court level, a smaller operation than the larger trial courts, conservative estimates for salary costs associated with lost or misplaced files were in the tens of thousands of dollars per year.

> **Even at the juvenile court level, a smaller operation than the larger trial courts, conservative estimates for salary costs associated with lost or misplaced files were in the tens of thousands of dollars per year.**

Lost files have other implications for the court manager, in the capacity as chief operating officer of the court, to consider. Courts hinder their operational effectiveness and risk liability because of missing files. Investigations could be hampered because of time lost due to the inability to locate needed court files. One goal of government agencies is to serve the public. Citizens lose confidence in a juvenile justice system that continually is unable to locate, in a timely manner, crucial court documents.

In addition to interrupting the judicial process, lost or misplaced files can lead to direct, negative economic consequences on the operating budget of the court. They can and do generate court hearing postponements and continuances. Due to strict and prompt hearing schedules mandated for juvenile hearings, the path of least resistance is to issue a postponement or continuance if files needed for the case are not available.[1] When outside-appointed attorneys are hired to represent indigent clients and the cases for these clients are repeatedly continued, fees paid to these outside-appointed attorneys can rise precipitously. Depending on the jurisdiction, outside attorney fees can be one of the largest single line-items in a court's budget, and court managers face increasing pressure to rein in this expense. In fiscal year 2004, the DeKalb County Juvenile Court experienced a major budgetary crisis stemming from substantial cost overruns in the account of attorney and legal fees for representation of indigent parents and children in dependency-abuse and neglect cases.

Judicial decision-making paralysis, cost pressures, and the inordinate allocation of labor and resources led the court to seek a solution to the lost and misplaced file problem. The court recognized that information is mission-critical and access to information is a strategic part of court operations. More important, it saw that lack of access to the information that drives crucial court operations costs money, saps productivity, and causes delays in judicial decision making that can impact people's lives.

The Solution

RFID is a wireless tracking system that uses radio frequency transmissions to convey data between a portable device and a personal computer. Anyone who has rolled through a tollbooth without having to toss change into a basket or stop and pay an attendant has experienced its inherent speed and efficiency. Sometimes called "bar-coding on steroids," RFID has many advantages over traditional bar codes, which are a line-of-sight technology, meaning a scanner has to "see" the bar code to read it. RFID tags can be read from different angles and through certain materials. They also ensure a 100 percent scanning achievement rate in the first pass of the item being scanned, and multiple tags can be read simultaneously.

RFID is widely discussed in the corporate press, primarily as a retail-based technology. For example, in 2005 Wal-Mart began requiring its top 100 suppliers to ship RFID-tagged pallets and cases to its distribution centers. Retailers apply and integrate RFID to capitalize on the data flow in supply chain management. The deployment of RFID has recently become more universal and mainstream:

- Delta Airlines announced plans to use RFID tags to track its luggage at U.S. airports.
- McCarran Airport in Las Vegas and Hong Kong International Airport announced plans to use RFID tags and readers for planned baggage-handling systems.
- Library systems around the country are looking to RFID to track holdings (including the DeKalb County Library System).
- The National Aeronautics and Space Administration is testing an RFID-based system that will monitor hazardous chemicals stored in various facilities.
- The U.S. Food and Drug Administration is using RFID technology to combat the spread of counterfeit prescription drugs.
- The U.S. Department of Homeland Security is evaluating RFID use at national borders.

The court recognized RFID as a tracking option and a proven tool in other sectors, but could the application work in a court setting? Perhaps. The court considered that Wal-Mart, Target, public libraries, and other organizations were employing RFID technology to track their high-value assets. By adopting this technology, the DeKalb County Juvenile Court would be doing the same thing: implementing an emerging technology to track its high-value assets—its files. Retail and manufacturing companies use their supply chain information to make timely decisions and to track individual products from manufacture to sale. Unlike retailers, courts don't move millions of products or pallets stacked with goods. A juvenile court's supply chain is its court case management flow. Why shouldn't RFID—which retailers use to identify the exact location of every asset on their production lines and to improve their business processes—help the DeKalb County Juvenile Court solve the problem of lost or misfiled files?

The court researched and studied various improvement alternatives and spoke with people throughout the court; a discussion with one its primary software vendors led the court to narrow its focus and put the adoption of RFID into high gear. The court's case management vendor, ACS, Inc., said that future software releases would be RFID-enabled. Since this is the primary software used by the records staff to maintain the court's electronic case file records, a solution to an exasperating and recurring problem for this court manager became clear.

The adoption of an RFID solution by the DeKalb County Juvenile Court has been, in governmental terms, rapid. In nine months, the entire process—from introduction of the technology, to procurement of an RFID tag/software vendor, to securing funding and resolving contract issues—has been completed. Pilot implementation at the DeKalb County Juvenile Court should be taking place as this article goes to print. The rapid facilitation was largely due to three factors:

1. A call to action from the judge to the court manager to develop and implement a technology-based solution for the problem of lost and misplaced files and the institutional support for the application of that solution.
2. Buy-in from the clerk of court, a thirty-year court veteran, who went through two demonstrations of the RFID technology, including one on-site demonstration in the central record room with live records, before becoming an advocate.
3. Recognition by the county's information systems director, who clearly understood the juvenile court's problem and the business case being made for deploying RFID technology to solve that problem. He is also strongly focused on document management for the entire county and foresees integrating RFID, imaging, and biometrics in the county's document management enterprise applications.

Implementation

This DeKalb County Juvenile Court technology project is utilizing a 3M RFID Tracking Solutions product, composed of a suite of products for courts, based on RFID technology that locates and identifies individual files via a tiny microchip and antenna. The microchip and antenna are inside a 3M RFID Tracking Tag affixed to each file, which allows the file to be easily tracked through the entire workflow. As a file moves from central file rooms, team rooms, or individual offices, a complete file history is tracked and can be easily viewed on any network computer. The court's RFID system will use labels with passive semiconductors from Texas Instruments that transmit on the 13.56-Mhz frequency. Readers, hand-held devices, and software will come from 3M.

The basic unit to be tracked will be the file folder. Each folder will receive a 3M RFID tag programmed with a unique file identifier and will be tracked separately, allowing the system to identify where each one is located. Two types of files will be tracked: the delinquent cases (these typically have only one folder) and dependency cases (these can have multiple case numbers and multiple folders). Initially, only the active files will be tagged and tracked.

The record room staff and selected judicial staffers will receive full system training from 3M. The 3M training process covers all system functions: software and hardware installation; software configuration; troubleshooting; tag programming; creating multivolume files; system administration; data import; creating and modifying item records, locations, and search lists; exporting from and importing to the hand-held device; and using the hand-held device for inventory, shelf order, and searching for items.

Challenges and Opportunities Ahead

How best to adapt the right emerging technology will always be an issue that faces court managers. Ultimately, adopting a strategic technology solution (in the case of the DeKalb County Juvenile Court, deploying RFID) means not choosing another, possibly equally valid, solution. For the court, the decision boiled down to the following:

- Major private-sector companies use this technology to track the vast quantity of goods in their supply chains.
- Large public agencies are finding viable RFID-based solutions for their tracking needs.
- Then, the court, which operates on a smaller scale, can use it to track its most vital information—its case files.
- Most important, RFID gives key decision makers immediate access and greatly improves the quality of justice delivered to the public.

Among the judges and other key players at the DeKalb County Juvenile Court, the preliminary indications are that RFID is the right technology to support court business needs and that it will improve primary court operations. The record room staff, which participated in the on-site demonstrations of RFID, is excited about the immediate, significant benefits of the system, including the reduction in stress and increase in productivity (hence, cost savings). They now have the ability to track items in real time as they move through the case record supply chain. The clerk of court has noticed increased customer satisfaction and reduced physical file costs.

Technologies are important for what they allow you to do and also for what they allow you to stop doing. In the case of the

DeKalb County Juvenile Court, RFID has allowed the clerk of court to stop giving one specific record room file clerk responsibility for a particular judge's files and to redeploy those staffers to complete more value-added job responsibilities.

As the RFID system becomes an integral part of court business operational processes, additional applications will become manifest and the court will strategically expand the use of the RFID application into those newly identified areas. The technology will become more pervasive, and, because of its inherent traceability, it will also shed light on how files are distributed throughout the court. New uses will emerge as the court staff becomes more comfortable with the technology.

Change is always stressful, partly because organizations comprise workers with different attitudes and tolerances for new ideas. The DeKalb County Juvenile Court is no exception. Trying to implement an innovative technology disrupts the status quo. To gain full staff commitment and involvement, the RFID tracking system is being implemented in small, simple, and selective steps through a pilot program. In addition, an RFID tracking system action and monitoring committee is being established, composed of cross-functional staff members from all divisions of the court, to guide and monitor the implementation process, to communicate activities and report on progress to all court staffers, and to document improved efficiencies.

As the RFID system is being implemented, the court should avoid autocratic groupthink and encourage thoughtful concerns and criticisms. During the planning phase, some saw RFID as only a stopgap and proposed adopting a more global solution, such as imaging or another system that would make the court's operations entirely paperless. The problem with that solution is that it assumes imaging systems have reached a level of standardization in counties or even within the various courts. Within DeKalb County departments, several concurrent imaging solutions are in vogue. One of these competing imaging solutions may eventually be adopted (at a much higher cost than RFID) enterprise-wide, but while the court waits for this to happen, the problem of lost and misplaced files would remain, further eroding confidence in the record retrieval process.

Unexpected Outcome

One unexpected outcome of the process was the strengthening of the strategic partnership between the information technology department and the court. Such a partnership is critical to creating value from technology investments. Also, the court discovered that, within a supportive organizational context, innovation by the court manager doesn't have to be risky. If properly managed and focused, the adoption of innovative practices is a sensible, not risky, course of action.

RFID is playing a central role in administrative actions focused on improving internal court operations and productivity. The court has stayed focused on its mission: to use the technology within a framework of establishing a more efficient and productive core business process—the tracking of files. RFID directly benefits the DeKalb County Juvenile Court because it is a relevant technology and is solving the problem it was intended to fix.

Note

1. In Georgia, once a child is taken into custody, a probable cause hearing must be held within forty-eight hours, and then a detentional hearing—to determine whether the child will be detained or released—must be held within seventy-two hours.

DALE PHILLIPS is the director of court services for the DeKalb County Juvenile Court in Decatur, Georgia. He can be reached at dpphilli@co.dekalb.ga.us.

From *The Public Manager*, Vol. 34, Number 2, Summer 2005, pp. 32–36. Copyright © 2005 by The Bureaucrat, Inc. Reprinted by permission.

E-Waste Epidemic

Legislators seek new ways to handle electronic waste, the growing byproduct of the Information Age.

SHERRY WATKINS

Computers have an average life expectancy of three to six years. After that, it's often time to pull the plug, leaving consumers with a problem: What does one do with the old when bringing in the new? Chances are the local landfill won't take it.

Computers, especially cathode ray tube (CRT) monitors, contain several elements harmful to the environment. The good news is that these elements are usually recyclable. The bad news is this costs money, and nonprofit companies that accept donations often get stuck with having to dispose of computer electronics in an environmentally safe and economically feasible way.

"Electronic waste is becoming a costly problem for us," said Christine Nyirjesy Bragale, spokeswoman of Goodwill Industries International Inc. "[In 2004] alone, we got more than 23 million pounds of electronic goods, and 10 to 30 percent of those donations were unusable."

As computer use continues to increase dramatically, the United States will face more and more electronic waste considered toxic and unfit for burial. For this reason, Congress initiated a working group to determine a course of action.

But devising federal legislation could take a while. In the meantime, a few states have enacted their own laws to effectively handle electronic waste.

California, Maine and Maryland have already created laws, but differing state laws mandating financial contributions from manufacturers scattered throughout the nation could create confusion for global electronics manufacturers, such as Hewlett-Packard (HP)—confusion that could be minimized or eliminated with a single, unified nationwide system.

"Our dream is that there is federal legislation harmonized at a worldwide level," said Renee St. Denis, director of Americas Product Take Back at HP. "That's probably a pipe dream, but we think federal legislation in the United States is probably— on some level—inevitable, because as states do their own thing, it's really tough to comply."

Multiple Methods

With federal legislation a future possibility, policymakers in Congress can start by considering the three states' laws to get working

knowledge of the different approaches. The most obvious disparity among them is who should be held responsible for recycling costs—consumers, manufacturers or the government.

In California, electronic recycling is funded by waste recycling fees assessed to the customer, which took effect on Jan. 1, 2005. Retailers collect between $6 and $10 per device, based on size at the time of purchase, and the fees are sent to the State Board of Equalization quarterly. The California Integrated Waste Management Board (CIWMB) administers the program and distributes the payments to recyclers to cover costs.

To be eligible to receive payment for recycling, recyclers must be approved by the CIWMB, a process that includes registering with the Department of Toxic Substances Control as a hazardous waste handler.

"It's not like handling explosive and toxic corrosive chemicals," said Chris Peck, CIWMB spokesman. "It's under the rubric of what's called universal waste, which has more general requirements for handling. But the department wants to know who's handling the materials, and they have to be inspected."

Maine's law mandates that manufacturers pay for transporting and collecting electronic waste, with municipalities responsible for the physical collection and transportation to consolidation centers. The consolidation centers prepare the electronic waste for shipment to recycling centers, and ultimately must ensure that each device is attributed to a manufacturer so each manufacturer can be billed appropriately.

In Maryland, local government and manufacturers share financial responsibility. Counties pay for the entire recycling process, but they can acquire funding assistance through grants drawn from the State Recycling Trust Fund, which comes from a $5,000 fee assessed annually to each manufacturer. Maryland also advocates the establishment of manufacturer take-back programs, which can reduce annual payments to $500, but only after the first year's full fee.

Some electronic manufacturers, such as HP, already provide their own recycling programs.

Private Interests

HP recycles almost 4 million pounds per month, said St. Denis.

"We take old products apart that HP owns, refurbish them and use them to support customers who have the same thing," she said. "It's standard industry process to use used parts in support. It's in the contractual terms."

Reusing selective computer parts creates unusable leftovers, and St. Denis was charged with researching options for disposing of or recycling those leftovers. She approached Noranda, a Canadian mining company already recycling precious metals for HP, to ask if additional metals or other materials in computer electronics could be recycled.

After extensive testing and new equipment, Noranda further broke down HP's e-waste into steel, aluminum, brass, zinc, nickel, plastic and glass.

Through research and active participation, St. Denis said HP developed a unique perspective on recycling policy issues.

"HP is positioned so we understand the operations side of [recycling], understand a lot of the customer side of it—what customers like and don't like about various services. We know the values of the materials coming back so we can understand what the costs are going to be," said St. Denis.

HP favors a manufacturer responsibility model to handle electronic waste, believing that manufacturers would manage the process like a business, and figure out alternatives to drive costs down and achieve set goals, according to St. Denis.

Directing responsibility at manufacturers motivates them to improve design to lower waste costs, said Jon Hinck, staff attorney of the Natural Resources Council of Maine (NRCM), the organization largely responsible for lobbying on behalf of Maine's legislation and seeing it through to enactment.

"If you have a more manufacturer responsibility-based approach, manufacturers will bring the efficiencies that private interests bring to getting something done," Hinck said.

He predicts, however, that some manufacturers will fight the manufacturer responsibility laws.

"Some of the opponents seem to feel—their lawyers and lobbyists feel—that anything that puts responsibility on them needs to be fought. I think that's an American industry approach, which makes it hard to get good input from them, because if it means any responsibility at all, they're against it," said Hinck.

But the costs generated from the Maine legislation are not large for any manufacturer, Hinck said. As a result, he said, the fight is symbolic.

"Opponents don't want Maine to work because other people might follow the model."

Consumers Pay

Opponents of Maine's model might consider California's law—charging advanced recovery fees (ARFs) to consumers upon purchasing electronics—the solution.

Using the ARF model nationwide might be a good thing if the fees were used efficiently, said St. Denis, but she expressed concern that the government lacks the efficiencies private interests bring to the table.

California collected an estimated $31 million via the electronic waste recycling program from its inception in January 2005 through July, according to Peck. The state pays out 48 cents per pound to recyclers that are approved to participate and can provide the documentation proving that the devices originated in California.

> **"To be a part of the system that the state set up, recyclers are required to offer free take-back once per year, and the requirement doesn't say anything about how big the event has to be, or what kind of advertising or reach you have to have."**
> **—Renee St. Denis, Director, American Product Take Back, Hewlett-Packard**

These recyclers are paid too much money, according to St. Denis, who said HP recycles at an average rate of 20 cents per pound, saving consumers money. She also said administering fees requires a lot of red tape and additional government support staff.

"I'm not saying government shouldn't raise money, but let's be honest about what they're doing: taxing our products to raise money that's probably going to be used ultimately for something else."

For instance, California doesn't have enough people to ensure that recyclers are doing their job the way they're contracted to, St. Denis said.

"They don't have a way to make sure CRTs are actually recycled in California and not exported to a third-world country where the raw material value versus the labor cost is so much lower."

Furthermore, St. Denis said many recycling centers in California—and some municipalities—are still charging customers to drop off electronic waste because there is nothing to prevent them from doing so.

"To be a part of the system that the state set up, recyclers are required to offer free take-back once per year, and the requirement doesn't say anything about how big the event has to be, or what kind of advertising or reach you have to have," said St. Denis. "The system is flawed because it doesn't police itself."

Peck admits participating collectors and recyclers aren't required to always take electronic waste for free, especially if their recycling costs exceed the state's reimbursement. Peck also said consumers are encouraged to shop around to determine when recyclers might have free take-back events.

California's approach is so new that there's still a learning curve, Peck said.

"We have only had about nine months of implementation in California, so to say that it's the way to go is perhaps a little premature," he said. "There are critics of the system, and there are also people who really like what we're doing in California. As the administering agency, we're just trying to make it work—which it seems to be doing so far."

The Buck Stops Where?

As for criticism of California's consumer responsibility model, Gerald Davis, chairman of the board at Goodwill, observed that there's no way to remove consumers from the financial equation—even with manufacturer responsibility.

"If you're going to put costs on the manufacturer, you are in essence putting them on the consumer because [manufacturers] just pass them on," Davis said.

HP doesn't deny that consumers must bear the costs, said St. Denis.

"Ultimately every time someone buys from us, they're paying for our costs—we're not under any misconceptions that customers aren't going to pay," she said. "The question for us is, *'How much* should the customers pay?'"

Despite apparently inevitable consumer responsibility, charging ARFs in Maine could financially jeopardize retailers in the state, said Hinck.

"In looking at the possibility of doing an advanced recovery fee approach, one problem particular to Maine is, if we were to put ARFs on products and neighboring states—notably New Hampshire—did not, retailers in Maine would take a hit," Hinck said.

In other words, Maine retailers could lose business to retailers in neighboring states.

Although federal legislation could address this issue, Hinck said legislators in Maine are not in support of an ARF approach at a national level.

Coming Together

As states enact their own laws, global manufacturers could face confusing and problematic regulations. But as landfills throughout the nation continue to ban electronic equipment, decisions must be made.

There are a few concerns to consider. For example, who would pay for orphan electronic equipment manufactured by organizations no longer in business? What about manufacturers who have been in business for a long time and have more equipment coming down the pipeline? The costs would certainly be more substantial for them.

"Any program we talk about is going to have details that need to be worked out and negotiated, so I don't want anyone to think that we say manufacturer responsibility and lickety-split, it's done," said St. Denis.

Goodwill has recently joined the bipartisan Congressional E-Waste Working Group, which consists of members of the U.S. House of Representatives and stakeholders, who discuss end-of-life management solutions that are mutually beneficial to all, said Davis.

"I'm optimistically pleased that the government seems to understand that nonprofits are being affected by this by inviting us to testify and having us in the group," he said.

The group brings people from different sectors together, all of whom have different concerns.

"The manufacturer sees this entirely differently than a consumer advocate or a charity," Davis said. "But we've all got to play in the same sandbox."

The goal is to educate members of Congress and their staff about the issues surrounding e-waste management and disposal, and to explore the role the federal government might play in regulating electronic waste, said Jay Hutchins, federal affairs manager of Goodwill.

"We are seeing more and more stakeholders express concern with a patchwork solution of each state adopting its own set of laws," Hutchins said. "It's too early to tell if there is one popular approach, but people are concerned about what will happen as each state adopts its own regulation."

SHERRY WATKINS is a freelance writer based in the Sacramento, Calif., area.

Find It Fast

Texas city turns to digital document management.

Adam Stone

There is no nice way to say it. There was paper *everywhere.* "There were a lot of hard paper files stored in file cabinets, taking up mountains of city space. Some people were using document warehousing and others used off-site storage," said Rocky Rodriguez, senior systems analyst of management information services for Garland, Texas.

Today that's changing. A tentative foray into digital documents management proved sufficiently successful that the city now is rolling out the technology to multiple departments, with an eye toward eventually digitizing all documents throughout city government.

In 2004 the municipal court system in this city of more than 250,000 went live with OnBase, a product of Hyland Software. OnBase is enterprise content management software that combines integrated document management, business process management and records management in a single, Web-enabled application.

A repository for data in nearly all formats, the software accommodates text files, PDFs, electronic drawings and scanned images of documents. Users can capture, store, manage and distribute documents across the extended government enterprise. Users can also search and retrieve documents, which can be structured and indexed to correspond with defined business processes.

With a 30-person MIS department, the city spent $250,000 implementing the system in the municipal court department, using funds appropriated by the City Council specifically for that purpose.

To expand into human resources and engineering, the council appropriated $500,000 more—a very good indicator that the trial run was impressive. At press time, the police and planning departments were next in line for expansion. The system will serve close to 350 users when all five departments are live.

Broad Experience

MIS selected the new test-bed departments largely due to the diversity of their operations.

"We were looking for a couple of pilot departments in different areas [of] the government, including something from the administrative side and something from the engineering side," Rodriguez said, explaining that the idea was to demonstrate the system's effectiveness in a range of settings.

"We knew each area would bring its own set of issues to the table," he said. "Engineering deals with large-scale maps and drawings, for instance, and we wanted to show that we could deliver the capability to handle that."

Engineering staff said the system makes a noticeable change in workflow efficiencies—plus they don't buy shoes nearly as often these days.

"Before, when we would do research, we would have to get up from our desks, go to the file room, then look at the map to see what we were looking for and then go to the drawers. We'd have to pull up a viewer to view the card, and then we could view it," said Supervisor of Engineering Records Daniel Nigo.

These days it's all desktop work. Type in a project number and a description, the record pops up and the printer spits it out.

"It is going to be a tremendous help," Nigo said.

The city has not done a return-on-investment study to calculate the exact man-hours saved, but Rodriquez said the time savings of having the documents more accessible is an obvious benefit over the old system of physically tracking down documents, which could take 30 minutes or more.

Quality of Service Issues

It wasn't just the sheer volume of paper that posed a problem. Even worse than the inconvenience it posed for city workers, the quality of customer service in some city departments steadily eroded because of the labor-intensive, paper-based system.

Fastfacts

Garland, Texas, is replacing paper documents with digital document handling.

The City Council spent $250,000 implementing the system in the municipal court department.

The council gave an additional $500,000 to expand the system to the human resources and engineering departments, with the police and planning departments next in line.

Rodriguez cited the municipal courts as an example.

"They would have people come up to the window and wait for 30 minutes or longer while they [looked] for the hard case file in the file room," Rodriguez said. "Eventually you would start to wonder if maybe the person had simply gone away on their lunch break."

"There were a lot of hard paper files stored in file cabinets, taking up mountains of city space."

—Rocky Rodriguez, senior systems analyst, Management Information Services, Garland, Texas

---

The issue here isn't merely between the city and its diverse clients. Paper-based systems take an equal toll on the ability of city agencies to work together.

"In most cities of any size, you will have multiple offices," said Jason Kupcak, vertical marketing manager for Hyland Software. "How hard is it for someone in office A to get a document from office B? Someone first has to get hold of that document, and it can take a lot of time and energy just to find that file."

The issue of information sharing is a high priority in Garland, where slow processes have hampered productivity. The engineering office, for example, wants to share drawings and plans with architects, construction agencies and others. In addition to swapping such documents in-house, Garland is also in the midst of implementing a Web-based interface so contractors and external offices can access relevant public documents.

While many city documents are available for public consumption, access can be tightly regulated for any set of information not open to public viewing. The MIS team first defines user groups within a given application, granting and restricting access based on need. Any such user group can cross departments for inter-office file sharing—police and municipal courts, for instance, might have access to many of the same documents.

Access can be controlled on a granular level.

"We can set everything down to the document level and even to a keyword level that we use as an index. It allows us to lock it down as tightly as we want," Rodriguez said.

Implementation Issues

Despite the problems it can solve, implementing a digital document management system is a serious undertaking.

The process first calls for an in-depth discovery phase, during which managers on the end-user side determine what documents are handled during various processes and whether it's necessary to convert some or all existing files. A business-process analysis can also help determine user level access.

Typically a reseller will help coordinate and execute these investigations, but it still takes internal effort to gain the big-picture view.

"You have to take your time to identify your needs, to make sure you are not going to implement this in a way that may conform to the needs of one department, but leaves you having to re-invent the wheel when you go to the next department," Rodriguez said. "You don't want to lock everything down at the start."

Then there are the mechanical logistics.

"We had to do a lot of third-party scanning and indexing," Nigo said. "We were so backlogged, we had no choice but to hire a contractor to get this done. We also had a lot of microfilm, and we weren't equipped to scan that in-house."

Finally a successful implementation depends largely on the IT team's ability not just to look at the present moment, but also at the wider landscape of pending events.

"The challenging part of expanding [to more than one department] is just the time factor," Rodriguez said. "It's one thing for us to set a timeline, but when you're dealing with different areas and different departments, it's complicated. People may not always have time when you have time. It can force you to move on to an area where everything is ready," he said, adding that the deployment team will only to have to circle back at a later date.

ADAM STONE writes on business and technology from Annapolis, Md.

Moving Medicine Forward

Electronic health records are key to transforming a fractured health-care system. Who's helping hospitals and physicians make the transition?

SHANE PETERSON

In July 2004, the U.S. Department of Health and Human Services (HHS) announced a landmark, 10-year plan to build a Nationwide Health Information Network (NHIN) to link health records nationwide. The plan's success, however, depends on eliminating paper medical files and creating an electronic health record (EHR) for every American. Developing EHRs—which, like traditional patient files, would contain detailed information about an individual's medical care and health history—is a high-visibility issue for the HHS because of skyrocketing health-care costs and the dramatic impact they have on public-sector budgets.

> **"I think this is probably what President Eisenhower faced when trying to grow an interstate highway system that all of us can use and travel on."**
>
> Pat Wise, vice president for Healthcare Information Systems, Healthcare Information and Management Systems Society

Studies over the past several years point to health IT as a tool for improving quality of care, reducing errors and delivering significant cost savings, according to the HHS, and the potential value of the interoperable exchange of health information among disparate entities is substantial.

National implementation of fully standardized interoperability of health information between providers and other health-care organizations could save $77.8 billion annually—approximately 5 percent of the projected $1.7 trillion spent on health care in the United States in 2003—according to the HHS Office of the National Coordinator for Health Information Technology (ONCHIT).

Other studies estimate that 20 percent to 30 percent of healthcare spending in the United States—up to $300 billion each year—goes to treatments that don't improve health status, are redundant, or are not appropriate for the patient's condition, said ONCHIT.

It's clear that EHRs and a national health IT strategy can play a huge role in streamlining the delivery of health care to patients across the country.

Roughly two years later, however, widespread adoption of EHRs is far from smooth. Making the transition is clearly a difficult process, but regional efforts within states appear to be accomplishing the most.

Texas and Massachusetts are strong advocates for EHRs, and have begun implementation in various health care facilities. The role of state government in this transition, however, remains unclear.

Next-Generation Records

Though the push toward a NHIN is decidedly top down, prodding physicians, hospitals and health systems to adopt EHRs is necessarily grass-roots.

The best person to persuade a roomful of skeptical doctors of EHRs' efficiency gains and enhanced access to health information is another physician. It's similar to the spread of e-government: State and local governments look to see the root of a particular trend, then talk to the officials from that jurisdiction to pick their brains.

"I think this is probably what President Eisenhower faced when trying to grow an interstate highway system that all of us can use and travel on," said Pat Wise, vice president for Healthcare Information Systems at the Healthcare Information and Management Systems Society (HIMSS).

Designing a highway system capable of carrying all sorts of traffic—local, regional and national—requires significant advance planning, Wise said, and EHR adoption is no different.

"You have to map out, in some fashion, how these documents should travel," she said. "And clearly, not only do some people want to travel from the East side of the nation to the West and from the North to the South, but the larger number of people just want to travel in and around the city themselves. They don't even want to go to another state."

This is because most health-care referral patterns are local, Wise explained, and physicians, hospitals and health systems in cities have begun building health information exchanges (HIEs), often funded by federal grant money. According to the HIMSS's latest data, approximately 137 HIEs dot the country, and more crop up every month.

The push behind the HIEs' creation is to improve and simplify health care. HIEs serve as the mechanism for physicians, hospitals and health systems to exchange patient information electronically—information that, so far, hasn't been readily shared by health-care providers.

"There are very few locales that can do it effectively yet, but they're all kind of at the starting line," she said. "They don't know what their strategies are. This is too new. There are not a lot of success stories out there. There's not a lot of, 'Do step one, then step two, then step three and then step four,' for locales to follow. They're all kind of feeling their way."

East-Coast EHRs

The Massachusetts e-Health Collaborative (MAEHC) kicked off its pilot with a conference called "EHR in Your Office— Let's Get Started!" to introduce physicians to EHRs. The conference focused on the fundamentals of implementation, the daily effect they make in the lives of clinicians and staff, and factors involved in making the transition. The pilot is made possible by a $50 million fund from Blue Cross Blue Shield Massachusetts, said Micky Tripathi, president and CEO of the MAEHC.

Hospital systems serving three regions in the state were selected to participate in the pilot. Physicians, health-care providers, administrators and selected staff from Brockton Hospital, the Good Samaritan Medical Center, Anna Jacques Hospital and North Adams Regional Hospital attended the October training conference.

Over the long term, the pilot will equip the practices of more than 600 physicians with EHR software, support tools and data-exchange capabilities to support patient care, Tripathi said.

In 2004, the Massachusetts physician community formed the MAEHC—composed of 33 organizations—to bring together the state's major health-care stakeholders and begin establishing an EHR system. The sole government entity is the Massachusetts Executive Office of Health and Human Services (EOHHS), which is on the board of directors and has representation in the MAEHC's executive committee.

"It's incredibly valuable to have the Executive Office of Health and Human Services at the table," Tripathi said. "So much of what we're doing is what I would call a public good issue. There are certain things that are good for society to get done, and if you depend on the individual actors to do those things, it's not in any actor's individual interest to do it. I would put EHRs in that category for physicians—particularly in small offices."

Because state government was created to consider societal benefits and the public good, the MAEHC needs that perspective as it starts making EHRs a reality in Massachusetts. In addition, the EOHHS is part of the MAEHC for a much more practical reason.

Because of the amount of money the state spends under its Medicaid program—MassHealth—it is an important individual stakeholder, Tripathi said, and stands to benefit as much as any commercial health plan.

Health-Care Foundation

In late February, Michigan Gov. Jennifer Granholm orchestrated the launch of the Michigan Health Information Network (MHIN). The governor convened a diverse group of representatives of health-care entities from across the state, such as health-care providers and purchasers, employers, health plans, patient advocacy groups, technology vendors, labor, and government officials.

"These 300 stakeholders—who come from all walks of both the health-care and information technology industries— have banded together for the first time to build the foundations of a statewide health information network that will ultimately bring our Michigan health-care system into the 21st century," Granholm said in a statement.

The goal is to create a framework that will eventually foster an interoperable MHIN to move medical records electronically with patients statewide, which should greatly improve their quality of care.

The Michigan Department of Community Health and the Michigan Department of Information Technology will provide guidance and leadership for the MHIN initiative.

The stakeholder group was formed to find ways to best use technology to improve health-care quality, increase patient safety, reduce health-care costs, and enable individuals and communities to make the best possible health decisions.

CyberMichigan, and its nonprofit parent organization, Altarum Institute, also joined Michigan officials in launching the MHIN. Altarum received a federal grant to facilitate this initial design activity.

Altarum Institute, based in Ann Arbor, is a nonprofit research and innovation institution that accelerates transformational change in health and health care, government and business enterprise systems, national security and environmental management.

"To the extent that any payer has issues with this and is also going to be a beneficiary of this, MassHealth is one of those payers," he said, adding that in a way, by sitting at the table almost as the CEO of a health plan, the EOHHS has a direct interest in this. "Similarly public health is another important angle in all this. There's no other organization that would speak for those issues, except for state and local public health organizations."

The infrastructure that's ultimately created to support statewide EHRs will also play a huge role in how public health agencies obtain and share information in times of emergency, and the EOHHS can give the MAEHC an important perspective on shaping that infrastructure.

East Texas EHRs

In Tyler, Texas, a Regional Health Information Organization (RHIO) called Access Medica is orchestrating the rollout of EHR software to 29 physicians in six independent clinics during the first phase of a regional deployment. The second stage will see 50 to 60 more physicians get the software by mid-2006.

Access Medica was founded in 2005 to provide health-care IT services to physicians, hospitals and patients of east Texas. The nonprofit RHIO includes members of the Physicians Contracting Organization of Texas and other independent practices.

The RHIO's infrastructure is being designed with the ultimate goal of connecting more than 600 regional physicians across 10 counties, said Dr. Kenneth Haygood, CEO of Access Medica. When complete, he said, it will be the first operational RHIO model in Texas.

Though the need to push for these sorts of IT changes in health care is widely accepted by the federal government, and increasingly by state governments, Haygood said, the actual movement in the EHR arena is much closer to the ground.

"If you look at places around the country where these efforts are taking hold and happening, it's really from physicians groups and medical practice associations—cooperating sometimes with their local hospitals—really coming together to make the investments in putting together these health information networks, or RHIOs," Haygood explained.

A RHIO can act as a neutral, central collaborator for all the diverse parties across the health-care community, whether that's physicians, medical clinics, hospitals, labs, governments and other entities with an interest in EHRs. One thing Access Medica could use is more funding, Haygood said, which isn't necessarily coming from government sources.

"We're really in a fortunate position because we have a lot of physicians here who realize the importance of making these changes," he continued. "They know that, one way or the other, they've got to make these changes for the benefit of their patients, for the benefit of their practices and to take the health care they provide to a higher level."

As a result, Haygood said, doctors have personally invested in moving toward EHRs. Access Medica has applied for several grants at the state and federal levels, and is waiting for approval.

"We're hoping for funding from places like that because the rate at which we could make progress is very dependent on our level of funding," he said. "As it is right now, we're *just* able to keep moving forward with our initial group of doctors."

Nonprofit EHRs

In Michigan, doctors can turn to the Virtual Community Health Center, owned and operated by the nonprofit Michigan Primary Care Association (MPCA), for help with making the transition to EHRs.

The VirtualCHC is a hosted service that offers a range of medical applications—practice management, electronic claims interface, general ledger and EHRs—on a subscription basis to physicians belonging to the MPCA, said Bruce Wiegand, the MPCA's IT director.

Five years ago, the MPCA tapped a federal grant to design and develop an infrastructure that used the Internet as the backbone for providing a centralized medical billing system for the state, Weigand said, and that infrastructure evolved into the VirtualCHC.

It's a way for physicians to get the benefits of modern medical software without having to buy it themselves.

"Seventy percent of EHR implementations to date have failed on two different fronts," he said. "On the IT side, you need a lot more IT than you could ever imagine to maintain EHRs. A lot of doctors went into EHRs thinking it was just paperless. What they ended up doing was putting paper under glass."

The problem is that making the move to EHRs necessitates a radical overhaul of the way physicians run their medical practices—including electronic interfaces between a doctor's office, pharmacies, labs and clinics; patient management software; and billing systems.

"We're trying to corral all these disparate systems into a single data center, which makes it easier to secure, provides better IT oversight, and we can better manage these interfaces between systems," Weigand said. "We're trying to suck the cost of IT out of health care."

A high-speed Internet connection is all that's needed, he said, and a primary care doctor can tap into the VirtualCHC for all his or her medical software applications needs. In part, the evolution to EHRs is hampered by the stand-alone medical software systems that physicians use.

"You have all these islands of needs," Weigand said. "Most EHRs don't do billing. Most billing systems don't do clinical. So you have to interface the two, and typically you're dealing with two different vendors with two different types of databases."

Need Is There

The medical community and its stakeholders, including the public sector, see the need to move to EHRs. But, as with any technological evolution, not everybody's on board.

Weigand said some older doctors, perhaps a year or two away from retiring, aren't rushing to modernize their practices. On the other hand, he said, younger doctors can't imagine a medical practice without EHRs and related technology.

We're trying to corral all these disparate systems into a single data center, which makes it easier to secure; provides better IT oversight, and we can better manage these interfaces between systems. We're trying to suck the cost of IT out of health care.

Bruce Wiegand,
IT Director, Michigan Primary Care Association

Health IT in Rhode Island

In 2001, the state's Attorney General formed the Rhode Island Quality Institute. The RIQI comprises diverse groups—the top leaders among hospital administrators, doctors, nurses, pharmacists, business, insurers, consumers, state government officials and academic institutions—committed to working together to revamp health care in the state.

Rhode Island began focusing on health IT with an electronic prescribing project in 2002. The statewide effort now includes electronic health records (EHRs) and a statewide health information network, said Laura Adams, the RIQI's president and CEO, and the most important thing the RIQI did was taking time to build the necessary relationships and trust between diverse groups.

"That has served us so well," Adams said. "We did not rush to technology. I think a lot of people believe it's all about the technology. This really is about human social systems, and the technology isn't really the biggest challenge."

It's not that mapping health data to standards and agreeing to standards won't be a challenge, she said, but spending time creating trust between the various groups turned out to be time very well spent.

State government is active in the RIQI's work, she said, and agencies took it upon themselves to play an early leadership role in RIQI's development of statewide strategies for health IT.

At the executive branch level, the efforts are focused on Rhode Island's health information network, Adams said, a crucial component of the overall strategy. It's easy to become fascinated with the power of EHRs and neglect building a way for clinical information to get to hospitals and doctors across a state, or vice versa.

"There are some problems with becoming enamored with either one of those separately," Adams said, "EHRs have a more immediate return on the promise. You can implement these in a physician's office and start imporving care very quickly.

"But the connectivity build-out is a longer, more arduous and difficult process that requires enormous amounts of buy-in, lots and lots of communication across entities," she continued. "It is really our long-term Holy Grail for care improvement."

To that end, Gov. Donald Carcieri proposed that $20 million in the Governor's Innovation Bond Fund to be earmarked for health IT.

In a statement, the governor said funds from the bond would use federal and private resources to secure hardware, software and the network capabilities necessary to share, secure and compile medical data. While more providers are adopting EHRs, state funding will play an important role supporting the design, implementation and stewardship of such a network.

"It's a tough nut to crack because there are so many variables," he said. "But now you have the feds pushing it. The states are pushing it. Pay for performance is coming down the pike. The reality is that the doctors moving to EHRs quicker are the ones that are going to survive and prosper."

Pay for performance is a new approach to the way the federal government pays for health care under Medicare.

The idea is to use Medicare reimbursements to reward innovative approaches to health care to get better patient outcomes at lower costs, according to the Centers for Medicare and Medicaid Services (CMS). To test pay for performance, the CMS announced in January 2005 that 10 large physician groups across the United States agreed to participate in the first pay-for-performance initiative for physicians under the Medicare program.

The problem is that Medicare's physician payment rates for a service are the same regardless of its quality, its impact on improving patient's health or its efficiency, said Herb Kuhn, director of the Center for Medicare Management, in testimony at a hearing before the Senate Committee on Finance in July 2005.

Kuhn said ample evidence shows that by anticipating patient needs—especially for patients with chronic diseases—healthcare teams that work more closely with patients can intervene before expensive procedures and hospitalizations are required.

Kuhn told the committee that, as a result of Medicare's payment practices, patients often end up seeing more physicians and using more medical services—but without obtaining positive results. This, of course, means the CMS spends more on medical care for Medicare members.

"Providers who want to improve quality of care find that Medicare's payment systems may not provide the flexibility to undertake activities that, if properly implemented, have the potential to improve quality and avoid unnecessary medical costs," Kuhn told the committee. "Linking a portion of Medicare payments to valid measures of quality and effective use of resources would give providers more direct incentives to implement the innovative ideas and approaches that actually result in improvements in the value of care that people with Medicare receive."

Private insurers also back pay for performance, and the trend toward this way of practicing medicine will drive physicians and hospitals to improve their electronic records and reporting capabilities to demonstrate positive outcomes in treating patients.

Physicians that lag behind, that can't show positive outcomes—that they're tackling diabetes, that they're tackling asthma, and that they're managing their patients—risk losing substantial payments from private insurers and the federal government, Weigand continued.

"There's no other way to do it than to have this stuff electronic—not in a Word document. You can't pull data out of a progress note, but you can out of an EHR," said Weigand. States have more vested interest today than just six months ago, he added, but the push to EHRs is still so new that the public sector is unsure of the outcome. One thing that is—patient information must be available to who needs it, in real time. States have begun exploring ways to map information sharing across geographical and political boundaries, but it's not an easy task.

"Another barrier to this has been how incredibly decentralized health care is, as opposed to almost every other industry you look at in the country," said the MAEHC's Tripathi. "The individual entities at the end are these one- and two-physician practices way out there who, up until now, have had absolutely nothing compelling them to be electronically connected with anything else."

From *Government Technology*, Vol. 19, Issue 4, April 2006, pp. 18–21. Copyright © 2006 by Government Technology. Reprinted by permission.

UNIT 6

Public Policy, Law, Community, and Environmental Planning

Unit Selections

Key Points to Consider

- What can you say about the current health care at the Veterans' (VA) hospitals? What was health care like at the VA hospitals 10 years ago, and how has health care at the VA hospitals changed over the last 10 years?

- What are the major issues in the immigration battle? Why is it so difficult to reach agreement on new legislation to address these issues?

- What is the impact of Florida's new law that requires governmental advocacy on local governments?

- What is "smart growth"? What are some of the positive and negative features of "smart growth"?

- What was the impact of state-mandated local government planning on coastal area resource protection in North Carolina?

- Identify and discuss the positive and negative factors associated with the closing of a mine on tribal lands. On balance, what is the "right" thing to do in this situation?

- Identify and discuss some of the planning principles that should be followed in the rebuilding of the city of New Orleans.

- What are some of the ways that local governments can create more affordable housing in their communities?

Student Web Site

www.mhcls.com/online

Internet References

Further information regarding these Web sites may be found in this book's preface or online.

Capitol Reports: Environmental News Link
http://www.caprep.com

Innovation Groups (IG)
http://www.ig.org

National Association of Counties
http://www.naco.org/counties/index.cfm

National League of Cities
http://www.nlc.org

The articles in this unit focus on public policy issues, community and environmental planning, and intergovernmental relations and the law. In the area of policy, we take a look at some of the major issues in public policy affecting public organizations today. Among these issues are immigration, health care, and social policy and welfare.

Community and environmental planning issues explored include rebuilding after a disaster such as hurricane Katrina, the tradeoffs between jobs, economic growth and environmental protection, and promoting affordable housing. Also explored in this section is how local governments can plan effectively through a variety of measures such as "smart growth" practices.

Public Policy and the Law

Veterans' hospitals have come a long way during the last 10 years. According to Phillip Longman in his article *The Best Care Anywhere,* the health care provided hit bottom in the mid-1990s and has since started a journey that has led to the establishment of a system that is now providing modern and convenient health care for veterans.

The attempts to solve the immigration issue through new national legislation have been characterized by a failure to satisfy any of the involved parties. Authors Abby Goodnough and Jennifer Steinhauer, in their article *Senate's Failure to Agree on Immigration Plan Angers Workers and Employers Alike*, explore the problems with proposed legislation that has been presented to the U.S. Senate. They also review the positions of the various sides of the immigration battle.

The Florida Supreme Court has concluded that in accordance with a Florida law that requires governmental advocacy, local governing bodies have not only the right but the duty to advocate on matters they believe are beneficial or detrimental to their constituents. In the article *Who's Advocating What Here?*, the authors Robert Meyers and Victoria Frigo review the implications for local governments of this new law and try to provide some guidance on how public managers can cope with the law and the court mandate.

Community & Environmental Planning

The article *Smart Growth: Why We Discuss It More Than We Do It* by Anthony Downs reviews and analyzes the positive and negative features of smart growth and planning. The author pays special attention to the factors that inhibit the success of smart growth initiatives and discusses what policy makers need to do in order to have some success with the smart growth initiatives.

The next article, *More and Better Local Planning* by Richard K. Norton, presents findings from an evaluation of state-mandated local planning in coastal North Carolina. According to the author, the planning efforts provided limited guidance for growth management, especially in terms of coastal area resource protection.

How do you rebuild New Orleans after its destruction by hurricane Katrina? Clay Risen, in his article *Rebuilding a Beautiful Mess*, cites the rebuilding efforts of other cities and identifies some of the planning principles that should be followed for a successful outcome.

Hurricane Katrina has resulted in the spending of tens of billions of dollars on disaster relief and billions more on repairing the infrastructure of the city of New Orleans. Craig Pittman, in his article *On the Gulf: Too Little, Too Late,* explores how prior planning could have made a big difference in limiting the amount of damage. The author explores what went wrong in prior planning and what can be done to avoid the mistakes made in the past.

The next article asks the question: How do you measure protection of the environment against jobs and economic development? John M. Broder, in his article *Closing of Mine on*

Tribal Lands Fuels Dispute over Air, Water and Jobs, reviews the positive and negative consequences of closing a coal mine on tribal Indian lands and discusses the need for environmental protection against a backdrop of job loss and a deteriorating economic situation for the local residents.

Examples of housing policies that emphasize affordable housing are reviewed by the author James B. Goodno in his article *Getting to Yes*. He also discusses some of the major constraints to achieving affordable housing in most communities in the United States.

The Best Care Anywhere

Ten years ago, veterans hospitals were dangerous, dirty, and scandal-ridden. Today, they're producing the highest quality care in the country. Their turnaround points the way toward solving America's health-care crisis.

PHILLIP LONGMAN

Quick. When you read "veterans hospital," what comes to mind? Maybe you recall the headlines from a dozen years ago about the three decomposed bodies found near a veterans medical center in Salem, Va. Two turned out to be the remains of patients who had wandered months before. The other body had been resting in place for more than 15 years. The Veterans Health Administration (VHA) admitted that its search for the missing patients had been "cursory."

Or maybe you recall images from movies like *Born on the Fourth of July*, in which Tom Cruise plays a wounded Vietnam vet who becomes radicalized by his shabby treatment in a crumbling, rat-infested veterans hospital in the Bronx. Sample dialogue: "This place is a fuckin' slum!"

By the mid-1990s, the reputation of veterans hospitals had sunk so low that conservatives routinely used their example as a kind of reductio ad absurdum critique of any move toward "socialized medicine." Here, for instance, is Jarret B. Wollstein, a right-wing activist/author, railing against the Clinton health-care plan in 1994: "To see the future of health care in America for you and your children under Clinton's plan," Wollstein warned, "just visit any Veterans Administration hospital. You'll find filthy conditions, shortages of everything, and treatment bordering on barbarism."

And so it goes today. If the debate is over health-care reform, it won't be long before some free-market conservative will jump up and say that the sorry shape of the nation's veterans hospitals just proves what happens when government gets into the health-care business. And if he's a true believer, he'll then probably go on to suggest, quoting William Safire and other free marketers, that the government should just shut down the whole miserable system and provide veterans with health-care vouchers.

Yet here's a curious fact that few conservatives or liberals know. Who do you think receives higher-quality health care. Medicare patients who are free to pick their own doctors and specialists? Or aging veterans stuck in those presumably filthy VA hospitals with their antiquated equipment, uncaring administrators, and incompetent staff? An answer came in 2003, when the prestigious *New England Journal of Medicine* published a study

that compared veterans health facilities on 11 measures of quality with fee-for-service Medicare. On all 11 measures, the quality of care in veterans facilities proved to be "significantly better."

Here's another curious fact. The *Annals of Internal Medicine* recently published a study that compared veterans health facilities with commercial managed-care systems in their treatment of diabetes patients. In seven out of seven measures of quality, the VA provided better care.

It gets stranger. Pushed by large employers who are eager to know what they are buying when they purchase health care for their employees, an outfit called the National Committee for Quality Assurance today ranks health-care plans on 17 different performance measures. These include how well the plans manage high blood pressure or how precisely they adhere to standard protocols of evidence-based medicine such as prescribing beta blockers for patients recovering from a heart attack. Winning NCQA's seal of approval is the gold standard in the health-care industry. And who do you suppose this year's winner is: Johns Hopkins? Mayo Clinic? Massachusetts General? Nope. In every single category, the VHA system outperforms the highest rated non-VHA hospitals.

Not convinced? Consider what vets themselves think. Sure, it's not hard to find vets who complain about difficulties in establishing eligibility. Many are outraged that the Bush administration has decided to deny previously promised health-care benefits to veterans who don't have service-related illnesses or who can't meet a strict means test. Yet these grievances are about access to the system, not about the quality of care received by those who get in. Veterans groups tenaciously defend the VHA and applaud its turnaround. "The quality of care is outstanding," says Peter Gayton, deputy director for veterans affairs and rehabilitation at the American Legion. In the latest independent survey, 81 percent of VHA hospital patients express satisfaction with the care they receive, compared to 77 percent of Medicare and Medicaid patients.

Outside experts agree that the VHA has become an industry leader in its safety and quality measures. Dr. Donald M. Berwick, president of the Institute for Health Care Improvement and one of the nation's top health-care quality experts, praises the VHA's information technology as "spectacular." The venerable Institute of Medicine notes that the VHA's "integrated health information system, including its framework for using performance measures to improve quality, is considered one of the best in the nation."

If this gives you cognitive dissonance, it should. The story of how and why the VHA became the benchmark for quality medicine in the United States suggests that much of what we think we know about health care and medical economics is just wrong. It's natural to believe that more competition and consumer choice in health care would lead to greater quality and lower costs, because in almost every other realm, it does. That's why the Bush administration—which has been promoting greater use of information technology and other quality improvement in health care—also wants to give individuals new tax-free "health savings accounts" and high-deductible insurance plans. Together, these measures are supposed to encourage patients to do more comparison shopping and haggling with their doctors; therefore, they create more market discipline in the system.

But when it comes to health care, it's a government bureaucracy that's setting the standard for maintaining best practices while reducing costs, and it's the private sector that's lagging in quality. That unexpected reality needs examining if we're to have any hope of understanding what's wrong with America's health-care system and how to fix it. It turns out that precisely because the VHA is a big, government-run system that has nearly a lifetime relationship with its patients, it has incentives for investing in quality and keeping its patients well—incentives that are lacking in for-profit medicine.

Hitting Bottom

By the mid-1990s, the veterans health-care system was in deep crisis. A quarter of its hospital beds were empty. Government audits showed that many VHA surgeons had gone a year without picking up a scalpel. The population of veterans was falling sharply, as aging World War II and Korean War vets began to pass away. At the same time, a mass migration of veterans from the Snowbelt to the Sunbelt overwhelmed hospitals in places such as Tampa with new patients, while those in places such as Pittsburgh had wards of empty beds.

Serious voices called for simply dismantling the VA system. Richard Cogan, a senior fellow at the Center on Budget and Policy Priorities in Washington, told *The New York Times* in 1994: "The real question is whether there should be a veterans health care system at all." At a time when the other health-care systems were expanding outpatient clinics, the VHA still required hospital stays for routine operations like cataract surgery. A patient couldn't even receive a pair of crutches without checking in. Its management system was so ossified and top-down that permission for such trivial expenditures as $9.82 for a computer cable had to be approved in Washington at the highest levels of the bureaucracy.

Yet few politicians dared to go up against the powerful veterans lobby, or against the many unions that represented much

of the VHA's workforce. Instead, members of Congress fought to have new veterans hospitals built in their districts, or to keep old ones from being shuttered. Three weeks before the 1996 presidential election, in part to keep pace with Bob Dole's promises to veterans, President Clinton signed a bill that planned, as he put it, to "furnish comprehensive medical services to all veterans," regardless of their income or whether they had service-related disabilities.

So, it may have been politics as usual that kept the floundering veterans health-care system going. Yet behind the scenes, a few key players within the VHA had begun to look at ways in which the system might heal itself. Chief among them was Kenneth W. Kizer, who in 1994 had become VHA's undersecretary for health, or, in effect, the system's CEO.

A physician trained in emergency medicine and public health, Kizer was an outsider who immediately started upending the VHA's entrenched bureaucracy. He oversaw a radical downsizing and decentralization of management power, implemented pay-for-performance contracts with top executives, and won the right to fire incompetent doctors. He and his team also began to transform the VHA from an acute care, hospital-based system into one that put far more resources into primary care and outpatient services for the growing number of aging veterans beset by chronic conditions.

By 1998, Kizer's shake-up of the VHA's operating system was already earning him management guru status in an era in which management gurus were practically demigods. His story appeared that year in a book titled *Straight from the CEO: The World's Top Business Leaders Reveal Ideas That Every Manager Can Use* published by Price Waterhouse and Simon & Schuster. Yet the most dramatic transformation of the VHA didn't just involve such trendy, 1990s ideas as downsizing and reengineering. It also involved an obsession with systematically improving quality and safety that to this day is still largely lacking throughout the rest of the private health-care system.

America's Worst Hospitals

To understand the larger lessons of the VHA's turnaround, it's necessary to pause for a moment to think about what comprises quality health care. The first criterion likely to come to mind is the presence of doctors who are highly trained, committed professionals. They should know a lot about biochemistry, anatomy, cellular and molecular immunology, and other details about how the human body works—and have the academic credentials to prove it. As it happens, the VHA has long had many doctors who answer to that description. Indeed, most VHA doctors have faculty appointments with academic hospitals.

But when you get seriously sick, it's not just one doctor who will be involved in your care. These days, chances are you'll see many doctors, including different specialists. Therefore, how well these doctors communicate with one another and work as a team matters a lot. "Forgetfulness is such a constant problem in the system," says Berwick of the Institute for Health Care Improvement. "It doesn't remember you. Doesn't remember that you were here and here and then there. It doesn't remember your story."

Are all your doctors working from the same medical record and making entries that are clearly legible? Do they have a reliable system to ensure that no doctor will prescribe drugs that will interact harmfully with medications prescribed by another doctor? Is any one of them going to take responsibility for coordinating your care so that, for example, you don't leave the hospital without the right follow-up medication or knowing how and when to take it? Just about anyone who's had a serious illness, or tried to be an advocate for a sick loved one, knows that all too often the answer is no.

Doctors aren't the only ones who define the quality of your health care. There are also many other people involved—nurses, pharmacists, lab technicians, orderlies, even custodians. Any one of these people could kill you if they were to do their jobs wrong. Even a job as lowly as changing a bedpan, if not done right, can spread a deadly infection throughout a hospital. Each of these people is part of an overall system of care, and if the system lacks cohesion and quality control, many people will be injured and many will die.

Just how many? In 1999, the Institute of Medicine issued a groundbreaking study, titled *To Err is Human*, that still haunts health care professionals. It found that up to 98,000 people die of medical errors in American hospitals each year. This means that as many as 4 percent of all deaths in the United States are caused by such lapses as improperly filled or administered prescription drugs—a death toll that exceeds that of AIDS, breast cancer, or even motor vehicle accidents.

Since then, a cavalcade of studies have documented how a lack of systematic attention not only to medical errors but to appropriate treatment has made putting yourself into a doctor's or hospital's care extraordinarily risky. The practice of medicine in the United States, it turns out, is only loosely based on any scientifically driven standards. The most recent and persuasive evidence came from study by Dartmouth Medical School published last October in *Health Affairs*. It found that even among the "best hospitals," as rated by *U.S. News & World Report*, Medicare patients with the same conditions receive strikingly different patterns and intensities of care from one another, with no measurable difference in their well-being.

For example, among patients facing their last six months of life, those who are checked into New York's renowned Mount Sinai Medical Center will receive an average of 53.9 visits from physicians, while those who are checked into Duke University Medical Center will receive only 20.9. Yet all those extra doctors' visits at Mount Sinai bring no gain in life expectancy, just more medical bills. By that measure of quality, many of the country's most highly rated hospitals are actually its shoddiest.

Worse, even when strong scientific consensus emerges about appropriate protocols and treatments, the health-care industry is extremely slow to implement them. For example, there is little controversy over the best way to treat diabetes; it starts with keeping close track of a patient's blood sugar levels. Yet if you have diabetes, your chances are only one-out-four that your health care system will actually monitor your blood sugar levels or teach you how to do it. According to a recent RAND Corp. study, this oversight causes an estimated 2,600 diabetics to go blind every year, and anther 29,000 to experience kidney failure.

All told, according to the same RAND study, Americans receive appropriate care from their doctors only about half of the time. The results are deadly. On top of the 98,000 killed by medical errors, another 126,000 die from their doctor's failure to observe evidence-based protocols for just four common conditions: hypertension, heart attacks, pneumonia, and colorectal cancer.

Now, you might ask, what's so hard about preventing these kinds of fatal lapses in health care? The airline industry, after all, also requires lots of complicated teamwork and potentially dangerous technology, but it doesn't wind up killing hundreds of thousands of its customers each year. Indeed, airlines, even when in bankruptcy, continuously improve their safety records. By contrast, the death toll from medical errors alone is equivalent to a fully loaded jumbo-jet crashing each day.

Laptop Medicine

Why doesn't this change? Well, much of it has changed in the veterans health-care system, where advanced information technology today serves not only to deeply reduce medical errors, but also to improve diagnoses and implement coordinated, evidence-based care. Or at least so I kept reading in the professional literature on health-care quality in the United States. I arranged to visit the VA Medical Center in Washington, D.C. to see what all these experts were so excited about.

The complex's main building is a sprawling, imposing structure located three miles north of the Capitol building. When it was built in 1972, it was in the heart of Washington's ghetto, a neighborhood dangerous enough though one nurse I spoke with remembered having to lock her car doors and drive as fast as she could down Irving Street when she went home at night.

Today, the surrounding area is rapidly gentrifying. And the medical center has evolved, too. Certain sights, to be sure, remind you of how alive the past still is here. In its nursing home facility, there are still a few veterans of World War I. Standing outside of the hospital's main entrance, I was moved by the sight of two elderly gentlemen, both standing at near attention, and sporting neatly pressed Veterans of Foreign Wars dress caps with MIA/POW insignias. One turned out to be a survivor of the Bataan Death March.

But while history is everywhere in this hospital, it is also among the most advanced, modern health-care facilities in the globe—a place that hosts an average of four visiting foreign delegations a week. The hospital has a spacious generic lobby with a food court, ATM machines, and a gift shop. But once you are in the wards, you notice something very different: doctors and nurses wheeling bed tables with wireless laptops attached down the corridors. How does this change the practice of medicine? Opening up his laptop, Dr. Ross Fletcher, an avuncular, white-haired cardiologist who led the hospital's adoption of information technology, begins a demonstration.

With a key stroke, Dr. Fletcher pulls up the medical records for one of his current patients—an 87-year-old veteran living in Montgomery County, Md. Normally, sharing such records with a reporter or anyone else would, of course, be highly unethical and illegal, but the patient, Dr. Fletcher explains, has given him permission.

Soon it becomes obvious why this patient feels that getting the word out about the VHA's information technology is important. Up pops a chart showing a daily record of his weight as it has fluctuated over a several-month period. The data for this chart, Dr. Fletcher explains, flows automatically from a special scale the patient uses in his home that sends a wireless signal to a modem.

Why is the chart important? Because it played a key role, Fletcher explains, in helping him to make a difficult diagnosis. While recovering from Lyme Disease and a hip fracture, the patient began periodically complaining of shortness of breath. Chest X-rays were ambiguous and confusing. They showed something amiss in one lung, but not the other, suggesting possible lung cancer. But Dr. Fletcher says he avoided having to chase down that possibility when he noticed a pattern jumping out of the graph generated from the patient's scale at home.

The chart clearly showed that the patient gained weight around the time he experienced shortness of breath. This pattern, along with the record of the hip fracture, helped Dr. Fletcher to form a hypothesis that turned out to be accurate. A buildup of fluid in the patient's lung was causing him to gain weight. The fluid gathered only in one lung because the patient was consistently sleeping on one side to cope with the pain from his hip fracture. The fluid in the lung indicated that the patient was in immediate need of treatment for congestive heart failure, and, fortunately, he received it in time.

The same software program, known as VistA, also plays a key role in preventing medical errors. Kay J. Craddock, who spent most of her 28 years with the VHA as a nurse, and who today coordinates the use of the information systems at the VA Medical Center, explains how. In the old days, pharmacists did their best to decipher doctors' handwritten prescription orders, while nurses, she says, did their best to keep track of which patients should receive which medicines by shuffling 3-by-5 cards.

Today, by contrast, doctors enter their orders into their laptops. The computer system immediately checks any order against the patient's records. If the doctors working with a patient have prescribed an inappropriate combination of medicines or overlooked the patient's previous allergic reaction to a drug, the computer sends up a red flag. Later, when hospital pharmacists fill those prescriptions, the computer system generates a bar code that goes on the bottle or intravenous bag and registers what the medicine is, who it is for, when it should be administered, in what dose, and by whom.

Each patient also has an ID bracelet with its own bar code, and so does each nurse. Before administering any drug, a nurse must first scan the patient's ID bracelet, then her own, and then the barcode on the medicine. If she has the wrong patient or the wrong medicine, the computer will tell her. The computer will also create a report if she's late in administering a dose, "and saying you were just too busy is not an excuse," says Craddock.

Craddock cracks a smile when she recalls how nurses reacted when they first were ordered to use the system. "One nurse tried to get the computer to accept her giving an IV, and when it wouldn't let her, she said, 'you see, I told you this thing is never going to work.' Then she looked down at the bag." She had mixed it up with another, and the computer had saved her

from a career-ending mistake. Today, says Craddock, some nurses still insist on getting paper printouts of their orders, but nearly all applaud the computer system and its protocols. "It keeps them from having to run back and forth to the nursing station to get the information they need, and, by keeping them from making mistakes, it helps them to protect their license." The VHA has now virtually eliminated dispensing errors.

In speaking with several of the young residents at the VA Medical Center, I realized that the computer system is also a great aid to efficiency. At the university hospitals where they had also trained, said the residents, they constantly had to run around trying to retrieve records—first upstairs to get X-rays from the radiology department, then downstairs to pick up lab results. By contrast, when making their rounds at the VA Medical Center, they just flip open their laptops when they enter a patient's room. In an instant, they can see not only all of the patient's latest data, but also a complete medical record going back as far as the mid-1980s, including records of care performed in any other VHA hospital or clinic.

Along with the obvious benefits this brings in making diagnoses, it also means that residents don't face impossibly long hours dealing with paperwork. "It lets these twentysomethings go home in time to do the things twentysomethings like to do," says Craddock. One neurologist practicing at both Georgetown University Hospital and the VA Medical Center reports that he can see as many patients in a few hours at the veterans hospital as he can all day at Georgetown.

By this summer, anyone enrolled in the VHA will be able to access his or her own complete medical records from a home computer, or give permission for others to do so. "Think what this means," says Dr. Robert M. Kolodner, acting chief health informatics officer for the VHA. "Say you're living on the West Coast, and you call up your aging dad back East. You ask him to tell you what his doctor said during his last visit and he mumbles something about taking a blue pill and white one. Starting this summer, you'll be able to monitor his medical record, and know exactly what pills he is supposed to be taking."

The same system reminds doctors to prescribe appropriate care for patients when they leave the hospital, such as beta blockers for heart attack victims, or eye exams for diabetics. It also keeps track of which vets are due for a flu shot, a breast cancer screen, or other follow-up care—a task virtually impossible to pull off using paper records. Another benefit of electronic records became apparent last September when the drug-maker Merck announced a recall of its popular arthritis medication, Vioxx. The VHA was able to identify which of its patients were on the drug within minutes, and to switch them to less dangerous substitutes within days.

Similarly, in the midst of a nationwide shortage of flu vaccine, the system has also allowed the VHA to identify, almost instantly, those veterans who are in greatest need of a flu shot and to make sure those patients have priority. One aging relative of mine—a man who has had cancer and had been in and out of nursing homes—wryly reports that he beat out 5,000 other veterans in the New London, Conn., area for a flu shot. He's happy that his local veterans hospital called him up to tell him he qualified, but somewhat alarmed by what this implies about his health.

The VistA system also helps to put more science into the practice of medicine. For example, electronic medical records collectively form a powerful database that enables researchers to look back and see which procedures work best without having to assemble and rifle through innumerable paper records. This database also makes it possible to discover emerging disease vectors quickly and effectively. For example, when a veterans hospital in Kansas City noticed an outbreak of a rare form of pneumonia among its patients, its computer system quickly spotted the problem: All the patients had been treated with what turned out to be the same bad batch of nasal spray.

Developed at taxpayer expense, the VistA program is available for free to anyone who cares to download it off the Internet. The link is to a demo, but the complete software is nonetheless available. You can try it out yourself by going to http://www1.va.gov/CPRSdemo/. Not surprisingly, it is currently being used by public health care systems in Finland, Germany, and Nigeria. There is even an Arabic language version up and running in Egypt. Yet VHA officials say they are unaware of any private health care system in the United States that uses the software. Instead, most systems are still drowning in paper, or else just starting to experiment with far more primitive information technologies.

Worse, some are even tearing out their electronic information systems. That's what happened at Cedars-Sinai Medical Center in Los Angeles, which in 2003 turned off its brand-new, computerized physician order entry system after doctors objected that it was too cumbersome. At least six other hospitals have done the same in recent years. Another example of the resistance to information technology among private practice doctors comes from the Hawaii Independent Physicians Association, which recently cancelled a program that offered its members $3,000 if they would adopt electronic medical records. In nine months, there were only two takers out of its 728 member doctors.

In July, Connecting for Health—a public-private cooperative of hospitals, health plans, employers and government agencies—found that persuading doctors in small- to medium-sized practices to adopt electronic medical records required offering bonuses of up to 10 percent of the doctors' annual income. This may partly be due to simple techno-phobia or resistance to change. But the broader reason, as we shall see, is that most individual doctors and managed care providers in the private sector often lack a financial incentive to invest for investing in electronic medical records and other improvements to the quality of the care they offer.

This is true even when it comes to implementing low-tech, easy-to-implement safety procedures. For example, you've probably heard about surgeons who operate on the wrong organ or limb. So-called "wrong site" surgery happens in about one out of 15,000 operations, with those performing foot and hand surgeries particularly likely to make the mistake. Most hospitals try to minimize this risk by having someone use a magic marker to show the surgeon where to cut. But about a third of time, the VHA has found, the root problem isn't that someone mixed up left with right; it's that the surgeon is not operating on the patient he thinks he is. How do you prevent that?

Obviously, in the VHA system, scanning the patient's ID bracelet and the surgical orders helps, but even that isn't foolproof. Drawing on his previous experience as a NASA astronaut and accident investigator, the VHA's safety director, Dr. James Bagian, has developed a five-step process that VHA surgical teams now use to verify both the identity of the patient and where they are supposed to operate. Though it's similar to the check lists astronauts go through before blast off, it is hardly rocket science. The most effective part of the drill, says Bagian, is simply to ask the patient, in language he can understand, who he is and what he's in for. Yet the efficacy of this and other simple quality-control measures adopted by the VHA makes one wonder all the more why the rest of the health-care system is so slow to follow.

Why Care About Quality?

Here's one big reason. As Lawrence P. Casalino, a professor of public health at the University of Chicago, puts it, "The U.S. medical market as presently constituted simply does not provide a strong business case for quality."

Casalino writes from his own experience as a solo practitioner, and on the basis of over 800 interviews he has since conducted with health-care leaders and corporate health care purchasers. While practicing medicine on his own in Half Moon Bay, Calif, Casalino had an idealistic commitment to following emerging best practices in medicine. That meant spending lots of time teaching patients about their diseases, arranging for careful monitoring and follow-up care, and trying to keep track of what prescriptions and procedures various specialists might be ordering.

Yet Casalino quickly found out that he couldn't sustain this commitment to quality, given the rules under which he was operating. Nobody paid him for the extra time he spent with his patients. He might have eased his burden by hiring a nurse to help with all the routine patient education and follow-up care that was keeping him at the office too late. Or he might have teamed up with other providers in the area to invest in computer technology that would allow them to offer the same coordinated care available in veterans hospitals and clinics today. Either step would have improved patient safety and added to the quality of care he was providing. But even had he managed to pull them off, he stood virtually no chance of seeing any financial return on his investment. As a private practice physician, he got paid for treating patients, not for keeping them well or helping them recover faster.

The same problem exists across all health-care markets, and its one main reason in explaining why the VHA has a quality performance record that exceeds that of private-sector providers. Suppose a private managed-care plan follows the VHA example and invests in a computer program to identify diabetics and keep track of whether they are getting appropriate follow-up care. The costs are all upfront, but the benefits may take 20 years to materialize. And by then, unlike in the VHA system, the patient will likely have moved on to some new health-care plan. As the chief financial officer of one health plan told

Casalino: "Why should I spend our money to save money for our competitors?"

Or suppose an HMO decides to invest in improving the quality of its diabetic care anyway. Then not only will it risk seeing the return on that investment go to a competitor, but it will also face another danger as well. What happens if word gets out that this HMO is the best place to go if you have diabetes? Then more and more costly diabetic patients will enroll there, requiring more premium increases, while its competitors enjoy a comparatively large supply of low-cost, healthier patients. That's why, Casalino says, you never see a billboard with an HMO advertising how good it is at treating one disease or another. Instead, HMO advertisements generally show only healthy families.

In many realms of health care, no investment in quality goes unpunished. A telling example comes from semi-rural Whatcom County, Wash. There, idealistic health-care providers banded together and worked to bring down rates of heart disease and diabetes in the country. Following best practices from around the country, they organized multi-disciplinary care teams to provide patients with counseling, education, and navigation through the health-care system. The providers developed disease protocols derived from evidence-based medicine. They used information technology to allow specialists to share medical records and to support disease management.

But a problem has emerged. Who will pay for the initiative? It is already greatly improving public health and promises to bring much more business to local pharmacies, as more people are prescribed medications to manage their chronic conditions and will also save Medicare lots of money. But projections show that, between 2001 and 2008, the initiative will cost the local hospital $7.7 million in lost revenue, and reduce the income of the county's medical specialists by $1.6 million. An idealistic commitment to best practices in medicine doesn't pay the bills. Today, the initiative survives only by attracting philanthropic support, and, more recently, a $500,000 grant from Congress.

For health-care providers outside the VHA system, improving quality rarely makes financial sense. Yes, a hospital may have a business case for purchasing the latest, most expensive imaging devices. The machines will help attract lots of highly-credentialed doctors to the hospital who will bring lots of patients with them. The machines will also induce lots of new demand for hospital services by picking up all sorts of so-called "pseudo-diseases." These are obscure, symptomless conditions, like tiny, slow-growing cancers, that patients would never have otherwise become aware of because they would have long since died of something else. If you're a fee-for-service health-care provider, investing in technology that leads to more treatment of pseudo-disease is a financial no-brainer.

But investing in any technology that ultimately serves to reduce hospital admissions, like an electronic medical record system that enables more effective disease management and reduces medical errors, is likely to take money straight from the bottom line. "The business case for safety … remains inadequate … [for] the task," concludes Robert Wachter, M.D., in a recent study for Health Affairs in which he surveyed quality control efforts across the U.S. health-care system.

If health care was like a more pure market, in which customers know the value of what they are buying, a business case for quality might exist more often. But purchasers of health care usually don't know, and often don't care about its quality, and so private health-care providers can't increase their incomes by offering it. To begin with, most people don't buy their own health care; their employers do. Consortiums of large employers may have the staff and the market power necessary to evaluate the quality of health-care plans and to bargain for greater commitments to patient safety and evidence-based medicine. And a few actually do so. But most employers are not equipped for this. Moreover, in these days of rapid turnover and vanishing post-retirement health-care benefits, few employers have any significant financial interest in their workers' long-term health.

That's why you don't see many employers buying insurance that covers smoking cessation programs or the various expensive drugs that can help people to quit the habit. If they did, they'd be being buying more years of healthy life per dollar than just about any other way they could use their money. But most of the savings resulting from reduced lung cancer, stroke, and heart attacks would go to future employers of their workers, and so such a move makes little financial sense.

Meanwhile, what employees value most in health care is maximum choice at minimal cost. They don't want the boss man telling them they must use this hospital or that one because it has the best demonstrated quality of care. They'll be their own judge of quality, thank-you, and they'll usually base their choice on criteria like: "My best friend recommended this hospital," or "This doctor agrees with my diagnosis and refills the prescriptions I want," or "I like this doctor's bedside manner." If more people knew how dangerous it can be to work with even a good doctor in a poorly run hospital or uncoordinated provider network, the premium on doctor choice would be much less decisive, but for now it still is.

And so we get results like what happened in Cleveland during the 1990s. There, a well-publicized initiative sponsored by local businesses, hospitals and physicians identified several hospitals as having significantly higher than expected mortality rates, longer than expected hospital stays, and worse patient satisfaction. Yet, not one of these hospitals ever lost a contract because of their poor performance. To the employers buying health care in the community, and presumably their employees as well, cost and choice counted for more than quality. Developing more and better quality measures in health care is a noble cause, but it's not clear that putting more information into health-care markets will change these hard truths.

Health for service

So what's left? Consider why, ultimately, the veterans health system is such an outlier in its commitment to quality. Partly it's because of timely, charismatic leadership. A quasi-military culture may also facilitate acceptance of new technologies and protocols. But there are also other important, underlying factors.

First, unlike virtually all other health-care systems in the United States, VHA has a near lifetime relationship with its patients. Its customers don't jump from one health plan to the next every few years. They start a relationship with the VHA as early as their teens, and it endures. That means that the VHA actually has an incentive to invest in prevention and more effective disease management. When it does so, it isn't just saving money for somebody else. It's maximizing its own resources.

The system's doctors are salaried, which also makes a difference. Most could make more money doing something else, so their commitment to their profession most often derives from a higher-than-usual dose of idealism. Moreover, because they are not profit maximizers, they have no need to be fearful of new technologies or new protocols that keep people well. Nor do they have an incentive to clamor for high-tech devices that don't improve the system's quality or effectiveness of care.

And, because it is a well-defined system, the VHA can act like one. It can systematically attack patient safety issues. It can systematically manage information using standard platforms and interfaces. It can systematically develop and implement evidence-based standards of care. It can systematically discover where its care needs improvement and take corrective measures. In short, it can do what the rest of the health-care sector can't seem to, which is to pursue quality systematically without threatening its own financial viability.

Hmm. That gives me an idea. No one knows how we're ever going to provide health care for all these aging baby boomers. Meanwhile, in the absence of any near-term major wars, the population of veterans in the United States will fall dramatically in the next decade. Instead of shuttering under-utilized VHA facilities, maybe we should build more. What if we expanded the veterans health-care system and allowed anyone who is either already a vet or who agrees to perform two years of community service a chance to buy in? Indeed, what if we said to young and middle-aged people, if you serve your community and your country, you can make your parents or other loved ones eligible for care in an expanded VHA system?

The system runs circles around Medicare in both cost and quality. Unlike Medicare, it's allowed by law to negotiate for deep drug discounts, and does. Unlike Medicare, it provides long-term nursing home care. And it demonstrably delivers some of the best, if not the best, quality health care in the United States with amazing efficiency. Between 1999 and 2003, the number of patients enrolled in the VHA system increased by 70 percent, yet funding (not adjusted for inflation) increased by only 41 percent. So the VHA has not only become the health care industry's best quality performer, it has done so while spending less and less on each patient. Decreasing cost and improving quality go hand and hand in industries like autos and computers—but in health care, such a relationship virtually unheard of. The more people we can get into the VHA, the more efficient and effective the American health-care system will be.

We could start with demonstration projects using VHA facilities that are currently under-utilized or slated to close. Last May, the VHA announced it was closing hospitals in Pittsburgh; Gulfport, Miss.; and Brecksville, Ohio. Even after the closures, the VHA will still have more than 4 million square feet of vacant or obsolete real estate. Beyond this, there are empty facilities available from bankrupt HMOs and public hospitals, such as the defunct D.C. General. Let the VHA take over these facilities, and apply its state-of-the-art information systems, safety systems, and protocols of evidence-based medicine.

Once fully implemented, the plan would allow Americans to avoid skipping from one health-care plan to the next over their lifetimes, with all the discontinuities in care and record keeping and disincentives to preventative care that this entails. No matter where you moved in the country, or how often you changed jobs, or where you might happen to come down with an illness, there would be a VHA facility nearby where your complete medical records would be available and the same evidence-based protocols of medicine would be practiced.

You might decide that such a plan is not for you. But, as with mass transit, an expanded VHA would offer you a benefit even if you didn't choose to use it. Just as more people riding commuter trains means fewer cars in your way, more people using the VHA would mean less crowding in your own, private doctor's waiting room, as well as more pressure on your private health-care network to match the VHA's performance on cost and quality.

Why make public service a requirement for receiving VHA care? Because it's in the spirit of what the veterans health-care system is all about. It's not an entitlement; it's recognition for those who serve. America may not need as many soldiers as in the past, but it has more need than ever for people who will volunteer to better their communities.

Would such a system stand in danger of becoming woefully under-funded, just as the current VHA system is today? Veterans comprise a declining share of the population, and the number of Americans who have personal contact with military life continues to shrink. It is therefore not surprising that veterans health-care issues barely register on the national agenda, even in times of war. But, as with any government benefit, the broader the eligibility, the more political support it is likely to receive. Many veterans will object to the idea of sharing their health care system with non-vets; indeed, many already have issues with the VHA treating vets who do not have combat-related disabilities. But in the long run, extending eligibility to non-vets may be the only way to ensure that more veterans get the care they were promised and deserve.

Does this plan seem too radical? Well, perhaps it does for now. We'll have to let the ranks of the uninsured further swell, let health-care costs consume larger and larger portions of payrolls and household budgets, let more and more Americans die from medical errors and mismanaged care, before any true reform of the health-care system becomes possible. But it is time that our debates over health care took the example of the veterans health-care system into account and tried to learn some lessons from it.

Today, the Bush administration is pushing hard, and so far without much success, to get health-care providers to adopt information technology. Bush's National Coordinator for Health Care Information Technology, Dr. David Brailer, estimates that if the U.S. health-care system as a whole would adopt electronic medical records and computerized prescription orders, it would save as much as 2 percent of GDP and also dramatically improve quality of care. Yet the VHA's extraordinary ability to outperform the private sector on both cost and quality suggests that the rest of the Bush administration's agenda on health care is in conflict with this goal.

The administration wants to move American health care from the current employer-based model, where companies chose health-care plans for their workers, to an "ownership" model, where individuals use much more of their own money to purchase their own health care. But shifting more costs on to patients, and encouraging them to bargain and haggle for the "best deal" will result in even more jumping from provider to provider. This, in turn, will give private sector providers even fewer incentives to invest in quality measures that pay off only over time. The Bush administration is right to question all the tax subsidies going to prop up employer-provided health insurance. But it is wrong to suppose that more choice and more competition will solve the quality problem in American health care.

VHA's success shows that Americans clearly could have higher-quality health care at lower cost. But if we presume—and it is safe to do so—that Americans are not going to accept the idea of government-run health care any time soon, it's still worth thinking about how the private health-care industry might be restructured to allow it to do what the VHA has done. For any private health-care plan to have enough incentive to match the VHA's performance on quality, it would have to be nearly as big as the VHA. It would have to have facilities and significant market share in nearly every market so that it could, like the VHA, stand a good chance of holding on to customers no matter where they moved.

It would also have to be big enough to achieve the VHA's economies of scale in information management and to create the volumes of patients needed to keep specialists current in performing specific operations and procedures. Not surprisingly, the next best performers on quality after the VHA are big national or near-national networks like Kaiser Permanente. Perhaps if every American had to join one such plan and had to pay a financial penalty for switching plans (as, in effect, do most customers of the VHA), then a business case for quality might exist more often in the private health-care market. Simply mandating that all health-care providers adopt electronic medical records and other quality protocols pioneered by the VHA might seem like a good idea. But in the absence of any other changes, it would likely lead to more hospital closings and bankrupt health-care plans.

As the health-care crisis worsens, and as more become aware of how dangerous and unscientific most of the U.S. health-care system is, maybe we will find a way to get our minds around these strange truths. Many Americans still believe that the U.S. health-care system is the best in the world, and that its only major problems are that it costs too much and leaves too many people uninsured. But the fact remains that Americans live shorter lives, with more disabilities, than people in countries that spend barely half as much per person on health care. Pouring more money into the current system won't change that. Nor will making the current system even more fragmented and driven by short-term profit motives. But learning from the lesson offered by the veterans health system could point the way to an all-American solution.

PHILLIP LONGMAN, a Schwartz Senior Fellow at the New America Foundation, is the author of *The Empty Cradle*; Basic Books, 2004.

Senate's Failure to Agree on Immigration Plan Angers Workers and Employers Alike

ABBY GOODNOUGH AND JENNIFER STEINHAUER

Until it collapsed on Friday, a compromise immigration plan in the Senate offered Rigoberto Morales a chance to reach his dream of becoming an American citizen.

Mr. Morales had worked eight years in the sun-baked fields of Immokalee, Fla., in the southern part of the state, picking tomatoes, evading the authorities, and sending most of his earnings to his mother and daughter in Mexico. The Senate plan would have allowed Mr. Morales, 25, to apply for permanent residency because he has lived here more than five years.

But as tantalizing as the possibility was, Mr. Morales said he never really believed Congress would solve his plight.

''It's a very bad thing because we're working very hard here and there's no support from the government,'' he said, standing outside a dreary shack where he lives with his wife and three other tomato pickers, all illegal immigrants from Mexico. ''We're only working. We're not committing a sin.''

Many of the nation's approximately 11 million illegal immigrants—as well as their employers—have long sought some of the major provisions in the Senate proposal, which failed amid partisan rancor.

In interviews, employers and illegal workers said the bill would have offered significant improvement, and several said the failure of the compromise was a lost opportunity.

''This is disappointing,'' said Edward Overdevest, president of Overdevest Nurseries in Bridgeton, N.J. ''I think it is a setback for reason, it is a setback for common sense.''

Mr. Overdevest said the Senate had failed to solve a problem that has been festering for years.

Mr. Overdevest and other employers who rely on an existing guest worker program that is smaller than what was proposed had hoped that the Senate would address the reams of red tape they say have plagued the program.

Antonia Fuentes, a Mexican who has picked tomatoes in Immokalee for two years, said legal status, even as a guest worker, would have allowed her to breathe easier even though life would have remained hard. ''We live here in fear,'' said Ms. Fuentes, 18. ''We fear Immigration will come, and many people just don't go out.''

Yet she and others were wary of a provision in the Senate plan that would have forced illegal immigrants who have been here from two to five years to return home and then apply for temporary work in the United States. A million immigrants who have been here illegally for less than two years would have had to leave with little promise of returning.

Paulino Pineda, a community college custodian in Perrysburg, Ohio, outside Toledo, said any bill that did not provide amnesty to all illegal immigrants was flawed.

''It's not a democratic solution,'' said Mr. Pineda, 65, who moved to the United States from the Dominican Republic in 1992 and sends money home to his 11 children. ''If people come here, work very hard, do everything they're told to do, and then when they're not needed anymore they're told to take your things and go back, they might as well be slaves.''

According to the Department of Labor, the United States economy will add about five million jobs in businesses like retail, food service and landscaping over the next decade, with not enough American workers to meet the need.

Many employers—especially in industries that rely on large numbers of unskilled laborers—had embraced the idea of a guest-worker program. They said it would stabilize the workforce, reduce the high cost of turnover and perhaps increase the number of workers available.

But others said an expanded guest-worker program would bring higher costs and more paperwork, and were cheered by the Senate bill's defeat.

''Yay!'' said Jay Taylor, president of Taylor & Fulton, a tomato grower in Florida, Maryland and Virginia, who said that the bill was too hastily drafted and that Congress had not grasped the complexity of the issue. Mr. Taylor said guest workers should be able to come and go as they pleased, with freedom to earn wages in this country but no promise of citizenship or benefits.

"It was a dinner cooked in a pressure cooker," said Mr. Taylor, who employs nearly 1,000 immigrants. "What we need is something that comes out of a crock pot. We need something that is well thought out, well planned and well executed, and in the atmosphere we are in today on this subject, we're not going to get that kind of situation."

Judith Ingalls, a vice president at Fortune Contract Inc., a carpet maker in Dalton, Ga., did not find many of the provisions in the Senate bill practical, particularly those that would have required longtime immigrants to learn English and to pay fines.

"It is crazy to listen to this whole debate when you live here and see what is happening," Ms. Ingalls said. "Nothing I have heard out of Washington works."

Many employers, too, oppose any provision that would penalize them for hiring illegal workers, knowingly or not. Some expressed concern about the provision that would have granted citizenship to immigrants who had been in the United States for at least five years, saying it might have encouraged them to quit or be less productive.

"The illegals are probably better workers than the legal ones," said Mike Gonya, who farms 2,800 acres of wheat and vegetables near Fremont, Ohio. "The legal ones know the system. They know legal recourse. The illegal ones will bust their butts."

Some employers, especially in agriculture, say keeping full operations in the United States will not be viable without an overhaul of the system.

Jack Vessey, who runs a garlic-production company in El Centro, Calif., said stricter border enforcement and competition with other agriculture businesses had lengthened his harvest season by months and left him shorthanded.

"We don't have the people to work," Mr. Vessey said.

Agricultural businesses, with their mostly migrant workforce, are the proverbial canaries in the coal mine of immigration. With some local governments searching for ways to stem illegal immigration, other businesses fear that time is running out.

"Disruptions in agriculture could cause disruptions in our own workforce," said John Gay, vice president for government affairs at the National Restaurant Association, which said it did not have enough workers to deal with the industry's projected growth over the next few years. "We have been muddling through with this don't-ask-don't-tell policy we've had, but it's not sustainable."

ABBY GOODNOUGH reported from Immokalee, Fla., for this article, and **JENNIFER STEINHAUER** from New York. Terry Aguayo contributed reporting from Immokalee, Brenda Goodman from Georgia and Chris Maag from Ohio.

Who's Advocating What Here?

ROBERT MEYERS AND VICTORIA FRIGO

Direct democracy, a concept employed by the Founding Fathers of the United States to present questions directly to the voters, has regained popularity recently, in the form of legislative referendums and citizen initiatives. But serious ethical issues may develop for city and county managers if their governments choose to promote or oppose ballot measures by using public dollars.

Some jurisdictions limit local government expenditures in this arena, requiring government actions—if allowable at all—to be balanced in viewpoint and strictly educational in purpose and tenor. Only a minority of jurisdictions holds that governments may spend public money to advocate for or against ballot questions, and even this minority adds the caveat that the issue being supported or opposed must have emerged from an elected body. (See Figure 1 for an overview of states' decisions.)

Less clear is whether localities have the right to oppose ballot questions arising from citizens' initiatives. Regardless of the degree to which local governments fund advocacy campaigns, however, their managers can maintain fairness, impartiality, and professionalism during referendum or initiative elections.

State Court Rulings
Florida Law Favors Government Advocacy

The Florida Supreme Court has concluded that local governing bodies have not only the right but also the duty to advocate on matters they believe are beneficial or detrimental to their constituents. In the 2004 election campaign, Miami-Dade County spent $800,000 to urge citizens to approve a $2.9 billion general-obligation bond program.

This project was intended to support the largest capital construction program in the history of Miami-Dade County (and the third-largest municipal bond program of its kind in the nation). Leaflets and other print advertising, funded with public dollars, asked citizens in three languages to make "Miami-Dade a better place to live, work, and play" by voting on eight bond questions aimed at improving the general infrastructure and certain cultural and recreational facilities.

The Miami-Dade County manager also enlisted business, religious, and civic leaders to serve as "ambassadors" to advance the bond program. Not only did these volunteers host more than 100 meetings extolling the benefits of the project, but individual organizations and newly formed political action committees also raised private funds to conduct economic impact studies, lead focus groups, poll the electorate, and buy TV ads.

A month before the election, one privately funded poll costing $200,000 showed that the number of voters undecided about supporting the bond issues was increasing. As a result, a business group dedicated an additional $400,000 of its own funds to television advertising.

The ads featured grade-school children urging their parents, in English and Spanish, to "Vote with your heart. Vote yes for each part." All eight referendums passed, by margins ranging from 58 to 71 percent. The Miami-Dade County manager attributed the success of the campaign to the innovative, grassroots approach that joined public and private efforts.

New Mexico Sidesteps a Decision

Less satisfactory were actions taken by the city of Las Cruces, New Mexico, during a special municipal election in August 1994. Following a decade-long battle with the local utility company, the city was advised that it could save 10 to 20 percent on electric rates if a buyout of the privately held transmission system could be negotiated.

The city spent $80,000 to hire advertising firms, conduct public opinion surveys, employ new personnel, and purchase brochures, yard signs, billboards, and advertising on television and radio and in newspapers to advocate for city ownership of the utility. Additionally, public employees were assigned to special advocacy tasks, and public facilities were made available for meetings. Voters approved the purchase by a vote of 9,672 to 5,159, and the state legislature authorized the sale of tax-exempt revenue bonds to finance the deal.

The Florida Supreme Court has concluded that local governing bodies have not only the right but also the duty to advocate on matters they believe are beneficial or detrimental to their constituents.

But the spending was far from over. The purchase price of the utility company was argued in a long court battle, and a citizen sued the city for wrongfully using public funds in a partisan

Figure 1. Comparison of States Limiting Government Advocacy

This table provides a synopsis of various rationales given by state and federal courts that have addressed the legality of publicly funded advocacy of referendums and initiatives.

State	Neutrality Required?	Legal Rationale
Alabama	No	The city of **Birmingham** was allowed to urge passage of a bond to provide funds for several public projects because the advertising costs were incidental to Birmingham's obligation "to determine the needs of its citizens and to provide funds to service those needs." A federal court concluded that a state subdivision has a right to self-advancement and self-protection. Therefore, a city's advocacy for passage of its own proposals is consistent with its role.
Arizona	No	A state court found that **Tucson** could legally publicize its support of two propositions with pamphlets, a Web site, and a television spot. The rationale was that the city did not employ "express advocacy," which the court defined as "communication that, taken as a whole, unambiguously urges a person to vote in a particular manner." The court concluded that reasonable minds could differ on whether the city *expressly advocated* or *unambiguously urged* a particular vote.
California	Yes	A California **parks department** could disseminate neutral information relevant to its purpose, but the government agency could not expend public funds to promote a partisan position in an election campaign. The California court stated, "A fundamental precept of this nation's democratic electoral process is that the government may not 'take sides' in election contests or bestow an unfair advantage on one of the several competing factions."
Colorado	Yes	The **state treasurer** could not expend public monies to compensate department staff for formulating and distributing press releases that opposed a ballot measure and urged voters to defeat it. Efforts by the director and his staff were considered "contributions in kind" and violated the Fair Campaign Promises Act, which limits state-employee contributions during elections to $50. The Colorado state court observed that "jurisdictions that have addressed the issue so far agree almost uniformly that, during an election, communication from the state may inform but not attempt to sway the electorate."
Washington, D.C.	Yes	The **District of Columbia** could not expend funds in an attempt to defeat a citizen-initiated petition requiring the city to provide overnight homeless shelters. A federal appellate court concluded that the money that D.C. had spent in trying to defeat the petition violated a congressional appropriation statute that expressly forbade D.C. from engaging in publicity or propaganda for the purpose of influencing legislation.
Florida	No	Public funds and county resources used by **Leon County** to advocate for passage of a bond referendum were legal, even though the state supreme court noted that the county's campaign slogans reflected a "slight lack of neutrality that should not be encouraged in ballot language." The court continued, "One duty of a democratic government is to lead the people to make informed choices through fair persuasion-Local governments are not bound to keep silent in the face of a controversial vote that will have profound consequences for the community."
Massachusetts	Yes	In spite of the city of **Boston's** broad authority under its home-rule charter, the city could not urge its inhabitants to vote for a proposed amendment to the state constitution because, "traditionally, municipalities have not appropriated funds to influence election results." The fact that local governments were not specifically mentioned in statutes governing elections indicated to the Massachusetts court that "the Legislature did not even contemplate such municipal action could occur."
New York	Yes	A state court found that the New York constitution prohibits giving or loaning "the money of the state" to aid "any private corporation or association, or private undertaking." The case involved then-Governor Mario Cuomo and the commissioner of the state **Office of Economic Development**, who directed that a newsletter be printed and distributed at state expense. The newsletter contained factual information, as well as a plea to oppose the alleged Republican position on welfare and Medicaid reform.
New Mexico	Unsettled	The city of **Las Cruces** expended $80,000 in public funds as part of a mass-media campaign to encourage voters to support the city's purchase of a private electric utility. The state appellate court did not rule because the election had passed, rendering the issue moot. In *dicta*, however, the court cited numerous jurisdictions that found support "for the general proposition that, at some threshold level, a public entity must refrain from spending public funds to promote a partisan position during an election campaign."
Oklahoma	Yes	Although the city of **Tulsa** impermissibly expended public money to promote passage of bond issues through activities such as developing voter surveys, compiling a campaign strategy manual, and paying for newspaper ads, an Oklahoma court concluded that the electoral process had not been "contaminated by these activities." Under the relevant state statute, the court stated that one must prove conclusively, by clear and convincing evidence, that the result of the election would have been substantialty different but for the unlawful acts of public officials.
Oregon	Yes	The **health department** could not use taxpayers' funds to engage in an aggressive anti-fluoridation policy. An Oregon court found that "excessive or questionable efforts by government to manufacture the consent of the governed calls the legitimacy of its action into question."

fashion. By 1999, the city had paid out nearly $8 million in legal fees. At this point, a deregulation law was on the books, and a newly elected city council no longer saw the merits of buying the utility.

Although some of the city's expenses were recovered, the $8 million figure did not include in-house costs, which, according to the Las Cruces city manager, were impossible to calculate. In the end, the New Mexico Court of Appeals refused to address the legality of spending public funds on the advocacy campaign because the controversy was moot.

California Restricts Advocacy

Public spending in California is limited to impact studies. Nevertheless, the stakes were especially high for cities and counties during the 2004 electoral cycle. The 2004 Local Taxpayers and Public Safety Act, or Proposition 1A, sought to prohibit the California legislature from snatching property taxes from cities, counties, and special districts. The proposed amendment would allow the state to borrow local funds but only if the governor had proclaimed a "significant state hardship" and only if the states previous loans from local governments had been repaid.

To avoid the ban on government advocacy before elections and, at the same time, to support the interests of cities and counties, the League of California Cities joined with coalition partners to found a nonprofit entity called LOCAL (Leave Our Community Assets Local). LOCAL raised more than $9 million in private donations to purchase television advertising and to fund other media events.

Proposition 1A was approved overwhelmingly by 83.6 percent of the voters. The league attributed the stunning victory to LOCAL efforts, but throughout the campaign, city and county managers had faced ongoing quandaries over the extent to which they could support the LOCAL coalition.

Considerations for Local Managers

Avoiding the Appearance of Divided Loyalties or Interests

Tenet 7 of the Code of Ethics adopted by the International City/County Management Association requires that members avoid political activities that might undermine their reputations for fairness, impartiality, and professionalism. This ethical principle was reiterated, specifically with the California dilemma in mind, in a February 2004 *PA Times* article by Elizabeth Kellar titled "Professionalism vs. Politics: What Are the Issues?"

The article advised California members that their role was to assist their governments in presenting the official position these localities had taken on Proposition 1A. Additionally, because California law allows public resources to be used lo evaluate a ballot measure's impact on the local government, managers could present information-based talks on the issues, as long as the presentations were fair and impartial. Finally, the article stated, although the ICMA Code of Ethics permits members to make contributions to causes, including ballot measures, ICMA

cautions members to consider how their personal support for a cause may be viewed in light of their official responsibilities.

What were the consequences of the managers' activism of Proposition 1A? In "California Pushes the Envelope on Advocacy," October 2005, *Public Management,* Kellar interviewed several California managers and observers. The consensus was that city and county managers did a good job of raising ethical issues before moving into action. Not a single complaint reached the executive director or legal counsel of the League of California Cities.

One issue that concerned some California managers, however, was that employees might feel obligated to make financial contributions when they know their boss is an advocate for a cause, even if the boss does not solicit contributions in the work place.

Additional Common-Sense Guidelines

Building on what was learned in California, here are six further recommendations that managers should follow when their local governments are engaged in initiatives and referendums, regardless of professional or jurisdictional limitations. (See also Figure 2 for a useful "self-questionnaire" that managers might employ in their decision making.)

1. Know the laws. Before taking any course of action, managers should consult their city or county attorneys for specific rules that may apply in their states. Once the limits of public spending are known, the local manager is in a good position to monitor time and other resources that can be allocated to supporting initiatives and referendums.

Specific restrictions may he found in home-rule charters, state campaign disclosure laws, ethics ordinances, court decisions, and attorney-general legal opinions. Several Florida attorney-general opinions, for example, address government involvement in referendums and initiatives. One opinion recognizes the authority of governing bodies composed of elected officials to spend public funds for advocacy but does not extend the same privilege to entities composed of appointed officials.

Special considerations involve both the federal Hatch Act and comparable state laws. Generally, these regulations prohibit government employees from engaging in political activity while on duty or in a government office. For instance, a local manager would not be permitted to solicit contributions from other employees to support a ballot issue. More particularly, soliciting contributions from subordinates might be viewed as coercive and a possible abuse of power. Numerous other restrictions under the Hatch Act and its state equivalents might also apply.

2. Know your constituents. Even if local law does not require it, the manager should encourage the gathering of legislative findings to identify the public interest to be served, as well as to justify the necessity of spending public funds for an educational or advocacy campaign.

3. Make it official. Once legislative findings have been obtained, the manager should encourage the legislative body to adopt a resolution formalizing the scope of the education or advocacy expenditure. In jurisdictions that do not allow government funding for political purposes, this prohibition should be clearly stated in

Figure 2. Self-Questionnaire

Here are some questions that can help local government managers assess their own localities' history of advocacy, as well as their own past behaviors regarding these campaigns and their attitudes toward advocacy.

1. Has your local government or a local government agency in your jurisdiction spent *public funds* before an election to educate voters (i.e., to disseminate neutral, balanced information) on an issue?

2. Has your local government or a local government agency in your jurisdiction spent *public funds* prior to an election to advocate (i.e., to actively campaign for or against) an issue?

3. If your local government has spent public funds to *educate* or *advocate*, what type of issue or issues were involved? Transportation? Health care? Housing? Gambling? Education? Other? (Describe.)

4. In general, what is the *range of money spent* from public funds on a typical neutral, *educational* campaign, including wages earned by government employees assigned to the task?

5. In general, what is the *range of money spent* from public funds on a typical *advocacy* campaign, including wages earned by government employees assigned to the task?

6. If your government has *collaborated* with *nongovernmental* organizations in educational or advocacy campaigns, briefly describe the nature of the collaboration(s).

7. If your government has engaged in *advocacy campaigns* (i.e.. taken a position for or against), have the campaigns been successful?

8. Have you *consulted a government attorney* on the legality of *government advocacy* for or against an issue in your jurisdiction?

9. Indicate any *legal or ethical prohibitions* that you believe would ban *government advocacy* in your jurisdiction.

10. Have you *advocated* for or against an issue before an election, in your individual capacity as a public manager—not as a candidate for office?

11. Is *government advocacy* (i.e., the spending of public funds to support or defeat an issue before the electorate) consistent with your *personal philosophy* about how government should operate?

12. Explain briefly *your personal position* on the merits and/or deficiencies of *government advocacy.*

Fast Facts

- 60 percent of local governments report developing a comprehensive homeland-security-related plan or amending an existing emergency management plan.
- 55 percent provide training for staff, such as administrative staff, who are not first responders.
- 54 percent have conducted a homeland-security-related drill or exercise.
- 91 percent of respondents report collaborating on homeland security issues with other local governments, 75 percent with the state government, and 60 percent with a regional organization.
- 61 percent have adopted the National Incident Management System (NIMS), a protocol developed by the Federal Emergency Management Agency to help ensure consistency of training and approach for first responders at all governmental levels.
- Nearly one-third of survey respondents have hired or appointed a manager to help coordinate intergovernmental security functions.
- Cities and counties have used their own funds for many homeland security activities, primarily for equipment (66 percent), disaster mitigation and preparedness (64 percent), drills and training exercises (63 percent), and disaster response (60 percent).
- Approximately 60 percent of respondents report requesting state and/or federal funding for equipment.
- 19 percent of local governments report that they experienced budget shortfalls during the past two fiscal years as a result of homeland security activities.

Source: ICMA's Homeland Security 2005 survey. Results are based on responses from 2,786 local governments nationwide with populations of more than 2,500. For more survey information, visit icma.org (click on Information Resources, then Survey Research, then Survey Results).

PM Web Resource

www.muninetguide.com

Features of the online publication *MuniNet Guide* include:
- A searchable database of Web sites by state, county, and local governments and public sector agencies, as well as other municipal-related topics.
- An interactive map that allows users to zero in on a specific state to see news, articles, and listings of Web sites for agencies, organizations, hospitals, housing authorities, airports, counties, and municipalities in that state.
- Feature articles that highlight Web site content for elected and appointed government officials, webmasters, municipal investors, and urban enthusiasts.
- Municipal Bond Calendar of upcoming bond sales, including links to issuers.
- Top Picks: an annual selection of Web sites that rise above the crowd.
- New & Noteworthy announcements of new state and local government and public sector agency Web sites, improved features, trends, and discoveries.
- Melange, a collection of favorite Web sites that are deemed most useful and interesting for everyday use—at work and at home—from time-management tips to famous quotations, and handy reference tools.

the resolution. If the law allows public money to be spent, however, the resolution should include sufficient safeguards to ensure that funds are distributed according to the intended purpose.

4. Clarify roles. To avoid misunderstandings, the manager should identify which elected officials and/or staff will be deciding the form and appearance of the education or advocacy campaign. In Las Cruces, New Mexico, during the 1990s, the biggest advocate for the purchase of the utility company was the mayor. Once he left office, however, others were not willing to oversee the project with the same fervor.

If government employees will be shifted to new tasks to deliver the message, the local manager must evaluate the impact that these shifts will have on the overall functioning of the government. During the "Better Place to Live, Work, and Play" advocacy campaign in Miami-Dade County, some county employees volunteered to speak in favor of the bond referendums "off the clock," and others were "on county time" when collaborating with grass-roots leaders and managing the county's own ad campaign.

5. Distinguish financial sources. Identify the type of public resources that can be used in the advocacy or educational campaign. Even when state and local laws support public spending, other factors, such as bond regulations, may prevent tapping into certain assets.

6. Minimize liabilities. Set guidelines to minimize the government's liabilities if responsibilities are transferred to third parties like public relations firms or ad agencies. Monitor the output of these parties regularly to ensure that all laws are being followed. In Florida, advocacy language used in campaign advertising must he "fair" and not distort the truth.

Discretion Is the Better Part of Valor

Although the law may be on your side, discretion is also advised. In one case, elected city commissioners in Coral Gables, Florida, had a legal mandate to advocate for a referendum to change the mayors term limits. But because they could not arrive at a unanimous decision, the commissioners chose instead to spend public dollars to educate the electorate on the pros and cons of the issue. In other situations, governments may choose to avoid taking a stand if the initiatives involve recalls or if competing, contradictory citizens' initiatives are presented during the same election cycle.

Another option that helps ascertain the level of community support for an issue and. at the same time, conserves public dollars is placing nonbinding straw ballots before the voters during a regular election cycle. This strategy has been used many times throughout Miami-Dade County.

In the 2004 election in the city of Miami Beach, 55 percent of the electorate supported the straw ballot to develop Bay Link, an electrically operated streetcar that would connect the harrier island to the mainland. Before the straw poll, public support for Bay Link had been unclear because of the strongly conflicting rhetoric of political factions, both on and off the Beach.

In conclusion, local managers can accrue many advantages for their communities during referendums and initiative elections if they are guided by relevant laws and ethical considerations.

ROBERT MEYERS (rmeyers@miamidade.gov) is executive director, and **VICTORIA FRIGO** (frigov@miamidade.gov) is staff attorney for the Commission on Ethics and Public Trust, Miami-Dade County, Florida.

Smart Growth

Why We Discuss It More than We Do It

The Smart Growth vision has a strong intellectual and emotional appeal, compared to more sprawl. However, though some places follow Smart Growth policies, they are outnumbered by those where such policies are commonly discussed but rarely practiced effectively. Why is this the case? Successful implementation requires adopting policies that give up long-established traditions, including local home rule and low-density living patterns. These intermediate steps are unappealing to most Americans. This article analyzes where Smart Growth advocates among urban planners, government officials, environmentalists, and real estate developers should focus their attention if they hope to move from vision to reality.

ANTHONY DOWNS

As I speak to audiences around the country about how to cope with growth, people often ask me, "Where is Smart Growth being implemented most effectively?" I usually reply, "Smart Growth is much more talked about than actually carried out in practice." That does not mean no regions are actually using Smart Growth policies. But it does mean that such regions are greatly outnumbered by others where Smart Growth principles are commonly discussed but not actually put into effect. Why is that the case?

The basic reason is that carrying out Smart Growth principles encounters many obstacles that are not obvious at the outset, but emerge strongly as advocates try to apply those principles. Those obstacles have inhibited the ability of urban planners, government officials, environmentalists, and real estate developers who promote Smart Growth to achieve their initial objectives. This article explores why I believe that is the case.

The Genesis and Nature of Smart Growth

Smart Growth was originally conceived as a reaction to what many planners believed were undesirable features of continuing growth through "suburban sprawl" (Burchell, Listokin, et al., 2000; Burchell, Lowenstein, et al., 2002; Downs, 2001a). Those undesirable features included the following:

- Unlimited outward and "leapfrog" expansion of low-density new development.
- Large-scale conversion of open space and environmentally sensitive lands to urban uses.
- Lack of choice among housing types and neighborhood configurations.

- Worsening traffic congestion and air pollution caused by more intensive use of automotive vehicles for ground travel.
- Costly requirements to expand roads, sewers, water systems, and other infrastructures outward rather than repairing and using those already in place.
- Failure to redevelop existing older neighborhoods.
- Segregation of land uses rather than a mixing of uses that reduces the need for travel.

Since Smart Growth was created to reduce or eliminate these perceived ills, its advocates tend to promote opposite principles of action. Thus, the most common principles of Smart Growth are the following:[1]

1. Limiting outward extension of new development in order to make settlements more compact and preserve open spaces. This can be done via urban growth boundaries or utility districts.
2. Raising residential densities in both new-growth areas and existing neighborhoods.
3. Providing for more mixed land uses and pedestrian friendly layouts to minimize the use of cars on short trips.
4. Loading the public costs of new development onto its consumers via impact fees rather than having those costs paid by the community in general.
5. Emphasizing public transit to reduce the use of private vehicles.
6. Revitalizing older existing neighborhoods.

Other Smart Growth principles less universally advocated include these:

7. Creating more affordable housing.
8. Reducing obstacles to developer entitlement.

9. Adopting more diverse regulations concerning aesthetics, street layouts, and design.

In reality, different groups in society emphasize different constellations of these elements, depending upon their own perspectives.[2] Thus, the real estate development community plays down limitations on outward development, big-city officials strongly favor redeveloping existing older areas plus repairing existing infrastructures, and urban planners and environmentalists accept all the above principles and stress using more public transit to cut down on vehicle trips and miles of travel.[3] Thus, Smart Growth does not mean the same thing to everyone. In reality, it has almost come to stand for "whatever form of growth I like best" in the opinion of whoever is speaking. Nevertheless, the first six principles set forth above are generally considered key elements of most Smart Growth programs actually being promoted across the nation.

Who Actually Originates Pressures to Implement Smart Growth Principles?

Pressures to put Smart Growth principles into practice tend to originate from three different groups. The first is *nongovernment environmentalists* who are appalled by sprawl and want to stop its absorption of so much open land. They normally operate out of private foundations and other groups that are not part of the public sector. The Sierra Club and the Nature Conservancy are examples of such groups. They function as private lobbyists trying to persuade the media, the public, and government officials to adopt broad Smart Growth policies (see, e.g., Benfield et al., 1999).

The second group consists of *urban planners and other local public officials* who work mainly for local governments. They seek to preserve local government fiscal resources and keep local taxes low. They believe Smart Growth principles will help them avoid building a lot of costly new roads and other infrastructures in outlying areas, shift new housing construction to higher densities that conserve land and infrastructure costs, and use land on in-fill sites easier to develop than far-out "greenfield" sites (see, e.g., American Planning Association, 2001, 2002; Meek, 2002). However, these officials are also susceptible to being influenced by local homeowning voters who want to keep housing prices rising by preventing large-scale new construction nearby, especially of lower-cost housing (Fischel, 2001). Finally, as local government officials, they are normally hostile to the idea of shifting any of their local authority over land uses to higher-level public agencies, such as regional agencies (Beaumont, 1999; Downs, 1994; Orfield, 1997).

The third group of Smart Growth promoters consists of *innovative private real estate developers* who are trying to get permission from local governments to build specific new projects. They promote Smart Growth principles to support their desires to create large-scale mixed-use projects, use higher densities than in surrounding areas, and create a variety of housing types in a single project. Their focus is almost always on a particular site, rather than on broad regional principles of development.

Such developers are more likely to be in large-scale firms than small-scale ones. The former have more resources with which to cope with local delays and regulatory barriers to large-scale innovative projects, which the developers believe are worth waiting for because of their great profit potential (see, e.g. National Association of Home Builders, 1999; National Association of Industrial and Office Parks, 1999).

One thing these three main sources of promotion for Smart Growth have in common is that they do *not* include significant numbers of plain citizens—especially local homeowners, who are the majority in most suburban communities. To put it another way, *most pressures to adopt Smart Growth policies do not come from the citizenry at large but from one or more of these special interest groups.* In almost every community, all three of these promotional groups are relatively small compared to the general citizenry. Hence these groups are all challenged by the need to persuade lots of "plain citizens" to agree with their views. Such persuasion is necessary in our democracy in order to shift a powerfully entrenched set of policies like those embodied in suburban sprawl to something quite different. It is a wise old saying that "You can't beat something with nothing!" Therefore, to beat sprawl, these groups must persuade significant numbers of local citizens to support adoption of a new and different set of growth-related policies—that is. Smart Growth policies. How to accomplish such persuasion is a critical aspect of getting Smart Growth policies actually put into practice.[4]

How Applying Smart Growth Principles Generates Problems

Given the widespread hostility to continued suburban sprawl in America among professional planners and environmentalists, and even among many real estate developers, it seems that the major principles of Smart Growth ought to be in the process of being vigorously applied in most metropolitan areas. Yet I do not believe that is the case. True, quite a few areas have effectively implemented one or two principles of Smart Growth—the ones least difficult to implement. But few regions have put into practice the most problematic principles. And almost no areas (not even Portland, Oregon) have implemented all of Smart Growth's principles.[5] The main reason is that carrying out those principles requires adopting one or more of eight other principles of action that are not nearly as widely praised nor as readily accepted by the American public. These obstacles are described below.

Redistributing Benefits and Costs of Development

Smart Growth policies differ fundamentally from the sprawl-related development processes long dominant in almost all U.S. metropolitan areas. Therefore, changing from sprawl to Smart Growth almost inevitably involves redistributing the benefits and costs associated with urban development generally. For example, preventing growth from moving outward without limits from built-up areas by shifting to more compact growth concentrated very close to built-up areas changes the location of future subdivisions. It reduces the chances that owners of far-outlying parcels will "capture" future subdivisions, thereby profiting from big increases in land values. At the same time, this shift increases the chances that owners of close-in sites will capture higher density projects, thereby benefiting from large increases in land values. In short, it greatly alters the potential benefit structure currently embodied in the status quo, turning some now-likely future gainers into losers, and vice versa. But every basic change in development strategy that causes such major shifts in who gains and who loses upsets widespread expectations among yesterday's potential gainers, thereby alienating them. This naturally makes those once-potential gainers hostile to the idea of such change. Moreover, a loss of a potential future benefit tends to be felt more intensely than the gain of such an uncertain benefit. True, this is nothing new; even just building a new highway also generates winners and losers among land owners affected by that road.

Long experience with human nature under an immense variety of circumstances indicates that most people resist major changes in the established status quo, unless it is clear that those changes will produce very specific benefits for them. Thus, a major problem with shifting federal finance from the existing income tax to a consumption tax is that such a shift would radically change who gains and who loses from federal fiscal operations. But most people are now accustomed to an income-tax-oriented regime. Therefore, they resist changing to a new regime that might affect them quite differently in ways they cannot foresee. The same problem plagues attempts to replace sprawl development with Smart Growth. Most Americans are accustomed to sprawl and its consequences, but they are not at all sure what would happen to them under Smart Growth. Faced with such uncertainty, they are reluctant to support such a major change, especially if they are among those groups who would lose existing benefits from sprawl. This is a serious difficulty associated with changing any fundamental arrangements in a complex society. It applies to almost all the specific obstacles described below.[6]

Shifting Power and Authority from Local to Regional Levels

Several key Smart Growth principles require government action at the regional or state level, not at the local government level where most powers over land use planning now reside. But achieving regional action requires shifting a significant degree of existing land use planning authority from local governments to some higher-level organization. In most metropolitan areas, no such higher-level organization exists, short of the state government itself. And even where such an organization does exist, most local governments do not want to yield any of their existing power over land use decisions to anyone else. "Home rule" powers are among the most vigorously defended of any authorities entrusted to local governments.

Yet this kind of power shift would be necessary for any real check on the outward expansion of urban development far beyond presently built-up areas. Although individual communities can adopt local urban growth boundaries, unless all such communities within a region adopt such boundaries that are closely coordinated (which almost never happens), no one community alone can stop growth from leaping out into open country beyond its boundaries. And even if all the localities in a metropolitan area adopted a coordinated set of urban growth limits, that would not prevent private developers from going outside the boundaries of that metropolitan area and starting new subdivisions in farther-out counties. This is precisely what is now happening in both the Washington, DC, and Minneapolis/St. Paul metropolitan areas. Only state governments are capable of *both* creating regional urban growth boundaries *and* stringently limiting growth outside those boundaries (as in Oregon), which can stop such long-distance "leapfrog" developments. But if these developments are not stopped, urban growth boundaries have only limited power to halt sprawl.

Federal law has already recognized the need for similar regional planning powers concerning transportation in the creation of Metropolitan Planning Organizations (MPOs) to supervise new major ground transportation facilities. In fact, rational development of strong public transit networks within any sizable metropolitan area requires controlling the placement of such facilities at the regional level. But planning highways and transit facilities regionally will not work well if that planning is not coordinated with the planning of where housing and other developments are to be located.

Yet currently that set of decisions is totally controlled at the local level by dozens of small governments through a process of "disjointed incrementalism." Moreover, there is very little willingness of local officials, or even state government officials, to shift any notable degree of power over local land use decisions from local to regional or state levels, even though such officials are among the strongest promoters of Smart Growth ideas. Until this changes, in the vast majority of U.S. metropolitan areas, most recent and likely fixture growth is going to continue to be in the form of outward sprawl unchecked by Smart Growth policies forcing development into more compact patterns.

The few American regions that have shifted significant land use planning power from local to regional bodies have done so primarily as the result of some situation perceived to be a crisis at the state level. In these cases, that perception galvanized the state government—which has ultimate legal power over local governments—to do what was necessary to overcome pervasive parochialism among local governments. Otherwise, each locality would have continued to act almost solely in what its officials perceived was the best interests of their own residents, without regard for the welfare of their entire region. In Florida, the crisis was the threat of development of the Everglades. In Oregon, it was imminent development of the Willamette River Valley. In New Jersey, it was a threat by the courts to end local zoning powers unless localities better met regional needs for housing for low-income households. In Georgia, it was the federal government's threat to withhold highway finances unless Atlanta's air pollution was reduced. But without such crises, few states have shifted enough power over land use planning from localities to regional bodies to make Smart Growth feasible. And even in regions where such a shift has occurred, it is arguable how much of an effect that shift has had upon urban form.

Increasing Residential Density

A second critical problem in carrying out Smart Growth principles involves an inherent conflict of views within the minds of millions of American homeowners. In 2004, homeowning households comprised 69% of all American households, according to the U.S. Gensus Bureau (2004). In most suburbs, they form a significant majority of all voters. Nearly all such households strongly desire to maintain the market values of the homes they occupy. In most cases, those homes are their largest single asset, and those assets have been rising in value significantly in the past few years. Thus, from 1999 to 2004, the median value of single-family homes sold across the U.S. rose from $133,300 to $184,100, or by 38.1% (National Association of Realtors, 2005).

In order to protect the values of their homes from possibly declining, most homeowners (especially in the suburbs) are reluctant to permit into their existing neighborhoods any entry of additional housing units that would sell for lower prices than their own homes. They fear such lower-cost homes would reduce the desirability (and therefore the prices) of their homes too. This normally means they do not want any additional low-cost for-sale units built there, or any rental units built in primarily ownership neighborhoods.[7]

This economic motive for preventing such changes in their neighborhoods is reinforced by the widespread American view that it is undesirable for lower-income households to move near them for social, educational, and security reasons. In addition, many households fear higher density would mean more traffic congestion and more crowded schools and other facilities.

These sources of hostility to local changes that might reduce home values are the foundation of NIMBYism. It is the belief that "although some changes in society are necessary. Not My Back Yard please!" This attitude frequently surfaces whenever any increases in neighborhood density are proposed in built-up areas.[8]

On the other hand, many suburban homeowners are also opposed to continued expansion of their metropolitan regions through more sprawl. They believe sprawl results in costlier tax bills to pay for the provision of infrastructures stretching out into open spaces. They also oppose more absorption of open land that they would like to have readily available to them. This hostility towards more sprawl is more general and abstract, however, than their hostility towards any increases in residential density near them. Thus, many suburban homeowners are likely to support Smart Growth in the abstract, but oppose its specific manifestations when the increases in density it calls for are planned near them (Fischel, 2001).

This internally conflicting attitude among homeowners towards continued sprawl is a major underlying problem for those interested in promoting Smart Growth policies. Those promoters are often encouraged by the general support of many homeowners in the overall area. But any specific steps towards implementing anti-sprawl increases in density encounter strong localized opposition from those homeowners residing nearby. Maryland's Governor Parris Glendening, who built his reputation on supporting Smart Growth and limiting sprawl, was able to get his policies passed easily in general. But then their partic-

ular applications were basically defeated at local levels by NIMBY resistance, according to detailed stories published in the *Washington Post* (e.g., Graig, 2004; Lewis, 2004; Whoriskey, 2004a, b, c). As a result, suburban growth in Maryland has continued in a sprawling manner, unchecked by the state's Smart Growth policies.

Raising Housing Prices

Yet another problem caused by Smart Growth policies is a tendency to raise housing prices. After all, Smart Growth proposes to locate more housing units on smaller total amounts of land than in the past as part of its making future growth more compact. Smart Growth also seeks to set aside large amounts of open space as unavailable for housing purposes. And Smart Growth wants to prevent "leapfrog" subdivisions where households looking for low cost homes on inexpensive far-out land can "keep driving until they qualify." This removes the least expensive land from availability for housing.

The resulting higher density on land still usable for housing is normally accompanied by higher land prices per gross acre. True, those higher land prices can be offset by smaller lots per dwelling, but there is no certainty that this will be the case. If the proportion of all housing units built shifts markedly towards higher shares of multifamily dwellings, as has happened in Portland, Oregon, then land costs per dwelling may not necessarily rise. But they still could rise even in that case. And if many residents continue to prefer detached single-family homes on their own lots, the land price per dwelling may rise considerably.

Unfortunately, it is difficult to determine what specific factors cause housing prices to rise, especially in a period when housing prices have been increasing markedly in almost all developed nations around the world. Yet that has been happening since the late 1990s. There have been intense arguments about whether the urban land boundary around Portland has been a major factor causing housing prices there to rise as substantially as they have. Defenders of Smart Growth even argue that home prices there have risen because Smart Growth policies have made Portland a more desirable place to live, thereby attracting more residents, rather than affecting prices by restricting the housing supply. However, there is little doubt that Smart Growth policies have caused housing prices to rise more than they otherwise would have in at least some communities where they have been applied. That is why some analysts have concluded that Smart Growth and affordable housing are inconsistent goals for a single community to pursue simultaneously.[9] Even defenders of Smart Growth admit that it is consistent with the creation of more affordable housing only under unusual circumstances when many strong measures are applied to insure that consistency. For example. Nelson and Wachter (2003) wrote that "Affordable housing policies can be a component of smart growth. Such policies, however, depend on local implementation that runs counter to both local home rule principles and local fiscal incentives" (p. 182). Thus, Smart Growth does not invariably produce higher housing prices, but it has a tendency to do so.

Of course, insofar as Smart Growth does raise the prices of existing housing units, it benefits the owners of those units. Therefore, this quality of Smart Growth can be considered an advantage from the viewpoint of homeowners seeking greater wealth in their home equities. Yet it is a disadvantage to renters and households who do not yet own a home but hope to buy one. In most suburban communities, the beneficiaries outnumber the losers, and the losers are mainly not yet present in the community to oppose Smart Growth policies. So this characteristic is by no means a net disadvantage for proponents of Smart Growth, though few openly state that they favor higher housing prices resulting from Smart Growth policies.

Failing to Reduce Traffic Congestion

A fourth problem generated by some Smart Growth policies is their inherent inability to achieve the results they promise. This defect is especially true concerning policies that promise to reduce traffic congestion by increasing public reliance upon public transit. My own extensive analysis of traffic congestion in *Still Stuck in Traffic* (Downs, 2004b) convinced me that such congestion is likely to get worse throughout the world as societies become wealthier and more populous. Experience in the United States in particular shows that building additional public transit facilities almost never reduces traffic congestion in a region, once that congestion has reached the point of serious slowdowns during major rush hours. For example, although Portland, Oregon, doubled the extent of its light rail system's tracks in the 1990s, and significantly increased ridership on that system, traffic congestion became more intense than before. Why? First, a high percentage of the new light rail riders shifted from buses rather than private vehicles. Second, population growth in the region overcame any slight improvements in traffic congestion caused by the added light rail facilities. Similarly, additions of light rail systems in San Diego, San Jose, Denver, Dallas, and many other American communities have not reduced the intensity of traffic congestion there. In the period from 1980 to 2000, the U.S. added 1.2 additional cars, trucks, or buses to the existing vehicle population for every 1.0 additional man, woman, or child added to the human population. As long as that ratio continues, and our human population keeps growing around 30 million per decade, no policies are likely to reduce traffic congestion in any major U.S. metropolitan areas.

True, some proponents of Smart Growth would counter that this "alarming increase" in vehicle ownership has been caused by public policies that promote car use. Those policies include designing communities to be mainly car dependent, and investing in roadway infrastructure and parking and other means of accommodating the car at the expense of investing in other modes of travel. Therefore, the relative utility of other modes of travel as compared to private cars is exceedingly low. Yet public investments in transit facilities are much greater in relation to their actual usage than public investments in auto-oriented facilities.[10]

Increasing the "Red Tape" of New Development

Shifting new development from an outward-oriented sprawl pattern into a more inward-oriented compact pattern typically increases the amount of "red tape" that developers must go through to complete projects, such as preparing environmental impact, endangered species, and historical preservation studies; getting applications processed by multiple departments in the local government; etc. This occurs because larger cities tend to have much more detailed and onerous permission processes for new projects than those outlying suburbs in which sprawl normally occurs. Moreover, many big cities also have strong construction labor unions that may impose higher wage costs upon projects within their boundaries than for projects in outlying suburban communities, where most housing is built with non-union labor. These conditions increase the resistance of developers to adopting more compact development strategies, other things equal. More compact development also favors large-scale real estate developers, who have deeper pockets than small-scale developers with which to bear the greater delays and higher costs of new in-city projects. That is why developers promoting projects based upon Smart Growth values tend to be largerscale developers. Small-scale developers are more likely to want to stick to building on suburban greenfield sites.

Restricting Profits for Owners of Outlying Land

The compact growth pattern dictated by Smart Growth principles restricts the ability of farmers and other owners of outlying land to take advantage of the higher land prices they could obtain from further sprawl development. By confining a lot of open outlying land to farming or open space. Smart Growth diminishes the capital gains the owners of such land can expect to receive from future development. On the other hand, Smart Growth increases the capital gains that owners of vacant land, or land covered with obsolete structures, within built-up areas are likely to receive from in-fill projects. However, the number of persons owning open land outside built-up areas who *might* profit from further sprawl is normally much larger than the number owning in-fill sites within built-up areas likely to profit from Smart Growth. That is because the amount of undeveloped open land outside built-up areas greatly exceeds the amount of land on usable in-fill or other close-in sites. Therefore, this obstacle tends to generate more voters resistant to Smart Growth strategies than voters supporting them.

In some regions, planners have attempted to offset the loss of potential gains from new development for owners of outlying land by creating transferable development rights (TDRs) for such owners. Under this arrangement, owners of outlying sites agree to limit future development on their land in return for receiving TDRs. The owners can then sell those TDRs to owners of closer-in land as a means of allowing the latter to increase permissible densities on their sites. However, this arrangement has not fully compensated most owners of outlying land for what they believe is the loss of future development profits when Smart Growth blocks development on their sites.

Replacing "Disjointed Incrementalism" with Regional Planning

There is a fundamental conflict between developing a single, overall plan to direct future population growth within a region and permitting such growth to occur through an unplanned, decentralized process of "disjointed incrementalism."[11] Many Americans consider the first approach to be excessively socialistic in nature. They prefer the traditional American method of allowing individual developers, landowners, and local communities to make unrelated choices of where to put fixture growth. The resulting absence of regional planning makes it difficult to carry out Smart Growth policies that depend on such planning, such as limiting outward expansion of new development, preserving outlying open space, and creating new high-density development clusters around fixed-rail transit stations. But others think such an unplanned approach will only exacerbate existing undesirable conditions generated by past sprawl, such as "excessive" absorption of open space by urbanization. This is not a purely ideological argument. Its outcome partly hinges on whether centralized or regional planners can anticipate future trends in population growth, technological change, and the market's locational preferences as well as, or better than, individual entrepreneurs creating particular new subdivisions without any overall plan. There is no clear evidence regarding which approach is more effective in the long run, partly because so few U.S. regions have tried any regional planning of their growth. However, up to now, the disjointed incrementalism approach to future growth remains the overwhelmingly dominant method used in American metropolitan areas, mainly because there are very few effective regional bodies with the authority to influence where future growth will occur.

How These Obstacles Inhibit Implementation of Smart Growth Policies

The eight obstacles to implementing Smart Growth policies set forth above have quite different impacts upon each of the nine Smart Growth policies described earlier. Each row in this chart represents one of the nine Smart Growth policies frequently advocated in various regions. Each column represents one of the eight obstacles to such policies that arise when trying to implement them. Therefore, each cell represents the probable interaction of one policy and one obstacle. Dark squares indicate that the particular obstacle concerned normally has a significant negative impact on implementation of that particular policy. For example, the first policy, limiting outward extension of growth, is strongly negatively affected by the second obstacle, the need to shift power from local to regional authorities. This occurs because so many local officials and other citizens ate opposed to shifting any of their local government authority over land use decisions to any regional or higher-level agency. So they tend to oppose limiting outward extensions of growth because doing so requires such a power shift.

Lighter squares indicate that the obstacle in that column has some negative impact on implementing the policy in that row, but not necessarily a decisively prohibitive impact. Diamonds show that the policy in that row actually reduces the negative impact of that obstacle on the implementation of that policy. Thus, the policy of creating more affordable housing tends to offset the impact of Smart Growth in raising housing prices, though that policy may also arouse hostility among homeowners who want home prices to rise higher.

Circles indicate no significant relationship between the policy in that row and the obstacle in that column. A significant relationship is lacking in 43 of the 72 cells in this matrix. Of course, the relationships described in all 72 cells represent my views—other observers may arrive at different conclusions concerning specific cells. Nevertheless, this matrix provides a clear way of relating each obstacle to each proposed Smart Growth policy.

This chart clearly shows that certain obstacles affect the implementation of far more Smart Growth policies than others. Thus, the obstacle "Shifting power" negatively affects implementation of six out of the nine Smart Growth policies. All six of those policies require some movement of power from local governments to more regional agencies. At the other extreme, the obstacle "Increasing red tape" only inhibits implementation of two Smart Growth policies, and then only partly. The obstacle "Raising housing prices" negatively affects four Smart Growth policies because they tend to raise housing prices. But the same obstacle also positively helps in the implementation of two other policies ("Creating more affordable housing" and "Reducing obstacles to developer entitlement") because they tend to reduce housing prices.

This chart also clearly shows that some Smart Growth policies are likely to encounter much more difficulty getting implemented than others. The policy of "Limiting outward extension of new developments" is likely to be hindered by five out of the eight obstacles, three of which will impose serious negative impacts. Conversely, the policy "Adopting more diverse regulations on aesthetics, street layouts, and design" is far more likely to be implemented because it helps reduce two obstacles and is not hindered by any others.

However, this matrix does not provide clear guidance about the degree of difficulty each Smart Growth policy is likely to encounter when advocates try to implement it. Why not? Because it does not quantify the interplay of different obstacles in relation to each specific policy. To provide more definite guidance of that type, a second chart is also presented. In Table 1, the rows again represent the nine Smart Growth policies described earlier, while the columns present a calculation of the resistance or support each policy is likely to encounter. The second column indicates which groups in society are likely to oppose each policy, while the third shows which groups are likely to support each one. The fourth column compares the strength of opposition and support among these groups, and the fifth arrives at a conclusion concerning how favorable the prospects for implementing each policy are likely to be. Again, the cells in this matrix represent only my best judgment, based upon my past experience and the literature on Smart Growth. Other ob-

Table 1. Likelihood of implementing Smart Growth policies.

Smart growth policy	Arouses opposition among these	Garners support among these	Opposition vs. support	Likelihood of implementation
1. Limiting outward extension of new developments	Owners of land in outlying areas now blocked from development; real estate developers	Owners of close-in in-fill parcels now emphasized for higher-density development	Losers likely to vastly outnumber winners, and may feel their losses more strongly than winners feel their gains	Very unlikely
2. Raising densities in both new-growth and existing neighborhoods	Homeowners living near where higher density is proposed in both new and existing neighborhoods	Environmentalists; owners of in-fill sites where high density is proposed	Local NIMBYs intensely oppose any higher densities near them, pressuring local officials to block higher densities	Very unlikely
3. Providing for more mixed land uses and pedestrian-friendly environments	Only a few residents who dislike mixed-use environments; also retail chain operating firms	New Urbanism supporters; public transit supporters; many existing residents	Opposition likely to be weak except for unwillingness of retail chain operators to run small neighborhood outlets	Likely
4. Loading public costs of new development onto residents of growth areas	Renters wanting to restrain housing costs; households seeking to buy first homes	Residents of most existing neighborhoods; local government officials	Supporters of passing most public costs onto new residents will almost always outnumber those who pay because they live in new areas	Very likely
5. Emphasizing public transit to reduce the use of private vehicles	Road builders who lose funds shifted to transit; trucking firms and auto companies	Supporters of more public transit facilities; builders of transit-oriented developments	Urban planners who favor transit tend to dominate MPOs; users of private vehicles do not feel harmed if others shift to transit	Somewhat likely
6. Revitalizing older existing neighborhoods	Developers of outlying sites competing with older neighborhoods for funds	Big-city labor union workers; big-city local officials; owners of in-fill sites and sites in older areas	Key factor is size of financing available to revitalize older areas; if it is great, resistance to revitalization will be low	Somewhat likely
7. Creating more affordable housing	Homeowners fearing lower-cost housing will reduce values of their homes; local officials responding to them	Renters and low-income households needing housing assistance; low-income housing advocates	Resistance to any large amount of relatively low-cost housing is likely to be great because of homeowner attitudes	Unlikely
8. Reducing obstacles to developer entitlement	Environmentalists; home-owners seeking to keep local prices rising; historic preservationists; big-city labor unions	Home builders and real estate developers; landowners of sites on which developers want to create new projects	Not clear which group will have the greatest political power, though changing existing rules is difficult	Unclear
9. Adopting more diverse regulations on aesthetics, street layouts, and design	Historic preservationists	New Urbanists; real estate developers; home builders; urban planners	The cost of broadening existing regulations is very low and supporters are strong	Very likely

servers may reach quite different conclusions. But this matrix should help anyone interested in this subject arrive at systematic conclusions about the likelihood any one policy will be adopted under "normal" circumstances.

This admittedly rough analysis shows the following results:

- Two Smart Growth policies—"Limiting outward extension of new developments" and "Raising densities in both new-growth and existing neighborhoods"—are *Very unlikely* to be implemented. Both require shifting considerable authority from local to regional bodies and would generate strong opposition from heavily affected groups.

- Implementation of "Creating more affordable housing" is considered *Unlikely* because it would arouse opposition from local homeowners trying to prevent the values of their own homes from being weakened by the appearance of lower-cost housing nearby.

- Two other Smart Growth policies—"Loading public costs of new development onto residents of growth areas" and "Adopting more diverse regulations on street layouts, aesthetics, and design"—are *Very likely* to be implemented. The first benefits existing residents, who vastly outnumber potential newcomers. The second has no significant negative costs.

- Implementation of three other Smart Growth policies is considered either *Likely* or *Somewhat likely*. "Providing or mixed land uses and pedestrian friendly environments," "Emphasizing public transit to reduce the use of private vehicles," and "Revitalizing older existing neighborhoods." However, the last is likely only when adequate public funds are available, and the second is not likely to change commuting behavior very much.

- Whether "Reducing obstacles to developer entitlement" will be readily implemented or not is *Unclear*.

This analysis indicates that prospects for a metropolitan area adopting an entire broad Smart Growth strategy are very low. The political resistance likely to be generated by shifting the requisite authority from local to regional bodies, by raising densities in most neighborhoods, and by blocking outward extension of future growth is too great to be easily overcome. Thus, the central idea of Smart Growth—constraining future development into more compact, higher-density patterns—is not very likely to be adopted by many regions.

On the other hand, changes in certain development rules within local governments designed to broaden housing styles, permit more mixed uses, create more pedestrian ways, and push most of the public costs of new development onto residents of new-growth areas are far more likely to be implemented. These policies can be carried out without having local governments lose any of their existing land use powers.

The Crucial Role of State Governments

An overall Smart Growth strategy that encompasses most of the specific policies discussed above cannot really be carried out in any U.S. metropolitan area without the active advocacy and strong support of the state government concerned. Only the state government has the Constitutional power to shift authority over certain types of land use planning from local governments to regional or statewide agencies with the scope to carry out many Smart Growth policies. Only the state government can both pressure metropolitan areas to agree upon a single urban growth boundary for the entire region, and then prohibit further development outside that boundary within reasonable commuting distance of the region. Without such a prohibition, developers will quickly leapfrog new subdivisions beyond the urban growth boundary into nearby counties outside the metropolitan area's legal limits. That will soon undermine the whole idea of confining future growth into a more compact area.

The state government's powers are also necessary for many other aspects of Smart Growth policies. Raising densities in both existing and new-growth areas on a consistent basis throughout a metropolitan area requires powers that go beyond those of individual local governments, which cannot alter what neighboring governments do. So does locating affordable housing throughout many parts of a region, rather than concentrating it within older central cities, as has often occurred in the past. Any attempts to shift more ground movement to public transit requires a regional plan for where new transit facilities should be located. That is in theory within the jurisdiction of the regional Metropolitan Planning Organization, but the state government's planning and condemnation powers will also be critical.

Past experience shows that state government is likely to become actively involved in implementing Smart Growth policies only if the state's governor assumes a powerful leadership role. The governor is best situated to coordinate the efforts of myriad state agencies related to growth, and to provide them with the incentives to make Smart Growth a reality. Even then, gubernatorial leadership may not be enough to overcome all the obstacles to implementing Smart Growth, as has been shown in Maryland. Yet without such leadership, chances of getting any specific region within a state to adopt an overall Smart Growth strategy are dim indeed.

This analysis also shows that getting effective Smart Growth policies adopted in a multistate metropolitan area will be extraordinarily difficult. Although individual county governments can try such policies, as in the Washington, DC, area, their efforts are likely to be undermined by the failure of all their neighboring counties to do likewise.[12]

Conclusion

Many Americans unhappy with several past results of sprawl development have devised an alternative approach that has come to be known as Smart Growth. The policies incorporated into the Smart Growth vision have a strong intellectual and emotional appeal, compared to more sprawl. But trying to implement those policies requires adopting a whole set of additional policies that are much less appealing to most Americans. Those intermediary policies include changing the powers and scope of long-established governmental traditions, especially local home rule and relatively low-density living patterns. Unless the proponents of Smart Growth realize the necessity of carrying out such intermediary policies and devise ways of getting more political support for doing so, Smart Growth is likely to remain a vision that is much more talked about than carried out in practice.

Acknowledgments

The views in this article are those solely of the author and not of the Brookings Institution, its trustees, or its other staff members.

Notes

1. The literature is by now extensive. For leading examples see Burchell, Listokin, et al. (2000). Downs (2001b, 2003b), Downs et al. (2002), and Urban Land Institute (1998, 1999). For recent state-level examples, see Governor's Sustainable Washington Advisory Panel (2003) and Michigan State University (2004).

2. The National Association of Homebuilders (NAHB) lists the following principles for its version of Smart Growth: (i) Planning for and accommodating anticipated growth in economic activity, population, and housing demand as well as ongoing changes in demographics and lifestyles while protecting the environment, (2) Providing for a wide range of housing types to suit the needs, preferences, and income levels of a community's diverse population, (3) Adopting a comprehensive land-use planning process at the local level that clearly identifies land uses, such as residential, commercial, recreational, and industrial as well as land to be set aside as meaningful open space, (4) Adopting balanced and reliable means to finance and pay for the construction and expansion of roads, schools, water and sewer facilities, and other infrastructure required to serve a prosperous community, (5) Using land more efficiently by allowing higher density development and innovative land use policies and encouraging mixed-use and pedestrian-friendly developments with access to open space and mass transit, (6) Revitalizing older suburban and inner-city markets and encouraging infill development, and (7) Planning should be the exclusive province of local units of government (NAHB, Z005).

3. The Sustainable Communities Network, funded in part by the Environmental Protection Agency, defines Smart Growth as consisting of the following principles: (1) Create range of housing opportunities and choices, (2) Create walkable neighborhoods, (3) Encourage community and stakeholder collaboration, (4) Foster distinctive, attractive communities with a strong sense of place, (5) Make development decisions predictable, fair, and cost-effective, (6) Mix land uses, (7) Preserve open space, farmland, natural beauty, and critical environmental areas, (8) Provide a variety of transportation choices, (9) Strengthen and direct development towards existing communities, and (10) Take advantage of compact building design (Smart Growth Network, n.d.).

4. In contrast, many "growth management" efforts indeed engage citizens actively. See Porter (1997).

5. Portland has not developed an effective program for creating affordable housing for its low-income citizens, though it has carried out to some degree most of the other principles described earlier.

6. I am indebted to my friend and colleague Robert Burchell of Rutgers University for pointing out this aspect to me.

7. This argument has been made most persuasively by Fischel (2001).

8. For an in-depth analysis of NIMBYism, see Advisory Commission on Regulatory Barriers to Affordable Housing (1991).

9. For several discussions of this subject, see Downs (2004a), in particular Nelson et al. (2004), Fischel (2004), Voith and Crawford (2004), and Schill (2004). See also a review of the issues by Downs (2003a) and potential approaches by Goldberg (2003).

10. Public transit receives a share of total government spending on transportation far in excess of the proportion of all trips that are made on public transit nationwide. See Downs (2004b, pp. 141–147).

11. Insofar as I know, the term *disjointed incrementalism* was invented by Charles E. Lindblom (Lindblom & Braybrooke, 1963) of Yale University.

12. For attempts to encourage leadership by states in these and related areas, see Downs (1973, 2000) and Pendall (2000).

References

Advisory Commission on Regulatory Barriers to Affordable Housing. (1991)."*Not In my backyard": Removing barriers to affordable housing.* Washington, DC: Government Printing Office.

American Planning Association. (2001). *Policy guide on smart growth.* Chicago: Author.

American Planning Association. (2002). *Growing smart user manual for the growing smart legislative guidebook: Model statutes for planning and the management of change 2002 edition.* Chicago: Author.

Beaumont, C. (Ed.). (1999). *Challenging sprawl: Organizational responses to a national problem.* Washington, DC: National Trust for Historic Preservation.

Benfield, K., Raimi, M. D., & Chen, D. D. T. (1999). *Once there were greenfields: How urban sprawl is undermining America's environment, economy, and social fabric.* Washington, DC: Natural Resources Defense Council and Surface Transportation Policy Project.

Burchell, R. W., Listokin, D., & Galley, C. C. (2000). Smart growth: More than a ghost of urban policy past, less than a bold new horizon. *Housing Policy Debate, 11,* 821-879.

Burchell, R., Lowenstein, C , Dolphin, W. R., Galley, C. C., Downs, A., Seskin, S., Still, K. G., & Moore, T. (2002). *Costs of sprawl 2000* (Transit Cooperative Research Program Report 74). Washington, DC: National Academy Press.

Craig, T. (2004, July 22). Maryland panel backs study of Route 32 widening; vote to by-pass "smart growth" angers activists. *Washington Post,* p. B04.

Downs, A. (1973). *Opening up the suburbs: An urban strategy for America.* New Haven, CT: Yale University Press.

Downs, A. (1994). *New visions for metropolitan America.* Washington, DC: Brookings Institution Press and the Lincoln Institute for Land Policy.

Downs, A. (2000). *Dealing effectively with fast growth* (Brookings Institution Policy Brief No. 67). Washington, DC: Brookings Institution.

Downs, A. (2001a). An approach to analyzing the impacts of "smart growth" upon economic development. *Economic Development Review, 17*(4)9–17.

Downs, A. (2001b). What does "smart growth" really mean? *Planning,* 20–25.

Downs, A. (2003a, May 29). *Growth management, smart growth, and affordable housing* (Keynote speech made at the Symposium on the Relationship Between Affordable Housing and Growth Management, Washington, DC). Available on-line at www.AnthonyDowns.com

Downs, A. (2003b, April 30). *The impacts of smart growth upon the economy* (Speech presented at a Land Use Institute of the New Jersey Institute for Continuing Legal Education, New Brunswick, NJ). Available on-line at www.AnthonyDowns.com

Downs, A. (Ed.). (2004a). *Growth management and affordable housing: Do they conflict?* Washington, DC: Brookings Institution Press.

Downs, A. (2004b). *Still stuck in traffic: Coping with peak-hour traffic congestion.* Washington, DC: Brookings Institution Press.

Downs, A., Burchell, R., Galley, C., & Listokin, D. (2002). The activities and benefits of smart growth. *Wharton Real Estate Review, VI*(1), 86–93.

Fischel, W. (2001). *The homevoter hypothesis: How home values influence local government taxation, school finance, and land-use policies.* Cambridge, MA: Harvard University Press.

Fischel, W. (2004). Comment on Nelson et al. In A. Downs (Ed.), *Growth management and affordable housing: Do they conflict?* (pp. 158–167). Washington, DC: Brookings Institution Press.

Goldberg, D. (2003, Summer). Smart growth techniques pave the way for affordable housing. *On Common Ground,* 18–23.

Governor's Sustainable Washington Advisory Panel. (2003). *A new path forward: Action plan for a sustainable Washington: Achieving longterm economic, social, and environmental vitality.* Olympia: Washington State Government. Available on-line at http://www.ofm.wa.gov/sustainability/panel.htm

Lewis R. K. (2004, August 21). Sprawl is here to stay as long as suburbs represent the American dream. *Washington Post,* p. F05.

Lindblom, C. E., & Braybrooke, D. (1963). *A Strategy of decision: Policy evaluation as a social process.* Glencoe, IL: Free Press.

Meek, S. (Ed.). (2002). *Growing smart legislative guidebook: Model statutes for planning and the management of change.* Chicago: American Planning Association.

Michigan State University. (2004). *Overcoming impediments to smart growth: Finding ways for land development professionals to help achieve sustainability.* East Lansing: Michigan Travel, Tourism, and Recreation Resource Center at Michigan State University and Planning & Zoning Center, Inc.

National Association of Home Builders. (1999). *Smart growth policy statement: Building better places to live, work, and play.* Washington, DC: Author.

National Association of Home Builders. (2005). *Smart growth.* Retrieved March 24, 2005, from http://www.nahb.org/generic.aspx?genericContentID=3519

National Association of Industrial and Office Parks. (1999). *Growing to greatness: Creating America's quality workplaces.* Herndon, VA: Author.

National Association of Realtors. (2005, January). *Existing home sales.* Available on-line at http://www.realtor.org/Research.nsf/Pages/EHSdata

Nelson, A., Pendall, R., Dawkins, C., & Knaap, G. (2004). The link between growth management and housing affordability: The academic evidence. In A. Downs (Ed.), *Growth management and affordable housing: Do they conflict?* (pp. 117–158). Washington, DC: Brookings Institution Press.

Nelson, A., & Wachter, S. (2003). Growth management and affordable housing policy. *Journal of Affordable Homing and Community Development Law, 12*(1), 173–187.

Orfield, M. (1997). *Metropolitics: A regional agenda for community and sustainability.* Washington, DC: Brookings Institution Press.

Pendall, R. (2000). Local land use regulation and the chain of exclusion. *Journal of the American Planning Association, 66,* 125–142.

Porter, D. (1997). *Managing growth in America's communities.* Washington, DC: Island Press.

Schill, M. (2004). Comment on Voith and Crawford. In A. Downs (Ed.), *Growth management and affordable housing: Do they conflict?* (pp. 102–105). Washington, DC: Brookings Institution Press.

Smart Growth Network, (n. d.). *Smart growth principles.* Available online at http://www.smartgrowth.org/library/prinlist.asp

Urban Land Institute. (1998). *Smart growth: Economy, community, environment.* Washington, DC: Author.

Urban Land Institute. (1999). *Smart growth: Myth and fact.* Washington, DC: Author.

U.S. Census Bureau. (2004). *Current population survey/housing vacancy survey, annual statistics 2004.* Available on-line at http://www.census.gov/hhes/www/housing/hvs/annualo4/ann0412.html

Voith, R., & Crawford, D. (2004). Smart growth and affordable housing. In A. Downs (Ed.), *Growth management and affordable housing: Do they conflict?* (pp. 82–101). Washington, DC: Brookings Institution Press.

Whoriskey, P. (2004a, August 8). Space for employers, not for homes; Residents driven farther out as D.C. suburbs lure business and limit housing. *Washington Post,* p. A01.

Whoriskey, P. (2004b, August 10). Planners' brains vs. public's brawn: Neighbors' hostility to dense projects impairs Md. land preservation. *Washington Post,* p. A01.

Whoriskey, P. (2004c, August 9). Washington's road to outward growth; Far-off houses are cheap, but drive carries costs: Time, traffic and pollution. *Washington Post,* p. A01.

ANTHONY DOWNS is a senior fellow at the Brookings Institution in Washington, DC, where he has been since 1977. Author or editor of 24 books, his latest are *Still Stuck in Traffic* and *Growth Management and Affordable Housing: Do They Conflict?* (both from Brookings Institution Press, 2004).

More and Better Local Planning

State-Mandated Local Planning in Coastal North Carolina

Academics, public officials, and citizens increasingly advocate more and better local planning as a central component of regional growth management. They assume that local plans will provide meaningful policy guidance to local officials when making land use-related policy decisions, and that local officials will implement their plans. This article presents findings from an evaluation of state-mandated local planning in coastal North Carolina during the mid 1990s. All 20 coastal counties and 72 municipalities were preparing plans consistent with the state's procedural requirements during this time, and many were using those plans to at least some extent when making land use-related policy decisions. Taken altogether, however, the plans were weak analytically and substantively, providing limited guidance for growth management, especially in terms of coastal area resource protection. The promise of state-mandated local planning for managing growth at the regional level is discussed in light of North Carolina's experiences.

RICHARD K. NORTON

O ver the last decade or so, a reinvigorated call has gone out for more and better local planning. It has been made by academics (e.g., Burby & Dalton, 1994); professional planners (American Planning Association, 2002); land use lawyers (e.g., Freilich, 1999); broad-based political action groups (Smart Growth Network, 2002); a host of national, state, and local action groups; and citizen activists. More and better local planning is even promoted by such ideologically opposed groups as the National Association of Home Builders (2000) and the Sierra Club (2000). For the most part, this movement is not so much about improving local planning for its own sake as it is about using improved local planning to improve regional growth management. Widely popularized as "smart growth," this response to the unhappy consequences of "sprawl" stems in part from concerns about the inefficient use of public infrastructure, increasing traffic congestion, decreasing affordable housing, and declining central cities. But it is especially animated by quality-of-life and environmental concerns stemming from the ongoing loss and fragmentation of arable farmland, natural open space, viable wildlife habitat, and functioning wetlands; the continuing decline of water quality from nonpoint sources of pollution; and the decreasing resilience of communities to natural hazards such as catastrophic forest fires and coastal storms (see, e.g., APA, 2000; Burby, 1998).

Calling for more and better local planning to address these kinds of concerns makes sense; they are all a function of land use, and local government has traditionally had the prerogative in managing local land development (see, e.g., Peck, 1998; Porter, 1997; U.S. Environmental Protection Agency, 1989). But advocates seem to be making some assumptions that ought to be clarified. First, they assume that more and better local planning

will yield plans that provide meaningful policy guidance for local officials as they make local development management decisions. Second, they assume that those policies will effectively address regional growth management concerns—especially quality of life and environmental concerns—as well as local concerns. Finally, they assume that local officials will actually use those plans for their decision making rather than leaving them on the proverbial shelf. Are these assumptions warranted?

This article reviews briefly the evolution of state/local growth management programs and recent scholarship addressing the successes and failures of local planning when required through those programs. Building on that scholarship, it then presents findings from a study of state-mandated local planning in coastal North Carolina, focusing in particular on the quality, policy focus, and use of local plans throughout the coastal region during the mid 1990s. It concludes by contemplating the promise of state-mandated local planning for regional growth management in light of coastal North Carolina's experiences.

More and Better Planning— For What and How Well?

The call for improved local planning as a way to improve growth management has in fact been made for some time. Since the dawn of a widespread environmental consciousness about four decades ago (see, e.g., Carson, 1962; McHarg, 1969), states and localities have been engaged in a complex, often contentious growth management debate, trying to find just the right balance between protecting the environment and promoting the economy (Bollens, 1992, 1993; Bosselman & Callies, 1971;

Porter, 1997). While early approaches were animated largely by environmental protection concerns, growth management advocates now articulate an array of co-equal principles addressing the economy, infrastructure efficiency, and quality of life, along with environmental protection (see APA, 2002).

Similarly, intergovernmental growth programs—particularly those incorporating state-mandated local planning—have evolved over time as states and localities have struggled to find just the right process to balance competing policy goals effectively and equitably. Early top-down, coercive approaches are now becoming more collaborative. Referred to variously as conjoint, co-production, or state/local partnership approaches to growth management, the collaborative model generally entails the state prescribing broad local planning procedures (whether madated or strongly encouraged) and establishing larger growth management goals, but leaving local governments great flexibility in deciding how much planning to undertake and which specific policies to adopt (see Berke, 1998; Bollens, 1992; Burby & May, 1997; Gale, 1992; Weitz, 1999).

Thus, advocates for improved growth management now largely embrace a policy-balancing, collaborative state/local approach that relies heavily on the use of more and better local planning to advance regional growth management goals. Yet something here does not quite square. During the very same decades when popular and political pressures pushed against the idea of managing growth primarily for environmental reasons, urbanization accelerated at a remarkable pace, yielding the host of increasingly troublesome environmental problems noted above. Moreover, even while these same pressures have pushed states to adopt more collaborative growth management programs, there remains broad agreement that a key reason behind continued unmanaged growth has been the continued parochial attitudes and actions of local governments (Burby & May, 1998). So juxtaposing the growing call for yet more and better planning against these seemingly remorseless trends and unyielding attitudes begs the question: Will more and better local planning really work?

Some states have been mandating local planning for regional growth management, and some researchers have been tackling questions about local planning outcomes since at least the 1970s (e.g., Alterman & Hill, 1978; Johnston et al., 1978), although their collective efforts over time have yielded relatively limited empirical results (Dalton & Burby, 1994). Despite the preeminence of Oregon's growth management program, for example, little is known "about the program's impact, effectiveness, and implementation experiences" (Howe, 1994, p. 275). Moreover, much of the work that has been done in Oregon and other growth management states has been based largely on single case studies that have collectively lacked a conceptual coherence (Baer, 1997; Bollens, 1993; Talen, 1996). Finally, most recent studies of growth management programs have generally assessed different growth management approaches (e.g., Gale, 1992), the administrative systems they employ (e.g., Weitz, 1999), or the land development patterns they appear to yield (e.g., Carruthers, 2002), not the quality and implementation of the local plans they engender.

Even so, considerable attention has been focused recently on the evaluation of local plan making and implementation outcomes within the context of managing growth to mitigate natural hazards, improve environmental governance, and promote sustainability (see, e.g., Burby & May, 1997, 1998; Deyle & Smith, 1998; Godschalk et al., 1999; May et al., 1996). But the findings from this work regarding the successes and failures of local planning have been decidedly mixed. A research team led by Raymond Burby and Peter May recently conducted a multi-state assessment of local planning for natural hazards mitigation, comparing states that mandated comprehensive local planning prior to 1990—California, Florida, and coastal North Carolina—against states that did not—Texas, Washington, and the mountain region of North Carolina (see Burby & May, 1997, which summarizes this work in a single source). They concluded that state mandates for local comprehensive planning make a difference, improving the quality of both local plans and local development management programs (Burby & Dalton, 1994; Burby & May, 1997; Dalton & Burby, 1994). This finding in particular suggests that the widespread call for more and better local planning—and in particular state-mandated local planning—is not misplaced.

These same researchers also found that the state planning mandate that yielded the highest quality local plans was North Carolina's coastal area planning mandate, producing plans that were better on average than those produced under both Florida's more coercive and California's less coercive mandates (Burby & May, 1997, pp. 105–106). North Carolina's mandate was crafted as a collaborative "state-local partnership," under which the state puts great emphasis on local planning and specifies general procedures and goals, but leaves considerable flexibility to the localities themselves in preparing the plans, adopting specific policies, and implementing them (Burby & May, 1997; North Carolina Division of Coastal Management [NCDCM], 1986; Owens, 1985). In addition, along with other federal coastal zone management programs, it was expressly designed to strike a balance between economic development and environmental protection rather than emphasizing primarily the environment (see Godschalk & Cousins, 1985; Lowry, 1985). As such, it represents an example of the "mature" growth management programs that seek to balance the competing substantive goals of environment and economy through the use of collaborative state/local planning processes (see Bollens, 1992, 1993). North Carolina's approach to coastal area growth management, along with Burby and May's finding that it yielded the highest quality local plans, thus suggests that calls for more and better local planning through the use of collaborative, policy-balancing state mandates do indeed show the most promise for achieving improved intergovernmental growth management.

But the story does not end there. While the Burby and May research team found that North Carolina's mandate yielded the highest quality plans relative to the other states studied, they also concluded that none of the states with comprehensive planning mandates did "a very good job of addressing natural hazards," including North Carolina's plans, which scored on average only a 1.35 out of a possible 5 points on a standardized index measure of plan quality (Burby & May, 1997, p. 105). Moreover, since the early 1990s, there has been substantial and growing evidence that North Carolina's coastal resources are continuing to decline despite more than two decades of local planning under the state's Coastal Area Management Act of 1974 (CAMA), not only in terms of coastal hazards mitigation but especially with regard to coastal habitat loss, wetland loss, estuarine shellfish bed closings, and coastal water quality degradation more generally (Mallin, Ensign, et al., 2001; Mallin & Wheeler, 2000; Mallin, Williams, et al., 2000; NC Coastal Futures Committee, 1994). This continued decline is attributable largely to cumulative impacts from ongoing low-density development occurring throughout the coastal region (see NCDCM, 1994).

The evidence taken altogether thus suggests that while collaborative, policy-balanced intergovernmental growth management programs can yield more and better local planning outcomes, especially relative to either highly coercive or minimally coercive programs, they are not yielding planning outcomes that are effectively addressing regional concerns, especially environmental protection concerns. It is not entirely clear, however, why this is so. Wanting to explore this and related questions in greater depth, I conducted a study of North Carolina's coastal area planning program.

State-Mandated Local Planning in Coastal North Carolina

North Carolina's coastal region, as defined by CAMA, encompasses the 20 coastal counties bordering the Atlantic Ocean and the Albemarle and Pamlico sounds. After 2 years of highly contentious debate, the state legislature enacted CAMA largely in response to impending threats to the region's resources from ongoing development (Heath, 1974; Heath & Owens, 1994). Designed expressly with the goal of striking a balance between the preservation of the coastal area's natural resource base and the orderly economic development of the coastal region (NCDCM, 1986), the program consists of four parts: a regulatory permitting program for statutorily defined "areas of environmental concern" (AECs); a state-mandated local planning program; a state-to-local grants-in-aid program; and a coastal area land acquisition program. The coastal region is the only region in the state where local planning is mandated. As of the mid 1990s, 72 municipalities and all 20 coastal counties were preparing CAMA land use plans.

The state addresses environmental protection issues under CAMA most directly through the regulatory permitting program for areas of environmental concern. AECs are formally designated on the ground in response to development permit requests and consist for the most part of the coastal water bodies themselves, coastal shorelines, relatively narrow shoreline buffers, and coastal wetlands (see NC Department of Environment, Health, & Natural Resources [NCDEHNR] State Guidelines for Areas of Environmental Concern, 2001). They comprise in total less than roughly 5–7% of the entire coastal region (Owens, 1985).[1] Local land use planning under CAMA, in contrast, is mandated for the entire coastal region. The state's Coastal Resources Commission (CRC), which administers the act, pre-

scribes the local planning process to be followed under administrative rules or "planning guidelines" (NCDEHNR Land Use Planning Guidelines, 2001). It is important to note that local planning is mandated in order to advance the state's full complement of growth management goals—including especially the goal of balancing economy and environment and to do so throughout the entire coastal region, including areas beyond the AECs (Heath, 1974, p. 371; Longest & Smith, 2000; NCDCM, 1986). However, because of a political compromise made during CAMA's enactment (Heath, 1974, p. 376), the Act specifically prohibits the CRC from compelling localities to actually implement their plans outside of designated areas of environmental concern (see Section 113A-111 of CAMA).

A state blue-ribbon commission released a report in 1994 that catalogued the continued decline of North Carolina's coastal resources and identified the need for more and better local CAMA planning as one of the key mechanisms to arrest that decline (NC Coastal Futures Committee, 1994). Building from that report, coastal environmental activists began pressing the state to demand more rigorous local plans and to compel local plan implementation. The program erupted in controversy in mid 1998 when the CRC temporarily refused to certify a local plan based on environmentalists' complaints. The CRC subsequently placed a moratorium on the local planning process and convened a stakeholder advisory group, called the Land Use Planning Review Team, to revisit its administrative rules (see NCDCM, 2000).[2] This turn of events, along with the prominence given to local planning in coastal North Carolina by the work of Burby and May and their colleagues, presented an ideal opportunity for study.

Methods
Research Questions and Design

Recent conceptual and empirical work on state-mandated local planning for intergovernmental growth management consistently points to several important and closely-related factors in explaining planning outcomes: the use and structure of planning mandates, the administration of those mandates by state officials, local fiscal and administrative capacity to plan, and local commitment (i.e., both to planning and to regional growth management goals; see Berke & French, 1994; Berke et al., 1996; Burby et al., 1993; Burby & May, 1997, 1998; Dalton & Burby, 1994; Deyle & Smith, 1998). Especially important, local commitment represents both an outcome of state growth management efforts and a key determinant of local planning outcomes, where higher levels of local commitment presumably yield more and better local plan making and plan implementation.[3]

Building on the conceptual and methodological work of Burby, May, and their colleagues, I addressed several research questions, including whether local CAMA plans provided meaningful policy guidance for development management, how those plans were actually balancing environment and economy—the express goal of CAMA (i.e., rather than focusing specifically on hazard mitigation)—and why local CAMA planning efforts were apparently not working to arrest the decline of the state's coastal

Table 1. Six measures of local CAMA planning outcomes (see Appendix).

Outcome	Measurement construct	Data source
Process-related planning outcomes		
Local elected officials' commitment to planning	Commitment by local elected officials to planning as a function of government for land use-related public policy decision making.	Survey of local administrators; asked to characterize local elected officials collectively during mid 1990s ($n = 36$).
Overall plan quality	Quality of a plan in terms of its articulation of values, goals, factual analyses, and policies; land suitability analysis; relationship between analysis and policies; and implementation, monitoring, and evaluation provisions.	Content evaluation of local CAMA plans of record during 1993-1998 ($n = 40$).
Plan use	Extent to which the plan played a role in guiding local elected officials' land use-related public policy decision making (e.g., ordinance adoption, site-specific ordinance revision, capital improvement program decisions).	Surveys of local administrators and local attorneys; asked to characterize local elected officials' collective use of the CAMA plan during mid 1990s ($n = 36$).
Substantive planning outcomes		
Local elected officials' policy trade-off preference	Clear evidence of a policy preference by local elected officials for economic development over environmental protection or vice versa.	Combined responses from surveys of local administrators, local attorneys, and state planners; asked to characterize local elected officials' policy preferences ($n = 36$).
Plan policy emphasis	Clear evidence of an emphasis in plan policies favoring economic development over environmental protection or vice versa.	Content evaluation of local CAMA plans of record during 1993-1998 ($n = 40$).
Plan use emphasis	Clear evidence that local elected officials tended to emphasize a plan's economic development policies over its environmental protection policies or vice versa when using the plan.	Survey of local administrators; asked to characterize local elected officials' collective use of the plan, adjusted for plan policy emphasis ($n = 36$).

resources. Also, given its pivotal importance, I focused especially on the question of local elected officials' commitment to CAMA planning. Finally, approaching planning as a mechanism to inform local decision making, I defined plan implementation as the role played by the plan (or use of the plan) when local elected officials engaged in land use-related policymaking (i.e., zoning and subdivision ordinance adoption or revision, site-specific decisions such as rezonings, and capital improvement program decisions), rather than as a factor influencing development management programs or land development patterns.

Thus, I focused on three process-related local planning outcomes, including local elected officials' commitment to planning, overall plan quality, and plan implementation (conceptualized as plan use). In order to better characterize how localities were striking the balance between economy and environment, I also focused on three substantive planning outcomes, including local elected officials' policy trade-off preferences, local plan policy emphasis, and plan use emphasis, all as between environment and economy. Table I summarizes the measurement constructs and data sources employed for these six variables, which are discussed in more detail below. Finally, CAMA requires localities to update their plans every 5 years, and a relatively recent review of the program suggested that local planning efforts had become well established, if not routine, by the mid 1990s (see Heath & Owens, 1994). Wanting

to evaluate the status of local planning in this settled state, but prior to the eruption of controversy over the program, I focused on the 5-year period between 1993 and 1998.[4]

Data Collection and Analysis

I employed two complementary data collection and analysis approaches for this study, both of which extended from late in 1998 through early 2001. First, I assessed systematically a cross-sectional sample of 36 coastal counties and municipalities, including 11 counties, 15 estuarine and inland communities, and 10 oceanfront or "beach" communities (referred to collectively as localities). Data were collected from several sources, including in-depth telephone surveys of local administrators and planning directors;[5] systematic content analyses of the local CAMA land use plans of record during the study period for 40 localities;[6] short mail surveys of the state's district planners and attorneys representing coastal localities; and demographic data for each locality collected from a variety of sources.

The measurement constructs and data sources used to operationalize the six key outcome variables summarized in Table I are detailed in the Appendix. Consistent with the Burby and May research team's approach, the local commitment and local plan implementation (plan use) variables evaluated for this study were drawn primarily from telephone and mail surveys (see Dalton & Burby, 1994). In order to obtain information on these variables efficiently, a single local administrator from each locality was asked to characterize his or her local elected officials collectively (i.e., the city council or county commission) using an 84-item telephone survey. In addition, I conducted shorter mail surveys of local attorneys and state planners in order to triangulate data sources for increased validity (see the Appendix). All of the telephone and mail survey instruments were designed, pretested, and administered following protocols prescribed by Dillman (1978) and Fowler (1995).

The local plan quality and policy emphasis variables were evaluated through plan content evaluations. In designing the evaluation protocol, I started with the conceptual framework employed by the Burby and May research team (see, e.g., Dalton & Burby, 1994). Drawing from this work and related studies, a plan can be characterized as a high-quality plan if it does the following:

- demonstrates a strong factual basis;
- provides clearly articulated goals;
- employs a land suitability analysis (LSA) that clearly identifies natural and built environment opportunities and constraints for development;
- establishes policies that are consistent with the LSA and that are directive rather than exhortative, are spatially specific, and that appear to be reasonably efficacious;
- satisfies several kinds of consistency (horizontal, vertical, internal, and implementation [see Weitz, 1999, pp. 198–205]);
- facilitates meaningful ongoing public participation; and
- designates implementation responsibilities and incorporates ongoing monitoring and implementation evaluation procedures (see, e.g., Berke et al., 1996; Burby & May, 1997; Kaiser et al., 1995).

I synthesized these general criteria with the specific requirements of North Carolina's CAMA planning mandate as of the mid 1990s, yielding a 400-plus-item evaluation protocol. Again, consistent with the Burby and May work (see, e.g., Dalton & Burby, 1994), plans were scored for the presence and strength of specified items, and indices were constructed to yield overall measures of plan quality and policy emphasis (see the Appendix).

The second data collection and analysis approach I employed entailed attending 20 of the 24 meetings conducted by a Land Use Planning Review Team, attending most of the Coastal Resource Commission's bi-monthly two-day meetings held throughout the region over the 18-month period spanning 1999 into 2001, and engaging in ongoing interviews and conversations with state officials, local officials, local government association representatives, chamber of commerce representatives, and local activists during that same period. I also reviewed a variety of reports, newsletters, memoranda, and other documentary data from a variety of sources. My involvement with the Land Use Planning Review Team in particular shifted over time from being merely an observer to a participant observer, as I provided comments and some limited analysis in response to conversations and specific requests for assistance. I used the ob-

servations I gained from these interactions to test and explicate the more quantitative measures of planning outcomes I was collecting concurrently.

Findings

The findings presented here include a detailed assessment of the six planning outcomes noted in Table I, which are then used to address the larger research questions noted above. Before discussing these results, a preliminary finding should be noted. At least some critics of the local CAMA planning program assert that one of the reasons for the program's problems stems from it being "consultant driven." Consultants do play a very large role in local CAMA planning efforts across the region. Thirty of the 40 plans evaluated for this study were prepared entirely or in part by private consultants, and the same firm prepared fully half of those. Several Councils of Government, effectively serving as consultants, prepared an additional five. Consultants are used so heavily because many of the localities in the region do not have large planning staffs, if any at all, and budgets for planning efforts appeared to be limited despite the availability of State-to-local grants (which averaged only $15,000 per community during the mid 1990s based on records provided by the State). Several of the larger localities with their own planning staffs also employed consultants for their technical specialties.

One of the clear results of this reliance on consultants was that many of the plans, when compared across localities, were formulaic in presentation. Even so, variation in use of consultants was so limited that it was difficult to discern a clear relationship between that use and variation in the quality of local planning efforts and outcomes. More significantly, a locality's decision to use a consultant was apparently less important than its decision of which consultant to use and why. Several local administrators commented during interviews that their local officials, in the words of one, "knew what they wanted out of the plan and they knew which consultant would give it to them, so that's who they used." The relationship between the use of consultants and planning outcomes across the region thus appears to have been a function of local capacity and commitment as much or more than a key causal relationship by itself. While deserving of more in-depth analysis, the issue was not addressed further for this study.

Planning Process: Local CAMA Planning Outcomes

Figure 2 presents frequency distributions for the three process-related local planning outcomes, including local elected officials' commitment to planning, overall plan quality, and plan use.

Local elected officials' commitment to planning. Local administrators generally indicated that their local elected officials were committed to land use planning and plan implementation. This finding is consistent with the perception of many State and local officials throughout the region but runs counter to the perceptions of many local environmental activists, who tended to see local commitment to CAMA planning as low or, at best, a calculated kind of commitment. Administrators' comments made

a. **Local elected officals'
commitment to planning**

Mean: 7.20

SD: 1.83

Possible range: 0–10

Actual range: 2–10

n = 36

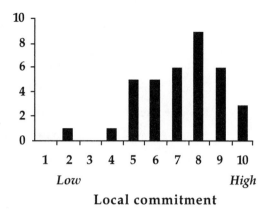

Local commitment

b. **Relative overall plan quality**

Mean: 25.35

SD: 4.8

Possible range: 8–37

Actual range: 18–36

n = 40

c. **Plan use**

Mean: 5.95

SD: 2.64

Possible range: 0–10

Actual range: 1–10

n = 36

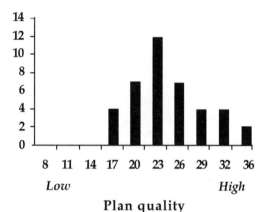

Plan use

Figure 2. Frequency distributions of process-related local CAMA planning outcomes during the mid 1990s.

during the telephone survey suggest that local commitment was in fact genuine; elected officials saw land use planning as a useful policymaking tool—although this conclusion is qualified based on the additional findings discussed below. In an historical context, this finding is especially significant in that local governments were the most vehement opponents of CAMA, and especially its local planning requirements, when the statute was enacted some 25 years ago (Heath, 1974).

Overall plan quality. Figures 2 (Graph b) and 3 illustrate the results from the plan content analysis, showing the distribution of scores for overall plan quality and the mean scores for eight of the criteria used to assess plan quality, respectively. These plan quality scores, although calculated using a criteria-based evaluation protocol, are appropriately viewed as relative

scores because quality was assessed primarily in a comparative fashion across this sample of plans.

The CAMA plans evaluated generally addressed the entire array of issues required of them by the State's planning mandate. In addition, taken altogether, the plans were generally good when considered as compiled sources of information about the localities, their histories, and development patterns. They were also generally good when considered as vision statements serving to characterize and focus on issues of greatest concern to the localities. Finally, a few of the CAMA plans evaluated were relatively strong overall in assessing locality-specific resource constraints, including both natural resource constraints and communities facilities constraints, and then linking those constraints in a transparent way to plan policies and future land use classifications. At the same time, however, important attributes of the plans taken

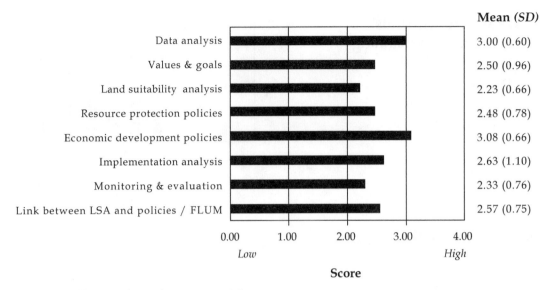

Mean (SD)

Data analysis — 3.00 (0.60)
Values & goals — 2.50 (0.96)
Land suitability analysis — 2.23 (0.66)
Resource protection policies — 2.48 (0.78)
Economic development policies — 3.08 (0.66)
Implementation analysis — 2.63 (1.10)
Monitoring & evaluation — 2.33 (0.76)
Link between LSA and policies / FLUM — 2.57 (0.75)

0.00   1.00   2.00   3.00   4.00
Low   *High*

Score

Maximum possible score for each criterion is 4.0
"LSA" = land suitability analysis
"FLUM" = future land use map

Figure 3. Mean relative overall plan quality scores for local CAMA land use plans by eight evaluation criteria ($n = 40$).

altogether were weak, including the clarity of their values and goals statements, land suitability analyses, resource protection policy statements, implementation analyses and provisions, and monitoring and evaluation provisions. Especially important, the link between land suitability analyses, on the one hand, and plan policies, future land use maps, and classifications on the other, was generally weak.

A number of the plans evaluated, particularly those for municipalities, stepped through the various required analyses for soils limitations, high hazards areas, floodplains, and fragile areas at the front of the plan and then classified much of the entire jurisdiction for future urban development at the end without reference to the earlier analyses. Many of the plans, including especially county plans, appeared to identify urban transition areas by simply expanding outward uniformly from existing developed areas. Altogether, the plans made classifications for future urban growth with little or no reference to their land suitability analyses. Moreover, they did so without discussion as to whether the classifications might cause environmental impacts and, if so, why they were warranted by other considerations nonetheless. They also made little or no attempt to address potential adverse environmental impacts from those classifications in their policy statements beyond citing compliance with the state's AEC permitting rules. Finally, beyond classifying currently developed land for continued urban development, the plans uniformly failed to employ their land suitability analyses to explain why the areas designated for future urban development were especially suitable for that designation.

In addition, reflecting market demand for oceanfront property and established development patterns, many of the beach community plans classified land for higher intensity development in nearly direct correspondence to increasing hazard zone designations (i.e., the highest hazard areas corresponded to the

areas classified for the highest density development and so on). Moreover, despite a Statewide policy of retreat in response to ongoing oceanfront shoreline erosion, only a few of the beach communities expressly adopted such a policy through their plans, and even those communities failed to present specific strategies for advancing such a policy.

Plan use. Local administrators reported that plan use— characterized as the extent to which the plan played a role in guiding local elected officials' land use decision making collectively— was moderately high or high for 19 of the 36 study localities (53%—see Figure 2 Graph c). Administrators also reported that local elected officials' efforts to address and implement specific plan policies were moderately high or high for 20 out of the 36 localities (55%). A number of administrators also volunteered that they, their staffs, and elected officials used the CAMA plan frequently as a convenient and comprehensive source of information about the locality. Conversely, 17 of the 36 study localities (47%) used their plans to a moderately low or low extent. Six additional localities were dropped from the study altogether when it was determined that they had in fact not used their plans at all during the study period because they had had no occasion to do so. Altogether, about half of the coastal localities were using their CAMA land use plans very little if at all during the mid 1990s, while about half used them to a moderate to high extent.

Administrators' comments suggested that, for at least some of the localities reporting high levels of plan use, that use referred to only one or two actions taken by local elected officials during the study period, where they took an action specifically to implement one of the plan's policies. Unfortunately, the operational construct used for measuring plan implementation for this study entailed characterizing the role played by the plan in local land use-related decision making but did not explicitly account for *frequency* of use. At least in some cases, it appears that

a. Local elected officials' policy trade-off preference

Clear preference for:

Economic development (ED):   13
Neither: 17
Environmental protection (EP): 6
n = 36

b. Plan policy emphasis

Clear preference for:

Economic development (ED):   13
Neither: 23
Environmental protection (EP): 4
n = 40

c. Plan use emphasis

Economic development (ED):   14
Neither: 13
Environmental protection (EP): 9
n = 36

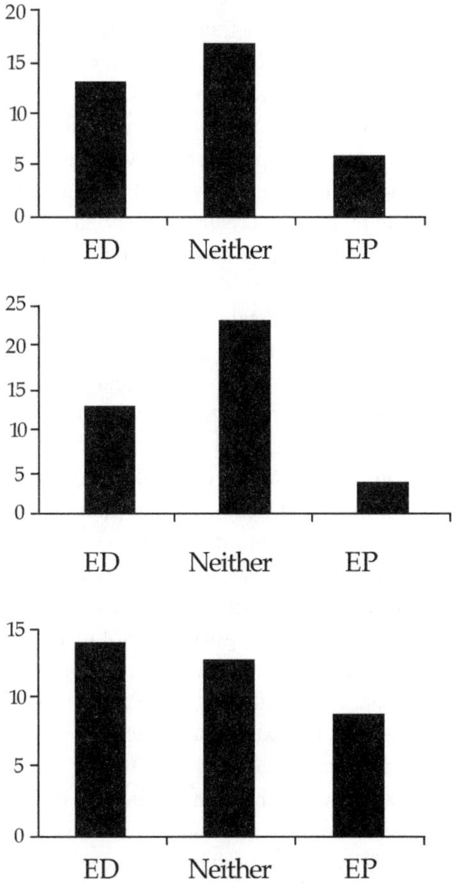

Figure 4.   Frequency distributions of substantive local CAMA planning outcomes during the mid 1990s.

the plans were not used all that often, but when they were, they played an important role. At the other extreme, for at least some localities the low levels of reported plan use may have been largely a function of not having to make many land use-related policy decisions, rather than local officials having kept the plan on the shelf despite its potential usefulness.[7]

Planning Substance: Local CAMA Policy Outcomes

Figure 4 presents frequency distributions for the three principal substantive planning policy outcomes: local elected officials' policy trade-off preferences; plan policy emphasis; and plan use emphasis. All three of these measures were constructed to yield one of three categories of outcomes for a given locality: a *clear* emphasis on economic development relative to environmental protection; a *clear* emphasis on environmental protection relative to economic development; or neither.

It could be argued that this conceptualization of policy emphasis is inherently biased, suggesting that a trade-off must be made between environment and economy when in fact none may be required. It is true that many planning scholars and others, particularly those exploring the concept of sustainable development, are working to develop policy and design techniques that do not force such a trade-off. Nonetheless, the perception that such trade-offs are often required is common,

and the fact that public officials often evidence discernable concern for one over the other is unremarkable. Moreover, coastal regions in particular represent one type of setting where such tradeoffs may in fact be required with some frequency, to the extent that development pressures are often greatest in the most ecologically fragile places.

In addition, like many other places, a common perception in coastal North Carolina is that, in the words of several state officials, "it's all about economic development" and "environmental protection is a luxury of a good economy." The apparent relationship between local administrators' assessments of the local economy and of local elected officials' policy preferences, based on a simple pairwise correlation, was in fact statistically significant, where a perceived stronger economy was moderately correlated with a preference for environmental protection over economic development (correlation coefficient = 0.4220, p-value = 0.0104). Interestingly, the correlation between the perceived strength of the economy and a plan emphasis favoring environmental protection was somewhat stronger (correlation coefficient = 0.5057, p-value = 0.0017). Thus, while there appears to be some merit to the assertion that an emphasis on environment comes with a strong economy, that relationship was not determinative.

Recognizing these limitations and qualifications, the conceptualization of policy emphasis between environment and economy described above was retained in light of the structure of the CAMA program mandate, using conceptual measures constructed so as to avoid measurement bias or an overstating of emphasis as described below and in the Appendix.

Local elected officials's policy trade-off preference. Local elected officials' policy trade-off preferences were determined by combining characterizations made by local administrators, local attorneys, and state planners. Survey respondents were asked to consider conversations they had had with elected officials, statements they had heard, or other such indications of a general policy preference by, the local officials. Using this measure, local officials for just under half of the coastal localities studied (17 out of 36 or 47%) demonstrated no clear policy preference between economic development and environmental protection, while officials for more than twice as many of the remaining localities showed a clear preference for economic development over environmental protection rather than vice versa (13 and 6 localities, respectively). In making this determination, respondents were asked specifically whether local officials tended to favor one policy over the other if a trade-off had to be made; the "no clear preference" category was not offered as a choice in order to discourage the easy characterization of "neither." While most respondents hesitated little if at all in characterizing local officials, the response was coded as "no clear preference" when the respondent could not do so.

Plan policy emphasis. All of the plans addressed both economic development issues and environmental protection issues as required by the State's planning guidelines. Like the distribution for local officials' policy preferences, most of the plans did not show a clear policy emphasis either way (see Figure 4 Graph b). Also like the distribution of local officials' policy preferences, of those plans for which a clear policy emphasis could be discerned, more plans showed a clear emphasis on economic and community development over environmental protection than vice versa (11 plans compared to 4, respectively).

Beyond this index measure of policy emphasis, local CAMA plans' resource protection policies collectively read more like goal statements—exhortative statements in support of the state's AEC program that were neither spatially specific nor directive, providing no clear policy guidance to local decision makers facing land use-related decisions. Moreover, while many plans called for efforts to address environmental issues in a generic way—articulating support for the use of agricultural best management practices, for example—none provided guidance on how and when those kinds of exhortative policies might be implemented. In contrast, economic development policies were generally more specific and more prescriptive. Counties (and to a lesser extent inland communities) tended to emphasize the need to expand and diversify their economic base, while the beach communities (and to a lesser extent inland communities) tended to emphasize community development issues such as the desire to maintain the community's family-oriented beach resort character and to avoid problems associated with neighboring land uses incompatible with one another (mostly beach cottages and concession shops).

One pressing environmental issue addressed by most of the plans—septic system failures and the corresponding need for centralized wastewater treatment—was typically addressed from a growth-accommodating perspective, or as a limitation on development that needed to be removed. While the plans often provided some discussion of the direct environmental benefits from expanded wastewater service, they almost uniformly failed to discuss the potential growth-inducing effects and resulting environmental impacts that come with such infrastructure expansions. Similarly, to the extent that the plans addressed stormwater control issues, they tended to focus on the need to improve stormwater drainage in order to address flooding problems and not on the water quality-related aspects of stormwater management.

Finally, in terms of environmental protection policies specifically, the plans taken as a whole relied almost entirely on the State. A number of the plans exceeded State AEC permitting standards on one or two issues, usually regarding the location and expansion of marinas. Nonetheless, almost uniformly, the plans made an exhortative statement about the need to ensure adequate environmental protection and then adopted policies that in essence pledged support for and the intent to comply with the State's minimum AEC permitting program (sometimes then stating a strong opposition to any further expansion of the AECs). Aside from one notable exception, a multi-county ecotourism-based initiative in the northern coastal region known as the "Partnership for the Sounds," none of the coastal localities' plans evaluated for this study actively promoted sustainable or low-environmental-impact economic development strategies such as ecotourism. Moreover, with a notable few exceptions, none of the CAMA plans contemplated any of a variety of well accepted site design requirements or other techniques for mitigating the environmental impacts from land development taking place outside of AECs (e.g., clustering requirements to reduce impervious surfaces and maintain open space).

Plan use emphasis. Administrators were asked to report whether their local elected officials tended to emphasize the CAMA plan's economic development or its environmental protection policies when using the plan. In contrast to local elected officials' policy trade-off preferences more generally, respondents were asked to make this characterization specifically with reference to elected officials' actual use of the plan. These responses were combined with plan policy emphasis in order to construct a single measure of plan use emphasis regarding these two policy goals.[8] Based on that measure, one relatively large group of localities showed no clear emphasis on either economy or environment when implementing plan policies, while an essentially equal number of localities clearly tended to emphasize economic development over environmental protection; a slightly smaller group of localities tended to emphasize environmental protection over economic development (i.e., 14, 13, and 9 localities, respectively).

Administrators indicated that local elected officials used their CAMA plans to address issues both directly and through staff analyses and recommendations. More importantly, their comments taken altogether suggested that the officials collectively used the plans primarily to address issues of local concern, and that those issues typically revolved around community development concerns, especially land use compatibility and public safety. This emphasis in use appeared to be primarily a function of local elected officials focusing on issues perceived to be in need of immediate attention. In explaining local use of the plan, for example, several administrators cited efforts to implement a specific plan policy identifying the need for additional public safety infrastructure, such as fire hydrants.

Based on these observations, as well as the analytical content, policy prescriptiveness, and policy focus of most of the CAMA plans taken collectively, coastal localities appear to have used their plans primarily to direct infrastructure decisions and land development so as to accommodate ongoing economic development while managing that development primarily to address public safety and land use compatibility concerns. That is, localities were using their plans by-and-large to promote the orderly economic development of their part of the coastal region. In doing so, most appear to have been willing to constrain individual development activities as necessary to address public safety needs, to ameliorate potential land use conflicts, and to undertake locally-initiated environmental restoration projects (e.g., waterway clean up projects, marshland restorations). Beyond acquiescing to the State's minimum environmental protection permitting requirements, however, they did not appear to be using their plans to manage individual development activities for the more controversial purpose of addressing regional environmental concerns, particularly concerns related to the cumulative and secondary impacts generated by land development activities.

Discussion

In an historical context, remarkable transitions have occurred in coastal North Carolina. The drafters of CAMA in 1974 recognized the challenge they faced and attempted to construct a program that would encourage not only local planning, but local planning that would advance regional growth management goals (Heath, 1974). They even titled their coastal program the Coastal *Area* Management Act rather than the Coastal *Zone* Management Act because the word zone was too close to the word *zoning*, which was a "dirty word" to be avoided (Heath, 1974, p. 350). To a substantial degree, they succeeded. Local officials in the region, at first among the CAMA local planning program's most vehement detractors, are now among its most ardent supporters. Indeed, localities prepare plans routinely and many use those plans at least to some extent when making land use-related policy decisions, even though the State cannot compel them to do so outside of designated areas of environmental concern.

Even so, most of those local officials, and some State officials, support CAMA planning primarily for the local benefits it has brought, as evidenced through the collective policy emphasis and use of the plans as detailed above. As of the mid 1990s, local planning efforts in coastal North Carolina have not achieved the promise of more and better local planning for improved regional growth management because they have largely failed to provide much meaningful policy guidance for local land use decision making and have focused mainly on addressing local economic and community development concerns while paying only minimal attention to regional environmental

protection concerns. Viewed another way, local planning efforts are procedurally strong, addressing the ranges of issues they are required to cover, but analytically and substantively weak, providing little meaningful growth management, especially with regard to regional coastal resource protection.

The coastal North Carolina experience highlights a troubling conundrum regarding the management of natural resources through the use of policy-balancing, collaborative processes—a conundrum that will likely confront more states as they attempt to craft policy-balancing, collaborative smart growth programs. That approach is founded on two fundamental premises: first, that we ought to strike a fair and reasonable balance between competing policy goals; and second, that our efforts will be more legitimate and efficacious if responsibilities are shared between state and locality. In practice this has meant ensuring an equitable distribution of opportunities to access resources in order to obtain wealth through continued economic growth. It also has meant respecting the development expectations of landowners and largely deferring to the political autonomy of local officials. Such an approach, furthermore, is defended against environmentalists' complaints as being environmentally benign given our technological capabilities. As one of the members of the Land Use Planning Review Team commented during a meeting, "There are no real environmental constraints because you can engineer your way out of anything; it's just a matter of how much you want to spend."

And yet adopting such an approach runs up against a harsh reality. The catch is that nature cares nothing for notions of fairness, the equitable distribution of resources, private property rights, local autonomy, or engineering prowess. No matter how well intentioned or compelling from the perspective of creating new jobs and providing diverse living choices, continuing land development that continues to fragment habitat and degrade water quality will have the remorseless effect of impairing viable ecological systems. Moreover, relying on engineering solutions to mitigate environmental impacts assumes that we in fact have the ability to successfully engineer ecological systems. The difficulties and failures we have had with constructing viable wetlands and engineering shoreline erosion controls give lie to that assumption (see, e.g., Dean, 1999).

Conclusions

Extending these observations yields two conclusions. First, if a fundamental reason for promoting more and better local planning is to ensure effective regional growth management, then a policy of balancing economy and environment in a "fair" way will not do enough. To yield truly sustainable outcomes—sustainable in the sense of sustaining the ecological systems upon which we depend for our survival—fair outcomes need be sought within the constraint of first ensuring the protection of those ecological systems. The unhappy consequences of pursuing growth for equitable reasons while ignoring the ecological consequences (or trying to engineer them away) are especially apparent in places like coastal North Carolina, which are both ecologically fragile and in such high demand for development, but they are not unique to those settings. Second, a collaborative or State/local partnership approach that compels local action procedurally but ultimately leaves substantive policy decisions at the local level will also not do enough. CAMA's planning mandate appears to have engendered commitment to local planning in coastal North Carolina, better local planning for the sake of addressing local land management concerns, and perhaps even better local planning for regional growth management than what would have been the case without CAMA. But North Carolinians are loving their coast to death, and while the State's coastal resource base continues to decline, State-mandated local CAMA plans are not doing enough to arrest that decline.

Based on this study alone, it is not possible to determine how generalizable coastal North Carolina's experiences are to other states. The findings presented here are largely consistent with conclusions drawn by Catlin (1997) regarding State-mandated local planning in Florida, however, a state conventionally seen as more demanding of localities than North Carolina. It could be that the growth management programs in states like Oregon and Washington, which also represent collaborative State/local programs but appear to demand more of localities in terms of substantive outcomes (see Abbott et al., 1994; Weitz, 1999), are yielding local planning efforts that address regional concerns more efficaciously, but detailed assessments of local efforts and outcomes parallel to the work presented here have apparently not been carried out. Coastal North Carolina's experiences and the problems they highlight are probably not unique, but more implementation analysis of local planning efforts and outcomes in other growth management states is needed to confirm that suspicion.

So if requiring local planning through a policy-balancing, collaborative approach to regional growth management is not achieving its full promise, at least in coastal North Carolina as of the mid 1990s, should we move on to other program designs? Perhaps not just yet. The work of Burby, May, and their colleagues strongly suggests that in general this approach yields better results than significantly more and less coercive designs. The challenge will be to refine State/local programs so that they yield more local planning that in fact does a better job of effectively addressing regional concerns, especially resource protection concerns. North Carolina recently amended its local planning mandate under CAMA to do just that based on recommendations made by its Land Use Planning Review Team. Proposed major revisions included a classification scheme to require more extensive planning from faster-growing localities and those encompassing substantial areas of environmental concern; more clear articulation of State growth management objectives and corresponding requirements that plans address those objectives; stronger land suitability analysis requirements; and stronger intergovernmental coordination requirements.[9] Time will tell whether these efforts to foster "more and better" local planning in coastal North Carolina engender the kinds of plan making and implementation outcomes that planning advocates envision.

Acknowledgments

Funding for this research was provided in part by the U.S. Environmental Protection Agency and by the Lincoln Institute of Land Policy.

Notes

1. This estimate reflects a recent expansion of the estuarine shoreline AEC (see Section 07H.200 of the NC DEHNR State Guidelines for Areas of Environmental Concern, 2001).

2. The North Carolina Division of Coastal Management provides a short history of the controversy and events leading to the land use planning moratorium and the formation of the Land Use Planning Review Team on-line at http://dcm2.enr.state.nc.us/Planning/history.htm.

3. In their conceptualizing about local commitment, plan quality, and plan implementation, Burby and May (1997) posited that higher quality plans, because of the information and analysis they provide, yield greater local commitment to state hazard mitigation mandates. They acknowledged that their empirical findings provide only weak support for this conceptualization at best, however, and that the relationship is likely reciprocal (1997, p. 142). While recognizing that high quality plans may in fact yield better knowledge of planning problems and higher commitment on the part of local officials, especially those coming to office with little direct knowledge of planning generally, I approached commitment as a key determinant of plan quality given the well established CAMA program and the flexibility built into its planning mandate.

4. Because plans are updated across the region every 5 years on a staggered basis, about two thirds of the plans evaluated had been adopted prior to the 5-year period of this study (some of which were in the process of being updated), while about one third had been updated and adopted during the study period. It could have been that turnover in elected officials led to one council adopting a plan and a second council—perhaps not inclined to follow the prior council's plan—having to implement it. Also, officials for localities with recently adopted plans would not have had much time to actually implement their policies. To address these issues, I asked early in the administrator survey whether the local council had changed substantially in membership during the study period and, if so, whether that change had led officials to address CAMA planning differently. Thirty of the 36 local councils had changed, by one or several members, but that change appeared to affect local commitment to or use of the plan in only three cases. While these issues of timing were present, they did not appear to be systematically problematic.

5. I approached administrators first with the expectation that they would provide the most disinterested assessment of their elected officials' commitment to and use of the local CAMA plan. Planning directors were interviewed for 8 localities either at the request of the administrator or because the administrator in office during the study period had since moved on and could not be located. I discerned no consistent difference in assessments between planning directors and managers. I attempted initially to assess all 60 localities with populations greater than 2,000 year-round or seasonal residents that participate in the CAMA planning program. I could not locate officials in office during the study period for 13 localities, however, while 5 administrators either declined to be interviewed or terminated the interview early. Finally, of the 42 remaining localities, 6 were dropped because they had not used their CAMA plans at all during the study period for lack of development activity. Based on multiple comparisons across means for selected factors between the 36 study localities and the 24 dropped localities, there appeared to be no systematic differences between the two groups. The telephone and mail survey instruments are available upon request.

6. Plans were evaluated for all 36 localities for which a telephone survey was successfully conducted, 3 pretest localities, and 1 additional locality for which the telephone survey was initiated but terminated early, yielding a sample size of 40 plans evaluated. The plan content evaluation instrument is available upon request.

7. Although several administrators volunteered that local officials and citizens used their plans very selectively, raising questions of post-hoc rationalization (see, e.g., Flyvbjerg, 1998; Throgmorton, 1993), that issue was not addressed systematically for this study.

8. This operational construct was employed for plan use emphasis to account for situations in which local elected officials did not clearly focus on one type of policy over another through the use of their plans, but the plans themselves showed a clear policy emphasis on one policy over the other. Without this adjustment, local administrators' responses regarding policy emphasis in plan use were not significantly correlated to local attorneys' responses (correlation coefficient = 0.2190, p-value = 0.3676); with this adjustment, plan use emphasis was moderately correlated with local attorneys' responses at a significance threshold of 0.10 (correlation coefficient = 0.4204, p-value = 0.0731). Recognizing that there is no perfect construct for the concept, this combined construct was employed as a plausible and reasonable measure of plan use emphasis accordingly.

9. The State's recently revised administrative rules can be accessed online at http://dcm2.enr.state.nc.us/Rules/current.htm.

Appendix

Concept measurements for six planning outcomes in coastal North Carolina.

Local Elected Officials' Commitment to Planning

Administrator response to the following question (telephone survey):

> In a general sense, to what extent do you think the majority of your local elected board members were committed [during the study period] to the idea that land use planning is an appropriate and desirable function of local government? Specifically, how would you characterize their commitment to land use planning generally on a scale from 0 to 10, where 0 indicates no commitment whatsoever to planning, 10 indicates a strong level of commitment, and 5 indicates a moderate level of commitment?

Overall Local CAMA Plan Quality

Scale constructed from the summation of plan content evaluation scores for nine plan attributes. The first eight plan attributes, each scored 1 (low) to 4 (high), included: data analysis; statements of values and goals; land suitability/carrying capacity analysis; environmental protection policy statements; economic and community development policy statements; implementation assessment (i.e., of past plan efforts); monitoring and evaluation provisions; and the clarity of the link between the plan's land suitability analysis and its policies and future land use classifications. In addition, comprehensiveness of coverage was scored 0 (low) to 5 (high) based on the extent to which the plan addressed the topics specified by the State's land use planning guidelines.

Local CAMA Plan Use

Scale constructed from responses to the following question (telephone survey and mail surveys):

> To what extent did the CAMA land use plan play a role in guiding the board's decision-making on average or as a general rule [during the study period]? Specifically, please try to take into account all of the ways the plan might have played into the board's thinking, such as through their use of staff analyses or as a part of their public debate, and tell me how much of a role the plan played in the process using a scale of 0 to 10, with 0 meaning the plan played no role at all in the decision-making, 10 indicating that the plan played the predominant role in the board's decision-making, and 5 indicating that the plan was important but not the driving factor.

This question was asked for each of three purposes for which the plan may have been used by the locality, including the enactment or substantial revision of land use-related ordinances (e.g., zoning), site-specific land use-related decision making (e.g., rezonings), and/or infrastructure or capital improvement program decision making. These same questions were asked of local attorneys through a mail survey. Given a moderately strong correlation between administrator and attorney responses with regard to elected officials' use of the plan for enacting ordinances (coefficient = 0.5459; p-value = 0.0664), and based on the assumption that local managers were in the best position to evaluate elected officials' use of the plan, the following protocol was used to construct the measure of "plan use":

- If the administrator reported that the locality had enacted an ordinance (22 cases), then the level of plan use for that activity as reported by the administrator was used to measure "plan use."
- If the administrator reported that the locality had not enacted an ordinance but had engaged in site-specific decision making (11 cases), then the level of use for that purpose as reported by the administrator was used to measure "plan use."
- If the administrator reported that the locality had neither enacted an ordinance nor engaged in site-specific decision making but that it had made infrastructure-related decisions (3 cases), then the level of use for that purpose as reported by the administrator was used to measure "plan use."

Local Elected Officials' Policy Trade-Off Preferences

Index measure constructed as follows:

Local administrator (telephone survey), local attorneys (mail survey), and state district planners (mail survey) were asked the following two questions:

To put these two ideas [i.e., commitment to economic development and commitment to environmental protection] in the form of a number, could you characterize [the board or commission of local elected officials during the study period] on a scale of 1 to 4, with 1 indicating that the board was primarily interested in economic development and 4 indicating that the board was primarily interested in environmental protection?

And when it comes to the trade-off between economic development and environmental protection, if one had to be made, would the local elected board [during the study period] have favored strong economic development even though it might have necessitated some environmental degradation or would it have favored strong environmental protection even though it might have limited economic development somewhat?

Responses were received from all three respondents for 19 of the 36 study localities and from two respondents for the remaining 17 localities. Comparing responses to these questions across respondents, a study site was coded as emphasizing economic development over environmental protection, or vice versa, or showing no clear emphasis, if there was complete or substantial agreement among the respondents (i.e., 3/4 or 5/6 of the responses or better) for any one of these three characterizations. The study locality was also coded as showing no clear emphasis if there was substantial disagreement among the respondents.

Local CAMA Plan Policy Emphasis

Index measure constructed by first scoring plans according to the two following attributes:

- **Plan policy emphasis on economic and community development** (0 to 2—low to high), based on whether a plan: called for providing infrastructure in order to accommodate or promote economic development; specifically called for public efforts to promote private economic and commercial activities; specifically called for public efforts to recruit private industry; or called for or expressed the goal of reducing regulatory barriers that might be hindering local economic development.
- **Plan policy emphasis on environmental protection** (0 to 2—low to high), based on whether the plan called for or referred to: local rules exceeding State standards such as shoreline setbacks or sediment and erosion controls; low density and/or impervious surface limits specifically for

the purpose of water quality protection; use-based restrictions more stringent than State restrictions (e.g., marina siting and design); or the use of local environmental impact assessment requirements.

Plan policy emphasis was determined by subtracting the environmental protection score from the economic and community development score, where a negative overall score indicated an emphasis on economic development over environmental protection, a positive overall score indicated an emphasis on environmental protection over economic development, and a score of 0 indicated no clear emphasis. Note that plans placing a uniform level of emphasis on both economic development and environmental protection (low or high) were coded as "no clear emphasis;" only those plans demonstrating a measurably higher level of emphasis on one policy goal relative to the other were coded as showing an emphasis.

Local CAMA Plan Use Emphasis

Index measure constructed by first asking local administrators (telephone survey) the following question:

Would you say that, when using the plan, your local elected board [during the study period] focused on implementing the plan's economic development policies more so than its environmental protection policies, or focused on implementing the plan's environmental protection policies more so than its economic development policies, or focused on both sets of policies to the same extent?

If the administrator indicated that the local officials clearly emphasized one policy goal over the other in using the plan, then plan use emphasis was coded accordingly (i.e., economic development or environmental protection). If the administrator indicated that the local officials focused on both sets of policies equally, then implementation emphasis was coded according to the score given the plan with regard to plan policy emphasis (i.e., economic development, environmental protection, or no clear emphasis). Six localities for which the administrator indicated an equal focus on plan policies were coded as emphasizing economic development, while three localities were coded as emphasizing environmental protection, accordingly. This adjustment was made to account for localities where the administrator noted no clear emphasis, but the plan itself embodied a clear emphasis.

References

Abbott, C., Howe, D., & Adler, S. (1994). *Planning the Oregon way: A twenty-year evaluation.* Corvallis: Oregon State University Press.

Alterman, R., & Hill, M. (1978). Implementation of urban land use plan. *Journal of the American Planning Association, 44*(3), 274–285.

American Planning Association. (2000). *Policy guide on planning for sustainability.* Chicago: Author.

American Planning Association. (2002). *Policy guide on smart growth.* Chicago: Author.

Baer, W. C. (1997). General plan evaluation criteria: An approach to making better plans. *Journal of the American Planning Association, 63*(3), 329–344.

Berke, P. R. (1998). Reducing natural hazard risks through state growth management. *Journal of the American Planning Association, 64*(1), 76–87.

Berke, P. R., & French, S. P. (1994). The influence of state planning mandates on local plan quality. *Journal of Planning Education and Research, 13*, 237–250.

Berke, P. R., Roenigk, D., Kaiser, E. J., & Burby, R. J. (1996). Enhancing plan quality: Evaluating the role of state planning mandates for natural hazard mitigation. *Journal of Environmental Planning and Management, 39*, 79–96.

Bollens, S. A. (1992). State growth management: Intergovernmental frameworks and policy objectives. *Journal of the American Planning Association, 58*(4), 454–466.

Bollens, S. A. (1993). Restructuring land use governance. *Journal of Planning Literature, 7*(3), 211–226.

Bosselman, F., & Callies, D. (1971). *The quiet revolution in land control*. Washington, DC: Council on Environmental Quality and Council of State Governments.

Burby, R. J. (Ed.). (1998). *Cooperating with nature: Confronting natural hazards with land-use planning for sustainable communities*. Washington, DC: Joseph Henry Press.

Burby, R. J., Berke, P. R., Dalton, L. C., DeGrove, J. M., French, S. P., Kaiser, E. J., et al. (1993). Is state-mandated planning effective? *Land Use Law and Zoning Digest, 45*(10), 3–9.

Burby, R. J., & Dalton, L. C. (1994). Plans can matter! The role of land use plans and state planning mandates in limiting development in hazardous areas. *Public Administration Review, 54*(3), 229–238.

Burby, R. J., & May, P. J. (1997). *Making governments plan: State experiments in managing land use*. Baltimore: Johns Hopkins University Press.

Burby, R. J., & May, P. J. (1998). Intergovernmental environmental planning: Addressing the commitment conundrum. *Journal of Environmental Planning and Management, 41*(1), 95–110.

Carruthers, J. I. (2002). The impacts of state growth management programmes: A comparative analysis. *Urban Studies, 39*(11), 1959–1982.

Carson, R. (1962). *Silent spring*. Boston: Houghton Mifflin.

Catlin, R. A. (1997). *Land use planning, environmental protection and growth management: The Florida experience*. Chelsea, MI: Ann Arbor Press.

Dalton, L. C., & Burby, R. J. (1994). Mandates, plans, and planners: Building local commitment to development management. *Journal of the American Planning Association, 60*(4), 444–461.

Dean, C. (1999). *Against the tide: The battle for America's beaches*. New York: Columbia University Press.

Deyle, R. E., & Smith, R. A. (1998). Local government compliance with state planning mandates: The effects of state implementation in Florida. *Journal of the American Planning Association, 64*(4), 457–469.

Dillman, D. A. (1978). *Mail and telephone surveys: The total design method*. New York: John Wiley & Sons.

Flyvbjerg, B. (1998). *Rationality and power: Democracy in practice*. Chicago: University of Chicago Press.

Fowler, F. J., Jr. (1995). *Improving survey questions: Design and evaluation*. Thousand Oaks, CA: Sage.

Freilich, R. H. (1999). *From sprawl to smart growth: Successful legal, planning, and environmental systems*. Chicago: American Bar Association.

Gale, D. E. (1992). Eight state-sponsored growth management programs: A comparative analysis. *Journal of the American Planning Association, 58*(4), 425–439.

Godschalk, D. R., Beatley, T., Berke, P. R., Brower, D. J., & Kaiser, E. J. (1999). *Natural hazard mitigation: Recasting disaster policy and planning*. Washington, DC: Island Press.

Godschalk, D. R., & Cousins, K. (1985). Coastal management: Planning on the edge. *Journal of the American Planning Association, 51*(3), 263–265.

Heath, M. S. (1974). A legislative history of the Coastal Area Management Act. *North Carolina Law Review, 52*(2), 345–398.

Heath, M. S., & Owens, D. W. (1994). Coastal management law in North Carolina 1974-1994. *North Carolina Law Review, 72*(6), 1413–1451.

Howe, D. (1994). A research agenda for Oregon planning: Problems and practice for the 1990s. In C. Abbott, D. Howe, & S. Adler (Eds.), *Planning the Oregon way: A twenty-year evaluation* (pp. 275–290). Corvallis: Oregon State University Press.

Johnston, R. A., Schwartz, S. I., & Klinkner, T. F. (1978). Successful plan implementation: The growth phasing program of Sacramento County. *Journal of the American Institute of Planners, 44*(4), 412–423.

Kaiser, E. J., Godschalk, D. R., & Chapin, S. F., Jr. (1995). *Urban land use planning* (4th ed.). Urbana: University of Illinois Press.

Longest, R., & Smith, R. (2000, July 26). Assistant Attorney General, State of North Carolina, and Assistant Secretary, NC Department of Environment, Health and Natural Resources (Untitled briefing for the Land Use Planning Review Team). Morehead City, NC.

Lowry, K. (1985). Assessing the implementation of federal coastal policy. *Journal of the American Planning Association, 51*(3), 288–298.

Mallin, M. A., Ensign, S. H., McIver, M. R., Shank, G. C., & Fowler, P. K. (2001). Demographic, landscape, and meteorological factors controlling the microbial pollution in coastal waters. *Hydrobiologia, 460*(1), 185–193.

Mallin, M. A., & Wheeler, T. L. (2000). Nutrient and fecal coliform discharge from coastal North Carolina golf courses. *Journal of Environmental Quality, 29*(3), 979–986.

Mallin, M. A., Williams, K. E., Esham, E. C., & Lowe, R. P. (2000). Effect of human development on bacteriological water quality in coastal watersheds. *Ecological Applications, 10*(4), 1047–1056.

May, P. J., Burby, R. J., Ericksen, N. J., Handmer, J. W., Dixon, J. E., Michaels, S., et al. (1996). *Environmental management and governance: Intergovernmental approaches to hazards and sustainability*. New York: Routledge.

McHarg, I. L. (1969). *Design with nature*. Garden City, NJ: Natural History Press.

National Association of Home Builders. (2000). *Smart growth: Building better places to live, work and play*. Washington, DC: Author.

North Carolina Coastal Area Management Act of 1974, 113A Gen. Stat. [§] 100 et seq. (1974 & Supp. 2001).

North Carolina Coastal Futures Committee. (1994). *Charting a course for our coast: A report to the governor*. Raleigh: North Carolina Division of Coastal Management.

North Carolina Department of Environment, Health, & Natural Resources Land Use Planning Guidelines, 15A NC Admin. Code 7B.0100 et seq. (2001).

North Carolina Department of Environment, Health, & Natural Resources State Guidelines for Areas of Environmental Concern, 15A NC Admin. Code 7H.201 et seq. (2001).

North Carolina Division of Coastal Management. (1986). *Protecting coastal water quality through local planning*. Raleigh, NC: Author.

North Carolina Division of Coastal Management. (1994). *Managing cumulative impacts in the North Carolina coastal area*. Raleigh, NC: Author.

North Carolina Division of Coastal Management. (2000). *Land use plan review team: Report to the Coastal Resources Commission*. Raleigh, NC: Author.

Owens, D. W. (1985). Coastal management in North Carolina: Building a regional consensus. *Journal of the American Planning Association, 51*(3), 322–329.

Peck, S. (1998). *Planning for biodiversity: Issues and examples.* Washington, DC: Island Press.

Porter, D. R. (1997). *Managing growth in America's communities.* Washington, DC: Island Press.

Smart Growth Network. (2002). *Getting to smart growth.* Washington, DC: Author.

Sierra Club. (2000). *Smart choices or sprawling growth: A 50-state survey of development.* San Francisco: Sierra Club Foundation.

Talen, E. (1996). Do plans get implemented? A review of evaluation in planning. *Journal of Planning Literature, 10*(3), 248–259.

Throgmorton, J. A. (1993). Survey research as rhetorical trope: Electric power planning arguments in Chicago. In F. Fischer & J. Forester (Eds.), *The argumentative turn in policy analysis and planning.* Durham, NC: Duke University Press.

U. S. Environmental Protection Agency. (1989). *Nonpoint sources: Agenda for the future.* Washington, DC: Author.

Weitz, J. (1999). *Sprawl busting: State programs to guide growth.* Chicago: American Planning Association.

RICHARD K. NORTON is an assistant professor in the urban and regional planning program at the University of Michigan. He teaches and conducts research on land use and environmental planning, sustainable development, intergovernmental growth management, and the legal aspects of planning.

From *Journal of the American Planning Association,* Vol. 71, Number 1, Winter 2005, pp. 55–71. Copyright © 2005 by American Planning Association. Reprinted by permission.

Rebuilding a Beautiful Mess

Plus Ca Change

CLAY RISEN

The only thing harder to imagine than rebuilding New Orleans is not rebuilding New Orleans. If the notion of reconstructing vast swaths of a city of 500,000 inhabitants, with all the economic and civic functions that go with it, seems daunting, imagine having to do it from scratch, somewhere else. New Orleans, despite its awful poverty, has one of the most vibrant urban cultures on the planet. And it is one of the world's busiest ports, not only because of its naturally advantageous position at the mouth of the Mississippi but also because, over the last two centuries, the country has spun a tight web of nationally linked infrastructure around the city. None of these attributes can simply be picked up and moved 100 miles away.

So, while a few politicians and pundits—House Speaker Dennis Hastert most famously—have suggested that New Orleans not be rebuilt, the question is really more about how to rebuild and what rebuilding means. Within city-planning literature, the most noted recent, near-total urban rebuilding efforts were in autocratic or semi-autocratic countries: Tangshan, China, wracked by an earthquake in 1976, and Mexico City, also hit by an earthquake in 1985. (The 1995 earthquake in Kobe, Japan, is a noteworthy exception, though even there the Japanese government was able to take liberties with private property rights in its rebuilding that we would never allow in the United States.) But how can a city be rebuilt in a free-market democracy, where the prior demands of property and constantly changing market forces are often at loggerheads with the need for rational urban planning?

The temptation is to call for a robust master plan that drastically restitches the urban fabric. But one need only to look at the post-September 11 efforts at the World Trade Center site to see how quickly planning ideals give way under the pressure of the market. Indeed, according to numerous urban-planning experts, there is always the impetus post-disaster to think big in the hopes that something good can come of something awful. But, they also warn, the results are almost always frustrating. "The record of almost every past precedent is that those who think we can start over again and do some grand plan find themselves frustrated," says Lawrence Vale, head of MIT's Department of Urban Studies and Planning and the co-author of *The Resilient City*. But, if overplanning is a recipe for frustration, doing nothing is a recipe for disaster. "We need to move quickly, but if the planning gets discarded, we will repeat the same mistakes," says Andrew Altman, former head of city planning for Washington, D.C., and CEO of Washington's Anacostia waterfront rebuilding initiative. So New Orleans must plan for a better future but do so humbly. The best proposal may be a modest one: a city that is better protected from future floods, a metropolis with upgraded infrastructure and less blight, but one that retains the better aspects of its essential character. New Orleans should not—and will not—become Disney World. But neither can it remain exactly as it was.

The impulse to rebuild a radically new city is especially pointed in New Orleans, punctuated as it is by a degraded infrastructure, corrupt politics, massive wealth disparities, and, in many neighborhoods, near-Third World living conditions. After a disaster like Hurricane Katrina, "for the first time, adequate resources become available for thorough physical and design studies," wrote the authors of a 1977 National Science Foundation-funded study on post-disaster reconstruction. "The impossible seems possible … the opportunity for comprehensive study and major change is at hand."

In fact, the idea of rebuilding a city "bigger and better" has a long—and disheartening—history. After the Great London Fire of 1666, the architect Sir Christopher Wren pushed city leaders to adopt his plan for an ordered city grid, with wide streets that would help slow a future fire. But even the man who built St. Paul's Cathedral had little impact on London's reconstruction. A similar story unfolded after the San Francisco earthquake of 1906, which destroyed over 50 percent of the city's housing stock and wiped out its commercial and industrial sectors. By coincidence, the year before the earthquake, the great architect and urban planner Daniel Burnham had drawn up a master plan for the San Francisco of the twentieth century. But, when the earthquake provided the perfect opportunity to put his plan into effect, it was completely overlooked. Even Chicago, which supposedly rebuilt itself according to exacting new construction codes after a fire wiped out much of its downtown in 1871, was actually first rebuilt in the same shoddy manner as before; it was only after a prolonged political battle that planners put tougher building codes in place.

The crux of the problem, planners admit, is that no city, even one as thoroughly devastated as New Orleans, emerges a tabula rasa. "There is already a plan for reconstruction, indelibly stamped in the perception of each resident—the plan of the pre-disaster city," wrote the authors of the NSF study. Not only does the will of the residents to "make it like it was" render any thought of relocation void, but it also makes it difficult to conceive of any urban design that varies too far from the old model—no matter how socially unjust that model may have been.

Perhaps even more of an obstacle to radical change is the vested interests of the powers that be. Any effort to rebuild a city in a markedly different fashion would inevitably require land redistribution, and, even with just compensation, it's unlikely that wealthy property owners would accept such a deal. After all, this was the essence of the struggle in 2002 and 2003 by some politicians in New York City to wrest control of the World Trade Center site from the Port Authority (PA), which owns the land, and Larry Silverstein, who owns the lease and claims a contractual obligation to rebuild the ten million square feet of office space that existed before September 11. Even a tentative offer by City Hall to swap Ground Zero for the land under the city's two airports, a roughly equal financial trade, did nothing to sway the PA and Silverstein. In the face of catastrophe, those with the most money involved will take the fewest risks.

But, even if big plans make for big failures, cities do in fact get rebuilt. And, if having too many big ideas means few are likely to be implemented, that doesn't mean that a few well-chosen rebuilding principles—and a few well-written rebuilding laws—can't have a decisive impact, laying the groundwork for the eventual, organic emergence of a more just society and more dynamic civic culture.

The first principle in rebuilding New Orleans should be to reduce the risk of future catastrophic flooding. The levee system that Katrina compromised was built to withstand a Category Three hurricane. Given the city's experience with Category Four Katrina, overengineering for a Category Five shouldn't be a question. Many of the most flooded neighborhoods will need to be bulldozed and the ground under them razed. A related idea should be to improve the sustainability of the bayous and barrier islands to the south of New Orleans, which will help sap the power of future hurricanes before they hit the city. And, while the city itself should obviously stay where it is, planners should be willing to consider relocating some of the most flood-prone neighborhoods (which also tend to be the poorest sections of town), perhaps even closing off East New Orleans and Chalmette to future development.

Beyond mere safety, the rebuilding process must inspire public confidence. While New Orleanians will undoubtedly want to return home, many will be hesitant to do so unless they can be assured that there is an unencumbered power structure in place to oversee the city's recovery. In some cases, it might be possible to place such power in the hands of local and state authorities. But New Orleans was, in many ways, a disaster before Katrina, the victim of decades of state neglect and local inepti-

tude. In this case, only Washington has the wherewithal to oversee the reconstruction. "There's really only one entity who can do that here, given the economic realities, and that's the federal government," says Thomas Campanella, a planning professor at the University of North Carolina, Chapel Hill, and Vale's co-author on The Resilient City. "There's going to be some private sector investment in certain areas, but as far as the vast infrastructure and housing for low-income residents, it has to come from the federal government."

But rebuilding physical structures isn't enough—residents need to know that they will have a way to make a living. Any rebuilding efforts should therefore include job prospects as well. New Orleans's largest employers, the shipping and tourism industries, won't fully recover for years. Thus, a corollary principle should be to use New Orleans residents as much as possible in the rebuilding effort, on construction crews, and in support staff, even if this requires some job training. This, in turn, will assure the commercial sector that it will have a labor force to draw from when it eventually returns.

Another principle should be to keep as many changes as possible in the background. Toughen up building codes, but in ways that take into account local architectural traditions. Push for more mixed-income neighborhoods, but recognize that residents will revolt if they are forced to move into drastically different living patterns. Push for a city with less corruption and crime, but also recognize that what made New Orleans such an attractive place to live was precisely its down-at-the-heels, not-quite-clean reputation. "I hope we don't end up with a sanitized New Orleans, with the French Quarter and the Garden District and tourist sites surrounded by acres of bulldozed shotgun and camelback houses," says Campanella. "I'm worried that a themeparking of New Orleans could take place," a result akin to the artificially aged "old town" sections of Cologne, Düsseldorf, and other German cities destroyed during World War II. Such a New Orleans may look more attractive to outsiders, but it will eviscerate the soul of the city.

And, while a strong federal role of unprecedented proportions is clearly necessary, it shouldn't be so large that it chokes off private investment. Oddly enough, it is often immediately after a disaster that a city experiences its greatest growth, not only because it is starting from close to zero but also because the opportunities for investment seem so wide open. Guiding these forces, rather than competing with them, should be at the center of any rebuilding effort.

Perhaps the most important principle is to respect the persistence of urban memory. A city is not just a collection of streets and buildings; it is a population of individuals who have strong attachments to their ways of life and patterns of living. Places like New Orleans's impoverished Eighth and Ninth Wards "were real and vital places with wonderful social fabrics, where the people had roots that went generations deep," says Campanella. Ignorance of local patterns of life led mid-century planners to tear down inner-city slums and toss residents into soulless projects. Contemporary planners recognize the need to study such patterns and incorporate them into new housing efforts, and the same should be done in New Orleans.

This is not to argue against trying to make the next New Orleans a more equitable place. But it is to say that overly ambitious planners may find their efforts thwarted by the very people they imagine they are helping. Ironically, the same attachments to place and lifestyle that militate so strongly against relocating New Orleans are the exact forces that will stand in the way of any effort to radically refashion the city as well. So the new New Orleans ought to look a lot like the old New Orleans—only better.

CLAY RISEN, a former assistant editor at *The New Republic*, is managing editor of *Democracy: A Journal of Ideas*.

On the Gulf: Too Little, Too Late

A wetlands buffer could have made a difference to New Orleans.

The suffering caused by Katrina has spurred Congress to authorize spending tens of billions of dollars on disaster relief—and billions more on repairing the city's infrastructure.

CRAIG PITTMAN

Forty years ago, Hurricane Betsy came howling in from the Gulf of Mexico and took dead aim at New Orleans. The Category 3 storm overwhelmed the levees with an eight- to 10-foot storm surge, putting the city's streets under seven feet of water.

After Betsy, Congress authorized a massive construction project to ensure the city's safety in case another Category 3 storm ever hit. The Army Corps of Engineers built and raised levees along Lake Pontchartrain, the city's northern boundary, and constructed floodgates and barriers to prevent storm surges from washing through the lake and overwhelming the city.

But the engineers neglected one thing that could have made a real difference when Hurricane Katrina—a far stronger Category 4 storm—smashed into the Gulf Coast on August 30 and inundated 80 percent of New Orleans. They did nothing to halt the loss of thousands of acres of wetlands in the Cajun country to the south.

Louisiana's vast coastal wetlands once buffered the Big Easy from gulf storms. The wetlands functioned like a sponge, absorbing a hurricane's destructive power before it reached the city. For years, Louisiana's marshes have been sinking beneath the waves at an astonishing rate—25 to 30 square miles a year, the equivalent of a football field every 15 minutes. As its wetlands buffer disappeared. New Orleans inched closer and closer to open water.

Back in 1965 when Betsy hit, "there were many more acres of wetlands than there are now," says Kerry St. Pé, a Louisiana native who directs the Barataria-Terrebonne National Estuary Program. "There is no question that those wetlands protected us."

With the disappearance of the wetlands, experts say, the city was much more exposed to the danger posed by a major hurricane like Katrina. "The storm surge was four to five feet higher than it would have been 50 years ago because of the loss of wetlands," says Shea Penland, a University of New Orleans geologist who has spent decades studying the Louisiana coastline.

The suffering caused by Katrina has spurred Congress to authorize spending tens of billions of dollars on disaster relief, and experts estimate it will cost hundreds of billions more to repair the damage.

Scientists say some of those appropriations should be spent on recreating the land that's been lost to the sea. Otherwise, the next hurricane could be even worse. "We can't rebuild New Orleans without rebuilding the barrier islands and the wetlands," Penland says.

Not everyone agrees. In a September op-ed column in the *New York Times,* geology professors Robert Young of Western Carolina University and David Bush of the University of West Georgia wrote: "We seriously doubt that any objective, scientific cost-benefit review would find that spending all that money in Louisiana makes sense."

'We starved our wetlands'

From its founding in 1718, New Orleans has lived with the threat of inundation. The mighty river that brought cotton and grain to its port, enriching its merchants, also brought frequent floods that swept away homes and required repeated rebuilding.

Residents grumbled about the destruction, but the floods actually helped the state. As the Mississippi River courses toward the gulf, it drains half the U.S. Local wags dubbed Louisiana "the re-United States" because the state is built on sediment from throughout the country that has washed its way downriver.

As the sediment collected on the rivers 2,000-mile journey was deposited throughout the delta, it built up the swampy land. Between floods, the land would slowly sink under its own muddy weight. Then after a few years, the next flood would sweep in with more sediment, building up the land once again.

Then came the great Mississippi flood of 1927 chat killed at least 1,000 people and drove nearly a million more from their homes, from Illinois south to the Gulf Coast. Such a widespread catastrophe spurred a frenzy of federally financed levee construction that continues to this day. The string of levees strait-jacketed the river, confining it to a single course.

Now, instead of sprinkling its sediment throughout the delta, the river rushes its load straight out to sea. Seventy million cubic yards of sediment a year shoot off the end of the continental

How the Dutch Do It

A two-day conference on "Sustainable Waterfronts: Learning from the Dutch Experience" drew a varied audience last month to the Illinois Institute of Technology in Chicago. At the last minute, organizers added a panel titled "New Orleans and the Netherlands—Living Below Sea Level."

In a small country (200 square miles and 16.3 million residents), where 26.7 percent of the land, including the most economically important parts. is below sea level, flood control is a national obsession. The Dutch speakers stressed that Holland is nothing if not prepared.

But Dico van Ooijen, senior adviser for dikes and dams for the Netherlands Ministry of Transport, Public Works, and Water Management, described a shift from a reliance on engineering solutions such as huge storm surge barriers and ever taller dikes to regulatory solutions such as housing on stilts.

Even with the dikes—first built in the 11th century—there have been catastrophes, notably a 1916 storm surge from the Zuiderzee in the north and a 1953 flood that killed more 1,800 people in the southeast. The latter led to the construction of a series of 13 projects known as Delta Works, which ended in 1997 with a storm surge barrier in the Rotterdam Harbor. Meanwhile, dikes were built and strengthened along the Rhine and Maas rivers, often requiring the demolition of adjacent neighborhoods.

Increasing local opposition ended the project, van Ooijen said. It's hard to muster political support "when there is no disaster," he noted.

In 2000, the government instituted a new, more sustainable approach: "Making room for the river." Peter Torbijn, director of national spatial planning policy for the Netherlands, explained. "We have made a conscious choice not to strengthen the dikes and to forbid most building in floodplains," he said, although some "alternative" structures such as floating housing are allowed.

Torbijn noted that this approach requires careful planning. And a water assessment is part of what the Dutch call "spatial planning," at every level, from the federal to the local. Even the Dutch crown prince has taken personal interest in water management and spatial planning, he said.

For the New Orleans area, Torbijn had this advice: "Take water into consideration when you allocate land uses. Compartmentalize so breeches of your flood defenses won't be fatal. And create an effective water management agency and give it power."

Ruth Knack, AICP

Knack is the executive editor of Planning.

Building in all the wrong places

Meanwhile, in New Orleans, low-lying land that flooded regularly through the 1800s became the site of new housing. To make sure that the land stayed dry, the city turned to a complex system of pumps.

At the turn of the 20th century, city officials built the first comprehensive water, sewer, and drainage system, says Craig Colten, a geography professor at Louisiana State University and author of *Unnatural Metropolis: Wresting New Orleans from Nature*. So even as New Orleans pumped water from the Mississippi for its residents to drink, it drained its wetlands to make room for development.

Before Katrina hit, New Orleans had the most sophisticated drainage network in the country, with almost 200 miles of canals and 22 pumping stations capable of pumping 35 billion gallons of water a day out of the city, all in the service of ensuring that its dry land would not turn back into swamps.

New Orleans's attitude toward its wetlands is not unusual. Through most of the 20th century, Americans thought of swamps and marshes as at best a waste of good farmland and at worst a source of disease. In a 1912 speech to the National Drainage Congress, held in New Orleans, the U.S. Geological Survey's chief hydrographer declared the nations wetlands to be the "greatest single menace that remains to public health" and "a source of weakness in our national economy."

The solution: Drain them. Ditch them. Fill them in. One way or another, convert them to dry land. No one knew then that wetlands were actually beneficial. They not only help to prevent flooding by retaining water, but they also filter pollution, recharge underground drinking water supplies, and provide a nursery for fish and shrimp.

But with the water pumped out. New Orleans's former wetlands settled even faster than they did when they were still damp. The bowl in which the city sits became deeper than ever. "New Orleans has sunk faster than the delta," Colten says. Even the levees built to protect the city slowly sank, requiring more construction to make them higher.

Things got so bad that houses built atop the city's peaty soil began to explode, Colten says. As the land sank, he explains, the process of settling would rip loose the gas lines below the house, followed shortly by a kaboom.

In the 1930s, the state's oil and gas industry began exploring Louisiana's coastal marshes south of New Orleans. Over the next several decades, as the industry extended its pipelines toward the gulf, the companies sliced 17,000 small navigational canals through the swamps. Wave action eroded the banks of the canals, widening them dramatically. As a result, even more wetlands sank into the gulf.

The largest canal is the 70-mile-long Mississippi River Gulf Outlet, nicknamed "Mr. Go." Dredged by the Army Corps of Engineers in the 1960s as a shortcut from the Port of New Orleans to the gulf, Mr. Go is too shallow to be used regularly by modern ships. But it's sure wide enough: Erosion has expanded the canal from 500 feet, its width when it was built, to 2,000 feet wide today. In the process it has eaten away local residents call a "hurricane superhighway" leading straight to the city. Sure enough,

shelf and into the fathomless deep, says St. Pé. A century ago, a hurricane barreling toward New Orleans would have had to traverse 50 miles of wetlands to reach the city. But with no floods and no sediment, the sinking wetlands could not be replenished, and now that buffer is only half as broad.

"We starved our wetlands," says St. Pé, whose Barataria-Terrebonne National Estuary Program is named for the two parishes south of New Orleans that have lost the most wetlands. "They became the fastest disappearing landmass on earth. Eighteen square miles a year changed from vegetated wetland masses to open water."

Katrina's storm surge swept right through Mr. Go and hit the first levee, breaching it.

The combined result of all these wetland damaging factors has been catastrophic. A 2003 study by the U.S. Geological Survey found that since the 1930s coastal Louisiana has lost some 1,900 square miles—an area about the size of Delaware swallowed up by the sea.

Finally, a plan

Scientists have known for 30 years that Louisiana's wetlands were vanishing, Colten says. They spotted the disappearance by comparing aerial photos taken in the 1940s with photos shot in the 1970s. Doing something about it was another story.

Since the 1980s, Louisiana officials have repeatedly asked Congress for money to rebuild the coastal wetlands. But no one could agree on exactly how to do it, and Congress was unwilling to spend much on a program where there were so many disagreements about solutions. "No one, the Corps, the state, the oil and gas community, the environmental community, the parishes, treated this with sufficient urgency," says Scott Faber, a spokesman for the activist group Environmental Defense.

Each year that passed brought warnings of the disaster to come. "Smaller storms were putting more water in people's yards than they got from Betsy and Camille" in the 1960s, Penland says.

In 1990, then-Sen. John Breaux (D-La.) persuaded his colleagues in Congress to approve a first step; the Coastal Wetlands Planning, Protection and Restoration Act, under which the federal government would spend $35 million a year and the state $15 million a year on small restoration projects.

The so-called Breaux Act produced some small successes, but not enough to turn the tide of whole sale wetland losses. Then, in 1998, Hurricane Georges came within a hair of slamming into New Orleans. The near-miss scared Louisianans into agreeing to work together. They drew up a far-reaching plan for restoration called Coast 2050, which proposed some 80 projects hat would use pipelines, pumps, and other engineering solutions to rebuild the wetlands.

Among the solutions: closing Mr. Go as soon as possible; diverting the Mississippi so it would once again deposit sediments in the marshes; building a sediment trap at the mouth of the river to halt the loss of material over the continental shelf; and constructing a 60-mile-long channel from the river to the marshes of Bayou Lafourche to create two new deltas there.

The plan had a $14 billion price tag. That's higher than the anticipated cost of restoring the Everglades, which Corps officials have called the largest environmental restoration project in history. But now the cost of carrying out Coast 2050 "suddenly looks like chump change compared to the cost of rebuilding New Orleans," Colten says.

Everglades model

Louisiana officials figured that they could take the same route as Florida officials did in their successful drive for federal funding for the Everglades. They boned the sprawling Coast 2050 plan into the more sharply defined Louisiana Coastal Area Ecosystem Restoration Plan. They signed a formal agreement with the Corps of Engineers and worked to get funding in the Water Resources Development Act, which finances Corps projects. They projected a completion date 40 years down the road.

But the 20-year, $8 billion Everglades plan passed Congress just before a hotly contested presidential election, when the federal budget had a surplus. Now the surplus is gone, and Louisiana's electoral votes haven't been nearly as crucial as Florida's. So while the Bush administration supported the Everglades plan, it balked at full funding for Louisiana wetland restoration.

Even after Hurricane Ivan gave Louisiana a bad scare last year before hitting Alabama and the Florida Panhandle instead. Congress failed to act on Louisiana's wetland funding, to the consternation of state officials.

"What is it going to take for Congress and the president to realize this is not just another project?" Sidney Coffee, an aide to Louisiana Gov. Kathleen Blanco, complained to the New Orleans *Times-Picayune* last year. "Would we have had to get hit by the big one?"

It's not as if the state didn't have some deep-pocketed partners working to convince Congress. In 2002, a sophisticated lobbying effort, backed by such sponsors as Shell Oil and the makers of Tabasco, came up with the idea of marketing the Louisiana delta as "America's Wetland" to drum up national support for restoration.

The award-winning publicity campaign pointed out that restoring the environment would he good for the economy. Louisiana's coastal wetlands produce a third of the nations commercial seafood—about a billion pounds of fish, crab, and oysters annually—the most in the lower 48 states.

The campaign produced some positive press, but the "America's Wetland" label failed to catch on, and federal funding continued to be elusive. This summer, however, as part of the energy bill. Congress approved giving Louisiana a share of federal oil and gas revenues—totaling $540 million over the next four years, far short of the $14 billion needed—to get the restoration started. The bill passed just a month before Katrina hit.

After the flood

Pumping all the floodwater out of New Orleans—not just from Katrina but also from the weaker Hurricane Rita that hit in mid-September—took until early October. Bourbon Street's strip clubs immediately reopened.

But rebuilding the rest of the drowned city is likely to take decades, and no one knows yet just what it will look like when its done. Mayor C. Ray Nagin announced the creation of a 17-member, racially mixed commission to draft a broad rebuilding plan by year's end. The commission will have its work cut out for it.

"We're finding some pretty startling issues," Nagin said. To begin with, there are some big problems with the infrastructure. During Katrina's onslaught, trees that were ripped out of the ground pulled loose underground pipes, rupturing sewer lines. The sewage treatment plant was also knocked out of commission. The sewer system was outdated to begin with, and restoring service is expected to be so difficult that the city's water and sewer board predicted in mid-September that it might have to pump raw sewage into the Mississippi for months.

The water system is contaminated throughout most of the city. Experts predicted in September that making the system functional again could take three months. Until then, what was coming through the pipes was untreated water from the Mississippi—which is where the city is pumping its untreated sewage.

Contaminated drinking water is not a new problem for New Orleans, Colten says. Because of concerns dating back to the 1960s about cancer-causing chemicals in the water the city draws from the Mississippi, "New Orleans has one of the highest bottled water consumption rates in the country," he notes.

Beyond infrastructure needs, there are some philosophical questions to wrestle with as well. For instance, what should be done with the low-lying parts of the city, which flooded after the storm? Would it be safe to build houses there again? Or would it be smarter to turn those areas back into wetlands in case of future levee breaks? Of course, that means finding new housing elsewhere for the people who lived in those neighborhoods.

"Relocation is probably the best long-term alternative," says David Godschalk, FAICP, professor of city and regional planning at the University of North Carolina. "It's very counterproductive to encourage people to stay in areas where their lives are in danger and their property's in danger."

The city's low-lying areas were for the most part occupied by low-income residents. Before the storm, 28 percent of the city's residents lived below the poverty line, and the population was 67 percent African American. Any decision to permanently relocate so many of the city's poor residents comes freighted with political and socioeconomic ramifications.

"Where do you think the musicians live who play in the clubs? They don't live in the French Quarter," Geoff Coats of the local advocacy group Urban Conservancy told the *Boston Globe*. Still, he added, "we may have to make very difficult choices as to whether some areas get rebuilt or not."

Another view

Relocating residents for the sake of flood protection doesn't necessarily mean moving thousands of people out of New Orleans, says Colten. "We could increase the density on the highest ground that was never inundated." Then, he adds, the former wetlands could be left as green space, rather than rebuilding houses that would always be at risk from future floods.

And what of the wetlands south of the city? They were hit hard by an estimated 40 oil spills from ruptured pipelines and damaged oil processing facilities. In all, the industry lost an estimated 193,000 barrels, a cumulative total that makes this the largest oil spill in Louisiana history. This too was a result of wetlands loss: The pipelines were originally buried under the marshes. As the wetlands disappeared, they became more exposed and thus more vulnerable to damage.

Meanwhile, the storm surges from Katrina and Rita combined for a one-two punch that hit Barataria and Terrebonne parishes hard. Saltwater washed into freshwater marshlands, burning the salt-intolerant vegetation and inundating even more acres of former swamps.

Still, St. Pé, who grew up among the Cajun shrimpers in this area, remains confident that the damaged wetlands can be rebuilt through some accelerated version of the plans the state had been pursuing before the storms. "There's a lot of foundation that was there before that's still there," he says. "There's still a platform on which we can rebuild."

The hurricane relief bill that Louisiana's congressional delegation filed seeking $250 billion in aid over the next decade includes a provision calling for $3 billion to $4 billion for coastal restoration. The money would be drawn from oil and gas revenues.

While Louisiana scientists and officials contend that now is the time to push for the billions the wetlands need, some scientists from other states are skeptical.

"We are being sold a giant engineering project intended to fix problems caused by engineering projects elsewhere on the river and the delta," geologists Young and Bush wrote in their *New York Times* column. They questioned how anyone could support rebuilding the wetlands while also arguing for more and higher levees.

Instead of spending all those billions on Louisiana wetlands, they contended, Congress would do better to spend the money on restoring wetlands all across the country.

As the debate begins over what to do, environmental advocates see in Louisiana's losses a lesson for other coastal states that could find themselves facing future Katrinas. "We should not countenance another acre of coastal wetlands loss anywhere," says Jim Tripp, an activist with the group Environmental Defense who serves on Gov. Kathleen Blanco's Advisory Commission on Coastal Restoration and Conservation. "It's foolhardy."

Resources

APA-New Orleans team. At the request of local officials, APA has assembled a team of experts to help New Orleans rebuild its planning function in the wake of Hurricane Katrina. The six team members are Fernando Costa, AICP, the team leader; Jane Brooks, FAICP; Chandra Foreman, AICP; Robert Lurcott, FAICP; Grover Mouton; and Richard Roths, AICP.

Working with the Planning Department, the City Planning Commission, and other local officials and citizens, the team will assess the city's planning needs and prepare recommendations. For more on the team's mission and its members, go to APA's website, www.planning.org.

Note: A special section of the APA website provides links to APA publications (including a chapter of a Planning Advisory Service report on disaster planning) and other articles. Check Interact for up-to-date information.

More to come. Watch *Planning* in the coming months for stories on rebuilding in New Orleans (December), housing for hurricane victims (January), evacuees in Texas towns (February), and transportation impacts (May).

San Antonio. Special sessions are being arranged for APA's National Planning Conference, April 22-26 in San Antonio. See the website for the latest information.

CRAIG PITTMAN covers the environment for the *St. Petersburg Times* in Florida.

Closing of Mine on Tribal Lands Fuels Dispute over Air, Water and Jobs

JOHN M. BRODER

Black Mesa, Ariz.—The gigantic earth-moving crane sits idle, a 5,500-ton behemoth stilled by a legal, cultural and environmental dispute playing out far from the rich vein of coal beneath the desert of remote northeastern Arizona.

The rig, known as a dragline, may never again scrape the earth's surface at the Black Mesa Mine to get at the coal beneath the Hopi and Navajo lands.

Some welcome the idling of the earth-gobbling beast, a symbol, they say, of the rape of the land and precious water below. Others, mostly American Indians who have come to depend on the high-paying jobs at the mine, are furious.

For 35 years, the Black Mesa Mine has produced coal for a power plant in southern Nevada. But it suspended operations at the end of December, ending the jobs of nearly 200 people.

Most of them are members of the Navajo Nation and the Hopi Tribe whose livelihood and dreams depend on work at the mine, jobs that pay as much as $80,000 a year in wages and benefits, 10 times the average annual income on the reservations.

The mine is ceasing work indefinitely because the sole power plant it supplies, the Mohave Generating Station 273 miles away in Laughlin, Nev., is shutting down under a legal agreement with environmental groups that sued because of repeated pollution violations.

The power plant is owned by four utilities that have balked at paying the estimated $1 billion in upgrades to comply with the court order and keep the plant operating.

One idled worker is Myrata Cody, 48, a heavy equipment operator at Black Mesa for the last 27 years. She is a Navajo and a single mother, providing support for three children and her aging parents. Her anger at losing her job drives her to tears.

"This income is the only thing I have," she said. "There is no power line to my house, no phone line, no running water. Everybody else has everything at the tip of their hands."

She reserved particular ire for the environmentalists who went after the owners of the power plant to try to stop the thick plume of smoke and noxious chemicals it has poured into the atmosphere for decades. The groups contended that the emissions fouled the air over the Grand Canyon and threatened the health of people who lived downwind.

"All those people protesting for the environmental groups, none of them live up here," Ms. Cody said. "If this plant shuts down, some of us are going to have to leave our elderly parents behind to go find work. Who's going to go out there and check on them, make sure they get their medication? Nobody from the environmental groups, that's for sure."

While many of the players are quick to point to villains—a heartless coal company, out-of-touch environmentalists, air-fouling utilities—the facts are more shaded and complex. The coal company has both exploited and enriched the reservations, the environmental groups are offering other sources of income for the tribes, and the utilities are seeking cleaner energy alternatives to the coal-burning Mohave plant.

The mine is operated by the Peabody Western Coal Company, a subsidiary of the Peabody Energy Corporation, the world's largest coal company, which has made tens of millions of dollars from the Black Mesa mine. But it has also poured millions of dollars into schools, community centers, roads and power lines on the Indian lands of northeastern Arizona, although basic services are still lacking in much of the tribal region.

It provides $89 million a year in payroll, lease payments, taxes and other benefits to this region, where unemployment among the Hopi and Navajo is nearly 40 percent.

Buck Woodward, the mine manager, called the closing of Black Mesa "a tragedy" that could hinder economic development on the reservations for years.

The environmental groups that sued Southern California Edison and the three other owners of the Mohave Generating Station agreed to give the plant operators six years to comply with the consent decree, which was signed in 1999.

The company was supposed to install scrubbers to clean its smokestacks of sulfur dioxide emissions and negotiate new coal and water supply agreements with Peabody and the tribes. But it decided not to, at least for now, after the original estimate of $400 million for compliance rose to $1 billion and it received no assurance that it could recover the cost from customers.

The plaintiffs said that they were willing to discuss an extension of the deadline to preserve the jobs but that the utilities chose not to negotiate.

The environmental groups—the Grand Canyon Trust, the Sierra Club and the National Parks Conservation Association— are also proposing alternative energy sources for the power companies and economic development programs for the tribes to cushion the impact of closing the mine and the power plant.

Roger Clark of the Grand Canyon Trust said Southern California Edison and the other plant owners would be eligible for as much as $50 million a year in pollution credits when the Mohave plant closed. He added that the utilities should send some of that money to the Hopi and Navajo as compensation.

The plant owners delayed the needed investment in Mohave in part because they had no assurance that Peabody and the tribes would agree on water and coal issues that would keep a reliable source of fuel coming to the plant over the next 20 years.

Southern California Edison has acknowledged that the Mohave plant is a serious polluter and is seeking cleaner alternatives. This month it announced that it was opening a natural-gas-fueled plant in California to replace two-thirds of the generating capacity lost with Mohave.

A poor region assesses the cost of cleaning up the environment.

And the tribes have fought among themselves for a generation over the wisdom of the coal agreement and the use of the water beneath their lands to transport the coal to Mohave. In an unusual process, the coal is ground into fine particles and mixed with water to form a slurry, which is carried by underground pipeline from Black Mesa to Mohave, where it is dried in large centrifuges and then burned to produce electricity.

The process uses 1.2 billion gallons of water a year from a water table known as the Navajo Aquifer, one of the highest-quality sources of water in the arid West. Some tribal leaders said sacred streams and springs had dried up because of the mine's water use and called its closing an undisguised blessing.

''Peabody has done us a favor by putting us in this situation,'' said Vernon Masayesva, 66, former Hopi chairman and longtime mine opponent. He said he sympathized with the workers, but added, ''It's time for us to cut the umbilical cord to the company store.''

Mr. Masayesva said that as a young man in the 1960's he listened to Hopi elders discussing the proposed mining of the coal beneath the Black Mesa, which gets its name from the low-slung pinyon trees that from a distance make the top of the 6,000-foot mesa look black. He said the elders believed that the coal could be of lasting value to the tribe, if mined at the right time, in the right way and for the right purpose.

But Mr. Masayesva said the agreements the Hopi and the Navajo struck with Peabody and the federal government were poor. ''We should have waited until we were educated, until we had our own hydrologists, our own engineers, our own lawyers and economists,'' he said.

He said the mining had been destructive and wasteful, to the land and to the water. ''Wasting water is criminal in our culture,'' he said. ''It is the tribe's covenant with the earth, and we broke it.''

Last, he said, the coal has been used for the wrong purpose. Rather than enriching the lives of all tribal members and contributing to a sustainable way of life, it is used to light the casinos of Las Vegas and heat the hot tubs of Los Angeles, he said.

''The benefits to the Hopi have been not much and not worth the price,'' he said. ''It's time for us to get aggressive and get smart about our own resources.''

Getting to Yes

Persuading the public about the need for affordable housing is a good first step.

My mother-in-law is a 72-year-old immigrant from the Philippines.

JAMES B. GOODNO

She spent her first decade or so in this country moving between relatives' houses, caring for children, preparing meals, and keeping house. In her late 60s, she finally became eager to live on her own. But market-rate housing in the San Francisco Bay Area was out of reach.

So, my wife's mother did what a growing number of elderly, low-income, and special-needs home hunters do: She put her name on waiting lists for subsidized senior housing in several East Bay communities. Then she waited, moving in with my sister-in-law and her husband and a college-aged grandson.

This story is not unusual. Low-cost housing providers maintain long waiting lists. Some of those lists are closed for years because the gap between supply and demand is so great. The problem occurs in small towns, prosperous suburbs, and big cities—and in every region of the nation.

"We have the same number of people on our waiting lists as we have total units," says Scott Minton, executive director of the Housing Opportunities Commission of Montgomery County in Maryland, the housing authority in that suburban Washington, D.C., county. The commission owns, manages, or has financed 23,649 housing units, and virtually all of them are occupied.

Despite the current shortfall, Montgomery County is something of a model for suburban affordable housing development. The county has long invested in affordable housing and has used local ordinances to get affordable units built by private developers. Today, smart growth is a goal as well, and new developments often are medium- to high-density, mixed-income complexes close to rail stations. But affordable housing has also met obstacles in the form of local opposition to higher density development, limited resources, and—for a time—a planning board that frowned on multifamily housing.

In Montgomery County and elsewhere, building affordable housing always involves politics. Selling public officials and their constituents on the importance of good housing policy is often just the first step towards selling good housing practices. In Montgomery County, it took the leadership of the county council,

the creation of a broad alliance of housing advocates, and the appointment of a pro-housing planning commission to clear a political logjam from the planning and permitting process.

My mother-in-law was lucky. Although neighborhood resistance to affordable housing is not unknown in Berkeley, the city does fairly well at getting affordable housing built. A pair of experienced affordable housing developers is active throughout Berkeley, and the city council is solidly behind the effort. Berkeley has also used density bonuses to add to its stock of units. As a result, Nanay, as Filipinos often call their mothers, started to get offers of units after nine months on the lists, and after 12 months the right apartment opened up. She moved in quickly.

Flawed policy

The wait for affordable housing varies from community to community, but in general it is longer for families and needy groups (the very poor, the chronically homeless, certain special-needs populations, and former convicts) than it is for the elderly or moderate-income workers.

For all these groups, the gap between income and housing costs is too wide. Economists call this gap a market failure. The problem is compounded by a political or social failure to respond well to the underlying economic problem.

National policy has allowed state and local governments the flexibility to design the appropriate response to unique problems, but federal financial support for affordable housing has failed to meet demand for more than three decades. "There's been a healthy amount of letting local flowers bloom," says Rolf Pendall, AICP, planning professor at Cornell University who has studied affordable housing policy for the Brookings Institution, "but not enough federal fertilizer to encourage growth."

Louisville, Kentucky, provides a case in point. It has used the federal HOPE VI program creatively and well, but questionable national support for the Department of Housing and Urban Development program casts doubt on the extent of the replicability of its efforts.

Fairness, Jersey Style

Ever since its highest court began issuing a series of sweeping decisions in the 1970s, New Jersey has been considered a national leader in the effort to build affordable housing. But for two decades, a controversial policy has gained popularity—one that allows richer communities to transfer their housing obligations to poorer towns.

Earlier this year, a coalition of religious leaders, environmentalists, and regional planners struck a blow against these regional contribution agreements—a tool that critics say reinforces racial segregation and helps to keep impoverished minorities in the inner cities. The group persuaded a relatively poor town to reject the housing units (and cash transfer) offered by a wealthy town in the same region.

Some background: In 1985, with many towns in open rebellion over the New Jersey Supreme Court's second affordable housing decision—known as *Mount Laurel II*—the legislature fashioned a compromise aimed at wresting the matter from the courts. It established a state agency, the Council on Affordable Housing, to oversee local housing plans. Towns that agreed to participate were given immunity from builders' lawsuits.

The council reduced by half the number of units for low- and moderate-income families that the courts had identified as a target. It also introduced a number of rules that the towns accepted—and that housing advocates considered loopholes. One of the most hotly debated was the rule covering regional contribution agreements, which allow towns to pay other jurisdictions—most often financially strapped cities—to build up to half of their required units.

In the years since the council was established, 36,698 affordable housing units have been built in New Jersey. An additional 9,792 units have been transferred from suburbs to cities—but some critics say that the price per unit was so low that many fewer units were actually built. Some $200 million changed hands in roughly 175 regional contribution agreement deals.

In a blistering speech last year at Princeton University, state assembly majority leader Joseph Roberts, one of South Jersey's most powerful politicians, ripped the agreements for fostering segregation. His speech came a year after advocates had asked the state supreme court to bar the use of the agreements—and the court had refused.

Supporters of the agreements note that cities, with a disproportionate number of poor people and decreasing federal assistance, desperately need the housing dollars. Many urban mayors have refused to discuss the issue with members of the New Jersey Regional Coalition, which lobbied behind the scenes to stop communities from entering into such deals.

The coalition won its first big battle earlier this year. In January, the wealthy Philadelphia suburb of Medford (pop. 23,600) in Burlington County, New Jersey, offered the gritty, working-class town of Pennsauken (pop. 35,600) some $2.9 million to assume 117 units of affordable housing. After fierce internal debate—and prodding from the regional coalition—Pennsauken rejected the offer.

"Morally, we might have been allowing Medford to shirk their responsibility," says Mayor Jack Killion. "But we could have really used the cash."

The coalition argues that building more affordable housing units in poor towns further concentrates poverty: It became aware of the pending deal because it was already pushing for more integration in Pennsauken, which has been suffering the effects of white flight largely because of its proximity to Camden, the state's poorest city.

Medford promptly moved on to the struggling town of Glassboro (pop. 19,200), which accepted the money. "The fact of the matter is that this is a legal approach to helping towns meet their obligations," says Medford township manager Alan Felt. "Towns that are receptive see it as a means of improving their housing stock, and that's fine."

Members of the regional coalition concede that the Pennsauken case was mainly a symbolic victory. They say it is evidence, however, that some people in New Jersey are changing their minds about the regional contribution agreements and what they represent.

In doing its research, the group worked with regional planning advocates—people like former Minnesota legislator Myron Orfield and David Rusk, the former mayor of Albuquerque. Its maps highlighted how the regional agreements had helped move affordable units out of wealthy communities and into poorer ones.

Coalition organizer Paul Scully says those maps have helped to make the case that the agreements are hurting some towns mid helping others—and that they should be abolished. He adds that the agreements are merely one of many state policies that work to preserve the status quo. But he also notes that people living at the edge of poverty are beginning to recognize the implications.

"Any town can go under," he says. "White flight can be rapidly triggered, and it is debilitating to a community."

Steve Chambers

Chambers is a reporter with the *Star-Ledger* in Newark, New Jersey.

Generally, HOPE VI has allowed local housing authorities to replace older, deteriorated housing projects with human-scale, often mixed-income housing, but critics have decried it for displacing poor residents and contributing to gentrification. When Louisville officials, planners, and housing specialists looked at HOPE VI, however, they saw a tool that could be used to replace a pair of 1940s housing projects while ensuring new housing for all the project residents—and for revitalizing several neighborhoods at the same time.

The city planning department and the local housing authority did a number of things right from the beginning, starting with the Park DuValle Revitalization. Early on, authorities decided to replace all the low-income units either on-site or in the neighborhood and to keep track of temporarily displaced residents. These issues have been problems in HOPE VI projects elsewhere.

Planners also combined HOPE VI's preference for new urbanist type development with a commitment to community planning. The planning process offered residents of the existing housing projects and the surrounding community numerous ways to get involved. Launched in 1995 and nearing completion at an estimated cost of $200 million (50 percent public funds, including $20 million in HOPE VI money, plus 50 percent private financing), Park DuValle will provide 1,213 units.

Louisville's second HOPE VI project, the Clarksdale Revitalization project, will use $40 million in HOPE VI funds (20 percent of the $200 million total project cost). When completed, the complex will encompass the old public housing site and off-site housing in surrounding neighborhoods. The old project housing will be torn down and replaced by a mixture of housing options designed to blend into the neighborhood. Amenities will include parks and commercial development.

Charles Cash, an architect who heads Louisville Metro Planning and Design Services, the city planning department, says the projects have succeeded for a number of reasons: The mayor has been a strong advocate of housing as a tool for neighborhood revitalization; various government entities have worked cooperatively on the projects; and neighborhood involvement has resulted in community buy-in and in planning and design that addresses community concerns. The end result, according to Cash, is quality housing for low- and moderate-income households, increased home ownership, and stronger communities.

It may be difficult to replicate Louisville's success. The Bush administration's fiscal 2006 budget zeroed out HOPE VI funding as part of a broader proposal to reduce and restructure federal support for affordable housing and community development. Congress appears likely to restore funding at somewhere between $60 million (the House-approved amount) and $150 million (the amount approved by the Senate Appropriations Committee) for the year. Fiscal 2005 funding was $144 million.

This is just one skirmish in the political battle that has raged on Capitol Hill since this spring, when the Bush administration proposed consolidating a variety of federal housing and community development programs within the Department of Commerce (most are currently run by HUD) and slashing or eliminating funding for several programs, including the widely used Community Development Block Grant program.

As of this writing, housing and community development advocates had done fairly well in staving off the shift to the Department of Commerce, persuading the House and the Senate committee to commit more than $4 billion in CDBG funding, and holding off the most severe cuts to other HUD programs. (The full Senate was expected to vote on the budget after its August recess.)

This victory reflects local officials' preference for the current menu of programs—and for HUD'S continued administration. But it's only a partial victory. The primary goal of the nation's affordable housing advocates—a major increase in federal funding for affordable housing development, perhaps through an affordable housing trust fund—remains a distant vision. And until then, much of the nitty-gritty policy work will take place on the state and local level.

States weigh in

California often gets credit for creating a climate conducive to affordable housing development. The state has a number of tools that help affordable housing to get built. State law mandates that local governments offer density bonuses of up to 35 percent, based on the percentage of affordable units in a development. It also exempts certain affordable housing projects from state environmental impact procedures and requires localities to streamline permitting on affordable housing development. In 2002, by a margin of 58 to 42 percent, California voters approved Proposition 46, a $2.1 billion affordable housing bond.

But success hasn't been complete. Rising costs and the raiding of Proposition 46 funds to close the state's budget gap have limited the impact of the bond. A recent *Sacramento Bee* investigation noted that Proposition 46 covers just 27 percent of costs for each rental housing project it supports, rather than the earlier estimate of 35 to 40 percent.

Kevin Zwick, housing development director for Berkeley's Affordable Housing Associates, a nonprofit developer active throughout the Bay Area, suggests another reason for the lag in building affordable units. "Generally, in California, people are more supportive of affordable housing the more theoretical it is," he says. Support for a bond measure doesn't necessarily translate into support for a housing development next door.

California may need the kind of stick being used in Massachusetts, which has a long history of supporting affordable housing. The Massachusetts Department of Housing and Community Development continues to provide financial support, management oversight, and design, construction, and development services to local housing authorities. Massachusetts also has a state affordable housing trust fund (recapitalization is currently being debated in the statehouse), and its primary regulatory tool for leveraging affordable housing where demand is greatest—in suburban communities with less than 10 percent of affordable housing stock—dates to 1969. Chapter 40B of the state's general laws (the state's well-known anti-snob zoning statute) allows a state board to override local zoning to allow the development of affordable housing.

Even Massachusetts has a housing crunch, however. The state has long depended on its status as the nation's education capital to attract brainy young adults and investment. But the high cost of housing is driving these young people away, says Aaron Gornstein, executive director of the Citizens Housing and Planning Association in Boston. "Starter homes in the suburbs simply don't exist," he says. "More and more young people don't see buying a home as an option, so the business community is very concerned about attracting and holding employees."

As a regulatory approach, 40B is effective. According to Gornstein, the law resulted in the construction of more than 35,000 units (22,000 reserved for people earning less than 80 percent of median income) between 1970 and 2004.

But even a statewide requirement may not suffice. "You can win the battle but lose the war," says Gornstein. "With 40B there is still a process to go through, negotiating with neighbors, negotiating with the town. If you act like a bully, it undermines support for affordable housing in the long run."

My Town Comes to Terms with Affordable Housing

I live in a suburb of Chicago where the median house price is $850,000. I'm a village trustee and until two years ago would have described our village government process as "consensus." But that was before the June 2003 passage of the Illinois Affordable Housing and Appeal Act. All hell has broken loose since then.

The Illinois law applies to communities with less than 10 percent of its housing units in the affordable category—defined as affordable for those earning 80 to 120 percent of the local area median income (about $57,000 for a family of four). Those communities were to adopt a plan by April 2005 indicating how they would go about achieving the 10 percent goal.

For our built-out village of 8,700 people, 3,200 housing units, and only 3.4 percent affordable housing, that meant finding ways to add close to 300 units of affordable housing. If a developer came to the village with an affordable housing project and the board turned him down, we could be taken before a "super-zoning" board in Springfield. The board could override a rejection, if it were found that we refused the developer because of a bias against affordable housing.

It seemed obvious that the village couldn't add 300 units. Teardown replacements are the only new construction here, our zoning precludes buildings taller than three stories, and the village itself owns very little land, all of it used. The trustees decided that our strategy would be to show the state our willingness to add what we could. Before the law passed, we scheduled a public meeting with a housing advocate and a local college professor to explain its provisions.

I shouldn't have been surprised at the outcome, but in fact, I was. The audience was so rude that the professor was unable to give his presentation and the advocate was peppered with questions about why this law was even considered. This should have been a hint about what was to come.

When the state law passed, the village president appointed me co-chair of a newly created affordable housing task force, a group of 15 that also included two homebuilders (who build outside the community), the president and former president of the local League of Women Voters chapter, four attorneys—one of whom served both as a trustee and co-chair of the task force—three long-time residents, a planning consultant, and a township official.

The first two meetings were informal and low key. We sat around a table, didn't follow strict procedure, and began to talk of how to structure our investigation. At least three members—all of them affordable housing supporters—openly discussed the impossibility of compliance with the law: The land in town is too expensive, they said, and there just wasn't room for the number of units required. But they were willing to look into the issues.

We should have been prepared for trouble when two opponents of affordable housing showed up at the second task force meeting. One was a founding member of an area wide organization that had worked against the law. The other had the fixed idea that the law was a backhanded way of forcing Section 8 housing on the suburbs. She later ran unsuccessfully against our incumbent state legislator, who had supported the law.

At the village board meeting held in August 2003, the room was filled with screaming, arm-waving opponents. They personally attacked those who had expressed an interest in following the law, adopting a housing plan, and trying to build more affordable housing units in the village-four trustees, including me, and a state legislator who had come to watch. Fears spilled out: Parks would be filled with multistory buildings, the state board would overturn our zoning, our tranquil village would be transformed overnight.

Lines were drawn very quickly. Opponents said that the village should ignore the law. Proponents responded by saying we should follow the law and that the law required a plan, not actual units. We also noted that no parks would be taken—a developer needed to own the land before offering any housing plan and we assumed that the park district wouldn't sell. We also pointed out that affordable units could benefit village employees and seniors.

There was no middle ground; civility was out the window. Eventually, the task force assumed a more formal manner, with the members sitting on a raised platform. Meetings were taped and shown on cable television, as were village board meetings.

As the heat rose, my co-chair invited our state senators to attend a public meeting. Later, the village president appointed him to lead a legislative action committee to recommend changes in the law. The aim was to secure our zoning and to protect the village if a case came before the state zoning board (where the appeal would be heard, and so on).

Ultimately, the village board did adopt a plan in time for the law's compliance deadline this April. The plan directs the planning and zoning commissions and the village board to examine existing codes and ordinances to make sure there are no barriers to affordable housing. It makes no promise of government subsidy. This year, too, the legislature passed amendments to the law that parallel what the legislative action committee recommended.

It may sound as if we worked out our problems, but the uproar seriously divided our community. The village president's pro-affordable housing attitude (among other issues) worked against him; he wasn't re-slated for office, and he unhappily retired. My co-chair ran for re-election and lost. It's unlikely that I will be slated for a second term as village trustee. Few people have come forward publicly to support affordable housing in the village, although one or two women have told me to "hang tight" on the issue.

Village residents have parted ways before—on home rule, tax increment financing, and school referendums. But rarely have we seen such vitriol, such nastiness both in person and in the local newspaper. I don't think my village differs from others that are equally affluent and lack affordable housing. For me, this story proves how hard it is to implement affordable housing policies—and how hard it is to change people's minds. But it also shows how this issue rips towns down to the bone, whether because people fear that their property values will decline, or because they fear anyone different from themselves. I just know that I don't wish this experience on any other public official.

Ellen Shubart

Shubart is manager of the Campaign for Sensible Growth at the Metropolitan Planning Council in Chicago. She has lived in Glencoe, Illinois, for 33 years.

Gornstein advises affordable housing developers in Massachusetts to tread lightly and build local support. His model is Bedford, a suburb of Boston, which recently passed the 10 percent affordable goal. Bedford did what needs to be done: "long-term commitment from political leadership and active citizens."

"It takes a critical mass of local people" to win support, he adds. "They may be outnumbered at first, but persistence has paid off."

"If a strong local group is involved, it can make for a better, non-confrontational process, and that's what we hope to achieve with the suburban initiative," adds Mathew Thall, senior program director with the Local Initiatives Support Corporation in greater Boston. LISC is working to strengthen housing groups in the city's suburbs. "Groups that take community organizing seriously have been able to build more housing with less opposition."

NIMBYs or not

How important is "not in my backyard" opposition when affordable housing is at issue?

"There is no such thing as a NIMBY," says Arthur Sullivan, program manager for ARCH Housing, a coalition of city and county governments that supports the production of affordable housing in suburban Seattle. Sullivan has successfully navigated the shoals of local politics in some of the country's most affluent and sophisticated communities, leading efforts to produce low- and moderate-income family housing, senior housing, special-needs housing, and transitional housing for people facing homelessness. And he's emphatic: To think of neighbors of a project as NIMBYs and their concerns as obstructionist is bad politics.

Many people involved in affordable housing development recommend a straightforward approach to working with neighbors. Be honest, they say, and show willingness to address legitimate concerns. Engage neighbors and members of the broader community through public meetings, door-to-door canvassing, and private discussions. Tours of existing developments, meetings with representatives of management companies, and discussions with architects and planners involved in a project can help break down rumors and myths.

"We can explain what contextual design is," says Joe Geller, a landscape architect and former selectman in Brookline, Massachusetts. In New England's history-rich landscape, Geller notes, neighborhood complaints about design can have a big impact on decision makers. "Anything you can do to make housing look like the neighborhood will make it easier to win local support."

When possible, the experts say, it's best to get a jump on community engagement before projects are on the drawing board.

Planner Troy Galloway, AICP, heads the community development department in Bentonville, Arkansas, a fast growing town that's best known as the headquarters of Wal-Mart. Bentonville hopes to address affordable housing concerns before the issue explodes, "The problem is just beginning; that's why we're trying to get our arms around it now," says Galloway.

Civic leaders and planners in Bentonville recognize the need to increase density in order to get more affordable units built.

Recently, they managed to tie the discussion of affordability to studies of downtown redevelopment. In public meetings, a local architect showed how traditional neighborhood design—and relatively high density—could enhance the historic downtown. A difference was drawn between affordable and cheap—and the notion seems to be selling. "There's been wide acceptance of the need [for more housing] and for tying it to the whole idea of revitalizing downtown," says Galloway.

The lesson from these and other experiences is that patience and compromise must be part of the political tool kit. In some cases, though, compromise is impossible. One developer working in the Northwest tells the story of a neighboring property owner who battled an affordable housing project he is developing in Montana after a deal to sell her land for the project collapsed.

Then there are cases—like one in California—that fit the classic NIMBY definition. Neighborhood objections gained little traction in 1999, when Resources for Community Development, an affordable housing developer in Berkeley, opened 16 units of housing for disabled residents on Sacramento Street.

But just a year later, when Affordable Housing Associates bought a neighboring property with the intention of building a 40-unit senior housing project, the neighborhood organization pulled out all the stops. It battled before local commissions, the city council, and in court.

Among other things, the group demanded that the city prepare an environmental impact report on the low-rise, infill project. The developer ultimately won, and construction started this May, but the experience conveyed some lessons in hardball politics.

"This was not typical of Berkeley," says AHA's Zwick. "It required us to think differently and to reframe the issue as a regional or community-wide issue. Affordable housing is an issue for the entire community and who should get a say is broader than a project's immediate neighbors." The project moved ahead despite fierce opposition because "the whole city came together behind it: environmentalists, seniors, business, the local council member," he says.

Building local support is an essential part of any affordable housing campaign, especially in suburban areas that may be unreceptive to affordable housing. In Montgomery County, political leaders, planning commissioners, and housing advocates say it's been very important to build broad support for affordable housing to move the issue ahead.

"Decision makers need to know there is a constituency for affordable housing if they're going to approve controversial projects," says Steve Silverman, a Montgomery County council member and housing advocate.

Refraining the issue?

The structure of power has an influence on affordable housing decision making. In Maryland, county government is the focal point of land-use politics. Plans are drafted at the county level, permits are issued there, and policies crafted. This results in decisions being made by elected officials with some sense of regional responsibility.

Massachusetts, on the other hand, has a long tradition of local self-rule, and decisions are made by each individual town. This frequently means the town as a whole at the annual town meeting. This living relic of an era of direct democracy has many positive attributes, but it also makes changing zoning for affordable housing a tough sell.

No matter what decision-making body is involved, one political fact remains remarkably consistent from place to place: The key task of affordable-housing advocates is to build public support for affordable-housing financing and development. And in recent years, it's become popular to talk about reframing the issue

"We need to see affordable housing as part of our infrastructure rather than as a social program that's nice but not essential," says Cornell's Pendall. "We need to see affordable housing as being as essential as water, sewers, and parks. We need to recognize the reality that affordable housing is essential to our regional economies."

Workforce housing is one of the buzzwords in this discussion. In Montgomery County, the county government is working on a series of strategies aimed at increasing the amount of housing affordable to teachers, police, fire fighters, and young professionals. The same thing is happening around the country. "This is a working person's problem," says Paul Williams, director of LISC programs in Minneapolis-St. Paul. "This is the message people are bringing to the suburbs."

In the Chicago area, Housing Illinois—part of the Chicago Rehab Network—decided to focus on workforce housing in a public relations campaign aimed at increasing awareness of affordable housing issues. "We have to ask, what leverage points are there to get people to change their minds?" says Hoy McConnell, a former advertising executive who headed the effort. "People need to be convinced that it would benefit them to have affordable housing in their community."

McConnell's group discovered that people want to know who is going to live in the affordable housing, what the housing is going to look like, and how well it will be maintained. In the Chicago suburbs, Housing Illinois found numerous misconceptions about affordable housing. "You say 'affordable housing' in Chicago, they say 'Cabrini-Green,'" McConnell says, referring to Chicago's notoriously impoverished and crime ridden housing project (now partly replaced by a HOPE VI development).

In response, Housing Illinois organized an advertising and public relations campaign around the issue of housing for teachers, medical workers, firefighters, and police officers. The pitch appeared in television and newspaper advertisements and in pamphlets and other handouts.

The campaign is ongoing, and while its impact has not yet been evaluated, McConnell says anecdotal evidence suggests a positive reaction. This is due, he believes, to the perception that the people who are being shown to need affordable housing opportunities "add to the fabric of the community." (For another view of the Illinois affordable housing requirement, see the accompanying sidebar, "My Town Comes to Terms With Affordable Housing.")

Common sense and anecdotal evidence from a variety of places in the country suggest that using pillars of the community—public safety officers, health care workers, and teachers—as representatives of the market for affordable housing makes political sense. Clearly, if the folks who make a community function can't afford to live in it, something is wrong.

But the approach has a drawback: It allows a community to imagine it is doing its part to meet the affordable housing challenge while it continues to ignore the plight of the neediest and those low-wage workers who make a community tick but don't have the sex appeal or respectability of the poster children: janitors, housekeepers, gardeners, day laborers, and other service workers.

Montgomery County is trying to get it right by layering workforce housing programs on top of existing affordable housing programs and by including a mix of incomes in various developments: affordable, workforce, and market. They are trying to make sure that regulatory, incentive, and funding programs benefit the less glamorous of our housing needy.

Resources

Advocates. Housing Opportunities Commission of Montgomery County: www.hocmc.org. Clarksdale Hope VI Revitalization: www.hal1.org. Click on the "Hope VI" link. Affordable Housing Advocates: www.housingadvocates.org. ARCH Housing: www.archhousing.org. Housing Illinois: www.chicagorehab.org.

JIM GOODNO is *Planning's* contributing editor.

UNIT 7

International Public Policy and Administration

Unit Selections

Key Points to Consider

- Discuss the history and the evolution of urban planning in China. Identify and discuss some of the major challenges that the Chinese face as they plan for their future.

- What are some of the major uses and benefits of the British Community Communication Network?

- Identify and discuss some of the major things that the government of South Africa has done in its efforts to curb corruption in that country.

- Identify and discuss some of the ways in which the Dutch provide quality housing for its citizens. Also discuss how the Dutch go about national planning. Do you agree or disagree with the way the Dutch conduct their planning and housing activities? Why or why not? Also, are there any lessons that Americans can learn from the Dutch in these areas?

Student Web Site

www.mhcls.com/online

Internet References

Further information regarding these Web sites may be found in this book's preface or online.

Division for Public Administration and Development Management
http://www.unpan.org/dpepa.asp

European Group of Public Administration (EGPA)
http://www.iiasiisa.be/egpa/agacc.htm

Governments on the WWW
http://www.gksoft.com/govt/en/

Institute of Public Administration of Canada (IPAC)
http://www.ipaciapc.ca

Latin American Center for Development Administration (CLAD)
http://www.clad.org.ve/siare/index.htm

Section on International and Comparative Administration (SICA)
http://www.uncc.edu/stwalker/sica/

UNPAN
http://www.unpan.org

The articles in this unit look at public administration and public policy issues around the world and try to provide some comparative information for public managers in the United States in areas such as housing, urban planning, communications technology, and ethics/values.

Professional planning in China is relatively new but has strong historical roots. According to the first article, planning efforts in China will concentrate on a variety of topics such as environmental protection, urban design, economic development, and physical development. Daniel Benjamin Abramson, in his article *Urban Planning in China: Continuity and Change*, also reviews the planning history of China and predicts that politics and the bureaucracy will continue to exert significant influence over the Chinese planning process.

The British have developed a new communications technology to help local officials get important information to constituents accurately and conveniently. The technology is known as the Community Communication Network (CCN). It consists of plasma video screens placed in a variety of public and private venues. The article *The Community Communication Network: New Technology for Public Engagement* by Louis Bezich reviews the advantages of building and locating these screens throughout a city.

The Republic of South Africa has enacted a variety of new measures in an effort to curb public sector corruption in that country. The authors I. W. Ferreira and M.S. Bayat, in their article *Curbing Corruption in the Republic of South Africa,* discuss methods such as ethics codes, whistle-blowing ordinances, and training initiatives that are making public officials more aware of the need for ethical conduct in their public dealings.

How the Dutch Do Housing, by Jane Holtz Kay, states that national planning is required not just for housing but also for the conservation of water, land, infrastructure, and forests. Such national planning is essential to Holland's existence and accounts for its progressive reputation. According to the author, the Netherlands does have something to offer to other countries in the way of excellent planning practices in all of these areas.

Urban Planning in China

Continuity and Change

Although professional planning in China is relatively new, Chinese urban planning has roots in governance practices that predate both Mao and the current era of market-oriented reform. Government and social responses to the unprecedented contradictions caused by current reforms suggest some likely future directions for planning in China. I expect the discipline of planning will diversify from the current emphasis on enabling economic growth to include a stronger regulatory function, greater emphasis on maintaining environmental quality, and stronger analytical, communicative, and advocacy roles. Efforts to revive and strengthen property rights and reformulate urban communities will affect planning practice, but I expect politics to be more influential than institutional or bureaucratic changes.

Daniel Benjamin Abramson

Chinese cities expanded and redeveloped at an astounding rate during the past two decades. The consequent rise in prices for energy and basic building materials, and the impacts on the environment and on global consumption, production, and trading patterns all became subjects for broad popular discussion (Fallows, 2005; Friedman, 2005; Liu & Diamond, 2005; Newman, 2005). Scholarship on Chinese urbanization grew in concert with the cities it described.[1] Most of it focused on examples of the transition from a planned to a market economy or of globalization (see, e.g., Bian & Logan, 1996; Logan, 2002; Ma & Wu, 2005; F. Wu, 2002a, 2002b, 2003a, 2003b, 2004; Wu & Yeh, 1999; T. Zhang, 2002b; Jieming Zhu, 2004). By contrast, Friedmann (2005) argued that China's urbanization is "an evolutionary process that is driven from within," as the country "perforce develops out of its own resources, traditions, and civilizational genius" (pp. xvi–xvii). Urban change in China is neither ahistorical nor historically deterministic. And it is both a local and a global phenomenon.

China's system of urban planning and governance, like urban planning everywhere, applies both conventional and experimental practices to current problems, within constraints created by existing institutions and values that are not always flexible. Any analysis of Chinese urban planning and its prospects must take historic conditions and motives of development into account. The challenge is to identify the pressures and opportunities facing Chinese urban development and planning as Chinese society navigates the global market and the Chinese government seeks to retain legitimacy after two centuries of profound deprivation and disorder.

This article focuses on planning-related institutions and values in China that appear particularly open to change, and anticipates which innovations have the best chance of guiding development in a positive direction. Of course, how the term "positive" is defined, and by whom, is resolvable only by political means, not by technical expertise (Ng & Wu, 1997). For example, Chinese planning discourse does not present the public good or social justice as normative goals of planning, and distinctions between public and private interests generally are not well articulated (Leaf, 1998). Because the Communist Party is defined as the champion of social justice, planning, as an arm of the Party-state, is assumed to advance the public good and follow the principles of social justice. In fact, where the state fails to pursue this mission, the technocratic quality of planning allows it to become a tool for abuse. Nevertheless, as diversity increases among socioeconomic strata and interests in Chinese society and even among levels of government, defining and defending the public good becomes a more and more obvious problem. These trends in society and the planning discipline lead to questioning the definition of "development," in both academic and popular circles. In response, Chinese urban planning is developing new expertise.

Yet change is incremental and difficult to predict, for a number of reasons. Questioning the value or manner of development challenges the state's political legitimacy, including both central and local Chinese Communist Party and government priorities and successes. Moreover, the state's own market-oriented rhetoric sometimes conflicts with other, earlier, sources of state legitimacy, weakening efforts to institutionalize planning reforms. Finally, in order to implement those market-oriented reforms on which the Party does agree, the state has decentralized much of its formal decision-making mechanisms, creating "local corporatist states" that can both encourage and obstruct planning progress, depending on what level of government initiates the innovation (Oi, 1995).

I describe how urban planning in China reflects both the persistence of historical practices and the adoption of new ones. Many emerging conflicts find expression in terms that are relatively new to the discourse of planning in China: environmental sustainability; individual and collective rights; property and community. These concepts nevertheless have broader historical relevance in China, and provide a basis for comparing Chinese practice to that elsewhere. I use an example from one city where I have watched this evolution over the course of 12 years. In the following section I outline historical practices that remain relevant to contemporary urban planning and governance, especially to the maintenance of state legitimacy and social control.

China's Urban Planning Legacy

The maintenance of political legitimacy may be one of the oldest motives for urban planning in China. Although China's society as a whole is urbanizing only now, its large cities and tradition of city planning are very old. Before the urbanization of the West in the 19th century, most large cities were in Asia, and China's dominance among these extended back nearly two millennia (Chandler, 1987). Four of the 10 largest cities in the world in the early 16th century were Chinese, and Beijing was the world's largest city in both 1500 and 1800. The largest cities in China were typically administrative capitals, not purely commercial centers, and were planned according to principles that legitimated the state through ritual and cosmology (Meyer, 1991; Wheatley, 1971; Wright, 1977; Jianfei Zhu, 2004; Zhu & Kwok, 1997). China's premodern planned megacities did not mean China was an urban society in a modern or economic sense, but rather that the state was powerful enough to unify its territory and mobilize its population, moving whole cities if necessary, and recreating familiar cityscapes in new locations (Steinhardt, 1990, p. 10).

Each new dynasty would essentially build a new capital, and it was not uncommon in the earlier dynasties to move capitals from one site to another to deal with immediate military or political challenges, or floods or changes in riverbeds. Joseph Rykwert has noted that "none of the ancient peoples—except the Egyptians perhaps—practised such changes as frequently" (1976, p. 184). At their most planned, these cities were organized according to social rank and resembled military camps more than market places (Heng, 1999). The planning of capital cities (and indeed the *drawing* of the plan) itself helped legitimate newly established dynasties. Conformance to a standard form of urban planning facilitated the creation of capitals from scratch, and lesser cities' conformance to planning principles symbolized imperial unity and power (Steinhardt, 1990, pp. 1–5).

Ancient Chinese planning is based on a canon of city layout that supposedly dates from the Zhou dynasty (11th to 3rd centuries BC), but should not be confused with the reality of Chinese cities on the ground. A number of empirical studies provide a more nuanced view of China's historically diverse urban geography and design (Gaubatz, 1996; Rowe, 1989; Skinner, Baker, & History E-Book Project, 1977; Y. Xu, 2000). The gap between canon and reality did indicate planning's symbolic importance, however, and dynasties justified planning decisions using precedent that existed only in the canon (Steinhardt, 1990, pp. ix–x).[2]

Given that planning conveyed legitimacy, the place of the market in China's traditional planning priorities was often problematic. The amount and distribution of space for market activity in Chinese cities fluctuated from period to period and dynasty to dynasty, as did the manner and degree of its regulation. Uniformity and regularity of urban space have been celebrated as an expression of state power and effectiveness in China since early times, often at the expense of commercial activity (see, e.g., Knechtges & Xiao, 1982, pp. 201–203). Nearly all dynasties (except the Song dynasty) established themselves through invasion, widespread rebellion, or victory in civil war, and then imposed sociospatial control on cities that loosened as the regime consolidated itself.[3]

These facts are not mere historical curiosities; they represent a legacy of practice that remains relevant to the state's modern struggles with civil war, the search for legitimacy, and conflicts between market impulses and popular mobilization. At the close of the last dynasty and into the Republican period in the early 20th century, cultural conservatives clung to traditional ritualistic planning methods (e.g., *feng shui*) more tightly than ever, and resisted innovative plans for fear that such departures would signal a wider breakdown in social and political order (M. Shi, 1993; L. Wang, 1963). By the end of the 20th century, of course, little remained of the specific principles of imperial city planning, but this ancient legacy persists in at least two general ways: first, in the conflict cities experience between their roles as local or regional economic centers and as administrative centers in a rigidly hierarchical system of national spatial government; second, in the hierarchical and cellular way that cities themselves are structured and designed, including the formation of urban communities and patterns of property disposition.

With respect to the former, cities in China have almost always served as seats of different levels of authority in the imperial or national hierarchy of administration (Skinner, 1977).[4] Not only do municipal governments have no autonomous legal authority outside this system, but there are no other forms of autonomous local jurisdiction either (e.g., comparable with school districts, water districts, port authorities, etc.). Historically, all rural areas were administered from a county-level urban center, which in turn answered either to a prefectural-level city or directly to the provincial government (which answered to the central government). This system remains in place today, and is so central to the governing structure of the country that it is rare for any city to be larger and more economically important than another city higher in the administrative hierarchy (Wong, 1997; see Figure 1).[5]

Recently, the administrative integration of countryside and cities has been strengthened by putting increasing numbers of counties under the jurisdiction of prefectural-level cities, to the point where most cities now administer a large rural hinterland (Chan, 1997).[6] However, this integration is of a top-down nature; population mobility between countryside and city has been severely restricted for most of the past half century by China's system of household registration (*hukou*), which has not only controlled the size of cities by assigning people to a specific res-

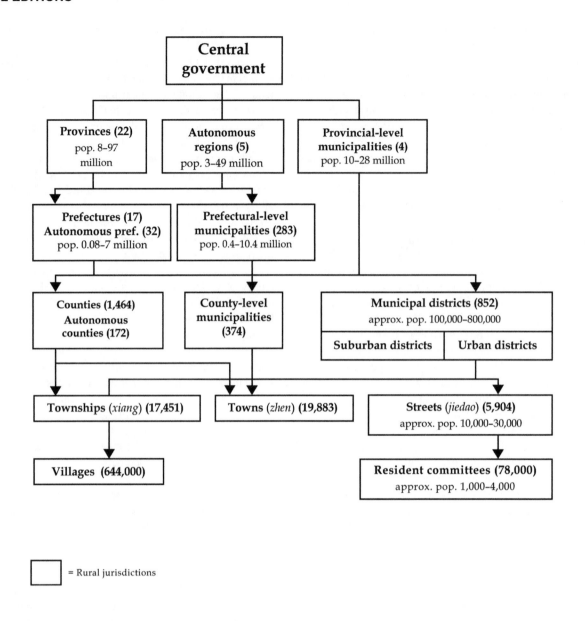

Figure 1. Hierachy of territorial administration in mainland China.

Source: People's Republic of China, Ministry of Civil Affairs, Department of Administrative Territorial Delineation and Place-naming, 2004.

Notes: "Autonomous" jurisdictions include a range of minority ethnic territories. Numbers in parentheses indicate the number of jurisdictions of a particular type, and are followed by the range of their population sizes.

idence in a particular city, but has also labeled people as either "rural" or "urban," designations that entail various privileges and restrictions (Chan, 1994). During the past two decades the *hukou* system has become increasingly irrelevant to labor mobility, but it continues to contribute to sociospatial inequality and it remains an important tool of state social control (F.-L. Wang, 2004). Another important consequence of Chinese cities' lack of legal autonomy is the central government's historic control of the location of commercial and industrial activities, and the conversion of rural land to other uses since 1949, although this control was always compromised by

power politics and has diminished in the transition to a market economy (Ding & Song, 2005; Fung, 1981).

There are also a number of historic patterns in how Chinese cities are internally structured and designed that persist into the present. The same administrative hierarchy that has bound cities into China's regional and national system of governance also extends below the municipal level down to urban districts, subdistricts or "streets" (*jiedao*, similar to wards in some American cities), and neighborhoods or "residents committees" (*jumin weiyuanhui*). Although hierarchies for administering urban space are found in many countries, the Chinese system is strikingly cellular (Gaubatz, 1995). Both premodern and modern Chinese cities have been organized to enable the government to monitor and mobilize urban populations, both by restricting residence and by making local communities responsible for their own internal law and order (Rowe, 1989; Wakeman, 1993; M. Wang, 2004). Until very recently, the very notion of "community" in China has been spatial. The word for community in Chinese is *shequ*, a compound of the characters for society/association/organization and for differentiate/region/area, or "society in a spatially defined area."

Premodern Chinese capital cities were divided into walled and patrolled wards (*fang*). With the establishment of the Manchu Qing dynasty capital in Beijing, for example, the Inner City was divided along social lines into large blocks assigned to different Banners, military units that maintained Manchu control over the empire and which became the basis of urban communities, with their own schools and local administration (Han, 1996; X. Li, 1995, p. 9). This cellularity broke down somewhat during the late Qing period and through the first half of the 20th century, but it was revived under Maoist socialism in the form of the work unit (*danwei*), which was a form of enclosed live-work community, often with complete educational, health, and recreational services (Bray, 2005; Lü & Perry, 1997). The physical layout of these communities and also of most new residential areas followed the Soviet model (the Chinese for "neighborhood unit," *xiao qu*, is a direct translation from the Russian *mikrorayon*), which itself evolved from housing in Weimar Germany in the 1920s (Bai, 1993, p. 32). Although China did use the neighborhood unit somewhat prior to 1949, it became the unvarying approach to all planned residential development afterwards (Lu, Rowe, & Zhang, 2001). In general, standardization in planning represents the state's ability to unify Chinese society following the century of turmoil that preceded the Communist Party's victory in 1949.

The work unit system under Mao worked in concert with the new restrictions on job choice and labor mobility, and with the replacement of the land market by state land allocation, to create cities with minimal commuting. However, state budgets were never adequate to house all urban residents in new work unit compounds, and therefore many urbanites still had to commute from crowded, unrehabilitated old neighborhoods to workplaces elsewhere in the city (G. Chen, 1994; W. Lu, 1994). Entire new cities, most notably those built as models of socialist production, as at Daqing, relied on premodern "traditional design ideals" and resembled military camps (Xie & Costa, 1991, pp. 281–286). Even after China again initiated urban land markets in the 1990s, the socialist planning and design standards that had evolved with the work unit system continued to influence the design of new residential areas, leaving the urban residential landscape dominated by gated communities (Abramson, 1997b; Huang, 2005).

Premodern Chinese urban structure also persists in the lack of an explicit cultural and legal notion of the public realm. While ownership of housing units (condominium-style), other fixed assets, and land use rights may be private, land itself is universally owned by the state. Private ownership of land, along with deeds, registries, contracts, and taxation systems, existed for centuries in China before all land came under the control of the state in the 1950s, but through much of China's history the state was assumed to have "ultimate ownership" or at least control of land (Clunas, 1996, pp. 26–27; Zelin, Ocko, & Gardella, 2004). Private homes were always subject to imperial restrictions and broad police powers that continue to the present. Resident committees retain rights to enter family compounds and mediate disputes between neighbors and even within families, and to represent the interests of the state on issues of public safety, public health, and family planning (Samuels, 1986, p. 61). Moreover, property use and disposition tended historically to be subject also to extensive informal and customary rules intended to maintain the integrity of extended families and clans and lineages, including requiring dividing property among all sons of a patriarch, providing space for ancestral worship, and allowing relatives and neighbors rights of first refusal in transactions (Clunas, 1996, pp. 200–201; Zelin et al., 2004, pp. 26–27). While few land use rights in large cities remain in the hands of private owners, most villages are still structured this way.

Public space, the complement of private space, was traditionally not a subject for architectural symbolism, nor was it the object of voluntary civic responsibility, except for temples and other spaces belonging to specific institutions but used informally for a variety of social activities (Clunas, 2004, p. 159; Y. Xu, 2000, pp. 191 ff.). In any case, spaces for informal gathering were not the subject of urban planning. Public parks and squares like Beijing's Tiananmen Square, the world's largest urban plaza, have appeared in China's cities only since the early 20th century, but their role in civil society is still disputed (Davis, Kraus, Naughton, & Perry, 1995; Feuchtwang, 2004; Wakeman, 1993). The public embellishments of China's cities today do not so much reflect civic pride as symbolize Modernist statism as described by James Scott (1998), and also hark back to periods of China's imperial history when planning practice favored symbolic structures and spaces at the expense of small-scale commercial activity and gathering places for a diverse citizenry.

Such priorities are reflected today in the sweeping away of informal markets; in the construction of remote, monumental municipal buildings surrounded by vast, empty plazas in nearly every city; in the attention given to energy- and water-wasting "nightscape" projects and wide expanses of grass; and local governments' efforts to use planning for propaganda (Broudehoux, 2004). Perhaps the most spectacular instance of this last is the Shanghai Urban Planning Exhibition Hall, next to the municipal government building in the heart of the city. In the lobby of the Hall, large bas-reliefs (in a heroic style reminiscent of much American public art during the New Deal) portray the demolition of old neighborhoods and the relocation of grateful residents and their modern home appliances to new apartment estates, when in fact such displacement is one of the most controversial aspects of urban policy in China today.

Historic preservation also fulfills many of the symbolic and legitimating functions of ancient planning. Urban heritage plans often aim to restore or copy the premodern ideal rather than preserve the historic reality (Abramson, 2001; Ke, 1991; Stille, 1998). The Maoist motto "let the past serve the present" applies not only to the planning of most capital cities in Chinese history, but also to contemporary preservation policy (Spence, 1992; Steinhardt, 1990, p. 1).

Professional Chinese planners and the public at large increasingly debate these problems. Both planners and the popular press now frequently criticize "political showcase projects" (*zhengji gongcheng*) as tasteless and wasteful of resources. Among the most recent examples is Beijing's hosting of a competition for the design of new buildings that would serve as "symbols of the city" (even though a number of such symbols already exist, including the Forbidden City, Tiananmen Square, the Temple of Heaven, the Summer Palace, etc.) In response, the official Xinhua News Agency published on the web a selection of caustic letters from the public calling the competition redundant, irrelevant, and wasteful (Fazhan Luntan [Development Forum], 2005).

Local leaders are primarily accountable to those above them rather than the people under their administration and they depend on symbolic projects for promotion. Nevertheless, such projects contradict other professed goals of the Party-state: increasingly to rely on the market to allocate resources, to downsize government, to conserve energy, to make communities self-reliant, and to privatize assets. The state continues to rely on hierarchical administration, cellular organization of communities, and ideological domination of public space to maintain social order and assert its legitimacy. Urban planning in China assists in these endeavors, but it also serves other ends that are more in conflict with its legacy.

Planning Challenges in Modern China

Urban planning as a profession in China today is inextricably linked to the national goal of market-oriented economic development, based on a Western-inspired definition of "modernization" and decentralized fiscal power. Planning practice in China fundamentally enables growth, especially export-oriented growth. It also is part of the reaction against Maoist principles of indigenous, self-sufficient, development. That approach to development was anti-urban and relied on a central command-control economy, and was deeply distrustful of professionalism in general. The rationalist tradition of professional planning that emerged in the West in the late 19th century also took root in 20th-century China, largely through the efforts of Republican-era municipal reformers and educators eager to modernize China's cities (Cook, 1998; M. Shi, 1993; Tsin, 2000). After 1949, the socialist regime adopted the Soviet practice of separating economic planning (*jihua*), carried out by the State Planning Commission, from physical/spatial planning (*guihua*), carried out by the Ministry of Construction. Though economic planning was considered more important, all forms of professional planning were made extremely difficult by consecutive political purges and campaigns (Fung, 1981, pp. 214–216; Ng & Wu, 1997, pp. 157–158).

Following Mao, Deng Xiaoping (called "The Chief Architect," in contrast to Mao's less technocratic sobriquet, "The Great Helmsman"), the Communist Party promoted physical

planning and especially architecture and engineering to make cities the engines of growth in a new export-oriented economy. In the early 1980s, municipal governments were given enhanced authority over rural hinterlands in a reformed hierarchy of administrative territories, as mentioned above. Additionally, formerly rural counties were promoted to "county-level cities" (Chan, 1997; see Figure 1) and the central government took responsibility for approving the development plans of a number of large cities well positioned to attract foreign investment, bypassing the provincial level.

All of these reforms gave cities significantly more leeway than previously to raise revenue, invest, and convert rural land to urban uses as they saw fit. Developers' "normal" business decisions were also freed from state oversight, beginning with those in urban residential districts, and tentative efforts were made to put housing units on the market (Canada Mortgage and Housing Corporation, 1996; Z. Lin, 1988, p. 3). In 1984, the State Council issued "Urban Planning Provisions" requiring all municipal and county governments to develop master plans (*zangti guihua*) to guide their physical development (State Council of the People's Republic of China, 1984). China's first City Planning Act was passed in 1989. By then, 96% of cities and 85% of county towns had prepared master plans, and the number of urban planners in the country had increased to 15,000 (Ng & Wu, 1997, p. 159).

The planning system that has emerged since the 1980s is very hierarchical, with the most conceptual plans prepared for large regions at the national and provincial levels, and increasingly detailed plans prepared at smaller scales by municipal, district, and project agencies. Typically, the central- and provincial-level plans have been made by provincial planning institutes (*guihua yuan*), by geography departments at universities, and by the Chinese Academy of Urban Planning and Design based in the Ministry of Construction itself. These are approved by the State Council (cabinet) of the central government. Municipal master plans and more detailed plans (district plans, "development control" plans, and project site plans) may also drawn up by these types of entities, or by municipal planning institutes, university urban planning departments, or urban planning consulting firms. Master plans are examined by the provincial government and approved by the State Council, and more detailed plans are approved by the municipal government. Once a plan is approved, municipal construction commissions (*jianshe weiyuanhui*) and/or planning bureaus (*guihua ju*) have responsibility for ensuring the developers build according to the plan. However, as described below, the more detailed plans are often tightly integrated with the development process itself, leaving little distinction between regulation and implementation; local governments often compromise the former in order to achieve the latter.

The Ministry of Construction still oversees urban spatial planning, but specific plans at the highest levels must be coordinated with the 5-year economic development plan created by what is now the Development and Reform Commission and its provincial and municipal branches. As the nation has moved away from a command-and-control economy, the economic and social planning bureaucracy has taken on more of a policy formulation function. Economic and social planning therefore do not necessarily coordinate with urban physical planning at lower levels. The social welfare and community governance bureaucracy, the Ministry of Civil Affairs, is responsible for democratic reforms at the village level, for issues of public accountability in government, and for basic services and governance down to the resident committee level. Given the impacts that urban redevelopment and urbanization of rural villages has had on China's local communities, Civil Affairs has increasing relevance to urban planning, and yet no institutional mechanisms reflect the relationship.

Although it appears that higher-level/larger-scale plans support policy, and lower-level/smaller-scale plans support regulation, this is deceptive. Increased fiscal autonomy on the part of municipalities has taken most of the teeth out of the national 5-year plan, and the sheer speed of growth has made long-term policy planning a low priority for most municipal leaders. As a result, much large-scale planning is a *pro forma* exercise. At the smaller scale, truly private development interests have not yet become widespread, and thus there is often no one for the local government to regulate other than its own development agencies. In the absence of a private real estate industry, most development "companies" in the 1990s were actually spun off from submunicipal (district or street committee) government agencies or from construction "brigades" that originally carried out central government directives. Under decentralized fiscal conditions, these companies enjoy both freedom to pursue profits as well as extremely tight collaborative relationships with the agencies that spawned them (Abramson, 1997a; T. Zhang, 2002b). State control of most urban land facilitates land assembly and further exacerbates this close relationship. Therefore local area plans tend either to be subverted or used as blueprints depending on the extent to which they anticipated and accommodated imminent development intentions when they were drawn up. They rarely serve as regulating tools.

One potential brake on state-driven, unregulated development is China's land management system, the domain of yet another branch of the government, the Ministry of Land Resources, which since 1998 includes the Land Management Bureau, the agency responsible for pricing land, approving conversion of rural to urban land uses, and allocating land to work units (Ho, 2001). This agency primarily regulates the conversion of agricultural land to other uses, with the goal of maintaining national food security (Chinese Academy of Social Science Institute of Finance and Trade Economics & Institute of Public Administration, 1992; Ding & Knaap, 2005, pp. 18–19; Lin & Ho, 2005, pp. III ff.). Given that most of China's arable land is located in its most prosperous city-regions, preserving farmland conflicts directly with allowing urban growth to drive the economy.

However, since the 1988 Land Administration Law, the attempt to regulate rural-urban land conversion while gradually marketizing land use rights transactions has created a "dual land market." The central government makes land available both through the old system of administratively allocating land use rights for supposedly public purposes, and by leasing land through the paid transfer of land use rights (Valletta, 2005; Yeh, 2005). Lease terms are typically 40 years for commercial use, 50 years

for industrial use, and 70 years for residential use (Hong, 2005). A significant black market has also emerged as work units that were responsible for managing land in the public interest transfer rights to developers for secretly negotiated fees. In the absence of a straightforward land taxation system, municipal governments rely heavily on one-time revenues from leasing land development rights or make land available to developers in exchange for in-kind contributions of road construction, public amenities, and other infrastructure (Dowall, 1993; Hong, 2005). The incentive for local governments to develop land quickly is thus very strong, and different branches and levels of the approving bureaucracy often have opposing interests in specific projects.

The combination of the dual land market and public revenues from land being limited to lump-sum payments, often in-kind, has produced inefficiencies, opportunities for corruption, and challenges for long-range planning (S. K. J. Chen, 2000; Yeh, 2005, pp. 48–51). Rapid urban change has also elevated the demand for design- and engineering-oriented planning, even as the state is shedding its economic and social planning function. Not only is social and economic planning increasingly unable to govern urban development, even municipal master plans are threatened with irrelevance (Ng & Tang, 2004). The state's response to uncontrolled development has been to call for more plans at the local level. The submunicipal "detailed development control plan" that regulates population density, land use, and building heights, density, and ground coverage for each parcel of urban land has been a national requirement since 1989. More recently, various non-mandated "strategic" plans at different scales, "half-hour (radius) metro-area plans," and sector-specific development plans and urban designs, have been added to the range of planning types carried out in China.

These plans set normative goals for physical development, but do not account for conflicts of interest among government agencies responsible for their implementation (Fang & Zhang, 2003; Leaf, 1998). Both inner-city redevelopment and the development of the urban fringe are extremely controversial because they benefit local government agencies and developers at the expense of residents and villagers who are dislocated. At its worst, such dislocation removes people from their livelihoods and basic services. At the least, it involves disputes over appropriate levels of compensation.

In China's city centers housing owned and managed by the local government occupies most land, having been appropriated from private owners during the collectivizing movements of the 1950s and 1960s. This has allowed local governments (sometimes even down to the resident committee level) to profit from relocating people in order to redevelop the centrally located, and newly valuable, land where they lived (Leaf, 1995). The conversion of agricultural land to urban use is similarly fraught with conflict (Guo, 2001). Rural "collective" ownership is vested in agricultural village governments supposedly answerable to all the villagers, but often able to act with impunity. Such governments on the urban fringe may sell land use rights to adjacent urban governments that then establish development zones on the village land and transfer the rights to developers.

The large-scale clearance of old neighborhoods in China is somewhat reminiscent of the extensive renewal of Western cities after 1950, and indeed even of earlier large-scale redevelopments as in 19th-century Paris and Vienna. As a political-economic process, China's urban redevelopment demonstrates much of the logic of regime theory, including especially the formation of "growth coalitions" between local government leaders acting with broad policy mandates, property owners (in China's case, holders of land use rights and other fixed assets), and firms and organizations able to mobilize labor and capital (T. Zhang, 2002b; Zhang & Fang, 2004). The sociospatial impacts, too, resemble those of Western European and North American inner-city redevelopment (Castells, 1977; Harvey, 1985; Jacobs, 1961; Rose, 1981): increasing amounts of space dedicated to the exclusive use of transportation; poorer residents resettled farther from the city center, often in large housing projects with inadequate services; older, demographically and socially diverse or poorer neighborhoods replaced with more exclusive, uniform, and expensive neighborhoods or commercial projects (Abramson, 1994; Logan, 2005). China's planning legacy tends to exacerbate these impacts.

Designs that rely on traditional axiality, regularity, and monumental scale must erase more of the historic human-scaled environment than more flexible designs would, and they tend to make the new public spaces particularly unhospitable to pedestrians (Fairfield, Manor, Perkes, & Tregoning, 2004). The lack of a tradition of planning specifically for the public realm and the continued cellular approach to designing and developing new neighborhoods and commercial areas has not only created homogenous gated communities (including those that concentrate lower-income residents together in poorly-served parts of the city), it has also inhibited planners from considering the interface of individual projects and the surrounding streets (Marshall, 2003, chs. 6 & 7; Miao, 2003). Such enclaves are usually now off limits to street vendors and others whose jobs provide inexpensive services to residents.

Also, since urban planning focuses entirely on enabling large-scale redevelopment rather than on regulating small-scale building activity, neighborhoods or villages not officially redeveloped proceed either to accelerated deterioration or to chaotic makeshift improvement and densification. Urban administration and economic policy since the early 1980s has done little to support a community-based, nonprofit, or self-help-enabling sector to "take up the slack" in areas that have been left behind by market-driven growth (Zhang, Zhao, & Tian, 2003). It is assumed that *all* areas of the city are to be brought up to standard, and quickly, but the reality is that as one part of the city is improved, other areas further away from the center are degraded. Villagers throughout the country have responded with protests that are increasingly violent (French, 2005).

This situation is especially acute at the urban fringe, to which factories are frequently relocated from the inner city, and where the greatest numbers of provincial migrants tend to concentrate even as the environment is rapidly degraded (Fan & Taubmann, 2002; Tang & Chung, 2002; W. Wu, 2005; L. Zhang, 2001, 2005). The problem of planning a durable physical environment when individuals are mobile, while familiar to modern cities in other societies, is a new challenge to China's traditional cellular mode of urban organization, which was previously enabled by the state's ability to control urban residence and rigid standards for housing development and urban spatial design.

Finally, the gravest challenge to urban planning and growth in the coming decades is likely to be an increasingly unyielding environment. Since the 1990s, energy shortages have increased, to the point that during summer peak energy-use periods in 2004 and 2005 cities resorted for the first time to planned blackouts. Ultimately, the effect of urbanization will be to increase the affluence of the population, creating consumers. When China reaches the current rate of consumption in developed countries (which many argue is already unsustainable) it will "approximately double the world's human resource use and environmental impact" (Liu & Diamond, 2005, p. 1185). This strongly suggests that planners in China and throughout the world should radically redefine "development" as a goal.

Policy Responses

Policy responses to the challenges listed above already appear capable of changing planning practice significantly, primarily by creating new potential clients for planners. Among these responses are efforts at "community-building" (*shequ jianshe*), and also the formation of private homeowners' associations and the turning over of the management of residential compounds to supposedly private and self-supporting property management companies. Community-building is an effort to restructure the lowest levels of urban governance and social service provision, mainly by reorganizing and consolidating resident committees into "communities" (*shequ*), which then are encouraged to involve residents in responsibility for community affairs, including managing urban space and maintaining social order in the face of dislocation, loss or change of jobs, or the transformation of the environment (Choate, 1998). Largely a top-down, policy-driven movement, community-building in China may be interpreted as an effort by the state both to shed its welfare responsibilities and to maintain a spatially cellular approach to governance (F. Xu, 2005).

Nevertheless, *shequ* have funds to carry out community improvement projects, including facilities for recreation, and activities for adult education, job training, and career placement. Planners have responded by taking commissions from some of the more established (but not especially privileged) communities to develop long-term plans (Zhao, 2003). After working only for higher level government agencies, work units, and developers throughout the entire period of reform, planners now working with this new type of client will be required to adopt new skills and to redefine their discipline.

A second important arena of recent national policy change is in property law and the rights of citizens to litigate. In 2004 China made revisions to its national constitution that give greater protections to private property, in the interest of facilitating the operation of the market and combating corruption. While the Chinese constitution is a frequently amended document compared with most Western constitutions (it is considered a programmatic rather than a rights-based constitution), this revision is momentous nevertheless, as it parallels a number of recent court decisions against local government agencies (including the Beijing Planning Bureau) in cases of land use rights expropriation for urban redevelopment (Phan, 2005). This new legal environment has shaken local governments' confidence in their abilities to carry out large-scale plans, and has fueled discussions over how to make planning a more transparent, democratic process (N. Shi, 2004). Government tolerance of these discussions varies, but the current legal trend appears likely to force Chinese planning practice to include broader and more open discussions in decision-making.[7]

Legal challenges have also been brought against local government officials and enterprises for environmental pollution. The central government has taken a pro-active stand on environmental matters, strengthening its regulatory role and attempting to cultivate a more progressive image internationally. China early established its own national Agenda 21 sustainable development policy following the United Nations Conference on Environment and Development held in Rio de Janeiro in 1992; ratified the Kyoto Protocol in 2002, and in 2005 began trial calculations of a new "green" Gross Domestic Product (GDP) measure in three of its largest cities (Beijing, Tianjin and Chongqing) and in seven provinces (Ray, 2005). From a domestic urban planning perspective, this last is particularly interesting. China uses GDP to measure economic performance for the nation and also for individual cities, which allows every expenditure to contribute to rapid economic growth, regardless of its efficiency or environmental cost. The "green" GDP attempts to take these problems into account and provide a better planning objective.

These responses indicate that planning in China is changing from being an enabler of growth to a more diversely conceived discipline. The need to resolve environmental and other conflicts have increased the analytical role of planning, requiring greater economic and other social science expertise (Abramson, Leaf, & Tan, 2002). The same pressures involve planners in conflict resolution and even advocacy. Planners in China already do advocate for the public interest as official "expert consultants" and members of commissions, and also in less official capacities, as respected professionals or academics whose signatures on petitions carry some weight (C. Xu, 2004; T. Zhang, 2002a). However, they do so only at the pleasure of the official leadership, and rarely in the interest of particular communities. Chinese planners' public influence continues to derive from their specialized and supposedly objective knowledge of the physical environment and their imagined distance from the particular interests affecting it (L. Wu, 1999, pp. 192–193).

The following section describes my own experience of planning in one historic neighborhood over a period of more than a decade. Although the planning I describe is at the neighborhood scale and focuses primarily on housing, urban design, and historic preservation (as opposed to regional economic, infrastructural, or environmental planning, for example), it illustrates the trends I outline above.

Return to West Street: 12 Years in the Planning of One Neighborhood

This example occurred in the prefectural-level city of Quanzhou, in Fujian Province on China's southeast coast. Quanzhou is a prosperous, medium-sized city by Chinese standards, and it has experienced the rapid economic and growth and physical development typical of coastal cities.[8] Quanzhou's economy is unusual, however, in that local families' retained private ownership of productive assets and benefited from remittances and investments sent by overseas relatives (*huaqiao*) even during the most radical periods of Maoist collectivization (C.-J. J. Chen, 1999; Leaf & Abramson, 2002; Y. Zhu, 2000). This is typical of diasporic hometowns along China's southeast coast, but Quanzhou is remarkable in that housing and residential land use rights in the inner city have remained in private hands continuously since before Mao because the local government took special measures to protect the popular transnational property interests that were the city's economic and cultural lifeblood (Jingsheng Wang, personal communication, June 15, 2000). Then, in the very earliest days of Deng Xiaoping's leadership, a series of court cases and negotiations brokered by local *huaqiao* advocates established a precedent for returning expropriated property to its original owners or otherwise generously compensating them. As a result, Quanzhou's planning diverged somewhat from standard practice elsewhere in China, while the city still enjoyed rapid urban growth (Abramson et al., 2002).

My own involvement in the city's planning began in 1993 when I participated on a team from Tsinghua University's department of urban planning commissioned by Quanzhou's inner-city district government to produce neighborhood-scaled plans for redeveloping the city's historic center. At the time, university teams of planning and architecture faculty and students often accepted short-term commissions to make surveys and draw up purely physical plans for such redevelopment projects. Taking its cue from major cities like Xiamen, Fuzhou, Guangzhou, Shanghai, and Beijing, the district government administering Quanzhou's old city center did not wait for a revision of the municipal master plan before it forged ahead with its own more detailed redevelopment planning. The master plan eventually proposed a broad expansion of the city into formerly agricultural lands, following a fairly standard pattern of wide streets, gated residential estates, and expansive monumental open spaces. Within the historic center it put a priority both on preservation and on widening streets to serve regional traffic. These conflicting goals are commonly left unreconciled in the master plans of historic Chinese cities, and would both have hampered the district government's goal to increase saleable floor area. The district government plan largely ignored the goal of preservation and increased the amount of city-center land area designated for redevelopment by the year 2000 from 56% in 1992 to 65% in 1993 (Tao, 1995).

However, the prevalence of privately-owned housing and land use rights prompted the city to adopt an unusually generous compensation policy for residents whose neighborhoods were to be redeveloped, requiring developers to provide owners of demolished housing with new units in their original neighborhood ("*chai yi pei yi, jiu di an zhi*"; S. Lu et al., 2004). This rather crude, in-kind compensation policy suited the complexity of ownership and the volatile real estate market of the mid 1990s well, as determining monetary "fair market value" would have been extremely difficult. It also prevented significant displacement, preserved communities, limited the opportunities to widen streets and create monumental open spaces, and reduced developers' profits. By the end of 1999, only about 17% of the old city had actually been rebuilt.

Among the redevelopment projects that the Tsinghua University team undertook was one that was never carried out, in the neighborhood of Xi Jie (West Street), an important but narrow and dilapidated thoroughfare that passed in front of Quanzhou's most important historic landmark and tourist attraction, the Kai Yuan Temple. (For an early 20th-century description of this Tang and Song dynasty temple's remarkable stone pagodas, see Ecke, 1935; Leaf et al., 1995). The initial 1994 plan called for the widening of the street, the demolition of all but a few structures valued for their especially characteristic architecture, and the relocation of most residents into new large apartment buildings on one side of the neighborhood. The historic quality of the temple would be respected by rebuilding the structures along West Street uniformly in Tang or Song period style. The official planning authorities had no interest in consulting or surveying the residents.

While an underlying obstacle to this and other redevelopment projects in Quanzhou was the difficulty of assembling land given the complex property ownership pattern, the more important problem in the eyes of Quanzhou's leadership was West Street's historical significance. On the suggestion of a top central government official concerned about the impact of redevelopment on the temple (Li Ruihuan, then Chairman of the national People's Political Consultative Conference), the local government delayed widening the street, for fear that doing so would destroy the pagodas' sense of monumentality and visual prominence. Although the residents of the street remained in limbo, since they did not know whether their buildings might be demolished, the delay allowed historic-architectural analyses of the street to conclude that no particular era (Tang, Song or even later dynasties) best represented the neighborhood's architectural character; it was a stylistically varied accretion of buildings, reflecting its eclectic ownership. Therefore recreating all the buildings as if they belonged to any single time period would not "preserve" the area as it had ever really existed.

In late 2004, the municipal government accepted this analysis, and provisionally decided to revitalize the street under existing ownership, and to explore policies that would encourage residents themselves to upgrade their houses according to the city's regulations for private house building in historic districts. The government paid the municipal planning institute to produce designs that would both provide improved living conditions and satisfy the regulations, and presented these to each household along the street. Residents demurred, however, finding the regulations were unreasonably restrictive (the rules essentially forbade any enlargement of existing building envelopes).

In effect, the local planners of Quanzhou had moved from an approach that mobilized resources for profitable redevelopment

(assembly of land and investment of large amounts of capital) to one that regulated private initiative in the interest of a public good, with limited potential to generate income. The definition of that good, preserving a heritage of private, on-going architectural innovation and monumental architecture, was informed by expert analysis as well as by the opinion of the highest level of the governmental hierarchy. However, given the penchant of the local government for fast, visible action, even these persuasive arguments might have fallen on deaf ears had not the political-economic realities of Quanzhou's private property structure also supported it. Ironically, now the residents themselves need convincing of the new regulatory approach; they actually prefer the favorable compensation that accompanies large-scale redevelopment, and do not share the planning authority's view of the street's historic architectural value.

It was at this point that I became involved again in the planning of West Street, 10 years after the first street-widening scheme was abandoned. In the meantime, I had been working with a team experimenting in participatory community planning and design in other neighborhoods in Quanzhou where residents and planning authorities faced similar conflicts (Abramson et al., 2001). In this work the project team initiated a tentative form of advocacy planning and mediation using design (Abramson, 2005).[9] The project concluded with participatory research involving students in design, policy, and anthropology. Hoping to draw on this experience for use in West Street, the Quanzhou Municipal Planning Bureau hired members of this project team to lead a small group of designers to work more directly with West Street households than the planning institute could before.

The planning bureau's primary goal for this project is to demonstrate to residents that, with appropriate design, they can both invest to improve the neighborhood and also live comfortably within the restrictions of the historic district regulations, which themselves may be refined by the process (Y. Li, 2005). By doing this, the planning bureau in effect opens discussion on the definition of "modern living" that drives so much of the planning for other areas of the city. There are also two other possible outcomes with profound implications: both residents and government may clarify and harmonize their understandings of the distinction between public/governmental and private/family realms and responsibilities; and residents themselves may find they have a communal interest in revitalizing the neighborhood, regardless of government priorities.

Regardless of how this on-going story unfolds, the evolution in planning attitudes and approaches towards West Street over the last decade is remarkable. When discussing the possibility of mass demolition and relocation from the neighborhood in 1995, local planners were extremely cavalier about resident reactions: "no need to be polite about it (*bu yong keqi*)," one said. In 2005, the planning authorities depend fundamentally on residents to participate in the revitalization process, and are stretching the limits of both their practice and their budgetary restrictions to engage with them by providing free design services to individual households. The purpose is to facilitate communication rather than state-sponsored construction. Perhaps most significant is the willingness of the local government to consider a different definition of "promotable" practice (i.e., practice that both has public propaganda value and counts toward promotion in the bureaucracy). Rather than continue with the street widenings, broad plazas, and ersatz "historic streets," the planning authorities hope to gain notoriety through practice that is progressive in terms of its process as much as its product.

Certainly there is much that has not changed: the monumental Kai Yuan Temple still looms over the project both physically and as a symbol of the government's priorities, representing traditional top-down decision making as well as a beloved local landmark. Residents in the neighborhood still chafe under the historic district restrictions they did not create that prevent them from rebuilding their houses as they wish. Also, the *de facto* protection of property rights in Quanzhou does not mean government encourages residents to participate in local environmental improvement as a community. Quanzhou has established new administrative *shequ* according to the community-building policy, but the planning bureau tends not to involve the *shequ* staff when it engages residents on this project, and has set up its own project headquarters in the neighborhood. The bureau's expectation that residents should pay to upgrade their own houses though it has not yet invested in the street itself also shows continuing lack of appreciation for the distinction between public and private space, and avoids state responsibility for local public goods. Residents often complain that the government expects them to adhere to rules that it routinely breaks.

It may be that community institutions and resident property rights will evolve to the point that government will redefine the goals and methods of planning to accommodate them. Formal property rights would be a prerequisite to establishing a viable property tax system, for example, which would better enable the city to establish a matching fund or other standard budget item for providing planning and construction assistance to local communities. But my story above illustrates how the goals and methods of planning in China are already being redefined, even without a formal, legally tested, new policy on property rights. This in turn has led the planning authorities to recognize the community in West Street, a community that is rooted in common interest rather than defined by territorial administration.

Conclusion

Quanzhou's political and economic conditions are unusual, but they are not unique. Other studies of local government behavior show varied communal institutions and webs of obligation (Oi & Walder, 1999). Other accounts of local planning practice in China would likely display variations on my general theme and contribute to a much more complex portrait of Chinese planning than the current one, which is dominated by the problems and achievements of only some of the largest and newest cities, mainly Beijing, Shanghai, Guangzhou, and Shenzhen. In the meantime, I suggest that near-term innovations in planning need not only emerge from major institutional reforms of China's political system, such as directly electing mayors or repealing restrictions on the formation of social organizations.

Planning practices are as subject to informal arrangements between central agencies, local governments, and citizens as they are to formal institutions of governance. Such arrangements often reflect local historically-rooted conditions that are officially ignored by the state, but are crucial in practice. Who planners represent, how their expertise is weighed, what sort of publicity their ideas receive, how they and others publicly define the goals of planning, all can change within the current governmental structure in China. Admittedly, government has formal powers to block changes or even reverse them, but once they enter the popular imagination, they often gain political momentum. At that point, the government will likely adopt new ideas much as previous dynasties did, to bolster its own legitimacy, even if this means declaring them to be ancient practice.

Acknowledgements

Michael Leaf accompanied me in nearly all the work I describe in Quanzhou, and his insights have been central in my attempt to make sense of it. John Friedmann encouraged me to write what I would have thought was far too ambitious a paper, and gave it repeated readings and constructive comments, as did four anonymous reviewers. Conversations with Alison Bailey, Feng Xu and Zhang Jie also assisted me greatly to hone the manuscript. Hao Xin's etymological inspiration added a final touch. To them all, and to my Chinese teachers and partners in the Quanzhou work, I give my heartfelt thanks.

Notes

1. A quick search on June 19, 2005, for all publications on "city planning" and "China" (excluding Hong Kong) in the Library of Congress catalog revealed only 43 monographs and edited books in English (out of a total of 379), of which 17 were published since 1999. Within the last 2 years, the Lincoln Institute of Land Policy has established a special research program on the People's Republic of China, with news on courses, research and consulting projects, and working papers in English and Chinese (see http://www.lincolninst.edu/aboutlincoln/prc.asp).

2. Beijing, "the ultimate crystallization of the planning and design of imperial capitals" (L. Wu, 1999, p. 4), was laid out in its current location by the Mongol emperor Khubilai Khan in 1267. To ensure his own legitimacy as ruler of an ethnically diverse people, he matched the design of his city more closely to "the classical tradition of Chinese urban planning than any city that had come before it" (Steinhardt, 1986, 1990, p. 158).

3. Heng (1999) describes a transition in city planning from the Tang to the Song dynasty as expressed in the closed, regulated, camp-like layout and administration of the Tang capital Changan (*Xi'an*) and the open, commercially vibrant Song capital Bianliang (*Kaifeng*). In another example, when the Ming dynasty succeeded the Yuan dynasty and moved the capital from Nanjing to Beijing, the Ming emperor sought to establish his supremacy and reproduce in Beijing attributes of his former palace, as well as shifting Beijing's center away from its market and drum tower, and dividing the city into greater numbers of walled segments, blocking the waterways that served as transport to the market (Hou, 1986, pp. 228–230; L. Wu, 1999, pp. 3–12). Indeed in cities throughout China, Ming dynasty urban planning expanded ceremonial administrative spaces at the expense of commercial spaces, in accordance with a revived Confucian ideology of social control

(Brook, 1985; M. Wang, 1995). Wu Hung (H. Wu, 2005, pp. 131–164) describes how Beijing's Drum and Bell Towers imposed social control on the city visually, aurally, and corporeally, through a combination of their prominence in the cityscape in daylight, their sound in the darkness at night, and their function as signals to gatekeepers throughout the city. They were actually silent during the day, and thus did not serve as time-keepers for the convenience of the citizens. Instead, at their sounding at dawn and sunset, movement would be freed or restricted by the opening or closing of "all the walled spaces within the city—palaces, offices, markets, temples and private homes." Thus they regulated the sociospatial cellularity of the city, and "focused public perception and brought about a sense of unification and standardization" (H. Wu, 2005, p. 145).

4. The ancient Chinese character for "city" is *yi*, written as a walled enclosure (*wei*) over an official seal (*jie*). This predates the modern word for "city," *chengshi* ("wall" plus "market") (see www.zhongwen.com for the etymology of *yi*).

5. Cities that most dramatically outgrew their historic political status in modern times have since been "promoted" to the status of "provincial-level cities" or "cities under central administration": Shanghai, Tianjin, and Chongqing. Going back many centuries, the hierarchical relationship between cities is better documented than the boundaries of the territories they administered (Berman, 2005).

6. In this article, "municipalities" and "municipal governments" refer to cities that are at either the prefectural level or directly under the central government (i.e., cities that are likely to administer a number of rural counties as well as one or more county-level cities).

7. The Conference on Democratization of the Urban Planning Decision-making Process in Quanzhou in July 2004 was a relatively open and relaxed event that included faculty and students from the U.S., Canada, and Taiwan as well as the P.R.C.; a conference on constitutionalism scheduled for the following May in 2005 at Beijing University, however, was cancelled on short notice.

8. According to a National Statistical Bureau survey at the end of 1989, Quanzhou municipality's 10,865 square kilometers of mountains and coastal plains (i.e., its prefectural-level municipally-administered region) had a total population of over 5.5 million, of which almost 620,000 were "non-agricultural" (National Bureau of Statistics Urban Social and Economic Survey Team, 1990 pp. 37 & 53). By 2000, the built-up urbanized area had quadrupled, and the Statistical Bureau count of Quanzhou's total population was about 6.5 million, of which 910,000 were nonagriculturally employed. However, according to the 2000 census, which included for the first time all people living in an area regardless whether they had registered residency (*hukou*) or not, Quanzhou's total population was almost 7.3 million (All China Marketing Research Co. Ltd. & University of Michigan China Data Center, 2002). The extra migrants who made up this larger figure are employed for the most part in industry, and therefore are essentially additional urban population. GDP for the entire prefectural-level municipality has grown at an annual rate of between 12 and 13% through the late 1990s and early 2000s. A useful general reference on Quanzhou's position in the overall development of Fujian Province are the contributions to *Fujian: A Coastal Province in Transition and Transformation*, edited by Y. M. Yeung and David K. Y. Chu (2000).

9. Project team members, from 1999 to 2004, included primarily Tan Ying, Lecturer at Tsinghua University in Beijing; Tao Tao, Senior Planner at the Chinese Academy of Urban Planning and Design; and Professor Michael Leaf and myself at the University of British Columbia. The project was independently funded by a grant from the Ford Foundation in Beijing.

References

Abramson, D. (1994). New housing in old Beijing: A comparative survey of projects completed to date—Beijing's old and dilapidated housing renewal (part V). *China City Planning Review, 10*(3), 42–56.

Abramson, D. (1997a). "Marketization" and institutions in Chinese inner-city neighborhood redevelopment: A commentary on "Beijing's old and dilapidated housing renewal" by Lü Junhua. *Cities, 14*(2), 71–75.

Abramson, D. (1997b). *Neighborhood redevelopment as a cultural problem: A western perspective on current plans for the old city of Beijing*. Unpublished doctoral dissertation, Tsinghua University, Beijing.

Abramson, D. (2001). Beijing's preservation policy and the fate of the siheyuan. *Traditional Design and Settlements Review, 13*(1) 7–22.

Abramson, D. B. (2005). The "studio abroad" as a mode of transcultural engagement in urban planning: A reflection on nine years of Sino-Canadian educational exchange. *Journal of Planning Education and Research, 25*(1), 89–102.

Abramson, D., Leaf, M., & Anderson, S., and the students of UBC course Plan 545B. (2001). *Governance and design: Participatory planning, residential design guidelines and historic preservation in Quanzhou, Fujian, China: A year 2000 studio report* (Asian Urban Research Network Working Paper No. WP27). Vancouver: UBC Centre for Human Settlements.

Abramson, D., Leaf, M., & Tan, Y. (2002). Social research and the localization of Chinese urban planning practice: Some ideas from Quanzhou, Fujian. In J. R. Logan (Ed.), *The new Chinese city: Globalization and market reform* (pp. 227–245). Oxford: Blackwell Publishers.

All China Marketing Research Co., Ltd., & University of Michigan China Data Center. (2002). *China data online: China 5th national province population census data in 2000, Fujian 2000 population census assembly, table 1–2* (Census Book FUJ2000000). Retrieved March 29, 2006, from http://141.211.142.26/eng/macro/census2000/#

Bai, D. (1993). *Juzhuqu guihua yu huanjing sheji* [Residential area planning and environmental design]. Beijing: Zhongguo Jianzhu Gongye Chubanshe.

Berman, M. L. (2005). Boundaries or networks in historical GIS: Concepts of measuring space and administrative geography in Chinese history. *Historical Geography, 33* (Special Issue: Emerging Trends in Historical GIS), 118–133.

Bian, Y., & Logan, J. R. (1996). Market transition and the persistence of power: The changing stratification system in urban China. *American Sociological Review, 61*(5), 739.

Bray, D. (2005). *Social space and governance in urban China: The danwei system from origins to reform*. Stanford, CA: Stanford University Press.

Brook, T. (1985). The spatial structure of Ming local administration. *Late Imperial China, 6*(1), 1–55.

Broudehoux, A.-M. (2004). *The making and selling of post-Mao Beijing*. New York: Routledge.

Canada Mortgage and Housing Corporation. (1996). *China housing market report*. Ottawa: Author.

Castells, M. (1977). *The urban question: A Marxist approach* (A. Sheridan, Trans. Rev., 2nd ed.). Cambridge, MA: MIT Press.

Chan, K. W. (1994). *Cities with invisible walls: Reinterpreting urbanization in post-1949 China.* New York: Oxford University Press.

Chan, K. W. (1997). Urbanization and urban infrastructure services in the P.R.C. In C. P. W. Wong (Ed.*), Financing local government in the People's Republic of China* (pp. 83–125). New York: Published for the Asian Development Bank by Oxford University Press.

Chandler, T. (1987). *Four thousand years of urban growth: An historical census.* Lewiston, NY: St. David's University Press.

Chen, C.-J. J. (1999). Local institutions and the transformation of property rights in southern Fujian. In J. C. Oi & A. G. Walder (Eds.*), Property rights and economic reform in China* (pp. 49–70). Stanford, CA: Stanford University Press.

Chen, G. (1994). Urban housing problems in China. In M. H. Choko & C. Guangting (Eds.), *China: The challenge of urban housing* (pp. 13–36). Quebec: Editions du Meridien.

Chen, S. K. J. (2000*). Land management practice in Fuzhou, People's Republic of China.* Unpublished master's thesis, University of British Columbia, Vancouver, Canada.

Chinese Academy of Social Science Institute of Finance and Trade Economics, & Institute of Public Administration. (1992). *Zhongguo chengshi tudi shiyong yu guanli. Zong bao gao* [Urban land use and management in China: Final report]. Beijing: Jingji Kexue Chubanshe.

Choate, A. C. (1998). *Local governance in China, part II: An assessment of urban residents' committees and municipal community development* (Working Paper No. 10). San Francisco: Asia Foundation.

Clunas, C. (1996). Fruitful sites: Garden culture in Ming dynasty China. Durham: Duke University Press.

Clunas, C. (2004). *Superfluous things: Material culture and social status in early modern China.* Honolulu: University of Hawaii Press.

Cook, J. A. (1998*). Bridges to modernity: Xiamen, overseas Chinese and southeast coastal modernization, 1843–1937.* Unpublished doctoral dissertation, University of California, San Diego.

Davis, D. S., Kraus, R., Naughton, B., & Perry, E. J. (Eds.). (1995). Urban *spaces in contemporary China: The potential for autonomy and community in post-Mao China.* New York: Cambridge University Press.

Ding, C., & Knaap, G. (2005). Urban land policy reform in China's transitional economy. In C. Ding & Y. Song (Eds.), *Emerging land and housing markets in China* (pp. 59–87). Cambridge, MA: Lincoln Institute of Land Policy.

Ding, C., & Song, Y. (Eds.). (2005). *Emerging land and housing markets in China.* Cambridge, MA: Lincoln Institute of Land Policy.

Dowall, D. E. (1993). Establishing urban land markets in the People's Republic of China. *Journal of the American Planning Association, 59*(2), 182–193.

Ecke, G. (1935). *The twin pagodas of Zayton: A study of later Buddhist sculpture in China.* Cambridge, MA: Harvard University Press.

Fairfield, S., Manor, O., Perkes, D., & Tregoning, H. (2004). Some observations on street life in Chinese cities. *Land Lines: Newsletter of the Lincoln Institute of Land Policy, 16*(4), 5–7.

Fallows, J. (2005). Countdown to a meltdown. *Atlantic Monthly, 296*(1), 51–64.

Fan, J., & Taubmann, W. (2002). Migrant enclaves in large Chinese cities. In J. R. Logan (Ed.), *The new Chinese city: Globalization and market reform* (pp. 183–197). Oxford, UK: Blackwell.

Fang, K., & Zhang, Y. (2003). Plan and market mismatch: Urban redevelopment in Beijing during a period of transition. *Asia Pacific Viewpoint, 44*(2), 149–162.

Fazhan Luntan [Development Forum]. (2005). *You xiang gai biaozhi jianzhu: Beijing ni you wan mei wan?* [Wanting to build yet more architectural landmarks: Beijing, will you ever be done?]. Retrieved 6 October, 2005, from http://news.xinhuanet.com/forum/2005-09/12/ content_3478247.htm

Feuchtwang, S. (2004). *Making place: State projects, globalisation and local responses in China.* London: University College London Press.

French, H. W. (2005, July 19). Riots in a village in China as pollution protest heats up. *New York Times,* p. A3.

Friedman, T. L. (2005). *The world is flat: A brief history of the twenty-first century.* New York: Farrar Straus and Giroux.

Friedmann, J. (2005). *China's urban transition.* Minneapolis: University of Minnesota Press.

Fung, K. I. (1981). Urban sprawl in China: Some causative factors. In L. J. C. Ma & E. W. Hanten (Eds.), *Urban development in modern China* (pp. 194–221). Boulder, CO: Westview Press.

Gaubatz, P. R. (1995). Urban transformation in post-Mao China: Impacts of the reform era on China's urban form. In D. S. Davis, R. Kraus, B. Naughton, & E. J. Perry (Eds.), *Urban spaces in contemporary China: The potential for autonomy and community in post-Mao China* (pp. 28–60). New York: Cambridge University Press.

Ganbatz, P. R. (1996). *Beyond the great wall: Urban form and transformation on the Chinese frontiers.* Stanford, CA: Stanford University Press.

Guo, X. (2001). Land expropriation and rural conflicts in China. *China Quarterly, 166,* 422–439.

Han, G. (1996). *Beijing lishi renkou dili* [Historical demographic geography of Beijing]. Beijing: Beijing Daxue Chubanshe.

Harvey, D. (1985*). Consciousness and the urban experience: Studies in the history and theory of capitalist urbanization.* Baltimore: John Hopkins University Press.

Heng, C. K. (1999). *Cities of aristocrats and bureaucrats: The development of medieval Chinese cityscapes.* Honolulu: University of Hawaii Press.

Ho, P. (2001). Who owns China's land? Policies, property rights and deliberate institutional ambiguity. *China Quarterly, 166,* 394–421.

Hong, Y.-H. (2005). Taxing publicly owned land in China: A paradox? *Land Lines: Newsletter of the Lincoln Institute of Land Policy, 17*(1), 9–10.

Hou, R. (1986). The transformation of the old city of Beijing, China: A concrete manifestation of new China's cultural reconstruction. In M. P. Conzen (Ed.), *World patterns of modern urban change: Essays in honor of Chauncy D. Harris* (pp. 217–239). Chicago: University of Chicago Department of Geography.

Huang, Y. (2005). From work-unit compounds to gated communities: Housing inequality and residential segregation in transitional Beijing. In L. J. C. Ma & F. Wu (Eds.), *Restructuring the Chinese city: Changing society, economy and space* (pp. 192–221). New York: Routledge.

Jacobs, J. (1961). *The death and life of great American cities.* New York: Random House.

Ke, H. (1991). Preservation and development of Beijing. *Building in China, 4*(4), 2–10.

Knechtges, D. R., & Xiao, T. (1982). *Wen xuan, or, selections of refined literature (Vol. I, Rhapsodies on metropolises and capitals).* Princeton, NJ: Princeton University Press.

Leaf, M. (1995). Inner city redevelopment in China: Implications for the city of Beijing. *Cities, 12*(3), 149–162.

Leaf, M. (1998). Urban planning and urban reality under Chinese economic reforms. *Journal of Planning Education and Research, 18*(2), 145–153.

Leaf, M., & Abramson, D. (2002). Global networks, civil society, and the transformation of the urban core in Quanzhou, China. In E. J. Heikkila & R. Pizarro (Eds.), *Southern California and the world* (pp. 153–178). Westport, CT: Praeger.

Leaf, M., and the students of UBC course Plan 545B. (1995). *Planning for urban redevelopment in Quanzhou, Fujian, China* (Asian Urban Research Network Working Paper Series #WP5). Vancouver: University of British Columbia, Centre for Human Settlements.

Li, X. (1995). Structure spatiale et identité culturelle des villes chinoises traditionnelles [Spatial Structure and Cultural Identity of Traditional Chinese Cities] (C. Lamoureux, Trans.). In *Histoire et identités urbaines: Nouvelles tendences de la recherche urbaine [History and Urban Identities: New Directions of Urban Research]*. Beijing: Table rondée organisée par les revues Dushu et Annales avec le soutien de l'Ambassade de France et de l'École française d'Extrême-Orient [Roundtable organized by Dushu and Annales with the support of the Embassy of France and the French School of the Far East].

Li, Y. (2005, November 9). Xijie zhengzhi baohu you le xin silu [New thinking for the upgrading and preservation of West Street]. *Haixia dushi bao [Strait News]* [electronic edition]. Retrieved December 15, 2005, from http://www.hxdsb.com/news/2005-11-09/20051123151736.html

Lin, G. C. S., & Ho, S. P. S. (2005). Land resources and land use change. In C. Ding & Y. Song (Eds.), *Emerging land and housing markets in China* (pp. 90–119). Cambridge, MA: Lincoln Institute of Land Policy.

Lin, Z. (1988). Comprehensive development of urban areas. *Building in China, 1*(2), 2–7.

Liu, J., & Diamond, J. (2005). China's environment in a globalizing world: How China and the rest of the world affect each other. *Nature, 435*(30), 1179–1186.

Logan, J. (2005). Socialism, market reform and neighborhood inequality in urban China. In C. Ding & Y. Song (Eds.), *Emerging land and housing markets in China* (pp. 233–248). Cambridge, MA: Lincoln Institute of Land Policy.

Logan, J. R. (Ed.). (2002). *The new Chinese city." Globalization and market reform.* Oxford, UK: Blackwell.

Lü, J., Rowe, P. G., & Zhang, J. (Eds.). (2001). *Modern urban housing in China, 1840–2000.* New York: Prestel.

Lu, S., Chen, Z., Li, Y., Xie, M., Yang, Q., & Zheng, J. (2004, July 22). Zhanwang Xijie weilai moyang—dui mei yi jia mei yi hu jinxing sheji [Looking ahead to the future appearance of Xijie—Carry out design for each family, each household]. *Haixia Dushi Bao [Strait News]*, p. A6.

Lu, W. (1994). Housing for low-income groups in China: Tianjin, a case study. In M. H. Choko & C. Guangting (Eds.), *China: The challenge of urban housing* (pp. 127–140). Quebec: Editions du Meridien.

Lü, X., & Perry, E. J. (1997). *Danwei: The changing Chinese workplace in historical and comparative perspective.* Armonk, NY: M. E. Sharpe.

Ma, L. J. C., & Wu, F. (2005). *Restructuring the Chinese city: Changing society, economy and space.* New York: Routledge.

Marshall, R. (2003). *Emerging urbanity: Global urban projects in the Asia Pacific Rim.* New York: Spon Press.

Meyer, J. F. (1991). *The dragons of Tiananmen: Beijing as a sacred city.* Columbia: University of South Carolina Press.

Miao, P. (2003). Deserted streets in a jammed town: The gated community in Chinese cities and its solution. *Journal of Urban Design, 8*(1), 45–66.

National Bureau of Statistics Urban Social and Economic Survey Team. (1990) *Zhongguo chengshi tongji nianjian* [China urban statistical yearbook]. Beijing: China Statistical Publishing House.

Newman, R. J. (2005). The rise of a new power; a communist economic juggernaut emerges to challenge the West; Shanghai (Special Report Cover Story). *U.S. News & World Report, 138*(23), 40.

Ng, M. K., & Tang, W.-S. (2004). The role of planning in the development of Shenzhen, China: Rhetoric and realities. *Eurasian Geography and Economics, 45*(3), 190–211.

Ng, M.-K., & Wu, F. (1997). Challenges and opportunities—Can Western planning theories inform changing Chinese urban planning practices? In A. G. O. Yeh, X. Xu, & X. Yan (Eds.), *Urban planning and planning education under economic reform in China* (pp. 147–170). Hong Kong: Centre of Urban Planning and Environmental Management, University of Hong Kong.

Oi, J. C. (1995). The role of the local state in China's transitional economy. *China Quarterly, 144* (Special Issue: China's Transitional Economy), 1132–1149.

Oi, J. C., & Walder, A. G. (Eds.). (1999). *Property rights and economic reform in China.* Stanford, CA: Stanford University Press.

People's Republic of China, Ministry of Civil Affairs, Department of Administrative Territorial Delineation and Place-naming (2004). Retrieved December 16, 2005, from http://www.xzqh.org/yange/2004.htm

Phan, P. N. (2005, June). Enriching the land or the political elite? Lessons from China on democratization of the urban renewal process. *Pacific Rim Law & Policy Journal, 14*, 607.

Ray, C. (2005, March 1). "Green GDP"; Trials start in 10 regions. *South China Morning Post*, p. 7.

Rose, D. (1981). Accumulation versus reproduction in the inner city: The recurrent crisis of London revisited. In M. Dear & A. J. Scott (Eds.), *Urbanization and urban planning in capitalist society* (pp. 339–381). New York: Methuen.

Rowe, W. T. (1989). *Hankow: Conflict and community in a Chinese city, 1796–1895.* Stanford, CA: Stanford University Press.

Rykwert, J. (1976). *The idea of a town: The anthropology of urban form in Rome, Italy and the ancient world.* Princeton, NJ: Princeton University Press.

Samuels, C. (1986). *Cultural ideology and the landscape of Confucian China: The traditional si he yuan.* Unpublished master's thesis, University of British Columbia, Vancouver, British Columbia, Canada.

Scott, J. C. (1998). *Seeing like a state: How certain schemes to improve the human condition have failed.* New Haven, CT: Yale University Press.

Shi, M. (1993). *Beijing transforms: Urban infrastructure, public works, and social change in the Chinese capital, 1900–1928.* Unpublished doctoral dissertation, Columbia University, New York.

Shi, N. (2004, July). *Opening address by the secretary general of the urban planning society of China.* Paper presented at the Chengshi Guihua Juece Minzhuhua Yantaohui [Conference on Democratization of the Urban Planning Decision-making Process], Quanzhou, Fujian.

Skinner, W. G. (1977). Cities and the hierarchy of local systems. In W. G. Skinner (Ed.), *The city in late imperial China* (pp. 275–352). Stanford, CA: Stanford University Press.

Skinner, W. G., Baker, H. D. R., & History E-Book Project. (1977). *The city in late imperial China.* Stanford, CA: Stanford University Press.

Spence, J. D. (1992). Let the past serve the present: The ideological claims of cultural relics works. *China Exchange News, 20*(2), 16–19.

State Council of the People's Republic of China. (1984). *Chengshi guihua tiaoli* [Urban planning provisions]. Beijing: Author.

Steinhardt, N. S. (1986). Why were Chang'an and Beijing so different? *Journal of the Society of Architectural Historians, 45*(4), 339–357.

Steinhardt, N. S. (1990). *Chinese imperial city planning.* Honolulu: University of Hawaii Press.

Stille, A. (1998). Faking it. *New Yorker, 74*(16), 36–42.

Tang, W.-S., & Chung, H. (2002). Rural-urban transition in China: Illegal land use and construction. *Asia Pacific Viewpoint, 43*(1), 43–62.

Tao, T. (1995, July). *Problems in the implementation of Quanzhou's old city redevelopment plan.* Paper presented at the International Conference on Renewal and Development in Housing Areas of Traditional Chinese and European Cities, Beijing, Quanzhou and Xi'an.

Tsin, M. (2000). Canton remapped. In J. W. Esherick (Ed.), *Remaking the Chinese city: Modernity and national identity, 1900–1950* (pp. 19–29). Honolulu: University of Hawaii Press.

Valletta, W. (2005). The land administration law of 1998 and its impact on urban development. In C. Ding & Y. Song (Eds.), *Emerging land and housing markets in China* (pp. 59–87). Cambridge, MA: Lincoln Institute of Land Policy.

Wakeman, F., Jr. (1993). The civil society and public sphere debate: Western reflections on Chinese political culture. *Modern China 19*(2), Symposium: "Public Sphere" "Civil Society" in China? Paradigmatic Issues in Chinese Studies, III), 108–138.

Wang, F.-L. (2004). Reformed migration control and new targeted people: China's *hukou* system in the 2000s. *The China Quarterly, 177*, 115–132.

Wang, L. (1963). Quanzhou chaicheng pilu yu shizheng gaikuang [A brief account of the demolition of the city walls and the clearing of land for roads in Quanzhou]. *Quanzhou wenshi ziliao [Quanzhou Cultural and Historical Materials], 8.*

Wang, M. (1995). Place, administration, and territorial cults in late imperial China: A case study from south Fujian. *Late Imperial China, 16*(1), 33–78.

Wang, M. (2004). Mapping "chaos": The dong xi fo feuds of Quanzhou, 1644–1839. In S. Feuchtwang (Ed*.), Making place: State projects, globalisation and local responses in China* (pp. 33–59). London: University College London Press.

Wheatley, P. (1971). *The pivot of the four quarters: A preliminary enquiry into the origins and character of the ancient Chinese city.* Chicago: Aldine.

Wong, C. (1997). Overview of issues in local public finance in the P.R.C. In C. Wong (Ed.), *Financing local government in the People's Republic of China* (pp. 27–60). New York: Published for the Asian Development Bank by Oxford University Press.

Wright, A. F. (1977). The cosmology of the Chinese city. In G. W. Skinner (Ed.), *The city in late imperial China* (pp. 22–74). Stanford, CA: Stanford University Press.

Wu, F. (2002a). China's changing urban governance in the transition towards a more market-oriented economy. *Urban Studies, 39*(7), 1071–1093.

Wu, F. (2002b). Review of the book *The transition of China's urban development: From plan-controlled to market-led. International Journal of Urban and Regional Research, 26*(4), 865–866.

Wu, F. (2003a). Globalization, place promotion and urban development in Shanghai. *Journal of Urban Affairs, 25*(1), 55–78

Wu, F. (2003b). The (post-) socialist entrepreneurial city as a state project: Shanghai's reglobalisation in question. *Urban Studies, 40*(9), 1673–1698.

Wu, F. (2004). Urban poverty and marginalization under market transition: The case of Chinese cities. *International Journal of Urban and Regional Research, 28*(2), 401–423.

Wu, F., & Yeh, A. G.-O. (1999). Urban spatial structure in a transitional economy: The case of Guangzhou, China. *Journal of the American Planning Association, 65*(4), 377–394.

Wu, H. (2005) *Remaking Beijing: Tiananmen Square and the creation of a political space.* Chicago: University of Chicago Press.

Wu, L. (1999). *Rehabilitating the old city of Beijing: A project in the ju'er hutong neighbourhood.* Vancouver: University of British Columbia Press.

Wu, W. (2005). Migrant residential distribution and metropolitan spatial development in Shanghai. In L. J. C. Ma & F. Wu (Eds.), *Restructuring the Chinese city: Changing society, economy and space* (pp. 222–242). New York: Routledge.

Xie, Y., & Costa, F. J. (1991). Urban design practice in socialist China. *Third World Planning Review, 13*(3), 277–296.

Xu, C. (2004, July). *Tamuo, gaige, chuangxin: Shenzhen chengshi guihua weiyuanhui zhidu de shixian* [Exploration, reform, innovation: The institutionalization of the Shenzhen municipal planning commission in practice]. Paper presented at the Chengshi Guihua Juece Minzhuhua Yantaohui [Conference on Democratization of the Urban Planning Decision-making Process], Quanzhou, Fujian.

Xu, F. (2005, December 8). *Building community in post-socialist China: Towards local democratic governance?* Paper presented at the China Studies Colloquium, University of Washington, Seattle.

Xu, Y. (2000). *The Chinese city in space and time: The development of urban form in Suzhou.* Honolulu: University of Hawaii Press.

Yeh, A. G. O. (2005). The dual land market and urban development in China. In C. Ding & Y. Song (Eds.), *Emerging land and housing markets in China* (pp. 40–57). Cambridge, MA: Lincoln Institute of Land Policy.

Yeung, Y.-M., & Chu, D. K. Y. (2000). *Fujian: A coastal province in transition and transformation.* Hong Kong: Chinese University Press.

Zelin, M., Ocko, J. K., & Gardella, R. (2004). *Contract and property in early modern China.* Stanford, CA: Stanford University Press.

Zhang, L. (2001. *Strangers in the city: Reconfigurations of space, power, and social networks within China 's floating population.* Stanford, CA: Stanford University Press.

Zhang, L. (2005). Migrant enclaves and impacts of redevelopment policy in Chinese cities. In L. J. C. Ma & F. Wu (Eds.), *Restructuring the Chinese city: Changing society, economy and space.* New York: Routledge.

Zhang, L., Zhao, S. X. B., & Tian, J. P. (2003). Self-help in housing and *chengzhongcun* in China's urbanization. *International Journal of Urban and Regional Research, 27*(4), 912–937.

Zhang, T. (2002a). Decentralization, localization, and the emergence of a quasi-participatory decision-making structure in urban development in Shanghai. *International Planning Studies, 7*(4), 303.

Zhang, T. (2002b). Urban development and a socialist pro-growth coalition in Shanghai. *Urban Affairs Review, 37*(4), 475–499.

Zhang, Y., & Fang, K. (2004). Is history repeating itself? From urban renewal in the United States to inner-city redevelopment in China. *Journal of Planning Education and Research, 23*(3), 286–298.

Zhao, M. (2003). *Shequ fazhan guihua: Lilun yu shixian* [Community development planning: Theory and practice]. Beijing: Zhongguo Jianzhu Gonghe Chubanshe.

Zhu, Jianfei (2004). *Chinese spatial strategies: Imperial Beijing, 1420–1911.* New York: RoutledgeCurzon.

Zhu, Jieming (2004). Local developmental state and order in China's urban development during transition. *International Journal of Urban and Regional Research, 28*(2), 424–447.

Zhu, Y. (2000). In situ urbanization in rural China: Case studies from Fujian province. *Development and Change, 31*(2), 413–434.

Zhu, Z., & Kwok, R. (1997). Beijing: The expression of national political ideology. In W. B. Kim, M. Douglass, S.-C. Choe, & K. C. Ho (Eds.), *Culture and the city in East Asia* (pp. 125–150). Oxford, UK: Oxford University Press.

DANIEL BENJAMIN ABRAMSON is an assistant professor of urban design and planning and a member of the China studies faculty at the University of Washington in Seattle. He received his doctoral degree in urban planning from Tsinghua University in Beijing in 1998 and continues to conduct research and consult on planning projects in China. He can be reached at abramson@u.washington.edu.

From *Journal of the American Planning Association,* Vol. 72, Number 2, Sprint 2006, pp. 197–215. Copyright © 2006 by American Planning Association. Reprinted by permission.

The Community Communication Network: New Technology for Public Engagement

LOUIS BEZICH

The British are coming, and this time they're bringing a new communications technology to help local officials with an age-old problem: getting important information to constituents accurately and conveniently.

Newsletters, cable channels, and the Internet give local government officials a means of reaching their constituents. Still, residents continually complain about a lack of public information, and public engagement—particularly on key issues—remains a challenge. While the media are certainly available, they present their own set of issues that make most officials shiver.

Officials in both urban and rural areas face additional problems like the digital divide. Residents of some larger cities or rural localities may not have access to computers or cable television. Language barriers further complicate the seemingly easy goal of public communication.

Community Communication Network (CCN) was developed in the United Kingdom to address the same need as American officials have, namely, getting critical information to their constituents. Its success has been recognized by a number of leading British officials, including Prime Minister Tony Blair. Its creators are now bringing it to the United States.

Through plasma video screens placed in a variety of public and private venues, CCN helps local officials get their messages directly to the public in a relatively eye-catching manner. High-impact screens are installed throughout the local community at venues where people remain in place for a few minutes, becoming a "static viewing audience." The screens are situated in positions that have been identified as giving maximum exposure and gaining maximum attention from members of the public within each venue.

The broadcast program plays public-service announcements on a continuous 30-minute loop, interspersed with daily news, weather, and sports updates as well as interesting facts and information relevant to the locality. Content is updated every 12 weeks to keep it fresh for those who are watching, and to enable government or other agencies to ensure that any new initiatives or local news reaches their communities regularly.

Local leaders can tailor public-service announcements and promotional messages to a variety of constituents: seniors, parents, children, students, veterans, job seekers, or commuters. Through the networks technology, the information on any one screen can be changed over the course of the day as the audience changes. A screen at a McDonald's, for example, can play senior-oriented messages in the early morning and switch to content aimed at teenagers after school. Each screen can be individually programmed to meet the needs of its venue. So, whether managers need to air a Spanish-language message at one location or to alter the playlist among locations, the technology is up to the task.

The system also has the capability of broadcasting emergency information, such as "amber" or terrorist alerts, quickly on a local or regional basis. Emergency broadcast templates allow local officials to e-mail critical information, like photos, to the operations center to have alerts broadcast within minutes. Although content is typically silent to avoid fatigue for workers in the venues, CCN can remotely activate sound as and when required for emergency purposes.

Residents don't need to read a newsletter, punch in a cable channel, or hunt for a Web site. This system requires no effort on their part. Placing the video screens in convenient locations draws a captured audience to short, punchy, 30-second messages while people wait or are engaged in some short-term activity. Locations typically include public and private sector locations like waiting rooms, fast-food restaurants, recreation centers, shopping malls, and public buildings.

The system uses solid-state technology provided by a company that has given CCN worldwide exclusivity for government applications. The system has no spinning hard drives or mechanical disk engines. A dial-out mechanism ensures that units cannot be directly dialed into or attached by hackers. Currently, all networks are supported by a U.K.-based network operations center offering day-to-day, proactive monitoring and customer help-desk service. Plans call for a U.S. center as new networks are established.

CCN grew out of a U.K. initiative called Public Safety Partnerships. In 1998, the Crime and Disorder Act required city councils, local police, and fire and emergency medical personnel to better coordinate their efforts to reduce crime in their constituencies. The initiative was successful and generated great results, but no one knew about it. Surveys showed that the fear of crime was rising while crime had actually fallen.

To combat this "information gap," local officials in Britain looked for a new way to convey their success stories and ensure future progress. The result was the Community Communication Network. Soon after the launching of the first few systems for the Public Safety Partnerships, other agencies saw the value of this direct link to citizens. The scope of the CCN networks has grown exponentially, and these now carry messages for all sorts of public programs, like recreation, education, health, and environmental affairs. Today, these networks are becoming an integral part of local government in the United Kingdom; most recently, they were used effectively to communicate emergency messages in a number of towns after the terrorist attacks in London. Today, more than a dozen British communities use this technology.

The CCN system costs between $13,000 and $18,000 per screen, depending on the length of a community's commitment. The costs include all hardware and programming for a year. A minimum of 10 screens is required, with the number of screens appropriate for a community being determined through a survey and assessment of local needs.

Content is controlled by the municipality or appropriate government agency. While the system's own producers create broadcast-quality product, the subject material is selected by local officials. As owners of the content, local government can also play messages on their local cable stations and on the municipal or government Web site, stretching the usefulness of the product.

In the United Kingdom, CCN is funded through a mixture of national government and local monies. To date, there has been no use of advertising to support program costs. To advance the concept in the United States, where there will not likely be federal or state funding (homeland security funding is being explored), company officials have begun a sponsorship model in which a business could sponsor a community's use of the technology, with recognition similar to that given on public television programming.

In addition to municipal governments, CCN-USA officials see widespread applications for county, state, and federal governments in the United States. Motor vehicle agencies, Social Security offices, rail-car installations, and intergovernmental partnerships that share a system are some of the possibilities under exploration.

Growing pressure to keep constituents informed, unprecedented public safety concerns, and an ever-increasing volume of public information have meant a demand for more extensive and diverse communications. New technology like CCN offers government leaders in U.S. communities a new means of getting accurate information directly to the public and meeting these critical needs.

LOUIS BEZICH is president of Public Solutions, Inc. (lbezich@publicsolutions.net), Haddonfield, New Jersey. He is a former municipal and county administrator in New Jersey. For more information on CCN, visit the Web site at www.ccnusa.tv. The United Kingdom Web site is at www.ccn.uk.net.

Curbing Corruption in the Republic of South Africa

Learn how new measures put in place since the 1996 Constitution, such as the drafting of codes of conduct, whistle-blowing, and training initiatives, are making public officials more aware of the need for ethical conduct in their public dealings.

I. W. Ferreira and M. S. Bayat

There is nothing new about corruption; it has been around for a long time. As far back as 300 B.C., Katilya, the then Prime Minister and Emperor Chandragupta of India, identified forty ways of embezzlement of funds by employees in the private sector, and he had this to say about government officials:

> Just as it is impossible not to taste the honey or the poison that finds itself at the tip of the tongue, so it is impossible for a government servant not to eat up at least a bit of the King's revenue.

Corruption is an increasingly important clandestine driving force in South Africa, and it is beginning to seriously undermine the faith of the citizens in the very foundations and fabric of society—in particular the market economy system, which is supposed to be free and fair. A democratic society expects to be ruled by a just and egalitarian government, and citizens are now questioning their public officials as well as the rule of law by an independent, corruption-free, and fair judicial system.

Evidence of corrupt practices is easily found:

- Ghost employees in the government service
- Fraud in the hospitals and school meals schemes
- Unauthorized use of credit cards by officials
- All manner of corruption in the police force
- Leaking of examination papers
- Issue of fraudulent university degrees and identity documents
- Electoral fraud
- False subsistence and transport claims by members of Parliament and medical doctors
- "Kickbacks" in tender procedures
- Pension payments to individuals under the age of sixty and to dead people
- Payment for submission of applications for employment.

And the list goes on.

In addition to media evidence and information from courts, official and unofficial reports suggest that corruption in South African society is not a matter of exceptional individual behavior, but a common practice affecting many sectors of public activity. Unfortunately, despite available evidence, corruption is substantially less visible than many other types of crime, and this is perhaps why it has not been attacked with the appropriate vigor. Corruption is a consensual crime in the sense that all participants are usually willing parties, who together have an interest in concealing it. Therefore, it involves fewer conscious victims and witnesses.

The sections that follow highlight key reports on corruption in South Africa. We then describe an organizational ethic that has begun to emerge since the 1996 Constitution, including anticorruption efforts, legislative and administrative measures, and, finally, the role of the Public Protector.

Reports on Corruption in South Africa

The Commission for Public Service Innovation (CPSI) published the following key statistics:

- In South Africa, 30 percent of the potentially economically active population are unemployed.
- Twenty percent of households earn less than R800 ($130) per month. In some provinces, notably the Free State and the Eastern Cape, the figure is as high as 46 percent.
- From 2002 to 2003, crime incidents totalled 2.7 million, or 6,000 crimes per 100,000 people per annum.
- Only 1.8 percent of Black-African households own a computer—limiting access to technology and information.

Corruption in the government service is the major concern among foreign investors. According to the CPSI, a survey of sixty-nine countries ranked corruption as the single largest obstacle to doing business with South Africa. Various bodies in South Africa concern themselves with the issue of corruption. The public media, particularly the popular press, regularly report on corrupt practices in government departments (agencies) throughout the nine provinces. Other bodies, some statutory, others not, act as watchdogs to report on the unethical behavior of public functionaries—including officials and politicians. Among these are the press, the Auditor-General (AG), and the Public Service Accountability Monitor (PSAM),[1] which incorporates the Eastern Cape Public Service Accountability Monitor and the KwaZulu-Natal (KZN) Provincial Internal Audit Unit, and a prominent consulting firm specializing in anticorruption measures, Heath Public Service Consultants. Brief examples of reports by these bodies follow.

The Press

A Sunday newspaper reported on a book, *The Crisis of Public Health Care in the Eastern Cape—The Post-Apartheid Challenges of Oversight and Accountability*, published by the PSAM, expounding on the reasons for the health care crisis in the Eastern Cape Province as follows:

> The way the Eastern Cape provincial government spent its health budget has significantly contributed to the public health care crisis in the province, demonstrated in a recently launched book. The book, produced by the PSAM, was launched during the People's Health Summit in East London. Key findings include:
>
> - That over eighty-one percent of the provincial health department's R25.2 billion budget from 1996 to 2003 was not properly accounted for. This amount (R20.6 billion) was issued with audit disclaimers by the Auditor-General.
>
> - That over R283 million (nineteen percent) of the infrastructure budget between 1999 and 2004 was unspent. This money should have gone towards maintenance of hospitals, clinics, and health centers in the province.
>
> - That between 2000 and 2003 the department failed to spend twenty-seven percent of its HIV-AIDS budget (R33 million)—and of the spent funds, R90 million was unaccounted for.

Auditor-General

The AG is the general watchdog of the government over administrative practices of government departments (agencies). Annual AG reports on two departments are described as examples: first, the Department of Defence (DOD) and, second, the South African Management and Development Institute (SAMDI), which is the official training division of the public service.

DOD

Among irregular financial management activities, accruals represent goods or services delivered without an invoice received from the supplier at year-end or with an invoice received but unpaid at year-end. Such information cannot be generated from the accounting systems of the DOD; thus, disclosed accruals are understated by an unknown amount. Also, various loss files could not be submitted for audit purposes, and the accuracy and

completeness of funds for irregularities and losses, as disclosed in the financial statements, could not be verified. Moreover, the security and general administration over vehicles are lacking, mainly because policies and procedures are not adequately applied or adhered to, resulting in the following:

- **Unauthorized trips.** The number of vehicles on hand materially differs from those reflected in the stock ledger.
- **Deteriorating vehicles.** Vehicles deteriorate to a condition beyond economical repair, mainly as a result of irregular servicing.
- **Irregular repair practices.** Vehicles sent for repairs are not serviced on time, and vehicles are stripped of their parts, causing further delays due to budget constraints.

An information systems audit of the general controls surrounding the Computer Aided Logistic Management Information Systems (CALMIS) and the Operational Support Information System (OSIS) revealed that the activities of the database administrators were not logged and monitored. This is a significant weakness as these administrators have the highest privilege available on the databases and also perform the incompatible system administrator functions. This weakness potentially allowed the databases to be changed without any record being kept. Such changes can then only be detected by comparing the data with source documents. No confirmation that this function was performed could be obtained. In addition, a number of accounts on the CALMIS UNIX servers do not have passwords.

According to the CRSI, a survey of sixty-nine countries ranked corruption as the single largest obstacle to doing business with South Africa.

On the basis of the above, no reliance could be placed on the general controls surrounding CALMIS for the regularity audit, and more extensive substantive testing had to be performed to obtain a higher audit assurance. The audit also indicated that limited progress has been made in addressing previously identified issues. Clearly, the report of the AG shows serious shortcomings in the financial management of the DOD that need to be addressed on a priority basis.

SAMDI

The AG report highlights a number of issues, including the following:

- Documentation relating to payments is missing.
- No framework for the allocation of expenditure exists, so no alternative audit procedures could be performed.
- The AG was unable to verify the completeness and accuracy of expenditures as accounted for in the financial statements.
- Amounts owed show differences between account records and SAMDI's financial statements that cannot be verified.

The European Commission is also investigating missing documentation relating to payments of R5 million since the commencement of the financial agreement until December 31, 2002.

The report of the AG shows serious shortcomings in the financial management of SAMDI, which need urgent attention, also on a parliamentary level.

PSAM

The PSAM published a number of lists detailing actual cases of corruption that took place during 2003–04 in the Eastern Cape provincial government (Table 1).

Examples of cases of corruption include the following:

- R15 million in pensions paid out to 2,400 under-60s.
- Twenty-nine officials implicated in a R2.8 million petrol scam.
- Eastern Cape Safety and Security spokesperson convicted of fraud.
- Transport official arrested for attempted fraud of R950,000.
- Two employees guilty of check theft.
- Health official arrested after cheques disappeared.
- Pensions paid out to bogus or dead people.

KZN Provincial Internal Audit Unit

Ernst and Young, in a fraud and corruption survey in South Africa, has confirmed the following statistically:

- More than 90 percent of fraud and corruption goes undetected.
- Insiders account for 85 percent of fraud and corruption, divided between staff (30 percent) and managers (55 percent).
- Of managers guilty of fraud and corruption, 85 percent have less than one year's service.
- The largest factor in fraud and corruption is weaknesses in internal control systems.

According to the Ernst and Young survey, the areas of prevalence of fraud and corruption in South Africa are bribes, inventory stock, fruitless expenditure, procurement, irregular expenditure, asset theft, unauthorized expenditure, leave, checks, claims, and payroll. The average global loss resulting from fraud per organization is R16.5 million ($2.75 million). The cost of forensic audits amounts to at least R40 million ($7 million) per annum. This money could have been used to alleviate poverty or create jobs.

Heath Consultants

According to Advocate W. H. Heath of Heath Consultants, democracy failed in the recent South African arms deal in that the call by the parliamentary oversight committee for an in-depth investigation by objective experts was never adhered to. In an abrupt about-face, members of the oversight committee completely changed their opinion regarding the investigation of the validity of the arms deal. The general view is that the executive instructed these members to "toe the (party) line." This violated the separation of powers and therefore democracy. The parliamentary oversight committee did not recommend that the contract be cancelled, but it did propose an investigation into

Table 1. Cases of Corruption in Eastern Cape Provincial Government (2003–04)

Variable	No. of Cases	No. Resolved	% Resolved
Corruption	345	28	8
Maladministration	170	3	2
Misconduct	179	28	15
Conflict of Interest	6	1	2

certain glaring flaws in the negotiating process that led to contracts governing the deal.

According to Heath, a complete investigation by the agency equipped for that purpose, as recommended by the committee, was not undertaken. This lack of adherence to recommendations of Parliament is the reason why controversy still looms over the deal, even though the contracts were signed by the government some years ago.

Red Flags

Heath Consultants identified scores of "red flags" in arms procurement contracts,[2] including the following:

1. High-ranking government officials establishing offshore companies and bank accounts.
2. Government officials paying for nonexistent goods and services to entities owned by a politician, his associates, or family members.
3. Politicians and government officials purchasing significant assets or investing in high-end real estate.
4. Members of government accumulating unexplained financial wealth, especially if inconsistent with information provided on public disclosure forms.
5. A lack of control over and total disregard for specified and general accounting procedures for purchases of government equipment and use of government funds.
6. Government paying individuals with no justification listed on the books, with checks cashed at exchange houses.
7. A single person in government or a limited group dominating operational, tendering, and financing decisions in defense procurement contracts.
8. An aggressive and dismissive attitude by politicians and arms manufacturing companies toward the findings and advice of independent consultants.
9. Governments not appointing or utilizing agencies established in terms of their constitutions for their designed purposes in large government contracts.
10. Arms manufacturing companies providing excessive incentives for government officials during the tendering process.
11. Governments of arms manufacturing companies assisting these companies financially and diplomatically to secure defense procurement contracts.
12. High-level politicians or arms manufacturing companies with questionable reputations.

13. Governments that are uncommitted to anticorruption measures and their implementation in arms contracts.
14. Lack of qualifications or incompetence of politicians—an easy target for syndicates or arms manufacturers with dubious intentions.
15. Government officials who vehemently retain authority in contracting processes and refuse to delegate to obvious officials within the government.
16. Government officials who override systems such as tendering processes.
17. Governments whose attitude is one of supreme power and little trust.
18. Governments that have little regard for the opinions of and issues raised by opposition parties and other stakeholders representing the interests of the community.
19. Internal government communications that are always from the top down—no proper reporting structures.
20. Politicians who are highly erratic and highly emotional—easily gauged by their public statements, etc.
21. Politicians with high personal debts or financial losses.
22. Politicians with extravagant lifestyles—beyond the means of their office.
23. Close relationships between politicians and certain tendering parties or publicly known relationships with certain private-sector institutions.
24. Too much trust placed in certain key members of government, without a proper review of their performance.
25. Reluctance by government to provide constitutionally established agencies with needed information to perform their legal duties.
26. Politicians who frequently rationalize failures in media statements, including rationalizing cost increases in defense and other government contracts.
27. Government officials who enter into regular significant transactions with the same parties on behalf of the state.
28. Failure to have a clear policy to require government officials and decision makers to disclose their interests.
29. Cabinet members (the executive) who have little regard for their accountability to the legislative.
30. Nepotism in government departments and in the tendering process.
31. Property misuse—using state assets to entertain and accommodate parties involved in the tendering process.
32. Many difficult and unexplainable accounting issues in the procurement process—difficult-to-audit financial and related records and difficult-to-establish audit trails.
33. Doubts regarding the independence of government officials and parties contracted by the state to facilitate procurement processes.
34. Payments made to government officials that are not disclosed for tax purposes.
35. A history of failure to record dishonest acts and disciplining of government officials.
36. Inadequate government policies with regard to internal controls in procurement processes.
37. Procurement contracts that are unduly complex and thereby lacking in transparency.
38. An urgent need by governments to report favorable elements of procurement contracts to the public.
39. Costs and expenses of procurement contracts outweighing the military needs of a specific country or its social welfare needs.
40. Contracts written to limit competition (for example, sole-source contracts).
41. The same manufacturer always winning contracts by small margins.
42. Contracts always going to the bid received last.
43. Splitting one purchase into multiples to avoid the approval process.
44. Paying above-market prices for defense packages.
45. Governments not employing independent consultants or advisors to conduct integrity and due diligence studies on parties in the tendering process.
46. Politicians and others in authority not conceding the problem of corruption.
47. Relative ease with which employees with dishonest intentions can get to know all the loopholes in an organization's control measures.

Development of an Organizational Ethic

According to the erstwhile Public Protector, efficiency improvements should not be achieved at the expense of high ethical standards. Moreover, a values-based approach alone is inadequate; corruption is as much about systems as about individual conduct. Thus, the country needs codes of conduct; administrative law mechanisms; whistle-blower protections; effective auditing, monitoring, and law enforcement systems; and training in and support of ethical conduct—all essential components of an ethical public-sector service-rendering environment.

The 1996 Constitution commits South Africa to implementing an ethical, accountable, and democratic system of governance. Indeed, the Department of Public Service and Administration (DPSA) is leading the process of transformation to ethical public servant behavior from within the public service. It is complemented by the Public Service Commission, as well as the Parliamentary Portfolio Committee on Public Service and Administration, which both play an essential oversight role.

Since the advent of the 1996 Constitution, the South African government has taken significant steps to ensure a clean and accountable administration. In 1999, the National Anti-Corruption Initiative was launched, initializing the creation of a National Anti-Corruption Forum, which contributes towards the establishment of a national consensus and coordination of sectoral strategies against corruption. Its role is to advise the government on national initiatives on the implementation of strategies to combat corruption, share information and best practices on sectoral anticorruption work, and advise sectors on the improvement of sectoral anticorruption strategies.

Legislative and Administrative Measures

The Constitution of the Republic of South Africa Act calls for a high standard of professional ethics—particularly in relation to administration in every sphere of government, organs of state, and public enterprises. It also calls for the following:

- Establishment of constitutionally independent bodies, such as the Auditor-General and the Public Protector (national parliamentary ombudsman)
- A Special Investigative Unit for investigating and recovering misappropriated public monies
- An Investigating Directorate on Corruption
- Establishment of inspectors-general within certain state departments (including the military and the police and intelligence services)
- The Executive Members' Ethics Act and its Code of Conduct governing the conduct of and disclosure of interests by members of the cabinet, including the president and deputy-president, deputy ministers, and members of provincial executive councils (cabinets)
- The Code of Conduct for public officials governing relationships with the legislature, executive, public, and colleagues, as well as performance, personal conduct, and disclosure of private interests
- Service contracts of heads of government departments (and soon their senior officials) requiring them to disclose their financial interests, protecting whistle-blowers in the public and private sectors, and other measures.

The Role of the Public Protector

The Public Protector of South Africa is an ombudsman in the classical sense of the word. The Public Protector has the power to investigate any conduct in state affairs, or in the public administration in any sphere of government, alleged or suspected to be improper or to result in any impropriety or prejudice. The Public Protector has been involved in, or supportive of, many of the developments in the anticorruption efforts described above. This was in furtherance of the constitutional injunction that the Public Protector is an institution to strengthen constitutional democracy in South Africa. The main contribution of the Public Protector is that of investigating, reporting, and taking appropriate remedial action, mostly by way of recommendations.

For present purposes it is convenient to distinguish the following "types" of corruption:

- Criminal corruption, where the perpetrator can be prosecuted for crimes, including the taking of bribes, fraud, or theft
- Corruption in the ethical sense, where the act does not constitute a crime, but is nevertheless unethical or in contravention of, for example, a code of conduct
- Corruption in the sense of a system not working or disintegrating because of, for example, incompetence or negligence.

As far as criminal corruption is concerned, the usual reaction to a complaint received by the Public Protector is to refer the matter to the police or prosecuting authorities, which are the appropriate institutions to deal with it. In his role as a receptacle for complaints from members of the public, the Public Protector often receives re-

ports of criminal corruption. However, the Public Protector has an important secondary role to play where the criminal corruption is the result of maladministration within the exploited state institution. A perfect example is the recently concluded Public Protector investigation into corruption in state subsidies paid for subeconomic housing. Private contractors are reportedly misappropriating such subsidies without providing proper housing in return. The Public Protector launched an investigation into the matter, but brought in the Director of Public Prosecutions to deal with the fraud investigations. The Public Protector concentrated his investigation on the procedures for the payment of subsidies in the relevant provincial housing department, and on the adherence to such procedures, with the aim to prevent similar crimes in future.

Conclusion

In this article, we examine corruption and the development of organizational ethic in the South African government and public service since the 1996 Constitution. We provide an overview of anticorruption measures taken by the government in response to widespread and varied corruption in South Africa. Almost ten years after the new Constitution, anticorruption initiatives have clearly become a major and broad government priority.

Notes

1. The PSAM, a nonstatutory body, is an independent monitoring and research organization based at Rhodes University, Grahamstown. South Africa. It monitors the way government departments, particularly those of the Eastern Cape provincial government, manage their resources, whether or not they provide effective service delivery, and the accountability of politicians and officials who run these departments.
2. A *red flag* is an advance warning or device that signals the potential for corruption and allows steps to avoid it.

References

Auditor-General. Report to Parliament on the Financial Statements of the South African Management and Development Institute (SAMDI) for the year ended 31 March 2003 and on the Financial Statements of the DOD for the year ended 31 March 2004.

Commission for Public Service Innovation. Report. 2003.

The Constitution of the Republic of South Africa Act 108 of 1996.

Public Service Accountability Monitor (PSAM) 2003–04. www.case.psam.ru.ac.za/cmwstypes.asp#Corruption.

Transparency International. Report. 2002.

DR I. W. (NAAS) FERREIRA is a senior lecturer, Faculty of Management, Cape Peninsula University of Technology, Cape Town, South Africa. He can be reached at ferreirai@cput.ac.za. **M. S. (SAHEED) BAYAT** is Dean of the Faculty and professor of Management, Cape Peninsula University of Technology, Cape Town, South Africa. He can be reached at bayatm@cput.ac.za. This article is excerpted from a presentation at the 66th Annual ASPA National Conference held in Milwaukee, Wisconsin, April 2–5, 2005. The full paper, including additional references and an extensive bibliography, can be found at www.thepublicmanager.org.

From *The Public Manager*, Vol. 34, Number 2, Summer 2005, pp. 15–21. Copyright © 2005 by The Bureaucrat, Inc. Reprinted by permission.

How the Dutch Do Housing...

Affordable Choices in the Netherlands

JANE HOLTZ KAY

Holland is a self-made nation. Smaller than Connecticut, more crowded than Japan,... the country has shaped its housing policies across a waterbound landscape, limited in everything but the need to plan. Both the acres of land reclaimed from the Zuider Zee since the 1930s and the number of housing units built by the government since World War II would dumbfound U.S. planners.

Add the newer designs by Dutch architects, and you have not only aesthetic flair but the "level-headed and pragmatic application of technology and planning," as *SuperDutch*, the aptly titled 2000 book by Bart Lootsmar, observes.

National planning, not just for housing but for the conservation of water, land, infrastructure, and forests, is essential to Holland's existence and accounts for its reputation. So do progressive policies like the postwar plan to set aside some 30 percent of dwelling places for "social" (public) housing.

Amsterdam's newest housing mecca, the Eastern Harbour, built on reclaimed land ("polders," in Dutch), is impressive. After a long planning process and a 1988 referendum to determine the national will, the Dutch transformed the docklands into four communities. The first step was the removal of a slaughterhouse on the industrial island of KNSM in 1988. Development followed on the islands, peninsulas really, of Java and Borneo Sporenburg.

By adroitly massing and individualizing rowhouses and outdoor space, the scheme for the new land set a pattern of unity and diversity. The rowhouses, behind splendid facades, offer light and views from patios and open space. Parking is out of sight. The result: compact but splendidly shaped surroundings that provide 8,000 homes for 17,000 people.

Borneo Sporenburg boasts the unique Scheepstimmermanstratt, an avenue of rowhouses, shoulder to shoulder along the canals. Last fall, it earned its creator, architect Adriaan Geuze of the firm West 8, Harvard's prestigious Veronica Rudge Green Prize for contributing to the public realm and urban life.

The Old Days

Recent Dutch housing hasn't always held to such high standards. *Spatial Planning and the Environment*, a recently published report by the Ministry of Housing, has the tone of an apologia. Noting the affluence and aging of the population and the shrinking size of the family, the document looks penitently at the last decades, when quantity of housing topped quality. The result, say the authors, was often shoddy, or at the least unfriendly, construction.

"By the late 1970s, it was clear that architecture was hemorrhaging," writes Lootsmar in *SuperDutch*. Plans for city centers languished. A visit bears that out. Like Europe and America, the Netherlands succumbed to Corbusian tower-in-the-park urban renewal, bland high-rise boxes, and sprawling suburbanization and is stuck with it.

Sterile mid-rises from the 1960s are the rule in Rotterdam's old harborfront neighborhood of Kop van Zuid, site of the barracks from which Dutch Jews were deported during World War II. And to walk through the Zuidoost center outside Amsterdam today is to see a grim, wind-whipped Edge City of towers; a drab sports arena; a glitzy, failed theater; and low-scale apartments—many in need of rehabilitation or even uprooting.

Even the supposed core city of Almere, a new town near Amsterdam, offers a grim, car-centered environment. The boxy, mid-rise buildings now under construction are chillingly bleak. Even the pleasant, single-family, canalside houses, designed by the architecture firm MVRVD on Almere's outskirts, and other buildings by well-known architects are devoid of shops and dependent on cars. Despite bike paths and bus-only lanes, such remote outposts give not even a nod to Amsterdam's transportation web.

Dutch architecture has changed dramatically in the last 20 years, with superstars like Rem Koolhaus grabbing the world stage. But housing design has not always kept pace. A decade ago, the national government's Fourth Report on Physical Planning called for new housing districts to be built at countless scattered sites.

The program was criticized for its dispersal and lack of public transportation. Now expanding, it is slated to create a total of 634,800 new dwellings by 2005. The good news is that it will locate roughly two-thirds of that housing in more central, urban zones.

Still, despite these cautionary notes, Holland's planners have an easier lot than their U.S. peers, who are bogged down by complicated and limited federal housing policies, a housing budget diminished by two-thirds in the '90s, and a disdain for city housing needs.

Changing Times

For all the Netherlands' planning pluses, its policies are shifting toward more market-oriented housing, as the country as a whole tilts toward the right. Last year's national election reflected this shift.

"Entering the real world of market-driven reality" has lessened government authority, says housing expert Arjen Oosterman. A government that once financed and dictated the course of housing corporations is letting go and loosening controls.

In an ironic twist, this change is occurring just as U.S. eyes turn eastward, seeking to absorb housing lessons from the Dutch, as U.S. planners have studied transportation in France and Germany. "New Design Paradigms for Housing," a program presented at New York's Van Alen Institute by the New Amsterdam Development Corporation, a group of Dutch developers, planners, and architects turning their attention to the city, attracted considerable interest from builders and others interested in the field.

In June, New York's Urban Center will kick off a six-city tour of examples of Dutch urban housing. The models, says Els Verbaken, the exhibit designer who assembled the show, "combine medium or high density with safety, ecology, and tranquility, qualities that are usually found in low-density circumstances."

Verbaken notes that most of the recent Dutch projects were financed by private money, contradicting the assumptions of many Americans about the key role of the government in housing, or at least in high style housing, in the Netherlands.

Who is Being Served?

In a late fall phone interview, Hans Huijsman, secretary of the Netherlands' central Board of Housing Assistance, looks back 100 years to describe Holland's slums, gradually eradicated by social housing, then skips forward to the last decade's movement toward deregulation. Today, he says, market orientation and financial self-sufficiency are the mode. Government policies that now force municipalities to sell 30 percent of any new development to individual owners for "custom-made" houses are a far cry from earlier public emphases.

"Things are changing quite drastically," he continues. With living space short, jammed cities like Amsterdam (once 80 percent subsidized housing) must shift from serving the hard-pressed to encouraging the comfortable. Today's focus on serving middle- and high-income groups to entice them to stay in cities can slight the disadvantaged. Likewise, stricter proof of legality from immigrants and performance agreements exacted from low-income renters squeeze the less fortunate.

"It was a good system," Huijsman says of the earlier subsidized housing requirements. But he's not opposed to the recent changes: "I think it was high time," he says of the shift in policy.

Others are more skeptical. There's more of a "free-for-all for developers," says Aaron Betsky, Dutch-born head of the Netherlands Architecture Institute in Rotterdam and former director of the San Francisco Museum of Art.

Still, some things haven't changed. The most densely built country in the world still has a pressing need to diagram its future, to look ahead, Betsky feels. "Every plan, every road becomes one giant three-D puzzle," he says. Nevertheless, the shift toward prioritizing private development is troublesome.

Some critics feel that the emphasis on "quality" and "free choice" in the latest Dutch housing survey, conducted by the ministry every fifth year, is a way of kowtowing to developers and serving the affluent. Even at Amsterdam's model Docklands development, planners succumbed to a supermarket developer's demand to exclude small shops for 10 years. And with few transit linkages, residents are left with a choice of 15-minute bike rides to get downtown or a slow crawl through increasing traffic jams.

Unsettled Future

How much and how fast will such shifts in thinking alter a nation that keeps 83 percent of its land mass green—for farms (70 percent) and open space (13 percent)? Compact development is still a political dictate in this dense nation, says Huijsman. That won't change, but imperfect implementation will make it hard to check "negative development"—homes heading out of designated central cities.

Harm Tilman, editor of *de Architect*, fears that planning in his country is no more immune to car dominance and polynuclear settlements than it was to the '60s high-rise craze. "We have had a very social kind of development," he says, "but now the old model is in revision." Private housing is promoted, and public spaces and social housing are less assured. A tilt to the right, and to the road, threatens Dutch life. "We have to rethink" what we are doing, he says.

Still, for all such shifts in social policy, the Dutch legacy and achievement in planning are remarkable—socially, quantitatively, and administratively. Spend time in Holland or count the reams of documents and designs, and the model seems alive and well. Factor in that these accomplishments have been achieved for a population of almost 16 million living on 7,000 square miles of mostly reclaimed land—75 percent since World War II—and admiration grows.

Despite the Netherlands' diminishing ratio of subsidized housing to market housing (already down to 30 percent from earlier 50-50 figures), the number of such dwellings would turn a U.S. housing activist green with envy. Equally enviable is the fact that the Dutch have sacrificed neither their social values, nor their urbanism, to that growth. Health care, public universities, and public schools reflect their progressive stance.

Densification

While the U.S. offers minimal direction to settlement or structure, Dutch law demands Bijlmermeur ("bundled deconcentration"), or densification. Thus, two-thirds of the nation's 6.5 million housing units consist of attached houses. Another third are in low-rise apartment buildings. Only a small number are single-family houses.

The Ministry of Housing still restricts half of all new housing to built-up areas within the Randstad—the western conurbation around Amsterdam, Rotterdam, the Hague, Utrecht, and the newer, less urban Almere—in order to preserve its "Green Heart."

The $450 million, 1990 Delta Metropolis plan for the area centered on the deltas of the Rhine, Mense, and Schelder rivers will be reinforced by the construction of some 190,000 homes between 2010 and 2030, all linked to a planned Deltametro light rail line. "It is sustainable development," Allard Jolles, architectural historian in Amsterdam's 75-year-old physical planning department, says of the plan that will add 50,000 new housing units in Amsterdam alone.

In plans for housing released after the United Nations summit conference in Johannesburg last year, the government spoke of "definitive urbanization accords" in 40 to 60 urban districts and 20 urban regions to accommodate an estimated million more people in the Delta Metropolis by 2030.

Always, strict building and design codes will set guidelines for everything from height to sustainability. And, despite change, the system of leasing the land, rather than outright purchase, will remain, benefiting "the community as a whole," says Jolles.

Still, housing advocates worry that the shift from social to speculative housing will drive out Holland's vaunted "polder" model of consensus, based on the historic need to join resources to reclaim a nation, and its imaginative design. Will the country maintain the social policies and tolerance that made it one of Europe's most progressive?

Whatever the outcome, what happens to Dutch housing matters. "If we are concerned about the future of the spatial debate, the Netherlands does have something to offer to other countries," says Betsky, as nations on both sides of the Atlantic look on.

Resources

Reading. *SuperDutch*, by Bart Lootsmar, published in 2000 by Princeton Architectural Press.

On the web. See the work of MVRDV (Maas, van Rijs and de Vries) at www.mvrdv.archined.nl/mvrdv.html.

JANE HOLTZ KAY is author of *Asphalt Nation* and *Lost Boston* and architecture critic for *The Nation*.

Index

Index

Test Your Knowledge Form

We encourage you to photocopy and use this page as a tool to assess how the articles in *Annual Editions* expand on the information in your textbook. By reflecting on the articles you will gain enhanced text information. You can also access this useful form on a product's book support Web site at *http://www.mhcls.com/online/*.

NAME: _____ DATE: _____

TITLE AND NUMBER OF ARTICLE: _____

BRIEFLY STATE THE MAIN IDEA OF THIS ARTICLE:

_____

LIST THREE IMPORTANT FACTS THAT THE AUTHOR USES TO SUPPORT THE MAIN IDEA:

_____

WHAT INFORMATION OR IDEAS DISCUSSED IN THIS ARTICLE ARE ALSO DISCUSSED IN YOUR TEXTBOOK OR OTHER READINGS THAT YOU HAVE DONE? LIST THE TEXTBOOK CHAPTERS AND PAGE NUMBERS:

_____

LIST ANY EXAMPLES OF BIAS OR FAULTY REASONING THAT YOU FOUND IN THE ARTICLE:

_____

LIST ANY NEW TERMS/CONCEPTS THAT WERE DISCUSSED IN THE ARTICLE, AND WRITE A SHORT DEFINITION:

We Want Your Advice

ANNUAL EDITIONS revisions depend on two major opinion sources: one is our Advisory Board, listed in the front of this volume, which works with us in scanning the thousands of articles published in the public press each year; the other is you—the person actually using the book. Please help us and the users of the next edition by completing the prepaid article rating form on this page and returning it to us. Thank you for your help!

ANNUAL EDITIONS: Public Policy and Administration 9/e

ARTICLE RATING FORM

Here is an opportunity for you to have direct input into the next revision of this volume.
We would like you to rate each of the articles listed below, using the following scale:

1. **Excellent: should definitely be retained**
2. **Above average: should probably be retained**
3. **Below average: should probably be deleted**
4. **Poor: should definitely be deleted**

Your ratings will play a vital part in the next revision.
Please mail this prepaid form to us as soon as possible.
Thanks for your help!

RATING	ARTICLE	RATING	ARTICLE
	1. What's New About the New Public Management?: Administrative Change in the Human Services		18. Enron/Andersen: Crisis in U.S. Accounting and Lessons for Government
	2. The State of Social Equity in American Public Administration		19. Huge Rise Looms for Health Care in Local Budgets
	3. A New Approach to Regulatory Reform		20. Privacy Concerns
	4. The Community of Inquiry: Classical Pragmatism and Public Administration		21. Strategic Applications of Technology: County-Level Case Study in the State of Georgia
	5. Performance Measurement: Test the Water Before You Dive In		22. E-Waste Epidemic
	6. Evidence-Based Management		23. Find It Fast
	7. Managing High-Risk Outsourcing		24. Moving Medicine Forward
	8. "There Was No Plan"—A Louisiana Perspective		25. The Best Care Anywhere
	9. Abu Ghraib: A Case of Moral and Administrative Failure		26. Senate's Failure to Agree on Immigration Plan Angers Workers and Employers Alike
	10. Twelve Obstacles to Ethical Decision Making: Rationalizations		27. Who's Advocating What Here?
	11. Follow the Money		28. Smart Growth: Why We Discuss It More Than We Do It
	12. Leadership in Your Midst: Tapping the Hidden Strengths of Minority Executives		29. More and Better Local Planning
	13. Organization Culture as an Explanation for Employee Discipline Practices		30. Rebuilding a Beautiful Mess
	14. The History of the Certified Public Manager		31. On the Gulf: Too Little, Too Late
	15. GovBenefits.gov: A Valuable E-Government Tool for Citizens		32. Closing of Mine on Tribal Lands Fuels Dispute over Air, Water and Jobs
	16. Governance and Risk Management: Challenges and Public Productivity		33. Getting to Yes
	17. Our Nation's Financial Condition and Fiscal Outlook: Shaping the Future of the Federal Government		34. Urban Planning in China: Continuity and Change
			35. The Community Communication Network: New Technology for Public Engagement
			36. Curbing Corruption in the Republic of South Africa
			37. How the Dutch Do Housing

BUSINESS REPLY MAIL
FIRST CLASS MAIL PERMIT NO. 551 DUBUQUE IA

POSTAGE WILL BE PAID BY ADDRESEE

McGraw-Hill Contemporary Learning Series
2460 KERPER BLVD
DUBUQUE, IA 52001-9902

ABOUT YOU

Name   Date

Are you a teacher? ❑   A student? ❑
Your school's name

Department

Address   City   State   Zip

School telephone #

YOUR COMMENTS ARE IMPORTANT TO US!

Please fill in the following information:
For which course did you use this book?

Did you use a text with this ANNUAL EDITION? ❑ yes ❑ no
What was the title of the text?

What are your general reactions to the *Annual Editions* concept?

Have you read any pertinent articles recently that you think should be included in the next edition? Explain.

Are there any articles that you feel should be replaced in the next edition? Why?

Are there any World Wide Web sites that you feel should be included in the next edition? Please annotate.

May we contact you for editorial input? ❑ yes ❑ no
May we quote your comments? ❑ yes ❑ no